THE C. S. LEWIS
SIGNATURE CLASSICS

BOOKS BY C. S. LEWIS

A Grief Observed
George MacDonald: An Anthology
Mere Christianity
Miracles
The Abolition of Man
The Great Divorce
The Problem of Pain
The Screwtape Letters (with "Screwtape Proposes a Toast")
The Weight of Glory
The Four Loves
Till We Have Faces
Surprised by Joy: The Shape of My Early Life
Reflections on the Psalms
Letters to Malcolm, Chiefly on Prayer
The Personal Heresy
The World's Last Night: And Other Essays
Poems
The Dark Tower: And Other Stories
Of Other Worlds: And Other Essays
Narrative Poems
A Mind Awake: An Anthology of C. S. Lewis
Letters of C. S. Lewis
All My Road Before Me
The Business of Heaven: Daily Readings from C. S. Lewis
Present Concerns: Journalistic Essays
Spirits in Bondage: A Cycle of Lyrics
On Stories: And Other Essays on Literature

ALSO AVAILABLE FROM HARPERCOLLINS
The Chronicles of Narnia
The Magician's Nephew
The Lion, the Witch and the Wardrobe
The Horse and His Boy
Prince Caspian
The Voyage of the Dawn Treader
The Silver Chair
The Last Battle

THE
C. S. LEWIS
SIGNATURE CLASSICS

HarperOne
An Imprint of HarperCollins*Publishers*

FIRST EDITION

Designed by Claudia Smelser

Illustrations by Kathleen Edwards

Library of Congress Cataloging-in-Publication Data is available upon request.

ISBN 978-0-06-257255-4 (hardcover)
ISBN 978-0-06-257254-7 (paperback)

19 20 21 LSC 10 9 8 7 6 5

THE C. S. LEWIS
SIGNATURE CLASSICS

CONTENTS

MERE CHRISTIANITY

MERE CHRISTIANITY
CONTENTS

PREFACE

THE CONTENTS OF this book were first given on the air, and then published in three separate parts as *Broadcast Talks* (1942), *Christian Behaviour* (1943) and *Beyond Personality* (1944). In the printed versions I made a few additions to what I had said at the microphone, but otherwise left the text much as it had been. A 'talk' on the radio should, I think, be as like real talk as possible, and should not sound like an essay being read aloud. In my talks I had therefore used all the contractions and colloquialisms I ordinarily use in conversation. In the printed version I reproduced this, putting *don't* and *we've* for *do not* and *we have*. And wherever, in the talks, I had made the importance of a word clear by the emphasis of my voice, I printed it in italics. I am now inclined to think that this was a mistake—an undesirable hybrid between the art of speaking and the art of writing. A talker ought to use variations of voice for emphasis because his medium naturally lends itself to that method: but a writer ought not to use italics for the same purpose. He has his own, different, means of bringing out the key words and ought to use them. In this edition I have expanded the contractions and replaced most of the italics by a recasting of the sentences in which they occurred: but without altering, I hope, the 'popular' or 'familiar' tone which I had all along intended. I have also added and deleted where I thought I understood any part of my subject better now than ten years ago or where I knew that the original version had been misunderstood by others.

The reader should be warned that I offer no help to anyone who is hesitating between two Christian 'denominations'. You will not learn from me whether you ought to become an Anglican, a Methodist, a Presbyterian, or a Roman Catholic. This omission is intentional (even in the list I have just given the order is alphabetical). There is no mystery about my own position. I am a very ordinary layman of the Church of England, not especially 'high', nor especially 'low', nor especially anything else. But in this book I am not trying to convert anyone to my own position. Ever since I became a Christian I have thought that the best, perhaps the only, service I could do for my unbelieving neighbours was to explain and defend the belief that has been common to nearly all Christians at all times. I had more than one reason for thinking this. In the first place, the questions which divide Christians from one another often involve points of high Theology or even of ecclesiastical history, which ought never to be treated except by real experts. I should have been out of my depth in such waters: more in need of help myself than able to help others. And secondly, I think we must admit that the discussion of these disputed points has no tendency at all to bring an outsider into the Christian fold. So long as we write and talk about them we are much more likely to deter him from entering any Christian communion than to draw him into our own. Our divisions should never be discussed except in the presence of those who have already come to believe that there is one God and that Jesus Christ is His only Son. Finally, I got the impression that far more, and more talented, authors were already engaged in such controversial matters than in the defence of what Baxter calls 'mere' Christianity. That part of the line where I thought I could serve best was also the part that seemed to be thinnest. And to it I naturally went.

So far as I know, these were my only motives, and I should be very glad if people would not draw fanciful inferences from my silence on certain disputed matters.

For example, such silence need not mean that I myself am sitting on the fence. Sometimes I am. There are questions at issue between Christians to which I do not think we have been told the answer. There are some to which I may never know the answer: if I asked them, even in a better world, I might (for all I know) be answered as a far greater questioner was answered: 'What is that to thee? Follow thou Me.' But there are other questions as to which I am definitely on one side of the fence, and yet say nothing. For I am not writing to expound something I could call 'my religion', but to expound 'mere' Christianity, which is what it is and what it was long before I was born and whether I like it or not.

Some people draw unwarranted conclusions from the fact that I never say more about the Blessed Virgin Mary than is involved in asserting the Virgin Birth of Christ. But surely my reason for not doing so is obvious? To say more would take me at once into highly controversial regions. And there is no controversy between Christians which needs to be so delicately touched as this. The Roman Catholic beliefs on that subject are held not only with the ordinary fervour that attaches to all sincere religious belief, but (very naturally) with the peculiar and, as it were, chivalrous sensibility that a man feels when the honour of his mother or his beloved is at stake. It is very difficult so to dissent from them that you will not appear to them a cad as well as a heretic. And contrariwise, the opposed Protestant beliefs on this subject call forth feelings which go down to the very roots of all Monotheism whatever. To radical Protestants it seems that the distinction between Creator and creature (however holy) is imperilled: that Polytheism is risen again. Hence it is hard so to dissent from them that you will not appear something worse than a heretic—a Pagan. If any topic could be relied upon to wreck a book about 'mere' Christianity—if any topic makes utterly unprofitable reading for those who do not yet believe that the Virgin's son is God—surely this is it.

Oddly enough, you cannot even conclude, from my silence on disputed points, either that I think them important or that I think them unimportant. For this is itself one of the disputed points. One of the things Christians are disagreed about is the importance of their disagreements. When two Christians of different denominations start arguing, it is usually not long before one asks whether such-and-such a point 'really matters' and the other replies: 'Matter? Why, it's absolutely essential.'

All this is said simply in order to make clear what kind of book I was trying to write; not in the least to conceal or evade responsibility for my own beliefs. About those, as I said before, there is no secret. To quote Uncle Toby: 'They are written in the Common-Prayer Book.'

The danger clearly was that I should put forward as common Christianity anything that was peculiar to the Church of England or (worse still) to myself. I tried to guard against this by sending the original script of what is now Book II to four clergymen (Anglican, Methodist, Presbyterian, Roman Catholic) and asking for their criticism. The Methodist thought I had not said enough about Faith, and the Roman Catholic thought I had gone rather too far about the comparative unimportance of theories in explanation of the Atonement. Otherwise all five of us were agreed. I did not have the remaining books similarly 'vetted' because in them, though differences might arise among Christians, these would be differences between individuals or schools of thought, not between denominations.

So far as I can judge from reviews and from the numerous letters written to me, the book, however faulty in other respects, did at least succeed in presenting an agreed, or common, or central, or 'mere' Christianity. In that way it may possibly be of some help in silencing the view that, if we omit the disputed points, we shall have left only a vague and bloodless H.C.F. The H.C.F. turns out to be something not only positive but pungent; divided from all non-Christian beliefs by a chasm to which the worst divisions inside Christendom are not really comparable at all. If I have not directly helped the cause of reunion, I have perhaps made it clear why we ought to be reunited. Certainly I have met with little of the fabled *odium theologicum* from convinced members of communions different from my own. Hostility has come more from borderline people whether within the Church of England or without it: men not exactly obedient to any communion. This I find curiously consoling. It is at her centre, where her truest children dwell, that each communion is really closest to every other in spirit, if not in doctrine. And this suggests that at the centre of each there is a something, or a Someone, who against all divergencies of belief, all differences of temperament, all memories of mutual persecution, speaks with the same voice.

So much for my omissions on doctrine. In Book III, which deals with morals, I have also passed over some things in silence, but for a different reason. Ever since I served as an infantryman in the First World War I have had a great dislike of people who, themselves in ease and safety, issue exhortations to men in the front line. As a result I have a reluctance to say much about temptations to which I myself am not exposed. No man, I suppose, is tempted to every sin. It so happens that the impulse which makes men gamble has been left out of my make-up; and, no doubt, I pay for this by lacking some good impulse of which it is the excess or perversion. I therefore did not feel myself qualified to give advice about permissible and impermissible gambling: if there is any permissible, for I do not claim to know even that. I have also said nothing about birth-control. I am not a woman nor even a married man, nor am I a priest. I did not think it my place to take a firm line about pains, dangers and expenses from which I am protected; having no pastoral office which obliged me to do so.

Far deeper objections may be felt—and have been expressed—against my use of the word *Christian* to mean one who accepts the common doctrines of Christianity. People ask: 'Who are you, to lay down who is, and who is not a Christian?' or 'May not many a man who cannot believe these doctrines be far more truly a Christian, far closer to the spirit of Christ, than some who do?' Now this objection is in one sense very right, very charitable, very spiritual, very sensitive. It has every available quality except that of being useful. We simply cannot, without disaster, use language as these objectors want us to use it. I will try to make this clear by the history of another, and very much less important, word.

The word *gentleman* originally meant something recognisable; one who had a coat of arms and some landed property. When you called someone 'a gentleman' you were not paying him a compliment, but merely stating a fact. If you said he was not 'a gentleman' you were not insulting him, but giving information. There was no contradiction in saying that John was a liar and a gentleman; any more than there now is in saying that James is a fool and an M.A. But then there came people who said—so rightly, charitably, spiritually, sensitively, so anything but usefully—'Ah, but surely the important thing about a gentleman is not the coat of arms and the land, but the behaviour? Surely he is the true gentleman who behaves as a gentleman should? Surely in that sense Edward is far more truly a gentleman than John?' They meant well. To be honourable and courteous and brave is of course a far better thing than to have a coat of arms. But it is not the same thing. Worse still, it is not a thing everyone will agree about. To call a man 'a gentleman' in this new, refined sense, becomes, in fact, not a way of giving information about him, but a way of praising him: to deny that he is 'a gentleman' becomes simply a way of insulting him. When a word ceases to be a term of description and becomes merely a term of praise, it no longer tells you facts about the object: it only tells you about the speaker's attitude to that object. (A 'nice' meal only means a meal the speaker likes.) A *gentleman,* once it has been spiritualised and refined out of its old coarse, objective sense, means hardly more than a man whom the speaker likes. As a result, *gentleman* is now a useless word. We had lots of terms of approval already, so it was not needed for that use; on the other hand if anyone (say, in a historical work) wants to use it in its old sense, he cannot do so without explanations. It has been spoiled for that purpose.

Now if once we allow people to start spiritualising and refining, or as they might say 'deepening', the sense of the word *Christian*, it too will speedily become a useless word. In the first place, Christians themselves will never be able to apply it to anyone. It is not for us to say who, in the deepest sense, is or is not close to the spirit of Christ. We do not see into men's hearts. We cannot judge, and are indeed forbidden to judge. It would be wicked arrogance for us to say that any man is, or is not, a Christian in this refined sense. And obviously a word which we can never apply is not going to be a very useful word. As for the unbelievers, they will no doubt cheerfully use the word in the refined sense. It will become in their mouths simply a term of praise. In calling anyone a Christian they will mean that they think him a good man. But that way of using the word will be no enrichment of the language, for we already have the word *good*. Meanwhile, the word *Christian* will have been spoiled for any really useful purpose it might have served.

We must therefore stick to the original, obvious meaning. The name *Christians* was first given at Antioch (Acts 11:26) to 'the disciples', to those who accepted the teaching of the apostles. There is no question of its being restricted to those who profited by that teaching as much as they should have. There is no question of its being extended to those who in some refined, spiritual, inward fashion were 'far closer to the spirit of Christ' than the less satisfactory of the disciples. The point is not a theological or moral one. It is only a question of using words so that we can all understand what is being said. When a man who accepts the Christian doctrine lives unworthily of it, it is much clearer to say he is a bad Christian than to say he is not a Christian.

I hope no reader will suppose that 'mere' Christianity is here put forward as an alternative to the creeds of the existing communions—as if a man could adopt it in preference to Congregationalism or Greek Orthodoxy or anything else. It is more like a hall out of which doors open into several rooms. If I can bring anyone into that hall I shall have done what I attempted. But it is in the rooms, not in the hall, that there are fires and chairs and meals. The hall is a place to wait in, a place from which to try the various doors, not a place to live in. For that purpose the worst of the rooms (whichever that may be) is, I think, preferable. It is true that some people may find they have to wait in the hall for a considerable time, while others feel certain almost at once which door they must knock at. I do not know why there is this difference, but I am sure God keeps no one waiting unless He sees that it is good for him to wait. When you do get into your room you will find that the long wait has done you some kind of good which you would not have had otherwise. But you must regard it as waiting, not as camping. You must keep on praying for light: and, of course, even in the hall, you must begin trying to obey the rules which are common to the whole house. And above all you must be asking which door is the true one; not which pleases you best by its paint and panelling. In plain language, the question should never be: 'Do I like that kind of service?' but 'Are these doctrines true: Is holiness here? Does my conscience move me towards this? Is my reluctance to knock at this door due to my pride, or my mere taste, or my personal dislike of this particular door-keeper?'

When you have reached your own room, be kind to those who have chosen different doors and to those who are still in the hall. If they are wrong they need your prayers all the more; and if they are your enemies, then you are under orders to pray for them. That is one of the rules common to the whole house.

BOOK ONE

Right and Wrong as a Clue to the Meaning of the Universe

I

THE LAW OF HUMAN NATURE

EVERY ONE HAS heard people quarrelling. Sometimes it sounds funny and sometimes it sounds merely unpleasant; but however it sounds, I believe we can learn something very important from listening to the kind of things they say. They say things like this: 'How'd you like it if anyone did the same to you?'—'That's my seat, I was there first'—'Leave him alone, he isn't doing you any harm'—'Why should you shove in first?'—'Give me a bit of your orange, I gave you a bit of mine'—'Come on, you promised.' People say things like that every day, educated people as well as uneducated, and children as well as grown-ups.

Now what interests me about all these remarks is that the man who makes them is not merely saying that the other man's behaviour does not happen to please him. He is appealing to some kind of standard of behaviour which he expects the other man to know about. And the other man very seldom replies: 'To hell with your standard.' Nearly always he tries to make out that what he has been doing does not really go against the standard, or that if it does there is some special excuse. He pretends there is some special reason in this particular case why the person who took the seat first should not keep it, or that things were quite different when he was given the bit of orange, or that something has turned up which lets him off keeping his promise. It looks, in fact, very much as if both parties had in mind some kind of Law or Rule of fair play or decent behaviour or morality or whatever you like to call it, about which they really agreed. And they have. If they had not, they might, of course, fight like animals, but they could not quarrel in the human sense of the word.

Quarrelling means trying to show that the other man is in the wrong. And there would be no sense in trying to do that unless you and he had some sort of agreement as to what Right and Wrong are; just as there would be no sense in saying that a footballer had committed a foul unless there was some agreement about the rules of football.

Now this Law or Rule about Right and Wrong used to be called the Law of Nature. Nowadays, when we talk of the 'laws of nature' we usually mean things like gravitation, or heredity, or the laws of chemistry. But when the older thinkers called the Law of Right and Wrong 'the Law of Nature', they really meant the Law of Human Nature. The idea was that, just as all bodies are governed by the law of gravitation, and organisms by biological laws, so the creature called man also had his law— with this great difference, that a body could not choose whether it obeyed the law of gravitation or not, but a man could choose either to obey the Law of Human Nature or to disobey it.

We may put this in another way. Each man is at every moment subjected to several different sets of law but there is only one of these which he is free to disobey. As a body, he is subjected to gravitation and cannot disobey it; if you leave him unsupported in mid-air, he has no more choice about falling than a stone has. As an organism, he is subjected to various biological laws which he cannot disobey any more than an animal can. That is, he cannot disobey those laws which he shares with other things; but the law which is peculiar to his human nature, the law he does not share with animals or vegetables or inorganic things, is the one he can disobey if he chooses.

This law was called the Law of Nature because people thought that every one knew it by nature and did not need to be taught it. They did not mean, of course, that you might not find an odd individual here and there who did not know it, just as you find a few people who are colour-blind or have no ear for a tune. But taking the race as a whole, they thought that the human idea of decent behaviour was obvious to every one. And I believe they were right. If they were not, then all the things we said about the war were nonsense. What was the sense in saying the enemy were in the wrong unless Right is a real thing which the Nazis at bottom knew as well as we did and ought to have practised? If they had had no notion of what we mean by right, then, though we might still have had to fight them, we could no more have blamed them for that than for the colour of their hair.

I know that some people say the idea of a Law of Nature or decent behaviour known to all men is unsound, because different civilisations and different ages have had quite different moralities.

But this is not true. There have been differences between their moralities, but these have never amounted to anything like a total difference. If anyone will take the trouble to compare the moral teaching of, say, the ancient Egyptians, Babylonians, Hindus, Chinese, Greeks and Romans, what will really strike him will be how very like they are to each other and to our own. Some of the evidence for this I have put together in the appendix of another book called *The Abolition of Man;* but for our present purpose I need only ask the reader to think what a totally different morality would mean. Think of a country where people were admired for running away in battle, or where a man felt proud of double-crossing all the people who had been kindest to him. You might just as well try to imagine a country where two and two made five. Men have differed as regards what people you ought to be unselfish to—whether it was only your own family, or your fellow countrymen, or every one. But they have always agreed that you ought not to put yourself first. Selfishness has never been admired. Men have differed as to whether you should have one wife or four. But they have always agreed that you must not simply have any woman you liked.

But the most remarkable thing is this. Whenever you find a man who says he does not believe in a real Right and Wrong, you will find the same man going back on this a moment later. He may break his promise to you, but if you try breaking one to him he will be complaining 'It's not fair' before you can say Jack Robinson. A nation may say treaties don't matter; but then, next minute, they spoil their case by saying that the particular treaty they want to break was an unfair one. But if treaties do not matter, and if there is no such thing as Right and Wrong—in other words, if there is no Law of Nature—what is the difference between a fair treaty and an unfair one? Have they not let the cat out of the bag and shown that, whatever they say, they really know the Law of Nature just like anyone else?

It seems, then, we are forced to believe in a real Right and Wrong. People may be sometimes mistaken about them, just as people sometimes get their sums wrong; but they are not a matter of mere taste and opinion any more than the multiplication table. Now if we are agreed about that, I go on to my next point, which is this. None of us are really keeping the Law of Nature. If there are any exceptions among you, I apologise to them. They had much better read some other book, for nothing I am going to say concerns them. And now, turning to the ordinary human beings who are left:

I hope you will not misunderstand what I am going to say. I am not preaching, and Heaven knows I do not pretend to be better than anyone else. I am only trying to call attention to a fact; the fact that this year, or this month, or, more likely, this very day, we have failed to practise ourselves the kind of behaviour we expect from other people. There may be all sorts of excuses for us. That time you were so unfair to the children was when you were very tired. That slightly shady business about the money—the one you have almost forgotten—came when you were very hard-up. And what you promised to do for old So-and-so and have never done—well, you never would have promised if you had known how frightfully busy you were going to be. And as for your behaviour to your wife (or husband) or sister (or brother) if I knew how irritating they could be, I would not wonder at it—and who the dickens am I, anyway? I am just the same. That is to say, I do not succeed in keeping the Law of Nature very well, and the moment anyone tells me I am not keeping it, there starts up in my mind a string of excuses as long as your arm. The question at the moment is not whether they are good excuses. The point is that they are one more proof of how deeply, whether we like it or not, we believe in the Law of Nature. If we do not believe in decent behaviour, why should we be so anxious to make excuses for not having behaved decently? The truth is, we believe in decency so much—we feel the Rule of Law pressing on us so—that we cannot bear to face the fact that we are breaking it, and consequently we try to shift the responsibility. For you notice that it is only for our bad behaviour that we find all these explanations. It is only our bad temper that we put down to being tired or worried or hungry; we put our good temper down to ourselves.

These, then, are the two points I wanted to make. First, that human beings, all over the earth, have this curious idea that they ought to behave in a certain way, and cannot really get rid of it. Secondly, that they do not in fact behave in that way. They know the Law of Nature; they break it. These two facts are the foundation of all clear thinking about ourselves and the universe we live in.

2

SOME OBJECTIONS

IF THEY ARE the foundation, I had better stop to make that foundation firm before I go on. Some of the letters I have had show that a good many people find it difficult to understand just what this Law of Human Nature, or Moral Law, or Rule of Decent Behaviour is.

For example, some people wrote to me saying, 'Isn't what you call the Moral Law simply our herd instinct and hasn't it been developed just like all our other instincts?' Now I do not deny that we may have a herd instinct: but that is not what I mean by the Moral Law. We all know what it feels like to be prompted by instinct—by mother love, or sexual instinct, or the instinct for food. It means that you feel a strong want or desire to act in a certain way. And, of course, we sometimes do feel just that sort of desire to help another person: and no doubt that desire is due to the herd instinct. But feeling a desire to help is quite different from feeling that you ought to help whether you want to or not. Supposing you hear a cry for help from a man in danger. You will probably feel two desires—one a desire to give help (due to your herd instinct), the other a desire to keep out of danger (due to the instinct for self-preservation). But you will find inside you, in addition to these two impulses, a third thing which tells you that you ought to follow the impulse to help, and suppress the impulse to run away. Now this thing that judges between two instincts, that decides which should be encouraged, cannot itself be either of them. You might as well say that the sheet of music which tells you, at a given moment, to play one note on the piano and not another, is itself one of the notes on the keyboard. The Moral Law tells us the tune we have to play: our instincts are merely the keys.

Another way of seeing that the Moral Law is not simply one of our instincts is this. If two instincts are in conflict, and there is nothing in a creature's mind except those two instincts, obviously the stronger of the two must win. But at those moments when we are most conscious of the Moral Law, it usually seems to be telling us to side with the weaker of the two impulses. You probably *want* to be safe much more than you want to help the man who is drowning: but the Moral Law tells you to help him all the same. And surely it often tells us to try to make the right impulse stronger than it naturally is? I mean, we often feel it our duty to stimulate the herd instinct, by waking up our imaginations and arousing our pity and so on, so as to get up enough steam for doing the right thing. But clearly we are not acting *from* instinct when we set about making an instinct stronger than it is. The thing that says to you, 'Your herd instinct is asleep. Wake it up,' cannot itself *be* the herd instinct. The thing that tells you which note on the piano needs to be played louder cannot itself be that note.

Here is a third way of seeing it. If the Moral Law was one of our instincts, we ought to be able to point to some one impulse inside us which was always what we call 'good,' always in agreement with the rule of right behaviour. But you cannot. There is none of our impulses which the Moral Law may not sometimes tell us to suppress, and none which it may not sometimes tell us to encourage. It is a mistake to think that some of our impulses—say mother love or patriotism—are good, and others, like sex or the fighting instinct, are bad. All we mean is that the occasions on which the fighting instinct or the sexual desire need to be restrained are rather more frequent than those for restraining mother love or patriotism. But there are situations in which it is the duty of a married man to encourage his sexual impulse and of a soldier to encourage the fighting instinct. There are also occasions on which a mother's love for her own children or a man's love for his own country have to be suppressed or they will lead to unfairness towards other people's children or countries. Strictly speaking, there are no such things as good and bad impulses. Think once again of a piano. It has not got two kinds of notes on it, the 'right' notes and the 'wrong' ones. Every single note is right at one time and wrong at another. The Moral Law is not any one instinct or set of instincts: it is something which makes a kind of tune (the tune we call goodness or right conduct) by directing the instincts.

By the way, the point is of great practical consequence. The most dangerous thing you can do is to take any one impulse of your own nature and set it up as the thing you ought to follow at all costs. There is not one of them which will not make us into devils if we set it up as an absolute guide. You might think love of humanity in general was safe, but it is not. If you leave out justice you will find yourself breaking agreements and faking evidence in trials 'for the sake of humanity', and become in the end a cruel and treacherous man.

Other people wrote to me saying, 'Isn't what you call the Moral Law just a social convention, something that is put into us by education?' I think there is a misunderstanding here. The people who ask that question are usually taking it for granted that if we have learned a thing from parents and teachers, then that thing must be merely a human invention. But, of course, that is not so. We all learned the multiplication table at school. A child who grew up alone on a desert island would not know it. But surely it does not follow that the multiplication table is simply a human convention, something human beings have made up for themselves and might have made different if they had liked? I fully agree that we learn the Rule of Decent Behaviour from parents and teachers, and friends and books, as we learn everything else. But some of the things we learn are mere conventions which might have been different—we learn to keep to the left of the road, but it might just as well have been the rule to keep to the right—and others of them, like mathematics, are real truths. The question is to which class the Law of Human Nature belongs.

There are two reasons for saying it belongs to the same class as mathematics. The first is, as I said in the first chapter, that though there are differences between the moral ideas of one time or country and those of another, the differences are not really very great—not nearly so great as most people imagine—and you can recognise the same law running through them all: whereas mere conventions, like the rule of the road or the kind of clothes people wear, may differ to any extent. The other reason is this. When you think about these differences between the morality of one people and another, do you think that the morality of one people is ever better or worse than that of another? Have any of the changes been improvements? If not, then of course there could never be any moral progress. Progress means not just changing, but changing for the better. If no set of moral ideas were truer or better than any other, there would be no sense in preferring civilised morality to savage morality, or Christian morality to Nazi morality. In fact, of course, we all do believe that some moralities are better than others. We do believe that some of the people who tried to change the moral ideas of their own age were what we would call Reformers or Pioneers—people who understood morality better than their neighbours did. Very well then. The moment you say that one set of moral ideas can be better than another, you are, in fact, measuring them both by a standard, saying that one of them conforms to that standard more nearly than the other. But the standard that measures two things is something different from either. You are, in fact, comparing them both with some Real Morality, admitting that there is such a thing as a real Right, independent of what people think, and that some people's ideas get nearer to that real Right than others. Or put it this way. If your moral ideas can be truer, and those of the Nazis less true, there must be something—some Real Morality—for them to be true about. The reason why your idea of New York can be truer or less true than mine is that New York is a real place, existing quite apart from what either of us thinks. If when each of us said 'New York' each means merely 'The town I am imagining in my own head', how could one of us have truer ideas than the other? There would be no question of truth or falsehood at all. In the same way, if the Rule of Decent Behaviour meant simply 'whatever each nation happens to approve', there would be no sense in saying that any one nation had ever been more correct in its approval than any other; no sense in saying that the world could ever grow morally better or morally worse.

I conclude then, that though the difference between people's ideas of Decent Behaviour often make you suspect that there is no real natural Law of Behaviour at all, yet the things we are bound to think about these differences really prove just the opposite. But one word before I end. I have met people who exaggerate the differences, because they have not distinguished between differences of morality and differences of belief about facts. For example, one man said to me, 'Three hundred years ago people in England were putting witches to death. Was that what you call the Rule of Human Nature or Right Conduct?' But surely the reason we do not execute witches is that we do not believe there are such things. If we did—if we really thought that there were people going about who had sold themselves to the devil and received supernatural powers from him in return and were using these powers to kill their neighbours or drive them mad or bring bad weather—surely we would all agree that if anyone deserved the death penalty, then these filthy quislings did? There is no difference of moral principle here: the difference is simply about matter of fact. It may be a great advance in knowledge not to believe in witches: there is no moral advance in not executing them when you do not think they are there. You would not call a man humane for ceasing to set mousetraps if he did so because he believed there were no mice in the house.

3

THE REALITY OF THE LAW

I NOW GO back to what I said at the end of the first chapter, that there were two odd things about the human race. First, that they were haunted by the idea of a sort of behaviour they ought to practise, what you might call fair play, or decency, or morality, or the Law of Nature. Second, that they did not in fact do so. Now some of you may wonder why I called this odd. It may seem to you the most natural thing in the world. In particular, you may have thought I was rather hard on the human race. After all, you may say, what I call breaking the Law of Right and Wrong or of Nature, only means that people are not perfect. And why on earth should I expect them to be? That would be a good answer if what I was trying to do was to fix the exact amount of blame which is due to us for not behaving as we expect others to behave. But that is not my job at all. I am not concerned at present with blame; I am trying to find out truth. And from that point of view the very idea of something being imperfect, of its not being what it ought to be, has certain consequences.

If you take a thing like a stone or a tree, it is what it is and there seems no sense in saying it ought to have been otherwise. Of course you may say a stone is 'the wrong shape' if you want to use it for a rockery, or that a tree is a bad tree because it does not give you as much shade as you expected. But all you mean is that the stone or the tree does not happen to be convenient for some purpose of your own. You are not, except as a joke, blaming them for that. You really know, that, given the weather and the soil, the tree could not have been any different. What we, from our point of view, call a 'bad' tree is obeying the laws of its nature just as much as a 'good' one.

Now have you noticed what follows? It follows that what we usually call the laws of nature—the way weather works on a tree for example—may not really be *laws* in the strict sense, but only in a manner of speaking. When you say that falling stones always obey the law of gravitation, is not this much the same as saying that the law only means 'what stones always do'? You do not really think that when a stone is let go, it suddenly remembers that it is under orders to fall to the ground. You only mean that, in fact, it does fall. In other words, you cannot be sure that there is anything over and above the facts themselves, any law about what ought to happen, as distinct from what does happen. The laws of nature, as applied to stones or trees, may only mean 'what Nature, in fact, does'. But if you turn to the Law of Human Nature, the Law of Decent Behaviour, it is a different matter. That law certainly does not mean 'what human beings, in fact, do'; for as I said before, many of them do not obey this law at all, and none of them obey it completely. The law of gravity tells you what stones do if you drop them; but the Law of Human Nature tells you what human beings ought to do and do not. In other words, when you are dealing with humans, something else comes in above and beyond the actual facts. You have the facts (how men do behave) and you also have something else (how they ought to behave). In the rest of the universe there need not be anything but the facts. Electrons and molecules behave in a certain way, and certain results follow, and that may be the whole story.* But men behave in a certain way and that is not the whole story, for all the time you know that they ought to behave differently.

Now this is really so peculiar that one is tempted to try to explain it away. For instance, we might try to make out that when you say a man ought not to act as he does, you only mean the same as when you say that a stone is the wrong shape; namely, that what he is doing happens to be inconvenient to you. But that is simply untrue. A man occupying the corner seat in the train because he got there first, and a man who slipped into it while my back was turned and removed my bag, are both equally inconvenient. But I blame the second man and do not blame the first. I am not

---

* I do not think it is the whole story, as you will see later. I mean that, as far as the argument has gone up to date, it may be.

angry—except perhaps for a moment before I come to my senses—with a man who trips me up by accident; I am angry with a man who tries to trip me up even if he does not succeed. Yet the first has hurt me and the second has not. Sometimes the behaviour which I call bad is not inconvenient to me at all, but the very opposite. In war, each side may find a traitor on the other side very useful. But though they use him and pay him they regard him as human vermin. So you cannot say that what we call decent behaviour in others is simply the behaviour that happens to be useful to us. And as for decent behaviour in ourselves, I suppose it is pretty obvious that it does not mean the behaviour that pays. It means things like being content with thirty shillings when you might have got three pounds, doing school work honestly when it would be easy to cheat, leaving a girl alone when you would like to make love to her, staying in dangerous places when you would rather go somewhere safer, keeping promises you would rather not keep, and telling the truth even when it makes you look a fool.

Some people say that though decent conduct does not mean what pays each particular person at a particular moment, still, it means what pays the human race as a whole; and that consequently there is no mystery about it. Human beings, after all, have some sense; they see that you cannot have any real safety or happiness except in a society where every one plays fair, and it is because they see this that they try to behave decently. Now, of course, it is perfectly true that safety and happiness can only come from individuals, classes, and nations being honest and fair and kind to each other. It is one of the most important truths in the world. But as an explanation of why we feel as we do about Right and Wrong it just misses the point. If we ask: 'Why ought I to be unselfish?' and you reply 'Because it is good for society,' we may then ask, 'Why should I care what's good for society except when it happens to pay *me* personally?' and then you will have to say, 'Because you ought to be unselfish'—which simply brings us back to where we started. You are saying what is true, but you are not getting any further. If a man asked what was the point of playing football, it would not be much good saying 'in order to score goals', for trying to score goals is the game itself, not the reason for the game, and you would really only be saying that football was football—which is true, but not worth saying. In the same way, if a man asks what is the point of behaving decently, it is no good replying, 'in order to benefit society', for trying to benefit society, in other words being unselfish (for 'society' after all only means 'other people'), is one of the things decent behaviour consists in; all you are really saying is that decent behaviour is decent behaviour. You would have said just as much if you had stopped at the statement, 'Men ought to be unselfish.'

And that is where I do stop. Men ought to be unselfish, ought to be fair. Not that men are unselfish, not that they like being unselfish, but that they ought to be. The Moral Law, or Law of Human Nature, is not simply a fact about human behaviour in the same way as the Law of Gravitation is, or may be, simply a fact about how heavy objects behave. On the other hand, it is not a mere fancy, for we cannot get rid of the idea, and most of the things we say and think about men would be reduced to nonsense if we did. And it is not simply a statement about how we should like men to behave for our own convenience; for the behaviour we call bad or unfair is not exactly the same as the behaviour we find inconvenient, and may even be the opposite. Consequently, this Rule of Right and Wrong, or Law of Human Nature, or whatever you call it, must somehow or other be a real thing—a thing that is really there, not made up by ourselves. And yet it is not a fact in the ordinary sense, in the same way as our actual behaviour is a fact. It begins to look as if we shall have to admit that there is more than one kind of reality; that, in this particular case, there is something above and beyond the ordinary facts of men's behaviour, and yet quite definitely real—a real law, which none of us made, but which we find pressing on us.

4

WHAT LIES BEHIND THE LAW

LET US SUM UP what we have reached so far. In the case of stones and trees and things of that sort, what we call the Laws of Nature may not be anything except a way of speaking. When you say that nature is governed by certain laws, this may only mean that nature does, in fact, behave in a certain way. The so-called laws may not be anything real—anything above and beyond the actual facts which we observe. But in the case of Man, we saw that this will not do. The Law of Human Nature, or of Right and Wrong, must be something above and beyond the actual facts of human behaviour. In this case, besides the actual facts, you have something else—a real law which we did not invent and which we know we ought to obey.

I now want to consider what this tells us about the universe we live in. Ever since men were able to think they have been wondering what this universe really is and how it came to be there. And, very roughly, two views have been held. First, there is what is called the materialist view. People who take that view think that matter and space just happen to exist, and always have existed, nobody knows why; and that the matter, behaving in certain fixed ways, has just happened, by a sort of fluke, to produce creatures like ourselves who are able to think. By one chance in a thousand something hit our sun and made it produce the planets; and by another thousandth chance the chemicals necessary for life, and the right temperature, occurred on one of these planets, and so some of the matter on this earth came alive; and then, by a very long series of chances, the living creatures developed into things like us. The other view is the religious view.* According to it, what is behind the universe is more like a mind than it is like anything else we know. That is to say, it is conscious, and has purposes, and prefers one thing to another. And on this view it made the universe, partly for purposes we do not know, but partly, at any rate, in order to produce creatures like itself—I mean, like itself to the extent of having minds. Please do not think that one of these views was held a long time ago and that the other has gradually taken its place. Wherever there have been thinking men both views turn up. And note this too. You cannot find out which view is the right one by science in the ordinary sense. Science works by experiments. It watches how things behave. Every scientific statement in the long run, however complicated it looks, really means something like, 'I pointed the telescope to such and such a part of the sky at 2.20 a.m. on January 15th and saw so-and-so,' or, 'I put some of this stuff in a pot and heated it to such-and-such a temperature and it did so-and-so.' Do not think I am saying anything against science: I am only saying what its job is. And the more scientific a man is, the more (I believe) he would agree with me that this is the job of science—and a very useful and necessary job it is too. But why anything comes to be there at all, and whether there is anything behind the things science observes—something of a different kind—this is not a scientific question. If there is 'Something Behind', then either it will have to remain altogether unknown to men or else make itself known in some different way. The statement that there is any such thing, and the statement that there is no such thing, are neither of them statements that science can make. And real scientists do not usually make them. It is usually the journalists and popular novelists who have picked up a few odds and ends of half-baked science from textbooks who go in for them. After all, it is really a matter of common sense. Supposing science ever became complete so that it knew every single thing in the whole universe. Is it not plain that the questions, 'Why is there a universe?' 'Why does it go on as it does?' 'Has it any meaning?' would remain just as they were?

Now the position would be quite hopeless but for this. There is one thing, and only one, in the whole universe which we know more about than we could learn from external observation. That one thing is Man. We do not merely observe men, we *are* men. In this case we have, so to speak, inside information; we are in the know. And because of that, we

---

* See Note at end of this chapter.

know that men find themselves under a moral law, which they did not make, and cannot quite forget even when they try, and which they know they ought to obey. Notice the following point. Anyone studying Man from the outside as we study electricity or cabbages, not knowing our language and consequently not able to get any inside knowledge from us, but merely observing what we did, would never get the slightest evidence that we had this moral law. How could he? for his observations would only show what we did, and the moral law is about what we ought to do. In the same way, if there were anything above or behind the observed facts in the case of stones or the weather, we, by studying them from outside, could never hope to discover it.

The position of the question, then, is like this. We want to know whether the universe simply happens to be what it is for no reason or whether there is a power behind it that makes it what it is. Since that power, if it exists, would be not one of the observed facts but a reality which makes them, no mere observation of the facts can find it. There is only one case in which we can know whether there is anything more, namely our own case. And in that one case we find there is. Or put it the other way round. If there was a controlling power outside the universe, it could not show itself to us as one of the facts inside the universe—no more than the architect of a house could actually be a wall or staircase or fireplace in that house. The only way in which we could expect it to show itself would be inside ourselves as an influence or a command trying to get us to behave in a certain way. And that is just what we do find inside ourselves. Surely this ought to arouse our suspicions? In the only case where you can expect to get an answer, the answer turns out to be Yes; and in the other cases, where you do not get an answer, you see why you do not. Suppose someone asked me, when I see a man in blue uniform going down the street leaving little paper packets at each house, why I suppose that they contain letters? I should reply, 'Because whenever he leaves a similar little packet for me I find it does contain a letter.' And if he then objected— 'But you've never seen all these letters which you think the other people are getting,' I should say, 'Of course not, and I shouldn't expect to, because they're not addressed to me. I'm explaining the packets I'm not allowed to open by the ones I am allowed to open.' It is the same about this question. The only packet I am allowed to open is Man. When I do, especially when I open that particular man called Myself, I find that I do not exist on my own, that I am under a law; that somebody or something wants me to behave in a certain way. I do not, of course, think that if I could get inside a stone or a tree I should find exactly the same thing, just as I do not think all the other people in the street get the same letters as I do. I should expect, for instance, to find that the stone had to obey the law of gravity—that whereas the sender of the letters merely tells me to obey the law of my human nature, he compels the stone to obey the laws of its stony nature. But I should expect to find that there was, so to speak, a sender of letters in both cases, a Power behind the facts, a Director, a Guide.

Do not think I am going faster than I really am. I am not yet within a hundred miles of the God of Christian theology. All I have got to is a Something which is directing the universe, and which appears in me as a law urging me to do right and making me feel responsible and uncomfortable when I do wrong. I think we have to assume it is more like a mind than it is like anything else we know—because after all the only other thing we know is matter and you can hardly imagine a bit of matter giving instructions. But, of course, it need not be very like a mind, still less like a person. In the next chapter we shall see if we can find out anything more about it. But one word of warning. There has been a great deal of soft soap talked about God for the last hundred years. That is not what I am offering. You can cut all that out.

NOTE: In order to keep this section short enough when it was given on the air, I mentioned only the Materialist view and the Religious view. But to be complete I ought to mention the In-between view called Life-Force philosophy, or Creative Evolution, or Emergent Evolution. The wittiest expositions of it come in the works of Bernard Shaw, but the most profound ones in those of Bergson. People who hold this view say that the small variations by which life on this planet 'evolved' from the lowest forms to Man were not due to chance but to the 'striving' or 'purposiveness' of a Life-Force. When people say this we must ask them whether by Life-Force they mean something with a mind or not. If they do, then 'a mind bringing life into existence and leading it to perfection' is really a God, and their view is thus identical with the Religious. If they do not, then what is the sense in saying that something without a mind 'strives' or has 'purposes'? This seems to me fatal to their view. One reason why many people find Creative Evolution so attractive is that it gives one much of the emotional comfort of believing in God and none of the less pleasant consequences. When you are feeling fit and the sun is shining and you do not want to believe that the whole universe is a mere mechanical dance of atoms, it is nice to be able to think of this great mysterious Force rolling on through the centuries and carrying you on its crest. If, on the other hand, you want to do something rather shabby, the Life-Force, being only a blind force, with no morals and no mind, will never interfere with you like that troublesome God we learned about when we were children. The Life-Force is a sort of tame God. You can switch it on when you want, but it will not bother you. All the thrills of religion and none of the cost. Is the Life-Force the greatest achievement of wishful thinking the world has yet seen?

5

WE HAVE CAUSE
TO BE UNEASY

I ENDED MY last chapter with the idea that in the Moral Law somebody or something from beyond the material universe was actually getting at us. And I expect when I reached that point some of you felt a certain annoyance. You may even have thought that I had played a trick on you— that I had been carefully wrapping up to look like philosophy what turns out to be one more 'religious jaw'. You may have felt you were ready to listen to me as long as you thought I had anything new to say; but if it turns out to be only religion, well, the world has tried that and you cannot put the clock back. If anyone is feeling that way I should like to say three things to him.

First, as to putting the clock back. Would you think I was joking if I said that you can put a clock back, and that if the clock is wrong it is often a very sensible thing to do? But I would rather get away from that whole idea of clocks. We all want progress. But progress means getting nearer to the place where you want to be. And if you have taken a wrong turning, then to go forward does not get you any nearer. If you are on the wrong road, progress means doing an about-turn and walking back to the right road; and in that case the man who turns back soonest is the most progressive man. We have all seen this when doing arithmetic. When I have started a sum the wrong way, the sooner I admit this and go back and start again, the faster I shall get on. There is nothing progressive about being pig headed and refusing to admit a mistake. And I think if you look at the present state of the world, it is pretty plain that humanity has been making some big mistake. We are on the wrong road. And if that is so, we must go back. Going back is the quickest way on.

Then, secondly, this has not yet turned exactly into a 'religious jaw'. We have not yet got as far as the God of any actual religion, still less the God of that particular religion called Christianity. We have only got as far as a Somebody or Something behind the Moral Law. We are not taking anything from the Bible or the Churches, we are trying to see what we can find out about this Somebody on our own steam. And I want to make it quite clear that what we find out on our own steam is something that gives us a shock. We have two bits of evidence about the Somebody. One is the universe He has made. If we used that as our only clue, then I think we should have to conclude that He was a great artist (for the universe is a very beautiful place), but also that He is quite merciless and no friend to man (for the universe is a very dangerous and terrifying place). The other bit of evidence is that Moral Law which He has put into our minds. And this is a better bit of evidence than the other, because it is inside information. You find out more about God from the Moral Law than from the universe in general just as you find out more about a man by listening to his conversation than by looking at a house he has built. Now, from this second bit of evidence we conclude that the Being behind the universe is intensely interested in right conduct—in fair play, unselfishness, courage, good faith, honesty and truthfulness. In that sense we should agree with the account given by Christianity and some other religions, that God is 'good'. But do not let us go too fast here. The Moral Law does not give us any grounds for thinking that God is 'good' in the sense of being indulgent, or soft, or sympathetic. There is nothing indulgent about the Moral Law. It is as hard as nails. It tells you to do the straight thing and it does not seem to care how painful, or dangerous, or difficult it is to do. If God is like the Moral Law, then He is not soft. It is no use, at this stage, saying that what you mean by a 'good' God is a God who can forgive. You are going too quickly. Only a Person can forgive. And we have not yet got as far as a personal God—only as far as a power, behind the Moral Law, and more like a mind than it is like anything else. But it may still be very unlike a Person. If it is pure impersonal mind, there may be no sense in asking it to make allowances for you or let you off, just as there is no sense in asking the multiplication table to let you off when you do your sums wrong. You are bound to get the wrong answer. And it is no use either saying that if there is a God of that sort—an impersonal absolute goodness—then you do not like Him and are not going to bother about Him. For the trouble is that one part of you is on His side and really agrees with his disapproval of human greed and trickery and exploitation. You may want Him to make an exception in your own case, to let you off this one time; but you know at bottom that unless the power behind the world really and unalterably detests that sort of behaviour, then He cannot be good. On the other hand, we know that if there does exist an absolute goodness it must hate most of what we do. This is the terrible fix we are in. If the universe is not governed by an absolute goodness, then all our efforts are in the long run hopeless. But if it is, then we are making ourselves enemies to that goodness every day, and are not in the least likely to do any better tomorrow, and so our case is hopeless again. We cannot do without it, and we cannot do with it. God is the only comfort, He is also the supreme terror: the thing we most need and the thing we most want to hide from. He is our only possible ally, and we have made ourselves His enemies. Some people talk as if meeting the gaze of absolute goodness would be fun. They need to think again. They are still only playing with religion. Goodness is either the great safety or the great danger—according to the way you react to it. And we have reacted the wrong way.

Now my third point. When I chose to get to my real subject in this roundabout way, I was not trying to play any kind of trick on you. I had a different reason. My reason was that Christianity simply does not make sense until you have faced the sort of facts I have been describing. Christianity tells people to repent and promises them forgiveness. It therefore has nothing (as far as I know) to say to people who do not know they have done anything to repent of and who do not feel that they need any forgiveness. It is after you have realized that there is a real Moral Law, and a Power behind the law, and that you have broken that law and put yourself wrong with that Power—it is after all this, and not a moment sooner, that Christianity begins to talk. When you know you are sick, you will listen to the doctor. When you have realised that our position is nearly desperate you will begin to understand what the Christians are talking about. They offer an explanation of how we got into our present state of both hating goodness and loving it. They offer an explanation of how God can be this impersonal mind at the back of the Moral Law and yet also a Person. They tell you how the demands of this law, which you and I cannot meet, have been met on our behalf, how God Himself becomes a man to save man from the disapproval of God. It is an old story and if you want to go into it you will no doubt consult people who have more authority to talk about it than I have. All I am doing is to ask people to face the facts—to understand the questions which Christianity claims to answer. And they are very terrifying facts. I wish it was possible to say something more agreeable. But I must say what I think true. Of course, I quite agree that the Christian religion is, in the long run, a thing of unspeakable comfort. But it does not begin in comfort; it begins in the dismay I have been describing, and it is no use at all trying to go on to that comfort without first going through that dismay. In religion, as in war and everything else, comfort is the one thing you cannot get by looking for it. If you look for truth, you may find comfort in the end: if you look for comfort you will not get either comfort or truth—only soft soap and wishful thinking to begin with and, in the end, despair. Most of us have got over the pre-war wishful thinking about international politics. It is time we did the same about religion.

BOOK TWO

What Christians Believe

I

THE RIVAL CONCEPTIONS
OF GOD

I HAVE BEEN asked to tell you what Christians believe, and I am going to begin by telling you one thing that Christians do not need to believe. If you are a Christian you do not have to believe that all the other religions are simply wrong all through. If you are an atheist you do have to believe that the main point in all the religions of the whole world is simply one huge mistake. If you are a Christian, you are free to think that all those religions, even the queerest ones, contain at least some hint of the truth. When I was an atheist I had to try to persuade myself that most of the human race have always been wrong about the question that mattered to them most; when I became a Christian I was able to take a more liberal view. But, of course, being a Christian does mean thinking that where Christianity differs from other religions, Christianity is right and they are wrong. As in arithmetic—there is only one right answer to a sum, and all other answers are wrong; but some of the wrong answers are much nearer being right than others.

The first big division of humanity is into the majority, who believe in some kind of God or gods, and the minority who do not. On this point, Christianity lines up with the majority—lines up with ancient Greeks and Romans, modern savages, Stoics, Platonists, Hindus, Mohammedans, etc., against the modern Western European materialist.

Now I go on to the next big division. People who all believe in God can be divided according to the sort of God they believe in. There are two very different ideas on this subject. One of them is the idea that He is beyond good and evil. We humans call one thing good and another thing bad. But according to some people that is merely our human point of view. These people would say that the wiser you become the less you would want to call anything good or bad, and the more clearly you would see that everything is good in one way and bad in another, and that nothing could have been different. Consequently, these people think that long before you got anywhere near the divine point of view the distinction would have disappeared altogether. We call a cancer bad, they would say, because it kills a man; but you might just as well call a successful surgeon bad because he kills a cancer. It all depends on the point of view. The other and opposite idea is that God is quite definitely 'good' or 'righteous', a God who takes sides, who loves love and hates hatred, who wants us to behave in one way and not in another. The first of these views—the one that thinks God beyond good and evil—is called Pantheism. It was held by the great Prussian philosopher Hegel and, as far as I can understand them, by the Hindus. The other view is held by Jews, Mohammedans and Christians.

And with this big difference between Pantheism and the Christian idea of God, there usually goes another. Pantheists usually believe that God, so to speak, animates the universe as you animate your body: that the universe almost *is* God, so that if it did not exist He would not exist either, and anything you find in the universe is a part of God. The Christian idea is quite different. They think God invented and made the universe—like a man making a picture or composing a tune. A painter is not a picture, and he does not die if his picture is destroyed. You may say, 'He's put a lot of himself into it,' but you only mean that all its beauty and interest has come out of his head. His skill is not in the picture in the same way that it is in his head, or even in his hands. I expect you see how this difference between Pantheists and Christians hangs together with the other one. If you do not take the distinction between good and bad very seriously, then it is easy to say that anything you find in this world is a part of God. But, of course, if you think some things really bad, and God really good, then you cannot talk like that. You must believe that God is separate from the world and that some of the things we see in it are contrary to His will. Confronted with a cancer or a slum the Pantheist can say, 'If you could only see it from the divine point of view, you would realise that this also is God.' The Christian replies, 'Don't talk damned nonsense.'* For Christianity is a fighting religion. It thinks God made the world—that space and time, heat and cold, and all the colours and tastes, and all the animals and vegetables, are things that God 'made up out of His head' as a man makes up a story. But it also thinks that a great many things have gone wrong with the world that God made and that God insists, and insists very loudly, on our putting them right again.

And, of course, that raises a very big question. If a good God made the world why has it gone wrong? And for many years I simply refused to listen to the Christian answers to this question, because I kept on feeling 'whatever you say, and however clever your arguments are, isn't it much simpler and easier to say that the world was not made by any intelligent power? Aren't all your arguments simply a complicated attempt to avoid the obvious?' But then that threw me back into another difficulty.

My argument against God was that the universe seemed so cruel and unjust. But how had I got this idea of *just* and *unjust*? A man does not call a line crooked unless he has some idea of a straight line. What was I comparing this universe with when I called it unjust? If the whole show was bad and senseless from A to Z, so to speak, why did I, who was supposed to be part of the show, find myself in such violent reaction against it? A man feels wet when he falls into water, because man is not a water animal: a fish would not feel wet. Of course I could have given up my idea of justice by saying it was nothing but a private idea of my own. But if I did that, then my argument against God collapsed too—for the argument depended on saying that the world was really unjust, not simply that it did not happen to please my fancies. Thus in the very act of trying to prove that God did not exist—in other words, that the whole of reality was senseless—I found I was forced to assume that one part of reality—namely my idea of justice—was full of sense. Consequently atheism turns out to be too simple. If the whole universe has no meaning, we should never have found out that it has no meaning: just as, if there were no light in the universe and therefore no creatures with eyes, we should never know it was dark. *Dark* would be a word without meaning.

---

* One listener complained of the word *damned* as frivolous swearing. But I mean exactly what I say—nonsense that is *damned* is under God's curse, and will (apart from God's grace) lead those who believe it to eternal death.

2

THE INVASION

VERY WELL THEN, atheism is too simple. And I will tell you another view that is also too simple. It is the view I call Christianity-and-water, the view which simply says there is a good God in Heaven and everything is all right—leaving out all the difficult and terrible doctrines about sin and hell and the devil, and the redemption. Both these are boys' philosophies.

It is no good asking for a simple religion. After all, real things are not simple. They look simple, but they are not. The table I am sitting at looks simple: but ask a scientist to tell you what it is really made of—all about the atoms and how the light waves rebound from them and hit my eye and what they do to the optic nerve and what it does to my brain—and, of course, you find that what we call 'seeing a table' lands you in mysteries and complications which you can hardly get to the end of. A child saying a child's prayer looks simple. And if you are content to stop there, well and good. But if you are not—and the modern world usually is not—if you want to go on and ask what is really happening—then you must be prepared for something difficult. If we ask for something more than simplicity, it is silly then to complain that the something more is not simple.

Very often, however, this silly procedure is adopted by people who are not silly, but who, consciously or unconsciously, want to destroy Christianity. Such people put up a version of Christianity suitable for a child of six and make that the object of their attack. When you try to explain the Christian doctrine as it is really held by an instructed adult, they then complain that you are making their heads turn round and that it is all too complicated and that if there really were a God they are sure He would have made 'religion' simple, because simplicity is so beautiful, etc. You must be on your guard against these people for they will change their ground every minute and only waste your time. Notice, too, their idea of God 'making religion simple'; as if 'religion' were something God invented, and not His statement to us of certain quite unalterable facts about His own nature.

Besides being complicated, reality, in my experience, is usually odd. It is not neat, not obvious, not what you expect. For instance, when you have grasped that the earth and the other planets all go round the sun, you would naturally expect that all the planets were made to match— all at equal distances from each other, say, or distances that regularly increased, or all the same size, or else getting bigger or smaller as you go further from the sun. In fact, you find no rhyme or reason (that we can see) about either the sizes or the distances; and some of them have one moon, one has four, one has two, some have none, and one has a ring.

Reality, in fact, is usually something you could not have guessed. That is one of the reasons I believe Christianity. It is a religion you could not have guessed. If it offered us just the kind of universe we had always expected, I should feel we were making it up. But, in fact, it is not the sort of thing anyone would have made up. It has just that queer twist about it that real things have. So let us leave behind all these boys' philosophies— these over-simple answers. The problem is not simple and the answer is not going to be simple either.

What is the problem? A universe that contains much that is obviously bad and apparently meaningless, but containing creatures like ourselves who know that it is bad and meaningless. There are only two views that face all the facts. One is the Christian view that this is a good world that has gone wrong, but still retains the memory of what it ought to have been. The other is the view called Dualism. Dualism means the belief that there are two equal and independent powers at the back of everything, one of them good and the other bad, and that this universe is the battlefield in which they fight out an endless war. I personally think that next to Christianity Dualism is the manliest and most sensible creed on the market. But it has a catch in it.

The two powers, or spirits, or gods—the good one and the bad one— are supposed to be quite independent. They both existed from all eternity. Neither of them made the other, neither of them has any more right than the other to call itself God. Each presumably thinks it is good and thinks the other bad. One of them likes hatred and cruelty, the other likes love and mercy, and each backs its own view. Now what do we mean when we call one of them the Good Power and the other the Bad Power? Either we are merely saying that we happen to prefer the one to the other—like preferring beer to cider—or else we are saying that, whatever the two powers think about it, and whichever we humans, at the moment, happen to like, one of them is actually wrong, actually mistaken, it regarding itself as good. Now if we mean merely that we happen to prefer the first, then we must give up talking about good and evil at all. For good means what you ought to prefer quite regardless of what you happen to like at any given moment. If 'being good' meant simply joining the side you happened to fancy, for no real reason, then good would not deserve to be called good. So we must mean that one of the two powers is actually wrong and the other actually right.

But the moment you say that, you are putting into the universe a third thing in addition to the two Powers: some law or standard or rule of good which one of the powers conforms to and the other fails to conform to. But since the two powers are judged by this standard, then this standard, or the Being who made this standard, is farther back and higher up than either of them, and He will be the real God. In fact, what we meant by calling them good and bad turns out to be that one of them is in a right relation to the real ultimate God and the other in a wrong relation to Him.

The same point can be made in a different way. If Dualism is true, then the bad Power must be a being who likes badness for its own sake. But in reality we have no experience of anyone liking badness just because it is bad. The nearest we can get to it is in cruelty. But in real life people are cruel for one of two reasons—either because they are sadists, that is, because they have a sexual perversion which makes cruelty a cause of sensual pleasure to them, or else for the sake of something they are going to get out of it—money, or power, or safety. But pleasure, money, power, and safety are all, as far as they go, good things. The badness consists in pursuing them by the wrong method, or in the wrong way, or too much. I do not mean, of course, that the people who do this are not desperately wicked. I do mean that wickedness, when you examine it, turns out to be the pursuit of some good in the wrong way. You can be good for the mere sake of goodness: you cannot be bad for the mere sake of badness. You can do a kind action when you are not feeling kind and when it gives you no pleasure, simply because kindness is right; but no one ever did a cruel action simply because cruelty is wrong—only because cruelty was pleasant or useful to him. In other words badness cannot succeed even in being bad in the same way in which goodness is good. Goodness is, so to speak, itself: badness is only spoiled goodness. And there must be something good first before it can be spoiled. We called sadism a sexual perversion; but you must first have the idea of a normal sexuality before you can talk of its being perverted; and you can see which is the perversion, because you can explain the perverted from the normal, and cannot explain the normal from the perverted. It follows that this Bad Power, who is supposed to be on an equal footing with the Good Power, and to love badness in the same way as the Good Power loves goodness, is a mere bogy. In order to be bad he must have good things to want and then to pursue in the wrong way: he must have impulses which were originally good in order to be able to pervert them. But if he is bad he cannot supply himself either with good things to desire or with good impulses to pervert. He must be getting both from the Good Power. And if so, then he is not independent. He is part of the Good Power's world: he was made either by the Good Power or by some power above them both.

Put it more simply still. To be bad, he must exist and have intelligence and will. But existence, intelligence and will are in themselves good. Therefore he must be getting them from the Good Power: even to be bad he must borrow or steal from his opponent. And do you now begin to see why Christianity has always said that the devil is a fallen angel? That is not a mere story for the children. It is a real recognition of the fact that evil is a parasite, not an original thing. The powers which enable evil to carry on are powers given it by goodness. All the things which enable a bad man to be effectively bad are in themselves good things—resolution, cleverness, good looks, existence itself. That is why Dualism, in a strict sense, will not work.

But I freely admit that real Christianity (as distinct from Christianity-and-water) goes much nearer to Dualism than people think. One of the things that surprised me when I first read the New Testament seriously was that it talked so much about a Dark Power in the universe—a mighty evil spirit who was held to be the Power behind death and disease, and sin. The difference is that Christianity thinks this Dark Power was created by God, and was good when he was created, and went wrong. Christianity agrees with Dualism that this universe is at war. But it does not think this is a war between independent powers. It thinks it is a civil war, a rebellion, and that we are living in a part of the universe occupied by the rebel.

Enemy-occupied territory—that is what this world is. Christianity is the story of how the rightful king has landed, you might say landed in disguise, and is calling us all to take part in a great campaign of sabotage. When you go to church you are really listening-in to the secret wireless from our friends: that is why the enemy is so anxious to prevent us from going. He does it by playing on our conceit and laziness and intellectual snobbery. I know someone will ask me, 'Do you really mean, at this time of day, to re-introduce our old friend the devil—hoofs and horns and all?' Well, what the time of day has to do with it I do not know. And I am not particular about the hoofs and horns. But in other respects my answer is 'Yes, I do.' I do not claim to know anything about his personal appearance. If anybody really wants to know him better I would say to that person, 'Don't worry. If you really want to, you will. Whether you'll like it when you do is another question.'

3

THE SHOCKING
ALTERNATIVE

CHRISTIANS, THEN, BELIEVE that an evil power has made himself
for the present the Prince of this World. And, of course, that raises problems. Is this state of affairs in accordance with God's will, or not? If it is,
He is a strange God, you will say: and if it is not, how can anything happen contrary to the will of a being with absolute power?

But anyone who has been in authority knows how a thing can be in
accordance with your will in one way and not in another. It may be quite
sensible for a mother to say to the children, 'I'm not going to go and make
you tidy the schoolroom every night. You've got to learn to keep it tidy
on your own.' Then she goes up one night and finds the Teddy bear and
the ink and the French Grammar all lying in the grate. That is against
her will. She would prefer the children to be tidy. But on the other hand,
it is her will which has left the children free to be untidy. The same thing
arises in any regiment, or trade union, or school. You make a thing voluntary and then half the people do not do it. That is not what you willed,
but your will has made it possible.

It is probably the same in the universe. God created things which had
free will. That means creatures which can go either wrong or right. Some
people think they can imagine a creature which was free but had no possibility of going wrong; I cannot. If a thing is free to be good it is also free
to be bad. And free will is what has made evil possible. Why, then, did
God give them free will? Because free will, though it makes evil possible,
is also the only thing that makes possible any love or goodness or joy

worth having. A world of automata—of creatures that worked like machines—would hardly be worth creating. The happiness which God designs for His higher creatures is the happiness of being freely, voluntarily united to Him and to each other in an ecstasy of love and delight compared with which the most rapturous love between a man and a woman on this earth is mere milk and water. And for that they must be free.

Of course God knew what would happen if they used their freedom the wrong way: apparently He thought it worth the risk. Perhaps we feel inclined to disagree with Him. But there is a difficulty about disagreeing with God. He is the source from which all your reasoning power comes: you could not be right and He wrong any more than a stream can rise higher than its own source. When you are arguing against Him you are arguing against the very power that makes you able to argue at all: it is like cutting off the branch you are sitting on. If God thinks this state of war in the universe a price worth paying for free will—that is, for making a live world in which creatures can do real good or harm and something of real importance can happen, instead of a toy world which only moves when He pulls the strings—then we may take it it is worth paying.

When we have understood about free will, we shall see how silly it is to ask, as somebody once asked me: 'Why did God make a creature of such rotten stuff that it went wrong?' The better stuff a creature is made of—the cleverer and stronger and freer it is—then the better it will be if it goes right, but also the worse it will be if it goes wrong. A cow cannot be very good or very bad; a dog can be both better and worse; a child better and worse still; an ordinary man, still more so; a man of genius, still more so; a superhuman spirit best—or worst—of all.

How did the Dark Power go wrong? Here, no doubt, we ask a question to which human beings cannot give an answer with any certainty. A reasonable (and traditional) guess, based on our own experiences of going wrong, can, however, be offered. The moment you have a self at all, there is a possibility of putting yourself first—wanting to be the centre—wanting to be God, in fact. That was the sin of Satan: and that was the sin he taught the human race. Some people think the fall of man had something to do with sex, but that is a mistake. (The story in the Book of Genesis rather suggests that some corruption in our sexual nature followed the fall and was its result, not its cause.) What Satan put into the heads of our remote ancestors was the idea that they could 'be like gods'—could set up on their own as if they had created themselves—be their own masters—invent some sort of happiness for themselves outside God, apart from God. And out of that hopeless attempt has come nearly all that we call human history—money, poverty, ambition, war, prostitution, classes, empires, slavery—the long terrible story of man trying to find something other than God which will make him happy.

The reason why it can never succeed is this. God made us: invented us as a man invents an engine. A car is made to run on petrol, and it would not run properly on anything else. Now God designed the human machine to run on Himself. He Himself is the fuel our spirits were designed to burn, or the food our spirits were designed to feed on. There is no other. That is why it is just no good asking God to make us happy in our own way without bothering about religion. God cannot give us a happiness and peace apart from Himself, because it is not there. There is no such thing.

That is the key to history. Terrific energy is expended—civilisations are built up—excellent institutions devised; but each time something goes wrong. Some fatal flaw always brings the selfish and cruel people to the top and it all slides back into misery and ruin. In fact, the machine conks. It seems to start up all right and runs a few yards, and then it breaks down. They are trying to run it on the wrong juice. That is what Satan has done to us humans.

And what did God do? First of all He left us conscience, the sense of right and wrong: and all through history there have been people trying (some of them very hard) to obey it. None of them ever quite succeeded. Secondly, He sent the human race what I call good dreams: I mean those queer stories scattered all through the heathen religions about a god who dies and comes to life again and, by his death, has somehow given new life to men. Thirdly, He selected one particular people and spent several centuries hammering into their heads the sort of God He was—that there was only one of Him and that He cared about right conduct. Those people were the Jews, and the Old Testament gives an account of the hammering process.

Then comes the real shock. Among these Jews there suddenly turns up a man who goes about talking as if He was God. He claims to forgive sins. He says He has always existed. He says He is coming to judge the world at the end of time. Now let us get this clear. Among Pantheists, like the

Indians, anyone might say that he was a part of God, or one with God: there would be nothing very odd about it. But this man, since He was a Jew, could not mean that kind of God. God, in their language, meant the Being outside the world, who had made it and was infinitely different from anything else. And when you have grasped that, you will see that what this man said was, quite simply, the most shocking thing that has ever been uttered by human lips.

One part of the claim tends to slip past us unnoticed because we have heard it so often that we no longer see what it amounts to. I mean the claim to forgive sins: any sins. Now unless the speaker is God, this is really so preposterous as to be comic. We can all understand how a man forgives offences against himself. You tread on my toes and I forgive you, you steal my money and I forgive you. But what should we make of a man, himself unrobbed and untrodden on, who announced that he forgave you for treading on other men's toes and stealing other men's money? Asinine fatuity is the kindest description we should give of his conduct. Yet this is what Jesus did. He told people that their sins were forgiven, and never waited to consult all the other people whom their sins had undoubtedly injured. He unhesitatingly behaved as if He was the party chiefly concerned, the person chiefly offended in all offences. This makes sense only if He really was the God whose laws are broken and whose love is wounded in every sin. In the mouth of any speaker who is not God, these words would imply what I can only regard as a silliness and conceit unrivalled by any other character in history.

Yet (and this is the strange, significant thing) even His enemies, when they read the Gospels, do not usually get the impression of silliness and conceit. Still less do unprejudiced readers. Christ says that He is 'humble and meek' and we believe Him; not noticing that, if He were merely a man, humility and meekness are the very last characteristics we could attribute to some of His sayings.

I am trying here to prevent anyone saying the really foolish thing that people often say about Him: 'I'm ready to accept Jesus as a great moral teacher, but I don't accept His claim to be God.' That is the one thing we must not say. A man who was merely a man and said the sort of things Jesus said would not be a great moral teacher. He would either be a lunatic—on a level with the man who says he is a poached egg—or else he would be the Devil of Hell. You must make your choice. Either this man was, and is, the Son of God: or else a madman or something worse. You can shut Him up for a fool, you can spit at Him and kill Him as a demon; or you can fall at His feet and call Him Lord and God. But let us not come with any patronising nonsense about His being a great human teacher. He has not left that open to us. He did not intend to.

4

THE PERFECT PENITENT

WE ARE FACED, then, with a frightening alternative. This man we are talking about either was (and is) just what He said or else a lunatic, or something worse. Now it seems to me obvious that He was neither a lunatic nor a fiend: and consequently, however strange or terrifying or unlikely it may seem, I have to accept the view that He was and is God. God has landed on this enemy-occupied world in human form.

And now, what was the purpose of it all? What did he come to do? Well, to teach, of course; but as soon as you look into the New Testament or any other Christian writing you will find they are constantly talking about something different—about His death and His coming to life again. It is obvious that Christians think the chief point of the story lies there. They think the main thing He came to earth to do was to suffer and be killed.

Now before I became a Christian I was under the impression that the first thing Christians had to believe was one particular theory as to what the point of this dying was. According to that theory God wanted to punish men for having deserted and joined the Great Rebel, but Christ volunteered to be punished instead, and so God let us off. Now I admit that even this theory does not seem to me quite so immoral and so silly as it used to; but that is not the point I want to make. What I came to see later on was that neither this theory nor any other is Christianity. The central Christian belief is that Christ's death has somehow put us right with God and given us a fresh start. Theories as to how it did this are another matter. A good many different theories have been held as to how it works;

what all Christians are agreed on is that it does work. I will tell you what I think it is like. All sensible people know that if you are tired and hungry a meal will do you good. But the modern theory of nourishment—all about the vitamins and proteins—is a different thing. People ate their dinners and felt better long before the theory of vitamins was ever heard of: and if the theory of vitamins is some day abandoned they will go on eating their dinners just the same. Theories about Christ's death are not Christianity: they are explanations about how it works. Christians would not all agree as to how important those theories are. My own church—the Church of England—does not lay down any one of them as the right one. The Church of Rome goes a bit further. But I think they will all agree that the thing itself is infinitely more important than any explanations that theologians have produced. I think they would probably admit that no explanation will ever be quite adequate to the reality. But as I said in the preface to this book, I am only a layman, and at this point we are getting into deep water. I can only tell you, for what it is worth, how I, personally, look at the matter.

In my view the theories are not themselves the thing you are asked to accept. Many of you no doubt have read Jeans or Eddington. What they do when they want to explain the atom, or something of that sort, is to give you a description out of which you can make a mental picture. But then they warn you that this picture is not what the scientists actually believe. What the scientists believe is a mathematical formula. The pictures are there only to help you to understand the formula. They are not really true in the way the formula is; they do not give you the real thing but only something more or less like it. They are only meant to help, and if they do not help you can drop them. The thing itself cannot be pictured, it can only be expressed mathematically. We are in the same boat here. We believe that the death of Christ is just that point in history at which something absolutely unimaginable from outside shows through into our own world. And if we cannot picture even the atoms of which our own world is built, of course we are not going to be able to picture this. Indeed, if we found that we could fully understand it, that very fact would show it was not what it professes to be—the inconceivable, the uncreated, the thing from beyond nature, striking down into nature like lightning. You may ask what good it will be to us if we do not understand it. But that is easily answered. A man can eat his dinner without understanding exactly how food nourishes him. A man can accept what Christ has done without knowing how it works: indeed, he certainly would not know how it works until he has accepted it.

We are told that Christ was killed for us, that His death has washed out our sins, and that by dying He disabled death itself. That is the formula. That is Christianity. That is what has to be believed. Any theories we build up as to how Christ's death did all this are, in my view, quite secondary: mere plans or diagrams to be left alone if they do not help us, and, even if they do help us, not to be confused with the thing itself. All the same, some of these theories are worth looking at.

The one most people have heard is the one I mentioned before—the one about our being let off because Christ has volunteered to bear a punishment instead of us. Now on the face of it that is a very silly theory. If God was prepared to let us off, why on earth did He not do so? And what possible point could there be in punishing an innocent person instead? None at all that I can see, if you are thinking of punishment in the police-court sense. On the other hand, if you think of a debt, there is plenty of point in a person who has some assets paying it on behalf of someone who has not. Or if you take 'paying the penalty', not in the sense of being punished, but in the more general sense of 'standing the racket' or 'footing the bill', then, of course, it is a matter of common experience that, when one person has got himself into a hole, the trouble of getting him out usually falls on a kind friend.

Now what was the sort of 'hole' man had got himself into? He had tried to set up on his own, to behave as if he belonged to himself. In other words, fallen man is not simply an imperfect creature who needs improvement: he is a rebel who must lay down his arms. Laying down your arms, surrendering, saying you are sorry, realising that you have been on the wrong track and getting ready to start life over again from the ground floor—that is the only way out of our 'hole'. This process of surrender—this movement full speed astern—is what Christians call repentance. Now repentance is no fun at all. It is something much harder than merely eating humble pie. It means unlearning all the self-conceit and self-will that we have been training ourselves into for thousands of years. It means killing part of yourself, undergoing a kind of death. In fact, it needs a good man to repent. And here comes the catch. Only a bad person needs to repent: only a good person can repent perfectly. The worse you are the more you need it and the less you can do it. The only person who could do it perfectly would be a perfect person—and he would not need it.

Remember, this repentance, this willing submission to humiliation and a kind of death, is not something God demands of you before He will take you back and which He could let you off if He chose: it is simply a description of what going back to Him is like. If you ask God to take you back without it, you are really asking Him to let you go back without going back. It cannot happen. Very well, then, we must go through with it. But the same badness which makes us need it, makes us unable to do it. Can we do it if God helps us? Yes, but what do we mean when we talk of God helping us? We mean God putting into us a bit of Himself, so to speak. He lends us a little of His reasoning powers and that is how we think: He puts a little of His love into us and that is how we love one another. When you teach a child writing, you hold its hand while it forms the letters: that is, it forms the letters because you are forming them. We love and reason because God loves and reasons and holds our hand while we do it. Now if we had not fallen, that would be all plain sailing. But unfortunately we now need God's help in order to do something which God, in His own nature, never does at all—to surrender, to suffer, to submit, to die. Nothing in God's nature corresponds to this process at all. So that the one road for which we now need God's leadership most of all is a road God, in His own nature, has never walked. God can share only what He has: this thing, in His own nature, He has not.

But supposing God became a man—suppose our human nature which can suffer and die was amalgamated with God's nature in one person—then that person could help us. He could surrender His will, and suffer and die, because He was man; and He could do it perfectly because He was God. You and I can go through this process only if God does it in us; but God can do it only if He becomes man. Our attempts at this dying will succeed only if we men share in God's dying, just as our thinking can succeed only because it is a drop out of the ocean of His intelligence: but we cannot share God's dying unless God dies; and He cannot die except by being a man. That is the sense in which He pays our debt, and suffers for us what He Himself need not suffer at all.

I have heard some people complain that if Jesus was God as well as man, then His sufferings and death lose all value in their eyes, 'because it must have been so easy for Him'. Others may (very rightly) rebuke the ingratitude and ungraciousness of this objection; what staggers me is the misunderstanding it betrays. In one sense, of course, those who make it are right. They have even understated their own case. The perfect submission, the perfect suffering, the perfect death were not only easier to Jesus because He was God, but were possible only because He was God. But surely that is a very odd reason for not accepting them? The teacher is able to form the letters for the child because the teacher is grown-up and knows how to write. That, of course, makes it easier for the teacher; and only because it is easier for him can he help the child. If it rejected him because 'it's easy for grown-ups' and waited to learn writing from another child who could not write itself (and so had no 'unfair' advantage), it would not get on very quickly. If I am drowning in a rapid river, a man who still has one foot on the bank may give me a hand which saves my life. Ought I to shout back (between my gasps) 'No, it's not fair! You have an advantage! You're keeping one foot on the bank'? That advantage—call it 'unfair' if you like—is the only reason why he can be of any use to me. To what will you look for help if you will not look to that which is stronger than yourself?

Such is my own way of looking at what Christians call the Atonement. But remember this is only one more picture. Do not mistake it for the thing itself: and if it does not help you, drop it.

5

THE PRACTICAL
CONCLUSION

THE PERFECT SURRENDER and humiliation were undergone by
Christ: perfect because He was God, surrender and humiliation because
He was man. Now the Christian belief is that if we somehow share the
humility and suffering of Christ we shall also share in His conquest of
death and find a new life after we have died and in it become perfect,
and perfectly happy, creatures. This means something much more than
our trying to follow His teaching. People often ask when the next step in
evolution—the step to something beyond man—will happen. But in the
Christian view, it has happened already. In Christ a new kind of man appeared: and the new kind of life which began in Him is to be put into us.

How is this to be done? Now, please remember how we acquired the
old, ordinary kind of life. We derived it from others, from our father and
mother and all our ancestors, without our consent—and by a very curious process, involving pleasure, pain, and danger. A process you would
never have guessed. Most of us spend a good many years in childhood
trying to guess it: and some children, when they are first told, do not believe it—and I am not sure that I blame them, for it is very odd. Now the
God who arranged that process is the same God who arranges how the
new kind of life—the Christ-life—is to be spread. We must be prepared
for it being odd too. He did not consult us when He invented sex: He has
not consulted us either when He invented this.

There are three things that spread the Christ-life to us: baptism, belief, and that mysterious action which different Christians call by differ-

ent names—Holy Communion, the Mass, the Lord's Supper. At least, those are the three ordinary methods. I am not saying there may not be special cases where it is spread without one or more of these. I have not time to go into special cases, and I do not know enough. If you are trying in a few minutes to tell a man how to get to Edinburgh you will tell him the trains: he can, it is true, get there by boat or by a plane, but you will hardly bring that in. And I am not saying anything about which of these three things is the most essential. My Methodist friend would like me to say more about belief and less (in proportion) about the other two. But I am not going into that. Anyone who professes to teach you Christian doctrine will, in fact, tell you to use all three, and that is enough for our present purpose.

I cannot myself see why these things should be the conductors of the new kind of life. But then, if one did not happen to know, I should never have seen any connection between a particular physical pleasure and the appearance of a new human being in the world. We have to take reality as it comes to us: there is no good jabbering about what it ought to be like or what we should have expected it to be like. But though I cannot see why it should be so, I can tell you why I believe it is so. I have explained why I have to believe that Jesus was (and is) God. And it seems plain as a matter of history that He taught His followers that the new life was communicated in this way. In other words, I believe it on His authority. Do not be scared by the word authority. Believing things on authority only means believing them because you have been told them by someone you think trustworthy. Ninety-nine per cent of the things you believe are believed on authority. I believe there is such a place as New York. I have not seen it myself. I could not prove by abstract reasoning that there must be such a place. I believe it because reliable people have told me so. The ordinary man believes in the Solar System, atoms, evolution, and the circulation of the blood on authority—because the scientists say so. Every historical statement in the world is believed on authority. None of us has seen the Norman Conquest or the defeat of the Armada. None of us could prove them by pure logic as you prove a thing in mathematics. We believe them simply because people who did see them have left writings that tell us about them: in fact, on authority. A man who jibbed at authority in other things as some people do in religion would have to be content to know nothing all his life.

Do not think I am setting up baptism and belief and the Holy Communion as things that will do instead of your own attempts to copy Christ. Your natural life is derived from your parents; that does not mean it will stay there if you do nothing about it. You can lose it by neglect, or you can drive it away by committing suicide. You have to feed it and look after it: but always remember you are not making it, you are only keeping up a life you got from someone else. In the same way a Christian can lose the Christ-life which has been put into him, and he has to make efforts to keep it. But even the best Christian that ever lived is not acting on his own steam—he is only nourishing or protecting a life he could never have acquired by his own efforts. And that has practical consequences. As long as the natural life is in your body, it will do a lot towards repairing that body. Cut it, and up to a point it will heal, as a dead body would not. A live body is not one that never gets hurt, but one that can to some extent repair itself. In the same way a Christian is not a man who never goes wrong, but a man who is enabled to repent and pick himself up and begin over again after each stumble—because the Christ-life is inside him, repairing him all the time, enabling him to repeat (in some degree) the kind of voluntary death which Christ Himself carried out.

That is why the Christian is in a different position from other people who are trying to be good. They hope, by being good, to please God if there is one; or—if they think there is not—at least they hope to deserve approval from good men. But the Christian thinks any good he does comes from the Christ-life inside him. He does not think God will love us because we are good, but that God will make us good because He loves us; just as the roof of a greenhouse does not attract the sun because it is bright, but becomes bright because the sun shines on it.

And let me make it quite clear that when Christians say the Christ-life is in them, they do not mean simply something mental or moral. When they speak of being 'in Christ' or of Christ being 'in them', this is not simply a way of saying that they are thinking about Christ or copying Him. They mean that Christ is actually operating through them; that the whole mass of Christians are the physical organism through which Christ acts—that we are His fingers and muscles, the cells of His body. And perhaps that explains one or two things. It explains why this new life is spread not only by purely mental acts like belief, but by bodily acts like baptism and Holy Communion. It is not merely the spreading of an idea;

it is more like evolution—a biological or superbiological fact. There is no good trying to be more spiritual than God. God never meant man to be a purely spiritual creature. That is why He uses material things like bread and wine to put the new life into us. We may think this rather crude and unspiritual. God does not: He invented eating. He likes matter. He invented it.

Here is another thing that used to puzzle me. Is it not frightfully unfair that this new life should be confined to people who have heard of Christ and been able to believe in Him? But the truth is God has not told us what His arrangements about the other people are. We do know that no man can be saved except through Christ; we do not know that only those who know Him can be saved through Him. But in the meantime, if you are worried about the people outside, the most unreasonable thing you can do is to remain outside yourself. Christians are Christ's body, the organism through which He works. Every addition to that body enables Him to do more. If you want to help those outside you must add your own little cell to the body of Christ who alone can help them. Cutting off a man's fingers would be an odd way of getting him to do more work.

Another possible objection is this. Why is God landing in this enemy-occupied world in disguise and starting a sort of secret society to undermine the devil? Why is He not landing in force, invading it? Is it that He is not strong enough? Well, Christians think He is going to land in force; we do not know when. But we can guess why He is delaying. He wants to give us the chance of joining His side freely. I do not suppose you and I would have thought much of a Frenchman who waited till the Allies were marching into Germany and then announced he was on our side. God will invade. But I wonder whether people who ask God to interfere openly and directly in our world quite realise what it will be like when He does. When that happens, it is the end of the world. When the author walks on to the stage the play is over. God is going to invade, all right: but what is the good of saying you are on His side then, when you see the whole natural universe melting away like a dream and something else—something it never entered your head to conceive—comes crashing in; something so beautiful to some of us and so terrible to others that none of us will have any choice left? For this time it will be God without disguise; something so overwhelming that it will strike either irresistible love or irresistible horror into every creature. It will be too late then to choose your side. There is no use saying you choose to lie down when it has become impossible to stand up. That will not be the time for choosing: it will be the time when we discover which side we really have chosen, whether we realised it before or not. Now, today, this moment, is our chance to choose the right side. God is holding back to give us that chance. It will not last for ever. We must take it or leave it.

BOOK THREE

Christian Behaviour

THE THREE PARTS
OF MORALITY

THERE IS A story about a schoolboy who was asked what he thought God was like. He replied that, as far as he could make out, God was 'the sort of person who is always snooping around to see if anyone is enjoying himself and then trying to stop it'. And I am afraid that is the sort of idea that the word Morality raises in a good many people's minds: something that interferes, something that stops you having a good time. In reality, moral rules are directions for running the human machine. Every moral rule is there to prevent a breakdown, or a strain, or a friction, in the running of that machine. That is why these rules at first seem to be constantly interfering with our natural inclinations. When you are being taught how to use any machine, the instructor keeps on saying, 'No, don't do it like that,' because, of course, there are all sorts of things that look all right and seem to you the natural way of treating the machine, but do not really work.

Some people prefer to talk about moral 'ideals' rather than moral rules and about moral 'idealism' rather than moral obedience. Now it is, of course, quite true that moral perfection is an 'ideal' in the sense that we cannot achieve it. In that sense every kind of perfection is, for us humans, an ideal; we cannot succeed in being perfect car drivers or perfect tennis players or in drawing perfectly straight lines. But there is another sense in which it is very misleading to call moral perfection an ideal. When a man says that a certain woman, or house, or ship, or garden is 'his ideal' he does not mean (unless he is rather a fool) that everyone else ought to have the same ideal. In such matters we are entitled to have different tastes and, therefore, different ideals. But it is dangerous to describe a man who tries very hard to keep the moral law as a 'man of high ideals', because this might lead you to think that moral perfection was a private taste of his own and that the rest of us were not called on to share it. This would be a disastrous mistake. Perfect behaviour may be as unattainable as perfect gear-changing when we drive; but it is a necessary ideal prescribed for all men by the very nature of the human machine just as perfect gear-changing is an ideal prescribed for all drivers by the very nature of cars. And it would be even more dangerous to think of oneself as a person 'of high ideals' because one is trying to tell no lies at all (instead of only a few lies) or never to commit adultery (instead of committing it only seldom) or not to be a bully (instead of being only a moderate bully). It might lead you to become a prig and to think you were rather a special person who deserved to be congratulated on his 'idealism'. In reality you might just as well expect to be congratulated because, whenever you do a sum, you try to get it quite right. To be sure, perfect arithmetic is 'an ideal'; you will certainly make some mistakes in some calculations. But there is nothing very fine about trying to be quite accurate at each step in each sum. It would be idiotic not to try; for every mistake is going to cause you trouble later on. In the same way every moral failure is going to cause trouble, probably to others and certainly to yourself. By talking about rules and obedience instead of 'ideals' and 'idealism' we help to remind ourselves of these facts.

Now let us go a step further. There are two ways in which the human machine goes wrong. One is when human individuals drift apart from one another, or else collide with one another and do one another damage, by cheating or bullying. The other is when things go wrong inside the individual—when the different parts of him (his different faculties and desires and so on) either drift apart or interfere with one another. You can get the idea plain if you think of us as a fleet of ships sailing in formation. The voyage will be a success only, in the first place, if the ships do not collide and get in one another's way; and, secondly, if each ship is seaworthy and has her engines in good order. As a matter of fact, you cannot have either of these two things without the other. If the ships keep on having collisions they will not remain seaworthy very long. On the other hand, if their steering gears are out of order they will not be able to avoid collisions. Or, if you like, think of humanity as a band playing a tune. To get a good result, you need two things. Each player's individual instrument must be in tune and also each must come in at the right moment so as to combine with all the others.

But there is one thing we have not yet taken into account. We have not asked where the fleet is trying to get to, or what piece of music the band is trying to play. The instruments might be all in tune and might all come in at the right moment, but even so the performance would not be a success if they had been engaged to provide dance music and actually played nothing but Dead Marches. And however well the fleet sailed, its voyage would be a failure if it were meant to reach New York and actually arrived at Calcutta.

Morality, then, seems to be concerned with three things. Firstly, with fair play and harmony between individuals. Secondly, with what might be called tidying up or harmonising the things inside each individual. Thirdly, with the general purpose of human life as a whole: what man was made for: what course the whole fleet ought to be on: what tune the conductor of the band wants it to play.

You may have noticed that modern people are nearly always thinking about the first thing and forgetting the other two. When people say in the newspapers that we are striving for Christian moral standards, they usually mean that we are striving for kindness and fair play between nations, and classes, and individuals; that is, they are thinking only of the first thing. When a man says about something he wants to do, 'It can't be wrong because it doesn't do anyone else any harm,' he is thinking only of the first thing. He is thinking it does not matter what his ship is like inside provided that he does not run into the next ship. And it is quite natural, when we start thinking about morality, to begin with the first thing, with social relations. For one thing, the results of bad morality in that sphere are so obvious and press on us every day: war and poverty and graft and lies and shoddy work. And also, as long as you stick to the first thing, there is very little disagreement about morality. Almost all people at all times have agreed (in theory) that human beings ought to be honest and kind and helpful to one another. But though it is natural to begin with all that, if our thinking about morality stops there, we might just as well not have thought at all. Unless we go on to the second thing—the tidying up inside each human being—we are only deceiving ourselves.

What is the good of telling the ships how to steer so as to avoid collisions if, in fact, they are such crazy old tubs that they cannot be steered at all? What is the good of drawing up, on paper, rules for social behaviour, if we know that, in fact, our greed, cowardice, ill temper, and self-conceit are going to prevent us from keeping them? I do not mean for a moment that we ought not to think, and think hard, about improvements in our social and economic system. What I do mean is that all that thinking will be mere moonshine unless we realise that nothing but the courage and unselfishness of individuals is ever going to make any system work properly. It is easy enough to remove the particular kinds of graft or bullying that go on under the present system: but as long as men are twisters or bullies they will find some new way of carrying on the old game under the new system. You cannot make men good by law: and without good men you cannot have a good society. That is why we must go on to think of the second thing: of morality inside the individual.

But I do not think we can stop there either. We are now getting to the point at which different beliefs about the universe lead to different behaviour. And it would seem, at first sight, very sensible to stop before we got there, and just carry on with those parts of morality that all sensible people agree about. But can we? Remember that religion involves a series of statements about facts, which must be either true or false. If they are true, one set of conclusions will follow about the right sailing of the human fleet: if they are false, quite a different set. For example, let us go back to the man who says that a thing cannot be wrong unless it hurts some other human being. He quite understands that he must not damage the other ships in the convoy, but he honestly thinks that what he does to his own ship is simply his own business. But does it not make a great difference whether his ship is his own property or not? Does it not make a great difference whether I am, so to speak, the landlord of my own mind and body, or only a tenant, responsible to the real landlord? If somebody else made me, for his own purposes, then I shall have a lot of duties which I should not have if I simply belonged to myself.

Again, Christianity asserts that every individual human being is going to live for ever, and this must be either true or false. Now there are a good many things which would not be worth bothering about if I were going to live only seventy years, but which I had better bother about very seriously if I am going to live for ever. Perhaps my bad temper or my jealousy are gradually getting worse—so gradually that the increase in seventy years will not be very noticeable. But it might be absolute hell in a million years: in fact, if Christianity is true, Hell is the precisely correct technical term for what it would be. And immortality makes this other difference, which, by the by, has a connection with the difference between totalitarianism and democracy. If individuals live only seventy years, then a state, or a nation, or a civilisation, which may last for a thousand years, is more important than an individual. But if Christianity is true, then the individual is not only more important but incomparably more important, for he is everlasting and the life of a state or a civilisation, compared with his, is only a moment.

It seems, then, that if we are to think about morality, we must think of all three departments: relations between man and man: things inside each man: and relations between man and the power that made him. We can all co-operate in the first one. Disagreements begin with the second and become more serious with the third. It is dealing with the third that the main differences between Christian and non-Christian morality come out. For the rest of this book I am going to assume the Christian point of view, and look at the whole picture as it will be if Christianity is true.

2

THE 'CARDINAL VIRTUES'

THE PREVIOUS SECTION was originally composed to be given as a short talk on the air.

If you are allowed to talk for only ten minutes, pretty well everything else has to be sacrificed to brevity. One of my chief reasons for dividing morality up into three parts (with my picture of the ships sailing in convoy) was that this seemed the shortest way of covering the ground. Here I want to give some idea of another way in which the subject has been divided by old writers, which was too long to use in my talk, but which is a very good one.

According to this longer scheme there are seven 'virtues'. Four of them are called 'Cardinal' virtues, and the remaining three are called 'Theological' virtues. The 'Cardinal' ones are those which all civilised people recognise: the 'Theological' are those which, as a rule, only Christians know about. I shall deal with the Theological ones later on: at present I am talking about the four Cardinal virtues. (The word 'cardinal' has nothing to do with 'Cardinals' in the Roman Church. It comes from a Latin word meaning 'the hinge of a door'. These were called 'cardinal' virtues because they are, as we should say, 'pivotal'.) They are PRUDENCE, TEMPERANCE, JUSTICE and FORTITUDE.

Prudence means practical common sense, taking the trouble to think out what you are doing and what is likely to come of it. Nowadays most people hardly think of Prudence as one of the 'virtues'. In fact, because Christ said we could only get into His world by being like children, many Christians have the idea that, provided you are 'good', it does not matter being a fool. But that is a misunderstanding. In the first place, most children show plenty of 'prudence' about doing the things they are really interested in, and think them out quite sensibly. In the second place, as St Paul points out, Christ never meant that we were to remain children in *intelligence*: on the contrary. He told us to be not only 'as harmless as doves', but also 'as wise as serpents'. He wants a child's heart, but a grown-up's head. He wants us to be simple, single-minded, affectionate, and teachable, as good children are; but He also wants every bit of intelligence we have to be alert at its job, and in first-class fighting trim. The fact that you are giving money to a charity does not mean that you need not try to find out whether that charity is a fraud or not. The fact that what you are thinking about is God Himself (for example, when you are praying) does not mean that you can be content with the same babyish ideas which you had when you were a five-year-old. It is, of course, quite true that God will not love you any the less, or have less use for you, if you happen to have been born with a very second-rate brain. He has room for people with very little sense, but He wants every one to use what sense they have. The proper motto is not 'Be good, sweet maid and let who can be clever,' but 'Be good, sweet maid, and don't forget that this involves being as clever as you can.' God is no fonder of intellectual slackers than of any other slackers. If you are thinking of becoming a Christian, I warn you, you are embarking on something which is going to take the whole of you, brains and all. But, fortunately, it works the other way round. Anyone who is honestly trying to be a Christian will soon find his intelligence being sharpened: one of the reasons why it needs no special education to be a Christian is that Christianity is an education itself. That is why an uneducated believer like Bunyan was able to write a book that has astonished the whole world.

Temperance is, unfortunately, one of those words that has changed its meaning. It now usually means teetotalism. But in the days when the second Cardinal virtue was christened 'Temperance', it meant nothing of the sort. Temperance referred not specially to drink, but to all pleasures; and it meant not abstaining, but going the right length and no further. It is a mistake to think that Christians ought all to be teetotallers; Mohammedanism, not Christianity, is the teetotal religion. Of course it may be the duty of a particular Christian, or of any Christian, at a particular time, to abstain from strong drink, either because he is the sort of man who cannot drink at all without drinking too much, or because he is with people who are inclined to drunkenness and must not encourage them by drinking himself. But the whole point is that he is abstaining, for a good reason, from something which he does not condemn and which he likes to see other people enjoying. One of the marks of a certain type of bad man is that he cannot give up a thing himself without wanting every one else to give it up. That is not the Christian way. An individual Christian may see fit to give up all sorts of things for special reasons—marriage, or meat, or beer, or the cinema; but the moment he starts saying the things are bad in themselves, or looking down his nose at other people who do use them, he has taken the wrong turning.

One great piece of mischief has been done by the modern restriction of the word Temperance to the question of drink. It helps people to forget that you can be just as intemperate about lots of other things. A man who makes his golf or his motor-bicycle the centre of his life, or a woman who devotes all her thoughts to clothes or bridge or her dog, is being just as 'intemperate' as someone who gets drunk every evening. Of course, it does not show on the outside so easily: bridge-mania or golf-mania do not make you fall down in the middle of the road. But God is not deceived by externals.

Justice means much more than the sort of thing that goes on in law courts. It is the old name for everything we should now call 'fairness'; it includes honesty, give and take, truthfulness, keeping promises, and all that side of life. And Fortitude includes both kinds of courage—the kind that faces danger as well as the kind that 'sticks it' under pain. 'Guts' is perhaps the nearest modern English. You will notice, of course, that you cannot practise any of the other virtues very long without bringing this one into play.

There is one further point about the virtues that ought to be noticed. There is a difference between doing some particular just or temperate action and being a just or temperate man. Someone who is not a good tennis player may now and then make a good shot. What you mean by a good player is a man whose eye and muscles and nerves have been so trained by making innumerable good shots that they can now be relied on. They have a certain tone or quality which is there even when he is not playing, just as a mathematician's mind has a certain habit and outlook which is there even when he is not doing mathematics. In the same way a man who perseveres in doing just actions gets in the end a certain quality of character. Now it is that quality rather than the particular actions which we mean when we talk of a 'virtue'.

This distinction is important for the following reason. If we thought only of the particular actions we might encourage three wrong ideas.

(1) We might think that, provided you did the right thing, it did not matter how or why you did it—whether you did it willingly or unwillingly, sulkily or cheerfully, through fear of public opinion or for its own sake. But the truth is that right actions done for the wrong reason do not help to build the internal quality or character called a 'virtue', and it is this quality or character that really matters. (If the bad tennis player hits very hard, not because he sees that a very hard stroke is required, but because he has lost his temper, his stroke might possibly, by luck, help him to win that particular game; but it will not be helping him to become a reliable player.)

(2) We might think that God wanted simply obedience to a set of rules: whereas He really wants people of a particular sort.

(3) We might think that the 'virtues' were necessary only for this present life—that in the other world we could stop being just because there is nothing to quarrel about and stop being brave because there is no danger. Now it is quite true that there will probably be no occasion for just or courageous acts in the next world, but there will be every occasion for being the sort of people that we can become only as the result of doing such acts here. The point is not that God will refuse you admission to His eternal world if you have not got certain qualities of character: the point is that if people have not got at least the beginnings of those qualities inside them, then no possible external conditions could make a 'Heaven' for them—that is, could make them happy with the deep, strong, unshakable kind of happiness God intends for us.

3

SOCIAL MORALITY

THE FIRST THING to get clear about Christian morality between man and man is that in this department Christ did not come to preach any brand new morality. The Golden Rule of the New Testament (Do as you would be done by) is a summing up of what every one, at bottom, had always known to be right. Really great moral teachers never do introduce new moralities: it is quacks and cranks who do that. As Dr Johnson said, 'People need to be reminded more often than they need to be instructed.' The real job of every moral teacher is to keep on bringing us back, time after time, to the old simple principles which we are all so anxious not to see; like bringing a horse back and back to the fence it has refused to jump or bringing a child back and back to the bit in its lesson that it wants to shirk.

The second thing to get clear is that Christianity has not, and does not profess to have, a detailed political programme for applying 'Do as you would be done by' to a particular society at a particular moment. It could not have. It is meant for all men at all times and the particular programme which suited one place or time would not suit another. And, anyhow, that is not how Christianity works. When it tells you to feed the hungry it does not give you lessons in cookery. When it tells you to read the Scriptures it does not give you lessons in Hebrew and Greek, or even in English grammar. It was never intended to replace or supersede the ordinary human arts and sciences: it is rather a director which will set them all to the right jobs, and a source of energy which will give them all new life, if only they will put themselves at its disposal.

People say, 'The Church ought to give us a lead.' That is true if they mean it in the right way, but false if they mean it in the wrong way. By the Church they ought to mean the whole body of practising Christians. And when they say that the Church should give us a lead, they ought to mean that some Christians—those who happen to have the right talents—should be economists and statesmen, and that all economists and statesmen should be Christians, and that their whole efforts in politics and economics should be directed to putting 'Do as you would be done by' into action. If that happened, and if we others were really ready to take it, then we should find the Christian solution for our own social problems pretty quickly. But, of course, when they ask for a lead from the Church most people mean they want the clergy to put out a political programme. That is silly. The clergy are those particular people within the whole Church who have been specially trained and set aside to look after what concerns us as creatures who are going to live for ever: and we are asking them to do a quite different job for which they have not been trained. The job is really on us, on the laymen. The application of Christian principles, say, to trade unionism or education, must come from Christian trade unionists and Christian schoolmasters: just as Christian literature comes from Christian novelists and dramatists—not from the bench of bishops getting together and trying to write plays and novels in their spare time.

All the same, the New Testament, without going into details, gives us a pretty clear hint of what a fully Christian society would be like. Perhaps it gives us more than we can take. It tells us that there are to be no passengers or parasites: if man does not work, he ought not to eat. Every one is to work with his own hands, and what is more, every one's work is to produce something good: there will be no manufacture of silly luxuries and then of sillier advertisements to persuade us to buy them. And there is to be no 'swank' or 'side', no putting on airs. To that extent a Christian society would be what we now call Leftist. On the other hand, it is always insisting on obedience—obedience (and outward marks of respect) from all of us to properly appointed magistrates, from children to parents, and (I am afraid this is going to be very unpopular) from wives to husbands. Thirdly, it is to be a cheerful society: full of singing and rejoicing, and regarding worry or anxiety as wrong. Courtesy is one of the Christian virtues; and the New Testament hates what it calls 'busybodies'.

If there were such a society in existence and you or I visited it, I think we should come away with a curious impression. We should feel that its economic life was very socialistic and, in that sense, 'advanced', but that its family life and its code of manners were rather old fashioned—perhaps even ceremonious and aristocratic. Each of us would like some bits of it, but I am afraid very few of us would like the whole thing. That is just what one would expect if Christianity is the total plan for the human machine. We have all departed from that total plan in different ways, and each of us wants to make out that his own modification of the original plan is the plan itself. You will find this again and again about anything that is really Christian: every one is attracted by bits of it and wants to pick out those bits and leave the rest. That is why we do not get much further: and that is why people who are fighting for quite opposite things can both say they are fighting for Christianity.

Now another point. There is one bit of advice given to us by the ancient heathen Greeks, and by the Jews in the Old Testament, and by the great Christian teachers of the Middle Ages, which the modern economic system has completely disobeyed. All these people told us not to lend money at interest; and lending money at interest—what we call investment—is the basis of our whole system. Now it may not absolutely follow that we are wrong. Some people say that when Moses and Aristotle and the Christians agreed in forbidding interest (or 'usury' as they called it), they could not foresee the joint stock company, and were only thinking of the private money-lender, and that, therefore, we need not bother about what they said. That is a question I cannot decide on. I am not an economist and I simply do not know whether the investment system is responsible for the state we are in or not. This is where we want the Christian economist. But I should not have been honest if I had not told you that three great civilisations had agreed (or so it seems at first sight) in condemning the very thing on which we have based our whole life.

One more point and I am done. In the passage where the New Testament says that every one must work, it gives as a reason 'in order that he may have something to give to those in need'. Charity—giving to the poor—is an essential part of Christian morality: in the frightening parable of the sheep and the goats it seems to be the point on which everything turns. Some people nowadays say that charity ought to be unnecessary and that instead of giving to the poor we ought to be producing a society in which there were no poor to give to. They may be quite right in saying that we ought to produce this kind of society. But if anyone thinks that, as a consequence, you can stop giving in the meantime, then he has parted company with all Christian morality. I do not believe one can settle how much we ought to give. I am afraid the only safe rule is to give more than we can spare. In other words, if our expenditure on comforts, luxuries, amusements, etc., is up to the standard common among those with the same income as our own, we are probably giving away too little. If our charities do not at all pinch or hamper us, I should say they are too small. There ought to be things we should like to do and cannot do because our charities expenditure excludes them. I am speaking now of 'charities' in the common way. Particular cases of distress among your own relatives, friends, neighbours or employees, which God, as it were, forces upon your notice, may demand much more: even to the crippling and endangering of your own position. For many of us the great obstacle to charity lies not in our luxurious living or desire for more money, but in our fear—fear of insecurity. This must often be recognised as a temptation. Sometimes our pride also hinders our charity; we are tempted to spend more than we ought on the showy forms of generosity (tipping, hospitality) and less than we ought on those who really need our help.

And now, before I end, I am going to venture on a guess as to how this section has affected any who have read it. My guess is that there are some Leftist people among them who are very angry that it has not gone further in that direction, and some people of an opposite sort who are angry because they think it has gone much too far. If so, that brings us right up against the real snag in all this drawing up of blueprints for a Christian society. Most of us are not really approaching the subject in order to find out what Christianity says: we are approaching it in the hope of finding support from Christianity for the views of our own party. We are looking for an ally where we are offered either a Master or—a Judge. I am just the same. There are bits in this section that I wanted to leave out. And that is why nothing whatever is going to come of such talks unless we go a much longer way round. A Christian society is not going to arrive until most of us really want it: and we are not going to want it until we become fully Christian. I may repeat 'Do as you would be done by' till I am black in the face, but I cannot really carry it out till I love my neighbour as myself: and I cannot learn to love my neighbour as myself till I learn to love God: and I cannot learn to love God except by learning to obey Him. And so, as I warned you, we are driven on to something more inward—driven on from social matters to religious matters. For the longest way round is the shortest way home.

4

MORALITY AND PSYCHOANALYSIS

I HAVE SAID that we should never get a Christian society unless most of us became Christian individuals. That does not mean, of course, that we can put off doing anything about society until some imaginary date in the far future. It means that we must begin both jobs at once—(1) the job of seeing how 'Do as you would be done by' can be applied in detail to modern society, and (2) the job of becoming the sort of people who really would apply it if we saw how. I now want to begin considering what the Christian idea of a good man is—the Christian specification for the human machine.

Before I come down to details there are two more general points I should like to make. First of all, since Christian morality claims to be a technique for putting the human machine right, I think you would like to know how it is related to another technique which seems to make a similar claim—namely, psychoanalysis.

Now you want to distinguish very clearly between two things: between the actual medical theories and technique of the psychoanalysts, and the general philosophical view of the world which Freud and some others have gone on to add to this. The second thing—the philosophy of Freud—is in direct contradiction to the other great psychologist, Jung. And furthermore, when Freud is talking about how to cure neurotics he is speaking as a specialist on his own subject, but when he goes on to talk general philosophy he is speaking as an amateur. It is therefore quite sensible to attend to him with respect in the one case and not in the other—and that is what I do. I am all the readier to do it because I have found that when he is talking off his own subject and on a subject I do know something about (namely, language) he is very ignorant. But psychoanalysis itself, apart from all the philosophical additions that Freud and others have made to it, is not in the least contradictory to Christianity. Its technique overlaps with Christian morality at some points and it would not be a bad thing if every person knew something about it: but it does not run the same course all the way, for the two techniques are doing rather different things.

When a man makes a moral choice two things are involved. One is the act of choosing. The other is the various feelings, impulses and so on which his psychological outfit presents him with, and which are the raw material of his choice. Now this raw material may be of two kinds. Either it may be what we would call normal: it may consist of the sort of feelings that are common to all men. Or else it may consist of quite unnatural feelings due to things that have gone wrong in his subconscious. Thus fear of things that are really dangerous would be an example of the first kind: an irrational fear of cats or spiders would be an example of the second kind. The desire of a man for a woman would be of the first kind: the perverted desire of a man for a man would be of the second. Now what psychoanalysis undertakes to do is to remove the abnormal feelings, that is, to give the man better raw material for his acts of choice; morality is concerned with the acts of choice themselves.

Put it this way. Imagine three men who go to a war. One has the ordinary natural fear of danger that any man has and he subdues it by moral effort and becomes a brave man. Let us suppose that the other two have, as a result of things in their subconscious, exaggerated, irrational fears, which no amount of moral effort can do anything about. Now suppose that a psychoanalyst comes along and cures these two: that is, he puts them both back in the position of the first man. Well it is just then that the psychoanalytical problem is over and the moral problem begins. Because, now that they are cured, these two men might take quite different lines. The first might say, 'Thank goodness I've got rid of all those doo-dahs. Now at last I can do what I always wanted to do—my duty to my country.' But the other might say, 'Well, I'm very glad that I now feel moderately cool under fire, but, of course, that doesn't alter the fact that I'm still jolly well determined to look after Number One and let the other chap do the dangerous job whenever I can. Indeed one of the good things about feeling less frightened is that I can now look after myself much more efficiently and can be much cleverer at hiding the fact from the others.' Now this difference is a purely moral one and psychoanalysis cannot do anything about it. However much you improve the man's raw material, you have still got something else: the real, free choice of the man, on the material presented to him, either to put his own advantage first or to put it last. And this free choice is the only thing that morality is concerned with.

The bad psychological material is not a sin but a disease. It does not need to be repented of, but to be cured. And by the way, that is very important. Human beings judge one another by their external actions. God judges them by their moral choices. When a neurotic who has a pathological horror of cats forces himself to pick up a cat for some good reason, it is quite possible that in God's eyes he has shown more courage than a healthy man may have shown in winning the V.C. When a man who has been perverted from his youth and taught that cruelty is the right thing, does some tiny little kindness, or refrains from some cruelty he might have committed, and thereby, perhaps, risks being sneered at by his companions, he may, in God's eyes, be doing more than you and I would do if we gave up life itself for a friend.

It is as well to put this the other way round. Some of us who seem quite nice people may, in fact, have made so little use of a good heredity and a good upbringing that we are really worse than those whom we regard as fiends. Can we be quite certain how we should have behaved if we had been saddled with the psychological outfit, and then with the bad upbringing, and then with the power, say, of Himmler? That is why Christians are told not to judge. We see only the results which a man's choices make out of his raw material. But God does not judge him on the raw material at all, but on what he has done with it. Most of the man's psychological makeup is probably due to his body: when his body dies all that will fall off him, and the real central man, the thing that chose, that made the best or the worst out of this material, will stand naked. All sorts of nice things which we thought our own, but which were really due to a good digestion, will fall off some of us: all sorts of nasty things which were due to complexes or bad health will fall off others. We shall then, for the first time, see every one as he really was. There will be surprises.

And that leads on to my second point. People often think of Christian morality as a kind of bargain in which God says, 'If you keep a lot of rules I'll reward you, and if you don't I'll do the other thing.' I do not think that is the best way of looking at it. I would much rather say that every time you make a choice you are turning the central part of you, the part of you that chooses, into something a little different from what it was before. And taking your life as a whole, with all your innumerable choices, all your life long you are slowly turning this central thing either into a heavenly creature or into a hellish creature: either into a creature that is in harmony with God, and with other creatures, and with itself, or else into one that is in a state of war and hatred with God, and with its fellow-creatures, and with itself. To be the one kind of creature is heaven: that is, it is joy and peace and knowledge and power. To be the other means madness, horror, idiocy, rage, impotence, and eternal loneliness. Each of us at each moment is progressing to the one state or the other.

That explains what always used to puzzle me about Christian writers; they seem to be so very strict at one moment and so very free and easy at another. They talk about mere sins of thought as if they were immensely important: and then they talk about the most frightful murders and treacheries as if you had only got to repent and all would be forgiven. But I have come to see that they are right. What they are always thinking of is the mark which the action leaves on that tiny central self which no one sees in this life but which each of us will have to endure—or enjoy—for ever. One man may be so placed that his anger sheds the blood of thousands, and another so placed that however angry he gets he will only be laughed at. But the little mark on the soul may be much the same in both. Each has done something to himself which, unless he repents, will make it harder for him to keep out of the rage next time he is tempted, and will make the rage worse when he does fall into it. Each of them, if he seriously turns to God, can have that twist in the central man straightened out again: each is, in the long run, doomed if he will not. The bigness or smallness of the thing, seen from the outside, is not what really matters.

One last point. Remember that, as I said, the right direction leads not only to peace but to knowledge. When a man is getting better he understands more and more clearly the evil that is still left in him. When a man is getting worse he understands his own badness less and less. A moderately bad man knows he is not very good: a thoroughly bad man thinks he is all right. This is common sense, really. You understand sleep when you are awake, not while you are sleeping. You can see mistakes in arithmetic when your mind is working properly: while you are making them you cannot see them. You can understand the nature of drunkenness when you are sober, not when you are drunk. Good people know about both good and evil: bad people do not know about either.

5

SEXUAL MORALITY

WE MUST NOW consider Christian morality as regards sex, what Christians call the virtue of chastity. The Christian rule of chastity must not be confused with the social rule of 'modesty' (in one sense of that word); i.e. propriety, or decency. The social rule of propriety lays down how much of the human body should be displayed and what subjects can be referred to, and in what words, according to the customs of a given social circle. Thus, while the rule of chastity is the same for all Christians at all times, the rule of propriety changes. A girl in the Pacific islands wearing hardly any clothes and a Victorian lady completely covered in clothes might both be equally 'modest', proper, or decent, according to the standards of their own societies: and both, for all we could tell by their dress, might be equally chaste (or equally unchaste). Some of the language which chaste women used in Shakespeare's time would have been used in the nineteenth century only by a woman completely abandoned. When people break the rule of propriety current in their own time and place, if they do so in order to excite lust in themselves or others, then they are offending against chastity. But if they break it through ignorance or carelessness they are guilty only of bad manners. When, as often happens, they break it defiantly in order to shock or embarrass others, they are not necessarily being unchaste, but they are being uncharitable: for it is uncharitable to take pleasure in making other people uncomfortable. I do not think that a very strict or fussy standard of propriety is any proof of chastity or any help to it, and I therefore regard the great relaxation and simplifying of the rule which has taken place in my own lifetime as a good thing. At its present stage, however, it has this inconvenience, that people of different ages and different types do not all acknowledge the same standard, and we hardly know where we are. While this confusion lasts I think that old, or old-fashioned, people should be very careful not to assume that young or 'emancipated' people are corrupt whenever they are (by the old standard) improper; and, in return, that young people should not call their elders prudes or puritans because they do not easily adopt the new standard. A real desire to believe all the good you can of others and to make others as comfortable as you can will solve most of the problems.

Chastity is the most unpopular of the Christian virtues. There is no getting away from it; the Christian rule is, 'Either marriage, with complete faithfulness to your partner, or else total abstinence.' Now this is so difficult and so contrary to our instincts, that obviously either Christianity is wrong or our sexual instinct, as it now is, has gone wrong. One or the other. Of course, being a Christian, I think it is the instinct which has gone wrong.

But I have other reasons for thinking so. The biological purpose of sex is children, just as the biological purpose of eating is to repair the body. Now if we eat whenever we feel inclined and just as much as we want, it is quite true most of us will eat too much: but not terrifically too much. One man may eat enough for two, but he does not eat enough for ten. The appetite goes a little beyond its biological purpose, but not enormously. But if a healthy young man indulged his sexual appetite whenever he felt inclined, and if each act produced a baby, then in ten years he might easily populate a small village. This appetite is in ludicrous and preposterous excess of its function.

Or take it another way. You can get a large audience together for a strip-tease act—that is, to watch a girl undress on the stage. Now suppose you come to a country where you could fill a theatre by simply bringing a covered plate on to the stage and then slowly lifting the cover so as to let every one see, just before the lights went out, that it contained a mutton chop or a bit of bacon, would you not think that in that country something had gone wrong with the appetite for food? And would not anyone who had grown up in a different world think there was something equally queer about the state of the sex instinct among us?

One critic said that if he found a country in which such strip-tease acts with food were popular, he would conclude that the people of that country were starving. He meant, of course, to imply that such things as the strip-tease act resulted not from sexual corruption but from sexual star-vation. I agree with him that if, in some strange land, we found that simi-lar acts with mutton chops were popular, one of the possible explanations which would occur to me would be famine. But the next step would be to test our hypothesis by finding out whether, in fact, much or little food was being consumed in that country. If the evidence showed that a good deal was being eaten, then of course we should have to abandon the hypoth-esis of starvation and try to think of another one. In the same way, before accepting sexual starvation as the cause of the strip-tease, we should have to look for evidence that there is in fact more sexual abstinence in our age than in those ages when things like the strip-tease were unknown. But surely there is no such evidence. Contraceptives have made sexual indulgence far less costly within marriage and far safer outside it than ever before, and public opinion is less hostile to illicit unions and even to perversion than it has been since Pagan times. Nor is the hypothesis of 'starvation' the only one we can imagine. Everyone knows that the sexual appetite, like our other appetites, grows by indulgence. Starving men may think much about food, but so do gluttons; the gorged, as well as the famished, like titillations.

Here is a third point. You find very few people who want to eat things that really are not food or to do other things with food instead of eating it. In other words, perversions of the food appetite are rare. But perversions of the sex instinct are numerous, hard to cure, and frightful. I am sorry to have to go into all these details but I must. The reason why I must is that you and I, for the last twenty years, have been fed all day long on good solid lies about sex. We have been told, till one is sick of hearing it, that sexual desire is in the same state as any of our other natural desires and that if only we abandon the silly old Victorian idea of hushing it up, ev-erything in the garden will be lovely. It is not true. The moment you look at the facts, and away from the propaganda, you see that it is not.

They tell you sex has become a mess because it was hushed up. But for the last twenty years it has not been. It has been chattered about all day long. Yet it is still in a mess. If hushing up had been the cause of the trouble, ventilation would have set it right. But it has not. I think it is the other way round. I think the human race originally hushed it up because it had become such a mess. Modern people are always saying, 'Sex is nothing to be ashamed of.' They may mean two things. They may mean 'There is nothing to be ashamed of in the fact that the human race reproduces itself in a certain way, nor in the fact that it gives pleasure.' If they mean that, they are right. Christianity says the same. It is not the thing, nor the pleasure, that is the trouble. The old Christian teachers said that if man had never fallen, sexual pleasure, instead of being less than it is now, would actually have been greater. I know some muddle-headed Christians have talked as if Christianity thought that sex, or the body, or pleasure, were bad in themselves. But they were wrong. Christianity is almost the only one of the great religions which thoroughly approves of the body—which believes that matter is good, that God Himself once took on a human body, that some kind of body is going to be given to us even in Heaven and is going to be an essential part of our happiness, or beauty and our energy. Christianity has glorified marriage more than any other religion: and nearly all the greatest love poetry in the world has been produced by Christians. If anyone says that sex, in itself, is bad, Christianity contradicts him at once. But, of course, when people say, 'Sex is nothing to be ashamed of,' they may mean 'the state into which the sexual instinct has now got is nothing to be ashamed of'.

If they mean that, I think they are wrong. I think it is everything to be ashamed of. There is nothing to be ashamed of in enjoying your food: there would be everything to be ashamed of if half the world made food the main interest of their lives and spent their time looking at pictures of food and dribbling and smacking their lips. I do not say you and I are individually responsible for the present situation. Our ancestors have handed over to us organisms which are warped in this respect: and we grow up surrounded by propaganda in favour of unchastity. There are people who want to keep our sex instinct inflamed in order to make money out of us. Because, of course, a man with an obsession is a man who has very little sales-resistance. God knows our situation; He will not judge us as if we had no difficulties to overcome. What matters is the sincerity and perseverance of our will to overcome them.

Before we can be cured we must want to be cured. Those who really wish for help will get it; but for many modern people even the wish is difficult. It is easy to think that we want something when we do not really want it. A famous Christian long ago told us that when he was a young man he prayed constantly for chastity; but years later he realised that while his lips had been saying, 'Oh Lord, make me chaste,' his heart had been secretly adding, 'But please don't do it just yet.' This may happen in prayers for other virtues too; but there are three reasons why it is now specially difficult for us to desire—let alone to achieve—complete chastity.

In the first place our warped natures, the devils who tempt us, and all the contemporary propaganda for lust, combine to make us feel that the desires we are resisting are so 'natural', so 'healthy', and so reasonable, that it is almost perverse and abnormal to resist them. Poster after poster, film after film, novel after novel, associate the idea of sexual indulgence with the ideas of health, normality, youth, frankness, and good humour. Now this association is a lie. Like all powerful lies, it is based on a truth—the truth, acknowledged above, that sex in itself (apart from the excesses and obsessions that have grown round it) is 'normal' and 'healthy', and all the rest of it. The lie consists in the suggestion that any sexual act to which you are tempted at the moment is also healthy and normal. Now this, on any conceivable view, and quite apart from Christianity, must be nonsense. Surrender to all our desires obviously leads to impotence, disease, jealousies, lies, concealment, and everything that is the reverse of health, good humour, and frankness. For any happiness, even in this world, quite a lot of restraint is going to be necessary; so the claim made by every desire, when it is strong, to be healthy and reasonable, counts for nothing. Every sane and civilised man must have some set of principles by which he chooses to reject some of his desires and to permit others. One man does this on Christian principles, another on hygienic principles, another on sociological principles. The real conflict is not between Christianity and 'nature', but between Christian principles and other principles in the control of 'nature'. For 'nature' (in the sense of natural desire) will have to be controlled anyway, unless you are going to ruin your whole life. The Christian principles are, admittedly, stricter than the others; but then we think you will get help towards obeying them which you will not get towards obeying the others.

In the second place, many people are deterred from seriously attempting Christian chastity because they think (before trying) that it is impossible. But when a thing has to be attempted, one must never think about possibility or impossibility. Faced with an optional question in an examination paper, one considers whether one can do it or not: faced with a compulsory question, one must do the best one can. You may get some marks for a very imperfect answer: you will certainly get none for leaving the question alone. Not only in examinations but in war, in mountain climbing, in learning to skate, or swim, or ride a bicycle, even in fastening a stiff collar with cold fingers, people quite often do what seemed impossible before they did it. It is wonderful what you can do when you have to.

We may, indeed, be sure that perfect chastity—like perfect charity—will not be attained by any merely human efforts. You must ask for God's help. Even when you have done so, it may seem to you for a long time that no help, or less help than you need, is being given. Never mind. After each failure, ask forgiveness, pick yourself up, and try again. Very often what God first helps us towards is not the virtue itself but just this power of always trying again. For however important chastity (or courage, or truthfulness, or any other virtue) may be, this process trains us in habits of the soul which are more important still. It cures our illusions about ourselves and teaches us to depend on God. We learn, on the one hand, that we cannot trust ourselves even in our best moments, and, on the other, that we need not despair even in our worst, for our failures are forgiven. The only fatal thing is to sit down content with anything less than perfection.

Thirdly, people often misunderstand what psychology teaches about 'repressions'. It teaches us that 'repressed' sex is dangerous. But 'repressed' is here a technical term: it does not mean 'suppressed' in the sense of 'denied' or 'resisted'. A repressed desire or thought is one which has been thrust into the subconscious (usually at a very early age) and can now come before the mind only in a disguised and unrecognisable form. Repressed sexuality does not appear to the patient to be sexuality at all. When an adolescent or an adult is engaged in resisting a conscious desire, he is not dealing with a repression nor is he in the least danger of creating a repression. On the contrary, those who are seriously attempting chastity are more conscious, and soon know a great deal more about their own sexuality than anyone else. They come to know their desires as Wellington knew Napoleon, or as Sherlock Holmes knew Moriarty; as a rat-catcher knows rats or a plumber knows about leaky pipes. Virtue—even attempted virtue—brings light; indulgence brings fog.

Finally, though I have had to speak at some length about sex, I want to make it as clear as I possibly can that the centre of Christian morality is not here. If anyone thinks that Christians regard unchastity as the supreme vice, he is quite wrong. The sins of the flesh are bad, but they are the least bad of all sins. All the worst pleasures are purely spiritual: the pleasure of putting other people in the wrong, of bossing and patronising and spoiling sport, and back-biting, the pleasures of power, of hatred. For there are two things inside me, competing with the human self which I must try to become. They are the Animal self, and the Diabolical self. The Diabolical self is the worse of the two. That is why a cold, self-righteous prig who goes regularly to church may be far nearer to hell than a prostitute. But, of course, it is better to be neither.

6

CHRISTIAN MARRIAGE

THE LAST CHAPTER was mainly negative. I discussed what was wrong with the sexual impulse in man, but said very little about its right working—in other words, about Christian marriage. There are two reasons why I do not particularly want to deal with marriage. The first is that the Christian doctrines on this subject are extremely unpopular. The second is that I have never been married myself, and, therefore, can speak only at second hand. But in spite of that, I feel I can hardly leave the subject out in an account of Christian morals.

The Christian idea of marriage is based on Christ's words that a man and wife are to be regarded as a single organism—for that is what the words 'one flesh' would be in modern English. And the Christians believe that when He said this He was not expressing a sentiment but stating a fact—just as one is stating a fact when one says that a lock and its key are one mechanism, or that a violin and a bow are one musical instrument. The inventor of the human machine was telling us that its two halves, the male and the female, were made to be combined together in pairs, not simply on the sexual level, but totally combined. The monstrosity of sexual intercourse outside marriage is that those who indulge in it are trying to isolate one kind of union (the sexual) from all the other kinds of union which were intended to go along with it and make up the total union. The Christian attitude does not mean that there is anything wrong about sexual pleasure, any more than about the pleasure of eating. It means that you must not isolate that pleasure and try to get it by itself, any more than you ought to try to get the pleasures of taste without swallowing and digesting, by chewing things and spitting them out again.

As a consequence, Christianity teaches that marriage is for life. There is, of course, a difference here between different Churches: some do not admit divorce at all; some allow it reluctantly in very special cases. It is a great pity that Christians should disagree about such a question; but for an ordinary layman the thing to notice is that the Churches all agree with one another about marriage a great deal more than any of them agrees with the outside world. I mean, they all regard divorce as something like cutting up a living body, as a kind of surgical operation. Some of them think the operation so violent that it cannot be done at all; others admit it as a desperate remedy in extreme cases. They are all agreed that it is more like having both your legs cut off than it is like dissolving a business partnership or even deserting a regiment. What they all disagree with is the modern view that it is a simple readjustment of partners, to be made whenever people feel they are no longer in love with one another, or when either of them falls in love with someone else.

Before we consider this modern view in its relation to chastity, we must not forget to consider it in relation to another virtue, namely justice. Justice, as I said before, includes the keeping of promises. Now everyone who has been married in a church has made a public, solemn promise to stick to his (or her) partner till death. The duty of keeping that promise has no special connection with sexual morality: it is in the same position as any other promise. If, as modern people are always telling us, the sexual impulse is just like all our other impulses, then it ought to be treated like all our other impulses; and as their indulgence is controlled by our promises, so should its be. If, as I think, it is not like all our other impulses, but is morbidly inflamed, then we should be specially careful not to let it lead us into dishonesty.

To this someone may reply that he regarded the promise made in church as a mere formality and never intended to keep it. Whom, then, was he trying to deceive when he made it? God? That was really very unwise. Himself? That was not very much wiser. The bride, or bridegroom, or the 'in-laws'? That was treacherous. More often, I think, the couple (or one of them) hoped to deceive the public. They wanted the respectability that is attached to marriage without intending to pay the price: that is, they were impostors, they cheated. If they are still contented cheats,

I have nothing to say to them: who would urge the high and hard duty of chastity on people who have not yet wished to be merely honest? If they have now come to their senses and want to be honest, their promise, already made, constrains them. And this, you will see, comes under the heading of justice, not that of chastity. If people do not believe in permanent marriage, it is perhaps better that they should live together unmarried than that they should make vows they do not mean to keep. It is true that by living together without marriage they will be guilty (in Christian eyes) of fornication. But one fault is not mended by adding another: unchastity is not improved by adding perjury.

The idea that 'being in love' is the only reason for remaining married really leaves no room for marriage as a contract or promise at all. If love is the whole thing, then the promise can add nothing; and if it adds nothing, then it should not be made. The curious thing is that lovers themselves, while they remain really in love, know this better than those who talk about love. As Chesterton pointed out, those who are in love have a natural inclination to bind themselves by promises. Love songs all over the world are full of vows of eternal constancy. The Christian law is not forcing upon the passion of love something which is foreign to that passion's own nature: it is demanding that lovers should take seriously something which their passion of itself impels them to do.

And, of course, the promise, made when I am in love and because I am in love, to be true to the beloved as long as I live, commits me to being true even if I cease to be in love. A promise must be about things that I can do, about actions: no one can promise to go on feeling in a certain way. He might as well promise never to have a headache or always to feel hungry. But what, it may be asked, is the use of keeping two people together if they are no longer in love? There are several sound, social reasons; to provide a home for their children, to protect the woman (who has probably sacrificed or damaged her own career by getting married) from being dropped whenever the man is tired of her. But there is also another reason of which I am very sure, though I find it a little hard to explain.

It is hard because so many people cannot be brought to realise that when B is better than C, A may be even better than B. They like thinking in terms of good and bad, not of good, better, and best, or bad, worse and worst. They want to know whether you think patriotism a good thing: if you reply that it is, of course, far better than individual selfishness, but that it is inferior to universal charity and should always give way to universal charity when the two conflict, they think you are being evasive. They ask what you think of duelling. If you reply that it is far better to forgive a man than to fight a duel with him, but that even a duel might be better than a lifelong enmity which expresses itself in secret efforts to 'do the man down', they go away complaining that you would not give them a straight answer. I hope no one will make this mistake about what I am now going to say.

What we call 'being in love' is a glorious state, and, in several ways, good for us. It helps to make us generous and courageous, it opens our eyes not only to the beauty of the beloved but to all beauty, and it subordinates (especially at first) our merely animal sexuality; in that sense, love is the great conqueror of lust. No one in his senses would deny that being in love is far better than either common sensuality or cold self-centredness. But, as I said before, 'the most dangerous thing you can do is to take any one impulse of our own nature and set it up as the thing you ought to follow at all costs'. Being in love is a good thing, but it is not the best thing. There are many things below it, but there are also things above it. You cannot make it the basis of a whole life. It is a noble feeling, but it is still a feeling. Now no feeling can be relied on to last in its full intensity, or even to last at all. Knowledge can last, principles can last, habits can last; but feelings come and go. And in fact, whatever people say, the state called 'being in love' usually does not last. If the old fairy-tale ending 'They lived happily ever after' is taken to mean 'They felt for the next fifty years exactly as they felt the day before they were married', then it says what probably never was nor ever would be true, and would be highly undesirable if it were. Who could bear to live in that excitement for even five years? What would become of your work, your appetite, your sleep, your friendships? But, of course, ceasing to be 'in love' need not mean ceasing to love. Love in this second sense—love as distinct from 'being in love'—is not merely a feeling. It is a deep unity, maintained by the will and deliberately strengthened by habit; reinforced by (in Christian marriages) the grace which both partners ask, and receive, from God. They can have this love for each other even at those moments when they do not like each other; as you love yourself even when you do not like yourself. They can retain this love even when each would easily, if they allowed themselves, be 'in love' with someone else. 'Being in love' first moved them to promise fidelity: this quieter love enables them to keep the promise. It is on this love that the engine of marriage is run: being in love was the explosion that started it.

If you disagree with me, of course, you will say, 'He knows nothing about it, he is not married.' You may quite possibly be right. But before you say that, make quite sure that you are judging me by what you really know from your own experience and from watching the lives of your friends, and not by ideas you have derived from novels and films. This is not so easy to do as people think. Our experience is coloured through and through by books and plays and the cinema, and it takes patience and skill to disentangle the things we have really learned from life for ourselves.

People get from books the idea that if you have married the right person you may expect to go on 'being in love' for ever. As a result, when they find they are not, they think this proves they have made a mistake and are entitled to a change—not realising that, when they have changed, the glamour will presently go out of the new love just as it went out of the old one. In this department of life, as in every other, thrills come at the beginning and do not last. The sort of thrill a boy has at the first idea of flying will not go on when he has joined the R.A.F. and is really learning to fly. The thrill you feel on first seeing some delightful place dies away when you really go to live there. Does this mean it would be better not to learn to fly and not to live in the beautiful place? By no means. In both cases, if you go through with it, the dying away of the first thrill will be compensated for by a quieter and more lasting kind of interest. What is more (and I can hardly find words to tell you how important I think this), it is just the people who are ready to submit to the loss of the thrill and settle down to the sober interest, who are then most likely to meet new thrills in some quite different direction. The man who has learned to fly and become a good pilot will suddenly discover music; the man who has settled down to live in the beauty spot will discover gardening.

This is, I think, one little part of what Christ meant by saying that a thing will not really live unless it first dies. It is simply no good trying to keep any thrill: that is the very worst thing you can do. Let the thrill go—let it die away—go on through that period of death into the quieter interest and happiness that follow—and you will find you are living in a world of new thrills all the time. But if you decide to make thrills your regular diet and try to prolong them artificially, they will all get weaker and weaker, and fewer and fewer, and you will be a bored, disillusioned old man for the rest of your life. It is because so few people understand this that you find many middle-aged men and women maundering about their lost youth, at the very age when new horizons ought to be appearing and new doors opening all round them. It is much better fun to learn to swim than to go on endlessly (and hopelessly) trying to get back the feeling you had when you first went paddling as a small boy.

Another notion we get from novels and plays is that 'falling in love' is something quite irresistible; something that just happens to one, like measles. And because they believe this, some married people throw up the sponge and give in when they find themselves attracted by a new acquaintance. But I am inclined to think that these irresistible passions are much rarer in real life than in books, at any rate when one is grown up. When we meet someone beautiful and clever and sympathetic, of course we ought, in one sense, to admire and love these good qualities. But is it not very largely in our own choice whether this love shall, or shall not, turn into what we call 'being in love'? No doubt, if our minds are full of novels and plays and sentimental songs, and our bodies full of alcohol, we shall turn any love we feel into that kind of love: just as if you have a rut in your path all the rainwater will run into that rut, and if you wear blue spectacles everything you see will turn blue. But that will be our own fault.

Before leaving the question of divorce, I should like to distinguish two things which are very often confused. The Christian conception of marriage is one: the other is the quite different question—how far Christians, if they are voters or Members of Parliament, ought to try to force their views of marriage on the rest of the community by embodying them in the divorce laws. A great many people seem to think that if you are a Christian yourself you should try to make divorce difficult for every one. I do not think that. At least I know I should be very angry if the Mohammedans tried to prevent the rest of us from drinking wine. My own view is that the Churches should frankly recognise that the majority of the British people are not Christians and, therefore, cannot be expected to live Christian lives. There ought to be two distinct kinds of marriage: one governed by the State with rules enforced on all citizens, the other governed by the Church with rules enforced by her on her own members. The distinction ought to be quite sharp, so that a man knows which couples are married in a Christian sense and which are not.

So much for the Christian doctrine about the permanence of marriage. Something else, even more unpopular, remains to be dealt with. Christian wives promise to obey their husbands. In Christian marriage the man is said to be the 'head'. Two questions obviously arise here. (1) Why should there be a head at all—why not equality? (2) Why should it be the man?

(1) The need for some head follows from the idea that marriage is permanent. Of course, as long as the husband and wife are agreed, no question of a head need arise; and we may hope that this will be the normal state of affairs in a Christian marriage. But when there is a real disagreement, what is to happen? Talk it over, of course; but I am assuming they have done that and still failed to reach agreement. What do they do next? They cannot decide by a majority vote, for in a council of two there can be no majority. Surely, only one or other of two things can happen: either they must separate and go their own ways or else one or other of them must have a casting vote. If marriage is permanent, one or other party must, in the last resort, have the power of deciding the family policy. You cannot have a permanent association without a constitution.

(2) If there must be a head, why the man? Well, firstly is there any very serious wish that it should be the woman? As I have said, I am not married myself, but as far as I can see, even a woman who wants to be the head of her own house does not usually admire the same state of things when she finds it going on next door. She is much more likely to say 'Poor Mr X! Why he allows that appalling woman to boss him about the way she does is more than I can imagine.' I do not think she is even very flattered if anyone mentions the fact of her own 'headship'. There must be something unnatural about the rule of wives over husbands, because the wives themselves are half ashamed of it and despise the husbands whom they rule. But there is also another reason; and here I speak quite frankly as a bachelor, because it is a reason you can see from outside even better than from inside. The relations of the family to the outer world— what might be called its foreign policy—must depend, in the last resort, upon the man, because he always ought to be, and usually is, much more just to the outsiders. A woman is primarily fighting for her own children and husband against the rest of the world. Naturally, almost, in a sense, rightly, their claims override, for her, all other claims. She is the special trustee of their interests. The function of the husband is to see that this natural preference of hers is not given its head. He has the last word in order to protect other people from the intense family patriotism of the wife. If anyone doubts this, let me ask a simple question. If your dog has bitten the child next door, or if your child has hurt the dog next door,

which would you sooner have to deal with, the master of that house or the mistress? Or, if you are a married woman, let me ask you this question. Much as you admire your husband, would you not say that his chief failing is his tendency not to stick up for his rights and yours against the neighbours as vigorously as you would like? A bit of an Appeaser?

7

FORGIVENESS

I SAID IN a previous chapter that chastity was the most unpopular of the Christian virtues. But I am not sure I was right. I believe there is one even more unpopular. It is laid down in the Christian rule, 'Thou shalt love thy neighbour as thyself.' Because in Christian morals 'thy neighbour' includes 'thy enemy', and so we come up against this terrible duty of forgiving our enemies.

Every one says forgiveness is a lovely idea, until they have something to forgive, as we had during the war. And then, to mention the subject at all is to be greeted with howls of anger. It is not that people think this too high and difficult a virtue: it is that they think it hateful and contemptible. 'That sort of talk makes them sick,' they say. And half of you already want to ask me, 'I wonder how you'd feel about forgiving the Gestapo if you were a Pole or a Jew?'

So do I. I wonder very much. Just as when Christianity tells me that I must not deny my religion even to save myself from death by torture, I wonder very much what I should do when it came to the point. I am not trying to tell you in this book what I could do—I can do precious little—I am telling you what Christianity is. I did not invent it. And there, right in the middle of it, I find 'Forgive us our sins as we forgive those that sin against us.' There is no slightest suggestion that we are offered forgiveness on any other terms. It is made perfectly clear that if we do not forgive we shall not be forgiven. There are no two ways about it. What are we to do?

It is going to be hard enough, anyway, but I think there are two things we can do to make it easier. When you start mathematics you do not begin with the calculus; you begin with simple addition. In the same way, if we really want (but all depends on really wanting) to learn how to forgive, perhaps we had better start with something easier than the Gestapo. One might start with forgiving one's husband or wife, or parents or children, or the nearest N.C.O., for something they have done or said in the last week. That will probably keep us busy for the moment. And secondly, we might try to understand exactly what loving your neighbour as yourself means. I have to love him as I love myself. Well, how exactly do I love myself?

Now that I come to think of it, I have not exactly got a feeling of fondness or affection for myself, and I do not even always enjoy my own society. So apparently 'Love your neighbour' does not mean 'feel fond of him' or 'find him attractive'. I ought to have seen that before, because, of course, you cannot feel fond of a person by trying. Do I think well of myself, think myself a nice chap? Well, I am afraid I sometimes do (and those are, no doubt, my worst moments) but that is not why I love myself. In fact it is the other way round: my self-love makes me think myself nice, but thinking myself nice is not why I love myself. So loving my enemies does not apparently mean thinking them nice either. That is an enormous relief. For a good many people imagine that forgiving your enemies means making out that they are really not such bad fellows after all, when it is quite plain that they are. Go a step further. In my most clear-sighted moments not only do I not think myself a nice man, but I know that I am a very nasty one. I can look at some of the things I have done with horror and loathing. So apparently I am allowed to loathe and hate some of the things my enemies do. Now that I come to think of it, I remember Christian teachers telling me long ago that I must hate a bad man's actions, but not hate the bad man: or, as they would say, hate the sin but not the sinner.

For a long time I used to think this a silly, straw-splitting distinction: how could you hate what a man did and not hate the man? But years later it occurred to me that there was one man to whom I had been doing this all my life—namely myself. However much I might dislike my own cowardice or conceit or greed, I went on loving myself. There had never been the slightest difficulty about it. In fact the very reason why I hated the things was that I loved the man. Just because I loved myself, I was sorry to find that I was the sort of man who did those things. Consequently, Christianity does not want us to reduce by one atom the hatred we feel for cruelty and treachery. We ought to hate them. Not one word of what we have said about them needs to be unsaid. But it does want us to hate them in the same way in which we hate things in ourselves: being sorry that the man should have done such things, and hoping, if it is anyway possible, that somehow, sometime, somewhere he can be cured and made human again.

The real test is this. Suppose one reads a story of filthy atrocities in the paper. Then suppose that something turns up suggesting that the story might not be quite true, or not quite so bad as it was made out. Is one's first feeling, 'Thank God, even they aren't quite so bad as that,' or is it a feeling of disappointment, and even a determination to cling to the first story for the sheer pleasure of thinking your enemies as bad as possible? If it is the second then it is, I am afraid, the first step in a process which, if followed to the end, will make us into devils. You see, one is beginning to wish that black was a little blacker. If we give that wish its head, later on we shall wish to see grey as black, and then to see white itself as black. Finally, we shall insist on seeing everything—God and our friends and ourselves included—as bad, and not be able to stop doing it: we shall be fixed for ever in a universe of pure hatred.

Now a step further. Does loving your enemy mean not punishing him? No, for loving myself does not mean that I ought not to subject myself to punishment—even to death. If you had committed a murder, the right Christian thing to do would be to give yourself up to the police and be hanged. It is, therefore, in my opinion, perfectly right for a Christian judge to sentence a man to death or a Christian soldier to kill an enemy. I always have thought so, ever since I became a Christian, and long before the war, and I still think so now that we are at peace. It is no good quoting 'Thou shalt not kill.' There are two Greek words: the ordinary word to *kill* and the word to *murder*. And when Christ quotes that commandment He uses the *murder* one in all three accounts, Matthew, Mark, and Luke. And I am told there is the same distinction in Hebrew. All killing is not murder any more than all sexual intercourse is adultery. When soldiers came to St John the Baptist asking what to do, he never remotely suggested that they ought to leave the army: nor did Christ when He met a Roman sergeant-major—what they called a centurion. The idea of the knight—the Christian in arms for the defence of a good cause—is one of the great Christian ideas. War is a dreadful thing, and I can respect an honest pacifist, though I think he is entirely mistaken. What I cannot understand is this sort of semi-pacifism you get nowadays which gives people the idea that though you have to fight, you ought to do it with a long face and as if you were ashamed of it. It is that feeling that robs lots of magnificent young Christians in the Services of something they have a right to, something which is the natural accompaniment of courage—a kind of gaiety and wholeheartedness.

I have often thought to myself how it would have been if, when I served in the First World War, I and some young German had killed each other simultaneously and found ourselves together a moment after death. I cannot imagine that either of us would have felt any resentment or even any embarrassment. I think we might have laughed over it.

I imagine somebody will say, 'Well, if one is allowed to condemn the enemy's acts, and punish him, and kill him, what difference is left between Christian morality and the ordinary view?' All the difference in the world. Remember, we Christians think man lives for ever. Therefore, what really matters is those little marks or twists on the central, inside part of the soul which are going to turn it, in the long run, into a heavenly or a hellish creature. We may kill if necessary, but we must not hate and enjoy hating. We may punish if necessary, but we must not enjoy it. In other words, something inside us, the feeling of resentment, the feeling that wants to get one's own back, must be simply killed. I do not mean that anyone can decide this moment that he will never feel it any more. That is not how things happen. I mean that every time it bobs its head up, day after day, year after year, all our lives long, we must hit it on the head. It is hard work, but the attempt is not impossible. Even while we kill and punish we must try to feel about the enemy as we feel about ourselves—to wish that he were not bad, to hope that he may, in this world or another, be cured: in fact, to wish his good. That is what is meant in the Bible by loving him: wishing his good, not feeling fond of him nor saying he is nice when he is not.

I admit that this means loving people who have nothing lovable about them. But then, has oneself anything lovable about it? You love it simply because it is yourself. God intends us to love all selves in the same way and for the same reason: but He has given us the sum ready worked out in our own case to show us how it works. We have then to go on and apply the rule to all the other selves. Perhaps it makes it easier if we remember that that is how He loves us. Not for any nice, attractive qualities we think we have, but just because we are the things called selves. For really there is nothing else in us to love: creatures like us who actually find hatred such a pleasure that to give it up is like giving up beer or tobacco . . .

8

THE GREAT SIN

I NOW COME to that part of Christian morals where they differ most sharply from all other morals. There is one vice of which no man in the world is free; which every one in the world loathes when he sees it in someone else; and of which hardly any people, except Christians, ever imagine that they are guilty themselves. I have heard people admit that they are bad-tempered, or that they cannot keep their heads about girls or drink, or even that they are cowards. I do not think I have ever heard anyone who was not a Christian accuse himself of this vice. And at the same time I have very seldom met anyone, who was not a Christian, who showed the slightest mercy to it in others. There is no fault which makes a man more unpopular, and no fault which we are more unconscious of in ourselves. And the more we have it ourselves, the more we dislike it in others.

The vice I am talking of is Pride or Self-Conceit: and the virtue opposite to it, in Christian morals, is called Humility. You may remember, when I was talking about sexual morality, I warned you that the centre of Christian morals did not lie there. Well, now, we have come to the centre. According to Christian teachers, the essential vice, the utmost evil, is Pride. Unchastity, anger, greed, drunkenness, and all that, are mere flea-bites in comparison: it was through Pride that the devil became the devil: Pride leads to every other vice: it is the complete anti-God state of mind.

Does this seem to you exaggerated? If so, think it over. I pointed out a moment ago that the more pride one had, the more one disliked pride in others. In fact, if you want to find out how proud you are the easiest way is to ask yourself, 'How much do I dislike it when other people snub me, or refuse to take any notice of me, or shove their oar in, or patronise me, or show off?' The point is that each person's pride is in competition with every one else's pride. It is because I wanted to be the big noise at the party that I am so annoyed at someone else being the big noise. Two of a trade never agree. Now what you want to get clear is that Pride is *essentially* competitive—is competitive by its very nature—while the other vices are competitive only, so to speak, by accident. Pride gets no pleasure out of having something, only out of having more of it than the next man. We say that people are proud of being rich, or clever, or good-looking, but they are not. They are proud of being richer, or cleverer, or better-looking than others. If everyone else became equally rich, or clever, or good-looking there would be nothing to be proud about. It is the comparison that makes you proud: the pleasure of being above the rest. Once the element of competition has gone, pride has gone. That is why I say that Pride is essentially competitive in a way the other vices are not. The sexual impulse may drive two men into competition if they both want the same girl. But that is only by accident; they might just as likely have wanted two different girls. But a proud man will take your girl from you, not because he wants her, but just to prove to himself that he is a better man than you. Greed may drive men into competition if there is not enough to go round; but the proud man, even when he has got more than he can possibly want, will try to get still more just to assert his power. Nearly all those evils in the world which people put down to greed or selfishness are really far more the result of Pride.

Take it with money. Greed will certainly make a man want money, for the sake of a better house, better holidays, better things to eat and drink. But only up to a point. What is it that makes a man with £10,000 a year anxious to get £20,000 a year? It is not the greed for more pleasure. £10,000 will give all the luxuries that any man can really enjoy. It is Pride—the wish to be richer than some other rich man, and (still more) the wish for power. For, of course, power is what Pride really enjoys: there is nothing makes a man feel so superior to others as being able to move them about like toy soldiers. What makes a pretty girl spread misery wherever she goes by collecting admirers? Certainly not her sexual instinct: that kind of girl is quite often sexually frigid. It is Pride. What is it that makes a political leader or a whole nation go on and on, demanding more and more? Pride again. Pride is competitive by its very nature: that is why it goes on and on. If I am a proud man, then, as long as there is one man in the whole world more powerful, or richer, or cleverer than I, he is my rival and my enemy.

The Christians are right: it is Pride which has been the chief cause of misery in every nation and every family since the world began. Other vices may sometimes bring people together: you may find good fellowship and jokes and friendliness among drunken people or unchaste people. But pride always means enmity—it *is* enmity. And not only enmity between man and man, but enmity to God.

In God you come up against something which is in every respect immeasurably superior to yourself. Unless you know God as that—and, therefore, know yourself as nothing in comparison—you do not know God at all. As long as you are proud you cannot know God. A proud man is always looking down on things and people: and, of course, as long as you are looking down, you cannot see something that is above you.

That raises a terrible question. How is it that people who are quite obviously eaten up with Pride can say they believe in God and appear to themselves very religious? I am afraid it means they are worshipping an imaginary God. They theoretically admit themselves to be nothing in the presence of this phantom God, but are really all the time imagining how He approves of them and thinks them far better than ordinary people: that is, they pay a pennyworth of imaginary humility to Him and get out of it a pound's worth of Pride towards their fellow-men. I suppose it was of those people Christ was thinking when He said that some would preach about Him and cast out devils in His name, only to be told at the end of the world that He had never known them. And any of us may at any moment be in this death-trap. Luckily, we have a test. Whenever we find that our religious life is making us feel that we are good—above all, that we are better than someone else—I think we may be sure that we are being acted on, not by God, but by the devil. The real test of being in the presence of God is, that you either forget about yourself altogether or see yourself as a small, dirty object. It is better to forget about yourself altogether.

It is a terrible thing that the worst of all the vices can smuggle itself into the very centre of our religious life. But you can see why. The other, and less bad, vices come from the devil working on us through our animal nature. But this does not come through our animal nature at all. It comes direct from Hell. It is purely spiritual: consequently it is far more subtle and deadly. For the same reason, Pride can often be used to beat down the simpler vices. Teachers, in fact, often appeal to a boy's Pride, or, as they call it, his self-respect, to make him behave decently: many a man has overcome cowardice, or lust, or ill-temper, by learning to think that they are beneath his dignity—that is, by Pride. The devil laughs. He is perfectly content to see you becoming chaste and brave and self-controlled provided, all the time, he is setting up in you the Dictatorship of Pride—just as he would be quite content to see your chilblains cured if he was allowed, in return, to give you cancer. For Pride is spiritual cancer: it eats up the very possibility of love, or contentment, or even common sense.

Before leaving this subject I must guard against some possible misunderstandings:

(1) Pleasure in being praised is not Pride. The child who is patted on the back for doing a lesson well, the woman whose beauty is praised by her lover, the saved soul to whom Christ says 'Well done,' are pleased and ought to be. For here the pleasure lies not in what you are but in the fact that you have pleased someone you wanted (and rightly wanted) to please. The trouble begins when you pass from thinking, 'I have pleased him; all is well,' to thinking, 'What a fine person I must be to have done it.' The more you delight in yourself and the less you delight in the praise, the worse you are becoming. When you delight wholly in yourself and do not care about the praise at all, you have reached the bottom. That is why vanity, though it is the sort of Pride which shows most on the surface, is really the least bad and most pardonable sort. The vain person wants praise, applause, admiration, too much and is always angling for it. It is a fault, but a child-like and even (in an odd way) a humble fault. It shows that you are not yet completely contented with your own admiration. You value other people enough to want them to look at you. You are, in fact, still human. The real black, diabolical Pride, comes when you look down on others so much that you do not care what they think of you. Of course, it is very right, and often our duty, not to care what people think of us, if we do so for the right reason; namely, because we care so incomparably more what God thinks. But the Proud man has a different reason for not caring. He says 'Why should I care for the applause of that rabble as if their opinion were worth anything? And even if their opinions were of value, am I the sort of man to blush with pleasure at a compliment like some chit of a girl at her first dance? No, I am an

integrated, adult personality. All I have done has been done to satisfy my own ideals—or my artistic conscience—or the traditions of my family—or, in a word, because I'm That Kind of Chap. If the mob like it, let them. They're nothing to me.' In this way real thorough-going pride may act as a check on vanity; for, as I said a moment ago, the devil loves 'curing' a small fault by giving you a great one. We must try not to be vain, but we must never call in our Pride to cure our vanity.

(2) We say in English that a man is 'proud' of his son, or his father, or his school, or regiment, and it may be asked whether 'pride' in this sense is a sin. I think it depends on what, exactly, we mean by 'proud of'. Very often, in such sentences, the phrase 'is proud of' means 'has a warm-hearted admiration for'. Such an admiration is, of course, very far from being a sin. But it might, perhaps, mean that the person in question gives himself airs on the ground of his distinguished father, or because he belongs to a famous regiment. This would, clearly, be a fault; but even then, it would be better than being proud simply of himself. To love and admire anything outside yourself is to take one step away from utter spiritual ruin; though we shall not be well so long as we love and admire anything more than we love and admire God.

(3) We must not think Pride is something God forbids because He is offended at it, or that Humility is something He demands as due to His own dignity—as if God Himself was proud. He is not in the least worried about His dignity. The point is, He wants you to know Him: wants to give you Himself. And He and you are two things of such a kind that if you really get into any kind of touch with Him you will, in fact, be humble—delightedly humble, feeling the infinite relief of having for once got rid of all the silly nonsense about your own dignity which has made you restless and unhappy all your life. He is trying to make you humble in order to make this moment possible: trying to take off a lot of silly, ugly, fancy-dress in which we have all got ourselves up and are strutting about like the little idiots we are. I wish I had got a bit further with humility myself: if I had, I could probably tell you more about the relief, the comfort, of taking the fancy-dress off—getting rid of the false self, with all its 'Look at me' and 'Aren't I a good boy?' and all its posing and posturing. To get even near it, even for a moment, is like a drink of cold water to a man in a desert.

(4) Do not imagine that if you meet a really humble man he will be what most people call 'humble' nowadays: he will not be a sort of greasy,

smarmy person, who is always telling you that, of course, he is nobody. Probably all you will think about him is that he seemed a cheerful, intelligent chap who took a real interest in what *you* said to *him*. If you do dislike him it will be because you feel a little envious of anyone who seems to enjoy life so easily. He will not be thinking about humility: he will not be thinking about himself at all.

If anyone would like to acquire humility, I can, I think, tell him the first step. The first step is to realise that one is proud. And a biggish step, too. At least, nothing whatever can be done before it. If you think you are not conceited, it means you are very conceited indeed.

9

CHARITY

I SAID IN an earlier chapter that there were four 'Cardinal' virtues and three 'Theological' virtues. The three Theological ones are Faith, Hope, and Charity. Faith is going to be dealt with in the last two chapters. Charity was partly dealt with in Chapter 7, but there I concentrated on that part of Charity which is called Forgiveness. I now want to add a little more.

First, as to the meaning of the word. 'Charity' now means simply what used to be called 'alms'—that is, giving to the poor. Originally it had a much wider meaning. (You can see how it got the modern sense. If a man has 'charity', giving to the poor is one of the most obvious things he does, and so people came to talk as if that were the whole of charity. In the same way, 'rhyme' is the most obvious thing about poetry, and so people come to mean by 'poetry' simply rhyme and nothing more.) Charity means 'Love, in the Christian sense'. But love, in the Christian sense, does not mean an emotion. It is a state not of the feelings but of the will; that state of the will which we have naturally about ourselves, and must learn to have about other people.

I pointed out in the chapter on Forgiveness that our love for ourselves does not mean that we *like* ourselves. It means that we wish our own good. In the same way Christian Love (or Charity) for our neighbours is quite a different thing from liking or affection. We 'like' or are 'fond of' some people, and not of others. It is important to understand that this natural 'liking' is neither a sin nor a virtue, any more than your likes and dislikes in food are a sin or a virtue. It is just a fact. But, of course, what we do about it is either sinful or virtuous.

Natural liking or affection for people makes it easier to be 'charitable' towards them. It is, therefore, normally a duty to encourage our affections—to 'like' people as much as we can (just as it is often our duty to encourage our liking for exercise or wholesome food)—not because this liking is itself the virtue of charity, but because it is a help to it. On the other hand, it is also necessary to keep a very sharp look-out for fear our liking for some one person makes us uncharitable, or even unfair, to someone else. There are even cases where our liking conflicts with our charity towards the person we like. For example, a doting mother may be tempted by natural affection to 'spoil' her child; that is, to gratify her own affectionate impulses at the expense of the child's real happiness later on.

But though natural likings should normally be encouraged, it would be quite wrong to think that the way to become charitable is to sit trying to manufacture affectionate feelings. Some people are 'cold' by temperament; that may be a misfortune for them, but it is no more a sin than having a bad digestion is a sin; and it does not cut them out from the chance, or excuse them from the duty, of learning charity. The rule for all of us is perfectly simple. Do not waste time bothering whether you 'love' your neighbour; act as if you did. As soon as we do this we find one of the great secrets. When you are behaving as if you loved someone, you will presently come to love him. If you injure someone you dislike, you will find yourself disliking him more. If you do him a good turn, you will find yourself disliking him less. There is, indeed, one exception. If you do him a good turn, not to please God and obey the law of charity, but to show him what a fine forgiving chap you are, and to put him in your debt, and then sit down to wait for his 'gratitude', you will probably be disappointed. (People are not fools: they have a very quick eye for anything like showing off, or patronage.) But whenever we do good to another self, just because it is a self, made (like us) by God, and desiring its own happiness as we desire ours, we shall have learned to love it a little more or, at least, to dislike it less.

Consequently, though Christian charity sounds a very cold thing to people whose heads are full of sentimentality, and though it is quite distinct from affection, yet it leads to affection. The difference between a Christian and a worldly man is not that the worldly man has only affections or 'likings' and the Christian has only 'charity'. The worldly man treats certain people kindly because he 'likes' them: the Christian, trying to treat every one kindly, finds himself liking more and more people as he goes on—including people he could not even have imagined himself liking at the beginning.

This same spiritual law works terribly in the opposite direction. The Germans, perhaps, at first ill-treated the Jews because they hated them: afterwards they hated them much more because they had ill-treated them. The more cruel you are, the more you will hate; and the more you hate, the more cruel you will become—and so on in a vicious circle for ever.

Good and evil both increase at compound interest. That is why the little decisions you and I make every day are of such infinite importance. The smallest good act today is the capture of a strategic point from which, a few months later, you may be able to go on to victories you never dreamed of. An apparently trivial indulgence in lust or anger today is the loss of a ridge or railway line or bridgehead from which the enemy may launch an attack otherwise impossible.

Some writers use the word charity to describe not only Christian love between human beings, but also God's love for man and man's love for God. About the second of these two, people are often worried. They are told they ought to love God. They cannot find any such feeling in themselves. What are they to do? The answer is the same as before. Act as if you did. Do not sit trying to manufacture feelings. Ask yourself, 'If I were sure that I loved God, what would I do?' When you have found the answer, go and do it.

On the whole, God's love for us is a much safer subject to think about than our love for Him. Nobody can always have devout feelings: and even if we could, feelings are not what God principally cares about. Christian Love, either towards God or towards man, is an affair of the will. If we are trying to do His will we are obeying the commandment, 'Thou shalt love the Lord thy God.' He will give us feelings of love if He pleases. We cannot create them for ourselves, and we must not demand them as a right. But the great thing to remember is that, though our feelings come and go, His love for us does not. It is not wearied by our sins, or our indifference; and, therefore, it is quite relentless in its determination that we shall be cured of those sins, at whatever cost to us, at whatever cost to Him.

10

HOPE

HOPE IS ONE of the Theological virtues. This means that a continual looking forward to the eternal world is not (as some modern people think) a form of escapism or wishful thinking, but one of the things a Christian is meant to do. It does not mean that we are to leave the present world as it is. If you read history you will find that the Christians who did most for the present world were just those who thought most of the next. The Apostles themselves, who set on foot the conversion of the Roman Empire, the great men who built up the Middle Ages, the English Evangelicals who abolished the Slave Trade, all left their mark on Earth, precisely because their minds were occupied with Heaven. It is since Christians have largely ceased to think of the other world that they have become so ineffective in this. Aim at Heaven and you will get earth 'thrown in': aim at earth and you will get neither. It seems a strange rule, but something like it can be seen at work in other matters. Health is a great blessing, but the moment you make health one of your main, direct objects you start becoming a crank and imagining there is something wrong with you. You are only likely to get health provided you want other things more—food, games, work, fun, open air. In the same way, we shall never save civilisation as long as civilisation is our main object. We must learn to want something else even more.

Most of us find it very difficult to want 'Heaven' at all—except in so far as 'Heaven' means meeting again our friends who have died. One reason for this difficulty is that we have not been trained: our whole education tends to fix our minds on this world. Another reason is that when the real want for Heaven is present in us, we do not recognise it. Most people, if they had really learned to look into their own hearts, would know that they do want, and want acutely, something that cannot be had in this world. There are all sorts of things in this world that offer to give it to you, but they never quite keep their promise. The longings which arise in us when we first fall in love, or first think of some foreign country, or first take up some subject that excites us, are longings which no marriage, no travel, no learning, can really satisfy. I am not now speaking of what would be ordinarily called unsuccessful marriages, or holidays, or learned careers. I am speaking of the best possible ones. There was something we grasped at, in that first moment of longing, which just fades away in the reality. I think everyone knows what I mean. The wife may be a good wife, and the hotels and scenery may have been excellent, and chemistry may be a very interesting job: but something has evaded us. Now there are two wrong ways of dealing with this fact, and one right one.

(1) The Fool's Way—He puts the blame on the things themselves. He goes on all his life thinking that if only he tried another woman, or went for a more expensive holiday, or whatever it is, then, this time, he really would catch the mysterious something we are all after. Most of the bored, discontented, rich people in the world are of this type. They spend their whole lives trotting from woman to woman (through the divorce courts), from continent to continent, from hobby to hobby, always thinking that the latest is 'the Real Thing' at last, and always disappointed.

(2) The Way of the Disillusioned 'Sensible Man'—He soon decides that the whole thing was moonshine. 'Of course,' he says, 'one feels like that when one's young. But by the time you get to my age you've given up chasing the rainbow's end.' And so he settles down and learns not to expect too much and represses the part of himself which used, as he would say, 'to cry for the moon'. This is, of course, a much better way than the first, and makes a man much happier, and less of a nuisance to society. It tends to make him a prig (he is apt to be rather superior towards what he calls 'adolescents'), but, on the whole, he rubs along fairly comfortably. It would be the best line we could take if man did not live for ever. But supposing infinite happiness really is there, waiting for us? Supposing one really can reach the rainbow's end? In that case it would be a pity to find out too late (a moment after death) that by our supposed 'common sense' we had stifled in ourselves the faculty of enjoying it.

(3) The Christian Way—The Christian says, 'Creatures are not born with desires unless satisfaction for those desires exists. A baby feels hunger: well, there is such a thing as food. A duckling wants to swim: well, there is such a thing as water. Men feel sexual desire: well, there is such a thing as sex. If I find in myself a desire which no experience in this world can satisfy, the most probable explanation is that I was made for another world. If none of my earthly pleasures satisfy it, that does not prove that the universe is a fraud. Probably earthly pleasures were never meant to satisfy it, but only to arouse it, to suggest the real thing. If that is so, I must take care, on the one hand, never to despise, or be unthankful for, these earthly blessings, and on the other, never to mistake them for the something else of which they are only a kind of copy, or echo, or mirage. I must keep alive in myself the desire for my true country, which I shall not find till after death; I must never let it get snowed under or turned aside; I must make it the main object of life to press on to that other country and to help others to do the same.'

There is no need to be worried by facetious people who try to make the Christian hope of 'Heaven' ridiculous by saying they do not want 'to spend eternity playing harps'. The answer to such people is that if they cannot understand books written for grown-ups, they should not talk about them. All the scriptural imagery (harps, crowns, gold, etc.) is, of course, a merely symbolical attempt to express the inexpressible. Musical instruments are mentioned because for many people (not all) music is the thing known in the present life which most strongly suggests ecstasy and infinity. Crowns are mentioned to suggest the fact that those who are united with God in eternity share His splendour and power and joy. Gold is mentioned to suggest the timelessness of Heaven (gold does not rust) and the preciousness of it. People who take these symbols literally might as well think that when Christ told us to be like doves, He meant that we were to lay eggs.

II

FAITH

I MUST TALK in this chapter about what the Christians call Faith.
Roughly speaking, the word Faith seems to be used by Christians in two
senses or on two levels, and I will take them in turn. In the first sense
it means simply Belief—accepting or regarding as true the doctrines of
Christianity. That is fairly simple. But what does puzzle people—at least
it used to puzzle me—is the fact that Christians regard faith in this sense
as a virtue. I used to ask how on earth it can be a virtue—what is there
moral or immoral about believing or not believing a set of statements?
Obviously, I used to say, a sane man accepts or rejects any statement, not
because he wants to or does not want to, but because the evidence seems
to him good or bad. If he were mistaken about the goodness or badness
of the evidence that would not mean he was a bad man, but only that he
was not very clever. And if he thought the evidence bad but tried to force
himself to believe in spite of it, that would be merely stupid.

Well, I think I still take that view. But what I did not see then—and
a good many people do not see still—was this. I was assuming that if
the human mind once accepts a thing as true it will automatically go on
regarding it as true, until some real reason for reconsidering it turns up.
In fact, I was assuming that the human mind is completely ruled by reason. But that is not so. For example, my reason is perfectly convinced
by good evidence that anaesthetics do not smother me and that properly
trained surgeons do not start operating until I am unconscious. But that
does not alter the fact that when they have me down on the table and clap
their horrible mask over my face, a mere childish panic begins inside me.

I start thinking I am going to choke, and I am afraid they will start cutting me up before I am properly under. In other words, I lose my faith in anaesthetics. It is not reason that is taking away my faith: on the contrary, my faith is based on reason. It is my imagination and emotions. The battle is between faith and reason on one side and emotion and imagination on the other.

When you think of it you will see lots of instances of this. A man knows, on perfectly good evidence, that a pretty girl of his acquaintance is a liar and cannot keep a secret and ought not to be trusted: but when he finds himself with her his mind loses its faith in that bit of knowledge and he starts thinking, 'Perhaps she'll be different this time,' and once more makes a fool of himself and tells her something he ought not to have told her. His senses and emotions have destroyed his faith in what he really knows to be true. Or take a boy learning to swim. His reason knows perfectly well that an unsupported human body will not necessarily sink in water: he has seen dozens of people float and swim. But the whole question is whether he will be able to go on believing this when the instructor takes away his hand and leaves him unsupported in the water—or whether he will suddenly cease to believe it and get in a fright and go down.

Now just the same thing happens about Christianity. I am not asking anyone to accept Christianity if his best reasoning tells him that the weight of the evidence is against it. That is not the point at which Faith comes in. But supposing a man's reason once decides that the weight of the evidence is for it. I can tell that man what is going to happen to him in the next few weeks. There will come a moment when there is bad news, or he is in trouble, or is living among a lot of other people who do not believe it, and all at once his emotions will rise up and carry out a sort of blitz on his belief. Or else there will come a moment when he wants a woman, or wants to tell a lie, or feels very pleased with himself, or sees a chance of making a little money in some way that is not perfectly fair: some moment, in fact, at which it would be very convenient if Christianity were not true. And once again his wishes and desires will carry out a blitz. I am not talking of moments at which any real new reasons against Christianity turn up. Those have to be faced and that is a different matter. I am talking about moments when a mere mood rises up against it.

Now Faith, in the sense in which I am here using the word, is the art of holding on to things your reason has once accepted, in spite of your changing moods. For moods will change, whatever view your reason takes. I know that by experience. Now that I am a Christian I do have moods in which the whole thing looks very improbable: but when I was an atheist I had moods in which Christianity looked terribly probable. This rebellion of your moods against your real self is going to come anyway. That is why Faith is such a necessary virtue: unless you teach your moods 'where they get off', you can never be either a sound Christian or even a sound atheist, but just a creature dithering to and fro, with its beliefs really dependent on the weather and the state of its digestion. Consequently one must train the habit of Faith.

The first step is to recognise the fact that your moods change. The next is to make sure that, if you have once accepted Christianity, then some of its main doctrines shall be deliberately held before your mind for some time every day. That is why daily prayers and religious readings and churchgoing are necessary parts of the Christian life. We have to be continually reminded of what we believe. Neither this belief nor any other will automatically remain alive in the mind. It must be fed. And as a matter of fact, if you examined a hundred people who had lost their faith in Christianity, I wonder how many of them would turn out to have been reasoned out of it by honest argument? Do not most people simply drift away?

Now I must turn to Faith in the second or higher sense: and this is the most difficult thing I have tackled yet. I want to approach it by going back to the subject of Humility. You may remember I said that the first step towards humility was to realise that one is proud. I want to add now that the next step is to make some serious attempt to practise the Christian virtues. A week is not enough. Things often go swimmingly for the first week. Try six weeks. By that time, having, as far as one can see, fallen back completely or even fallen lower than the point one began from, one will have discovered some truths about oneself. No man knows how bad he is till he has tried very hard to be good. A silly idea is current that good people do not know what temptation means. This is an obvious lie. Only those who try to resist temptation know how strong it is. After all, you find out the strength of the German army by fighting against it, not by giving in. You find out the strength of a wind by trying to walk against it, not by lying down. A man who gives in to temptation after five minutes simply does not know what it would have been like an hour later. That is why bad people, in one sense, know very little about badness. They have lived a sheltered life by always giving in. We never find out the strength of the evil impulse inside us until we try to fight it: and Christ, because He was the only man who never yielded to temptation, is also the only man who knows to the full what temptation means—the only complete realist. Very well, then. The main thing we learn from a serious attempt to practise the Christian virtues is that we fail. If there was any idea that God had set us a sort of exam. and that we might get good marks by deserving them, that has to be wiped out. If there was any idea of a sort of bargain—any idea that we could perform our side of the contract and thus put God in our debt so that it was up to Him, in mere justice, to perform His side—that has to be wiped out.

I think every one who has some vague belief in God, until he becomes a Christian, has the idea of an exam. or of a bargain in his mind. The first result of real Christianity is to blow that idea into bits. When they find it blown into bits, some people think this means that Christianity is a failure and give up. They seem to imagine that God is very simple-minded. In fact, of course, He knows all about this. One of the very things Christianity was designed to do was to blow this idea to bits. God has been waiting for the moment at which you discover that there is no question of earning a pass mark in this exam. or putting Him in your debt.

Then comes another discovery. Every faculty you have, your power of thinking or of moving your limbs from moment to moment, is given you by God. If you devoted every moment of your whole life exclusively to His service you could not give Him anything that was not in a sense His own already. So that when we talk of a man doing anything for God or giving anything to God, I will tell you what it is really like. It is like a small child going to its father and saying, 'Daddy, give me sixpence to buy you a birthday present.' Of course, the father does, and he is pleased with the child's present. It is all very nice and proper, but only an idiot would think that the father is sixpence to the good on the transaction. When a man has made these two discoveries God can really get to work. It is after this that real life begins. The man is awake now. We can now go on to talk of Faith in the second sense.

12

FAITH

I WANT TO start by saying something that I would like every one to notice carefully. It is this. If this chapter means nothing to you, if it seems to be trying to answer questions you never asked, drop it at once. Do not bother about it at all. There are certain things in Christianity that can be understood from the outside, before you have become a Christian. But there are a great many things that cannot be understood until after you have gone a certain distance along the Christian road. These things are purely practical, though they do not look as if they were. They are directions for dealing with particular cross-roads and obstacles on the journey and they do not make sense until a man has reached those places. Whenever you find any statement in Christian writings which you can make nothing of, do not worry. Leave it alone. There will come a day, perhaps years later, when you suddenly see what it meant. If one could understand it now, it would only do one harm.

Of course, all this tells against me as much as anyone else. The thing I am going to try to explain in this chapter may be ahead of me. I may be thinking I have got there when I have not. I can only ask instructed Christians to watch very carefully, and tell me when I go wrong; and others to take what I say with a grain of salt—as something offered, because it may be a help, not because I am certain that I am right.

I am trying to talk about Faith in the second sense, the higher sense. I said just now that the question of Faith in this sense arises after a man has tried his level best to practise the Christian virtues, and found that he fails, and seen that even if he could he would only be giving back to

God what was already God's own. In other words, he discovers his bankruptcy. Now, once again, what God cares about is not exactly our actions. What he cares about is that we should be creatures of a certain kind or quality—the kind of creatures He intended us to be—creatures related to Himself in a certain way. I do not add 'and related to one another in a certain way', because that is included: if you are right with Him you will inevitably be right with all your fellow-creatures, just as if all the spokes of a wheel are fitted rightly into the hub and the rim they are bound to be in the right positions to one another. And as long as a man is thinking of God as an examiner who has set him a sort of paper to do, or as the opposite party in a sort of bargain—as long as he is thinking of claims and counter-claims between himself and God—he is not yet in the right relation to Him. He is misunderstanding what he is and what God is. And he cannot get into the right relation until he has discovered the fact of our bankruptcy.

When I say 'discovered', I mean really discovered: not simply said it parrot-fashion. Of course, any child, if given a certain kind of religious education, will soon learn to say that we have nothing to offer to God that is not already His own and that we find ourselves failing to offer even that without keeping something back. But I am talking of really discovering this: really finding out by experience that it is true.

Now we cannot, in that sense, discover our failure to keep God's law except by trying our very hardest (and then failing). Unless we really try, whatever we say there will always be at the back of our minds the idea that if we try harder next time we shall succeed in being completely good. Thus, in one sense, the road back to God is a road of moral effort, of trying harder and harder. But in another sense it is not trying that is ever going to bring us home. All this trying leads up to the vital moment at which you turn to God and say, 'You must do this. I can't.' Do not, I implore you, start asking yourselves, 'Have I reached that moment?' Do not sit down and start watching your own mind to see if it is coming along. That puts a man quite on the wrong track. When the most important things in our life happen we quite often do not know, at the moment, what is going on. A man does not always say to himself, 'Hullo! I'm growing up.' It is often only when he looks back that he realises what has happened and recognises it as what people call 'growing up'. You can see it even in simple matters. A man who starts anxiously watching to see whether he is going to sleep is very likely to remain wide awake. As well, the thing I am talking of now may not happen to every one in a sudden flash—as it did to St Paul or Bunyan: it may be so gradual that no one could ever point to a particular hour or even a particular year. And what matters is the nature of the change in itself, not how we feel while it is happening. It is the change from being confident about our own efforts to the state in which we despair of doing anything for ourselves and leave it to God.

I know the words 'leave it to God' can be misunderstood, but they must stay for the moment. The sense in which a Christian leaves it to God is that he puts all his trust in Christ: trusts that Christ will somehow share with him the perfect human obedience which He carried out from His birth to His crucifixion: that Christ will make the man more like Himself and, in a sense, make good his deficiencies. In Christian language, He will share His 'sonship' with us, will make us, like Himself, 'Sons of God': in Book IV I shall attempt to analyse the meaning of those words a little further. If you like to put it that way, Christ offers something for nothing: He even offers everything for nothing. In a sense, the whole Christian life consists in accepting that very remarkable offer. But the difficulty is to reach the point of recognising that all we have done and can do is nothing. What we should have liked would be for God to count our good points and ignore our bad ones. Again, in a sense, you may say that no temptation is ever overcome until we stop trying to overcome it—throw up the sponge. But then you could not 'stop trying' in the right way and for the right reason until you had tried your very hardest. And, in yet another sense, handing everything over to Christ does not, of course, mean that you stop trying. To trust Him means, of course, trying to do all that He says. There would be no sense in saying you trusted a person if you would not take his advice. Thus if you have really handed yourself over to Him, it must follow that you are trying to obey Him. But trying in a new way, a less worried way. Not doing these things in order to be saved, but because He has begun to save you already. Not hoping to get to Heaven as a reward for your actions, but inevitably wanting to act in a certain way because a first faint gleam of Heaven is already inside you.

Christians have often disputed as to whether what leads the Christian home is good actions, or Faith in Christ. I have no right really to speak on such a difficult question, but it does seem to me like asking which blade in a pair of scissors is most necessary. A serious moral effort is the only thing that will bring you to the point where you throw up the sponge.

Faith in Christ is the only thing to save you from despair at that point: and out of that Faith in Him good actions must inevitably come. There are two parodies of the truth which different sets of Christians have, in the past, been accused by other Christians of believing: perhaps they may make the truth clearer. One set were accused of saying, 'Good actions are all that matters. The best good action is charity. The best kind of charity is giving money. The best thing to give money to is the Church. So hand us over £10,000 and we will see you through.' The answer to that nonsense, of course, would be that good actions done for that motive, done with the idea that Heaven can be bought, would not be good actions at all, but only commercial speculations. The other set were accused of saying, 'Faith is all that matters. Consequently, if you have faith, it doesn't matter what you do. Sin away, my lad, and have a good time and Christ will see that it makes no difference in the end.' The answer to that nonsense is that, if what you call your 'faith' in Christ does not involve taking the slightest notice of what He says, then it is not Faith at all—not faith or trust in Him, but only intellectual acceptance of some theory about Him.

The Bible really seems to clinch the matter when it puts the two things together into one amazing sentence. The first half is, 'Work out your own salvation with fear and trembling'—which looks as if everything depended on us and our good actions: but the second half goes on, 'For it is God who worketh in you'—which looks as if God did everything and we nothing. I am afraid that is the sort of thing we come up against in Christianity. I am puzzled, but I am not surprised. You see, we are now trying to understand, and to separate into water-tight compartments, what exactly God does and what man does when God and man are working together. And, of course, we begin by thinking it is like two men working together, so that you could say, 'He did this bit and I did that.' But this way of thinking breaks down. God is not like that. He is inside you as well as outside: even if we could understand who did what, I do not think human language could properly express it. In the attempt to express it different Churches say different things. But you will find that even those who insist most strongly on the importance of good actions tell you you need Faith; and even those who insist most strongly on Faith tell you to do good actions. At any rate that is as far as I can go.

I think all Christians would agree with me if I said that though Christianity seems at the first to be all about morality, all about duties and rules and guilt and virtue, yet it leads you on, out of all that, into something beyond. One has a glimpse of a country where they do not talk of those things, except perhaps as a joke. Every one there is filled full with what we should call goodness as a mirror is filled with light. But they do not call it goodness. They do not call it anything. They are not thinking of it. They are too busy looking at the source from which it comes. But this is near the stage where the road passes over the rim of our world. No one's eyes can see very far beyond that: lots of people's eyes can see further than mine.

BOOK FOUR

Beyond Personality:
or First Steps in the Doctrine of the Trinity

I

MAKING AND BEGETTING

EVERYONE HAS WARNED me not to tell you what I am going to tell you in this last book. They all say 'the ordinary reader does not want Theology; give him plain practical religion'. I have rejected their advice. I do not think the ordinary reader is such a fool. Theology means 'the science of God', and I think any man who wants to think about God at all would like to have the clearest and most accurate ideas about Him which are available. You are not children: why should you be treated like children?

In a way I quite understand why some people are put off by Theology. I remember once when I had been giving a talk to the R.A.F., an old, hard-bitten officer got up and said, 'I've no use for all that stuff. But, mind you, I'm a religious man too. I know there's a God. I've felt Him: out alone in the desert at night: the tremendous mystery. And that's just why I don't believe all your neat little dogmas and formulas about Him. To anyone who's met the real thing they all seem so petty and pedantic and unreal!'

Now in a sense I quite agreed with that man. I think he had probably had a real experience of God in the desert. And when he turned from that experience to the Christian creeds, I think he really was turning from something real to something less real. In the same way, if a man has once looked at the Atlantic from the beach, and then goes and looks at a map of the Atlantic, he also will be turning from something real to something less real: turning from real waves to a bit of coloured paper. But here comes the point. The map is admittedly only coloured paper, but there are two things you have to remember about it. In the first place, it is based on what hundreds and thousands of people have found out by sailing the real Atlantic. In that way it has behind it masses of experience just as real as the one you could have from the beach; only, while yours would be a single glimpse, the map fits all those different experiences together. In the second place, if you want to go anywhere, the map is absolutely necessary. As long as you are content with walks on the beach, your own glimpses are far more fun than looking at a map. But the map is going to be more use than walks on the beach if you want to get to America.

Now, Theology is like the map. Merely learning and thinking about the Christian doctrines, if you stop there, is less real and less exciting than the sort of thing my friend got in the desert. Doctrines are not God: they are only a kind of map. But that map is based on the experience of hundreds of people who really were in touch with God—experiences compared with which any thrills or pious feelings you and I are likely to get on our own are very elementary and very confused. And secondly, if you want to get any further, you must use the map. You see, what happened to that man in the desert may have been real, and was certainly exciting, but nothing comes of it. It leads nowhere. There is nothing to do about it. In fact, that is just why a vague religion—all about feeling God in nature, and so on—is so attractive. It is all thrills and no work: like watching the waves from the beach. But you will not get to Newfoundland by studying the Atlantic that way, and you will not get eternal life by simply feeling the presence of God in flowers or music. Neither will you get anywhere by looking at maps without going to sea. Nor will you be very safe if you go to sea without a map.

In other words, Theology is practical: especially now. In the old days, when there was less education and discussion, perhaps it was possible to get on with a very few simple ideas about God. But it is not so now. Everyone reads, everyone hears things discussed. Consequently, if you do not listen to Theology, that will not mean that you have no ideas about God. It will mean that you have a lot of wrong ones—bad, muddled, out-of-date ideas. For a great many of the ideas about God which are trotted out as novelties today are simply the ones which real Theologians tried centuries ago and rejected. To believe in the popular religion of modern England is retrogression—like believing the earth is flat.

For when you get down to it, is not the popular idea of Christianity simply this: that Jesus Christ was a great moral teacher and that if only we took His advice we might be able to establish a better social order and avoid another war? Now, mind you, that is quite true. But it tells you much less than the whole truth about Christianity and it has no practical importance at all.

It is quite true that if we took Christ's advice we should soon be living in a happier world. You need not even go as far as Christ. If we did all that Plato or Aristotle or Confucius told us, we should get on a great deal better than we do. And so what? We never have followed the advice of the great teachers. Why are we likely to begin now? Why are we more likely to follow Christ than any of the others? Because He is the best moral teacher? But that makes it even less likely that we shall follow Him. If we cannot take the elementary lessons, is it likely we are going to take the most advanced one? If Christianity only means one more bit of good advice, then Christianity is of no importance. There has been no lack of good advice for the last four thousand years. A bit more makes no difference.

But as soon as you look at any real Christian writings, you find that they are talking about something quite different from this popular religion. They say that Christ is the Son of God (whatever that means). They say that those who give Him their confidence can also become Sons of God (whatever that means). They say that His death saved us from our sins (whatever that means).

There is no good complaining that these statements are difficult. Christianity claims to be telling us about another world, about something behind the world we can touch and hear and see. You may think the claim false, but if it were true, what it tells us would be bound to be difficult— at least as difficult as modern Physics, and for the same reason.

Now the point in Christianity which gives us the greatest shock is the statement that by attaching ourselves to Christ, we can 'become Sons of God'. One asks 'Aren't we Sons of God already? Surely the fatherhood of God is one of the main Christian ideas?' Well, in a certain sense, no doubt we are sons of God already. I mean, God has brought us into existence and loves us and looks after us, and in that way is like a father. But when the Bible talks of our 'becoming' Sons of God, obviously it must mean something different. And that brings us up against the very centre of Theology.

One of the creeds says that Christ is the Son of God 'begotten, not created'; and it adds 'begotten by his Father before all worlds'. Will you please get it quite clear that this has nothing to do with the fact that when

Christ was born on earth as a man, that man was the son of a virgin? We are not now thinking about the Virgin Birth. We are thinking about something that happened before Nature was created at all, before time began. 'Before all worlds' Christ is begotten, not created. What does it mean?

We don't use the words *begetting* or *begotten* much in modern English, but everyone still knows what they mean. To beget is to become the father of: to create is to make. And the difference is this. When you beget, you beget something of the same kind as yourself. A man begets human babies, a beaver begets little beavers and a bird begets eggs which turn into little birds. But when you make, you make something of a different kind from yourself. A bird makes a nest, a beaver builds a dam, a man makes a wireless set—or he may make something more like himself than a wireless set: say, a statue. If he is a clever enough carver he may make a statue which is very like a man indeed. But, of course, it is not a real man; it only looks like one. It cannot breathe or think. It is not alive.

Now that is the first thing to get clear. What God begets is God; just as what man begets is man. What God creates is not God; just as what man makes is not man. That is why men are not Sons of God in the sense that Christ is. They may be like God in certain ways, but they are not things of the same kind. They are more like statues or pictures of God.

A statue has the shape of a man but is not alive. In the same way, man has (in a sense I am going to explain) the 'shape' or likeness of God, but he has not got the kind of life God has. Let us take the first point (man's resemblance to God) first. Everything God has made has some likeness to Himself. Space is like Him in its hugeness: not that the greatness of space is the same kind of greatness as God's, but it is a sort of symbol of it, or a translation of it into non-spiritual terms. Matter is like God in having energy: though, again, of course, physical energy is a different kind of thing from the power of God. The vegetable world is like Him because it is alive, and He is the 'living God'. But life, in this biological sense, is not the same as the life there is in God: it is only a kind of symbol or shadow of it. When we come on to the animals, we find other kinds of resemblance in addition to biological life. The intense activity and fertility of the insects, for example, is a first dim resemblance to the unceasing activity and the creativeness of God. In the higher mammals we get the beginnings of instinctive affection. That is not the same thing as the love that exists in God: but it is like it—rather in the way that a picture drawn on a flat piece of paper can nevertheless be 'like' a landscape. When we come to man, the highest of the animals, we get the completest resemblance to God which we know of. (There may be creatures in other worlds who are more like God than man is, but we do not know about them.) Man not only lives, but loves and reasons: biological life reaches its highest known level in him.

But what man, in his natural condition, has not got, is Spiritual life—the higher and different sort of life that exists in God. We use the same word *life* for both: but if you thought that both must therefore be the same sort of thing, that would be like thinking that the 'greatness' of space and the 'greatness' of God were the same sort of greatness. In reality, the difference between Biological life and Spiritual life is so important that I am going to give them two distinct names. The Biological sort which comes to us through Nature, and which (like everything else in Nature) is always tending to run down and decay so that it can only be kept up by incessant subsidies from Nature in the form of air, water, food, etc., is *Bios*. The Spiritual life which is in God from all eternity, and which made the whole natural universe, is *Zoe*. *Bios* has, to be sure, a certain shadowy or symbolic resemblance to *Zoe*: but only the sort of resemblance there is between a photo and a place, or a statue and a man. A man who changed from having *Bios* to having *Zoe* would have gone through as big a change as a statue which changed from being a carved stone to being a real man.

And that is precisely what Christianity is about. This world is a great sculptor's shop. We are the statues and there is a rumour going round the shop that some of us are some day going to come to life.

2

THE THREE-PERSONAL GOD

THE LAST CHAPTER was about the difference between begetting and making. A man begets a child, but he only makes a statue. God begets Christ but He only makes men. But by saying that, I have illustrated only one point about God, namely, that what God the Father begets is God, something of the same kind as Himself. In that way it is like a human father begetting a human son. But not quite like it. So I must try to explain a little more.

A good many people nowadays say, 'I believe in a God, but not in a personal God.' They feel that the mysterious something which is behind all other things must be more than a person. Now the Christians quite agree. But the Christians are the only people who offer any idea of what a being that is beyond personality could be like. All the other people, though they say that God is beyond personality, really think of Him as something impersonal: that is, as something less than personal. If you are looking for something super-personal, something more than a person, then it is not a question of choosing between the Christian idea and the other ideas. The Christian idea is the only one on the market.

Again, some people think that after this life, or perhaps after several lives, human souls will be 'absorbed' into God. But when they try to explain what they mean, they seem to be thinking of our being absorbed into God as one material thing is absorbed into another. They say it is like a drop of water slipping into the sea. But of course that is the end of the drop. If that is what happens to us, then being absorbed is the same as ceasing to exist. It is only the Christians who have any idea of how human souls can be taken into the life of God and yet remain themselves—in fact, be very much more themselves than they were before.

I warned you that Theology is practical. The whole purpose for which we exist is to be thus taken into the life of God. Wrong ideas about what that life is will make it harder. And now, for a few minutes, I must ask you to follow rather carefully.

You know that in space you can move in three ways—to left or right, backwards or forwards, up or down. Every direction is either one of these three or a compromise between them. They are called the three Dimensions. Now notice this. If you are using only one dimension, you could draw only a straight line. If you are using two, you could draw a figure: say, a square. And a square is made up of four straight lines. Now a step further. If you have three dimensions, you can then build what we call a solid body: say, a cube—a thing like a dice or a lump of sugar. And a cube is made up of six squares.

Do you see the point? A world of one dimension would be a straight line. In a two-dimensional world, you still get straight lines, but many lines make one figure. In a three-dimensional world, you still get figures but many figures make one solid body. In other words, as you advance to more real and more complicated levels, you do not leave behind you the things you found on the simpler levels: you still have them, but combined in new ways—in ways you could not imagine if you knew only the simpler levels.

Now the Christian account of God involves just the same principle. The human level is a simple and rather empty level. On the human level one person is one being, and any two persons are two separate beings—just as, in two dimensions (say on a flat sheet of paper) one square is one figure, and any two squares are two separate figures. On the Divine level you still find personalities; but up there you find them combined in new ways which we, who do not live on that level, cannot imagine. In God's dimension, so to speak, you find a being who is three Persons while remaining one Being, just as a cube is six squares while remaining one cube. Of course we cannot fully conceive a Being like that: just as, if we were so made that we perceived only two dimensions in space we could never properly imagine a cube. But we can get a sort of faint notion of it. And when we do, we are then, for the first time in our lives, getting some positive idea, however faint, of something super-personal—something more than a person. It is something we could never have guessed, and yet, once we have been told, one almost feels one ought to have been able to guess it because it fits in so well with all the things we know already.

You may ask, 'if we cannot imagine a three-personal Being, what is the good of talking about Him?' Well, there isn't any good talking about Him. The thing that matters is being actually drawn into that three-personal life, and that may begin any time—tonight, if you like.

What I mean is this. An ordinary simple Christian kneels down to say his prayers. He is trying to get into touch with God. But if he is a Christian he knows that what is prompting him to pray is also God: God, so to speak, inside him. But he also knows that all his real knowledge of God comes through Christ, the Man who was God—that Christ is standing beside him, helping him to pray, praying for him. You see what is happening. God is the thing to which he is praying—the goal he is trying to reach. God is also the thing inside him which is pushing him on—the motive power. God is also the road or bridge along which he is being pushed to that goal. So that the whole threefold life of the three-personal Being is actually going on in that ordinary little bedroom where an ordinary man is saying his prayers. The man is being caught up into the higher kinds of life—what I called *Zoe* or spiritual life: he is being pulled into God, by God, while still remaining himself.

And that is how Theology started. People already knew about God in a vague way. Then came a man who claimed to be God; and yet He was not the sort of man you could dismiss as a lunatic. He made them believe Him. They met Him again after they had seen Him killed. And then, after they had been formed into a little society or community, they found God somehow inside them as well: directing them, making them able to do things they could not do before. And when they worked it all out they found they had arrived at the Christian definition of the three-personal God.

This definition is not something we have made up; Theology is, in a sense, an experimental science. It is simple religions that are the made-up ones. When I say it is an experimental science 'in a sense', I mean that it is like the other experimental sciences in some ways, but not in all. If you are a geologist studying rocks, you have to go and find the rocks. They will not come to you, and if you go to them they cannot run away. The initiative lies all on your side. They cannot either help or hinder. But suppose you are a zoologist and want to take photos of wild animals in their native haunts. That is a bit different from studying rocks. The wild animals will not come to you: but they can run away from you. Unless you keep very quiet, they will. There is beginning to be a tiny little trace of initiative on their side.

Now a stage higher; suppose you want to get to know a human person. If he is determined not to let you, you will not get to know him. You have to win his confidence. In this case the initiative is equally divided— it takes two to make a friendship.

When you come to knowing God, the initiative lies on His side. If He does not show Himself, nothing you can do will enable you to find Him. And, in fact, He shows much more of Himself to some people than to others—not because He has favourites, but because it is impossible for Him to show Himself to a man whose whole mind and character are in the wrong condition. Just as sunlight, though it has no favourites, cannot be reflected in a dusty mirror as clearly as in a clean one.

You can put this another way by saying that while in other sciences the instruments you use are things external to yourself (things like microscopes and telescopes), the instrument through which you see God is your whole self. And if a man's self is not kept clean and bright, his glimpse of God will be blurred—like the Moon seen through a dirty telescope. That is why horrible nations have horrible religions: they have been looking at God through a dirty lens.

God can show Himself as He really is only to real men. And that means not simply to men who are individually good, but to men who are united together in a body, loving one another, helping one another, showing Him to one another. For that is what God meant humanity to be like; like players in one band, or organs in one body.

Consequently, the one really adequate instrument for learning about God is the whole Christian community, waiting for Him together. Christian brotherhood is, so to speak, the technical equipment for this science—the laboratory outfit. That is why all these people who turn up every few years with some patent simplified religion of their own as a substitute for the Christian tradition are really wasting time. Like a man who has no instrument but an old pair of field glasses setting out to put all the real astronomers right. He may be a clever chap—he may be cleverer than some of the real astronomers, but he is not giving himself a chance. And two years later everyone has forgotten all about him, but the real science is still going on.

If Christianity was something we were making up, of course we could make it easier. But it is not. We cannot compete, in simplicity, with people who are inventing religions. How could we? We are dealing with Fact. Of course anyone can be simple if he has no facts to bother about.

3

TIME AND BEYOND TIME

IT IS A very silly idea that in reading a book you must never 'skip'. All sensible people skip freely when they come to a chapter which they find is going to be no use to them. In this chapter I am going to talk about something which may be helpful to some readers, but which may seem to others merely an unnecessary complication. If you are one of the second sort of readers, then I advise you not to bother about this chapter at all but to turn on to the next.

In the last chapter I had to touch on the subject of prayer, and while that is still fresh in your mind and my own, I should like to deal with a difficulty that some people find about the whole idea of prayer. A man put it to me by saying 'I can believe in God all right, but what I cannot swallow is the idea of Him attending to several hundred million human beings who are all addressing Him at the same moment.' And I have found that quite a lot of people feel this.

Now, the first thing to notice is that the whole sting of it comes in the words *at the same moment*. Most of us can imagine God attending to any number of applicants if only they came one by one and He had an endless time to do it in. So what is really at the back of this difficulty is the idea of God having to fit too many things into one moment of time.

Well that is of course what happens to us. Our life comes to us moment by moment. One moment disappears before the next comes along: and there is room for very little in each. That is what Time is like. And of course you and I tend to take it for granted that this Time series—this arrangement of past, present and future—is not simply the way life comes to us but the way all things really exist. We tend to assume that the whole universe and God Himself are always moving on from past to future just as we do. But many learned men do not agree with that. It was the Theologians who first started the idea that some things are not in Time at all: later the Philosophers took it over: and now some of the scientists are doing the same.

Almost certainly God is not in Time. His life does not consist of moments following one another. If a million people are praying to Him at ten-thirty tonight, He need not listen to them all in that one little snippet which we call ten-thirty. Ten-thirty—and every other moment from the beginning of the world—is always the Present for Him. If you like to put it that way, He has all eternity in which to listen to the split second of prayer put up by a pilot as his plane crashes in flames.

That is difficult, I know. Let me try to give something, not the same, but a bit like it. Suppose I am writing a novel. I write 'Mary laid down her work; next moment came a knock at the door!' For Mary who has to live in the imaginary time of my story there is no interval between putting down the work and hearing the knock. But I, who am Mary's maker, do not live in that imaginary time at all. Between writing the first half of that sentence and the second, I might sit down for three hours and think steadily about Mary. I could think about Mary as if she were the only character in the book and for as long as I pleased, and the hours I spent in doing so would not appear in Mary's time (the time inside the story) at all.

This is not a perfect illustration, of course. But it may give just a glimpse of what I believe to be the truth. God is not hurried along in the Time-stream of this universe any more than an author is hurried along in the imaginary time of his own novel. He has infinite attention to spare for each one of us. He does not have to deal with us in the mass. You are as much alone with Him as if you were the only being He had ever created. When Christ died, He died for you individually just as much as if you had been the only man in the world.

The way in which my illustration breaks down is this. In it the author gets out of one Time-series (that of the novel) only by going into another Time-series (the real one). But God, I believe, does not live in a Time-series at all. His life is not dribbled out moment by moment like ours: with Him it is, so to speak, still 1920 and already 1960. For His life is Himself.

If you picture Time as a straight line along which we have to travel, then you must picture God as the whole page on which the line is drawn. We come to the parts of the line one by one: we have to leave A behind before we get to B, and cannot reach C until we leave B behind. God, from above or outside or all round, contains the whole line, and sees it all.

The idea is worth trying to grasp because it removes some apparent difficulties in Christianity. Before I became a Christian one of my objections was as follows. The Christians said that the eternal God who is everywhere and keeps the whole universe going, once became a human being. Well, then, said I, how did the whole universe keep going while He was a baby, or while He was asleep? How could He at the same time be God who knows everything and also a man asking his disciples 'Who touched me?' You will notice that the sting lay in the *time* words: '*While* He was a baby'—How could He *at the same time?*' In other words I was assuming that Christ's life as God was in time, and that His life as the man Jesus in Palestine was a shorter period taken out of that time—just as my service in the army was a shorter period taken out of my total life. And that is how most of us perhaps tend to think about it. We picture God living through a period when His human life was still in the future: then coming to a period when it was present: then going on to a period when He could look back on it as something in the past. But probably these ideas correspond to nothing in the actual facts. You cannot fit Christ's earthly life in Palestine into any time-relations with His life as God beyond all space and time. It is really, I suggest, a timeless truth about God that human nature, and the human experience of weakness and sleep and ignorance, are somehow included in His whole divine life. This human life in God is from our point of view a particular period in the history of our world (from the year A.D. one till the Crucifixion). We therefore imagine it is also a period in the history of God's own existence. But God has no history. He is too completely and utterly real to have one. For, of course, to have a history means losing part of your reality (because it has already slipped away into the past) and not yet having another part (because it is still in the future): in fact having nothing but the tiny little present, which has gone before you can speak about it. God forbid we should think God was like that. Even we may hope not to be always rationed in that way.

Another difficulty we get if we believe God to be in time is this. Everyone who believes in God at all believes that He knows what you and I are going to do tomorrow. But if He knows I am going to do so-and-so, how can I be free to do otherwise? Well, here once again, the difficulty comes from thinking that God is progressing along the Time-line like us: the only difference being that He can see ahead and we cannot. Well, if that were true, if God *foresaw* our acts, it would be very hard to understand how we could be free not to do them. But suppose God is outside and above the Time-line. In that case, what we call 'tomorrow' is visible to Him in just the same way as what we call 'today'. All the days are 'Now' for Him. He does not remember you doing things yesterday; He simply sees you doing them, because, though you have lost yesterday, He has not. He does not 'foresee' you doing things tomorrow; He simply sees you doing them: because, though tomorrow is not yet there for you, it is for Him. You never supposed that your actions at this moment were any less free because God knows what you are doing. Well, He knows your tomorrow's actions in just the same way—because He is already in tomorrow and can simply watch you. In a sense, He does not know your action till you have done it: but then the moment at which you have done it is already 'Now' for Him.

This idea has helped me a good deal. If it does not help you, leave it alone. It is a 'Christian idea' in the sense that great and wise Christians have held it and there is nothing in it contrary to Christianity. But it is not in the Bible or any of the creeds. You can be a perfectly good Christian without accepting it, or indeed without thinking of the matter at all.

4

GOOD INFECTION

I BEGIN THIS chapter by asking you to get a certain picture clear in your minds. Imagine two books lying on a table one on top of the other. Obviously the bottom book is keeping the other one up—supporting it. It is because of the underneath book that the top one is resting, say, two inches from the surface of the table instead of touching the table. Let us call the underneath book A and the top one B. The position of A is causing the position of B. That is clear? Now let us imagine—it could not really happen, of course, but it will do for an illustration—let us imagine that both books have been in that position for ever and ever. In that case B's position would always have been resulting from A's position. But all the same, A's position would not have existed before B's position. In other words the result does not come after the cause. Of course, results usually do: you eat the cucumber first and have the indigestion afterwards. But it is not so with all causes and results. You will see in a moment why I think this important.

I said a few pages back that God is a Being which contains three Persons while remaining one Being, just as a cube contains six squares while remaining one body. But as soon as I begin trying to explain how these Persons are connected I have to use words which make it sound as if one of them was there before the others. The First Person is called the Father and the Second the Son. We say that the First begets or produces the second; we call it *begetting*, not *making*, because what He produces is of the same kind as Himself. In that way the word Father is the only word to use. But unfortunately it suggests that He is there first—just as a human father exists before his son. But that is not so. There is no before and after about it. And that is why I think it important to make clear how one thing can be the source, or cause, or origin, of another without being there before it. The Son exists because the Father exists: but there never was a time before the Father produced the Son.

Perhaps the best way to think of it is this. I asked you just now to imagine those two books, and probably most of you did. That is, you made an act of imagination and as a result you had a mental picture. Quite obviously your act of imagining was the cause and the mental picture the result. But that does not mean that you first did the imagining and then got the picture. The moment you did it, the picture was there. Your will was keeping the picture before you all the time. Yet that act of will and the picture began at exactly the same moment and ended at the same moment. If there were a Being who had always existed and had always been imagining one thing, his act would always have been producing a mental picture; but the picture would be just as eternal as the act.

In the same way we must think of the Son always, so to speak, streaming forth from the Father, like light from a lamp, or heat from a fire, or thoughts from a mind. He is the self-expression of the Father—what the Father has to say. And there never was a time when He was not saying it. But have you noticed what is happening? All these pictures of light or heat are making it sound as if the Father and Son were two things instead of two Persons. So that after all, the New Testament picture of a Father and a Son turns out to be much more accurate than anything we try to substitute for it. That is what always happens when you go away from the words of the Bible. It is quite right to go away from them for a moment in order to make some special point clear. But you must always go back. Naturally God knows how to describe Himself much better than we know how to describe Him. He knows that Father and Son is more like the relation between the First and Second Persons than anything else we can think of. Much the most important thing to know is that it is a relation of love. The Father delights in His Son; the Son looks up to His Father.

Before going on, notice the practical importance of this. All sorts of people are fond of repeating the Christian statement that 'God is love'. But they seem not to notice that the words 'God is love' have no real meaning unless God contains at least two Persons. Love is something that one person has for another person. If God was a single person, then before the world was made, He was not love. Of course, what these people mean when they say that God is love is often something quite different: they really mean 'Love is God'. They really mean that our feelings of love, however and wherever they arise, and whatever results they produce, are to be treated with great respect. Perhaps they are: but that is something quite different from what Christians mean by the statement 'God is love'. They believe that the living, dynamic activity of love has been going on in God forever and has created everything else.

And that, by the way, is perhaps the most important difference between Christianity and all other religions: that in Christianity God is not a static thing—not even a person—but a dynamic, pulsating activity, a life, almost a kind of drama. Almost, if you will not think me irreverent, a kind of dance. The union between the Father and the Son is such a live concrete thing that this union itself is also a Person. I know this is almost inconceivable, but look at it thus. You know that among human beings, when they get together in a family, or a club, or a trade union, people talk about the 'spirit' of that family, or club, or trade union. They talk about its 'spirit' because the individual members, when they are together, do really develop particular ways of talking and behaving which they would not have if they were apart.* It is as if a sort of communal personality came into existence. Of course, it is not a real person: it is only rather like a person. But that is just one of the differences between God and us. What grows out of the joint life of the Father and Son is a real Person, is in fact the Third of the three Persons who are God.

This third Person is called, in technical language, the Holy Ghost or the 'spirit' of God. Do not be worried or surprised if you find it (or Him) rather vaguer or more shadowy in your mind than the other two. I think there is a reason why that must be so. In the Christian life you are not usually looking *at* Him. He is always acting through you. If you think of the Father as something 'out there', in front of you, and of the Son as someone standing at your side, helping you to pray, trying to turn you into another son, then you have to think of the third Person as something inside you, or behind you. Perhaps some people might find it easier to

---

* This corporate behaviour may, of course, be either better or worse than their individual behaviour.

begin with the third Person and work backwards. God is love, and that love works through men—especially through the whole community of Christians. But this spirit of love is, from all eternity, a love going on between the Father and the Son.

And now, what does it all matter? It matters more than anything else in the world. The whole dance, or drama, or pattern of this three-Personal life is to be played out in each one of us: or (putting it the other way round) each one of us has got to enter that pattern, take his place in that dance. There is no other way to the happiness for which we were made. Good things as well as bad, you know, are caught by a kind of infection. If you want to get warm you must stand near the fire: if you want to be wet you must get into the water. If you want joy, power, peace, eternal life, you must get close to, or even into, the thing that has them. They are not a sort of prize which God could, if He chose, just hand out to anyone. They are a great fountain of energy and beauty spurting up at the very centre of reality. If you are close to it, the spray will wet you: if you are not, you will remain dry. Once a man is united to God, how could he not live forever? Once a man is separated from God, what can he do but wither and die?

But how is he to be united to God? How is it possible for us to be taken into the three-Personal life?

You remember what I said in Chapter 1 about *begetting* and *making*. We are not begotten by God, we are only made by Him: in our natural state we are not sons of God, only (so to speak) statues. We have not got *Zoe* or spiritual life: only *Bios* or biological life which is presently going to run down and die. Now the whole offer which Christianity makes is this: that we can, if we let God have His way, come to share in the life of Christ. If we do, we shall then be sharing a life which was begotten, not made, which always has existed and always will exist. Christ is the Son of God. If we share in this kind of life we also shall be sons of God. We shall love the Father as He does and the Holy Ghost will arise in us. He came to this world and became a man in order to spread to other men the kind of life He has—by what I call 'good infection'. Every Christian is to become a little Christ. The whole purpose of becoming a Christian is simply nothing else.

5

THE OBSTINATE
TOY SOLDIERS

THE SON OF GOD became a man to enable men to become sons of God. We do not know—anyway, I do not know—how things would have worked if the human race had never rebelled against God and joined the enemy. Perhaps every man would have been 'in Christ', would have shared the life of the Son of God, from the moment he was born. Perhaps the Bios or natural life would have been drawn up into the Zoe, the un-created life, at once and as a matter of course. But that is guesswork. You and I are concerned with the way things work now.

And the present state of things is this. The two kinds of life are now not only different (they would always have been that) but actually op-posed. The natural life in each of us is something self-centred, something that wants to be petted and admired, to take advantage of other lives, to exploit the whole universe. And especially it wants to be left to itself: to keep well away from anything better or stronger or higher than it, any-thing that might make it feel small. It is afraid of the light and air of the spiritual world, just as people who have been brought up to be dirty are afraid of a bath. And in a sense it is quite right. It knows that if the spir-itual life gets hold of it, all its self-centredness and self-will are going to be killed and it is ready to fight tooth and nail to avoid that.

Did you ever think, when you were a child, what fun it would be if your toys could come to life? Well suppose you could really have brought them to life. Imagine turning a tin soldier into a real little man. It would involve turning the tin into flesh. And suppose the tin soldier did not like it. He is not interested in flesh: all he sees is that the tin is being spoilt. He thinks you are killing him. He will do everything he can to prevent you. He will not be made into a man if he can help it.

What you would have done about that tin soldier I do not know. But what God did about us was this. The Second Person in God, the Son, became human Himself: was born into the world as an actual man—a real man of a particular height, with hair of a particular colour, speaking a particular language, weighing so many stone. The Eternal Being, who knows everything and who created the whole universe, became not only a man but (before that) a baby, and before that a *foetus* inside a Woman's body. If you want to get the hang of it, think how you would like to become a slug or a crab.

The result of this was that you now had one man who really was what all men were intended to be: one man in whom the created life, derived from His Mother, allowed itself to be completely and perfectly turned into the begotten life. The natural human creature in Him was taken up fully into the divine Son. Thus in one instance humanity had, so to speak, arrived: had passed into the life of Christ. And because the whole difficulty for us is that the natural life has to be, in a sense, 'killed', He chose an earthly career which involved the killing of His human desires at every turn—poverty, misunderstanding from His own family, betrayal by one of His intimate friends, being jeered at and manhandled by the Police, and execution by torture. And then, after being thus killed—killed every day in a sense—the human creature in Him, because it was united to the divine Son, came to life again. The Man in Christ rose again: not only the God. That is the whole point. For the first time we saw a real man. One tin soldier—real tin, just like the rest—had come fully and splendidly alive.

And here, of course, we come to the point where my illustration about the tin soldier breaks down. In the case of real toy soldiers or statues, if one came to life, it would obviously make no difference to the rest. They are all separate. But human beings are not. They look separate because you see them walking about separately. But then, we are so made that we can see only the present moment. If we could see the past, then of course it would look different. For there was a time when every man was part of his mother, and (earlier still) part of his father as well: and when they were part of his grandparents. If you could see humanity spread out in time, as God sees it, it would not look like a lot of separate things dotted about. It would look like one single growing thing—rather like a very complicated tree. Every individual would appear connected with every other. And not only that. Individuals are not really separate from God any more than from one another. Every man, woman, and child all over the world is feeling and breathing at this moment only because God, so to speak, is 'keeping him going'.

Consequently, when Christ becomes man it is not really as if you could become one particular tin soldier. It is as if something which is always affecting the whole human mass begins, at one point, to affect the whole human mass in a new way. From that point the effect spreads through all mankind. It makes a difference to people who lived before Christ as well as to people who lived after Him. It makes a difference to people who have never heard of Him. It is like dropping into a glass of water one drop of something which gives a new taste or a new colour to the whole lot. But, of course, none of these illustrations really works perfectly. In the long run God is no one but Himself and what He does is like nothing else. You could hardly expect it to be otherwise.

What, then, is the difference which He has made to the whole human mass? It is just this; that the business of becoming a son of God, of being turned from a created thing into a begotten thing, of passing over from the temporary biological life into timeless 'spiritual' life, has been done for us. Humanity is already 'saved' in principle. We individuals have to appropriate that salvation. But the really tough work—the bit we could not have done for ourselves—has been done for us. We have not got to try to climb up into spiritual life by our own efforts; it has already come down into the human race. If we will only lay ourselves open to the one Man in whom it was fully present, and who, in spite of being God, is also a real man, He will do it in us and for us. Remember what I said about 'good infection'. One of our own race has this new life: if we get close to Him we shall catch it from Him.

Of course, you can express this in all sorts of different ways. You can say that Christ died for our sins. You may say that the Father has forgiven us because Christ has done for us what we ought to have done. You may say that we are washed in the blood of the Lamb. You may say that Christ has defeated death. They are all true. If any of them do not appeal to you, leave it alone and get on with the formula that does. And, whatever you do, do not start quarrelling with other people because they use a different formula from yours.

6

TWO NOTES

IN ORDER TO avoid misunderstanding I here add notes on two points arising out of the last chapter.

(1) One sensible critic wrote asking me why, if God wanted sons instead of 'toy soldiers', He did not *beget* many sons at the outset instead of first *making* toy soldiers and then bringing them to life by such a difficult and painful process. One part of the answer to this question is fairly easy: the other part is probably beyond all human knowledge. The easy part is this. The process of being turned from a creature into a son would not have been difficult or painful if the human race had not turned away from God centuries ago. They were able to do this because He gave them free will: He gave them free will because a world of mere automata could never love and therefore never know infinite happiness. The difficult part is this. All Christians are agreed that there is, in the full and original sense, only one 'Son of God'. If we insist on asking 'But could there have been many?' we find ourselves in very deep water. Have the words 'Could have been' any sense at all when applied to God? You can say that one particular finite thing 'could have been' different from what it is, because it would have been different if something else had been different, and the something else would have been different if some third thing had been different, and so on. (The letters on this page would have been red if the printer had used red ink, and he would have used red ink if he had been instructed to, and so on.) But when you are talking about God—i.e. about the rock bottom, irreducible Fact on which all other facts depend— it is nonsensical to ask if it could have been otherwise. It is what it is, and

there is an end of the matter. But quite apart from this, I find a difficulty about the very idea of the Father begetting many sons from all eternity. In order to be many they would have to be somehow different from one another. Two pennies have the same shape. How are they two? By occupying different places and containing different atoms. In other words, to think of them as different, we have had to bring in space and matter; in fact we have had to bring in 'Nature' or the created universe. I can understand the distinction between the Father and the Son without bringing in space or matter, because the one begets and the other is begotten. The Father's relation to the Son is not the same as the Son's relation to the Father. But if there were several sons they would all be related to one another and to the Father in the same way. How would they differ from one another? One does not notice the difficulty at first, of course. One thinks one can form the idea of several 'sons'. But when I think closely, I find that the idea seemed possible only because I was vaguely imagining them as human forms standing about together in some kind of space. In other words, though I pretended to be thinking about something that exists before any universe was made, I was really smuggling in the picture of a universe and putting that something *inside* it. When I stop doing that and still try to think of the Father begetting many sons 'before all worlds' I find I am not really thinking of anything. The idea fades away into mere words. (Was Nature—space and time and matter—created precisely in order to make many-ness possible? Is there perhaps no other way of getting many eternal spirits except by first making many natural creatures, in a universe, and then spiritualising them? But of course all this is guesswork.)

(2) The idea that the whole human race is, in a sense, one thing—one huge organism, like a tree—must not be confused with the idea that individual differences do not matter or that real people, Tom and Nobby and Kate, are somehow less important than collective things like classes, races, and so forth. Indeed the two ideas are opposites. Things which are parts of a single organism may be very different from one another: things which are not, may be very alike. Six pennies are quite separate and very alike: my nose and my lungs are very different but they are only alive at all because they are parts of my body and share its common life. Christianity thinks of human individuals not as mere members of a group or items in a list, but as organs in a body—different from one another and each contributing what no other could. When you find yourself wanting

to turn your children, or pupils, or even your neighbours, into people exactly like yourself, remember that God probably never meant them to be that. You and they are different organs, intended to do different things. On the other hand, when you are tempted not to bother about someone else's troubles because they are 'no business of yours', remember that though he is different from you he is part of the same organism as you. If you forget that he belongs to the same organism as yourself you will become an Individualist. If you forget that he is a different organ from you, if you want to suppress differences and make people all alike, you will become a Totalitarian. But a Christian must not be either a Totalitarian or an Individualist.

I feel a strong desire to tell you—and I expect you feel a strong desire to tell me—which of these two errors is the worse. That is the devil getting at us. He always sends errors into the world in pairs—pairs of opposites. And he always encourages us to spend a lot of time thinking which is the worse. You see why, of course? He relies on your extra dislike of the one error to draw you gradually into the opposite one. But do not let us be fooled. We have to keep our eyes on the goal and go straight through between both errors. We have no other concern than that with either of them.

7

LET'S PRETEND

MAY I ONCE again start by putting two pictures, or two stories rather, into your minds? One is the story you have all read called *Beauty and the Beast*. The girl, you remember, had to marry a monster for some reason. And she did. She kissed it as if it were a man. And then, much to her relief, it really turned into a man and all went well. The other story is about someone who had to wear a mask; a mask which made him look much nicer than he really was. He had to wear it for years. And when he took it off he found his own face had grown to fit it. He was now really beautiful. What had begun as disguise had become a reality. I think both these stories may (in a fanciful way, of course) help to illustrate what I have to say in this chapter. Up till now, I have been trying to describe facts— what God is and what He has done. Now I want to talk about practice— what do we do next? What difference does all this theology make? It can start making a difference tonight. If you are interested enough to have read thus far you are probably interested enough to make a shot at saying your prayers: and, whatever else you say, you will probably say the Lord's Prayer.

Its very first words are *Our Father*. Do you now see what those words mean? They mean quite frankly, that you are putting yourself in the place of a son of God. To put it bluntly, you are *dressing up as Christ*. If you like, you are pretending. Because, of course, the moment you realise what the words mean, you realise that you are not a son of God. You are not a being like The Son of God, whose will and interests are at one with those of the Father: you are a bundle of self-centred fears, hopes, greeds, jealousies, and self-conceit, all doomed to death. So that, in a way, this dressing up as Christ is a piece of outrageous cheek. But the odd thing is that He has ordered us to do it.

Why? What is the good of pretending to be what you are not? Well, even on the human level, you know, there are two kinds of pretending. There is a bad kind, where the pretence is there instead of the real thing; as when a man pretends he is going to help you instead of really helping you. But there is also a good kind, where the pretence leads up to the real thing. When you are not feeling particularly friendly but know you ought to be, the best thing you can do, very often, is to put on a friendly manner and behave as if you were a nicer person than you actually are. And in a few minutes, as we have all noticed, you will be really feeling friendlier than you were. Very often the only way to get a quality in reality is to start behaving as if you had it already. That is why children's games are so important. They are always pretending to be grown-ups—playing soldiers, playing shop. But all the time, they are hardening their muscles and sharpening their wits so that the pretence of being grown-up helps them to grow up in earnest.

Now, the moment you realise 'Here I am, dressing up as Christ,' it is extremely likely that you will see at once some way in which at that very moment the pretence could be made less of a pretence and more of a reality. You will find several things going on in your mind which would not be going on there if you were really a son of God. Well, stop them. Or you may realise that, instead of saying your prayers, you ought to be downstairs writing a letter, or helping your wife to wash-up. Well, go and do it.

You see what is happening. The Christ Himself, the Son of God who is man (just like you) and God (just like His Father) is actually at your side and is already at that moment beginning to turn your pretence into a reality. This is not merely a fancy way of saying that your conscience is telling you what to do. If you simply ask your conscience, you get one result; if you remember that you are dressing up as Christ, you get a different one. There are lots of things which your conscience might not call definitely wrong (specially things in your mind) but which you will see at once you cannot go on doing if you are seriously trying to be like Christ. For you are no longer thinking simply about right and wrong; you are trying to catch the good infection from a Person. It is more like painting a portrait than like obeying a set of rules. And the odd thing is that while in one way it is much harder than keeping rules, in another way it is far easier.

The real Son of God is at your side. He is beginning to turn you into the same kind of thing as Himself. He is beginning, so to speak, to 'inject' His kind of life and thought, His *Zoe,* into you; beginning to turn the tin soldier into a live man. The part of you that does not like it is the part that is still tin.

Some of you may feel that this is very unlike your own experience. You may say 'I've never had the sense of being helped by an invisible Christ, but I often have been helped by other human beings.' That is rather like the woman in the first war who said that if there were a bread shortage it would not bother her house because they always ate toast. If there is no bread there will be no toast. If there were no help from Christ, there would be no help from other human beings. He works on us in all sorts of ways: not only through what we think our 'religious life'. He works through Nature, through our own bodies, through books, sometimes through experiences which seem (at the time) *anti*-Christian. When a young man who has been going to church in a routine way honestly realises that he does not believe in Christianity and stops going—provided he does it for honesty's sake and not just to annoy his parents—the spirit of Christ is probably nearer to him then than it ever was before. But above all, He works on us through each other.

Men are mirrors, or 'carriers' of Christ to other men. Sometimes unconscious carriers. This 'good infection' can be carried by those who have not got it themselves. People who were not Christians themselves helped me to Christianity. But usually it is those who know Him that bring Him to others. That is why the Church, the whole body of Christians showing Him to one another, is so important. You might say that when two Christians are following Christ together there is not twice as much Christianity as when they are apart, but sixteen times as much.

But do not forget this. At first it is natural for a baby to take its mother's milk without knowing its mother. It is equally natural for us to see the man who helps us without seeing Christ behind him. But we must not remain babies. We must go on to recognise the real Giver. It is madness not to. Because, if we do not, we shall be relying on human beings. And that is going to let us down. The best of them will make mistakes; all of them will die. We must be thankful to all the people who have helped us, we must honour them and love them. But never, never pin your whole faith on any human being: not if he is the best and wisest in the whole world. There are lots of nice things you can do with sand: but do not try building a house on it.

And now we begin to see what it is that the New Testament is always talking about. It talks about Christians 'being born again'; it talks about them 'putting on Christ'; about Christ 'being formed in us'; about our coming to 'have the mind of Christ'.

Put right out of your head the idea that these are only fancy ways of saying that Christians are to read what Christ said and try to carry it out—as a man may read what Plato or Marx said and try to carry it out. They mean something much more than that. They mean that a real Person, Christ, here and now, in that very room where you are saying your prayers, is doing things to you. It is not a question of a good man who died two thousand years ago. It is a living Man, still as much a man as you, and still as much God as He was when He created the world, really coming and interfering with your very self; killing the old natural self in you and replacing it with the kind of self He has. At first, only for moments. Then for longer periods. Finally, if all goes well, turning you permanently into a different sort of thing; into a new little Christ, a being which, in its own small way, has the same kind of life as God; which shares in His power, joy, knowledge and eternity. And soon we make two other discoveries.

(1) We begin to notice, besides our particular sinful acts, our sinfulness; begin to be alarmed not only about what we do, but about what we are. This may sound rather difficult, so I will try to make it clear from my own case. When I come to my evening prayers and try to reckon up the sins of the day, nine times out of ten the most obvious one is some sin against charity; I have sulked or snapped or sneered or snubbed or stormed. And the excuse that immediately springs to my mind is that the provocation was so sudden and unexpected; I was caught off my guard, I had not time to collect myself. Now that may be an extenuating circumstance as regards those particular acts: they would obviously be worse if they had been deliberate and premeditated. On the other hand, surely what a man does when he is taken off his guard is the best evidence for what sort of a man he is? Surely what pops out before the man has time to put on a disguise is the truth? If there are rats in a cellar you are most likely to see them if you go in very suddenly. But the suddenness does not create the rats: it only prevents them from hiding. In the same way the

suddenness of the provocation does not make me an ill-tempered man; it only shows me what an ill-tempered man I am. The rats are always there in the cellar, but if you go in shouting and noisily they will have taken cover before you switch on the light. Apparently the rats of resentment and vindictiveness are always there in the cellar of my soul. Now that cellar is out of reach of my conscious will. I can to some extent control my acts: I have no direct control over my temperament. And if (as I said before) what we are matters even more than what we do—if, indeed, what we do matters chiefly as evidence of what we are—then it follows that the change which I most need to undergo is a change that my own direct, voluntary efforts cannot bring about. And this applies to my good actions too. How many of them were done for the right motive? How many for fear of public opinion, or a desire to show off? How many from a sort of obstinacy or sense of superiority which, in different circumstances, might equally have led to some very bad act? But I cannot, by direct moral effort, give myself new motives. After the first few steps in the Christian life we realise that everything which really needs to be done in our souls can be done only by God. And that brings us to something which has been very misleading in my language up to now.

(2) I have been talking as if it were we who did everything. In reality, of course, it is God who does everything. We, at most, allow it to be done to us. In a sense you might even say it is God who does the pretending. The Three-Personal God, so to speak, sees before Him in fact a self-centred, greedy, grumbling, rebellious human animal. But He says 'Let us pretend that this is not a mere creature, but our Son. It is like Christ in so far as it is a Man, for He became Man. Let us pretend that it is also like Him in Spirit. Let us treat it as if it were what in fact it is not. Let us pretend in order to make the pretence into a reality.' God looks at you as if you were a little Christ: Christ stands beside you to turn you into one. I daresay this idea of a divine make-believe sounds rather strange at first. But, is it so strange really? Is not that how the higher thing always raises the lower? A mother teaches her baby to talk by talking to it as if it understood long before it really does. We treat our dogs as if they were 'almost human': that is why they really become 'almost human' in the end.

8

IS CHRISTIANITY HARD
OR EASY?

IN THE PREVIOUS chapter we were considering the Christian idea of 'putting on Christ', or first 'dressing up' as a son of God in order that you may finally become a real son. What I want to make clear is that this is not one among many jobs a Christian has to do; and it is not a sort of special exercise for the top class. It is the whole of Christianity. Christianity offers nothing else at all. And I should like to point out how it differs from ordinary ideas of 'morality' and 'being good'.

The ordinary idea which we all have before we become Christians is this. We take as starting point our ordinary self with its various desires and interests. We then admit that something else—call it 'morality' or 'decent behaviour', or 'the good of society'—has claims on this self: claims which interfere with its own desires. What we mean by 'being good' is giving in to those claims. Some of the things the ordinary self wanted to do turn out to be what we call 'wrong': well, we must give them up. Other things, which the self did not want to do, turn out to be what we call 'right': well, we shall have to do them. But we are hoping all the time that when all the demands have been met, the poor natural self will still have some chance, and some time, to get on with its own life and do what it likes. In fact, we are very like an honest man paying his taxes. He pays them all right, but he does hope that there will be enough left over for him to live on. Because we are still taking our natural self as the starting point.

As long as we are thinking that way, one or other of two results is likely to follow. Either we give up trying to be good, or else we become very unhappy indeed. For, make no mistake: if you are really going to try to meet all the demands made on the natural self, it will not have enough left over to live on. The more you obey your conscience, the more your conscience will demand of you. And your natural self, which is thus being starved and hampered and worried at every turn, will get angrier and angrier. In the end, you will either give up trying to be good, or else become one of those people who, as they say, 'live for others' but always in a discontented, grumbling way—always wondering why the others do not notice it more and always making a martyr of yourself. And once you have become that you will be a far greater pest to anyone who has to live with you than you would have been if you had remained frankly selfish.

The Christian way is different: harder, and easier. Christ says 'Give me All. I don't want so much of your time and so much of your money and so much of your work: I want You. I have not come to torment your natural self, but to kill it. No half-measures are any good. I don't want to cut off a branch here and a branch there, I want to have the whole tree down. I don't want to drill the tooth, or crown it, or stop it, but to have it out. Hand over the whole natural self, all the desires which you think innocent as well as the ones you think wicked—the whole outfit. I will give you a new self instead. In fact, I will give you Myself: my own will shall become yours.'

Both harder and easier than what we are all trying to do. You have noticed, I expect, that Christ Himself sometimes describes the Christian way as very hard, sometimes as very easy. He says, 'Take up your Cross'—in other words, it is like going to be beaten to death in a concentration camp. Next minute he says, 'My yoke is easy and my burden light.' He means both. And one can just see why both are true.

Teachers will tell you that the laziest boy in the class is the one who works hardest in the end. They mean this. If you give two boys, say, a proposition in geometry to do, the one who is prepared to take trouble will try to understand it. The lazy boy will try to learn it by heart because, for the moment, that needs less effort. But six months later, when they are preparing for an exam, that lazy boy is doing hours and hours of miserable drudgery over things the other boy understands, and positively enjoys, in a few minutes. Laziness means more work in the long run. Or look at it this way. In a battle, or in mountain climbing, there is often one thing which it takes a lot of pluck to do; but it is also, in the long run, the safest thing to do. If you funk it, you will find yourself, hours later, in far worse danger. The cowardly thing is also the most dangerous thing.

It is like that here. The terrible thing, the almost impossible thing, is to hand over your whole self—all your wishes and precautions—to Christ. But it is far easier than what we are all trying to do instead. For what we are trying to do is to remain what we call 'ourselves', to keep personal happiness as our great aim in life, and yet at the same time be 'good'. We are all trying to let our mind and heart go their own way—centred on money or pleasure or ambition—and hoping, in spite of this, to behave honestly and chastely and humbly. And that is exactly what Christ warned us you could not do. As He said, a thistle cannot produce figs. If I am a field that contains nothing but grass-seed, I cannot produce wheat. Cutting the grass may keep it short: but I shall still produce grass and no wheat. If I want to produce wheat, the change must go deeper than the surface. I must be ploughed up and re-sown.

That is why the real problem of the Christian life comes where people do not usually look for it. It comes the very moment you wake up each morning. All your wishes and hopes for the day rush at you like wild animals. And the first job each morning consists simply in shoving them all back; in listening to that other voice, taking that other point of view, letting that other larger, stronger, quieter life come flowing in. And so on, all day. Standing back from all your natural fussings and frettings; coming in out of the wind.

We can only do it for moments at first. But from those moments the new sort of life will be spreading through our system: because now we are letting Him work at the right part of us. It is the difference between paint, which is merely laid on the surface, and a dye or stain which soaks right through. He never talked vague, idealistic gas. When He said, 'Be perfect,' He meant it. He meant that we must go in for the full treatment. It is hard; but the sort of compromise we are all hankering after is harder—in fact, it is impossible. It may be hard for an egg to turn into a bird: it would be a jolly sight harder for it to learn to fly while remaining an egg. We are like eggs at present. And you cannot go on indefinitely being just an ordinary, decent egg. We must be hatched or go bad.

May I come back to what I said before? This is the whole of Christianity. There is nothing else. It is so easy to get muddled about that. It is easy to think that the Church has a lot of different objects—education, building, missions, holding services. Just as it is easy to think the State has a lot of different objects—military, political, economic, and what not. But in a way things are much simpler than that. The State exists simply to promote and to protect the ordinary happiness of human beings in this life. A husband and wife chatting over a fire, a couple of friends having a game of darts in a pub, a man reading a book in his own room or digging in his own garden—that is what the State is there for. And unless they are helping to increase and prolong and protect such moments, all the laws, parliaments, armies, courts, police, economics, etc., are simply a waste of time. In the same way the Church exists for nothing else but to draw men into Christ, to make them little Christs. If they are not doing that, all the cathedrals, clergy, missions, sermons, even the Bible itself, are simply a waste of time. God became Man for no other purpose. It is even doubtful, you know, whether the whole universe was created for any other purpose. It says in the Bible that the whole universe was made for Christ and that everything is to be gathered together in Him. I do not suppose any of us can understand how this will happen as regards the whole universe. We do not know what (if anything) lives in the parts of it that are millions of miles away from this Earth. Even on this Earth we do not know how it applies to things other than men. After all, that is what you would expect. We have been shown the plan only in so far as it concerns ourselves.

I sometimes like to imagine that I can just see how it might apply to other things. I think I can see how the higher animals are in a sense drawn into Man when he loves them and makes them (as he does) much more nearly human than they would otherwise be. I can even see a sense in which the dead things and plants are drawn into Man as he studies them and uses and appreciates them. And if there were intelligent creatures in other worlds they might do the same with their worlds. It might be that when intelligent creatures entered into Christ they would, in that way, bring all the other things in along with them. But I do not know: it is only a guess.

What we have been told is how we men can be drawn into Christ—can become part of that wonderful present which the young Prince of the universe wants to offer to His Father—that present which is Himself and therefore us in Him. It is the only thing we were made for. And there are strange, exciting hints in the Bible that when we are drawn in, a great many other things in Nature will begin to come right. The bad dream will be over: it will be morning.

9

COUNTING THE COST

I FIND A good many people have been bothered by what I said in the previous chapter about Our Lord's words, 'Be ye perfect'. Some people seem to think this means 'Unless you are perfect, I will not help you'; and as we cannot be perfect, then, if He meant that, our position is hopeless. But I do not think He did mean that. I think He meant 'The only help I will give is help to become perfect. You may want something less: but I will give you nothing less.'

Let me explain. When I was a child I often had toothache, and I knew that if I went to my mother she would give me something which would deaden the pain for that night and let me get to sleep. But I did not go to my mother—at least, not till the pain became very bad. And the reason I did not go was this. I did not doubt she would give me the aspirin; but I knew she would also do something else. I knew she would take me to the dentist next morning. I could not get what I wanted out of her without getting something more, which I did not want. I wanted immediate relief from pain: but I could not get it without having my teeth set permanently right. And I knew those dentists: I knew they started fiddling about with all sorts of other teeth which had not yet begun to ache. They would not let sleeping dogs lie, if you gave them an inch they took an ell.

Now, if I may put it that way, Our Lord is like the dentists. If you give Him an inch, He will take an ell. Dozens of people go to Him to be cured of some one particular sin which they are ashamed of (like masturbation or physical cowardice) or which is obviously spoiling daily life (like bad temper or drunkenness). Well, He will cure it all right: but He will not stop there. That may be all you asked; but if once you call Him in, He will give you the full treatment.

That is why He warned people to 'count the cost' before becoming Christians. 'Make no mistake,' He says, 'if you let me, I will make you perfect. The moment you put yourself in My hands, that is what you are in for. Nothing less, or other, than that. You have free will, and if you choose, you can push Me away. But if you do not push Me away, understand that I am going to see this job through. Whatever suffering it may cost you in your earthly life, whatever inconceivable purification it may cost you after death, whatever it costs Me, I will never rest, nor let you rest, until you are literally perfect—until my Father can say without reservation that He is well pleased with you, as He said He was well pleased with me. This I can do and will do. But I will not do anything less.'

And yet—this is the other and equally important side of it—this Helper who will, in the long run, be satisfied with nothing less than absolute perfection, will also be delighted with the first feeble, stumbling effort you make tomorrow to do the simplest duty. As a great Christian writer (George MacDonald) pointed out, every father is pleased at the baby's first attempt to walk: no father would be satisfied with anything less than a firm, free, manly walk in a grown-up son. In the same way, he said, 'God is easy to please, but hard to satisfy.'

The practical upshot is this. On the one hand, God's demand for perfection need not discourage you in the least in your present attempts to be good, or even in your present failures. Each time you fall He will pick you up again. And He knows perfectly well that your own efforts are never going to bring you anywhere near perfection. On the other hand, you must realise from the outset that the goal towards which He is beginning to guide you is absolute perfection; and no power in the whole universe, except you yourself, can prevent Him from taking you to that goal. That is what you are in for. And it is very important to realise that. If we do not, then we are very likely to start pulling back and resisting Him after a certain point. I think that many of us, when Christ has enabled us to overcome one or two sins that were an obvious nuisance, are inclined to feel (though we do not put it into words) that we are now good enough. He has done all we wanted Him to do, and we should be obliged if He would now leave us alone. As we say 'I never expected to be a saint, I only wanted to be a decent ordinary chap.' And we imagine when we say this that we are being humble.

But this is the fatal mistake. Of course we never wanted, and never asked, to be made into the sort of creatures He is going to make us into. But the question is not what we intended ourselves to be, but what He intended us to be when He made us. He is the inventor, we are only the machine. He is the painter, we are only the picture. How should we know what He means us to be like? You see, He has already made us something very different from what we were. Long ago, before we were born, when we were inside our mothers' bodies, we passed through various stages. We were once rather like vegetables, and once rather like fish: it was only at a later stage that we became like human babies. And if we had been conscious at those earlier stages, I daresay we should have been quite contented to stay as vegetables or fish—should not have wanted to be made into babies. But all the time He knew His plan for us and was determined to carry it out. Something the same is now happening at a higher level. We may be content to remain what we call 'ordinary people': but He is determined to carry out a quite different plan. To shrink back from that plan is not humility: it is laziness and cowardice. To submit to it is not conceit or megalomania; it is obedience.

Here is another way of putting the two sides of the truth. On the one hand we must never imagine that our own unaided efforts can be relied on to carry us even through the next twenty-four hours as 'decent' people. If He does not support us, not one of us is safe from some gross sin. On the other hand, no possible degree of holiness or heroism which has ever been recorded of the greatest saints is beyond what He is determined to produce in every one of us in the end. The job will not be completed in this life; but He means to get us as far as possible before death.

That is why we must not be surprised if we are in for a rough time. When a man turns to Christ and seems to be getting on pretty well (in the sense that some of his bad habits are now corrected) he often feels that it would now be natural if things went fairly smoothly. When troubles come along—illnesses, money troubles, new kinds of temptation—he is disappointed. These things, he feels, might have been necessary to rouse him and make him repent in his bad old days; but why now? Because God is forcing him on, or up, to a higher level: putting him into situations where he will have to be very much braver, or more patient, or more loving, than he ever dreamed of being before. It seems to us all unnecessary: but that is because we have not yet had the slightest notion of the tremendous thing He means to make of us.

I find I must borrow yet another parable from George MacDonald. Imagine yourself as a living house. God comes in to rebuild that house. At first, perhaps, you can understand what He is doing. He is getting the drains right and stopping the leaks in the roof and so on: you knew that those jobs needed doing and so you are not surprised. But presently he starts knocking the house about in a way that hurts abominably and does not seem to make sense. What on earth is He up to? The explanation is that He is building quite a different house from the one you thought of—throwing out a new wing here, putting on an extra floor there, running up towers, making courtyards. You thought you were going to be made into a decent little cottage: but He is building a palace. He intends to come and live in it Himself.

The command *Be ye perfect* is not idealistic gas. Nor is it a command to do the impossible. He is going to make us into creatures that can obey that command. He said (in the Bible) that we were 'gods' and He is going to make good His words. If we let Him—for we can prevent Him, if we choose—He will make the feeblest and filthiest of us into a god or goddess, a dazzling, radiant, immortal creature, pulsating all through with such energy and joy and wisdom and love as we cannot now imagine, a bright stainless mirror which reflects back to God perfectly (though, of course, on a smaller scale) His own boundless power and delight and goodness. The process will be long and in parts very painful, but that is what we are in for. Nothing less. He meant what He said.

NICE PEOPLE OR NEW MEN

HE MEANT WHAT He said. Those who put themselves in His hands will become perfect, as He is perfect—perfect in love, wisdom, joy, beauty, and immortality. The change will not be completed in this life, for death is an important part of the treatment. How far the change will have gone before death in any particular Christian is uncertain.

I think this is the right moment to consider a question which is often asked: If Christianity is true why are not all Christians obviously nicer than all non-Christians? What lies behind that question is partly something very reasonable and partly something that is not reasonable at all. The reasonable part is this. If conversion to Christianity makes no improvement in a man's outward actions—if he continues to be just as snobbish or spiteful or envious or ambitious as he was before—then I think we must suspect that his 'conversion' was largely imaginary; and after one's original conversion, every time one thinks one has made an advance, that is the test to apply. Fine feelings, new insights, greater interest in 'religion' mean nothing unless they make our actual behaviour better; just as in an illness 'feeling better' is not much good if the thermometer shows that your temperature is still going up. In that sense the outer world is quite right to judge Christianity by its results. Christ told us to judge by results. A tree is known by its fruit; or, as we say, the proof of the pudding is in the eating. When we Christians behave badly, or fail to behave well, we are making Christianity unbelievable to the outside world. The war-time posters told us that Careless Talk costs Lives. It is equally true that Careless Lives cost Talk. Our careless lives set the outer world talking; and we give them grounds for talking in a way that throws doubt on the truth of Christianity itself.

But there is another way of demanding results in which the outer world may be quite illogical. They may demand not merely that each man's life should improve if he becomes a Christian: they may also demand before they believe in Christianity that they should see the whole world neatly divided into two camps—Christian and non-Christian—and that all the people in the first camp at any given moment should be obviously nicer than all the people in the second. This is unreasonable on several grounds.

(1) In the first place the situation in the actual world is much more complicated than that. The world does not consist of 100 per cent. Christians and 100 per cent. non-Christians. There are people (a great many of them) who are slowly ceasing to be Christians but who still call themselves by that name: some of them are clergymen. There are other people who are slowly becoming Christians though they do not yet call themselves so. There are people who do not accept the full Christian doctrine about Christ but who are so strongly attracted by Him that they are His in a much deeper sense than they themselves understand. There are people in other religions who are being led by God's secret influence to concentrate on those parts of their religion which are in agreement with Christianity, and who thus belong to Christ without knowing it. For example, a Buddhist of good will may be led to concentrate more and more on the Buddhist teaching about mercy and to leave in the background (though he might still say he believed) the Buddhist teaching on certain other points. Many of the good Pagans long before Christ's birth may have been in this position. And always, of course, there are a great many people who are just confused in mind and have a lot of inconsistent beliefs all jumbled up together. Consequently, it is not much use trying to make judgments about Christians and non-Christians in the mass. It is some use comparing cats and dogs, or even men and women, in the mass, because there one knows definitely which is which. Also, an animal does not turn (either slowly or suddenly) from a dog into a cat. But when we are comparing Christians in general with non-Christians in general, we are usually not thinking about real people whom we know at all, but only about two vague ideas which we have got from novels and newspapers. If you want to compare the bad Christian and the good Atheist, you must think about two real specimens whom you have actually met. Unless we come down to brass tacks in that way, we shall only be wasting time.

(2) Suppose we have come down to brass tacks and are now talking not about an imaginary Christian and an imaginary non-Christian, but about two real people in our own neighbourhood. Even then we must be careful to ask the right question. If Christianity is true then it ought to follow *(a)* That any Christian will be nicer than the same person would be if he were not a Christian. *(b)* That any man who becomes a Christian will be nicer than he was before. Just in the same way, if the advertisements of Whitesmile's toothpaste are true it ought to follow *(a)* That anyone who uses it will have better teeth than the same person would have if he did not use it. *(b)* That if anyone begins to use it his teeth will improve. But to point out that I, who use Whitesmile's (and also have inherited bad teeth from both my parents) have not got as fine a set as some healthy young negro who never used any toothpaste at all, does not, by itself, prove that the advertisements are untrue. Christian Miss Bates may have an unkinder tongue than unbelieving Dick Firkin. That, by itself, does not tell us whether Christianity works. The question is what Miss Bates's tongue would be like if she were not a Christian and what Dick's would be like if he became one. Miss Bates and Dick, as a result of natural causes and early upbringing, have certain temperaments: Christianity professes to put both temperaments under new management if they will allow it to do so. What you have a right to ask is whether that management, if allowed to take over, improves the concern. Everyone knows that what is being managed in Dick Firkin's case is much 'nicer' than what is being managed in Miss Bates's. That is not the point. To judge the management of a factory, you must consider not only the output but the plant. Considering the plant at Factory A it may be a wonder that it turns out anything at all; considering the first-class outfit at Factory B its output, though high, may be a great deal lower than it ought to be. No doubt the good manager at Factory A is going to put in new machinery as soon as he can, but that takes time. In the meantime low output does not prove that he is a failure.

(3) And now, let us go a little deeper. The manager is going to put in new machinery: before Christ has finished with Miss Bates, she is going to be very 'nice' indeed. But if we left it at that, it would sound as though Christ's only aim was to pull Miss Bates up to the same level on which Dick had been all along. We have been talking, in fact, as if Dick were all right; as if Christianity was something nasty people needed and nice ones could afford to do without; and as if niceness was all that God de-

manded. But this would be a fatal mistake. The truth is that in God's eyes Dick Firkin needs 'saving' every bit as much as Miss Bates. In one sense (I will explain what sense in a moment) niceness hardly comes into the question.

You cannot expect God to look at Dick's placid temper and friendly disposition exactly as we do. They result from natural causes which God Himself creates. Being merely temperamental, they will all disappear if Dick's digestion alters. The niceness, in fact, is God's gift to Dick, not Dick's gift to God. In the same way, God has allowed natural causes, working in a world spoiled by centuries of sin, to produce in Miss Bates the narrow mind and jangled nerves which account for most of her nastiness. He intends, in His own good time, to set that part of her right. But that is not, for God, the critical part of the business. It presents no difficulties. It is not what He is anxious about. What He is watching and waiting and working for is something that is not easy even for God, because, from the nature of the case, even He cannot produce it by a mere act of power. He is waiting and watching for it both in Miss Bates and in Dick Firkin. It is something they can freely give Him or freely refuse to Him. Will they, or will they not, turn to Him and thus fulfil the only purpose for which they were created? Their free will is trembling inside them like the needle of a compass. But this is a needle that can choose. It *can* point to its true North; but it need not. Will the needle swing round, and settle, and point to God?

He can help it to do so. He cannot force it. He cannot, so to speak, put out His own hand and pull it into the right position, for then it would not be free will any more. Will it point North? That is the question on which all hangs. Will Miss Bates and Dick offer their natures to God? The question whether the natures they offer or withhold are, at that moment, nice or nasty ones, is of secondary importance. God can see to that part of the problem.

Do not misunderstand me. Of course God regards a nasty nature as a bad and deplorable thing. And, of course, He regards a nice nature as a good thing—good like bread, or sunshine, or water. But these are the good things which He gives and we receive. He created Dick's sound nerves and good digestion, and there is plenty more where they came from. It costs God nothing, so far as we know, to create nice things: but to convert rebellious wills cost His crucifixion. And because they are wills they can—in nice people just as much as in nasty ones—refuse His request. And then, because that niceness in Dick was merely part of nature, it will all go to pieces in the end. Nature herself will all pass away. Natural causes come together in Dick to make a pleasant psychological pattern, just as they come together in a sunset to make a pleasant pattern of colours. Presently (for that is how nature works) they will fall apart again and the pattern in both cases will disappear. Dick has had the chance to turn (or rather, to allow God to turn) that momentary pattern into the beauty of an eternal spirit: and he has not taken it.

There is a paradox here. As long as Dick does not turn to God, he thinks his niceness is his own, and just as long as he thinks that, it is not his own. It is when Dick realises that his niceness is not his own but a gift from God, and when he offers it back to God—it is just then that it begins to be really his own. For now Dick is beginning to take a share in his own creation. The only things we can keep are the things we freely give to God. What we try to keep for ourselves is just what we are sure to lose.

We must, therefore, not be surprised if we find among the Christians some people who are still nasty. There is even, when you come to think it over, a reason why nasty people might be expected to turn to Christ in greater numbers than nice ones. That was what people objected to about Christ during His life on earth: He seemed to attract 'such awful people'. That is what people still object to and always will. Do you not see why? Christ said 'Blessed are the poor' and 'How hard it is for the rich to enter the Kingdom,' and no doubt He primarily meant the economically rich and economically poor. But do not His words also apply to another kind of riches and poverty? One of the dangers of having a lot of money is that you may be quite satisfied with the kinds of happiness money can give and so fail to realise your need for God. If everything seems to come simply by signing cheques, you may forget that you are at every moment totally dependent on God. Now quite plainly, natural gifts carry with them a similar danger. If you have sound nerves and intelligence and health and popularity and a good upbringing, you are likely to be quite satisfied with your character as it is. 'Why drag God into it?' you may ask. A certain level of good conduct comes fairly easily to you. You are not one of those wretched creatures who are always being tripped up by sex, or dipsomania, or nervousness, or bad temper. Everyone says you are a nice chap and (between ourselves) you agree with them. You are quite likely to believe that all this niceness is your own doing: and you may easily not feel the need for any better kind of goodness. Often people who have all these natural kinds of goodness cannot be brought to recognise their need for Christ at all until, one day, the natural goodness lets them down and their self-satisfaction is shattered. In other words, it is hard for those who are 'rich' in this sense to enter the Kingdom.

It is very different for the nasty people—the little, low, timid, warped, thin-blooded, lonely people, or the passionate, sensual, unbalanced people. If they make any attempt at goodness at all, they learn, in double quick time, that they need help. It is Christ or nothing for them. It is taking up the cross and following—or else despair. They are the lost sheep; He came specially to find them. They are (in one very real and terrible sense) the 'poor': He blessed them. They are the 'awful set' He goes about with—and of course the Pharisees say still, as they said from the first, 'If there were anything in Christianity those people would not be Christians.'

There is either a warning or an encouragement here for every one of us. If you are a nice person—if virtue comes easily to you—beware! Much is expected from those to whom much is given. If you mistake for your own merits what are really God's gifts to you through nature, and if you are contented with simply being nice, you are still a rebel: and all those gifts will only make your fall more terrible, your corruption more complicated, your bad example more disastrous. The Devil was an archangel once; his natural gifts were as far above yours as yours are above those of a chimpanzee.

But if you are a poor creature—poisoned by a wretched upbringing in some house full of vulgar jealousies and senseless quarrels—saddled, by no choice of your own, with some loathsome sexual perversion—nagged day in and day out by an inferiority complex that makes you snap at your best friends—do not despair. He knows all about it. You are one of the poor whom He blessed. He knows what a wretched machine you are trying to drive. Keep on. Do what you can. One day (perhaps in another world, but perhaps far sooner than that) He will fling it on the scrap-heap and give you a new one. And then you may astonish us all—not least yourself: for you have learned your driving in a hard school. (Some of the last will be first and some of the first will be last).

'Niceness'—wholesome, integrated personality—is an excellent thing. We must try by every medical, educational, economic, and political means in our power to produce a world where as many people as possible grow up 'nice'; just as we must try to produce a world where all have plenty to eat. But we must not suppose that even if we succeeded in making everyone nice we should have saved their souls. A world of nice people, content in their own niceness, looking no further, turned away from God, would be just as desperately in need of salvation as a miserable world—and might even be more difficult to save.

For mere improvement is not redemption, though redemption always improves people even here and now and will, in the end, improve them to a degree we cannot yet imagine. God became man to turn creatures into sons: not simply to produce better men of the old kind but to produce a new kind of man. It is not like teaching a horse to jump better and better but like turning a horse into a winged creature. Of course, once it has got its wings, it will soar over fences which could never have been jumped and thus beat the natural horse at its own game. But there may be a period, while the wings are just beginning to grow, when it cannot do so: and at that stage the lumps on the shoulders—no one could tell by looking at them that they are going to be wings—may even give it an awkward appearance.

But perhaps we have already spent too long on this question. If what you want is an argument against Christianity (and I well remember how eagerly I looked for such arguments when I began to be afraid it was true) you can easily find some stupid and unsatisfactory Christian and say, 'So there's your boasted new man! Give me the old kind.' But if once you have begun to see that Christianity is on other grounds probable, you will know in your heart that this is only evading the issue. What can you ever really know of other people's souls—of their temptations, their opportunities, their struggles? One soul in the whole creation you do know: and it is the only one whose fate is placed in your hands. If there is a God, you are, in a sense, alone with Him. You cannot put Him off with speculations about your next door neighbours or memories of what you have read in books. What will all that chatter and hearsay count (will you even be able to remember it?) when the anaesthetic fog which we call 'nature' or 'the real world' fades away and the Presence in which you have always stood becomes palpable, immediate, and unavoidable?

11

THE NEW MEN

IN THE LAST chapter I compared Christ's work of making New Men to the process of turning a horse into a winged creature. I used that extreme example in order to emphasise the point that it is not mere improvement but Transformation. The nearest parallel to it in the world of nature is to be found in the remarkable transformations we can make in insects by applying certain rays to them. Some people think this is how Evolution worked. The alterations in creatures on which it all depends may have been produced by rays coming from outer space. (Of course once the alterations are there, what they call 'Natural Selection' gets to work on them: i.e. the useful alterations survive and the other ones get weeded out.)

Perhaps a modern man can understand the Christian idea best if he takes it in connection with Evolution. Everyone now knows about Evolution (though, of course, some educated people disbelieve it): everyone has been told that man has evolved from lower types of life. Consequently, people often wonder 'What is the next step? When is the thing beyond man going to appear?' Imaginative writers try sometimes to picture this next step—the 'Superman' as they call him; but they usually only succeed in picturing someone a good deal nastier than man as we know him and then try to make up for that by sticking on extra legs or arms. But supposing the next step was to be something even more different from the earlier steps than they ever dreamed of? And is it not very likely it would be? Thousands of centuries ago huge, very heavily armoured creatures were evolved. If anyone had at that time been watching the course of

Evolution he would probably have expected that it was going to go on to heavier and heavier armour. But he would have been wrong. The future had a card up its sleeve which nothing at that time would have led him to expect. It was going to spring on him little, naked, unarmoured animals which had better brains: and with those brains they were going to master the whole planet. They were not merely going to have more power than the prehistoric monsters, they were going to have a new kind of power. The next step was not only going to be different, but different with a new kind of difference. The stream of Evolution was not going to flow on in the direction in which he saw it flowing: it was in fact going to take a sharp bend.

Now it seems to me that most of the popular guesses at the Next Step are making just the same sort of mistake. People see (or at any rate they think they see) men developing great brains and getting greater mastery over nature. And because they think the stream is flowing in that direction, they imagine it will go on flowing in that direction. But I cannot help thinking that the Next Step will be really new; it will go off in a direction you could never have dreamed of. It would hardly be worth calling a New Step unless it did. I should expect not merely difference but a new kind of difference. I should expect not merely change but a new method of producing the change. Or, to make an Irish bull, I should expect the next stage in Evolution not to be a stage in Evolution at all: should expect that Evolution itself as a method of producing change will be superseded. And finally, I should not be surprised if, when the thing happened, very few people noticed that it was happening.

Now, if you care to talk in these terms, the Christian view is precisely that the Next Step has already appeared. And it is really new. It is not a change from brainy men to brainier men: it is a change that goes off in a totally different direction—a change from being creatures of God to being sons of God. The first instance appeared in Palestine two thousand years ago. In a sense, the change is not 'Evolution' at all, because it is not something arising out of the natural process of events but something coming into nature from outside. But that is what I should expect. We arrived at our idea of 'Evolution' from studying the past. If there are real novelties in store then of course our idea, based on the past, will not really cover them. And in fact this New Step differs from all previous ones not only in coming from outside nature but in several other ways as well.

(1) It is not carried on by sexual reproduction. Need we be surprised at that? There was a time before sex had appeared; development used to go on by different methods. Consequently, we might have expected that there would come a time when sex disappeared, or else (which is what is actually happening) a time when sex, though it continued to exist, ceased to be the main channel of a development.

(2) At the earlier stages living organisms have had either no choice or very little choice about taking the new step. Progress was, in the main, something that happened to them, not something that they did. But the new step, the step from being creatures to being sons, is voluntary. At least, voluntary in one sense. It is not voluntary in the sense that we, of ourselves, could have chosen to take it or could even have imagined it; but it is voluntary in the sense that when it is offered to us, we can refuse it. We can, if we please, shrink back; we can dig in our heels and let the new Humanity go on without us.

(3) I have called Christ the 'first instance' of the new man. But of course He is something much more than that. He is not merely a new man, one specimen of the species, but *the* new man. He is the origin and centre and life of all the new men. He came into the created universe, of His own will, bringing with Him the *Zoe,* the new life. (I mean new to us, of course: in its own place *Zoe* has existed for ever and ever.) And He transmits it not by heredity but by what I have called 'good infection'. Everyone who gets it gets it by personal contact with Him. Other men become 'new' by being 'in Him'.

(4) This step is taken at a different speed from the previous ones. Compared with the development of man on this planet, the diffusion of Christianity over the human race seems to go like a flash of lightning—for two thousand years is almost nothing in the history of the universe. (Never forget that we are all still 'the early Christians'. The present wicked and wasteful divisions between us are, let us hope, a disease of infancy: we are still teething. The outer world, no doubt, thinks just the opposite. It thinks we are dying of old age. But it has thought that very often before. Again and again it has thought Christianity was dying, dying by persecutions from without and corruptions from within, by the rise of Mohammedanism, the rise of the physical sciences, the rise of great anti-Christian revolutionary movements. But every time the world has been disappointed. Its first disappointment was over the crucifixion. The Man came to life again. In a sense—and I quite realise how frightfully unfair it must

seem to them—that has been happening ever since. They keep on killing the thing that He started: and each time, just as they are patting down the earth on its grave, they suddenly hear that it is still alive and has even broken out in some new place. No wonder they hate us.)

(5) The stakes are higher. By falling back at the earlier steps a creature lost, at the worst, its few years of life on this earth: very often it did not lose even that. By falling back at this step we lose a prize which is (in the strictest sense of the word) infinite. For now the critical moment has arrived. Century by century God has guided nature up to the point of producing creatures which can (if they will) be taken right out of nature, turned into 'gods'. Will they allow themselves to be taken? In a way, it is like the crisis of birth. Until we rise and follow Christ we are still parts of Nature, still in the womb of our great mother. Her pregnancy has been long and painful and anxious, but it has reached its climax. The great moment has come. Everything is ready. The Doctor has arrived. Will the birth 'go off all right'? But of course it differs from an ordinary birth in one important respect. In an ordinary birth the baby has not much choice: here it has. I wonder what an ordinary baby would do if it had the choice. It might prefer to stay in the dark and warmth and safety of the womb. For of course it would think the womb meant safety. That would be just where it was wrong; for if it stays there it will die.

On this view the thing has happened: the new step has been taken and is being taken. Already the new men are dotted here and there all over the earth. Some, as I have admitted, are still hardly recognisable: but others can be recognised. Every now and then one meets them. Their very voices and faces are different from ours: stronger, quieter, happier, more radiant. They begin where most of us leave off. They are, I say, recognisable; but you must know what to look for. They will not be very like the idea of 'religious people' which you have formed from your general reading. They do not draw attention to themselves. You tend to think that you are being kind to them when they are really being kind to you. They love you more than other men do, but they need you less. (We must get over wanting to be needed: in some goodish people, specially women, that is the hardest of all temptations to resist.) They will usually seem to have a lot of time: you will wonder where it comes from. When you have recognised one of them, you will recognise the next one much more easily. And I strongly suspect (but how should I know?) that they recognise one another immediately and infallibly, across every barrier of colour, sex, class, age, and even of creeds. In that way, to become holy is rather like joining a secret society. To put it at the very lowest, it must be great *fun*.

But you must not imagine that the new men are, in the ordinary sense, all alike. A good deal of what I have been saying in this last book might make you suppose that that was bound to be so. To become new men means losing what we now call 'ourselves'. Out of our selves, into Christ, we must go. His will is to become ours and we are to think His thoughts, to 'have the mind of Christ' as the Bible says. And if Christ is one, and if He is thus to be 'in' us all, shall we not be exactly the same? It certainly sounds like it; but in fact it is not so.

It is difficult here to get a good illustration; because, of course, no other two things are related to each other just as the Creator is related to one of His creatures. But I will try two very imperfect illustrations which may give a hint of the truth. Imagine a lot of people who have always lived in the dark. You come and try to describe to them what light is like. You might tell them that if they come into the light that same light would fall on them all and they would all reflect it and thus become what we call visible. Is it not quite possible that they would imagine that, since they were all receiving the same light, and all reacting to it in the same way (i.e. all reflecting it), they would all look alike? Whereas you and I know that the light will in fact bring out, or show up, how different they are. Or again, suppose a person who knew nothing about salt. You give him a pinch to taste and he experiences a particular strong, sharp taste. You then tell him that in your country people use salt in all their cookery. Might he not reply 'In that case I suppose all your dishes taste exactly the same: because the taste of that stuff you have just given me is so strong that it will kill the taste of everything else.' But you and I know that the real effect of salt is exactly the opposite. So far from killing the taste of the egg and the tripe and the cabbage, it actually brings it out. They do not show their real taste till you have added the salt. (Of course, as I warned you, this is not really a very good illustration, because you can, after all, kill the other tastes by putting in too much salt, whereas you cannot kill the taste of a human personality by putting in too much Christ. I am doing the best I can.)

It is something like that with Christ and us. The more we get what we now call 'ourselves' out of the way and let Him take us over, the more truly ourselves we become. There is so much of Him that millions and millions of 'little Christs', all different, will still be too few to express

Him fully. He made them all. He invented—as an author invents characters in a novel—all the different men that you and I were intended to be. In that sense our real selves are all waiting for us in Him. It is no good trying to 'be myself' without Him. The more I resist Him and try to live on my own, the more I become dominated by my own heredity and upbringing and surroundings and natural desires. In fact what I so proudly call 'Myself' becomes merely the meeting place for trains of events which I never started and which I cannot stop. What I call 'My wishes' become merely the desires thrown up by my physical organism or pumped into me by other men's thoughts or even suggested to me by devils. Eggs and alcohol and a good night's sleep will be the real origins of what I flatter myself by regarding as my own highly personal and discriminating decision to make love to the girl opposite to me in the railway carriage. Propaganda will be the real origin of what I regard as my own personal political ideas. I am not, in my natural state, nearly so much of a person as I like to believe: most of what I call 'me' can be very easily explained. It is when I turn to Christ, when I give myself up to His Personality, that I first begin to have a real personality of my own.

At the beginning I said there were Personalities in God. I will go further now. There are no real personalities anywhere else. Until you have given up your self to Him you will not have a real self. Sameness is to be found most among the most 'natural' men, not among those who surrender to Christ. How monotonously alike all the great tyrants and conquerors have been: how gloriously different are the saints.

But there must be a real giving up of the self. You must throw it away 'blindly' so to speak. Christ will indeed give you a real personality: but you must not go to Him for the sake of that. As long as your own personality is what you are bothering about you are not going to Him at all. The very first step is to try to forget about the self altogether. Your real, new self (which is Christ's and also yours, and yours just because it is His) will not come as long as you are looking for it. It will come when you are looking for Him. Does that sound strange? The same principle holds, you know, for more everyday matters. Even in social life, you will never make a good impression on other people until you stop thinking about what sort of impression you are making. Even in literature and art, no man who bothers about originality will ever be original: whereas if you simply try to tell the truth (without caring twopence how often it has been told before) you will, nine times out of ten, become original without ever having noticed it. The principle runs through all life from top to bottom. Give up yourself, and you will find your real self. Lose your life and you will save it. Submit to death, death of your ambitions and favourite wishes every day and death of your whole body in the end: submit with every fibre of your being, and you will find eternal life. Keep back nothing. Nothing that you have not given away will be really yours. Nothing in you that has not died will ever be raised from the dead. Look for yourself, and you will find in the long run only hatred, loneliness, despair, rage, ruin, and decay. But look for Christ and you will find Him, and with Him everything else thrown in.

THE END

THE SCREWTAPE
LETTERS

with

SCREWTAPE PROPOSES A TOAST

To J. R. R. Tolkien

The best way to drive out the devil, if he will not yield to texts of Scripture, is to jeer and flout him, for he cannot bear scorn.

LUTHER

The devil . . . the prowde spirite . . . cannot endure to be mocked.

THOMAS MORE

PREFACE

I HAVE NO intention of explaining how the correspondence which I now offer to the public fell into my hands.

There are two equal and opposite errors into which our race can fall about the devils. One is to disbelieve in their existence. The other is to believe, and to feel an excessive and unhealthy interest in them. They themselves are equally pleased by both errors and hail a materialist or a magician with the same delight. The sort of script which is used in this book can be very easily obtained by anyone who has once learned the knack; but ill-disposed or excitable people who might make a bad use of it shall not learn it from me.

Readers are advised to remember that the devil is a liar. Not everything that Screwtape says should be assumed to be true even from his own angle. I have made no attempt to identify any of the human beings mentioned in the letters; but I think it very unlikely that the portraits, say, of Fr Spike or the patient's mother, are wholly just. There is wishful thinking in Hell as well as on Earth.

In conclusion, I ought to add that no effort has been made to clear up the chronology of the letters. Number 17 appears to have been composed before rationing became serious; but in general the diabolical method of dating seems to bear no relation to terrestrial time and I have not attempted to reproduce it. The history of the European War, except in so far as it happens now and then to impinge upon the spiritual condition of one human being, was obviously of no interest to Screwtape.

C. S. LEWIS
MAGDALEN COLLEGE,
5 JULY 1941

I

MY DEAR WORMWOOD,

I note what you say about guiding your patient's reading and taking care that he sees a good deal of his materialist friend. But are you not being a trifle *naïve?* It sounds as if you supposed that *argument* was the way to keep him out of the Enemy's clutches. That might have been so if he had lived a few centuries earlier. At that time the humans still knew pretty well when a thing was proved and when it was not; and if it was proved they really believed it. They still connected thinking with doing and were prepared to alter their way of life as the result of a chain of reasoning. But what with the weekly press and other such weapons we have largely altered that. Your man has been accustomed, ever since he was a boy, to have a dozen incompatible philosophies dancing about together inside his head. He doesn't think of doctrines as primarily 'true' or 'false', but as 'academic' or 'practical', 'outworn' or 'contemporary', 'conventional' or 'ruthless'. Jargon, not argument, is your best ally in keeping him from the Church. Don't waste time trying to make him think that materialism is *true!* Make him think it is strong, or stark, or courageous—that it is the philosophy of the future. That's the sort of thing he cares about.

The trouble about argument is that it moves the whole struggle on to the Enemy's own ground. He can argue too; whereas in really practical propaganda of the kind I am suggesting He has been shown for centuries to be greatly the inferior of Our Father Below. By the very act of arguing, you awake the patient's reason; and once it is awake, who can foresee the result? Even if a particular train of thought can be twisted so as to end in our favour, you will find that you have been strengthening in your patient the fatal habit of attending to universal issues and withdrawing his attention from the stream of immediate sense experiences. Your business is to fix his attention on the stream. Teach him to call it 'real life' and don't let him ask what he means by 'real'.

Remember, he is not, like you, a pure spirit. Never having been a human (Oh that abominable advantage of the Enemy's!) you don't realise how enslaved they are to the pressure of the ordinary. I once had a patient, a sound atheist, who used to read in the British Museum. One day, as he sat reading, I saw a train of thought in his mind beginning to go the wrong way. The Enemy, of course, was at his elbow in a moment. Before I knew where I was I saw my twenty years' work beginning to totter. If I had lost my head and begun to attempt a defence by argument I should have been undone. But I was not such a fool. I struck instantly at the part of the man which I had best under my control and suggested that it was just about time he had some lunch. The Enemy presumably made the counter-suggestion (you know how one can never *quite* overhear what He says to them?) that this was more important than lunch. At least I think that must have been His line for when I said 'Quite. In fact much *too* important to tackle at the end of a morning,' the patient brightened up considerably; and by the time I had added 'Much better come back after lunch and go into it with a fresh mind,' he was already half way to the door. Once he was in the street the battle was won. I showed him a newsboy shouting the midday paper, and a No. 73 bus going past, and before he reached the bottom of the steps I had got into him an unalterable conviction that, whatever odd ideas might come into a man's head when he was shut up alone with his books, a healthy dose of 'real life' (by which he meant the bus and the newsboy) was enough to show him that all 'that sort of thing' just couldn't be true. He knew he'd had a narrow escape and in later years was fond of talking about 'that inarticulate sense for actuality which is our ultimate safeguard against the aberrations of mere logic'. He is now safe in Our Father's house.

You begin to see the point? Thanks to processes which we set at work in them centuries ago, they find it all but impossible to believe in the unfamiliar while the familiar is before their eyes. Keep pressing home on him the *ordinariness* of things. Above all, do not attempt to use science (I mean, the real sciences) as a defence against Christianity. They will positively encourage him to think about realities he can't touch and see. There have been sad cases among the modern physicists. If he must dabble in science, keep him on economics and sociology; don't let him get away from that invaluable 'real life'. But the best of all is to let him read no science but to give him a grand general idea that he knows it all and that everything he happens to have picked up in casual talk and reading is 'the results of modern investigation'. Do remember you are there to fuddle him. From the way some of you young fiends talk, anyone would suppose it was our job to *teach!*

Your affectionate uncle
SCREWTAPE

2

MY DEAR WORMWOOD,

I note with grave displeasure that your patient has become a Christian. Do not indulge the hope that you will escape the usual penalties; indeed, in your better moments, I trust you would hardly even wish to do so. In the meantime we must make the best of the situation. There is no need to despair; hundreds of these adult converts have been reclaimed after a brief sojourn in the Enemy's camp and are now with us. All the *habits* of the patient, both mental and bodily, are still in our favour.

One of our great allies at present is the Church itself. Do not misunderstand me. I do not mean the Church as we see her spread out through all time and space and rooted in eternity, terrible as an army with banners. That, I confess, is a spectacle which makes our boldest tempters uneasy. But fortunately it is quite invisible to these humans. All your patient sees is the half-finished, sham Gothic erection on the new building estate. When he goes inside, he sees the local grocer with rather an oily expression on his face bustling up to offer him one shiny little book containing a liturgy which neither of them understands, and one shabby little book containing corrupt texts of a number of religious lyrics, mostly bad, and in very small print. When he gets to his pew and looks round him he sees just that selection of his neighbours whom he has hitherto avoided. You want to lean pretty heavily on those neighbours. Make his mind flit to and fro between an expression like 'the body of Christ' and the actual faces in the next pew. It matters very little, of course, what kind of people that next pew really contains. You may know one of them to be a great warrior on the Enemy's side. No matter. Your patient, thanks to Our Father Below, is a fool. Provided that any of those neighbours sing out of tune, or have boots that squeak, or double chins, or odd clothes, the patient will quite easily believe that their religion must therefore be somehow ridiculous. At his present stage, you see, he has an idea of 'Christians' in his mind which he supposes to be spiritual but which, in fact, is largely pictorial. His mind is full of togas and sandals and armour and bare legs and the mere fact that the other people in church wear modern clothes is a real—though of course an unconscious—difficulty to him. Never let it come to the surface; never let him ask what he expected them to look like. Keep everything hazy in his mind now, and you will have all eternity wherein to amuse yourself by producing in him the peculiar kind of clarity which Hell affords.

Work hard, then, on the disappointment or anticlimax which is certainly coming to the patient during his first few weeks as a churchman. The Enemy allows this disappointment to occur on the threshold of every human endeavour. It occurs when the boy who has been enchanted in the nursery by *Stories from the Odyssey* buckles down to really learning Greek. It occurs when lovers have got married and begin the real task of learning to live together. In every department of life it marks the transition from dreaming aspiration to laborious doing. The Enemy takes this risk because He has a curious fantasy of making all these disgusting little human vermin into what He calls His 'free' lovers and servants—'sons' is the word He uses, with His inveterate love of degrading the whole spiritual world by unnatural liaisons with the two-legged animals. Desiring their freedom, He therefore refuses to carry them, by their mere affections and habits, to any of the goals which He sets before them: He leaves them to 'do it on their own'. And there lies our opportunity. But also, remember, there lies our danger. If once they get through this initial dryness successfully, they become much less dependent on emotion and therefore much harder to tempt.

I have been writing hitherto on the assumption that the people in the next pew afford no *rational* ground for disappointment. Of course if they do—if the patient knows that the woman with the absurd hat is a fanatical bridge-player or the man with squeaky boots a miser and an extortioner—then your task is so much the easier. All you then have to do is to keep out of his mind the question 'If I, being what I am, can consider that

I am in some sense a Christian, why should the different vices of those people in the next pew prove that their religion is mere hypocrisy and convention?' You may ask whether it is possible to keep such an obvious thought from occurring even to a human mind. It is, Wormwood, it is! Handle him properly and it simply won't come into his head. He has not been anything like long enough with the Enemy to have any real humility yet. What he says, even on his knees, about his own sinfulness is all parrot talk. At bottom, he still believes he has run up a very favourable credit-balance in the Enemy's ledger by allowing himself to be converted, and thinks that he is showing great humility and condescension in going to church with these 'smug', commonplace neighbours at all. Keep him in that state of mind as long as you can,

Your affectionate uncle
SCREWTAPE

3

MY DEAR WORMWOOD,

I am very pleased by what you tell me about this man's relations with his mother. But you must press your advantage. The Enemy will be working from the centre outwards, gradually bringing more and more of the patient's conduct under the new standard, and may reach his behaviour to the old lady at any moment. You want to get in first. Keep in close touch with our colleague Glubose who is in charge of the mother, and build up between you in that house a good settled habit of mutual annoyance; daily pinpricks. The following methods are useful.

1. Keep his mind on the inner life. He thinks his conversion is something *inside* him and his attention is therefore chiefly turned at present to the states of his own mind—or rather to that very expurgated version of them which is all you should allow him to see. Encourage this. Keep his mind off the most elementary duties by directing it to the most advanced and spiritual ones. Aggravate that most useful human characteristic, the horror and neglect of the obvious. You must bring him to a condition in which he can practise self-examination for an hour without discovering any of those facts about himself which are perfectly clear to anyone who has ever lived in the same house with him or worked in the same office.

2. It is, no doubt, impossible to prevent his praying for his mother, but we have means of rendering the prayers innocuous. Make sure that they are always very 'spiritual', that he is always concerned with the state of her soul and never with her rheumatism. Two advantages will follow. In

the first place, his attention will be kept on what he regards as her sins, by which, with a little guidance from you, he can be induced to mean any of her actions which are inconvenient or irritating to himself. Thus you can keep rubbing the wounds of the day a little sorer even while he is on his knees; the operation is not at all difficult and you will find it very entertaining. In the second place, since his ideas about her soul will be very crude and often erroneous, he will, in some degree, be praying for an imaginary person, and it will be your task to make that imaginary person daily less and less like the real mother—the sharp-tongued old lady at the breakfast table. In time, you may get the cleavage so wide that no thought or feeling from his prayers for the imagined mother will ever flow over into his treatment of the real one. I have had patients of my own so well in hand that they could be turned at a moment's notice from impassioned prayer for a wife's or son's 'soul' to beating or insulting the real wife or son without a qualm.

3. When two humans have lived together for many years it usually happens that each has tones of voice and expressions of face which are almost unendurably irritating to the other. Work on that. Bring fully into the consciousness of your patient that particular lift of his mother's eyebrows which he learned to dislike in the nursery, and let him think how much he dislikes it. Let him assume that she knows how annoying it is and does it to annoy—if you know your job he will not notice the immense improbability of the assumption. And, of course, never let him suspect that he has tones and looks which similarly annoy her. As he cannot see or hear himself, this is easily managed.

4. In civilised life domestic hatred usually expresses itself by saying things which would appear quite harmless on paper (the *words* are not offensive) but in such a voice, or at such a moment, that they are not far short of a blow in the face. To keep this game up you and Glubose must see to it that each of these two fools has a sort of double standard. Your patient must demand that all his own utterances are to be taken at their face value and judged simply on the actual words, while at the same time judging all his mother's utterances with the fullest and most over-sensitive interpretation of the tone and the context and the suspected intention. She must be encouraged to do the same to him. Hence from every quarrel they can both go away convinced, or very nearly convinced, that they are quite innocent. You know the kind of thing: 'I simply ask her what time dinner will be and she flies into a temper.' Once this habit is well estab-

lished you have the delightful situation of a human saying things with the express purpose of offending and yet having a grievance when offence is taken.

Finally, tell me something about the old lady's religious position. Is she at all jealous of the new factor in her son's life?—at all piqued that he should have learned from others, and so late, what she considers she gave him such good opportunity of learning in childhood? Does she feel he is making a great deal of 'fuss' about it—or that he's getting in on very easy terms? Remember the elder brother in the Enemy's story?

Your affectionate uncle
SCREWTAPE

4

MY DEAR WORMWOOD,

The amateurish suggestions in your last letter warn me that it is high time for me to write to you fully on the painful subject of prayer. You might have spared the comment that my advice about his prayers for his mother 'proved singularly unfortunate'. That is not the sort of thing that a nephew should write to his uncle—nor a junior tempter to the under-secretary of a department. It also reveals an unpleasant desire to shift responsibility; you must learn to pay for your own blunders.

The best thing, where it is possible, is to keep the patient from the serious intention of praying altogether. When the patient is an adult recently reconverted to the Enemy's party, like your man, this is best done by encouraging him to remember, or to think he remembers, the parrot-like nature of his prayers in childhood. In reaction against that, he may be persuaded to aim at something entirely spontaneous, inward, informal, and unregularised; and what this will actually mean to a beginner will be an effort to produce in himself a vaguely devotional *mood* in which real concentration of will and intelligence have no part. One of their poets, Coleridge, has recorded that he did not pray 'with moving lips and bended knees' but merely 'composed his spirit to love' and indulged 'a sense of supplication'. That is exactly the sort of prayer we want; and since it bears a superficial resemblance to the prayer of silence as practised by those who are very far advanced in the Enemy's service, clever and lazy patients can be taken in by it for quite a long time. At the very least, they can be persuaded that the bodily position makes no difference to their prayers; for they constantly forget, what you must always remember, that they are animals and that whatever their bodies do affects their souls. It is funny how mortals always picture us as putting things into their minds: in reality our best work is done by keeping things out.

If this fails, you must fall back on a subtler misdirection of his intention. Whenever they are attending to the Enemy Himself we are defeated, but there are ways of preventing them from doing so. The simplest is to turn their gaze away from Him towards themselves. Keep them watching their own minds and trying to produce *feelings* there by the action of their own wills. When they meant to ask Him for charity, let them, instead, start trying to manufacture charitable feelings for themselves and not notice that this is what they are doing. When they meant to pray for courage, let them really be trying to feel brave. When they say they are praying for forgiveness, let them be trying to feel forgiven. Teach them to estimate the value of each prayer by their success in producing the desired feeling; and never let them suspect how much success or failure of that kind depends on whether they are well or ill, fresh or tired, at the moment.

But of course the Enemy will not meantime be idle. Whenever there is prayer, there is danger of His own immediate action. He is cynically indifferent to the dignity of His position, and ours, as pure spirits, and to human animals on their knees He pours out self-knowledge in a quite shameless fashion. But even if He defeats your first attempt at misdirection, we have a subtler weapon. The humans do not start from that direct perception of Him which we, unhappily, cannot avoid. They have never known that ghastly luminosity, that stabbing and searing glare which makes the background of permanent pain to our lives. If you look into your patient's mind when he is praying, you will not find *that*. If you examine the object to which he is attending, you will find that it is a composite object containing many quite ridiculous ingredients. There will be images derived from pictures of the Enemy as He appeared during the discreditable episode known as the Incarnation: there will be vaguer—perhaps quite savage and puerile—images associated with the other two Persons. There will even be some of his own reverence (and of bodily sensations accompanying it) objectified and attributed to the object revered. I have known cases where what the patient called his 'God' was actually *located*—up and to the left at the corner of the bedroom ceiling, or inside his own head, or in a crucifix on the wall. But whatever the nature of the composite object, you must keep him praying to *it*—to the thing that he has made, not to the Person who has made him. You may even encourage him to attach great importance to the correction and improvement of his composite object, and to keeping it steadily before his imagination during the whole prayer. For if he ever comes to make the distinction, if ever he consciously directs his prayers 'Not to what I think thou art but to what thou knowest thyself to be', our situation is, for the moment, desperate. Once all his thoughts and images have been flung aside or, if retained, retained with a full recognition of their merely subjective nature, and the man trusts himself to the completely real, external, invisible Presence, there with him in the room and never knowable by him as he is known by it—why, then it is that the incalculable may occur. In avoiding this situation—this real nakedness of the soul in prayer—you will be helped by the fact that the humans themselves do not desire it as much as they suppose. There's such a thing as getting more than they bargained for!

Your affectionate uncle
SCREWTAPE

5

MY DEAR WORMWOOD,

It is a little bit disappointing to expect a detailed report on your work and to receive instead such a vague rhapsody as your last letter. You say you are 'delirious with joy' because the European humans have started another of their wars. I see very well what has happened to you. You are not delirious; you are only drunk. Reading between the lines in your very unbalanced account of the patient's sleepless night, I can reconstruct your state of mind fairly accurately. For the first time in your career you have tasted that wine which is the reward of all our labours—the anguish and bewilderment of a human soul—and it has gone to your head. I can hardly blame you. I do not expect old heads on young shoulders. Did the patient respond to some of your terror-pictures of the future? Did you work in some good self-pitying glances at the happy past?—some fine thrills in the pit of his stomach, were there? You played your violin prettily, did you? Well, well, it's all very natural. But do remember, Wormwood, that duty comes before pleasure. If any present self-indulgence on your part leads to the ultimate loss of the prey, you will be left eternally thirsting for that draught of which you are now so much enjoying your first sip. If, on the other hand, by steady and cool-headed application here and now you can finally secure his soul, he will then be yours forever— a brim-full living chalice of despair and horror and astonishment which you can raise to your lips as often as you please. So do not allow any temporary excitement to distract you from the real business of undermining faith and preventing the formation of virtues. Give me without fail in your next letter a full account of the patient's reactions to the war, so that we can consider whether you are likely to do more good by making him an extreme patriot or an ardent pacifist. There are all sorts of possibilities. In the meantime, I must warn you not to hope too much from a war.

Of course a war is entertaining. The immediate fear and suffering of the humans is a legitimate and pleasing refreshment for our myriads of toiling workers. But what permanent good does it do us unless we make use of it for bringing souls to Our Father Below? When I see the temporal suffering of humans who finally escape us, I feel as if I had been allowed to taste the first course of a rich banquet and then denied the rest. It is worse than not to have tasted it at all. The Enemy, true to His barbarous methods of warfare, allows us to see the short misery of His favourites only to tantalise and torment us—to mock the incessant hunger which, during this present phase of the great conflict, His blockade is admittedly imposing. Let us therefore think rather how to use, than how to enjoy, this European war. For it has certain tendencies inherent in it which are, in themselves, by no means in our favour. We may hope for a good deal of cruelty and unchastity. But, if we are not careful, we shall see thousands turning in this tribulation to the Enemy, while tens of thousands who do not go so far as that will nevertheless have their attention diverted from themselves to values and causes which they believe to be higher than the self. I know that the Enemy disapproves many of these causes. But that is where He is so unfair. He often makes prizes of humans who have given their lives for causes He thinks bad on the monstrously sophistical ground that the humans thought them good and were following the best they knew. Consider too what undesirable deaths occur in wartime. Men are killed in places where they knew they might be killed and to which they go, if they are at all of the Enemy's party, prepared. How much better for us if *all* humans died in costly nursing homes amid doctors who lie, nurses who lie, friends who lie, as we have trained them, promising life to the dying, encouraging the belief that sickness excuses every indulgence, and even, if our workers know their job, withholding all suggestion of a priest lest it should betray to the sick man his true condition! And how disastrous for us is the continual remembrance of death which war enforces. One of our best weapons, contented worldliness, is rendered useless. In wartime not even a human can believe that he is going to live forever.

I know that Scabtree and others have seen in wars a great opportunity for attacks on faith, but I think that view was exaggerated. The Enemy's human partisans have all been plainly told by Him that suffering is an essential part of what He calls Redemption; so that a faith which is destroyed by a war or a pestilence cannot really have been worth the trouble of destroying. I am speaking now of diffused suffering over a long period such as the war will produce. Of course, at the precise moment of terror, bereavement, or physical pain, you may catch your man when his reason is temporarily suspended. But even then, if he applies to Enemy headquarters, I have found that the post is nearly always defended,

Your affectionate uncle
SCREWTAPE

6

I am delighted to hear that your patient's age and profession make it possible, but by no means certain, that he will be called up for military service. We want him to be in the maximum uncertainty, so that his mind will be filled with contradictory pictures of the future, every one of which arouses hope or fear. There is nothing like suspense and anxiety for barricading a human's mind against the Enemy. He wants men to be concerned with what they do; our business is to keep them thinking about what will happen to them.

Your patient will, of course, have picked up the notion that he must submit with patience to the Enemy's will. What the Enemy means by this is primarily that he should accept with patience the tribulation which has actually been dealt out to him—the present anxiety and suspense. It is about *this* that he is to say 'Thy will be done', and for the daily task of bearing *this* that the daily bread will be provided. It is your business to see that the patient never thinks of the present fear as his appointed cross, but only of the things he is afraid of. Let him regard them as his crosses: let him forget that, since they are incompatible, they cannot all happen to him, and let him try to practise fortitude and patience to them all in advance. For real resignation, at the same moment, to a dozen different and hypothetical fates, is almost impossible, and the Enemy does not greatly assist those who are trying to attain it: resignation to present and actual suffering, even where that suffering consists of fear, is easier and is usually helped by this direct action.

An important spiritual law is here involved. I have explained that you can weaken his prayers by diverting his attention from the Enemy Himself to his own states of mind about the Enemy. On the other hand fear becomes easier to master when the patient's mind is diverted from the thing feared to the fear itself, considered as a present and undesirable state of his own mind; and when he regards the fear as his appointed cross he will inevitably think of it as a state of mind. One can therefore formulate the general rule; in all activities of mind which favour our cause, encourage the patient to be unself-conscious and to concentrate on the object, but in all activities favourable to the Enemy bend his mind back on itself. Let an insult or a woman's body so fix his attention outward that he does not reflect 'I am now entering into the state called Anger—or the state called Lust.' Contrariwise let the reflection 'My feelings are now growing more devout, or more charitable' so fix his attention inward that he no longer looks beyond himself to see our Enemy or his own neighbours.

As regards his more general attitude to the war, you must not rely too much on those feelings of hatred which the humans are so fond of discussing in Christian, or anti-Christian, periodicals. In his anguish, the patient can, of course, be encouraged to revenge himself by some vindictive feelings directed towards the German leaders, and that is good so far as it goes. But it is usually a sort of melodramatic or mythical hatred directed against imaginary scapegoats. He has never met these people in real life—they are lay figures modelled on what he gets from newspapers. The results of such fanciful hatred are often most disappointing, and of all humans the English are in this respect the most deplorable milksops. They are creatures of that miserable sort who loudly proclaim that torture is too good for their enemies and then give tea and cigarettes to the first wounded German pilot who turns up at the back door.

Do what you will, there is going to be some benevolence, as well as some malice, in your patient's soul. The great thing is to direct the malice to his immediate neighbours whom he meets every day and to thrust his benevolence out to the remote circumference, to people he does not know. The malice thus becomes wholly real and the benevolence largely imaginary. There is no good at all in inflaming his hatred of Germans if, at the same time, a pernicious habit of charity is growing up between him and his mother, his employer, and the man he meets in the train. Think of your man as a series of concentric circles, his will being the innermost, his intellect coming next, and finally his fantasy. You can hardly hope, at once, to exclude from all the circles everything that smells of the Enemy: but you must keep on shoving all the virtues outward till they are finally located in the circle of fantasy, and all the desirable qualities inward into the Will. It is only in so far as they reach the Will and are there embodied in habits that the virtues are really fatal to us. (I don't, of course, mean what the patient mistakes for his Will, the conscious fume and fret of resolutions and clenched teeth, but the real centre, what the Enemy calls the Heart.) All sorts of virtues painted in the fantasy or approved by the intellect or even, in some measure, loved and admired, will not keep a man from Our Father's house: indeed they may make him more amusing when he gets there,

Your affectionate uncle
SCREWTAPE

7

MY DEAR WORMWOOD,

I wonder you should ask me whether it is essential to keep the patient in ignorance of your own existence. That question, at least for the present phase of the struggle, has been answered for us by the High Command. Our policy, for the moment, is to conceal ourselves. Of course this has not always been so. We are really faced with a cruel dilemma. When the humans disbelieve in our existence we lose all the pleasing results of direct terrorism and we make no magicians. On the other hand, when they believe in us, we cannot make them materialists and sceptics. At least, not yet. I have great hopes that we shall learn in due time how to emotionalise and mythologise their science to such an extent that what is, in effect, a belief in us (though not under that name) will creep in while the human mind remains closed to belief in the Enemy. The 'Life Force', the worship of sex, and some aspects of Psychoanalysis, may here prove useful. If once we can produce our perfect work—the Materialist Magician, the man, not using, but veritably worshipping, what he vaguely calls 'Forces' while denying the existence of 'spirits'—then the end of the war will be in sight. But in the meantime we must obey our orders. I do not think you will have much difficulty in keeping the patient in the dark. The fact that 'devils' are predominantly *comic* figures in the modern imagination will help you. If any faint suspicion of your existence begins to arise in his mind, suggest to him a picture of something in red tights, and persuade him that since he cannot believe in that (it is an old textbook method of confusing them) he therefore cannot believe in you.

I had not forgotten my promise to consider whether we should make the patient an extreme patriot or an extreme pacifist. All extremes, except extreme devotion to the Enemy, are to be encouraged. Not always, of course, but at this period. Some ages are lukewarm and complacent, and then it is our business to soothe them yet faster asleep. Other ages, of which the present is one, are unbalanced and prone to faction, and it is our business to inflame them. Any small coterie, bound together by some interest which other men dislike or ignore, tends to develop inside itself a hothouse mutual admiration, and towards the outer world, a great deal of pride and hatred which is entertained without shame because the 'Cause' is its sponsor and it is thought to be impersonal. Even when the little group exists originally for the Enemy's own purposes, this remains true. We want the Church to be small not only that fewer men may know the Enemy but also that those who do may acquire the uneasy intensity and the defensive self-righteousness of a secret society or a clique. The Church herself is, of course, heavily defended and we have never yet quite succeeded in giving her *all* the characteristics of a faction; but subordinate factions within her have often produced admirable results, from the parties of Paul and of Apollos at Corinth down to the High and Low parties in the Church of England.

If your patient can be induced to become a conscientious objector he will automatically find himself one of a small, vocal, organised, and unpopular society, and the effects of this, on one so new to Christianity, will almost certainly be good. But only *almost* certainly. Has he had serious doubts about the lawfulness of serving in a just war before this present war began? Is he a man of great physical courage—so great that he will have no half-conscious misgivings about the real motives of his pacifism? Can he, when nearest to honesty (no human is ever *very* near), feel fully convinced that he is actuated wholly by the desire to obey the Enemy? If he is that sort of man, his pacifism will probably not do us much good, and the Enemy will probably protect him from the usual consequences of belonging to a sect. Your best plan, in that case, would be to attempt a sudden, confused, emotional crisis from which he might emerge as an uneasy convert to patriotism. Such things can often be managed. But if he is the man I take him to be, try Pacifism.

Whichever he adopts, your main task will be the same. Let him begin by treating the Patriotism or the Pacifism as a part of his religion. Then let him, under the influence of partisan spirit, come to regard it as the most important part. Then quietly and gradually nurse him on to the stage at which the religion becomes merely part of the 'cause', in which Christianity is valued chiefly because of the excellent arguments it can produce in favour of the British war-effort or of Pacifism. The attitude which you want to guard against is that in which temporal affairs are treated primarily as material for obedience. Once you have made the World an end, and faith a means, you have almost won your man, and it makes very little difference what kind of worldly end he is pursuing. Provided that meetings, pamphlets, policies, movements, causes, and crusades, matter more to him than prayers and sacraments and charity, he is ours—and the more 'religious' (on those terms) the more securely ours. I could show you a pretty cageful down here,

Your affectionate uncle
SCREWTAPE

8

MY DEAR WORMWOOD,

So you 'have great hopes that the patient's religious phase is dying away', have you? I always thought the Training College had gone to pieces since they put old Slubgob at the head of it, and now I am sure. Has no one ever told you about the law of Undulation?

Humans are amphibians—half spirit and half animal. (The Enemy's determination to produce such a revolting hybrid was one of the things that determined Our Father to withdraw his support from Him.) As spirits they belong to the eternal world, but as animals they inhabit time. This means that while their spirit can be directed to an eternal object, their bodies, passions, and imaginations are in continual change, for to be in time means to change. Their nearest approach to constancy, therefore, is undulation—the repeated return to a level from which they repeatedly fall back, a series of troughs and peaks. If you had watched your patient carefully you would have seen this undulation in every department of his life—his interest in his work, his affection for his friends, his physical appetites, all go up and down. As long as he lives on earth periods of emotional and bodily richness and liveliness will alternate with periods of numbness and poverty. The dryness and dullness through which your patient is now going are not, as you fondly suppose, your workmanship; they are merely a natural phenomenon which will do us no good unless you make a good use of it.

To decide what the best use of it is, you must ask what use the Enemy wants to make of it, and then do the opposite. Now it may surprise you to learn that in His efforts to get permanent possession of a soul, He relies on the troughs even more than on the peaks; some of His special favourites have gone through longer and deeper troughs than anyone else. The reason is this. To us a human is primarily food; our aim is the absorption of its will into ours, the increase of our own area of selfhood at its expense. But the obedience which the Enemy demands of men is quite a different thing. One must face the fact that all the talk about His love for men, and His service being perfect freedom, is not (as one would gladly believe) mere propaganda, but an appalling truth. He really *does* want to fill the universe with a lot of loathsome little replicas of Himself—creatures whose life, on its miniature scale, will be qualitatively like His own, not because He has absorbed them but because their wills freely conform to His. We want cattle who can finally become food; He wants servants who can finally become sons. We want to suck in, He wants to give out. We are empty and would be filled; He is full and flows over. Our war aim is a world in which Our Father Below has drawn all other beings into himself: the Enemy wants a world full of beings united to Him but still distinct.

And that is where the troughs come in. You must have often wondered why the Enemy does not make more use of His power to be sensibly present to human souls in any degree He chooses and at any moment. But you now see that the Irresistible and the Indisputable are the two weapons which the very nature of His scheme forbids Him to use. Merely to override a human will (as His felt presence in any but the faintest and most mitigated degree would certainly do) would be for Him useless. He cannot ravish. He can only woo. For His ignoble idea is to eat the cake and have it; the creatures are to be one with Him, but yet themselves; merely to cancel them, or assimilate them, will not serve. He is prepared to do a little overriding at the beginning. He will set them off with communications of His presence which, though faint, seem great to them, with emotional sweetness, and easy conquest over temptation. But He never allows this state of affairs to last long. Sooner or later He withdraws, if not in fact, at least from their conscious experience, all those supports and incentives. He leaves the creature to stand up on its own legs—to carry out from the will alone duties which have lost all relish. It is during such

trough periods, much more than during the peak periods, that it is growing into the sort of creature He wants it to be. Hence the prayers offered
in the state of dryness are those which please Him best. We can drag our
patients along by continual tempting, because we design them only for
the table, and the more their will is interfered with the better. He cannot
'tempt' to virtue as we do to vice. He wants them to learn to walk and
must therefore take away His hand; and if only the will to walk is really
there He is pleased even with their stumbles. Do not be deceived, Wormwood. Our cause is never more in danger than when a human, no longer
desiring, but still intending, to do our Enemy's will, looks round upon
a universe from which every trace of Him seems to have vanished, and
asks why he has been forsaken, and still obeys.

But of course the troughs afford opportunities to our side also. Next
week I will give you some hints on how to exploit them,

Your affectionate uncle
SCREWTAPE

9

MY DEAR WORMWOOD,

I hope my last letter has convinced you that the trough of dullness or 'dryness' through which your patient is going at present will not, of itself, give you his soul, but needs to be properly exploited. What forms the exploitation should take I will now consider.

In the first place I have always found that the trough periods of the human undulation provide excellent opportunity for all sensual temptations, particularly those of sex. This may surprise you, because, of course, there is more physical energy, and therefore more potential appetite, at the peak periods; but you must remember that the powers of resistance are then also at their highest. The health and spirits which you want to use in producing lust can also, alas, be very easily used for work or play or thought or innocuous merriment. The attack has a much better chance of success when the man's whole inner world is drab and cold and empty. And it is also to be noted that the trough sexuality is subtly different in quality from that of the peak—much less likely to lead to the milk and water phenomenon which the humans call 'being in love', much more easily drawn into perversions, much less contaminated by those generous and imaginative and even spiritual concomitants which often render human sexuality so disappointing. It is the same with other desires of the flesh. You are much more likely to make your man a sound drunkard by pressing drink on him as an anodyne when he is dull and weary than by encouraging him to use it as a means of merriment among his friends when he is happy and expansive. Never forget that when we are dealing with any pleasure in its healthy and normal and satisfying form, we are, in a sense, on the Enemy's ground. I know we have won many a soul through pleasure. All the same, it is His invention, not ours. He made the pleasures: all our research so far has not enabled us to produce one. All we can do is to encourage the humans to take the pleasures which our Enemy has produced, at times, or in ways, or in degrees, which He has forbidden. Hence we always try to work away from the natural condition of any pleasure to that in which it is least natural, least redolent of its Maker, and least pleasurable. An ever increasing craving for an ever diminishing pleasure is the formula. It is more certain; and it's better *style*. To get the man's soul and give him *nothing* in return—that is what really gladdens Our Father's heart. And the troughs are the time for beginning the process.

But there is an even better way of exploiting the trough; I mean through the patient's own thoughts about it. As always, the first step is to keep knowledge out of his mind. Do not let him suspect the law of undulation. Let him assume that the first ardours of his conversion might have been expected to last, and ought to have lasted, forever, and that his present dryness is an equally permanent condition. Having once got this misconception well fixed in his head, you may then proceed in various ways. It all depends on whether your man is of the desponding type who can be tempted to despair, or of the wishful-thinking type who can be assured that all is well. The former type is getting rare among the humans. If your patient should happen to belong to it, everything is easy. You have only got to keep him out of the way of experienced Christians (an easy task nowadays), to direct his attention to the appropriate passages in scripture, and then to set him to work on the desperate design of recovering his old feelings by sheer will-power, and the game is ours. If he is of the more hopeful type your job is to make him acquiesce in the present low temperature of his spirit and gradually become content with it, persuading himself that it is not so low after all. In a week or two you will be making him doubt whether the first days of his Christianity were not, perhaps, a little excessive. Talk to him about 'moderation in all things'. If you can once get him to the point of thinking that 'religion is all very well up to a point', you can feel quite happy about his soul. A moderated religion is as good for us as no religion at all—and more amusing.

Another possibility is that of direct attack on his faith. When you have caused him to assume that the trough is permanent, can you not persuade him that 'his religious phase' is just going to die away like all his previous phases? Of course there is no conceivable way of getting by reason from the proposition 'I am losing interest in this' to the proposition 'This is false'. But, as I said before, it is jargon, not reason, you must rely on. The mere word *phase* will very likely do the trick. I assume that the creature has been through several of them before—they all have—and that he always feels superior and patronising to the ones he has emerged from, not because he has really criticised them but simply because they are in the past. (You keep him well fed on hazy ideas of Progress and Development and the Historical Point of View, I trust, and give him lots of modern Biographies to read? The people in them are always emerging from Phases, aren't they?)

You see the idea? Keep his mind off the plain antithesis between True and False. Nice shadowy expressions—'It was a phase'—'I've been through all that'—and don't forget the blessed word 'Adolescent',

Your affectionate uncle
SCREWTAPE

10

MY DEAR WORMWOOD,

I was delighted to hear from Triptweeze that your patient has made some very desirable new acquaintances and that you seem to have used this event in a really promising manner. I gather that the middle-aged married couple who called at his office are just the sort of people we want him to know—rich, smart, superficially intellectual, and brightly sceptical about everything in the world. I gather they are even vaguely pacifist, not on moral grounds but from an ingrained habit of belittling anything that concerns the great mass of their fellow men and from a dash of purely fashionable and literary communism. This is excellent. And you seem to have made good use of all his social, sexual, and intellectual vanity. Tell me more. Did he commit himself deeply? I don't mean the words. There is a subtle play of looks and tones and laughs by which a mortal can imply that he is of the same party as those to whom he is speaking. That is the kind of betrayal you should specially encourage, because the man does not fully realise it himself; and by the time he does you will have made withdrawal difficult.

No doubt he must very soon realise that his own faith is in direct opposition to the assumptions on which all the conversation of his new friends is based. I don't think that matters much provided that you can persuade him to postpone any open acknowledgement of the fact, and this, with the aid of shame, pride, modesty and vanity, will be easy to do. As long as the postponement lasts he will be in a false position. He will be silent when he ought to speak and laugh when he ought to be silent. He will assume, at first only by his manner, but presently by his words, all sorts of cynical and sceptical attitudes which are not really his. But if you play him well, they may become his. All mortals tend to turn into the thing they are pretending to be. This is elementary. The real question is how to prepare for the Enemy's counterattack.

The first thing is to delay as long as possible the moment at which he realises this new pleasure as a temptation. Since the Enemy's servants have been preaching about 'the World' as one of the great standard temptations for two thousand years, this might seem difficult to do. But fortunately they have said very little about it for the last few decades. In modern Christian writings, though I see much (indeed more than I like) about Mammon, I see few of the old warnings about Worldly Vanities, the Choice of Friends, and the Value of Time. All that, your patient would probably classify as 'Puritanism'—and may I remark in passing that the value we have given to that word is one of the really solid triumphs of the last hundred years? By it we rescue annually thousands of humans from temperance, chastity, and sobriety of life.

Sooner or later, however, the real nature of his new friends must become clear to him, and then your tactics must depend on the patient's intelligence. If he is a big enough fool you can get him to realise the character of the friends only while they are absent; their presence can be made to sweep away all criticism. If this succeeds, he can be induced to live, as I have known many humans live, for quite long periods, two parallel lives; he will not only appear to be, but actually be, a different man in each of the circles he frequents. Failing this, there is a subtler and more entertaining method. He can be made to take a positive pleasure in the perception that the two sides of his life are inconsistent. This is done by exploiting his vanity. He can be taught to enjoy kneeling beside the grocer on Sunday just because he remembers that the grocer could not possibly understand the urbane and mocking world which he inhabited on Saturday evening; and contrariwise, to enjoy the bawdy and blasphemy over the coffee with these admirable friends all the more because he is aware of a 'deeper', 'spiritual' world within him which they cannot understand. You see the idea—the worldly friends touch him on one side and the grocer on the other, and he is the complete, balanced, complex man who sees round them all. Thus, while being permanently treacherous to at least two sets of people, he will feel, instead of shame, a continual undercurrent of self-satisfaction. Finally, if all else fails, you can persuade him, in defiance of conscience, to continue the new acquaintance on the ground that he is, in some unspecified way, doing these people 'good' by the mere fact of drinking their cocktails and laughing at their jokes, and that to cease to do so would be 'priggish', 'intolerant', and (of course) 'Puritanical'.

Meanwhile you will of course take the obvious precaution of seeing that this new development induces him to spend more than he can afford and to neglect his work and his mother. Her jealousy, and alarm, and his increasing evasiveness or rudeness, will be invaluable for the aggravation of the domestic tension,

Your affectionate uncle
SCREWTAPE

11

MY DEAR WORMWOOD,

Everything is clearly going very well. I am specially glad to hear that the two new friends have now made him acquainted with their whole set. All these, as I find from the record office, are thoroughly reliable people; steady, consistent scoffers and worldlings who without any spectacular crimes are progressing quietly and comfortably towards Our Father's house. You speak of their being great laughers. I trust this does not mean that you are under the impression that laughter as such is always in our favour. The point is worth some attention.

I divide the causes of human laughter into Joy, Fun, the Joke Proper, and Flippancy. You will see the first among friends and lovers reunited on the eve of a holiday. Among adults some pretext in the way of Jokes is usually provided, but the facility with which the smallest witticisms produce laughter at such a time shows that they are not the real cause. What that real cause is we do not know. Something like it is expressed in much of that detestable art which the humans call Music, and something like it occurs in Heaven—a meaningless acceleration in the rhythm of celestial experience, quite opaque to us. Laughter of this kind does us no good and should always be discouraged. Besides, the phenomenon is of itself disgusting and a direct insult to the realism, dignity, and austerity of Hell.

Fun is closely related to Joy—a sort of emotional froth arising from the play instinct. It is very little use to us. It can sometimes be used, of course, to divert humans from something else which the Enemy would like them to be feeling or doing: but in itself it has wholly undesirable tendencies; it promotes charity, courage, contentment, and many other evils.

The Joke Proper, which turns on sudden perception of incongruity, is a much more promising field. I am not thinking primarily of indecent or bawdy humour, which, though much relied upon by second-rate tempters, is often disappointing in its results. The truth is that humans are pretty clearly divided on this matter into two classes. There are some to whom 'no passion is as serious as lust' and for whom an indecent story ceases to produce lasciviousness precisely in so far as it becomes funny: there are others in whom laughter and lust are excited at the same moment and by the same things. The first sort joke about sex because it gives rise to many incongruities: the second cultivate incongruities because they afford a pretext for talking about sex. If your man is of the first type, bawdy humour will not help you—I shall never forget the hours which I wasted (hours to me of unbearable tedium) with one of my early patients in bars and smoking-rooms before I learned this rule. Find out which group the patient belongs to—and see that he does *not* find out.

The real use of Jokes or Humour is in quite a different direction, and it is specially promising among the English who take their 'sense of humour' so seriously that a deficiency in this sense is almost the only deficiency at which they feel shame. Humour is for them the all-consoling and (mark this) the all-excusing, grace of life. Hence it is invaluable as a means of destroying shame. If a man simply lets others pay for him, he is 'mean'; if he boasts of it in a jocular manner and twits his fellows with having been scored off, he is no longer 'mean' but a comical fellow. Mere cowardice is shameful; cowardice boasted of with humorous exaggerations and grotesque gestures can be passed off as funny. Cruelty is shameful—unless the cruel man can represent it as a practical joke. A thousand bawdy, or even blasphemous, jokes do not help towards a man's damnation so much as his discovery that almost anything he wants to do can be done, not only without the disapproval but with the admiration of his fellows, if only it can get itself treated as a Joke. And this temptation can be almost entirely hidden from your patient by that English seriousness about Humour. Any suggestion that there might be too much of it can be represented to him as 'Puritanical' or as betraying a 'lack of humour'.

But flippancy is the best of all. In the first place it is very economical. Only a clever human can make a real Joke about virtue, or indeed about anything else; any of them can be trained to talk *as if* virtue were funny. Among flippant people the Joke is always assumed to have been made. No one actually makes it; but every serious subject is discussed in a manner which implies that they have already found a ridiculous side to it. If prolonged, the habit of Flippancy builds up around a man the finest armour-plating against the Enemy that I know, and it is quite free from the dangers inherent in the other sources of laughter. It is a thousand miles away from joy: it deadens, instead of sharpening, the intellect; and it excites no affection between those who practise it,

Your affectionate uncle
SCREWTAPE

12

MY DEAR WORMWOOD,

Obviously you are making excellent progress. My only fear is lest in attempting to hurry the patient you awaken him to a sense of his real position. For you and I, who see that position as it really is, must never forget how totally different it ought to appear to him. We know that we have introduced a change of direction in his course which is already carrying him out of his orbit around the Enemy; but he must be made to imagine that all the choices which have effected this change of course are trivial and revocable. He must not be allowed to suspect that he is now, however slowly, heading right away from the sun on a line which will carry him into the cold and dark of utmost space.

For this reason I am almost glad to hear that he is still a churchgoer and a communicant. I know there are dangers in this; but anything is better than that he should realise the break he has made with the first months of his Christian life. As long as he retains externally the habits of a Christian he can still be made to think of himself as one who has adopted a few new friends and amusements but whose spiritual state is much the same as it was six weeks ago. And while he thinks that, we do not have to contend with the explicit repentance of a definite, fully recognised, sin, but only with his vague, though uneasy, feeling that he hasn't been doing very well lately.

This dim uneasiness needs careful handling. If it gets too strong it may wake him up and spoil the whole game. On the other hand, if you suppress it entirely—which, by the by, the Enemy will probably not allow you to do—we lose an element in the situation which can be turned to good account. If such a feeling is allowed to live, but not allowed to become irresistible and flower into real repentance, it has one invaluable tendency. It increases the patient's reluctance to think about the Enemy. All humans at nearly all times have some such reluctance; but when thinking of Him involves facing and intensifying a whole vague cloud of half-conscious guilt, this reluctance is increased tenfold. They hate every idea that suggests Him, just as men in financial embarrassment hate the very sight of a pass-book. In this state your patient will not omit, but he will increasingly dislike, his religious duties. He will think about them as little as he feels he decently can beforehand, and forget them as soon as possible when they are over. A few weeks ago you had to *tempt* him to unreality and inattention in his prayers: but now you will find him opening his arms to you and almost begging you to distract his purpose and benumb his heart. He will *want* his prayers to be unreal, for he will dread nothing so much as effective contact with the Enemy. His aim will be to let sleeping worms lie.

As this condition becomes more fully established, you will be gradually freed from the tiresome business of providing Pleasures as temptations. As the uneasiness and his reluctance to face it cut him off more and more from all real happiness, and as habit renders the pleasures of vanity and excitement and flippancy at once less pleasant and harder to forgo (for that is what habit fortunately does to a pleasure) you will find that anything or nothing is sufficient to attract his wandering attention. You no longer need a good book, which he really likes, to keep him from his prayers or his work or his sleep; a column of advertisements in yesterday's paper will do. You can make him waste his time not only in conversation he enjoys with people whom he likes, but in conversations with those he cares nothing about on subjects that bore him. You can make him do nothing at all for long periods. You can keep him up late at night, not roistering, but staring at a dead fire in a cold room. All the healthy and out-going activities which we want him to avoid can be inhibited and *nothing* given in return, so that at least he may say, as one of my own patients said on his arrival down here, 'I now see that I spent most of my life in doing *neither* what I ought *nor* what I liked.' The Christians describe the Enemy as one 'without whom Nothing is strong'. And Nothing is very strong: strong enough to steal away a man's best years not in sweet sins but in a dreary flickering of the mind over it knows not what and knows not why, in the gratification of curiosities so feeble that the man is only half aware of them, in drumming of fingers and kicking of heels, in whistling tunes that he does not like, or in the long, dim labyrinth of reveries that have not even lust or ambition to give them a relish, but which, once chance association has started them, the creature is too weak and fuddled to shake off.

You will say that these are very small sins; and doubtless, like all young tempters, you are anxious to be able to report spectacular wickedness. But do remember, the only thing that matters is the extent to which you separate the man from the Enemy. It does not matter how small the sins are provided that their cumulative effect is to edge the man away from the Light and out into the Nothing. Murder is no better than cards if cards can do the trick. Indeed the safest road to Hell is the gradual one—the gentle slope, soft underfoot, without sudden turnings, without milestones, without signposts,

Your affectionate uncle
SCREWTAPE

13

MY DEAR WORMWOOD,

It seems to me that you take a great many pages to tell a very simple story. The long and the short of it is that you have let the man slip through your fingers. The situation is very grave, and I really see no reason why I should try to shield you from the consequences of your inefficiency. A repentance and renewal of what the other side call 'grace' on the scale which you describe is a defeat of the first order. It amounts to a second conversion—and probably on a deeper level than the first.

As you ought to have known, the asphyxiating cloud which prevented your attacking the patient on his walk back from the old mill, is a well-known phenomenon. It is the Enemy's most barbarous weapon, and generally appears when He is directly present to the patient under certain modes not yet fully classified. Some humans are permanently surrounded by it and therefore inaccessible to us.

And now for your blunders. On your own showing you first of all allowed the patient to read a book he really enjoyed, because he enjoyed it and not in order to make clever remarks about it to his new friends. In the second place, you allowed him to walk down to the old mill and have tea there—a walk through country he really likes, and taken alone. In other words you allowed him two real positive Pleasures. Were you so ignorant as not to see the danger of this? The characteristic of Pains and Pleasures is that they are unmistakably real, and therefore, as far as they go, give the man who feels them a touchstone of reality. Thus if you had been trying to damn your man by the Romantic method—by making him a kind of Childe Harold or Werther submerged in self-pity for imaginary distresses—you would try to protect him at all costs from any real pain; because, of course, five minutes' genuine toothache would reveal the romantic sorrows for the nonsense they were and unmask your whole stratagem. But you were trying to damn your patient by the World, that is by palming off vanity, bustle, irony, and expensive tedium as pleasures. How can you have failed to see that a *real* pleasure was the last thing you ought to have let him meet? Didn't you foresee that it would just kill by contrast all the trumpery which you have been so laboriously teaching him to value? And that the sort of pleasure which the book and the walk gave him was the most dangerous of all? That it would peel off from his sensibility the kind of crust you have been forming on it, and make him feel that he was coming home, recovering himself? As a preliminary to detaching him from the Enemy, you wanted to detach him from himself, and had made some progress in doing so. Now, all that is undone.

Of course I know that the Enemy also wants to detach men from themselves, but in a different way. Remember always, that He really likes the little vermin, and sets an absurd value on the distinctness of every one of them. When He talks of their losing their selves, He only means abandoning the clamour of self-will; once they have done that, He really gives them back all their personality, and boasts (I am afraid, sincerely) that when they are wholly His they will be more themselves than ever. Hence, while He is delighted to see them sacrificing even their innocent wills to His, He hates to see them drifting away from their own nature for any other reason. And we should always encourage them to do so. The deepest likings and impulses of any man are the raw material, the starting-point, with which the Enemy has furnished him. To get him away from those is therefore always a point gained; even in things indifferent it is always desirable to substitute the standards of the World, or convention, or fashion, for a human's own real likings and dislikings. I myself would carry this very far. I would make it a rule to eradicate from my patient any strong personal taste which is not actually a sin, even if it is something quite trivial such as a fondness for county cricket or collecting stamps or drinking cocoa. Such things, I grant you, have nothing of virtue in them; but there is a sort of innocence and humility and self-forgetfulness about them which I distrust. The man who truly and disinterestedly enjoys any one thing in the world, for its own sake, and without caring two-pence what other people say about it, is by that very fact fore-armed against some of our subtlest modes of attack. You should always try to make the patient abandon the people or food or books he really likes in favour of the 'best' people, the 'right' food, the 'important' books. I have known a human defended from strong temptations to social ambition by a still stronger taste for tripe and onions.

It remains to consider how we can retrieve this disaster. The great thing is to prevent his doing anything. As long as he does not convert it into action, it does not matter how much he thinks about this new repentance. Let the little brute wallow in it. Let him, if he has any bent that way, write a book about it; that is often an excellent way of sterilising the seeds which the Enemy plants in a human soul. Let him do anything but act. No amount of piety in his imagination and affections will harm us if we can keep it out of his will. As one of the humans has said, active habits are strengthened by repetition but passive ones are weakened. The more often he feels without acting, the less he will be able ever to act, and, in the long run, the less he will be able to feel,

Your affectionate uncle
SCREWTAPE

14

MY DEAR WORMWOOD,

The most alarming thing in your last account of the patient is that he is making none of those confident resolutions which marked his original conversion. No more lavish promises of perpetual virtue, I gather; not even the expectation of an endowment of 'grace' for life, but only a hope for the daily and hourly pittance to meet the daily and hourly temptation! This is very bad.

I see only one thing to do at the moment. Your patient has become humble; have you drawn his attention to the fact? All virtues are less formidable to us once the man is aware that he has them, but this is specially true of humility. Catch him at the moment when he is really poor in spirit and smuggle into his mind the gratifying reflection, 'By jove! I'm being humble', and almost immediately pride—pride at his own humility—will appear. If he awakes to the danger and tries to smother this new form of pride, make him proud of his attempt—and so on, through as many stages as you please. But don't try this too long, for fear you awake his sense of humour and proportion, in which case he will merely laugh at you and go to bed.

But there are other profitable ways of fixing his attention on the virtue of Humility. By this virtue, as by all the others, our Enemy wants to turn the man's attention away from self to Him, and to the man's neighbours. All the abjection and self-hatred are designed, in the long run, solely for this end; unless they attain this end they do us little harm; and they may even do us good if they keep the man concerned with himself, and, above all, if self-contempt can be made the starting-point for contempt of other selves, and thus for gloom, cynicism, and cruelty.

You must therefore conceal from the patient the true end of Humility. Let him think of it not as self-forgetfulness but as a certain kind of opinion (namely, a low opinion) of his own talents and character. Some talents, I gather, he really has. Fix in his mind the idea that humility consists in trying to believe those talents to be less valuable than he believes them to be. No doubt they *are* in fact less valuable than he believes, but that is not the point. The great thing is to make him value an opinion for some quality other than truth, thus introducing an element of dishonesty and make-believe into the heart of what otherwise threatens to become a virtue. By this method thousands of humans have been brought to think that humility means pretty women trying to believe they are ugly and clever men trying to believe they are fools. And since what they are trying to believe may, in some cases, be manifest nonsense, they cannot succeed in believing it and we have the chance of keeping their minds endlessly revolving on themselves in an effort to achieve the impossible. To anticipate the Enemy's strategy, we must consider His aims. The Enemy wants to bring the man to a state of mind in which he could design the best cathedral in the world, and know it to be the best, and rejoice in the fact, without being any more (or less) or otherwise glad at having done it than he would be if it had been done by another. The Enemy wants him, in the end, to be so free from any bias in his own favour that he can rejoice in his own talents as frankly and gratefully as in his neighbour's talents—or in a sunrise, an elephant, or a waterfall. He wants each man, in the long run, to be able to recognise all creatures (even himself) as glorious and excellent things. He wants to kill their animal self-love as soon as possible; but it is His long-term policy, I fear, to restore to them a new kind of self-love—a charity and gratitude for all selves, including their own; when they have really learned to love their neighbours as themselves, they will be allowed to love themselves as their neighbours. For we must never forget what is the most repellent and inexplicable trait in our Enemy; He *really* loves the hairless bipeds He has created and always gives back to them with His right hand what He has taken away with His left.

His whole effort, therefore, will be to get the man's mind off the subject of his own value altogether. He would rather the man thought himself a great architect or a great poet and then forgot about it, than that he should spend much time and pains trying to think himself a bad one. Your efforts to instil either vain-glory or false modesty into the patient will therefore be met from the Enemy's side with the obvious reminder that a man is not usually called upon to have an opinion of his own talents at all, since he can very well go on improving them to the best of his ability without deciding on his own precise niche in the temple of Fame. You must try to exclude this reminder from the patient's consciousness at all costs. The Enemy will also try to render real in the patient's mind a doctrine which they all profess but find it difficult to bring home to their feelings—the doctrine that they did not create themselves, that their talents were given them, and that they might as well be proud of the colour of their hair. But always and by all methods the Enemy's aim will be to get the patient's mind off such questions, and yours will be to fix it on them. Even of his sins the Enemy does not want him to think too much: once they are repented, the sooner the man turns his attention outward, the better the Enemy is pleased,

Your affectionate uncle
SCREWTAPE

15

MY DEAR WORMWOOD,

I had noticed, of course, that the humans were having a lull in their European war—what they naïvely call '*The War*!'—and am not surprised that there is a corresponding lull in the patient's anxieties. Do we want to encourage this, or to keep him worried? Tortured fear and stupid confidence are both desirable states of mind. Our choice between them raises important questions.

The humans live in time but our Enemy destines them to eternity. He therefore, I believe, wants them to attend chiefly to two things, to eternity itself, and to that point of time which they call the Present. For the Present is the point at which time touches eternity. Of the present moment, and of it only, humans have an experience analogous to the experience which our Enemy has of reality as a whole; in it alone freedom and actuality are offered them. He would therefore have them continually concerned either with eternity (which means being concerned with Him) or with the Present—either meditating on their eternal union with, or separation from, Himself, or else obeying the present voice of conscience, bearing the present cross, receiving the present grace, giving thanks for the present pleasure.

Our business is to get them away from the eternal, and from the Present. With this in view, we sometimes tempt a human (say a widow or a scholar) to live in the Past. But this is of limited value, for they have some real knowledge of the past and it has a determinate nature and, to that extent, resembles eternity. It is far better to make them live in the Future. Biological necessity makes all their passions point in that direction already, so that thought about the Future inflames hope and fear. Also, it is unknown to them, so that in making them think about it we make them think of unrealities. In a word, the Future is, of all things, the thing *least like* eternity. It is the most completely temporal part of time—for the Past is frozen and no longer flows, and the Present is all lit up with eternal rays. Hence the encouragement we have given to all those schemes of thought such as Creative Evolution, Scientific Humanism, or Communism, which fix men's affections on the Future, on the very core of temporality. Hence nearly all vices are rooted in the future. Gratitude looks to the past and love to the present; fear, avarice, lust, and ambition look ahead. Do not think lust an exception. When the present pleasure arrives, the sin (which alone interests us) is already over. The pleasure is just the part of the process which we regret and would exclude if we could do so without losing the sin; it is the part contributed by the Enemy, and therefore experienced in a Present. The sin, which is our contribution, looked forward.

To be sure, the Enemy wants men to think of the Future too—just so much as is necessary for *now* planning the acts of justice or charity which will probably be their duty tomorrow. The duty of planning the morrow's work is *today's* duty; though its material is borrowed from the future, the duty, like all duties, is in the Present. This is now straw splitting. He does not want men to give the Future their hearts, to place their treasure in it. We do. His ideal is a man who, having worked all day for the good of posterity (if that is his vocation), washes his mind of the whole subject, commits the issue to Heaven, and returns at once to the patience or gratitude demanded by the moment that is passing over him. But we want a man hag-ridden by the Future—haunted by visions of an imminent heaven or hell upon earth—ready to break the Enemy's commands in the present if by so doing we make him think he can attain the one or avert the other—dependent for his faith on the success or failure of schemes whose end he will not live to see. We want a whole race perpetually in pursuit of the rainbow's end, never honest, nor kind, nor happy *now*, but always using as mere fuel wherewith to heap the altar of the future every real gift which is offered them in the Present.

It follows then, in general, and other things being equal, that it is better for your patient to be filled with anxiety or hope (it doesn't much matter which) about this war than for him to be living in the present. But the phrase 'living in the present' is ambiguous. It may describe a process which is really just as much concerned with the Future as anxiety itself. Your man may be untroubled about the Future, not because he is concerned with the Present, but because he has persuaded himself that the Future is going to be agreeable. As long as that is the real cause of his tranquillity, his tranquillity will do us good, because it is only piling up more disappointment, and therefore more impatience, for him when his false hopes are dashed. If, on the other hand, he is aware that horrors may be in store for him and is praying for the virtues, wherewith to meet them, and meanwhile concerning himself with the Present because there, and there alone, all duty, all grace, all knowledge, and all pleasure dwell, his state is very undesirable and should be attacked at once. Here again, our Philological Arm has done good work; try the word 'complacency' on him. But, of course, it is most likely that he is 'living in the Present' for none of these reasons but simply because his health is good and he is enjoying his work. The phenomenon would then be merely natural. All the same, I should break it up if I were you. No natural phenomenon is really in our favour. And anyway, why *should* the creature be happy?

Your affectionate uncle
SCREWTAPE

16

MY DEAR WORMWOOD,

You mentioned casually in your last letter that the patient has continued to attend one church, and one only, since he was converted, and that he is not wholly pleased with it. May I ask what you are about? Why have I no report on the causes of his fidelity to the parish church? Do you realise that unless it is due to indifference it is a very bad thing? Surely you know that if a man can't be cured of churchgoing, the next best thing is to send him all over the neighbourhood looking for the church that 'suits' him until he becomes a taster or connoisseur of churches.

The reasons are obvious. In the first place the parochial organisation should always be attacked, because, being a unity of place and not of likings, it brings people of different classes and psychology together in the kind of unity the Enemy desires. The congregational principle, on the other hand, makes each church into a kind of club, and finally, if all goes well, into a coterie or faction. In the second place, the search for a 'suitable' church makes the man a critic where the Enemy wants him to be a pupil. What He wants of the layman in church is an attitude which may, indeed, be critical in the sense of rejecting what is false or unhelpful, but which is wholly uncritical in the sense that it does not appraise—does not waste time in thinking about what it rejects, but lays itself open in uncommenting, humble receptivity to any nourishment that is going. (You see how grovelling, how unspiritual, how irredeemably vulgar He is!) This attitude, especially during sermons, creates the condition (most hostile to our whole policy) in which platitudes can become really audible to a human soul. There is hardly any sermon, or any book, which may not be dangerous to us if it is received in this temper. So pray bestir yourself and send this fool the round of the neighbouring churches as soon as possible. Your record up to date has not given us much satisfaction.

The two churches nearest to him, I have looked up in the office. Both have certain claims. At the first of these the Vicar is a man who has been so long engaged in watering down the faith to make it easier for a supposedly incredulous and hard-headed congregation that it is now he who shocks his parishioners with his unbelief, not *vice versa*. He has undermined many a soul's Christianity. His conduct of the services is also admirable. In order to spare the laity all 'difficulties' he has deserted both the lectionary and the appointed psalms and now, without noticing it, revolves endlessly round the little treadmill of his fifteen favourite psalms and twenty favourite lessons. We are thus safe from the danger that any truth not already familiar to him and to his flock should ever reach them through Scripture. But perhaps your patient is not quite silly enough for this church—or not yet?

At the other church we have Fr Spike. The humans are often puzzled to understand the range of his opinions—why he is one day almost a Communist and the next not far from some kind of theocratic Fascism—one day a scholastic, and the next prepared to deny human reason altogether—one day immersed in politics, and, the day after, declaring that all states of this world are *equally* 'under judgment'. We, of course, see the connecting link, which is Hatred. The man cannot bring himself to preach anything which is not calculated to shock, grieve, puzzle, or humiliate his parents and their friends. A sermon which such people could accept would be to him as insipid as a poem which they could scan. There is also a promising streak of dishonesty in him; we are teaching him to say 'The teaching of the Church is' when he really means 'I'm almost sure I read recently in Maritain or someone of that sort'. But I must warn you that he has one fatal defect: he really believes. And this may yet mar all.

But there is one good point which both these churches have in common—they are both party churches. I think I warned you before that if your patient can't be kept out of the Church, he ought at least to be violently attached to some party within it. I don't mean on really doctrinal issues; about those, the more lukewarm he is the better. And it isn't the doctrines on which we chiefly depend for producing malice. The real fun is working up hatred between those who *say* 'mass' and those who *say* 'holy communion' when neither party could possibly state the difference between, say, Hooker's doctrine and Thomas Aquinas', in any form which would hold water for five minutes. And all the purely indifferent things—candles and clothes and what not—are an admirable ground for our activities. We have quite removed from men's minds what that pestilent fellow Paul used to teach about food and other unessentials—namely, that the human without scruples should always give in to the human with scruples. You would think they could not fail to see the application. You would expect to find the 'low' churchman genuflecting and crossing himself lest the weak conscience of his 'high' brother should be moved to irreverence, and the 'high' one refraining from these exercises lest he should betray his 'low' brother into idolatry. And so it would have been but for our ceaseless labour. Without that the variety of usage within the Church of England might have become a positive hotbed of charity and humility,

Your affectionate uncle
SCREWTAPE

17

MY DEAR WORMWOOD,

The contemptuous way in which you spoke of gluttony as a means of catching souls, in your last letter, only shows your ignorance. One of the great achievements of the last hundred years has been to deaden the human conscience on that subject, so that by now you will hardly find a sermon preached or a conscience troubled about it in the whole length and breadth of Europe. This has largely been effected by concentrating all our efforts on gluttony of Delicacy, not gluttony of Excess. Your patient's mother, as I learn from the dossier and you might have learned from Glubose, is a good example. She would be astonished—one day, I hope, *will* be—to learn that her whole life is enslaved to this kind of sensuality, which is quite concealed from her by the fact that the quantities involved are small. But what do quantities matter, provided we can use a human belly and palate to produce querulousness, impatience, uncharitableness, and self-concern? Glubose has this old woman well in hand. She is a positive terror to hostesses and servants. She is always turning from what has been offered her to say with a demure little sigh and a smile 'Oh please, please . . . *all* I want is a cup of tea, weak but not too weak, and the teeniest weeniest bit of really crisp toast.' You see? Because what she wants is smaller and less costly than what has been set before her, she never recognises as gluttony her determination to get what she wants, however troublesome it may be to others. At the very moment of indulging her appetite she believes that she is practising temperance. In a crowded restaurant she gives a little scream at the plate which some over-worked waitress has set before her and says, 'Oh, that's far, far too much! Take it away and bring me about a quarter of it.' If challenged, she would say she was doing this to avoid waste; in reality she does it because the particular shade of delicacy to which we have enslaved her is offended by the sight of more food than she happens to want.

The real value of the quiet, unobtrusive work which Glubose has been doing for years on this old woman can be gauged by the way in which her belly now dominates her whole life. The woman is in what may be called the 'All-I-want' state of mind. *All* she wants is a cup of tea prop-erly made, or an egg properly boiled, or a slice of bread properly toasted. But she never finds any servant or any friend who can do these simple things 'properly'—because her 'properly' conceals an insatiable demand for the exact, and almost impossible, palatal pleasures which she imagines she remembers from the past; a past described by her as 'the days when you could get good servants' but known to us as the days when her senses were more easily pleased and she had pleasures of other kinds which made her less dependent on those of the table. Meanwhile, the daily dis-appointment produces daily ill temper: cooks give notice and friendships are cooled. If ever the Enemy introduces into her mind a faint suspicion that she is too interested in food, Glubose counters it by suggesting to her that she doesn't mind what she eats herself but 'does like to have things nice for her boy'. In fact, of course, her greed has been one of the chief sources of his domestic discomfort for many years.

Now your patient is his mother's son. While working your hardest, quite rightly, on other fronts, you must not neglect a little quiet infiltra-tion in respect of gluttony. Being a male, he is not so likely to be caught by the '*All* I want' camouflage. Males are best turned into gluttons with the help of their vanity. They ought to be made to think themselves very knowing about food, to pique themselves on having found the only res-taurant in the town where steaks are really 'properly' cooked. What be-gins as vanity can then be gradually turned into habit. But, however you approach it, the great thing is to bring him into the state in which the denial of any one indulgence—it matters not which, champagne or tea, *sole colbert* or cigarettes—'puts him out', for then his charity, justice, and obedience are all at your mercy.

Mere excess in food is much less valuable than delicacy. Its chief use is as a kind of artillery preparation for attacks on chastity. On that, as on every other subject, keep your man in a condition of false spirituality. Never let him notice the medical aspect. Keep him wondering what pride or lack of faith has delivered him into your hands when a simple enquiry into what he has been eating or drinking for the last twenty-four hours would show him whence your ammunition comes and thus enable him by a very little abstinence to imperil your lines of communication. If he *must* think of the medical side of chastity, feed him the grand lie which we have made the English humans believe, that physical exercise in excess and consequent fatigue are specially favourable to this virtue. How they can believe this, in face of the notorious lustfulness of sailors and soldiers, may well be asked. But we used the schoolmasters to put the story about—men who were really interested in chastity as an excuse for games and therefore recommended games as an aid to chastity. But this whole business is too large to deal with at the tail-end of a letter,

Your affectionate uncle
SCREWTAPE

18

MY DEAR WORMWOOD,

Even under Slubgob you must have learned at college the routine technique of sexual temptation, and since, for us spirits, this whole subject is
one of considerable tedium (though necessary as part of our training) I
will pass it over. But on the larger issues involved I think you have a good
deal to learn.

The Enemy's demand on humans takes the form of a dilemma; *either*
complete abstinence *or* unmitigated monogamy. Ever since our Father's
first great victory, we have rendered the former very difficult to them.
The latter, for the last few centuries, we have been closing up as a way of
escape. We have done this through the poets and novelists by persuading the humans that a curious, and usually shortlived, experience which
they call 'being in love' is the only respectable ground for marriage; that
marriage can, and ought to, render this excitement permanent; and that
a marriage which does not do so is no longer binding. This idea is our
parody of an idea that came from the Enemy.

The whole philosophy of Hell rests on recognition of the axiom that
one thing is not another thing, and, specially, that one self is not another
self. My good is my good and your good is yours. What one gains another loses. Even an inanimate object is what it is by excluding all other
objects from the space it occupies; if it expands, it does so by thrusting
other objects aside or by absorbing them. A self does the same. With
beasts the absorption takes the form of eating; for us, it means the suck-

ing of will and freedom out of a weaker self into a stronger. 'To be' *means* 'to be in competition'.

Now the Enemy's philosophy is nothing more nor less than one continued attempt to evade this very obvious truth. He aims at a contradiction. Things are to be many, yet somehow also one. The good of one self is to be the good of another. This impossibility He calls *love*, and this same monotonous panacea can be detected under all He does and even all He is—or claims to be. Thus He is not content, even Himself, to be a sheer arithmetical unity; He claims to be three as well as one, in order that this nonsense about Love may find a foothold in His own nature. At the other end of the scale, He introduces into matter that obscene invention the organism, in which the parts are perverted from their natural destiny of competition and made to co-operate.

His real motive for fixing on sex as the method of reproduction among humans is only too apparent from the use He has made of it. Sex might have been, from our point of view, quite innocent. It might have been merely one more mode in which a stronger self preyed upon a weaker— as it is, indeed, among the spiders where the bride concludes her nuptials by eating the groom. But in the humans the Enemy has gratuitously associated affection between the parties with sexual desire. He has also made the offspring dependent on the parents and given the parents an impulse to support it—thus producing the Family, which is like the organism, only worse; for the members are more distinct, yet also united in a more conscious and responsible way. The whole thing, in fact, turns out to be simply one more device for dragging in Love.

Now comes the joke. The Enemy described a married couple as 'one flesh'. He did not say 'a happily married couple' or 'a couple who married because they were in love', but you can make the humans ignore that. You can also make them forget that the man they call Paul did not confine it to *married* couples. Mere copulation, for him, makes 'one flesh'. You can thus get the humans to accept as rhetorical eulogies of 'being in love' what were in fact plain descriptions of the real significance of sexual intercourse. The truth is that wherever a man lies with a woman, there, whether they like it or not, a transcendental relation is set up between them which must be eternally enjoyed or eternally endured. From the true statement that this transcendental relation was intended to produce, and, if obediently entered into, too often *will* produce, affection and the family, humans can be made to infer the false belief that the blend of affection, fear, and desire which they call 'being in love' is the only thing that makes marriage either happy or holy. The error is easy to produce because 'being in love' does very often, in Western Europe, precede marriages which are made in obedience to the Enemy's designs, that is, with the intention of fidelity, fertility and good will; just as religious emotion very often, but not always, attends conversion. In other words, the humans are to be encouraged to regard as the basis for marriage a highly-coloured and distorted version of something the Enemy really promises as its result. Two advantages follow. In the first place, humans who have not the gift of continence can be deterred from seeking marriage as a solution because they do not find themselves 'in love', and, thanks to us, the idea of marrying with any other motive seems to them low and cynical. Yes, they think that. They regard the intention of loyalty to a partnership for mutual help, for the preservation of chastity, and for the transmission of life, as something lower than a storm of emotion. (Don't neglect to make your man think the marriage-service very offensive.) In the second place any sexual infatuation whatever, so long as it intends marriage, will be regarded as 'love', and 'love' will be held to excuse a man from all the guilt, and to protect him from all the consequences, of marrying a heathen, a fool, or a wanton. But more of this in my next,

Your affectionate uncle
SCREWTAPE

19

MY DEAR WORMWOOD,

I have been thinking very hard about the question in your last letter. If, as I have clearly shown, all selves are by their very nature in competition, and therefore the Enemy's idea of Love is a contradiction in terms, what becomes of my reiterated warning that He really loves the human vermin and really desires their freedom and continued existence? I hope, my dear boy, you have not shown my letters to anyone. Not that it matters of course. Anyone would see that the appearance of heresy into which I have fallen is purely accidental. By the way, I hope you understood, too, that some apparently uncomplimentary references to Slubgob were purely jocular. I really have the highest respect for him. And, of course, some things I said about not shielding you from the authorities were not seriously meant. You can trust me to look after your interests. But do keep everything under lock and key.

The truth is I slipped by mere carelessness into saying that the Enemy really loves the humans. That, of course, is an impossibility. He is one being, they are distinct from Him. Their good cannot be His. All His talk about Love must be a disguise for something else—He must have some *real* motive for creating them and taking so much trouble about them. The reason one comes to talk as if He really had this impossible Love is our utter failure to find out that real motive. What does He stand to make out of them? That is the insoluble question. I do not see that it can do any harm to tell you that this very problem was a chief cause of Our Father's quarrel with the Enemy. When the creation of man was first mooted and when, even at that stage, the Enemy freely confessed that He foresaw a certain episode about a cross, Our Father very naturally sought an interview and asked for an explanation. The Enemy gave no reply except to produce the cock-and-bull story about disinterested love which He has been circulating ever since. This Our Father naturally could not accept. He implored the Enemy to lay His cards on the table, and gave Him every opportunity. He admitted that he felt a real anxiety to know the secret; the Enemy replied 'I wish with all my heart that you did.' It was, I imagine, at this stage in the interview that Our Father's disgust at such an unprovoked lack of confidence caused him to remove himself an infinite distance from the Presence with a suddenness which has given rise to the ridiculous Enemy story that he was forcibly thrown out of Heaven. Since then, we have begun to see why our Oppressor was so secretive. His throne depends on the secret. Members of His faction have frequently admitted that if ever we came to understand what He means by love, the war would be over and we should re-enter Heaven. And there lies the great task. We know that He cannot really love: nobody can: it doesn't make sense. If we could only find out what He is *really* up to! Hypothesis after hypothesis has been tried, and still we can't find out. Yet we must never lose hope; more and more complicated theories, fuller and fuller collections of data, richer rewards for researchers who make progress, more and more terrible punishments for those who fail—all this, pursued and accelerated to the very end of time, cannot, surely, fail to succeed.

You complain that my last letter does not make it clear whether I regard *being in love* as a desirable state for a human or not. But really, Wormwood, that is the sort of question one expects *them* to ask! Leave them to discuss whether 'Love', or patriotism, or celibacy, or candles on altars, or teetotalism, or education, are 'good' or 'bad'. Can't you see there's no answer? Nothing matters at all except the tendency of a given state of mind, in given circumstances, to move a particular patient at a particular moment nearer to the Enemy or nearer to us. Thus it would be quite a good thing to make the patient decide that 'Love' is 'good' or 'bad'. If he is an arrogant man with a contempt for the body really based on delicacy but mistaken by him for purity—and one who takes pleasure in flouting what most of his fellows approve—by all means let him decide against love. Instil into him an overweening asceticism and then, when you have separated his sexuality from all that might humanise it, weigh in on him with it in some much more brutal and cynical form. If, on the other hand, he is an emotional, gullible man, feed him on minor poets and fifth-rate novelists of the old school until you have made him believe that 'Love' is both irresistible and somehow intrinsically meritorious. This belief is not much help, I grant you, in producing casual unchastity; but it is an incomparable recipe for prolonged, 'noble', romantic, tragic adulteries, ending, if all goes well, in murders and suicides. Failing that, it can be used to steer the patient into a useful marriage. For marriage, though the Enemy's invention, has its uses. There must be several young women in your patient's neighbourhood who would render the Christian life intensely difficult to him if only you could persuade him to marry one of them. Please send me a report on this when you next write. In the meantime, get it quite clear in your own mind that this state of *falling in love* is not, in itself, necessarily favourable either to us or to the other side. It is simply an occasion which we and the Enemy are both trying to exploit. Like most of the other things which humans are excited about, such as health and sickness, age and youth, or war and peace, it is, from the point of view of the spiritual life, mainly raw material,

Your affectionate uncle
SCREWTAPE

20

MY DEAR WORMWOOD,

I note with great displeasure that the Enemy has, for the time being, put a forcible end to your direct attacks on the patient's chastity. You ought to have known that He always does in the end, and you ought to have stopped before you reached that stage. For as things are, your man has now discovered the dangerous truth that these attacks don't last forever; consequently you cannot use again what is, after all, our best weapon— the belief of ignorant humans, that there is no hope of getting rid of us except by yielding. I suppose you've tried persuading him that chastity is unhealthy?

I haven't yet got a report from you on young women in the neighbourhood. I should like it at once, for if we can't use his sexuality to make him unchaste we must try to use it for the promotion of a desirable marriage. In the meantime I would like to give you some hint about the type of woman—I mean the physical type—which he should be encouraged to fall in love with if 'falling in love' is the best we can manage.

In a rough and ready way, of course, this question is decided for us by spirits far deeper down in the Lowerarchy than you and I. It is the business of these great masters to produce in every age a general misdirection of what may be called sexual 'taste'. This they do by working through the small circle of popular artists, dressmakers, actresses and advertisers who determine the fashionable type. The aim is to guide each sex away from those members of the other with whom spiritually helpful, happy, and fertile marriages are most likely. Thus we have now for many centuries triumphed over nature to the extent of making certain secondary characteristics of the male (such as the beard) disagreeable to nearly all the females—and there is more in that than you might suppose. As regards the male taste we have varied a good deal. At one time we have directed it to the statuesque and aristocratic type of beauty, mixing men's vanity with their desires and encouraging the race to breed chiefly from the most arrogant and prodigal women. At another, we have selected an exaggeratedly feminine type, faint and languishing, so that folly and cowardice, and all the general falseness and littleness of mind which go with them, shall be at a premium. At present we are on the opposite tack. The age of jazz has succeeded the age of the waltz, and we now teach men to like women whose bodies are scarcely distinguishable from those of boys. Since this is a kind of beauty even more transitory than most, we thus aggravate the female's chronic horror of growing old (with many excellent results) and render her less willing and less able to bear children. And that is not all. We have engineered a great increase in the licence which society allows to the representation of the apparent nude (not the real nude) in art, and its exhibition on the stage or the bathing beach. It is all a fake, of course; the figures in the popular art are falsely drawn; the real women in bathing suits or tights are actually pinched in and propped up to make them appear firmer and more slender and more boyish than nature allows a full-grown woman to be. Yet at the same time, the modern world is taught to believe that it is being 'frank' and 'healthy' and getting back to nature. As a result we are more and more directing the desires of men to something which does not exist—making the rôle of the eye in sexuality more and more important and at the same time making its demands more and more impossible. What follows you can easily forecast!

That is the general strategy of the moment. But inside the framework you will still find it possible to encourage your patient's desires in one of two directions. You will find, if you look carefully into any human's heart, that he is haunted by at least two imaginary women—a terrestrial and an infernal Venus, and that his desire differs qualitatively according to its object. There is one type for which his desire is such as to be naturally amenable to the Enemy—readily mixed with charity, readily obedient to marriage, coloured all through with that golden light of reverence and naturalness which we detest; there is another type which he desires brutally, and desires to desire brutally, a type best used to draw him away from marriage altogether but which, even within marriage, he would tend to treat as a slave, an idol, or an accomplice. His love for the first might involve what the Enemy calls evil, but only accidentally; the man would wish that she was not someone else's wife and be sorry that he could not love her lawfully. But in the second type, the felt evil is what he wants; it is that 'tang' in the flavour which he is after. In the face, it is the visible animality, or sulkiness, or craft, or cruelty which he likes, and in the body, something quite different from what he ordinarily calls Beauty, something he may even, in a sane hour, describe as ugliness, but which, by our art, can be made to play on the raw nerve of his private obsession.

The real use of the infernal Venus is, no doubt, as prostitute or mistress. But if your man is a Christian, and if he has been well trained in nonsense about irresistible and all-excusing 'Love', he can often be induced to marry her. And that is very well worth bringing about. You will have failed as regards fornication and solitary vice; but there are other, and more indirect, methods of using a man's sexuality to his undoing. And, by the way, they are not only efficient, but delightful; the unhappiness produced is of a very lasting and exquisite kind,

Your affectionate uncle
SCREWTAPE

21

MY DEAR WORMWOOD,

Yes. A period of sexual temptation is an excellent time for working in a subordinate attack on the patient's peevishness. It may even be the main attack, as long as he thinks it the subordinate one. But here, as in everything else, the way must be prepared for your moral assault by darkening his intellect.

Men are not angered by mere misfortune but by misfortune conceived as injury. And the sense of injury depends on the feeling that a legitimate claim has been denied. The more claims on life, therefore, that your patient can be induced to make, the more often he will feel injured and, as a result, ill-tempered. Now you will have noticed that nothing throws him into a passion so easily as to find a tract of time which he reckoned on having at his own disposal unexpectedly taken from him. It is the unexpected visitor (when he looked forward to a quiet evening), or the friend's talkative wife (turning up when he looked forward to a tête-à-tête with the friend), that throw him out of gear. Now he is not yet so uncharitable or slothful that these small demands on his courtesy are *in themselves* too much for it. They anger him because he regards his time as his own and feels that it is being stolen. You must therefore zealously guard in his mind the curious assumption 'My time is my own'. Let him have the feeling that he starts each day as the lawful possessor of twenty-four hours. Let him feel as a grievous tax that portion of this property which he has to make over to his employers, and as a generous donation that further portion which he allows to religious duties. But what he must never be permitted to doubt is that the total from which these deductions have been made was, in some mysterious sense, his own personal birthright.

You have here a delicate task. The assumption which you want him to go on making is so absurd that, if once it is questioned, even we cannot find a shred of argument in its defence. The man can neither make, nor retain, one moment of time; it all comes to him by pure gift; he might as well regard the sun and moon as his chattels. He is also, in theory, committed to a total service of the Enemy; and if the Enemy appeared to him in bodily form and demanded that total service for even one day, he would not refuse. He would be greatly relieved if that one day involved nothing harder than listening to the conversation of a foolish woman; and he would be relieved almost to the pitch of disappointment if for one half-hour in that day the Enemy said 'Now you may go and amuse yourself'. Now if he thinks about his assumption for a moment, even he is bound to realise that he is actually in this situation every day. When I speak of preserving this assumption in his mind, therefore, the last thing I mean you to do is to furnish him with arguments in its defence. There aren't any. Your task is purely negative. Don't let his thoughts come anywhere near it. Wrap a darkness about it, and in the centre of that darkness let his sense of ownership-in-Time lie silent, uninspected, and operative.

The sense of ownership in general is always to be encouraged. The humans are always putting up claims to ownership which sound equally funny in Heaven and in Hell and we must keep them doing so. Much of the modern resistance to chastity comes from men's belief that they 'own' their bodies—those vast and perilous estates, pulsating with the energy that made the worlds, in which they find themselves without their consent and from which they are ejected at the pleasure of Another! It is as if a royal child whom his father has placed, for love's sake, in titular command of some great province, under the real rule of wise counsellors, should come to fancy he really owns the cities, the forests, and the corn, in the same way as he owns the bricks on the nursery floor.

We produce this sense of ownership not only by pride but by confusion. We teach them not to notice the different senses of the possessive pronoun—the finely graded differences that run from 'my boots' through 'my dog', 'my servant', 'my wife', 'my father', 'my master' and 'my country', to 'my God'. They can be taught to reduce all these senses to that of 'my boots', the 'my' of ownership. Even in the nursery a child can be taught to mean by 'my teddy bear' *not* the old imagined recipient of affection to whom it stands in a special relation (for that is what the Enemy will teach them to mean if we are not careful) but 'the bear I can pull to pieces if I like'. And at the other end of the scale, we have taught men to say 'my God' in a sense not really very different from 'my boots', meaning 'the God on whom I have a claim for my distinguished services and whom I exploit from the pulpit—the God I have done a corner in'.

And all the time the joke is that the word 'Mine' in its fully possessive sense cannot be uttered by a human being about anything. In the long run either Our Father or the Enemy will say 'Mine' of each thing that exists, and specially of each man. They will find out in the end, never fear, to whom their time, their souls, and their bodies really belong—certainly not to *them*, whatever happens. At present the Enemy says 'Mine' of everything on the pedantic, legalistic ground that He made it: Our Father hopes in the end to say 'Mine' of all things on the more realistic and dynamic ground of conquest,

Your affectionate uncle
SCREWTAPE

22

MY DEAR WORMWOOD,

So! Your man is in love—and in the worst kind he could possibly have fallen into—and with a girl who does not even appear in the report you sent me. You may be interested to learn that the little misunderstanding with the Secret Police which you tried to raise about some unguarded expressions in one of my letters has been tidied over. If you were reckoning on that to secure my good offices, you will find yourself mistaken. You shall pay for that as well as for your other blunders. Meanwhile I enclose a little booklet, just issued, on the new House of Correction for Incompetent Tempters. It is profusely illustrated and you will not find a dull page in it.

I have looked up this girl's dossier and am horrified at what I find. Not only a Christian but such a Christian—a vile, sneaking, simpering, demure, monosyllabic, mouse-like, watery, insignificant, virginal, bread-and-butter miss. The little brute. She makes me vomit. She stinks and scalds through the very pages of the dossier. It drives me mad, the way the world has worsened. We'd have had her to the arena in the old days. That's what her sort is made for. Not that she'd do much good there, either. A two-faced little cheat (I know the sort) who looks as if she'd faint at the sight of blood and then dies with a smile. A cheat every way. Looks as if butter wouldn't melt in her mouth and yet has a satirical wit. The sort of creature who'd find *ME* funny! Filthy insipid little prude—and yet ready to fall into this booby's arms like any other breeding animal. Why doesn't the Enemy blast her for it, if He's so moonstruck by virginity—instead of looking on there, grinning?

He's a hedonist at heart. All those fasts and vigils and stakes and crosses are only a façade. Or only like foam on the seashore. Out at sea, out in His sea, there is pleasure, and more pleasure. He makes no secret of it; at His right hand are 'pleasures for evermore'. Ugh! I don't think He has the least inkling of that high and austere mystery to which we rise in the Miserific Vision. He's vulgar, Wormwood. He has a bourgeois mind. He has filled His world full of pleasures. There are things for humans to do all day long without His minding in the least—sleeping, washing, eating, drinking, making love, playing, praying, working. Everything has to be *twisted* before it's any use to us. We fight under cruel disadvantages. Nothing is naturally on our side. (Not that that excuses *you*. I'll settle with you presently. You have always hated me and been insolent when you dared.)

Then, of course, he gets to know this woman's family and whole circle. Could you not see that the very house she lives in is one that he ought never to have entered? The whole place reeks of that deadly odour. The very gardener, though he has only been there five years, is beginning to acquire it. Even guests, after a weekend visit, carry some of the smell away with them. The dog and the cat are tainted with it. And a house full of the impenetrable mystery. We are certain (it is a matter of first principles) that each member of the family must in some way be making capital out of the others—but we can't find out how. They guard as jealously as the Enemy Himself the secret of what really lies behind this pretence of disinterested love. The whole house and garden is one vast obscenity. It bears a sickening resemblance to the description one human writer made of Heaven: 'the regions where there is only life and therefore all that is not music is silence'.

Music and silence—how I detest them both! How thankful we should be that ever since Our Father entered Hell—though longer ago than humans, reckoning in light years, could express—no square inch of infernal space and no moment of infernal time has been surrendered to either of those abominable forces, but all has been occupied by Noise—Noise, the grand dynamism, the audible expression of all that is exultant, ruthless, and virile—Noise which alone defends us from silly qualms, despairing scruples and impossible desires. We will make the whole universe a noise in the end. We have already made great strides in this direction as regards the Earth. The melodies and silences of Heaven will be shouted down in the end. But I admit we are not yet loud enough, or anything like it. Research is in progress. Meanwhile *you*, disgusting little—

[Here the MS breaks off and is resumed in a different hand.]

In the heat of composition I find that I have inadvertently allowed myself to assume the form of a large centipede. I am accordingly dictating the rest to my secretary. Now that the transformation is complete I recognise it as a periodical phenomenon. Some rumour of it has reached the humans and a distorted account of it appears in the poet Milton, with the ridiculous addition that such changes of shape are a 'punishment' imposed on us by the Enemy. A more modern writer—someone with a name like Pshaw—has, however, grasped the truth. Transformation proceeds from within and is a glorious manifestation of that Life Force which Our Father would worship if he worshipped anything but himself. In my present form I feel even more anxious to see you, to unite you to myself in an indissoluble embrace,

(Signed) TOADPIPE

For his Abysmal Sublimity Under
Secretary Screwtape, TE, BS, etc.

23

MY DEAR WORMWOOD,

Through this girl and her disgusting family the patient is now getting to know more Christians every day, and very intelligent Christians too. For a long time it will be quite impossible to *remove* spirituality from his life. Very well then; we must *corrupt* it. No doubt you have often practised transforming yourself into an angel of light as a parade-ground exercise. Now is the time to do it in the face of the Enemy. The World and the Flesh have failed us; a third Power remains. And success of this third kind is the most glorious of all. A spoiled saint, a Pharisee, an inquisitor, or a magician, makes better sport in Hell than a mere common tyrant or debauchee.

Looking round your patient's new friends I find that the best point of attack would be the borderline between theology and politics. Several of his new friends are very much alive to the social implications of their religion. That, in itself, is a bad thing; but good can be made out of it.

You will find that a good many Christian-political writers think that Christianity began going wrong, and departing from the doctrine of its Founder, at a very early stage. Now this idea must be used by us to encourage once again the conception of a 'historical Jesus' to be found by clearing away later 'accretions and perversions' and then to be contrasted with the whole Christian tradition. In the last generation we promoted the construction of such a 'historical Jesus' on liberal and humanitarian lines; we are now putting forward a new 'historical Jesus' on Marxian, catastrophic, and revolutionary lines. The advantages of these constructions, which we intend to change every thirty years or so, are manifold. In the first place they all tend to direct men's devotion to something which does not exist, for each 'historical Jesus' is unhistorical. The documents say what they say and cannot be added to; each new 'historical Jesus' therefore has to be got out of them by suppression at one point and exaggeration at another, and by that sort of guessing (*brilliant* is the adjective we teach humans to apply to it) on which no one would risk ten shillings in ordinary life, but which is enough to produce a crop of new Napoleons, new Shakespeares, and new Swifts, in every publisher's autumn list. In the second place, all such constructions place the importance of their historical Jesus in some peculiar theory He is supposed to have promulgated. He has to be a 'great man' in the modern sense of the word— one standing at the terminus of some centrifugal and unbalanced line of thought—a crank vending a panacea. We thus distract men's minds from who He is, and what He did. We first make Him solely a teacher, and then conceal the very substantial agreement between His teachings and those of all other great moral teachers. For humans must not be allowed to notice that all great moralists are sent by the Enemy not to inform men but to remind them, to restate the primeval moral platitudes against our continual concealment of them. We make the Sophists: He raises up a Socrates to answer them. Our third aim is, by these constructions, to destroy the devotional life. For the real presence of the Enemy, otherwise experienced by men in prayer and sacrament, we substitute a merely probable, remote, shadowy, and uncouth figure, one who spoke a strange language and died a long time ago. Such an object cannot in fact be worshipped. Instead of the Creator adored by its creature, you soon have merely a leader acclaimed by a partisan, and finally a distinguished character approved by a judicious historian. And fourthly, besides being unhistorical in the Jesus it depicts, religion of this kind is false to history in another sense. No nation, and few individuals, are really brought into the Enemy's camp by the historical study of the biography of Jesus, simply as biography. Indeed materials for a full biography have been withheld from men. The earliest converts were converted by a single historical fact (the Resurrection) and a single theological doctrine (the Redemption) operating on a sense of sin which they already had—and sin, not against some new fancy-dress law produced as a novelty by a 'great man', but against the old, platitudinous, universal moral law which they had been taught by their nurses and mothers. The 'Gospels' come later and were written not to make Christians but to edify Christians already made.

The 'historical Jesus' then, however dangerous He may seem to be to us at some particular point, is always to be encouraged. About the general connection between Christianity and politics, our position is more delicate. Certainly we do not want men to allow their Christianity to flow over into their political life, for the establishment of anything like a really just society would be a major disaster. On the other hand we do want, and want very much, to make men treat Christianity as a means; preferably, of course, as a means to their own advancement, but, failing that, as a means to anything—even to social justice. The thing to do is to get a man at first to value social justice as a thing which the Enemy demands, and then work him on to the stage at which he values Christianity because it may produce social justice. For the Enemy will not be used as a convenience. Men or nations who think they can revive the Faith in order to make a good society might just as well think they can use the stairs of Heaven as a short cut to the nearest chemist's shop. Fortunately it is quite easy to coax humans round this little corner. Only today I have found a passage in a Christian writer where he recommends his own version of Christianity on the ground that 'only such a faith can outlast the death of old cultures and the birth of new civilisations'. You see the little rift? 'Believe this, not because it is true, but for some other reason.' That's the game,

Your affectionate uncle
SCREWTAPE

24

I have been in correspondence with Slumtrimpet who is in charge of your patient's young woman, and begin to see the chink in her armour. It is an unobtrusive little vice which she shares with nearly all women who have grown up in an intelligent circle united by a clearly defined belief; and it consists in a quite untroubled assumption that the outsiders who do not share this belief are really too stupid and ridiculous. The males, who habitually meet these outsiders, do not feel that way; their confidence, if they are confident, is of a different kind. Hers, which she supposes to be due to Faith, is in reality largely due to the mere colour she has taken from her surroundings. It is not, in fact, very different from the conviction she would have felt at the age of ten that the kind of fish-knives used in her father's house were the proper or normal or 'real' kind, while those of the neighbouring families were 'not real fish-knives' at all. Now the element of ignorance and naïvety in all this is so large, and the element of spiritual pride so small, that it gives us little hope of the girl herself. But have you thought of how it can be made to influence your own patient?

It is always the novice who exaggerates. The man who has risen in society is over-refined, the young scholar is pedantic. In this new circle your patient is a novice. He is there daily meeting Christian life of a quality he never before imagined and seeing it all through an enchanted glass because he is in love. He is anxious (indeed the Enemy commands him) to imitate this quality. Can you get him to imitate this *defect* in his mistress and to exaggerate it until what was venial in her becomes in him the strongest and most beautiful of the vices—Spiritual Pride?

The conditions seem ideally favourable. The new circle in which he finds himself is one of which he is tempted to be proud for many reasons other than its Christianity. It is a better educated, more intelligent, more agreeable society than any he has yet encountered. He is also under some degree of illusion as to his own place in it. Under the influence of 'love' he may still think himself unworthy of the girl, but he is rapidly ceasing to think himself unworthy of the others. He has no notion how much in him is forgiven because they are charitable and made the best of because he is now one of the family. He does not dream how much of his conversation, how many of his opinions, are recognised by them all as mere echoes of their own. Still less does he suspect how much of the delight he takes in these people is due to the erotic enhancement which the girl, for him, spreads over all her surroundings. He thinks that he likes their talk and way of life because of some congruity between their spiritual state and his, when in fact they are so far beyond him that if he were not in love he would be merely puzzled and repelled by much which he now accepts. He is like a dog which should imagine it understood fire-arms because its hunting instinct and love for its master enable it to enjoy a day's shooting!

Here is your chance. While the Enemy, by means of sexual love and of some very agreeable people far advanced in His service, is drawing the young barbarian up to levels he could never otherwise have reached, you must make him feel that he is finding his *own* level—that these people are 'his sort' and that, coming among them, he has come home. When he turns from them to other society he will find it dull; partly because almost any society within his reach is, in fact, much less entertaining, but still more because he will miss the enchantment of the young woman. You must teach him to mistake this contrast between the circle that delights and the circle that bores him for the contrast between Christians and unbelievers. He must be made to feel (he'd better not put it into words) 'how different we Christians are'; and by 'we Christians' he must really, but unknowingly, mean 'my set'; and by 'my set' he must mean not 'The people who, in their charity and humility, have accepted me', but 'The people with whom I associate by right'.

Success here depends on confusing him. If you try to make him explicitly and professedly proud of being a Christian, you will probably fail; the Enemy's warnings are too well known. If, on the other hand, you let the idea of 'we Christians' drop out altogether and merely make him complacent about 'his set', you will produce not true spiritual pride but mere social vanity which, by comparison, is a trumpery, puny little sin. What you want is to keep a sly self-congratulation mixing with all his thoughts and never allow him to raise the question 'What, precisely, am I congratulating myself *about?*' The idea of belonging to an inner ring, of being in a secret, is very sweet to him. Play on that nerve. Teach him, using the influence of this girl when she is silliest, to adopt an air of *amusement* at the things the unbelievers say. Some theories which he may meet in modern Christian circles may here prove helpful; theories, I mean, that place the hope of society in some inner ring of 'clerks', some trained minority of theocrats. It is no affair of yours whether those theories are true or false; the great thing is to make Christianity a mystery religion in which he feels himself one of the initiates.

Pray do not fill your letters with rubbish about this European War. Its final issue is, no doubt, important, but that is a matter for the High Command. I am not in the least interested in knowing how many people in England have been killed by bombs. In what state of mind they died, I can learn from the office at this end. That they were going to die sometime, I knew already. Please keep your mind on your work,

Your affectionate uncle
SCREWTAPE

25

MY DEAR WORMWOOD,

The real trouble about the set your patient is living in is that it is *merely* Christian. They all have individual interests, of course, but the bond remains mere Christianity. What we want, if men become Christians at all, is to keep them in the state of mind I call 'Christianity And'. You know— Christianity and the Crisis, Christianity and the New Psychology, Christianity and the New Order, Christianity and Faith Healing, Christianity and Psychical Research, Christianity and Vegetarianism, Christianity and Spelling Reform. If they must be Christians let them at least be Christians with a difference. Substitute for the faith itself some Fashion with a Christian colouring. Work on their horror of the Same Old Thing.

The horror of the Same Old Thing is one of the most valuable passions we have produced in the human heart—an endless source of heresies in religion, folly in counsel, infidelity in marriage, and inconstancy in friendship. The humans live in time, and experience reality successively. To experience much of it, therefore, they must experience many different things; in other words, they must experience change. And since they need change, the Enemy (being a hedonist at heart) has made change pleasurable to them, just as He has made eating pleasurable. But since He does not wish them to make change, any more than eating, an end in itself, He has balanced the love of change in them by a love of permanence. He has contrived to gratify both tastes together in the very world He has made, by that union of change and permanence which we call Rhythm.

He gives them the seasons, each season different yet every year the same, so that spring is always felt as a novelty yet always as the recurrence of an immemorial theme. He gives them in His Church a spiritual year; they change from a fast to a feast, but it is the same feast as before.

Now just as we pick out and exaggerate the pleasure of eating to produce gluttony, so we pick out this natural pleasantness of change and twist it into a demand for absolute novelty. This demand is entirely our workmanship. If we neglect our duty, men will be not only contented but transported by the mixed novelty and familiarity of snowdrops *this* January, sunrise *this* morning, plum pudding *this* Christmas. Children, until we have taught them better, will be perfectly happy with a seasonal round of games in which conkers succeed hopscotch as regularly as autumn follows summer. Only by our incessant efforts is the demand for infinite, or unrhythmical, change kept up.

This demand is valuable in various ways. In the first place it diminishes pleasure while increasing desire. The pleasure of novelty is by its very nature more subject than any other to the law of diminishing returns. And continued novelty costs money, so that the desire for it spells avarice or unhappiness or both. And again, the more rapacious this desire, the sooner it must eat up all the innocent sources of pleasure and pass on to those the Enemy forbids. Thus by inflaming the horror of the Same Old Thing we have recently made the Arts, for example, less dangerous to us than perhaps, they have ever been, 'low-brow' and 'high-brow' artists alike being now daily drawn into fresh, and still fresh, excesses of lasciviousness, unreason, cruelty, and pride. Finally, the desire for novelty is indispensable if we are to produce Fashions or Vogues.

The use of Fashions in thought is to distract the attention of men from their real dangers. We direct the fashionable outcry of each generation against those vices of which it is least in danger and fix its approval on the virtue nearest to that vice which we are trying to make endemic. The game is to have them all running about with fire extinguishers whenever there is a flood, and all crowding to that side of the boat which is already nearly gunwale under. Thus we make it fashionable to expose the dangers of enthusiasm at the very moment when they are all really becoming worldly and lukewarm; a century later, when we are really making them all Byronic and drunk with emotion, the fashionable outcry is directed against the dangers of the mere 'understanding'. Cruel ages are put on their guard against Sentimentality, feckless and idle ones against

Respectability, lecherous ones against Puritanism; and whenever all men are really hastening to be slaves or tyrants we make Liberalism the prime bogey.

But the greatest triumph of all is to elevate this horror of the Same Old Thing into a philosophy so that nonsense in the intellect may reinforce corruption in the will. It is here that the general Evolutionary or Historical character of modern European thought (partly our work) comes in so useful. The Enemy loves platitudes. Of a proposed course of action He wants men, so far as I can see, to ask very simple questions; is it righteous? is it prudent? is it possible? Now if we can keep men asking 'Is it in accordance with the general movement of our time? Is it progressive or reactionary? Is this the way that History is going?' they will neglect the relevant questions. And the questions they *do* ask are, of course, unanswerable; for they do not know the future, and what the future will be depends very largely on just those choices which they now invoke the future to help them to make. As a result, while their minds are buzzing in this vacuum, we have the better chance to slip in and bend them to the action *we* have decided on. And great work has already been done. Once they knew that some changes were for the better, and others for the worse, and others again indifferent. We have largely removed this knowledge. For the descriptive adjective 'unchanged' we have substituted the emotional adjective 'stagnant'. We have trained them to think of the Future as a promised land which favoured heroes attain—not as something which everyone reaches at the rate of sixty minutes an hour, whatever he does, whoever he is,

> Your affectionate uncle
> SCREWTAPE

26

MY DEAR WORMWOOD,

Yes; courtship is the time for sowing those seeds which will grow up ten years later into domestic hatred. The enchantment of unsatisfied desire produces results which the humans can be made to mistake for the results of charity. Avail yourself of the ambiguity in the word 'Love': let them think they have solved by Love problems they have in fact only waived or postponed under the influence of the enchantment. While it lasts you have your chance to foment the problems in secret and render them chronic.

The grand problem is that of 'Unselfishness'. Note, once again, the admirable work of our Philological Arm in substituting the negative unselfishness for the Enemy's positive Charity. Thanks to this you can, from the very outset, teach a man to surrender benefits not that others may be happy in having them but that he may be unselfish in forgoing them. That is a great point gained. Another great help, where the parties concerned are male and female, is the divergence of view about Unselfishness which we have built up between the sexes. A woman means by Unselfishness chiefly taking trouble for others; a man means not giving trouble to others. As a result, a woman who is quite far gone in the Enemy's service will make a nuisance of herself on a larger scale than any man except those whom Our Father has dominated completely; and, conversely, a man will live long in the Enemy's camp before he undertakes as much spontaneous work to please others as a quite ordinary woman may do every day. Thus while the woman thinks of doing good offices and the man of respecting other people's rights, each sex, without any obvious unreason, can and does regard the other as radically selfish.

On top of these confusions you can now introduce a few more. The erotic enchantment produces a mutual complaisance in which each is *really* pleased to give in to the wishes of the other. They also know that the Enemy demands of them a degree of charity which, if attained, would result in similar actions. You must make them establish as a Law for their whole married life that degree of mutual self-sacrifice which is at present sprouting naturally out of the enchantment, but which, when the enchantment dies away, they will not have charity enough to enable them to perform. They will not see the trap, since they are under the double blindness of mistaking sexual excitement for charity and of thinking that the excitement will last.

When once a sort of official, legal, or nominal Unselfishness has been established as a rule—a rule for the keeping of which their emotional resources have died away and their spiritual resources have not yet grown—the most delightful results follow. In discussing any joint action, it becomes obligatory that A should argue in favour of B's supposed wishes and against his own, while B does the opposite. It is often impossible to find out either party's real wishes; with luck, they end by doing something that neither wants, while each feels a glow of self-righteousness and harbours a secret claim to preferential treatment for the unselfishness shown and a secret grudge against the other for the ease with which the sacrifice has been accepted. Later on you can venture on what may be called the Generous Conflict Illusion. This game is best played with more than two players, in a family with grown-up children for example. Something quite trivial, like having tea in the garden, is proposed. One member takes care to make it quite clear (though not in so many words) that he would rather not but is, of course, prepared to do so out of 'Unselfishness'. The others instantly withdraw their proposal, ostensibly through their 'Unselfishness', but really because they don't want to be used as a sort of lay figure on which the first speaker practises petty altruisms. But he is not going to be done out of his debauch of Unselfishness either. He insists on doing 'what the others want'. They insist on doing what he wants. Passions are roused. Soon someone is saying 'Very well then, I won't have any tea at all!', and a real quarrel ensues with bitter resentment on both sides. You see how it is done? If each side had been frankly contending for its own real wish, they would all have kept within the bounds of reason and courtesy; but just because the contention is reversed and each side is fighting the other side's battle, all the bitterness which really flows from thwarted self-righteousness and obstinacy and the accumulated grudges of the last ten years is concealed from them by the nominal or official 'Unselfishness' of what they are doing or, at least, held to be excused by it. Each side is, indeed, quite alive to the cheap quality of the adversary's Unselfishness and of the false position into which he is trying to force them; but each manages to feel blameless and ill-used itself, with no more dishonesty than comes natural to a human.

A sensible human once said, 'If people knew how much ill-feeling Unselfishness occasions, it would not be so often recommended from the pulpit'; and again, 'She's the sort of woman who lives for others— you can always tell the others by their hunted expression.' All this can be begun even in the period of courtship. A little *real* selfishness on your patient's part is often of less value in the long run, for securing his soul, than the first beginnings of that elaborate and self-conscious unselfishness which may one day blossom into the sort of thing I have described. Some degree of mutual falseness, some surprise that the girl does not always notice just how Unselfish he is being, can be smuggled in already. Cherish these things, and, above all, don't let the young fools notice them. If they notice them they will be on the road to discovering that 'Love' is not enough, that charity is needed and not yet achieved and that no external law can supply its place. I wish Slumtrimpet could do something about undermining that young woman's sense of the ridiculous,

Your affectionate uncle
SCREWTAPE

27

MY DEAR WORMWOOD,

You seem to be doing very little good at present. The use of his 'love' to distract his mind from the Enemy is, of course, obvious, but you reveal what poor use you are making of it when you say that the whole question of distraction and the wandering mind has now become one of the chief subjects of his prayers. That means you have largely failed. When this, or any other distraction, crosses his mind you ought to encourage him to thrust it away by sheer will power and to try to continue the normal prayer as if nothing had happened; once he accepts the distraction as his present problem and lays *that* before the Enemy and makes it the main theme of his prayers and his endeavours, then, so far from doing good, you have done harm. Anything, even a sin, which has the total effect of moving him close up to the Enemy, makes against us in the long run.

A promising line is the following. Now that he is in love, a new idea of *earthly* happiness has arisen in his mind: and hence a new urgency in his purely petitionary prayers—about this war and other such matters. Now is the time for raising intellectual difficulties about prayer of that sort. False spirituality is always to be encouraged. On the seemingly pious ground that 'praise and communion with God is the true prayer', humans can often be lured into direct disobedience to the Enemy who (in His usual flat, commonplace, uninteresting way) has definitely told them to pray for their daily bread and the recovery of their sick. You will, of course, conceal from him the fact that the prayer for daily bread, interpreted in a 'spiritual sense', is really just as crudely petitionary as it is in any other sense.

But since your patient has contracted the terrible habit of obedience, he will probably continue such 'crude' prayers whatever you do. But you can worry him with the haunting suspicion that the practice is absurd and can have no objective result. Don't forget to use the 'heads I win, tails you lose' argument. If the thing he prays for doesn't happen, then that is one more proof that petitionary prayers don't work; if it does happen, he will, of course, be able to see some of the physical causes which led up to it, and 'therefore it would have happened anyway', and thus a granted prayer becomes just as good a proof as a denied one that prayers are ineffective.

You, being a spirit, will find it difficult to understand how he gets into this confusion. But you must remember that he takes Time for an ultimate reality. He supposes that the Enemy, like himself, sees some things as present, remembers others as past, and anticipates others as future; or even if he believes that the Enemy does not see things that way, yet, in his heart of hearts, he regards this as a peculiarity of the Enemy's mode of perception—he doesn't really think (though he would say he did) that things as the Enemy sees them are things as they are! If you tried to explain to him that men's prayers today are one of the innumerable co-ordinates with which the Enemy harmonises the weather of tomorrow, he would reply that then the Enemy always knew men were going to make those prayers and, if so, they did not pray freely but were predestined to do so. And he would add that the weather on a given day can be traced back through its causes to the original creation of matter itself—so that the whole thing, both on the human and on the material side, is given 'from the word go'. What he ought to say, of course, is obvious to us; that the problem of adapting the particular weather to the particular prayers is merely the appearance, at two points in his temporal mode of perception, of the total problem of adapting the whole spiritual universe to the whole corporeal universe; that creation in its entirety operates at every point of space and time, or rather that their kind of consciousness forces them to encounter the whole, self-consistent creative act as a series of successive events. *Why* that creative act leaves room for their free will is the problem of problems, the secret behind the Enemy's nonsense about 'Love'. *How* it does so is no problem at all; for the Enemy does not *foresee* the humans making their free contributions in a future, but *sees* them doing so in His unbounded Now. And obviously to watch a man doing something is not to make him do it.

It may be replied that some meddlesome human writers, notably Boethius, have let this secret out. But in the intellectual climate which we have at last succeeded in producing throughout Western Europe, you needn't bother about that. Only the learned read old books and we have now so dealt with the learned that they are of all men the least likely to acquire wisdom by doing so. We have done this by inculcating the Historical Point of View. The Historical Point of View, put briefly, means that when a learned man is presented with any statement in an ancient author, the one question he never asks is whether it is true. He asks who influenced the ancient writer, and how far the statement is consistent with what he said in other books, and what phase in the writer's development, or in the general history of thought, it illustrates, and how it affected later writers, and how often it has been misunderstood (specially by the learned man's own colleagues) and what the general course of criticism on it has been for the last ten years, and what is the 'present state of the question'. To regard the ancient writer as a possible source of knowledge—to anticipate that what he said could possibly modify your thoughts or your behaviour—this would be rejected as unutterably simple-minded. And since we cannot deceive the whole human race all the time, it is most important thus to cut every generation off from all others; for where learning makes a free commerce between the ages there is always the danger that the characteristic errors of one may be corrected by the characteristic truths of another. But thanks be to Our Father and the Historical Point of View, great scholars are now as little nourished by the past as the most ignorant mechanic who holds that 'history is bunk',

Your affectionate uncle
SCREWTAPE

28

MY DEAR WORMWOOD,

When I told you not to fill your letters with rubbish about the war, I meant, of course, that I did not want to have your rather infantile rhapsodies about the death of men and the destruction of cities. In so far as the war really concerns the spiritual state of the patient, I naturally want full reports. And on this aspect you seem singularly obtuse. Thus you tell me with glee that there is reason to expect heavy air raids on the town where the creature lives. This is a crying example of something I have complained about already—your readiness to forget the main point in your immediate enjoyment of human suffering. Do you not know that bombs kill men? Or do you not realise that the patient's death, at this moment, is precisely what we want to avoid? He has escaped the worldly friends with whom you tried to entangle him; he has 'fallen in love' with a very Christian woman and is temporarily immune from your attacks on his chastity; and the various methods of corrupting his spiritual life which we have been trying are so far unsuccessful. At the present moment, as the full impact of the war draws nearer and his worldly hopes take a proportionately lower place in his mind, full of his defence work, full of the girl, forced to attend to his neighbours more than he has ever done before and liking it more than he expected, 'taken out of himself' as the humans say, and daily increasing in conscious dependence on the Enemy, he will almost certainly be lost to us if he is killed tonight. This is so obvious that I am ashamed to write it. I sometimes wonder if you young fiends are not kept out on temptation-duty too long at a time—if you are not in some danger of becoming infected by the sentiments and values of the humans among whom you work. They, of course, do tend to regard death as the prime evil and survival as the greatest good. But that is because we have taught them to do so. Do not let us be infected by our own propaganda. I know it seems strange that your chief aim at the moment should be the very same thing for which the patient's lover and his mother are praying—namely his bodily safety. But so it is; you should be guarding him like the apple of your eye. If he dies now, you lose him. If he survives the war, there is always hope. The Enemy has guarded him from you through the first great wave of temptations. But, if only he can be kept alive, you have time itself for your ally. The long, dull, monotonous years of middle-aged prosperity or middle-aged adversity are excellent campaigning weather. You see, it is so hard for these creatures to *persevere*. The routine of adversity, the gradual decay of youthful loves and youthful hopes, the quiet despair (hardly felt as pain) of ever overcoming the chronic temptations with which we have again and again defeated them, the drabness which we create in their lives and the inarticulate resentment with which we teach them to respond to it—all this provides admirable opportunities of wearing out a soul by attrition. If, on the other hand, the middle years prove prosperous, our position is even stronger. Prosperity knits a man to the World. He feels that he is 'finding his place in it', while really it is finding its place in him. His increasing reputation, his widening circle of acquaintances, his sense of importance, the growing pressure of absorbing and agreeable work, build up in him a sense of being really at home in earth, which is just what we want. You will notice that the young are generally less unwilling to die than the middle-aged and the old.

The truth is that the Enemy, having oddly destined these mere animals to life in His own eternal world, has guarded them pretty effectively from the danger of feeling at home anywhere else. That is why we must often wish long life to our patients; seventy years is not a day too much for the difficult task of unravelling their souls from Heaven and building up a firm attachment to the earth. While they are young we find them always shooting off at a tangent. Even if we contrive to keep them ignorant of explicit religion, the incalculable winds of fantasy and music and poetry—the mere face of a girl, the song of a bird, or the sight of a horizon—are always blowing our whole structure away. They *will* not apply themselves steadily to worldly advancement, prudent connections, and the policy of safety first. So inveterate is their appetite for Heaven that our best method, at this stage, of attaching them to earth is to make them believe that earth can be turned into Heaven at some future date by politics or eugenics or 'science' or psychology, or what not. Real worldliness is a work of time—assisted, of course, by pride, for we teach them to describe the creeping death as good sense or Maturity or Experience. *Experience*, in the peculiar sense we teach them to give it, is, by the by, a most useful word. A great human philosopher nearly let our secret out when he said that where Virtue is concerned 'Experience is the mother of illusion'; but thanks to a change in Fashion, and also, of course, to the Historical Point of View, we have largely rendered his book innocuous.

How valuable time is to us may be gauged by the fact that the Enemy allows us so little of it. The majority of the human race dies in infancy; of the survivors, a good many die in youth. It is obvious that to Him human birth is important chiefly as the qualification for human death, and death solely as the gate to that other kind of life. We are allowed to work only on a selected minority of the race, for what humans call a 'normal life' is the exception. Apparently He wants some—but only a very few—of the human animals with which He is peopling Heaven to have had the experience of resisting us through an earthly life of sixty or seventy years. Well, there is our opportunity. The smaller it is, the better we must use it. Whatever you do, keep your patient as safe as you possibly can,

Your affectionate uncle
SCREWTAPE

29

MY DEAR WORMWOOD,

Now that it is certain the German humans will bombard your patient's town and that his duties will keep him in the thick of the danger, we must consider our policy. Are we to aim at cowardice—or at courage, with consequent pride—or at hatred of the Germans?

Well, I am afraid it is no good trying to make him brave. Our research department has not yet discovered (though success is hourly expected) how to produce *any* virtue. This is a serious handicap. To be greatly and effectively wicked a man needs some virtue. What would Attila have been without his courage, or Shylock without self-denial as regards the flesh? But as we cannot supply these qualities ourselves, we can only use them as supplied by the Enemy—and this means leaving Him a kind of foothold in those men whom, otherwise, we have made most securely our own. A very unsatisfactory arrangement, but, I trust, we shall one day learn to do better.

Hatred we can manage. The tension of human nerves during noise, danger, and fatigue, makes them prone to any violent emotion and it is only a question of guiding this susceptibility into the right channels. If conscience resists, muddle him. Let him say that he feels hatred not on his own behalf but on that of the women and children, and that a Christian is told to forgive his own, not other people's enemies. In other words let him consider himself sufficiently identified with the women and children to feel hatred on their behalf, but *not* sufficiently identified to regard their enemies as his own and therefore proper objects of forgiveness.

But hatred is best combined with Fear. Cowardice, alone of all the vices, is purely painful—horrible to anticipate, horrible to feel, horrible to remember; Hatred has its pleasures. It is therefore often the *compensation* by which a frightened man reimburses himself for the miseries of Fear. The more he fears, the more he will hate. And Hatred is also a great anodyne for shame. To make a deep wound in his charity, you should therefore first defeat his courage.

Now this is a ticklish business. We have made men proud of most vices, but not of cowardice. Whenever we have almost succeeded in doing so, the Enemy permits a war or an earthquake or some other calamity, and at once courage becomes so obviously lovely and important even in human eyes that all our work is undone, and there is still at least one vice of which they feel genuine shame. The danger of inducing cowardice in our patients, therefore, is lest we produce real self-knowledge and self-loathing with consequent repentance and humility. And in fact, in the last war, thousands of humans, by discovering their own cowardice, discovered the whole moral world for the first time. In peace we can make many of them ignore good and evil entirely; in danger, the issue is forced upon them in a guise to which even we cannot blind them. There is here a cruel dilemma before us. If we promoted justice and charity among men, we should be playing directly into the Enemy's hands; but if we guide them to the opposite behaviour, this sooner or later produces (for He permits it to produce) a war or a revolution, and the undisguisable issue of cowardice or courage awakes thousands of men from moral stupor.

This, indeed, is probably one of the Enemy's motives for creating a dangerous world—a world in which moral issues really come to the point. He sees as well as you do that courage is not simply *one* of the virtues, but the form of every virtue at the testing point, which means, at the point of highest reality. A chastity or honesty, or mercy, which yields to danger will be chaste or honest or merciful only on conditions. Pilate was merciful till it became risky.

It is therefore possible to lose as much as we gain by making your man a coward; he may learn too much about himself! There is, of course, always the chance, not of chloroforming the shame, but of aggravating it and producing Despair. This would be a great triumph. It would show that he had believed in, and accepted, the Enemy's forgiveness of his other sins only because he himself did not fully feel their sinfulness—that in respect of the one vice which he really understands in its full depth of dishonour he cannot seek, nor credit, the Mercy. But I fear you have already let him get too far in the Enemy's school, and he knows that Despair is a greater sin than any of the sins which provoke it.

As to the actual technique of temptations to cowardice, not much need be said. The main point is that precautions have a tendency to increase fear. The precautions publicly enjoined on your patient, however, soon become a matter of routine and this effect disappears. What you must do is to keep running in his mind (side by side with the conscious intention of doing his duty) the vague idea of all sorts of things he can do or not do, *inside* the framework of the duty, which seem to make him a little safer. Get his mind off the simple rule ('I've got to stay here and do so-and-so') into a series of imaginary life lines ('If A happened—though I very much hope it won't—I could do B—and if the worst came to the worst, I could always do C'). Superstitions, if not recognised as such, can be awakened. The point is to keep him feeling that he has *something*, other than the Enemy and courage the Enemy supplies, *to fall back on,* so that what was intended to be a total commitment to duty becomes honeycombed all through with little unconscious reservations. By building up a series of imaginary expedients to prevent 'the worst coming to the worst' you may produce, at that level of his will which he is not aware of, a determination that the worst *shall not* come to the worst. Then, at the moment of real terror, rush it out into his nerves and muscles and you may get the fatal act done before he knows what you're about. For remember, the *act* of cowardice is all that matters; the emotion of fear is, in itself, no sin and, though we enjoy it, does us no good,

Your affectionate uncle
SCREWTAPE

30

MY DEAR WORMWOOD,

I sometimes wonder whether you think you have been sent into the world for your own amusement. I gather, not from your miserably inadequate report but from that of the Infernal Police, that the patient's behaviour during the first raid has been the worst possible. He has been very frightened and thinks himself a great coward and therefore feels no pride; but he has done everything his duty demanded and perhaps a bit more. Against this disaster all you can produce on the credit side is a burst of ill temper with a dog that tripped him up, some excessive cigarette smoking, and the forgetting of a prayer. What is the use of whining to me about your difficulties? If you are proceeding on the Enemy's idea of 'justice' and suggesting that your opportunities and intentions should be taken into account, then I am not sure that a charge of heresy does not lie against you. At any rate, you will soon find that the justice of Hell is purely realistic, and concerned only with results. Bring us back food, or be food yourself.

The only constructive passage in your letter is where you say that you still expect good results from the patient's fatigue. That is well enough. But it won't fall into your hands. Fatigue *can* produce extreme gentleness, and quiet of mind, and even something like vision. If you have often seen men led by it into anger, malice and impatience, that is because those men have had efficient tempters. The paradoxical thing is that moderate fatigue is a better soil for peevishness than absolute exhaustion. This depends partly on physical causes, but partly on something else. It is not fatigue simply as such that produces the anger, but unexpected demands on a man already tired. Whatever men expect they soon come to think they have a right to: the sense of disappointment can, with very little skill on our part, be turned into a sense of injury. It is after men have given in to the irremediable, after they have despaired of relief and ceased to think even a half-hour ahead, that the dangers of humbled and gentle weariness begin. To produce the best results from the patient's fatigue, therefore, you must feed him with false hopes. Put into his mind plausible reasons for believing that the air raid will not be repeated. Keep him comforting himself with the thought of how much he will enjoy his bed next night. Exaggerate the weariness by making him think it will soon be over; for men usually feel that a strain could have been endured no longer at the very moment when it is ending, or when they think it is ending. In this, as in the problem of cowardice, the thing to avoid is the total commitment. Whatever he *says*, let his inner resolution be not to bear whatever comes to him, but to bear it 'for a reasonable period'— and let the reasonable period be shorter than the trial is likely to last. It need not be *much* shorter; in attacks on patience, chastity, and fortitude, the fun is to make the man yield just when (had he but known it) relief was almost in sight.

I do not know whether he is likely to meet the girl under conditions of strain or not. If he does, make full use of the fact that up to a certain point, fatigue makes women talk more and men talk less. Much secret resentment, even between lovers, can be raised from this.

Probably the scenes he is now witnessing will not provide material for an *intellectual* attack on his faith—your previous failures have put that out of your power. But there is a sort of attack on the emotions which can still be tried. It turns on making him *feel*, when first he sees human remains plastered on a wall, that this is 'what the world is *really* like' and that all his religion has been a fantasy. You will notice that we have got them completely fogged about the meaning of the word 'real'. They tell each other, of some great spiritual experience, 'All that *really* happened was that you heard some music in a lighted building'; here 'real' means the bare physical facts, separated from the other elements in the experience they actually had. On the other hand, they will also say 'It's all very well discussing that high dive as you sit here in an armchair, but wait till you get up there and see what it's *really* like': here 'real' is being used in the opposite sense to mean, not the physical facts (which they know already while discussing the matter in armchairs) but the emotional effect those facts will have on a human consciousness. Either application of the word could be defended; but our business is to keep the two going at once so that the emotional value of the word 'real' can be placed now on one side of the account, now on the other, as it happens to suit us. The general rule which we have now pretty well established among them is that in all experiences which can make them happier or better only the physical facts are 'real' while the spiritual elements are 'subjective'; in all experiences which can discourage or corrupt them the spiritual elements are the main reality and to ignore them is to be an escapist. Thus in birth the blood and pain are 'real', the rejoicing a mere subjective point of view; in death, the terror and ugliness reveal what death 'really means'. The hatefulness of a hated person is 'real'—in hatred you see men as they are, you are disillusioned; but the loveliness of a loved person is merely a subjective haze concealing a 'real' core of sexual appetite or economic association. Wars and poverty are 'really' horrible; peace and plenty are mere physical facts about which men happen to have certain sentiments. The creatures are always accusing one another of wanting 'to eat the cake and have it'; but thanks to our labours they are more often in the predicament of paying for the cake and not eating it. Your patient, properly handled, will have no difficulty in regarding his emotion at the sight of human entrails as a revelation of Reality and his emotion at the sight of happy children or fair weather as mere sentiment,

Your affectionate uncle
SCREWTAPE

31

MY DEAR, MY VERY DEAR, WORMWOOD, MY POPPET, MY PIGSNIE,

How mistakenly now that all is lost you come whimpering to ask me whether the terms of affection in which I address you meant nothing from the beginning. Far from it! Rest assured, my love for you and your love for me are as like as two peas. I have always desired you, as you (pitiful fool) desired me. The difference is that I am the stronger. I think they will give you to me now; or a bit of you. Love you? Why, yes. As dainty a morsel as ever I grew fat on.

You have let a soul slip through your fingers. The howl of sharpened famine for that loss re-echoes at this moment through all the levels of the Kingdom of Noise down to the very Throne itself. It makes me mad to think of it. How well I know what happened at the instant when they snatched him from you! There was a sudden clearing of his eyes (was there not?) as he saw you for the first time, and recognised the part you had had in him and knew that you had it no longer. Just think (and let it be the beginning of your agony) what he felt at that moment; as if a scab had fallen from an old sore, as if he were emerging from a hideous, shell-like tetter, as if he shuffled off for good and all a defiled, wet, clinging garment. By Hell, it is misery enough to see them in their mortal days taking off dirtied and uncomfortable clothes and splashing in hot water and giving little grunts of pleasure—stretching their eased limbs. What, then, of this final stripping, this complete cleansing?

The more one thinks about it, the worse it becomes. He got through so easily! No gradual misgivings, no doctor's sentence, no nursing home, no operating theatre, no false hopes of life; sheer, instantaneous liberation. One moment it seemed to be all our world; the scream of bombs, the fall of houses, the stink and taste of high explosive on the lips and in the lungs, the feet burning with weariness, the heart cold with horrors, the brain reeling, the legs aching; next moment all this was gone, gone like a bad dream, never again to be of any account. Defeated, out-manoeuvred fool! Did you mark how naturally—as if he'd been born for it—the earth-born vermin entered the new life? How all his doubts became, in the twinkling of an eye, ridiculous? I know what the creature was saying to itself! 'Yes. Of course. It always was like this. All horrors have followed the same course, getting worse and worse and forcing you into a kind of bottle-neck till, at the very moment when you thought you must be crushed, behold! you were out of the narrows and all was suddenly well. The extraction hurt more and more and then the tooth was out. The dream became a nightmare and then you woke. You die and die and then you are beyond death. How could I ever have doubted it?'

As he saw you, he also saw Them. I know how it was. You reeled back dizzy and blinded, more hurt by them than he had ever been by bombs. The degradation of it!—that this thing of earth and slime could stand upright and converse with spirits before whom you, a spirit, could only cower. Perhaps you had hoped that the awe and strangeness of it would dash his joy. But that is the cursed thing; the gods are strange to mortal eyes, and yet they are not strange. He had no faintest conception till that very hour of how they would look, and even doubted their existence. But when he saw them he knew that he had always known them and realised what part each one of them had played at many an hour in his life when he had supposed himself alone, so that now he could say to them, one by one, not 'Who *are* you?' but 'So it was *you* all the time.' All that they were and said at this meeting woke memories. The dim consciousness of friends about him which had haunted his solitudes from infancy was now at last explained; that central music in every pure experience which had always just evaded memory was now at last recovered. Recognition made him free of their company almost before the limbs of his corpse became quiet. Only you were left outside.

He saw not only Them; he saw Him. This animal, this thing begotten in a bed, could look on Him. What is blinding, suffocating fire to you, is now cool light to him, is clarity itself, and wears the form of a Man. You would like, if you could, to interpret the patient's prostration in the Presence, his self-abhorrence and utter knowledge of his sins (yes, Wormwood, a clearer knowledge even than yours) on the analogy of your own choking and paralysing sensations when you encounter the deadly air that breathes from the heart of Heaven. But it's all nonsense. Pains he may still have to encounter, but they *embrace* those pains. They would not barter them for any earthly pleasure. All the delights of sense, or heart, or intellect, with which you could once have tempted him, even the delights of virtue itself, now seem to him in comparison but as the half nauseous attractions of a raddled harlot would seem to a man who hears that his true beloved whom he has loved all his life and whom he had believed to be dead is alive and even now at his door. He is caught up into that world where pain and pleasure take on transfinite values and all our arithmetic is dismayed. Once more, the inexplicable meets us. Next to the curse of useless tempters like yourself the greatest curse upon us is the failure of our Intelligence Department. If only we could find out what He is really up to! Alas, alas, that knowledge, in itself so hateful and mawkish a thing, should yet be necessary for Power! Sometimes I am almost in despair. All that sustains me is the conviction that our Realism, our rejection (in the face of all temptations) of all silly nonsense and claptrap, *must* win in the end. Meanwhile, I have you to settle with. Most truly do I sign myself

Your increasingly and
ravenously affectionate uncle
SCREWTAPE

SCREWTAPE
PROPOSES A TOAST

PREFACE

From the collection of essays
"Screwtape Proposes a Toast"

C. S. LEWIS had finished putting this book together shortly before his death on 22 November 1963. It is devoted almost entirely to religion and the pieces are derived from various sources. Some of them have appeared in *They Asked for a Paper* (Geoffrey Bles, London 1962), a collection whose subjects included literature, ethics and theology. 'Screwtape Proposes a Toast' was initially published in Great Britain as part of a hard-covered book called *The Screwtape Letters and Screwtape Proposes a Toast* (Geoffrey Bles, London 1961). This consisted of the original 'The Screwtape Letters', together with the 'Toast', and also a new preface by Lewis. Meantime, 'Screwtape Proposes a Toast' had already appeared in the United States, first as an article in *The Saturday Evening Post* and then during 1960 in a hard-covered collection, *The World's Last Night* (Harcourt Brace and World, New York).

In the new preface for *The Screwtape Letters and Screwtape Proposes a Toast*, which we have reprinted in this book, Lewis explains the conception and birth of the 'Toast'. It would be quite wrong to call the address 'another Screwtape letter'. What he described as the technique of 'diabolical ventriloquism' is indeed still there: Screwtape's whites are our blacks and whatever he welcomes we should dread. But, whilst the form still broadly persists, there its affinity to the original *Letters* ends. They were mainly concerned with the moral life of an individual; in the 'Toast' the substance of the quest is now rather the need to respect and foster the mind of the young boy and girl.

'A Slip of the Tongue' (a sermon preached in Magdalene College Chapel) appears in a book for the first time. 'The Inner Ring' was a Memorial Oration delivered at King's College, University of London in 1944; 'Is Theology Poetry?' and 'On Obstinacy in Belief' were both papers read to the Socratic Club, subsequently first appearing in the 'Socratic Digest' in 1944 and 1955 respectively. 'Transposition' is a slightly fuller version of a sermon preached in Mansfield College, Oxford; whilst 'The Weight of Glory' was a sermon given in the Church of St Mary the Virgin, Oxford, and first published by SPCK. All these five papers were published by kind permission in *They Asked for a Paper*. 'Good Work and Good Works' first appeared in *The Catholic Art Quarterly* and then in *The World's Last Night*.

At the end of his preface to *They Asked for a Paper*, Lewis wrote: 'Since these papers were composed at various times during the last twenty years, passages in them which some readers may find reminiscent of my later work are in fact anticipatory and embryonic. I have allowed myself to be persuaded that such overlaps were not a fatal objection to their republication.' We are delighted that he allowed himself to be persuaded in the same way over this paperback collection of pieces on religious themes.

J.E.G.

SCREWTAPE PROPOSES A TOAST

I WAS OFTEN asked or advised to add to the original 'Screwtape Letters', but for many years I felt not the least inclination to do it. Though I had never written anything more easily, I never wrote with less enjoyment. The ease came, no doubt, from the fact that the device of diabolical letters, once you have thought of it, exploits itself spontaneously, like Swift's big and little men, or the medical and ethical philosophy of 'Erewhon', as Anstey's Garuda Stone. It would run away with you for a thousand pages if you gave it its head. But though it was easy to twist one's mind into the diabolical attitude, it was not fun, or not for long. The strain produced a sort of spiritual cramp. The world into which I had to project myself while I spoke through Screwtape was all dust, grit, thirst and itch. Every trace of beauty, freshness and geniality had to be excluded. It almost smothered me before I was done. It would have smothered my readers if I had prolonged it.

I had, moreover, a sort of grudge against my book for not being a different book which no one could write. Ideally, Screwtape's advice to Wormwood should have been balanced by archangelical advice to the patient's guardian angel. Without this the picture of human life is lop-sided. But who could supply the deficiency? Even if a man—and he would have to be a far better man than I—could scale the spiritual heights required, what 'answerable style' could he use? For the style would really be part of the content. Mere advice would be no good; every sentence would have to smell of Heaven. And nowadays even if you could write prose like Traherne's, you wouldn't be allowed to, for the canon of 'func-tionalism' has disabled literature for half its functions. (At bottom, every ideal of style dictates not only how we should say things but what sort of things we may say.)

Then, as years went on and the stifling experience of writing the 'Let-ters' became a weaker memory, reflections on this and that which seemed somehow to demand Screwtapian treatment began to occur to me. I was resolved never to write another 'Letter'. The idea of something like a lecture or 'address' hovered vaguely in my mind, now forgotten, now recalled, never written. Then came an invitation from *The Saturday Evening Post,* and that pressed the trigger.

C.S.L.

THE SCENE is in Hell at the annual dinner of the Tempters' Training College for young Devils. The Principal, Dr Slubgob, has just proposed the health of the guests. Screwtape, who is the guest of honour, rises to reply:

Mr Principal, your Imminence, your Disgraces, my Thorns, Shadies, and Gentledevils: It is customary on these occasions for the speaker to address himself chiefly to those among you who have just graduated and who will very soon be posted to official Tempterships on Earth. It is a custom I willingly obey. I well remember with what trepidation I awaited my own first appointment. I hope, and believe, that each one of you has the same uneasiness tonight. Your career is before you. Hell expects and demands that it should be—as Mine was—one of unbroken success. If it is not, you know what awaits you.

I have no wish to reduce the wholesome and realistic element of terror, the unremitting anxiety, which must act as the lash and spur to your endeavours. How often you will envy the humans their faculty of sleep! Yet at the same time I would wish to put before you a moderately encouraging view of the strategical situation as a whole.

Your dreaded Principal has included in a speech full of points something like an apology for the banquet which he has set before us. Well, gentledevils, no one blames *him*. But it would be vain to deny that the human souls on whose anguish we have been feasting tonight were of pretty poor quality. Not all the most skilful cookery of our tormentors could make them better than insipid.

Oh to get one's teeth again into a Farinata, a Henry VIII, or even a Hitler! There was real crackling there; something to crunch; a rage, an egotism, a cruelty only just less robust than our own. It put up a delicious resistance to being devoured. It warmed your innards when you'd got it down.

Instead of this, what have we had tonight? There was a municipal authority with Graft sauce. But personally I could not detect in him the flavour of a really passionate and brutal avarice such as delighted one in the great tycoons of the last century. Was he not unmistakably a Little Man—a creature of the petty rake-off pocketed with a petty joke in private and denied with the stalest platitudes in his public utterances—a grubby little nonentity who had drifted into corruption, only just realising that he was corrupt, and chiefly because everyone else did it? Then there was the lukewarm Casserole of Adulterers. Could you find in it any trace of a fully inflamed, defiant, rebellious, insatiable lust? I couldn't. They all tasted to me like under-sexed morons who had blundered or trickled into the wrong beds in automatic response to sexy advertisements, or to make themselves feel modern and emancipated, or to reassure themselves about their virility or their 'normalcy', or even because they had nothing else to do. Frankly, to me who have tasted Messalina and Casanova, they were nauseating. The Trade Unionist garnished with Claptrap was perhaps a shade better. He had done some real harm. He had, not quite unknowingly, worked for bloodshed, famine, and the extinction of liberty. Yes, in a way. But what a way! He thought of those ultimate objectives so little. Toeing the party line, self-importance, and above all mere routine, were what really dominated his life.

But now comes the point. Gastronomically, all this is deplorable. But I hope none of us puts gastronomy first. Is it not, in another and far more serious way, full of hope and promise?

Consider, first, the mere quantity. The quality may be wretched; but we never had souls (of a sort) in more abundance.

And then the triumph. We are tempted to say that such souls—or such residual puddles of what once was soul—are hardly worth damning. Yes, but the Enemy (for whatever inscrutable and perverse reason) thought them worth trying to save. Believe me, He did. You youngsters who have not yet been on active service have no idea with what labour, with what delicate skill, each of these miserable creatures was finally captured.

The difficulty lay in their very smallness and flabbiness. Here were vermin so muddled in mind, so passively responsive to environment, that it was very hard to raise them to that level of clarity and deliberateness at which mortal sin becomes possible. To raise them just enough; but not that fatal millimetre of 'too much'. For then, of course, all would possibly have been lost. They might have seen; they might have repented. On the other hand, if they had been raised too little, they would very possibly have qualified for Limbo, as creatures suitable neither for Heaven nor for Hell; things that, having failed to make the grade, are allowed to sink into a more or less contented sub-humanity forever.

In each individual choice of what the Enemy would call the 'wrong' turning such creatures are at first hardly, if at all, in a state of full spiritual responsibility. They do not understand either the source or the real character of the prohibitions they are breaking. Their consciousness hardly exists apart from the social atmosphere that surrounds them. And of course we have contrived that their very language should be all smudge and blur; what would be a *bribe* in someone else's profession is a *tip* or a *present* in theirs. The first job of their Tempters was to harden these choices of the Hell-ward roads into a habit by steady repetition. But then (and this was all-important) to turn the habit into a principle—a principle the creature is prepared to defend. After that, all will go well. Conformity to the social environment, at first merely instinctive or even mechani-cal—how should a *jelly* not conform?—now becomes an unacknowl-edged creed or ideal of Togetherness or Being like Folks. Mere ignorance of the law they break now turns into a vague theory about it—remember they know no history—a theory expressed by calling it *conventional* or *puritan* or *bourgeois* 'morality'. Thus gradually there comes to exist at the centre of the creature a hard, tight, settled core of resolution to go on being what it is, and even to resist moods that might tend to alter it. It is a very small core; not at all reflective (they are too ignorant) nor defi-ant (their emotional and imaginative poverty excludes that); almost, in its own way, prim and demure; like a pebble, or a very young cancer. But it will serve our turn. Here at last is a real and deliberate, though not fully articulate, rejection of what the Enemy calls Grace.

These, then, are two welcome phenomena. First, the abundance of our captures; however tasteless our fare, we are in no danger of famine.

And secondly, the triumph; the skill of our Tempters has never stood higher. But the third moral, which I have not yet drawn, is the most important of all.

The sort of souls on whose despair and ruin we have—well, I won't say feasted, but at any rate subsisted—tonight are increasing in numbers and will continue to increase. Our advices from Lower Command assure us that this is so; our directives warn us to orient all our tactics in view of this situation. The 'great' sinners, those in whom vivid and genial passions have been pushed beyond the bounds and in whom an immense concentration of will has been devoted to objects which the Enemy abhors, will not disappear. But they will grow rarer. Our catches will be ever more numerous; but they will consist increasingly of trash—trash which we should once have thrown to Cerberus and the hell-hounds as unfit for diabolical consumption. And there are two things I want you to understand about this. First, that however depressing it may seem, it is really a change for the better. And secondly, I would draw your attention to the means by which it has been brought about.

It is a change for the better. The great (and toothsome) sinners are made out of the very same material as those horrible phenomena, the great Saints. The virtual disappearance of such material may mean insipid meals for us. But is it not utter frustration and famine for the Enemy? He did not create the humans—He did not become one of them and die among them by torture—in order to produce candidates for Limbo; 'failed' humans. He wanted to make Saints; gods; things like Himself. Is the dullness of your present fare not a very small price to pay for the delicious knowledge that His whole great experiment is petering out? But not only that. As the great sinners grow fewer, and the majority lose all individuality, the great sinners become far more effective agents for us. Every dictator or even demagogue—almost every film-star or crooner—can now draw tens of thousands of the human sheep with him. They give themselves (what there is of them) to him; in him, to us. There may come a time when we shall have no need to bother about *individual* temptation at all, except for the few. Catch the bell-wether and his whole flock comes after him.

But do you realise how we have succeeded in reducing so many of the human race to the level of ciphers? This has not come about by accident. It has been our answer—and a magnificent answer it is—to one of the most serious challenges we ever had to face.

Let me recall to your minds what the human situation was in the latter half of the nineteenth century—the period at which I ceased to be a practising Tempter and was rewarded with an administrative post. The great movement towards liberty and equality among men had by then borne solid fruit and grown mature. Slavery had been abolished. The American War of Independence had been won. The French Revolution had succeeded. Religious toleration was almost everywhere on the increase. In that movement there had originally been many elements which were in our favour. Much Atheism, much Anti-Clericalism, much envy and thirst for revenge, even some (rather absurd) attempts to revive Paganism, were mixed in it. It was not easy to determine what our own attitude should be. On the one hand it was a bitter blow to us—it still is—that any sort of men who had been hungry should be fed or any who had long worn chains should have them struck off. But on the other hand, there was in the movement so much rejection of faith, so much materialism, secularism, and hatred, that we felt we were bound to encourage it.

But by the latter part of the century the situation was much simpler, and also much more ominous. In the English sector (where I saw most of my front-line service) a horrible thing had happened. The Enemy, with His usual sleight of hand, had largely appropriated this progressive or liberalising movement and perverted it to His own ends. Very little of its old anti-Christianity remained. The dangerous phenomenon called Christian Socialism was rampant. Factory owners of the good old type who grew rich on sweated labour, instead of being assassinated by their workpeople—we could have used that—were being frowned upon by their own class. The rich were increasingly giving up their powers not in the face of revolution and compulsion, but in obedience to their own consciences. As for the poor who benefited by this, they were behaving in a most disappointing fashion. Instead of using their new liberties—as we reasonably hoped and expected—for massacre, rape, and looting, or even for perpetual intoxication, they were perversely engaged in becoming cleaner, more orderly, more thrifty, better educated, and even more virtuous. Believe me, gentledevils, the threat of something like a really healthy state of society seemed then perfectly serious.

Thanks to Our Father Below the threat was averted. Our counter-attack was on two levels. On the deepest level our dealers contrived to call into full life an element which had been implicit in the movement from its earliest days. Hidden in the heart of this striving for Liberty there was also a deep hatred of personal freedom. That invaluable man Rousseau first revealed it. In his perfect democracy, you remember, only the state religion is permitted, slavery is restored, and the individual is told that he has really willed (though he didn't know it) whatever the Government tells him to do. From that starting point, *via* Hegel (another indispensable propagandist on our side) we easily contrived both the Nazi and the Communist state. Even in England we were pretty successful. I heard the other day that in that country a man could not, without a permit, cut down his own tree with his own axe, make it into planks with his own saw, and use the planks to build a tool-shed in his own garden.

Such was our counter-attack on one level. You, who are mere beginners, will not be entrusted with work of that kind. You will be attached as Tempters to private persons. Against them, or through them, our counter-attack takes a different form.

Democracy is the word with which you must lead them by the nose. The good work which our philological experts have already done in the corruption of human language makes it unnecessary to warn you that they should never be allowed to give this word a clear and definable meaning. They won't. It will never occur to them that *Democracy* is properly the name of a political system, even a system of voting, and that this has only the most remote and tenuous connection with what you are trying to sell them. Nor, of course, must they ever be allowed to raise Aristotle's question: whether 'democratic behaviour' means the behaviour that democracies like or the behaviour that will preserve a democracy. For if they did, it could hardly fail to occur to them that these need not be the same.

You are to use the word purely as an incantation; if you like, purely for its selling power. It is a name they venerate. And of course it is connected with the political ideal that men should be equally treated. You then make a stealthy transition in their minds from this political ideal to a factual belief that all men *are* equal. Especially the man you are working on. As a result you can use the word *Democracy* to sanction in his thought the most degrading (and also the least enjoyable) of all human feelings. You can get him to practise, not only without shame but with a positive glow of self-approval, conduct which, if undefended by the magic word, would be universally derided.

The feeling I mean is of course that which prompts a man to say *I'm as good as you.*

The first and most obvious advantage is that you thus induce him to enthrone at the centre of his life a good, solid resounding lie. I don't mean merely that his statement is false in fact, that he is no more equal to everyone he meets in kindness, honesty, and good sense than in height or waist-measurement. I mean that he does not believe it himself. No man who says *I'm as good as you* believes it. He would not say it if he did. The St Bernard never says it to the toy dog, nor the scholar to the dunce, nor the employable to the bum, nor the pretty woman to the plain. The claim to equality, outside the strictly political field, is made only by those who feel themselves to be in some way inferior. What it expresses is precisely the itching, smarting, writhing awareness of an inferiority which the patient refuses to accept.

And therefore resents. Yes, and therefore resents every kind of superiority in others; denigrates it; wishes its annihilation. Presently he suspects every mere difference of being a claim to superiority. No one must be different from himself in voice, clothes, manners, recreations, choice of food. 'Here is someone who speaks English rather more clearly and euphoniously than I—it must be a vile, upstage, lah-di-dah affectation. Here's a fellow who says he doesn't like hot dogs—thinks himself too good for them no doubt. Here's a man who hasn't turned on the jukebox—he must be one of those highbrows and is doing it to show off. If they were the right sort of chaps they'd be like me. They've no business to be different. It's undemocratic.'

Now this useful phenomenon is in itself by no means new. Under the name of Envy it has been known to the humans for thousands of years. But hitherto they always regarded it as the most odious, and also the most comical, of vices. Those who were aware of feeling it felt it with shame; those who were not gave it no quarter in others. The delightful novelty of the present situation is that you can sanction it—make it respectable and even laudable—by the incantatory use of the word *democratic*.

Under the influence of this incantation those who are in any or every way inferior can labour more wholeheartedly and successfully than ever before to pull down everyone else to their own level. But that is not all. Under the same influence, those who come, or could come, nearer to a full humanity, actually draw back from it for fear of being *undemocratic*. I am credibly informed that young humans now sometimes suppress an incipient taste for classical music or good literature because it might prevent their Being like Folks; that people who would really wish to be—and are offered the Grace which would enable them to be—honest, chaste, or temperate, refuse it. To accept might make them Different, might offend again the Way of Life, take them out of Togetherness, impair their Integration with the Group. They might (horror of horrors!) become individuals.

All is summed up in the prayer which a young female human is said to have uttered recently: 'Oh God, make me a normal twentieth-century girl!' Thanks to our labours, this will mean increasingly, 'Make me a minx, a moron, and a parasite'.

Meanwhile, as a delightful by-product, the few (fewer every day) who will not be made Normal and Regular and Like Folks and Integrated, increasingly tend to become in reality the prigs and cranks which the rabble would in any case have believed them to be. For suspicion often creates what it suspects. ('Since, whatever I do, the neighbours are going to think me a witch, or a Communist agent, I might as well be hanged for a sheep as a lamb and become one in reality.') As a result we now have an intelligentsia which, though very small, is very useful to the cause of Hell.

But that is a mere by-product. What I want to fix your attention on is the vast, overall movement towards the discrediting, and finally the elimination, of every kind of human excellence—moral, cultural, social, or intellectual. And is it not pretty to notice how *Democracy* (in the incantatory sense) is now doing for us the work that was once done by the most ancient Dictatorships, and by the same methods? You remember how one of the Greek Dictators (they called them 'tyrants' then) sent an envoy to another Dictator to ask his advice about the principles of government. The second Dictator led the envoy into a field of corn, and there he snicked off with his cane the top of every stalk that rose an inch or so above the general level. The moral was plain. Allow no pre-eminence among your subjects. Let no man live who is wiser, or better, or more famous, or even handsomer than the mass. Cut them all down to a level; all slaves, all ciphers, all nobodies. All equals. Thus Tyrants could practise, in a sense, 'democracy'. But now 'democracy' can do the same work without any other tyranny than her own. No one need now go through the field with a cane. The little stalks will now of themselves bite the tops off the big ones. The big ones are beginning to bite off their own in their desire to Be Like Stalks.

I have said that to secure the damnation of these little souls, these creatures that have almost ceased to be individual, is a laborious and tricky work. But if proper pains and skill are expended, you can be fairly confident of the result. The great sinners *seem* easier to catch. But then they are incalculable. After you have played them for seventy years, the Enemy may snatch them from your claws in the seventy-first. They are capable, you see, of real repentance. They are conscious of real guilt. They are, if things take the wrong turn, as ready to defy the social pressures around them for the Enemy's sake as they were to defy them for ours. It is in some ways more troublesome to track and swat an evasive wasp than to shoot, at close range, a wild elephant. But the elephant is more troublesome if you miss.

My own experience, as I have said, was mainly on the English sector, and I still get more news from it than from any other. It may be that what I am now going to say will not apply so fully to the sectors in which some of you may be operating. But you can make the necessary adjustments when you get there. Some application it will almost certainly have. If it has too little, you must labour to make the country you are dealing with more like what England already is.

In that promising land the spirit of *I'm as good as you* has already become something more than a generally social influence. It begins to work itself into their educational system. How far its operations there have gone at the present moment, I would not like to say with certainty. Nor does it matter. Once you have grasped the tendency, you can easily predict its future developments; especially as we ourselves will play our part in the developing. The basic principle of the new education is to be that dunces and idlers must not be made to feel inferior to intelligent and industrious pupils. That would be 'undemocratic'. These differences between the pupils—for they are obviously and nakedly *individual* differences—must be disguised. This can be done on various levels. At universities, examinations must be framed so that nearly all the students get good marks. Entrance examinations must be framed so that all, or nearly all, citizens can go to universities, whether they have any power (or wish) to profit by higher education or not. At schools, the children who are too stupid or lazy to learn languages and mathematics and elementary science can be set to doing the things that children used to do in their spare time. Let them, for example, make mud-pies and call it modelling. But all the time there must be no faintest hint that they are inferior to the children who are at work. Whatever nonsense they are engaged in must have—I believe the English already use the phrase—'parity of esteem'. An even more drastic scheme is not impossible. Children who are fit to proceed to a higher class may be artificially kept back, because the others would get a *trauma*—Beelzebub, what a useful word!—by being left behind. The bright pupil thus remains democratically fettered to his own age-group throughout his school career, and a boy who would be capable of tackling Aeschylus or Dante sits listening to his coeval's attempts to spell out A CAT SAT ON THE MAT.

In a word, we may reasonably hope for the virtual abolition of education when *I'm as good as you* has fully had its way. All incentives to learn and all penalties for not learning will vanish. The few who might want to learn will be prevented; who are they to overtop their fellows? And anyway the teachers—or should I say, nurses?—will be far too busy re-assuring the dunces and patting them on the back to waste any time on real teaching. We shall no longer have to plan and toil to spread imperturbable conceit and incurable ignorance among men. The little vermin themselves will do it for us.

Of course this would not follow unless all education became state education. But it will. That is part of the same movement. Penal taxes, designed for that purpose, are liquidating the Middle Class, the class who were prepared to save and spend and make sacrifices in order to have their children privately educated. The removal of this class, besides linking up with the abolition of education, is, fortunately, an inevitable effect of the spirit that says *I'm as good as you*. This was, after all, the social group which gave to the humans the overwhelming majority of their scientists, physicians, philosophers, theologians, poets, artists, composers, architects, jurists, and administrators. If ever there was a bunch of tall stalks that needed their tops knocked off, it was surely they. As an English politician remarked not long ago, 'A democracy does not want great men.'

It would be idle to ask of such a creature whether by *want* it means 'need' or 'like'. But you had better be clear. For here Aristotle's question comes up again.

We, in Hell, would welcome the disappearance of Democracy in the strict sense of that word; the political arrangement so called. Like all forms of government it often works to our advantage; but on the whole less often than other forms. And what we must realise is that 'democracy' in the diabolical sense (*I'm as good as you*, Being like Folks, Togetherness) is the finest instrument we could possibly have for extirpating political Democracies from the face of the earth.

For 'democracy' or the 'democratic spirit' (diabolical sense) leads to a nation without great men, a nation mainly of subliterates, morally flaccid from lack of discipline in youth, full of the cocksureness which flattery breeds on ignorance, and soft from lifelong pampering. And that is what Hell wishes every democratic people to be. For when such a nation meets in conflict a nation where children have been made to work at school, where talent is placed in high posts, and where the ignorant mass are allowed no say at all in public affairs, only one result is possible.

One Democracy was surprised lately when it found that Russia had got ahead of it in science. What a delicious specimen of human blindness! If the whole tendency of their society is opposed to every sort of excellence, why did they expect their scientists to excel?

It is our function to encourage the behaviour, the manners, the whole attitude of mind, which democracies naturally like and enjoy, because these are the very things which, if unchecked, will destroy democracy. You would almost wonder that even humans don't see it themselves. Even if they don't read Aristotle (that would be undemocratic) you would have thought the French Revolution would have taught them that the behaviour aristocrats naturally like is not the behaviour that preserves aristocracy. They might then have applied the same principle to all forms of government.

But I would not end on that note. I would not—Hell forbid!—encourage in your own minds that delusion which you must carefully foster in the minds of your human victims. I mean the delusion that the fate of nations is *in itself* more important than that of individual souls. The overthrow of free peoples and the multiplication of slave-states are for us a means (besides, of course, being fun); but the real end is the destruction of individuals. For only individuals can be saved or damned, can become sons of the Enemy or food for us. The ultimate value, for us, of any revolution, war, or famine lies in the individual anguish, treachery, hatred, rage, and despair which it may produce. *I'm as good as you* is a useful means for the destruction of democratic societies. But it has a far deeper value as an end in itself, as a state of mind, which necessarily excluding humility, charity, contentment, and all the pleasures of gratitude or admiration, turns a human being away from almost every road which might finally lead him to Heaven.

But now for the pleasantest part of my duty. It falls to my lot to propose on behalf of the guests the health of Principal Slubgob and the Tempters' Training College. Fill your glasses. What is this I see? What is this delicious bouquet I inhale? Can it be? Mr Principal, I unsay all my hard words about the dinner. I see, and smell, that even under wartime conditions the College cellar still has a few dozen of sound old vintage *Pharisee*. Well, well, well. This is like old times. Hold it beneath your nostrils for a moment, gentledevils. Hold it up to the light. Look at those fiery streaks that writhe and tangle in its dark heart, as if they were contending. And so they are. You know how this wine is blended? Different types of Pharisee have been harvested, trodden, and fermented together to produce its subtle flavour. Types that were most antagonistic to one another on earth. Some were all rules and relics and rosaries; others were all drab clothes, long faces, and petty traditional abstinences from wine or cards or the theatre. Both had in common their self-righteousness and the almost infinite distance between their actual outlook and anything the Enemy really is or commands. The wickedness of other religions was the really live doctrine in the religion of each; slander was its gospel and denigration its litany. How they hated each other up there where the sun shone! How much more they hate each other now that they are forever conjoined but not reconciled. Their astonishment, their resentment, at the combination, the festering of their eternally impenitent spite, passing into our spiritual digestion, will work like fire. Dark fire. All said and done, my friends, it will be an ill day for us if what most humans mean by 'religion' ever vanishes from the Earth. It can still send us the truly delicious sins. The fine flower of unholiness can grow only in the close neighbourhood of the Holy. Nowhere do we tempt so successfully as on the very steps of the altar.

Your Imminence, your Disgraces, my Thorns, Shadies, and Gentledevils: I give you the toast of—Principal Slubgob and the College!

MIRACLES

A Preliminary Study

To Cecil and Daphne Harwood

Among the hills a meteorite
Lies huge; and moss has overgrown,
And wind and rain with touches light
Made soft, the contours of the stone.

Thus easily can Earth digest
A cinder of sidereal fire,
And make her translunary guest
The native of an English shire.

Nor is it strange these wanderers
Find in her lap their fitting place,
For every particle that's hers
Came at the first from outer space.

All that is Earth has once been sky;
Down from the sun of old she came,
Or from some star that travelled by
Too close to his entangling flame.

Hence, if belated drops yet fall
From heaven, on these her plastic power
Still works as once it worked on all
The glad rush of the golden shower.

C.S.L.

Reprinted by permission of *Time and Tide*

MIRACLES
CONTENTS

I

THE SCOPE OF THIS BOOK

Those who wish to succeed must ask
the right preliminary questions.

ARISTOTLE, *METAPHYSICS*, II, (III), I.

IN ALL MY life I have met only one person who claims to have seen a ghost.
And the interesting thing about the story is that that person disbelieved in
the immortal soul before she saw the ghost and still disbelieves after seeing
it. She says that what she saw must have been an illusion or a trick of the
nerves. And obviously she may be right. Seeing is not believing.

For this reason, the question whether miracles occur can never be answered simply by experience. Every event which might claim to be a miracle is, in the last resort, something presented to our senses, something
seen, heard, touched, smelled, or tasted. And our senses are not infallible. If anything extraordinary seems to have happened, we can always
say that we have been the victims of an illusion. If we hold a philosophy
which excludes the supernatural, this is what we always shall say. What
we learn from experience depends on the kind of philosophy we bring to
experience. It is therefore useless to appeal to experience before we have
settled, as well as we can, the philosophical question.

If immediate experience cannot prove or disprove the miraculous, still
less can history do so. Many people think one can decide whether a miracle occurred in the past by examining the evidence 'according to the ordi-

nary rules of historical inquiry'. But the ordinary rules cannot be worked until we have decided whether miracles are possible, and if so, how probable they are. For if they are impossible, then no amount of historical evidence will convince us. If they are possible but immensely improbable, then only mathematically demonstrative evidence will convince us: and since history never provides that degree of evidence for any event, history can never convince us that a miracle occurred. If, on the other hand, miracles are not intrinsically improbable, then the existing evidence will be sufficient to convince us that quite a number of miracles have occurred. The result of our historical enquiries thus depends on the philosophical views which we have been holding before we even began to look at the evidence. This philosophical question must therefore come first.

Here is an example of the sort of thing that happens if we omit the preliminary philosophical task, and rush on to the historical. In a popular commentary on the Bible you will find a discussion of the date at which the Fourth Gospel was written. The author says it must have been written after the execution of St Peter, because, in the Fourth Gospel, Christ is represented as predicting the execution of St Peter. 'A book', thinks the author, 'cannot be written *before* events which it refers to'. Of course it cannot—unless real predictions ever occur. If they do, then this argument for the date is in ruins. And the author has not discussed at all whether real predictions are possible. He takes it for granted (perhaps unconsciously) that they are not. Perhaps he is right: but if he is, he has not discovered this principle by historical inquiry. He has brought his disbelief in predictions to his historical work, so to speak, ready made. Unless he had done so his historical conclusion about the date of the Fourth Gospel could not have been reached at all. His work is therefore quite useless to a person who wants to know *whether* predictions occur. The author gets to work only after he has already answered that question in the negative, and on grounds which he never communicates to us.

This book is intended as a preliminary to historical inquiry. I am not a trained historian and I shall not examine the historical evidence for the Christian miracles. My effort is to put my readers in a position to do so. It is no use going to the texts until we have some idea about the possibility or probability of the miraculous. Those who assume that miracles cannot happen are merely wasting their time by looking into the texts: we know in advance what results they will find for they have begun by begging the question.

2

THE NATURALIST AND
THE SUPERNATURALIST

'Gracious!' exclaimed Mrs Snip, 'and is there a place
where people venture to live above ground?' 'I never
heard of people living under *ground, " replied Tim,*
'before I came to Giant-Land'. 'Came to Giant-Land!'
cried Mrs Snip, 'why, isn't everywhere Giant-Land?'

ROLAND QUIZZ, *GIANT-LAND*, CHAP XXXII.

I USE THE word *Miracle* to mean an interference with Nature by supernatural power.[1] Unless there exists, in addition to Nature, something
else which we may call the supernatural, there can be no miracles. Some
people believe that nothing exists except Nature; I call these people *Natu-*
ralists. Others think that, besides Nature, there exists something else: I
call them *Supernaturalists.* Our first question, therefore, is whether the
Naturalists or the Supernaturalists are right. And here comes our first
difficulty.

---

[1] This definition is not that which would be given by many theologians. I am adopting it not
because I think it an improvement upon theirs but precisely because, being crude and 'popular', it
enables me most easily to treat those questions which 'the common reader' probably has in mind
when he takes up a book on Miracles.

Before the Naturalist and the Supernaturalist can begin to discuss their difference of opinion, they must surely have an agreed definition both of Nature and of Supernature. But unfortunately it is almost impossible to get such a definition. Just because the Naturalist thinks that nothing but Nature exists, the word *Nature* means to him merely 'everything' or 'the whole show' or 'whatever there is'. And if that is what we mean by Nature, then of course nothing else exists. The real question between him and the Supernaturalist has evaded us. Some philosophers have defined Nature as 'What we perceive with our five senses'. But this also is unsatisfactory; for we do not perceive our own emotions in that way, and yet they are presumably 'natural' events. In order to avoid this deadlock and to discover what the Naturalist and the Supernaturalist are really differing about, we must approach our problem in a more roundabout way.

I begin by considering the following sentences (1) Are those his natural teeth or a set? (2) The dog in his natural state is covered with fleas. (3) I love to get away from tilled lands and metalled roads and be alone with Nature. (4) Do be natural. Why are you so affected? (5) It may have been wrong to kiss her but it was very natural.

A common thread of meaning in all these usages can easily be discovered. The natural teeth are those which grow in the mouth; we do not have to design them, make them, or fit them. The dog's natural state is the one he will be in if no one takes soap and water and prevents it. The countryside where Nature reigns supreme is the one where soil, weather and vegetation produce their results unhelped and unimpeded by man. Natural behaviour is the behaviour which people would exhibit if they were not at pains to alter it. The natural kiss is the kiss which will be given if moral or prudential considerations do not intervene. In all the examples Nature means what happens 'of itself' or 'of its own accord': what you do not need to labour for; what you will get if you take no measures to stop it. The Greek word for Nature (Physis) is connected with the Greek verb for 'to grow'; Latin *Natura*, with the verb 'to be born'. The Natural is what springs up, or comes forth, or arrives, or goes on, *of its own accord:* the given, what is there already: the spontaneous, the unintended, the unsolicited.

What the Naturalist believes is that the ultimate Fact, the thing you can't go behind, is a vast process in space and time which is *going on of its own accord*. Inside that total system every particular event (such as your sitting reading this book) happens because some other event has happened; in the long run, because the Total Event is happening. Each particular thing (such as this page) is what it is because other things are what they are; and so, eventually, because the whole system is what it is. All the things and events are so completely interlocked that no one of them can claim the slightest independence from 'the whole show'. None of them exists 'on its own' or 'goes on of its own accord' except in the sense that it exhibits, at some particular place and time, that general 'existence on its own' or 'behaviour of its own accord' which belongs to 'Nature' (the great total interlocked event) as a whole. Thus no thoroughgoing Naturalist believes in free will: for free will would mean that human beings have the power of independent action, the power of doing something more or other than what was involved by the total series of events. And any such separate power of originating events is what the Naturalist denies. Spontaneity, originality, action 'on its own', is a privilege reserved for 'the whole show', which he calls *Nature*.

The Supernaturalist agrees with the Naturalist that there must be something which exists in its own right; some basic Fact whose existence it would be nonsensical to try to explain because this Fact is itself the ground or starting-point of all explanations. But he does not identify this Fact with 'the whole show'. He thinks that things fall into two classes. In the first class we find either things or (more probably) One Thing which is basic and original, which exists on its own. In the second we find things which are merely derivative from that One Thing. The one basic Thing has caused all the other things to be. It exists on its own; they exist because it exists. They will cease to exist if it ever ceases to maintain them in existence; they will be altered if it ever alters them.

The difference between the two views might be expressed by saying that Naturalism gives us a democratic, Supernaturalism a monarchical, picture of reality. The Naturalist thinks that the privilege of 'being on its own' resides in the total mass of things, just as in a democracy sovereignty resides in the whole mass of the people. The Supernaturalist thinks that this privilege belongs to some things or (more probably) One Thing and not to others—just as, in a real monarchy, the king has sovereignty and the people have not. And just as, in a democracy, all citizens are equal, so for the Naturalist one thing or event is as good as another, in the sense that they are all equally dependent on the total system of things. Indeed each of them is only the way in which the character of that total system exhibits itself at a particular point in space and time. The Supernaturalist, on the other hand, believes that the one original or self-existent thing is on a different level from, and more important than, all other things.

At this point a suspicion may occur that Supernaturalism first arose from reading into the universe the structure of monarchical societies. But then of course it may with equal reason be suspected that Naturalism has arisen from reading into it the structure of modern democracies. The two suspicions thus cancel out and give us no help in deciding which theory is more likely to be true. They do indeed remind us that Supernaturalism is the characteristic philosophy of a monarchical age and Naturalism of a democratic, in the sense that Supernaturalism, even if false, would have been believed by the great mass of unthinking people four hundred years ago, just as Naturalism, even if false, will be believed by the great mass of unthinking people today.

Everyone will have seen that the One Self-existent Thing—or the small class of self-existent things—in which Supernaturalists believe, is what we call God or the gods. I propose for the rest of this book to treat only that form of Supernaturalism which believes in one God; partly because polytheism is not likely to be a live issue for most of my readers, and partly because those who believed in many gods very seldom, in fact, regarded their gods as creators of the universe and as self-existent. The gods of Greece were not really supernatural in the strict sense which I am giving to the word. They were products of the total system of things and included within it. This introduces an important distinction.

The difference between Naturalism and Supernaturalism is not exactly the same as the difference between belief in a God and disbelief. Naturalism, without ceasing to be itself, could admit a certain kind of God. The great interlocking event called Nature might be such as to produce at some stage a great cosmic consciousness, an indwelling 'God' arising from the whole process as human mind arises (according to the Naturalists) from human organisms. A Naturalist would not object to that sort of God. The reason is this. Such a God would not stand outside Nature or the total system, would not be existing 'on his own'. It would still be 'the whole show' which was the basic Fact, and such a God would merely be one of the things (even if he were the most interesting) which the basic Fact contained. What Naturalism cannot accept is the idea of a God who stands outside Nature and made it.

We are now in a position to state the difference between the Naturalist and the Supernaturalist despite the fact that they do not mean the same by the word Nature. The Naturalist believes that a great process, of 'becoming', exists 'on its own' in space and time, and that nothing else exists—what we call particular things and events being only the parts into which we analyse the great process or the shapes which that process takes at given moments and given points in space. This single, total reality he calls Nature. The Supernaturalist believes that one Thing exists on its own and has produced the framework of space and time and the procession of systematically connected events which fill them. This framework, and this filling, he calls Nature. It may, or may not, be the only reality which the one Primary Thing has produced. There might be other systems in addition to the one we call Nature.

In that sense there might be several 'Natures'. This conception must be kept quite distinct from what is commonly called 'plurality of worlds'—i.e. different solar systems or different galaxies, 'island universes' existing in widely separated parts of a single space and time. These, however remote, would be parts of the same Nature as our own sun: it and they would be interlocked by being in relations to one another, spatial and temporal relations and casual relations as well. And it is just this reciprocal interlocking within a system which makes it what we call a Nature. Other Natures might not be spatio-temporal at all: or, if any of them were, their space and time would have no spatial or temporal relation to ours. It is just this discontinuity, this failure of interlocking, which would justify us in calling them different Natures. This does not mean that there would be absolutely no relation between them; they would be related by their common derivation from a single Supernatural source. They would, in this respect, be like different novels by a single author; the events in one story have no relation to the events in another *except* that they are invented by the same author. To find the relation between them you must go right back to the author's mind: there is no cutting across from anything Mr Pickwick says in *Pickwick Papers* to anything Mrs Gamp hears in *Martin Chuzzlewit*. Similarly there would be no normal cutting across from an event in one Nature to an event in any other. By a 'normal' relation I mean one which occurs in virtue of the character of the two systems. We have to put in the qualification 'normal' because we do not know in advance that God might not bring two Natures into partial contact at some particular point: that is, He might allow *selected* events in the one to produce results in the other. There would thus be, at certain points, a partial interlocking; but this would not turn the two Natures into one, for the total reciprocity which makes a Nature would still be lacking, and the anomalous interlockings would arise not from what either system was in itself but from the Divine act which was bringing them together. If this occurred each of the two Natures would be 'supernatural' in relation to the other: but the fact of their contact would be supernatural in a more absolute sense—not as being beyond this or that Nature but beyond any and every Nature. It would be one kind of miracle. The other kind would be Divine 'interference' not by the bringing together of two Natures, but simply.

All this is, at present purely speculative. It by no means follows from Supernaturalism that Miracles of any sort do in fact occur. God (the primary thing) may never in fact interfere with the natural system He has created. If He has created more natural systems than one, He may never cause them to impinge on one another.

But that is a question for further consideration. If we decide that Nature is not the only thing there is, then we cannot say in advance whether she is safe from miracles or not. There are things outside her: we do not yet know whether they can get in. The gates may be barred, or they may not. But if Naturalism is true, then we do know in advance that miracles are impossible: nothing can come into Nature from the outside because there is nothing outside to come in, Nature being everything. No doubt, events which we in our ignorance should mistake for miracles might occur: but they would in reality be (just like the commonest events) an inevitable result of the character of the whole system.

Our first choice, therefore, must be between Naturalism and Supernaturalism.

3

THE CARDINAL DIFFICULTY
OF NATURALISM

*We cannot have it both ways, and no sneers at the
limitations of logic . . . amend the dilemma.*

I. A. RICHARDS, *PRINCIPLES OF LITERARY
CRITICISM*, CHAP. XXV.

IF NATURALISM IS true, every finite thing or event must be (in principle) explicable in terms of the Total System. I say 'explicable *in principle*' because of course we are not going to demand that naturalists, at
any given moment, should have found the detailed explanation of every
phenomenon. Obviously many things will only be explained when the
sciences have made further progress. But if Naturalism is to be accepted
we have a right to demand that every single thing should be such that we
see, in general, how it could be explained in terms of the Total System.
If any one thing exists which is of such a kind that we see in advance the
impossibility of ever giving it *that kind* of explanation, then Naturalism
would be in ruins. If necessities of thought force us to allow to any one
thing any degree of independence from the Total System—if any one
thing makes good a claim to be on its own, to be something more than an
expression of the character of Nature as a whole—then we have abandoned Naturalism. For by Naturalism we mean the doctrine that only

Nature—the whole interlocked system—exists. And if that were true, every thing and event would, if we knew enough, be explicable without remainder (no *heel-taps*) as a necessary product of the system. The whole system being what it is, it ought to be a contradiction in terms if you were not reading this book at the moment; and, conversely, the only cause why you are reading it ought to be that the whole system, at such and such a place and hour, was bound to take that course.

One threat against strict Naturalism has recently been launched on which I myself will base no argument, but which it will be well to notice. The older scientists believed that the smallest particles of matter moved according to strict laws: in other words, that the movements of each particle were 'interlocked' with the total system of Nature. Some modern scientists seem to think—if I understand them—that this is not so. They seem to think that the individual unit of matter (it would be rash to call it any longer a 'particle') moves in an indeterminate or random fashion; moves, in fact, 'on its own' or 'of its own accord'. The regularity which we observe in the movements of the smallest visible bodies is explained by the fact that each of these contains millions of units and that the law of averages therefore levels out the idiosyncrasies of the individual unit's behaviour. The movement of one unit is incalculable, just as the result of tossing a coin once is incalculable: the majority movement of a billion units can however be predicted, just as, if you tossed a coin a billion times, you could predict a nearly equal number of heads and tails. Now it will be noticed that if this theory is true we have really admitted something other than Nature. If the movements of the individual units are events 'on their own', events which do not interlock with all other events, then these movements are not part of Nature. It would be, indeed, too great a shock to our habits to describe them as *super*-natural. I think we should have to call them *sub*-natural. But all our confidence that Nature has no doors, and no reality outside herself for doors to open on, would have disappeared. There is apparently *something* outside her, the Subnatural; it is indeed from this Subnatural that all events and all 'bodies' are, as it were, fed into her. And clearly if she thus has a back door opening on the Subnatural, it is quite on the cards that she may also have a front door opening on the Supernatural—and events might be fed into her at that door too.

I have mentioned this theory because it puts in a fairly vivid light certain conceptions which we shall have to use later on. But I am not, for my own part, assuming its truth. Those who like myself have had a philosophical rather than a scientific education find it almost impossible to believe that the scientists really mean what they seem to be saying. I cannot help thinking they mean no more than that the movements of individual units are permanently incalculable *to us*, not that they are in themselves random and lawless. And even if they mean the latter, a layman can hardly feel any certainty that some new scientific development may not tomorrow abolish this whole idea of a lawless Subnature. For it is the glory of science to progress. I therefore turn willingly to other ground.

It is clear that everything we know, beyond our own immediate sensations, is inferred from those sensations. I do not mean that we begin as children, by regarding our sensations as 'evidence' and thence arguing consciously to the existence of space, matter, and other people. I mean that if, after we are old enough to understand the question, our confidence in the existence of anything else (say, the solar system or the Spanish Armada) is challenged, our argument in defence of it will have to take the form of inferences from our immediate sensations. Put in its most general form the inference would run, 'Since I am presented with colours, sounds, shapes, pleasures and pains which I cannot perfectly predict or control, and since the more I investigate them the more regular their behaviour appears, therefore there must exist something other than myself and it must be systematic'. Inside this very general inference, all sorts of special trains of inference lead us to more detailed conclusions. We infer Evolution from fossils: we infer the existence of our own brains from what we find inside the skulls of other creatures like ourselves in the dissecting room.

All possible knowledge, then, depends on the validity of reasoning. If the feeling of certainty which we express by words like *must be* and *therefore* and *since* is a real perception of how things outside our own minds really 'must' be, well and good. But if this certainty is merely a feeling *in* our own minds and not a genuine insight into realities beyond them—if it merely represents the way our minds happen to work—then we can have no knowledge. Unless human reasoning is valid no science can be true.

It follows that no account of the universe can be true unless that account leaves it possible for our thinking to be a real insight. A theory which explained everything else in the whole universe but which made it impossible to believe that our thinking was valid, would be utterly out of court. For that theory would itself have been reached by thinking, and if thinking is not valid that theory would, of course, be itself demolished.

It would have destroyed its own credentials. It would be an argument which proved that no argument was sound—a proof that there are no such things as proofs—which is nonsense.

Thus a strict materialism refutes itself for the reason given long ago by Professor Haldane: 'If my mental processes are determined wholly by the motions of atoms in my brain, I have no reason to suppose that my beliefs are true . . . and hence I have no reason for supposing my brain to be composed of atoms.' (*Possible Worlds*, p. 209)

But Naturalism, even if it is not purely materialistic, seems to me to involve the same difficulty, though in a somewhat less obvious form. It discredits our processes of reasoning or at least reduces their credit to such a humble level that it can no longer support Naturalism itself.

The easiest way of exhibiting this is to notice the two senses of the word *because*. We can say, 'Grandfather is ill today *because* he ate lobster yesterday.' We can also say, 'Grandfather must be ill today *because* he hasn't got up yet (and we know he is an invariably early riser when he is well).' In the first sentence *because* indicates the relation of Cause and Effect: The eating made him ill. In the second, it indicates the relation of what logicians call Ground and Consequent. The old man's late rising is not the cause of his disorder but the reason why we believe him to be disordered. There is a similar difference between 'He cried out *because* it hurt him' (Cause and Effect) and 'It must have hurt him *because* he cried out' (Ground and Consequent). We are especially familiar with the Ground and Consequent *because* in mathematical reasoning: 'A = C *because*, as we have already proved, they are both equal to B.'

The one indicates a dynamic connection between events or 'states of affairs'; the other, a logical relation between beliefs or assertions.

Now a train of reasoning has no value as a means of finding truth unless each step in it is connected with what went before in the Ground-Consequent relation. If our B does not follow logically from our A, we think in vain. If what we think at the end of our reasoning is to be true, the correct answer to the question, 'Why do you think this?' must begin with the Ground-Consequent *because*.

On the other hand, every event in Nature must be connected with previous events in the Cause and Effect relation. But our acts of thinking are events. Therefore the true answer to 'Why do you think this?' must begin with the Cause-Effect *because*.

Unless our conclusion is the logical consequent from a ground it will be worthless and could be true only by a fluke. Unless it is the effect of a cause, it cannot occur at all. It looks therefore, as if, in order for a train of thought to have any value, these two systems of connection must apply simultaneously to the same series of mental acts.

But unfortunately the two systems are wholly distinct. To be caused is not to be proved. Wishful thinkings, prejudices, and the delusions of madness, are all caused, but they are ungrounded. Indeed to be caused is so different from being proved that we behave in disputation as if they were mutually exclusive. The mere existence of causes for a belief is popularly treated as raising a presumption that it is groundless, and the most popular way of discrediting a person's opinions is to explain them causally—'You say that *because* (Cause and Effect) you are a capitalist, or a hypochondriac, or a mere man, or only a woman'. The implication is that if causes fully account for a belief, then, since causes work inevitably, the belief would have had to arise whether it had grounds or not. We need not, it is felt, consider grounds for something which can be fully explained without them.

But even if grounds do exist, what exactly have they got to do with the actual occurrence of the belief as a psychological event? If it is an event it must be caused. It must in fact be simply one link in a causal chain which stretches back to the beginning and forward to the end of time. How could such a trifle as lack of logical grounds prevent the belief's occurrence or how could the existence of grounds promote it?

There seems to be only one possible answer. We must say that just as one way in which a mental event causes a subsequent mental event is by Association (when I think of parsnips I think of my first school), so another way in which it can cause it, is simply by being a ground for it. For then being a cause and being a proof would coincide.

But this, as it stands, is clearly untrue. We know by experience that a thought does not necessarily cause all, or even any, of the thoughts which logically stand to it as Consequents to Ground. We should be in a pretty pickle if we could never think 'This is glass' without drawing all the inferences which could be drawn. It is impossible to draw them all; quite often we draw none. We must therefore amend our suggested law. One thought can cause another not by *being*, but by being *seen to be*, a ground for it.

If you distrust the sensory metaphor in *seen*, you may substitute *apprehended* or *grasped* or simply *known*. It makes little difference for all these words recall us to what thinking really is. Acts of thinking are no doubt events; but they are a very special sort of events. They are 'about' something other than themselves and can be true or false. Events in general are not 'about' anything and cannot be true or false. (To say 'these events, or facts are false' means of course that someone's account of them is false). Hence acts of inference can, and must, be considered in two different lights. On the one hand they are subjective events, items in somebody's psychological history. On the other hand, they are insights into, or knowings of, something other than themselves. What from the first point of view is the psychological transition from thought A to thought B, at some particular moment in some particular mind, is, from the thinker's point of view a perception of an implication (if A, then B). When we are adopting the psychological point of view we may use the past tense. 'B *followed* A in my thoughts.' But when we assert the implication we always use the present—'B *follows* from A'. If it ever 'follows from' in the logical sense, it does so always. And we cannot possibly reject the second point of view as a subjective illusion without discrediting all human knowledge. For we can know nothing, beyond our own sensations at the moment unless the act of inference is the real insight that it claims to be.

But it can be this only on certain terms. An act of knowing must be determined, in a sense, solely by what is known; we must know it to be thus solely because it *is* thus. That is what knowing means. You may call this a Cause and Effect *because*, and call 'being known' a mode of causation if you like. But it is a unique mode. The act of knowing has no doubt various conditions, without which it could not occur: attention, and the states of will and health which this presupposes. But its positive character must be determined by the truth it knows. If it were totally explicable from other sources it would cease to be knowledge, just as (to use the sensory parallel) the ringing in my ears ceases to be what we mean by 'hearing' if it can be fully explained from causes other than a noise in the outer world—such as, say, the *tinnitus* produced by a bad cold. If what seems an act of knowledge is partially explicable from other sources, then the knowing (properly so called) in it is just what they leave over, just what demands, for its explanation, the thing known, as real hearing is what is left after you have discounted the *tinnitus*. Any thing which professes to explain our reasoning fully without introducing an act of knowing thus solely determined by what is known, is really a theory that there is no reasoning.

But this, as it seems to me, is what Naturalism is bound to do. It offers what professes to be a full account of our mental behaviour; but this account, on inspection, leaves no room for the acts of knowing or insight on which the whole value of our thinking, as a means to truth, depends.

It is agreed on all hands that reason, and even sentience, and life itself are late comers in Nature. If there is nothing but Nature, therefore, reason must have come into existence by a historical process. And of course, for the Naturalist, this process was not designed to produce a mental behaviour that can find truth. There was no Designer; and indeed, until there were thinkers, there was no truth or falsehood. The type of mental behaviour we now call rational thinking or inference must therefore have been 'evolved' by natural selection, by the gradual weeding out of types less fitted to survive.

Once, then, our thoughts were not rational. That is, all our thoughts once were, as many of our thoughts still are, merely subjective events, not apprehensions of objective truth. Those which had a cause external to ourselves at all were (like our pains) responses to stimuli. Now natural selection could operate only by eliminating responses that were biologically hurtful and multiplying those which tended to survival. But it is not conceivable that any improvement of responses could ever turn them into acts of insight, or even remotely tend to do so. The relation between response and stimulus is utterly different from that between knowledge and the truth known. Our physical vision is a far more useful response to light than that of the cruder organisms which have only a photosensitive spot. But neither this improvement nor any possible improvements we can suppose could bring it an inch nearer to being a knowledge of light. It is admittedly something without which we could not have had that knowledge. But the knowledge is achieved by experiments and inferences from them, not by refinement of the response. It is not men with specially good eyes who know about light, but men who have studied the relevant sciences. In the same way our psychological responses to our environment—our curiosities, aversions, delights, expectations—could be indefinitely improved (from the biological point of view) without becoming anything more than responses. Such perfection of the non-rational responses, far from amounting to their conversion into valid inferences, might be conceived as a different method of achieving survival—an alternative to reason. A conditioning which secured that we never felt delight except in the useful nor aversion save from the dangerous, and that the degrees of both were exquisitely proportional to the degree of real utility or danger in the object, might serve us as well as reason or in some circumstances better.

Besides natural selection there is, however, experience—experience originally individual but handed on by tradition and instruction. It might be held that this, in the course of millennia, could conjure the mental behaviour we call reason—in other words, the practice of inference—out of a mental behaviour which was originally not rational. Repeated experiences of finding fire (or the remains of fire) where he had seen smoke would condition a man to expect fire whenever he saw smoke. This expectation, expressed in the form 'If smoke, then fire' becomes what we call inference. Have all our inferences originated in that way?

But if they did they are all invalid inferences. Such a process will no doubt produce expectation. It will train men to expect fire when they see smoke in just the same way as it trained them to expect that all swans would be white (until they saw a black one) or that water would always boil at 212° (until someone tried a picnic on a mountain). Such expectations are not inferences and need not be true. The assumption that things which have been conjoined in the past will always be conjoined in the future is the guiding principle not of rational but of animal behaviour. Reason comes in precisely when you make the inference 'Since always conjoined, therefore probably connected' and go on to attempt the discovery of the connection. When you have discovered what smoke is you may then be able to replace the mere expectation of fire by a genuine inference. Till this is done reason recognises the expectation as a mere expectation. Where this does not need to be done—that is, where the inference depends on an axiom—we do not appeal to past experience at all. My belief that things which are equal to the same thing are equal to one another is not at all based on the fact that I have never caught them behaving otherwise. I see that it 'must' be so. That some people nowadays call axioms tautologies seems to me irrelevant. It is by means of such 'tautologies' that we advance from knowing less to knowing more. And to call them tautologies is another way of saying that they are completely and certainly known. To see fully that A implies B does (once you have seen it) involve the admission that the assertion of A and the assertion of B are at bottom in the same assertion. The degree to which any true proportion is a tautology depends on the degree of your insight into it. $9 \times 7 = 63$ is a tautology to the perfect arithmetician, but not to the child learning its tables nor to the primitive calculator who reached it, perhaps, by adding seven nines together. If Nature is a totally interlocked system, then every true statement about her (e.g. there was a hot summer in 1959) would be a tautology to an intelligence that could grasp that system in its entirety. 'God is love' may be a tautology to the seraphim; not to men.

'But', it will be said, 'it is incontestable that we do in fact reach truths by inferences'. Certainly. The Naturalist and I both admit this. We could not discuss anything unless we did. The difference I am submitting is that he gives, and I do not, a history of the evolution of reason which is inconsistent with the claims that he and I both have to make for inference as we actually practise it. For his history is, and from the nature of the case can only be, an account, in Cause and Effect terms, of how people came to think the way they do. And this of course leaves in the air the quite different question of how they could possibly be justified in so thinking. This imposes on him the very embarrassing task of trying to show how the evolutionary product which he has described could also be a power of 'seeing' truths.

But the very attempt is absurd. This is best seen if we consider the humblest and almost the most despairing form in which it could be made. The Naturalist might say, 'Well, perhaps we cannot exactly see—not yet—how natural selection would turn sub-rational mental behaviour into inferences that reach truth. But we are certain that this in fact has happened. For natural selection is bound to preserve and increase useful behaviour. And we also find that our habits of inference are in fact useful. And if they are useful they must reach truth'. But notice what we are doing. Inference itself is on trial: that is, the Naturalist has given an account of what we thought to be our inferences which suggests that they are not real insights at all. We, and he, want to be reassured. And the reassurance turns out to be one more inference (if useful, then true)—as if this inference were not, once we accept his evolutionary picture, under the same suspicion as all the rest. If the value of our reasoning is in doubt, you cannot try to establish it by reasoning. If, as I said above, a proof that there are no proofs is nonsensical, so is a proof that there are proofs. Reason is our starting point. There can be no question either of attacking or defending it. If by treating it as a mere phenomenon you put yourself outside it, there is then no way, except by begging the question, of getting inside again.

A still humbler position remains. You may, if you like, give up all claim to truth. You may say simply 'Our way of thinking is useful'—without adding, even under your breath, 'and therefore true'. It enables us to set a bone and build a bridge and make a Sputnik. And that is good enough. The old, high pretensions of reason must be given up. It is a behaviour evolved entirely as an aid to practice. That is why, when we use it simply for practice, we get along pretty well; but when we fly off into speculation and try to get general views of 'reality' we end in the endless, useless, and probably merely verbal, disputes of the philosopher. We will be humbler in future. Goodbye to all that. No more theology, no more ontology, no more metaphysics . . .

But then, equally, no more Naturalism. For of course Naturalism is a prime specimen of that towering speculation, discovered from practice and going far beyond experience, which is now being condemned. Nature is not an object that can be presented either to the senses or the imagination. It can be reached only by the most remote inferences. Or not reached, merely approached. It is the hoped for, the assumed, unification in a single interlocked system of all the things inferred from our scientific experiments. More than that, the Naturalist, not content to assert this, goes on to the sweeping negative assertion. 'There is nothing except this'—an assertion surely, as remote from practice, experience, and any conceivable verification as has ever been made since men began to use their reason speculatively. Yet on the present view, the very first step into such a use was an abuse, the perversion of a faculty merely practical, and the source of all chimeras.

On these terms the Theist's position must be a chimera nearly as outrageous as the Naturalist's. (Nearly, not quite; it abstains from the crowning audacity of a huge negative). But the Theist need not, and does not, grant these terms. He is not committed to the view that reason is a comparatively recent development moulded by a process of selection which can select only the biologically useful. For him, reason—the reason of God—is older than Nature, and from it the orderliness of Nature, which alone enables us to know her, is derived. For him, the human mind in the act of knowing is illuminated by the Divine reason. It is set free, in the measure required, from the huge nexus of non-rational causation; free from this to be determined by the truth known. And the preliminary processes within Nature which led up to this liberation, if there were any, were designed to do so.

To call the act of knowing—the act, not of remembering that something was so in the past, but of 'seeing' that it must be so always and in any possible world—to call this act 'supernatural', is some violence to our ordinary linguistic usage. But of course we do not mean by this that it is spooky, or sensational, or even (in any religious sense) 'spiritual'. We mean only that it 'won't fit in'; that such an act, to be what it claims to be—and if it is not, all our thinking is discredited—cannot be merely the exhibition at a particular place and time of that total, and largely mindless, system of events called 'Nature'. It must break sufficiently free from that universal chain in order to be determined by what it knows.

It is of some importance here to make sure that, if vaguely spatial imagery intrudes (and in many minds it certainly will), it should not be of the wrong kind. We had better not envisage our acts of reason as something 'above' or 'behind' or 'beyond' Nature. Rather 'this side of Nature'—if you must picture spatially, picture them between us and her. It is by inferences that we build up the idea of Nature at all. Reason is given before Nature and on reason our concept of Nature depends. Our acts of inference are prior to our picture of Nature almost as the telephone is prior to the friend's voice we hear by it. When we try to fit these acts into the picture of Nature we fail. The item which we put into that picture and label 'Reason' always turns out to be somehow different from the reason we ourselves are enjoying and exercising while we put it in. The description we have to give of thought as an evolutionary phenomenon always makes a tacit exception in favour of the thinking which we ourselves perform at that moment. For the one can only, like any other particular feat, exhibit, at particular moments in particular consciousnesses, the general and for the most part non-rational working of the whole interlocked system. The other, our present act, claims and must claim, to be an act of insight, a knowledge sufficiently free from non-rational causation to be determined (positively) only by the truth it knows. But the imagined thinking which we put into the picture depends—because our whole idea of Nature depends—on the thinking we are actually doing, not vice versa. This is the prime reality, on which the attribution of reality to anything else rests. If it won't fit into Nature, we can't help it. We will certainly not, on that account, give it up. If we do, we should be giving up Nature too.

4

NATURE AND SUPERNATURE

*Throughout the long tradition of European thought it
has been said, not by everyone but by most people, or
at any rate by most of those who have proved that they
have a right to be heard, that Nature, though it is a
thing that really exists, is not a thing that exists in itself
or in its own right, but a thing which depends for its
existence upon something else.*

R. G. COLLINGWOOD, *THE IDEA OF
NATURE*, III III.

IF OUR ARGUMENT has been sound, acts of reasoning are not interlocked with the total interlocking system of Nature as all its other items
are interlocked with one another. They are connected with it in a different way; as the understanding of a machine is certainly connected with
the machine but not in the way the parts of the machine are connected
with each other. The knowledge of a thing is not one of the thing's parts.
In this sense something beyond Nature operates whenever we reason. I
am not maintaining that consciousness as a whole must necessarily be put
in the same position. Pleasures, pains, fears, hopes, affections and mental images need not. No absurdity would follow from regarding them
as parts of Nature. The distinction we have to make is not one between
'mind' and 'matter', much less between 'soul' and 'body' (hard words, all

322

four of them) but between Reason and Nature: the frontier coming not where the 'outer world' ends and what I should ordinarily call 'myself' begins, but between reason and the whole mass of non-rational events whether physical or psychological.

At that frontier we find a great deal of traffic but it is all one-way traffic. It is a matter of daily experience that rational thoughts induce and enable us to alter the course of Nature—of physical nature when we use mathematics to build bridges, or of psychological nature when we apply arguments to alter our own emotions. We succeed in modifying physical nature more often and more completely than we succeed in modifying psychological nature, but we do at least a little to both. On the other hand, Nature is quite powerless to produce rational thought: not that she never modifies our thinking but that the moment she does so, it ceases (for that very reason) to be rational. For, as we have seen, a train of thought loses all rational credentials as soon as it can be shown to be wholly the result of non-rational causes. When Nature, so to speak, attempts to do things to rational thoughts she only succeeds in killing them. That is the peculiar state of affairs at the frontier. Nature can only raid Reason to kill; but Reason can invade Nature to take prisoners and even to colonise. Every object you see before you at this moment—the walls, ceiling, and furniture, the book, your own washed hands and cut fingernails, bears witness to the colonisation of Nature by Reason: for none of this matter would have been in these states if Nature had had her way. And if you are attending to my argument as closely as I hope, that attention also results from habits which Reason has imposed on the natural ramblings of consciousness. If, on the other hand, a toothache or an anxiety is at this very moment preventing you from attending, then Nature is indeed interfering with your consciousness: but not to produce some new variety of reasoning, only (as far as in her lies) to suspend Reason altogether.

In other words the relation between Reason and Nature is what some people call an Unsymmetrical Relation. Brotherhood is a symmetrical relation because if A is the brother of B, B is the brother of A. Father-and-son is an unsymmetrical relation because if A is the father of B, B is *not* the father of A. The relation between Reason and Nature is of this kind. Reason is not related to Nature as Nature is related to Reason.

I am only too well aware how shocking those who have been brought up to Naturalism will find the picture which begins to show itself. It is, frankly, a picture in which Nature (at any rate on the surface of our own planet) is perforated or pock-marked all over by little orifices at each of which something of a different kind from herself—namely reason—can do things to her. I can only beg you, before you throw the book away, to consider seriously whether your instinctive repugnance to such a conception is really rational, or whether it is only emotional or aesthetic. I know that the hankering for a universe which is all of a piece, and in which everything is the same sort of thing as everything else—a continuity, a seamless web, a democratic universe—is very deep-seated in the modern heart: in mine, no less than in yours. But have we any real assurance that things are like that? Are we mistaking for an intrinsic probability what is really a human desire for tidiness and harmony? Bacon warned us long ago that 'the human understanding is of its own nature prone to suppose the existence of more order and regularity in the world than it finds. And though there be many things which are singular and unmatched, yet it devises for them parallels and conjugates and relatives which do not exist. Hence the fiction that all celestial bodies move in perfect circles' (*Novum Organum*, 1, 45). I think Bacon was right. Science itself has already made reality appear less homogeneous than we expected it to be: Newtonian atomism was much more the sort of thing we expected (and desired) than Quantum physics.

If you can, even for the moment, endure the suggested picture of Nature, let us now consider the other factor—the Reasons, or instances of Reason, which attack her. We have seen that rational thought is not part of the system of Nature. Within each man there must be an area (however small) of activity which is outside or independent of her. In relation to Nature, rational thought goes on 'of its own accord' or exists 'on its own'. It does not follow that rational thought exists *absolutely* on its own. It might be independent of Nature by being dependent on something else. For it is not dependence simply but dependence on the non-rational which undermines the credentials of thought. One man's reason has been led to see things by the aid of another man's reason, and is none the worse for that. It is thus still an open question whether each man's reason exists absolutely on its own or whether it is the result of some (rational) cause—in fact, of some other Reason. That other Reason might conceivably be found to depend on a third, and so on; it would not matter how far this process was carried provided you found Reason coming from Reason at each stage. It is only when you are asked to believe in Reason coming from non-reason that you must cry Halt, for, if you don't, all thought is discredited. It is therefore obvious that sooner or later you must admit a Reason which exists absolutely on its own. The problem is whether you or I can be such a self-existent Reason.

This question almost answers itself the moment we remember what existence 'on one's own' means. It means that kind of existence which Naturalists attribute to 'the whole show' and Supernaturalists attribute to God. For instance, what exists on its own must have existed from all eternity; for if anything else could make it begin to exist then it would not exist on its own but because of something else. It must also exist incessantly: that is, it cannot cease to exist and then begin again. For having once ceased to be, it obviously could not recall itself to existence, and if anything else recalled it it would then be a dependent being. Now it is clear that my Reason has grown up gradually since my birth and is interrupted for several hours each night. I therefore cannot be that eternal self-existent Reason which neither slumbers nor sleeps. Yet if any thought is valid, such a Reason must exist and must be the source of my own imperfect and intermittent rationality. Human minds, then, are not the only supernatural entities that exist. They do not come from nowhere. Each has come into Nature from Supernature: each has its tap-root in an eternal, self-existent, rational Being, whom we call God. Each is an offshoot, or spearhead, or incursion of that Supernatural reality into Nature.

Some people may here raise the following question. If Reason is sometimes present in my mind and sometimes not, then, instead of saying that 'I' am a product of eternal Reason, would it not be wiser to say simply that eternal Reason itself occasionally works through my organism, leaving me a merely natural being? A wire does not become something other than a wire because an electric current has passed through it. But to talk thus is, in my opinion, to forget what reasoning is like. It is not an object which knocks against us, nor even a sensation which we feel. Reasoning doesn't 'happen to' us: we *do* it. Every train of thought is accompanied by what Kant called 'the *I think*'. The traditional doctrine that I am a creature to whom God has given reason but who is distinct from God seems to me much more philosophical than the theory that what appears to be my thinking is only God's thinking through me. On the latter view it is very difficult to explain what happens when I think correctly but reach a false conclusion because I have been misinformed about facts. Why God—who presumably knows the real facts—should be at the pains to think one of His perfectly rational thoughts through a mind in which it is bound to produce error, I do not understand. Nor indeed do I understand why, if all 'my' valid thinking is really God's, He should either Himself mistake it for mine or cause me to mistake it for mine. It seems much more likely that human thought is not God's but God-kindled.

I must hasten, however, to add that this is a book about miracles, not about everything. I am attempting no full doctrine of man:[1] and I am not in the least trying to smuggle in an argument for the 'immortality of the soul'. The earliest Christian documents give a casual and unemphatic assent to the belief that the supernatural part of a man survives the death of the natural organism. But they are very little interested in the matter. What they are intensely interested in is the restoration or 'resurrection' of the whole composite creature by a miraculous divine act: and until we have come to some conclusion about miracles in general we shall certainly not discuss that. At this stage the supernatural element in man concerns us solely as evidence that something beyond Nature exists. The dignity and destiny of man have, at present, nothing to do with the argument. We are interested in man only because his rationality is the little tell-tale rift in Nature which shows that there is something beyond or behind her.

In a pond whose surface was completely covered with scum and floating vegetation, there might be a few water-lilies. And you might of course be interested in them for their beauty. But you might also be interested in them because from their structure you could deduce that they had stalks underneath which went down to roots in the bottom. The Naturalist thinks that the pond (Nature—the great event in space and time) is of an indefinite depth—that there is nothing but water however far you go down. My claim is that some of the things on the surface (i.e. in our experience) show the contrary. These things (rational minds) reveal, on inspection, that they at least are not floating but attached by stalks to the bottom. Therefore the pond has a bottom. It is not pond, pond for ever. Go deep enough and you will come to something that is not pond—to mud and earth and then to rock and finally the whole bulk of Earth and the subterranean fire.

At this point it is tempting to try whether Naturalism cannot still be saved. I pointed out in Chapter II that one could remain a Naturalist and yet believe in a certain kind of God—a cosmic consciousness to which 'the whole show' somehow gave rise: what we might call an *Emergent*

---
[1] See Appendix A.

God. Would not an Emergent God give us all we need? Is it really necessary to bring in a *super*-natural God, distinct from and outside the whole interlocked system? (Notice, Modern Reader, how your spirits rise— how much more at home you would feel with an emergent, than with a transcendent, God—how much less primitive, repugnant, and naïf the emergent conception seems to you. For by that, as you will see later, there hangs a tale).

But I am afraid it will not do. It is, of course, possible to suppose that when all the atoms of the universe got into a certain relation (which they were bound to get into sooner or later) they would give rise to a universal consciousness. And it might have thoughts. And it might cause those thoughts to pass through our minds. But unfortunately its own thoughts, on this supposition, would be the product of non-rational causes and therefore, by the rule which we use daily, they would have no validity. This cosmic mind would be, just as much as our own minds, the product of mindless Nature. We have not escaped from the difficulty, we have only put it a stage further back. The cosmic mind will help us only if we put it at the beginning, if we suppose it to be, not the product of the total system, but the basic, original, self-existent Fact which exists in its own right. But to admit *that* sort of cosmic mind is to admit a God outside Nature, a transcendent and supernatural God. This route, which looked like offering an escape, really leads us round again to the place we started from.

There is, then, a God who is not a part of Nature. But nothing has yet been said to show that He must have created her. Might God and Nature be both self-existent and totally independent of each other? If you thought they were you would be a Dualist and would hold a view which I consider manlier and more reasonable than any form of Naturalism. You might be many worse things than a Dualist, but I do not think Dualism is true. There is an enormous difficulty in conceiving two things which simply co-exist and have no other relation. If this difficulty sometimes escapes our notice, that is because we are the victims of picture-thinking. We really imagine them side by side in some kind of space. But of course if they were both in a common space, or a common time, or in any kind of common medium whatever, they would both be parts of a system, in fact of a 'Nature'. Even if we succeed in eliminating such pictures, the mere fact of our trying to think of them together slurs over the real difficulty because, for that moment anyway, our own mind is the common medium. If there can be such a thing as sheer 'otherness', if things can co-exist and no more, it is at any rate a conception which my mind cannot form. And in the present instance it seems specially gratuitous to try to form it, for we already know that God and Nature have come into a certain relation. They have, at the very least, a relation—almost, in one sense, a common frontier—in every human mind.

The relations which arise at that frontier are indeed of a most complicated and intimate sort. That spearhead of the Supernatural which I call my reason links up with all my natural contents—my sensations, emotions, and the like—so completely that I call the mixture by the single word 'me'. Again, there is what I have called the unsymmetrical character of the frontier relations. When the physical state of the brain dominates my thinking, it produces only disorder. But my brain does not become any less a brain when it is dominated by Reason: nor do my emotions and sensations become any the less emotions and sensations. Reason saves and strengthens my whole system, psychological and physical, whereas that whole system, by rebelling against Reason, destroys both Reason and itself. The military metaphor of a spearhead was apparently ill-chosen. The supernatural Reason enters my natural being not like a weapon—more like a beam of light which illuminates or a principle of organisation which unifies and develops. Our whole picture of Nature being 'invaded' (as if by a foreign enemy) was wrong. When we actually examine one of these invasions it looks much more like the arrival of a king among his own subjects or a mahout visiting his own elephant. The elephant may run amuck, Nature may be rebellious. But from observing what happens when Nature obeys it is almost impossible not to conclude that it is her very 'nature' to be a subject. All happens *as if* she had been designed for that very role.

To believe that Nature produced God, or even the human mind, is, as we have seen, absurd. To believe that the two are both independently self-existent is impossible: at least the attempt to do so leaves me unable to say that I am thinking of anything at all. It is true that Dualism has a certain theological attraction; it seems to make the problem of evil easier. But if we cannot, in fact, think Dualism out to the end, this attractive promise can never be kept, and I think there are better solutions of the problem of evil. There remains, then, the belief that God created Nature. This at once supplies a relation between them and gets rid of the difficulty of sheer 'otherness'. This also fits in with the observed frontier situation, in which everything looks as if Nature were not resisting an alien invader but rebelling against a lawful sovereign. This, and perhaps this alone, fits in with the fact that Nature, though not apparently intelligent, is intelligible—that events in the remotest parts of space appear to obey the laws of rational thought. Even the act of creation itself presents none of the intolerable difficulties which seem to meet us on every other hypothesis. There is in our own human minds something that bears a faint resemblance to it. We can imagine: that is, we can cause to exist the mental pictures of material objects, and even human characters, and events. We fall short of creation in two ways. In the first place we can only re-combine elements borrowed from the real universe: no one can imagine a new primary colour or a sixth sense. In the second place, what we imagine exists only for our own consciousness—though we can, by words, induce other people to build for themselves pictures in their own minds which may be roughly similar to it. We should have to attribute to God the power both of producing the basic elements, of inventing not only colours but colour itself, the senses themselves, space, time and matter themselves, and also of imposing what He has invented on created minds. This seems to me no intolerable assumption. It is certainly easier than the idea of God and Nature as wholly unrelated entities, and far easier than the idea of Nature producing valid thought.

I do not maintain that God's creation of Nature can be proved as rigorously as God's existence, but it seems to me overwhelmingly probable, so probable that no one who approached the question with an open mind would very seriously entertain any other hypothesis. In fact one seldom meets people who have grasped the existence of a supernatural God and yet deny that He is the Creator. All the evidence we have points in that direction, and difficulties spring up on every side if we try to believe otherwise. No philosophical theory which I have yet come across is a radical improvement on the words of Genesis, that 'In the beginning God made Heaven and Earth'. I say 'radical' improvement, because the story in Genesis—as St Jerome said long ago—is told in the manner 'of a popular poet', or as we should say, in the form of folk tale. But if you compare it with the creation legends of other peoples—with all these delightful absurdities in which giants to be cut up and floods to be dried up are made to exist *before* creation—the depth and originality of this Hebrew folk tale will soon be apparent. The idea of *creation* in the rigorous sense of the word is there fully grasped.

5

A FURTHER DIFFICULTY
IN NATURALISM

*Even as rigorous a determinist as Karl Marx, who at
times described the social behaviour of the bourgeoisie in
terms which suggested a problem in social physics, could
subject it at other times to a withering scorn which only
the presupposition of moral responsibility could justify.*

R. NIEBUHR, *AN INTERPRETATION OF CHRISTIAN
ETHICS,* CHAP. III.

SOME PEOPLE REGARD logical thinking as the deadest and driest of
our activities and may therefore be repelled by the privileged position I
gave it in the last chapter. But logical thinking—Reasoning—had to be
the pivot of the argument because, of all the claims which the human mind
puts forward, the claim of Reasoning to be valid is the only one which
the Naturalist cannot deny without (philosophically speaking) cutting his
own throat. You cannot, as we saw, prove that there are no proofs. But you
can if you wish regard all human ideals as illusions and all human loves as
biological by-products. That is, you can do so without running into flat
self-contradiction and nonsense. Whether you can do so without extreme
unplausibility—without accepting a picture of things which no one really
believes—is another matter.

Besides reasoning about matters of fact, men also make moral judge-ments—'I ought to do this'—'I ought not to do that'—'This is good'—'That is evil.' Two views have been held about moral judgements. Some people think that when we make them we are not using our Reason, but are employing some different power. Other people think that we make them by our Reason. I myself hold this second view. That is, I believe that the primary moral principles on which all others depend are ration-ally perceived. We 'just see' that there is no reason why my neighbour's happiness should be sacrificed to my own, as we 'just see' that things which are equal to the same thing are equal to one another. If we can-not prove either axiom, that is not because they are irrational but because they are self-evident and all proofs depend on them. Their intrinsic rea-sonableness shines by its own light. It is because all morality is based on such self-evident principles that we say to a man, when we would recall him to right conduct, 'Be reasonable.'

But this is by the way. For our present purpose it does not matter which of these two views you adopt. The important point is to notice that moral judgements raise the same sort of difficulty for Naturalism as any other thoughts. We always assume in discussions about morality, as in all other discussions, that the other man's views are worthless if they can be fully accounted for by some non-moral and non-rational cause. When two men differ about good and evil we soon hear this principle being brought into play. 'He believes in the sanctity of property because he's a millionaire'—'He believes in Pacifism because he's a coward'—'He ap-proves of corporal punishment because he's a sadist.' Such taunts may often be untrue: but the mere fact that they are made by the one side, and hotly rebutted by the other, shows clearly what principle is being used. Neither side doubts that if they were true they would be decisive. No one (in real life) pays attention to any moral judgement which can be shown to spring from non-moral and non-rational causes. The Freudian and the Marxist attack traditional morality precisely on this ground—and with wide success. All men accept the principle.

But, of course, what discredits particular moral judgements must equally discredit moral judgement as a whole. If the fact that men have such ideas as *ought* and *ought not* at all can be fully explained by irrational and non-moral causes, then those ideas are an illusion. The Naturalist is ready to explain how the illusion arose. Chemical conditions produce life. Life, under the influence of natural selection, produces consciousness. Conscious organisms which behave in one way live longer than those which behave in another. Living longer, they are more likely to have offspring. Inheritance, and sometimes teaching as well, pass on their mode of behaviour to their young. Thus in every species a pattern of behaviour is built up. In the human species conscious teaching plays a larger part in building it up, and the tribe further strengthens it by killing individuals who don't conform. They also invent gods who are said to punish departures from it. Thus, in time, there comes to exist a strong human impulse to conform. But since this impulse is often at variance with the other impulses, a mental conflict arises, and the man expresses it by saying 'I want to do A but I ought to do B.'

This account may (or may not) explain why men do in fact make moral judgements. It does not explain how they could be right in making them. It excludes, indeed, the very possibility of their being right. For when men say 'I ought' they certainly think they are saying something, and something true, about the nature of the proposed action, and not merely about their own feelings. But if Naturalism is true, 'I ought' is the same sort of statement as 'I itch' or 'I'm going to be sick.' In real life when a man says 'I ought' we may reply, 'Yes. You're right. That *is* what you ought to do,' or else, 'No. I think you're mistaken.' But in a world of Naturalists (if Naturalists really remembered their philosophy out of school) the only sensible reply would be, 'Oh, are you?' All moral judgements would be statements about the speaker's feelings, mistaken by him for statements about something else (the real moral quality of actions) which does not exist.

Such a doctrine, I have admitted, is not flatly self-contradictory. The Naturalist can, if he chooses, brazen it out. He can say, 'Yes. I quite agree that there is no such thing as wrong and right. I admit that no moral judgement can be "true" or "correct" and, consequently, that no one system of morality can be better or worse than another. All ideas of good and evil are hallucinations—shadows cast on the outer world by the impulses which we have been conditioned to feel.' Indeed many Naturalists are delighted to say this.

But then they must stick to it; and fortunately (though inconsistently) most real Naturalists do not. A moment after they have admitted that good and evil are illusions, you will find them exhorting us to work for posterity, to educate, revolutionise, liquidate, live and die for the good of the human race. A Naturalist like Mr H. G. Wells spent a long life doing so with passionate eloquence and zeal. But surely this is very odd? Just as all the books about spiral nebulae, atoms and cave men would really have led you to suppose that the Naturalists claimed to be able to know something, so all the books in which Naturalists tell us what we ought to do would really make you believe that they thought some ideas of good (their own, for example) to be somehow preferable to others. For they write with indignation like men proclaiming what is good in itself and denouncing what is evil in itself, and not at all like men recording that they personally like mild beer but some people prefer bitter. Yet if the 'oughts' of Mr Wells and, say, Franco are both equally the impulses which Nature has conditioned each to have and both tell us nothing about any objective right or wrong, whence is all the fervour? Do they remember while they are writing thus that when they tell us we 'ought to make a better world' the words 'ought' and 'better' must, on their own showing, refer to an irrationally conditioned impulse which cannot be true or false any more than a vomit or a yawn?

My idea is that sometimes they do forget. That is their glory. Holding a philosophy which excludes humanity, they yet remain human. At the sight of injustice they throw all their Naturalism to the winds and speak like men and like men of genius. They know far better than they think they know. But at other times, I suspect they are trusting in a supposed way of escape from their difficulty.

It works—or *seems* to work—like this. They say to themselves, 'Ah, yes. Morality'—or 'bourgeois morality' or 'conventional morality' or 'traditional morality' or some such addition—'Morality *is* an illusion. But we have found out what modes of behaviour will in fact preserve the human race alive. That is the behaviour we are pressing you to adopt. Pray don't mistake us for moralists. We are under an entirely new management' . . . just as if this would help. It would help only if we grant, firstly, that life is better than death and, secondly, that we ought to care for the lives of our descendants as much as, or more than, for our own. And both these are moral judgements which have, like all others, been explained away by Naturalism. Of course, having been conditioned by Nature in a certain way, we do feel thus about life and about posterity. But the Naturalists have cured us of mistaking these feelings for insights into what we once called 'real value'. Now that I know that my impulse to serve posterity is just the same kind of thing as my fondness for cheese—now that its transcendental pretensions have been exposed for a sham—do you think I shall pay much attention to it? When it happens to be strong (and it has grown considerably weaker since you explained to me its real nature) I suppose I shall obey it. When it is weak, I shall put my money into cheese. There can be no reason for trying to whip up and encourage the one impulse rather than the other. Not now that I know what they both are. The Naturalists must not destroy all my reverence for conscience on Monday and expect to find me still venerating it on Tuesday.

There is no escape along those lines. If we are to continue to make moral judgements (and whatever we say we shall in fact continue) then we must believe that the conscience of man is not a product of Nature. It can be valid only if it is an offshoot of some absolute moral wisdom, a moral wisdom which exists absolutely 'on its own' and is not a product of non-moral, non-rational Nature. As the argument of the last chapter led us to acknowledge a supernatural source for rational thought, so the argument of this leads us to acknowledge a supernatural source for our ideas of good and evil. In other words, we now know something more about God. If you hold that moral judgement is a different thing from Reasoning you will express this new knowledge by saying, 'We now know that God has at least one other attribute than rationality.' If, like me, you hold that moral judgement is a kind of Reasoning, then you will say, 'We now know more about the Divine Reason.'

And with this we are almost ready to begin our main argument. But before doing so it will be well to pause for the consideration of some misgivings or misunderstandings which may have already arisen.

6

ANSWERS TO MISGIVINGS

*For as bats' eyes are to daylight so is our intellectual eye
to those truths which are, in their own nature, the most
obvious of all.*

ARISTOTLE, METAPHYSICS, I (BREVIOR) I.

IT MUST BE clearly understood that the argument so far leads to no
conception of 'souls' or 'spirits' (words I have avoided) floating about in
the realm of Nature with no relation to their environment. Hence we do
not deny—indeed we must welcome—certain considerations which are
often regarded as proofs of Naturalism. We can admit, and even insist,
that Rational Thinking can be shown to be conditioned in its exercise by
a natural object (the brain). It is temporarily impaired by alcohol or a
blow on the head. It wanes as the brain decays and vanishes when the
brain ceases to function. In the same way the moral outlook of a community can be shown to be closely connected with its history, geographi-
cal environment, economic structure, and so forth. The moral ideas of
the individual are equally related to his general situation: it is no accident that parents and schoolmasters so often tell us that they can stand
any vice rather than lying, the lie being the only defensive weapon of the
child. All this, far from presenting us with a difficulty, is exactly what we
should expect.

The rational and moral element in each human mind is a point of force from the Supernatural working its way into Nature, exploiting at each point those conditions which Nature offers, repulsed where the conditions are hopeless and impeded when they are unfavourable. A man's Rational thinking is *just so much* of his share in eternal Reason as the state of his brain allows to become operative: it represents, so to speak, the bargain struck or the frontier fixed between Reason and Nature at that particular point. A nation's moral outlook is just so much of its share in eternal Moral Wisdom as its history, economics etc. lets through. In the same way the voice of the Announcer is just so much of a human voice as the receiving set lets through. Of course it varies with the state of the receiving set, and deteriorates as the set wears out and vanishes altogether if I throw a brick at it. It is conditioned by the apparatus but not originated by it. If it were—if we knew that there was no human being at the microphone—we should not attend to the news. The various and complex conditions under which Reason and Morality appear are the twists and turns of the frontier between Nature and Supernature. That is why, if you wish, you can always ignore Supernature and treat the phenomena purely from the Natural side; just as a man studying on a map the boundaries of Cornwall and Devonshire can always say, 'What you call a bulge in Devonshire is really a dent in Cornwall.' And in a sense you can't refute him. What we call a bulge in Devonshire always *is* a dent in Cornwall. What we call rational thought in a man always involves a state of the brain, in the long run a relation of atoms. But Devonshire is none the less something more than 'where Cornwall ends', and Reason is something more than cerebral biochemistry.

I now turn to another possible misgiving. To some people the great trouble about any argument for the Supernatural is simply the fact that argument should be needed at all. If so stupendous a thing exists, ought it not to be obvious as the sun in the sky? Is it not intolerable, and indeed incredible, that knowledge of the most basic of all Facts should be accessible only by wire-drawn reasonings for which the vast majority of men have neither leisure nor capacity? I have great sympathy with this point of view. But we must notice two things.

When you are looking at a garden from a room upstairs it is obvious (once you think about it) that you are looking through a window. But if it is the garden that interests you, you may look at it for a long time without thinking of the window. When you are reading a book it is obvious (once you attend to it) that you are using your eyes: but unless your eyes begin to hurt you, or the book is a text book on optics, you may read all evening without once thinking of eyes. When we talk we are obviously using language and grammar: and when we try to talk a foreign language we may be painfully aware of the fact. But when we are talking English we don't notice it. When you shout from the top of the stairs, 'I'm coming in half a moment,' you are not usually conscious that you have made the singular *am* agree with the singular *I*. There is indeed a story told about a Redskin who, having learned several other languages, was asked to write a grammar of the language used by his own tribe. He replied, after some thought, that it had no grammar. The grammar he had used all his life had escaped his notice all his life. He knew it (in one sense) so well that (in another sense) he did not know it existed.

All these instances show that the fact which is in one respect the most obvious and primary fact, and through which alone you have access to all the other facts, may be precisely the one that is most easily forgotten—forgotten not because it is so remote or abstruse but because it is so near and so obvious. And that is exactly how the Supernatural has been forgotten. The Naturalists have been engaged in thinking about Nature. They have not attended to the fact that they were *thinking*. The moment one attends to this it is obvious that one's own thinking cannot be merely a natural event, and that therefore something other than Nature exists. The Supernatural is not remote and abstruse: it is a matter of daily and hourly experience, as intimate as breathing. Denial of it depends on a certain absent-mindedness. But this absent-mindedness is in no way surprising. You do not need—indeed you do not wish—to be always thinking about windows when you are looking at gardens or always thinking about eyes when you are reading. In the same way the proper procedure for all limited and particular inquiries is to ignore the fact of your own thinking, and concentrate on the object. It is only when you stand back from particular inquiries and try to form a complete philosophy that you must take it into account. For a complete philosophy must get in *all* the facts. In it you turn away from specialised or truncated thought to total thought: and one of the facts total thought must think about is Thinking itself. There is thus a tendency in the study of Nature to make us forget the most obvious fact of all. And since the sixteenth century, when Science was born, the minds of men have been increasingly turned outward, to know Nature and to master her. They have been increasingly engaged on those specialised inquiries for which truncated thought is the correct method. It is therefore not in the least astonishing that they should have forgotten the evidence for the Supernatural. The deeply ingrained habit of truncated thought—what we call the 'scientific' habit of mind—was indeed certain to lead to Naturalism, unless this tendency were continually corrected from some other source. But no other source was at hand, for during the same period men of science were coming to be metaphysically and theologically uneducated.

That brings me to the second consideration. The state of affairs in which ordinary people can discover the Supernatural only by abstruse reasoning is recent and, by historical standards, abnormal. All over the world, until quite modern times, the direct insight of the mystics and the reasonings of the philosophers percolated to the mass of the people by authority and tradition; they could be received by those who were no great reasoners themselves in the concrete form of myth and ritual and the whole pattern of life. In the conditions produced by a century or so of Naturalism, plain men are being forced to bear burdens which plain men were never expected to bear before. We must get the truth for ourselves or go without it. There may be two explanations for this. It might be that humanity, in rebelling against tradition and authority, has made a ghastly mistake; a mistake which will not be the less fatal because the corruptions of those in authority rendered it very excusable. On the other hand, it may be that the Power which rules our species is at this moment carrying out a daring experiment. Could it be intended that the whole mass of the people should now move forward and occupy for themselves those heights which were once reserved only for the sages? Is the distinction between wise and simple to disappear because all are now expected to become wise? If so, our present blunderings would be but growing pains. But let us make no mistake about our necessities. If we are content to go back and become humble plain men obeying a tradition, well. If we are ready to climb and struggle on till we become sages ourselves, better still. But the man who will neither obey wisdom in others nor adventure for her/himself is fatal. A society where the simple many obey the few seers can live: a society where all were seers could live even more fully. But a society where the mass is still simple and the seers are no longer attended to can achieve only superficiality, baseness, ugliness, and in the end extinction. On or back we must go; to stay here is death.

One other point that may have raised doubt or difficulty should here be dealt with. I have advanced reasons for believing that a supernatural element is present in every rational man. The presence of human rationality in the world is therefore a Miracle by the definition given in Chapter II. On realising this the reader may excusably say, 'Oh, if *that's* all he means by a Miracle . . .' and fling the book away. But I ask him to have patience. Human Reason and Morality have been mentioned not as instances of Miracle (at least, not of the kind of Miracle you wanted to hear about) but as proofs of the Supernatural: not in order to show that Nature ever is invaded but that there is a possible invader. Whether you choose to call the regular and familiar invasion by human Reason a Miracle or not is largely a matter of words. Its regularity—the fact that it regularly enters by the same door, human sexual intercourse—may incline you not to do so. It looks as if it were (so to speak) the very nature of Nature to suffer *this* invasion. But then we might later find that it was the very nature of Nature to suffer Miracles in general. Fortunately the course of our argument will allow us to leave this question of terminology on one side. We are going to be concerned with other invasions of Nature—with what everyone would call Miracles. Our question could, if you liked, be put in the form, 'Does Supernature ever produce particular results in space and time *except* through the instrumentality of human brains acting on human nerves and muscles?'

I have said '*particular* results' because, on our view, Nature as a whole is herself one huge result of the Supernatural: God created her. God pierces her wherever there is a human mind. God presumably maintains her in existence. The question is whether He ever does anything else to her. Does He, besides all this, ever introduce into her events of which it would not be true to say, 'This is simply the working out of the general character which He gave to Nature as a whole in creating her'? Such events are what are popularly called Miracles: and it will be in this sense only that the word Miracle will be used for the rest of the book.

7

A CHAPTER OF RED HERRINGS

Thence came forth Maul, *a giant. This* Maul *did use to spoil young Pilgrims with sophistry.*

BUNYAN

FROM THE ADMISSION that God exists and is the author of Nature, it by no means follows that miracles must, or even can, occur. God Himself might be a being of such a kind that it was contrary to His character to work miracles. Or again, He might have made Nature the sort of thing that cannot be added to, subtracted from, or modified. The case against Miracles accordingly relies on two different grounds. You either think that the character of God excludes them or that the character of Nature excludes them. We will begin with the second which is the more popular ground. In this chapter I shall consider forms of it which are, in my opinion, very superficial—which might even be called misunderstandings or Red Herrings.

The first Red Herring is this. Any day you may hear a man (and not necessarily a disbeliever in God) say of some alleged miracle, 'No. Of course I don't believe that. We know it is contrary to the laws of Nature. People could believe it in olden times because they didn't know the laws of Nature. We know now that it is a scientific impossibility'.

By the 'laws of Nature' such a man means, I think, the observed course of Nature. If he means anything more than that he is not the plain man I take him for but a philosophic Naturalist and will be dealt with in the next chapter. The man I have in view believes that mere experience (and specially those artificially contrived experiences which we call Experiments) can tell us what regularly happens in Nature. And he thinks that what we have discovered excludes the possibility of Miracle. This is a confusion of mind.

Granted that miracles *can* occur, it is, of course, for experience to say whether one has done so on any given occasion. But mere experience, even if prolonged for a million years, cannot tell us whether the thing is possible. Experiment finds out what regularly happens in Nature: the norm or rule to which she works. Those who believe in miracles are not denying that there is such a norm or rule: they are only saying that it can be suspended. A miracle is by definition an exception. How can the discovery of the rule tell you whether, granted a sufficient cause, the rule can be suspended? If we said that the rule was A, then experience might refute us by discovering that it was B. If we said that there was no rule, then experience might refute us by observing that there is. But we are saying neither of these things. We agree that there is a rule and that the rule is B. What has that got to do with the question whether the rule can be suspended? You reply, 'But experience shows that it never has'. We reply, 'Even if that were so, this would not prove that it never can. But does experience show that it never has? The world is full of stories of people who say they have experienced miracles. Perhaps the stories are false: perhaps they are true. But before you can decide on that historical question, you must first (as was pointed out in Chapter 1) discover whether the thing is possible, and if possible, how probable'.

The idea that the progress of science has somehow altered this question is closely bound up with the idea that people 'in olden times' believe in them 'because they didn't know the laws of Nature'. Thus you will hear people say, 'The early Christians believed that Christ was the son of a virgin, but we know that this is a scientific impossibility'. Such people seem to have an idea that belief in miracles arose at a period when men were so ignorant of the course of nature that they did not perceive a miracle to be contrary to it. A moment's thought shows this to be nonsense: and the story of the Virgin Birth is a particularly striking example. When

St Joseph discovered that his fiancée was going to have a baby, he not unnaturally decided to repudiate her. Why? Because he knew just as well as any modern gynaecologist that in the ordinary course of nature women do not have babies unless they have lain with men. No doubt the modern gynaecologist knows several things about birth and begetting which St Joseph did not know. But those things do not concern the main point—that a virgin birth is contrary to the course of nature. And St Joseph obviously knew *that*. In any sense in which it is true to say now, 'The thing is scientifically impossible', he would have said the same: the thing always was, and was always known to be, impossible *unless* the regular processes of nature were, in this particular case, being over-ruled or supplemented by something from beyond nature. When St Joseph finally accepted the view that his fiancée's pregnancy was due not to unchastity but to a miracle, he accepted the miracle as something contrary to the known order of nature. All records of miracles teach the same thing. In such stories the miracles excite fear and wonder (that is what the very word *miracle* implies) among the spectators, and are taken as evidence of supernatural power. If they were not known to be contrary to the laws of nature how could they suggest the presence of the supernatural? How could they be surprising unless they were seen to be exceptions to the rules? And how can anything be seen to be an exception till the rules are known? If there ever were men who did not know the laws of nature *at all*, they would have no idea of a miracle and feel no particular interest in one if it were performed before them. Nothing can seem extraordinary until you have discovered what is ordinary. Belief in miracles, far from depending on an ignorance of the laws of nature, is only possible in so far as those laws are known. We have already seen that if you begin by ruling out the supernatural you will perceive no miracles. We must now add that you will equally perceive no miracles until you believe that nature works according to regular laws. If you have not yet noticed that the sun always rises in the East you will see nothing miraculous about his rising one morning in the West.

If the miracles were offered us as events that normally occurred, then the progress of science, whose business is to tell us what normally occurs, would render belief in them gradually harder and finally impossible. The progress of science has in just this way (and greatly to our benefit) made all sorts of things incredible which our ancestors believed; man-eating ants and gryphons in Scythia, men with one single gigantic foot, magnetic islands that draw all ships towards them, mermaids and fire-breathing dragons. But those things were never put forward as supernatural interruptions of the course of nature. They were put forward as items within her ordinary course—in fact as 'science'. Later and better science has therefore rightly removed them. Miracles are in a wholly different position. If there were fire-breathing dragons our big-game hunters would find them: but no one ever pretended that the Virgin Birth or Christ's walking on the water could be reckoned on to recur. When a thing professes from the very outset to be a unique invasion of Nature by something from outside, increasing knowledge of Nature can never make it either more or less credible than it was at the beginning. In this sense it is mere confusion of thought to suppose that advancing science has made it harder for us to accept miracles. We always knew they were contrary to the natural course of events; we know still that if there is something beyond Nature, they are possible. Those are the bare bones of the question; time and progress and science and civilisation have not altered them in the least. The grounds for belief and disbelief are the same today as they were two thousand—or ten thousand—years ago. If St Joseph had lacked faith to trust God or humility to perceive the holiness of his spouse, he could have disbelieved in the miraculous origin of her Son as easily as any modern man; and any modern man who believes in God can accept the miracle as easily as St Joseph did. You and I may not agree, even by the end of this book, as to whether miracles happen or not. But at least let us not talk nonsense. Let us not allow vague rhetoric about the march of science to fool us into supposing that the most complicated account of birth, in terms of genes and spermatozoa, leaves us any more convinced than we were before that *nature* does not send babies to young women who 'know not a man'.

The second Red Herring is this. Many people say, 'They could believe in miracles in olden times because they had a false conception of the universe. They thought the Earth was the largest thing in it and Man the most important creature. It therefore seemed reasonable to suppose that the Creator was specially interested in Man and might even interrupt the course of Nature for his benefit. But now that we know the real immensity of the universe—now that we perceive our own planet and even the whole Solar System to be only a speck—it becomes ludicrous to believe in them any longer. We have discovered our significance and can no longer suppose that God is so drastically concerned in our petty affairs'.

Whatever its value may be as an argument, it may be stated at once that this view is quite wrong about facts. The immensity of the universe is not a recent discovery. More than seventeen hundred years ago Ptolemy taught that in relation to the distance of the fixed stars the whole Earth must be regarded as a point with no magnitude. His astronomical system was universally accepted in the Dark and Middle Ages. The insignificance of Earth was as much a commonplace to Boethius, King Alfred, Dante, and Chaucer as it is to Mr H. G. Wells or Professor Haldane. Statements to the contrary in modern books are due to ignorance.

The real question is quite different from what we commonly suppose. The real question is why the spatial insignificance of Earth, after being asserted by Christian philosophers, sung by Christian poets, and commented on by Christian moralists for some fifteen centuries, without the slightest suspicion that it conflicted with their theology, should suddenly in quite modern times have been set up as a stock argument against Christianity and enjoyed, in that capacity, a brilliant career. I will offer a guess at the answer to this question presently. For the moment, let us consider the strength of this stock argument.

When the doctor at a post-mortem looks at the dead man's organs and diagnoses poison he has a clear idea of the different state in which the organs would have been if the man had died a natural death. If from the vastness of the universe and the smallness of Earth we diagnose that Christianity is false we ought to have a clear idea of the sort of universe we should have expected if it were true. But have we? Whatever space may really be, it is certain that our perceptions make it appear three dimensional; and to a three-dimensional space no boundaries are conceivable. By the very forms of our perceptions therefore we must feel as if we lived somewhere in infinite space: and whatever size the Earth happens to be, it must of course be very small in comparison with infinity. And this infinite space must either be empty or contain bodies. If it were empty, if it contained nothing but our own Sun, then that vast vacancy would certainly be used as an argument against the very existence of God. Why, it would be asked, should He create one speck and leave all the rest of space to nonentity? If, on the other hand, we find (as we actually do) countless bodies floating in space, they must be either habitable or uninhabitable. Now the odd thing is that *both* alternatives are equally used as objections to Christianity. If the universe is teeming with life other than ours, then this, we are told, makes it quite ridiculous to believe that God should be so concerned with the human race as to 'come down from Heaven' and be made man for its redemption. If, on the other hand, our planet is really unique in harbouring organic life, then this is thought to prove that life is only an accidental by-product in the universe and so again to disprove our religion. We treat God as the policeman in the story treated the suspect; whatever he does 'will be used in evidence against Him'. This kind of objection to the Christian faith is not really based on the observed nature of the actual universe at all. You can make it without waiting to find out what the universe is like, for it will fit any kind of universe we choose to imagine. The doctor here can diagnose poison without looking at the corpse for he has a theory of poison which he will maintain *whatever* the state of the organs turns out to be.

The reason why we cannot even imagine a universe so built as to exclude these objections is, perhaps, as follows. Man is a finite creature who has sense enough to know that he is finite: therefore, on any conceivable view, he finds himself dwarfed by reality as a whole. He is also a derivative being: the cause of his existence lies not in himself but (immediately) in his parents and (ultimately) *either* in the character of Nature as a whole *or* (if there is a God) in God. But there must be something, whether it be God or the totality of Nature, which exists in its own right or goes on 'of its own accord'; not as the product of causes beyond itself, but simply because it does. In the face of that something, whichever it turns out to be, man must feel his own derived existence to be unimportant, irrelevant, almost accidental. There is no question of religious people fancying that all exists for man and scientific people discovering that it does not. Whether the ultimate and inexplicable being—that which simply *is*—turns out to be God or 'the whole show', of course it does not exist for us. On either view we are faced with something which existed before the human race appeared and will exist after the Earth has become uninhabitable; which is utterly independent of us though we are totally dependent on it; and which, through vast ranges of its being, has no relevance to our own hopes and fears. For no man was, I suppose, ever so mad as to think that man, or all creation, *filled* the Divine Mind; if we are a small thing to space and time, space and time are a much smaller thing to God. It is a profound mistake to imagine that Christianity ever intended to dissipate the bewilderment and even the terror, the sense of our own nothingness, which come upon us when we think about the nature of things. It comes to intensify them. Without such sensations there is no religion. Many a man, brought up in the glib profession of some shallow form of Christianity, who comes through reading Astronomy to realise for the first time how majestically indifferent most reality is to man, and who perhaps abandons his religion on that account, may at that moment be having his first genuinely religious experience.

Christianity does not involve the belief that all things were made for man. It does involve the belief that God loves man and for his sake became man and died. I have not yet succeeded in seeing how what we know (and have known since the days of Ptolemy) about the size of the universe affects the credibility of this doctrine one way or the other.

The sceptic asks how we can believe that God so 'came down' to this one tiny planet. The question would be embarrassing if we knew (1) that there are rational creatures on any of the other bodies that float in space; (2) that they have, like us, fallen and need redemption; (3) that their redemption must be in the same mode as ours; (4) that redemption in this mode has been withheld from them. But we know none of them. The universe may be full of happy lives that never needed redemption. It may be full of lives that have been redeemed in modes suitable to their condition, of which we can form no conception. It may be full of lives that have been redeemed in the very same mode as our own. It may be full of things quite other than life in which God is interested though we are not.

If it is maintained that anything so small as the Earth must, in any event, be too unimportant to merit the love of the Creator, we reply that no Christian ever supposed we did merit it. Christ did not die for men because they were intrinsically worth dying for, but because He is intrinsically love, and therefore loves infinitely. And what, after all, does the *size* of a world or a creature tell us about its 'importance' or value?

There is no doubt that we all *feel* the incongruity of supposing, say, that the planet Earth might be more important than the Great Nebula in Andromeda. On the other hand, we are all equally certain that only a lunatic would think a man six-feet high necessarily more important than a man five-feet high, or a horse necessarily more important than a man, or a man's legs than his brain. In other words this supposed ratio of size to importance feels plausible only when one of the sizes involved is very great. And that betrays the true basis of this type of thought. When a relation is perceived by Reason, it is perceived to hold good universally. If our Reason told us that size was proportional to importance, then small differences in size would be accompanied by small differences in importance just as surely as great differences in size were accompanied by great differences in importance. Your six-foot man would have to be slightly more valuable than the man of five feet, and your leg slightly more important than your brain—which everyone knows to be nonsense. The conclusion is inevitable: the importance we attach to great differences of size is an affair not of reason but of emotion—of that peculiar emotion which superiorities in size begin to produce in us only after a certain point of absolute size has been reached.

We are inveterate poets. When a quantity is very great we cease to regard it as a mere quantity. Our imaginations awake. Instead of mere quantity, we now have a quality—the Sublime. But for this, the merely arithmetical greatness of the Galaxy would be no more impressive than the figures in an account book. To a mind which did not share our emotions and lacked our imaginative energies, the argument against Christianity from the size of the universe would be simply unintelligible. It is therefore from ourselves that the material universe derives its power to overawe us. Men of sensibility look up on the night sky with awe: brutal and stupid men do not. When the silence of the eternal spaces terrified Pascal, it was Pascal's own greatness that enabled them to do so; to be frightened by the bigness of the nebulae is, almost literally, to be frightened at our own shadow. For light years and geological periods are mere arithmetic until the shadow of man, the poet, the maker of myths, falls upon them. As a Christian I do not say we are wrong to tremble at that shadow, for I believe it to be the shadow of an image of God. But if the vastness of Nature ever threatens to overcrow our spirits, we must remember that it is only Nature spiritualised by human imagination which does so.

This suggests a possible answer to the question raised a few pages ago—why the size of the universe, known for centuries, should first in modern times become an argument against Christianity. Has it perhaps done so because in modern times the imagination has become more sensitive to bigness? From this point of view the argument from size might almost be regarded as a by-product of the Romantic Movement in poetry. In addition to the absolute increase of imaginative vitality on this topic, there has pretty certainly been a decline on others. Any reader of old poetry can see that brightness appealed to ancient and medieval man more than bigness, and more than it does to us. Medieval thinkers believed that the stars must be somehow superior to the Earth because they looked bright and it did not. Moderns think that the Galaxy ought to be more important than the Earth because it is bigger. Both states of mind can produce good poetry. Both can supply mental pictures which rouse very respectable emotions—emotions of awe, humility, or exhilaration. But taken as serious philosophical argument both are ridiculous. The atheist's argument from size is, in fact, an instance of just that picture-thinking to which, as we shall see in a later chapter, the Christian is *not* committed. It is the particular mode in which picture-thinking appears in the twentieth century: for what we fondly call 'primitive' errors do not pass away. They merely change their form.

8

MIRACLES AND
THE LAWS OF NATURE

It's a very odd thing –
As odd as can be –
That whatever Miss T. eats
Turns into Miss T.

W. DE LA MARE

HAVING CLEARED OUT of the way those objections which are based
on a popular and confused notion that the 'progress of science' has somehow made the world safe against Miracle, we must now consider the subject on a somewhat deeper level. The question is whether Nature can be
known to be of such a kind that supernatural interferences with her are
impossible. She is already known to be, in general, regular: she behaves
according to fixed laws, many of which have been discovered, and which
interlock with one another. There is, in this discussion, no question of
mere failure or inaccuracy to keep these laws on the part of Nature,
no question of chancy or spontaneous variation.[1] The only question is

---

[1] If any region of reality is in fact chancy or lawless then it is a region which, so far from admitting Miracle with special ease, renders the word 'Miracle' meaningless throughout that region.

349

whether, granting the existence of a Power outside Nature, there is any intrinsic absurdity in the idea of its intervening to produce within Nature events which the regular 'going on' of the whole natural system would never have produced.

Three conceptions of the 'Laws' of Nature have been held. (1) That they are mere brute facts, known only by observation, with no discoverable rhyme or reason about them. We know *that* Nature behaves thus and thus; we do not know why she does and can see no reason why she should not do the opposite. (2) That they are applications of the law of averages. The foundations of Nature are in the random and lawless. But the number of units we are dealing with are so enormous that the behaviour of these crowds (like the behaviour of very large masses of men) can be calculated with practical accuracy. What we call 'impossible events' are events so overwhelmingly improbable—by actuarial standards—that we do not need to take them into account. (3) That the fundamental laws of Physics are really what we call 'necessary truths' like the truths of mathematics—in other words, that if we clearly understand what we are saying we shall see that the opposite would be meaningless nonsense. Thus it is a 'law' that when one billiard ball shoves another the amount of momentum lost by the first ball must exactly equal the amount gained by the second. People who hold that the laws of Nature are necessary truths would say that all we have done is to split up the single events into two halves (adventures of ball A, and adventures of ball B) and then discover that 'the two sides of the account balance'. When we understand this we see that of course they *must* balance. The fundamental laws are in the long run merely statements that every event is itself and not some different event.

It will at once be clear that the first of these three theories gives no assurance against Miracles—indeed no assurance that, even apart from Miracles, the 'laws' which we have hitherto observed will be obeyed tomorrow. If we have no notion why a thing happens, then of course we know no reason why it should not be otherwise, and therefore have no certainty that it might not some day be otherwise. The second theory, which depends on the law of averages, is in the same position. The assurance it gives us is of the same general kind as our assurance that a coin tossed a thousand times will not give the same result, say, nine hundred times: and that the longer you toss it the more nearly the numbers of Heads and Tails will come to being equal. But this is so only provided the coin is an honest coin. If it is a loaded coin our expectations may be disappointed. But the people who believe in miracles are maintaining precisely that the coin *is* loaded. The expectations based on the law of averages will work only for *undoctored* Nature. And the question whether miracles occur is just the question whether Nature is ever doctored.

The third view (that laws of Nature are necessary truths) seems at first sight to present an insurmountable obstacle to miracle. The breaking of them would, in that case, be a self-contradiction and not even Omnipotence can do what is self-contradictory. Therefore the Laws cannot be broken. And therefore, we shall conclude, no miracle can ever occur?

We have gone too quickly. It is certain that the billiard balls will behave in a particular way, just as it is certain that if you divided a shilling unequally between two recipients then A's share must exceed the half and B's share fall short of it by exactly the same amount. Provided, of course, that A does not by sleight of hand steal some of B's pennies at the very moment of the transaction. In the same way, you know what will happen to the two billiard balls—provided nothing interferes. If one ball encounters a roughness in the cloth which the other does not, their motion will not illustrate the law in the way you had expected. Of course what happens as a result of the roughness in the cloth will illustrate the law in some other way, but your original prediction will have been false. Or again, if I snatch up a cue and give one of the balls a little help, you will get a third result: and that third result will equally illustrate the laws of physics, and equally falsify your prediction. I shall have 'spoiled the experiment'. All interferences leave the law perfectly true. But every prediction of what will happen in a given instance is made under the proviso 'other things being equal' or 'if there are no interferences'. Whether other things *are equal* in a given case and whether interferences may occur is another matter. The arithmetician, as an arithmetician, does not know how likely A is to steal some of B's pennies when the shilling is being divided; you had better ask a criminologist. The physicist, as a physicist, does not know how likely I am to catch up a cue and 'spoil' his experiment with the billiard balls: you had better ask someone who knows *me*. In the same way the physicist, as such, does not know how likely it is that some supernatural power is going to interfere with them: you had better ask a metaphysician. But the physicist does know, just because he is a physicist, that if the billiard balls are tampered with by any agency, natural or supernatural, which he has not taken into account, then their behaviour must differ from what he expected. Not because the law is false, but because it is true. The more certain we are of the law the more clearly we know that if new factors have been introduced the result will vary accordingly. What we do not know, as physicists, is whether Supernatural power might be one of the new factors.

If the laws of Nature are necessary truths, no miracle can break them: but then no miracle needs to break them. It is with them as with the laws of arithmetic. If I put six pennies into a drawer on Monday and six more on Tuesday, the laws decree that—*other things being equal*—I shall find twelve pennies there on Wednesday. But if the drawer has been robbed I may in fact find only two. Something will have been broken (the lock of the drawer or the laws of England) but the laws of arithmetic will not have been broken. The new situation created by the thief will illustrate the laws of arithmetic just as well as the original situation. But if God comes to work miracles, He comes 'like a thief in the night'. Miracle is, from the point of view of the scientist, a form of doctoring, tampering, (if you like) cheating. It introduces a new factor into the situation, namely supernatural force, which the scientist had not reckoned on. He calculates what will happen, or what must have happened on a past occasion, in the belief that the situation, at that point of space and time, is or was A. But if supernatural force has been added, then the situation really is or was AB. And no one knows better than the scientist that AB *cannot* yield the same result as A. The necessary truth of the laws, far from making it impossible that miracles should occur, makes it certain that if the Supernatural is operating they must occur. For if the natural situation by itself, and the natural situation *plus* something else, yielded only the same result, it would be then that we should be faced with a lawless and unsystematic universe. The better you know that two and two make four, the better you know that two and three don't.

This perhaps helps to make a little clearer what the laws of Nature really are. We are in the habit of talking as if they caused events to happen; but they have never caused any event at all. The laws of motion do not set billiard balls moving: they analyse the motion after something else (say, a man with a cue, or a lurch of the liner, or, perhaps, supernatural power) has provided it. They produce no events: they state the pattern to which every event—if only it can be induced to happen—must conform, just as the rules of arithmetic state the pattern to which all transactions with money must conform—if only you can get hold of any money. Thus in one sense the laws of Nature cover the whole field of space and time; in another, what they leave out is precisely the whole real universe—the incessant torrent of actual events which makes up true history. That must come from somewhere else. To think the laws can produce it is like thinking that you can create real money by simply doing sums. For every law, in the last resort, says 'If you have A, then you will get B'. But first catch your A: the laws won't do it for you.

It is therefore inaccurate to define a miracle as something that breaks the laws of Nature. It doesn't. If I knock out my pipe I alter the position of a great many atoms: in the long run, and to an infinitesimal degree, of all the atoms there are. Nature digests or assimilates this event with perfect ease and harmonises it in a twinkling with all other events. It is one more bit of raw material for the laws to apply to, and they apply. I have simply thrown one event into the general cataract of events and it finds itself at home there and conforms to all other events. If God annihilates or creates or deflects a unit of matter He has created a new situation at that point. Immediately all Nature domiciles this new situation, makes it at home in her realm, adapts all other events to it. It finds itself conforming to all the laws. If God creates a miraculous spermatozoon in the body of a virgin, it does not proceed to break any laws. The laws at once take it over. Nature is ready. Pregnancy follows, according to all the normal laws, and nine months later a child is born. We see every day that physical nature is not in the least incommoded by the daily inrush of events from biological nature or from psychological nature. If events ever come from beyond Nature altogether, she will be no more incommoded by them. Be sure she will rush to the point where she is invaded, as the defensive forces rush to a cut in our finger, and there hasten to accommodate the newcomer. The moment it enters her realm it obeys all her laws. Miraculous wine will intoxicate, miraculous conception will lead to pregnancy, inspired books will suffer all the ordinary processes of textual corruption, miraculous bread will be digested. The divine art of miracle is not an art of suspending the pattern to which events conform but of feeding new events into that pattern. It does not violate the law's proviso, 'If A, then B': it says, 'But this time instead of A, A2,' and Nature, speaking through all her laws, replies 'Then B2' and naturalises the immigrant, as she well knows how. She is an accomplished hostess.

A miracle is emphatically not an event without cause or without results. Its cause is the activity of God: its results follow according to

Natural law. In the forward direction (i.e. during the time which follows its occurrence) it is interlocked with all Nature just like any other event. Its peculiarity is that it is not in that way interlocked backwards, interlocked with the previous history of Nature. And this is just what some people find intolerable. The reason they find it intolerable is that they start by taking Nature to be the whole of reality. And they are sure that all reality must be interrelated and consistent. I agree with them. But I think they have mistaken a partial system within reality, namely Nature, for the whole. That being so, the miracle and the previous history of Nature may be interlocked after all but not in the way the Naturalist expected: rather in a much more roundabout fashion. The great complex event called Nature, and the new particular event introduced into it by the miracle, are related by their common origin in God, and doubtless, if we knew enough, most intricately related in His purpose and design, so that a Nature which had had a different history, and therefore been a different Nature, would have been invaded by different miracles or by none at all. In that way the miracles and the previous course of Nature are as well interlocked as any other two realities, but you must go back as far as their common Creator to find the interlocking. You will not find it *within* Nature. The same sort of thing happens with any partial system. The behaviour of fishes which are being studied in a tank makes a relatively closed system. Now suppose that the tank is shaken by a bomb in the neighbourhood of the laboratory. The behaviour of the fishes will now be no longer fully explicable by what was going on in the tank before the bomb fell: there will be a failure of backward interlocking. This does not mean that the bomb and the previous history of events within the tank are totally and finally unrelated. It does mean that to find their relation you must go back to the much larger reality which includes both the tank and the bomb—the reality of wartime England in which bombs are falling but some laboratories are still at work. You would never find it within the history of the tank. In the same way, the miracle is not *naturally* interlocked in the backward direction. To find out how it is interlocked with the previous history of Nature you must replace both Nature and the miracle in a larger context. Everything *is* connected with everything else: but not all things are connected by the short and straight roads we expected.

The rightful demand that all reality should be consistent and systematic does not therefore exclude miracles: but it has a very valuable contribution to make to our conception of them. It reminds us that miracles, if they occur, must, like all events, be revelations of that total harmony of all that exists. Nothing arbitrary, nothing simply 'stuck on' and left unreconciled with the texture of total reality, can be admitted. By definition, miracles must of course interrupt the usual course of Nature; but if they are real they must, in the very act of so doing, assert all the more the unity and self-consistency of total reality at some deeper level. They will not be like unmetrical lumps of prose breaking the unity of a poem; they will be like that crowning metrical audacity which, though it may be paralleled nowhere else in the poem, yet, coming just where it does, and effecting just what it effects, is (to those who understand) the supreme revelation of the unity in the poet's conception. If what we call Nature is modified by supernatural power, then we may be sure that the capability of being so modified is of the essence of Nature—that the total events, if we could grasp it, would turn out to involve, by its very character, the possibility of such modifications. If Nature brings forth miracles then doubtless it is as 'natural' for her to do so when impregnated by the masculine force beyond her as it is for a woman to bear children to a man. In calling them miracles we do not mean that they are contradictions or outrages; we mean that, left to her own resources, she could never produce them.

9

A CHAPTER NOT STRICTLY NECESSARY

*And there we saw the giants, the sons of Anak; which
come of the giants: and we were in our own sight as
grasshoppers, and so we were in their sight*

NUMBERS 13:33

THE LAST TWO chapters have been concerned with objections to Miracle, made, so to speak, from the side of Nature; made on the ground that she is the sort of system which could not admit miracles. Our next step, if we followed a strict order, would be to consider objections from the opposite side—in fact, to inquire whether what is beyond Nature can reasonably be supposed to be the sort of being that could, or would, work miracles. But I find myself strongly disposed to turn aside and face first an objection of a different sort. It is a purely emotional one; severer readers may skip this chapter. But I know it is one which weighed very heavily with me at a certain period of my life, and if others have passed through the same experience they may care to read of it.

One of the things that held me back from Supernaturalism was a deep repugnance to the view of Nature which, as I thought, Supernaturalism entailed. I passionately desired that Nature should exist 'on her own'. The idea that she had been made, and could be altered, by God, seemed to take from her all that spontaneity which I found so refreshing. In order to breathe freely I wanted to feel that in Nature one reached at last something that simply *was:* the thought that she had been manufactured or 'put there', and put there with a purpose, was suffocating. I wrote a poem in those days about a sunrise, I remember, in which, after describing the scene, I added that some people liked to believe there was a Spirit behind it all and that this Spirit was communicating with them. But, said I, that was exactly what I did not want. The poem was not much good and I have forgotten most of it: but it ended up by saying how much rather I would feel

> That in their own right earth and sky
> Continually do dance
> For their own sakes—and here crept I
> To watch the world by chance.

'*By chance!*'—one could not bear to feel that the sunrise had been in any way 'arranged' or had anything to do with oneself. To find that it had not simply happened, that it had been somehow contrived, would be as bad as finding that the fieldmouse I saw beside some lonely hedge was really a clockwork mouse put there to amuse me, or (worse still) to point some moral lesson. The Greek poet asks, 'If water sticks in your throat, what will you take to wash it down?' I likewise asked, 'If Nature herself proves artificial, where will you go to seek wildness? Where is the real out-of-doors?' To find that all the woods, and small streams in the middle of the woods, and odd corners of mountain valleys, and the wind and the grass were only a sort of *scenery,* only backcloths for some kind of play, and that play perhaps one with a moral—what flatness, what an anticlimax, what an unendurable bore!

The cure of this mood began years ago: but I must record that the cure was not complete until I began to study this question of Miracles. At every stage in the writing of this book I have found my idea of Nature becoming more vivid and more concrete. I set out on a work which seemed to involve reducing her status and undermining her walls at every turn: the paradoxical result is a growing sensation that if I am not very careful she will become the heroine of my book. She has never seemed to me more great or more real than at this moment.

The reason is not far to seek. As long as one is a Naturalist, 'Nature' is only a word for 'everything'. And Everything is not a subject about which anything very interesting can be said or (save by illusion) felt. One aspect of things strikes us and we talk of the 'peace' of Nature; another strikes us and we talk of her cruelty. And then, because we falsely take her for the ultimate and self-existent Fact and cannot quite repress our high instinct to worship the Self-existent, we are all at sea and our moods fluctuate and Nature means to us whatever we please as the moods select and slur. But everything becomes different when we recognise that Nature is a *creature*, a created thing, with its own particular tang or flavour. There is no need any longer to select and slur. It is not in her, but in Something far beyond her, that all lines meet and all contrasts are explained. It is no more baffling that the creature called Nature should be both fair and cruel than that the first man you meet in the train should be a dishonest grocer and a kind husband. For she is not the Absolute: she is one of the creatures, with her good points and her bad points and her own unmistakable flavour running through them all.

To say that God has created her is not to say that she is unreal, but precisely that she is real. Would you make God less creative than Shakespeare or Dickens? What He creates is created in the round: it is far more concrete than Falstaff or Sam Weller. The theologians certainly tell us that He created Nature freely. They mean that He was not forced to do so by any external necessity. But we must not interpret freedom negatively, as if Nature were a mere construction of parts arbitrarily stuck together. God's creative freedom is to be conceived as the freedom of a poet: the freedom to create a consistent, positive thing with its own inimitable flavour. Shakespeare need not create Falstaff: but if he does, Falstaff *must* be fat. God need not create this Nature. He might have created others, He may have created others. But granted *this* Nature, then doubtless no smallest part of her is there except because it expresses the character He chose to give her. It would be a miserable error to suppose that the dimensions of space and time, the death and rebirth of vegetation, the unity in multiplicity of organisms, the union in opposition of sexes, and the colour of each particular apple in Herefordshire this autumn, were merely a collection of useful devices forcibly welded together. They are the very idiom, almost the facial expression, the smell or taste, of an individual thing. The *quality* of Nature is present in them all just as the Latinity of Latin is present in every inflection or the 'Correggiosity' of Correggio in every stroke of the brush.

Nature is by human (and probably by Divine) standards partly good and partly evil. We Christians believe that she has been corrupted. But the same tang or flavour runs through both her corruptions and her excellences. Everything is in character. Falstaff does not sin in the same way as Othello. Othello's fall bears a close relation to his virtues. If Perdita had fallen she would not have been bad in the same way as Lady Macbeth: if Lady Macbeth had remained good her goodness would have been quite different from that of Perdita. The evils we see in Nature are, so to speak, the evils proper to *this* Nature. Her very character decreed that if she were corrupted the corruption would take this form and not another. The horrors of parasitism and the glories of motherhood are good and evil worked out of the same basic scheme or idea.

I spoke just now about the Latinity of Latin. It is more evident to us than it can have been to the Romans. The Englishness of English is audible only to those who know some other language as well. In the same way and for the same reason, only Supernaturalists really see Nature. You must go a little away from her, and then turn round, and look back. Then at last the true landscape will become visible. You must have tasted, however briefly, the pure water from beyond the world before you can be distinctly conscious of the hot, salty tang of Nature's current. To treat her as God, or as Everything, is to lose the whole pith and pleasure of her. Come out, look back, and then you will see . . . this astonishing cataract of bears, babies, and bananas: this immoderate deluge of atoms, orchids, oranges, cancers, canaries, fleas, gases, tornadoes and toads. How could you ever have thought this was the ultimate reality? How could you ever have thought that it was merely a stage-set for the moral drama of men and women? She is herself. Offer her neither worship nor contempt. Meet her and know her. If we are immortal, and if she is doomed (as the scientists tell us) to run down and die, we shall miss this half-shy and half-flamboyant creature, this ogress, this hoyden, this incorrigible fairy, this dumb witch. But the theologians tell us that she, like ourselves, is to be redeemed. The 'vanity' to which she was subjected was her disease, not her essence. She will be cured in character: not tamed (Heaven forbid) nor sterilised. We shall still be able to recognise our old enemy, friend, playfellow and foster-mother, so perfected as to be not less, but more, herself. And that will be a merry meeting.

10

'HORRID RED THINGS'

We can call the attempt to refute theism by displaying
the continuity of the belief in God with primitive
delusion the method of Anthropological intimidation.

EDWYN BEVAN, *SYMBOLISM AND BELIEF*,
CHAP. II.

I HAVE ARGUED that there is no security against Miracle to be found by
the study of Nature. She is not the whole of reality but only a part; for all
we know she might be a small part. If that which is outside her wishes to
invade her she has, so far as we can see, no defences. But of course many
who disbelieve in Miracles would admit all this. Their objection comes
from the other side. They think that the Supernatural would not invade:
they accuse those who say that it has done so of having a childish and
unworthy notion of the Supernatural. They therefore reject all forms of
Supernaturalism which assert such interference and invasions: and specially the form called Christianity, for in it the Miracles, or at least some
Miracles, are more closely bound up with the fabric of the whole belief
than in any other. All the essentials of Hinduism would, I think, remain
unimpaired if you subtracted the miraculous, and the same is almost true
of Mohammedanism. But you cannot do that with Christianity. It is precisely the story of a great Miracle. A naturalistic Christianity leaves out
all that is specifically Christian.

The difficulties of the unbeliever do not begin with questions about this or that particular miracle; they begin much further back. When a man who has had only the ordinary modern education looks into any authoritative statement of Christian doctrine, he finds himself face to face with what seems to him a wholly 'savage' or 'primitive' picture of the universe. He finds that God is supposed to have had a 'Son', just as if God were a mythological deity like Jupiter or Odin. He finds that this 'Son' is supposed to have 'come down from Heaven', just as if God had a palace in the sky from which He had sent down His 'Son' like a parachutist. He finds that this 'Son' then 'descended into Hell'—into some land of the dead under the surface of a (presumably) flat earth—and thence 'ascended' again, as if by a balloon, into his Father's sky-palace, where He finally sat down in a decorated chair placed a little to His Father's right. Everything seems to presuppose a conception of reality which the increase of our knowledge has been steadily refuting for the last two thousand years and which no honest man in his senses could return to today.

It is this impression which explains the contempt, and even disgust, felt by many people for the writings of modern Christians. When once a man is convinced that Christianity *in general* implies a local 'Heaven', a flat earth, and a God who can have children, he naturally listens with impatience to our solutions of particular difficulties and our defences against particular objections. The more ingenious we are in such solutions and defences the more perverse we seem to him. 'Of course,' he says, 'once the doctrines are there, clever people can invent clever arguments to defend them, just as, when once a historian has made a blunder he can go on inventing more and more elaborate theories to make it appear that it was not a blunder. But the real point is that none of these elaborate theories would have been thought of if he had read his documents correctly in the first instance. In the same way, is it not clear that Christian theology would never have come into existence at all if the writers of the New Testament had had the slightest knowledge of what the real universe is actually like?' Thus, at any rate, I used to think myself. The very man who taught me to think—a hard, satirical atheist (ex-Presbyterian) who doted on the *Golden Bough* and filled his house with the products of the Rationalist Press Association—thought in the same way; and he was a man as honest as the daylight, to whom I here willingly acknowledge an immense debt. His attitude to Christianity was for me the starting point of adult thinking; you may say it is bred in my bones. And yet, since those days, I have come to regard that attitude as a total misunderstanding.

Remembering, as I do, from within, the attitude of the impatient sceptic, I realise very well how he is forearmed against anything I may say for the rest of this chapter. 'I know exactly what this man is going to do,' he murmurs. 'He is going to start explaining all these mythological statements away. It is the invariable practice of these Christians. On any matter whereon science has not yet spoken and on which they cannot be checked, they will tell you some preposterous fairytale. And then, the moment science makes a new advance and shows (as it invariably does) their statement to be untrue, they suddenly turn round and explain that they didn't mean what they said, that they were using a poetic metaphor or constructing an allegory, and that all they really intended was some harmless moral platitude. We are sick of this theological thimble-rigging'. Now I have a great deal of sympathy with that sickness and I freely admit that 'modernist' Christianity has constantly played just the game of which the impatient sceptic accuses it. But I also think there is a kind of explaining which is not explaining away. In one sense I am going to do just what the sceptic thinks I am going to do: that is, I am going to distinguish what I regard as the 'core' or 'real meaning' of the doctrines from that in their expression which I regard as inessential and possibly even capable of being changed without damage. But then, what will drop away from the 'real meaning' under my treatment will precisely *not* be the miraculous. It is the core itself, the core scraped as clean of inessentials as we can scrape it, which remains for me entirely miraculous, supernatural—nay, if you will, 'primitive' and even 'magical'.

In order to explain this I must now touch on a subject which has an importance quite apart from our present purpose and of which everyone who wishes to think clearly should make himself master as soon as he possibly can. And he ought to begin by reading Mr Owen Barfield's *Poetic Diction* and Mr Edwyn Bevan's *Symbolism and Belief*. But for the present argument it will be enough to leave the deeper problems on one side and proceed in a 'popular' and unambitious manner.

When I think about London I usually see a mental picture of Euston Station. But when I think (as I do) that London has several million inhabitants, I do not mean that there are several million images of people contained in my image of Euston Station. Nor do I mean that several millions of real people live in the real Euston Station. In fact though I have the image while I am thinking about London, what I think or say is not *about* that image, and would be manifest nonsense if it were. It makes sense because it is not about my own mental pictures but about the real London, outside my imagination, of which no one can have an adequate mental picture at all. Or again, when we say that the Sun is ninety-odd million miles away, we understand perfectly clearly what we mean by this number; we can divide and multiply it by other numbers and we can work out how long it would take to travel that distance at any given speed. But this clear *thinking* is accompanied by *imagining* which is ludicrously false to what we know that the reality must be.

To think, then, is one thing, and to imagine is another. What we think or say can be, and usually is, quite different from what we imagine or picture; and what we mean may be true when the mental images that accompany it are entirely false. It is, indeed, doubtful whether anyone except an extreme visualist who is also a trained artist ever has mental images which are particularly like the things he is thinking about.

In these examples the mental image is not only unlike the reality but is known to be unlike it, at least after a moment's reflection. I know that London is not merely Euston Station. Let us now go on to a slightly different predicament. I once heard a lady tell her young daughter that you would die if you ate too many tablets of aspirin. 'But why?' asked the child, 'it isn't poisonous'. 'How do you know it isn't poisonous?' said the mother. 'Because', said the child, 'when you crush an aspirin tablet you don't find horrid red things inside it'. Clearly, when this child thought of poison she had a mental picture of Horrid Red Things, just as I have a picture of Euston when I think of London. The difference is that whereas I know my image to be very unlike the real London, the child thought that poison was *really red*. To that extent she was mistaken. But this does not mean that everything she thought or said about poison was necessarily nonsensical. She knew perfectly well that a poison was something which killed you or made you ill if you swallowed it; and she knew, to some extent, which of the substances in her mother's house were poisonous. If a visitor to that house had been warned by the child, 'Don't drink that. Mother says it is poison', he would have been ill advised to neglect the warning on the ground that 'This child has a primitive idea of poison as Horrid Red Things, which my adult scientific knowledge has long since refuted.'

We can now add to our previous statement (that thinking may be sound where the images that accompany it are false) the further statement: thinking may be sound in certain respects where it is accompanied not only by false images but by false images mistaken for true ones.

There is still a third situation to be dealt with. In our two previous examples we have been concerned with thought and imagination, but not with language. I had to picture Euston Station, but I did not need to *mention* it; the child thought that poison was Horrid Red Things, but she could talk about poison without saying so. But very often when we are talking about something which is not perceptible by the five senses we use words which, in one of their meanings, refer to things or actions that are. When a man says that he grasps an argument he is using a verb (*grasp*) which literally means to take something in the hands, but he is certainly not thinking that his mind has hands or that an argument can be seized like a gun. To avoid the word *grasp* he may change the form of expression and say, 'I see your point,' but he does not mean that a pointed object has appeared in his visual field. He may have a third shot and say, 'I follow you,' but he does not mean that he is walking behind you along a road. Everyone is familiar with this linguistic phenomenon and the grammarians call it metaphor. But it is a serious mistake to think that metaphor is an optional thing which poets and orators may put into their work as a decoration and plain speakers can do without. The truth is that if we are going to talk at all about things which are not perceived by the senses, we are forced to use language metaphorically. Books on psychology or economics or politics are as continuously metaphorical as books of poetry or devotion. There is no other way of talking, as every philologist is aware. Those who wish can satisfy themselves on the point by reading the books I have already mentioned and the other books to which those two will lead them on. It is a study for a lifetime and I must here content myself with the mere statement; all speech about supersensibles is, and must be, metaphorical in the highest degree.

We have now three guiding principles before us. (1) That thought is distinct from the imagination which accompanies it. (2) That thought may be in the main sound even when the false images that accompany it are mistaken by the thinker for true ones. (3) That anyone who talks about things that cannot be seen, or touched, or heard, or the like, must inevitably talk as *if they could be* seen or touched or heard (e.g. must talk of 'complexes' and 'repressions' *as if* desires could really be tied up in bundles or shoved back; of 'growth' and 'development' *as if* institutions could really grow like trees or unfold like flowers; of energy being 're-leased' *as if* it were an animal let out of a cage).

Let us now apply this to the 'savage' or 'primitive' articles of the Christian creed. And let us admit at once that many Christians (though by no means all) when they make these assertions do have in mind just those crude mental pictures which so horrify the sceptic. When they say that Christ 'came down from Heaven' they do have a vague image of something shooting or floating downwards out of the sky. When they say that Christ is the 'Son' of 'the Father' they may have a picture of two human forms, the one looking rather older than the other. But we now know that the mere presence of these mental pictures does not, of itself, tell us anything about the reasonableness or absurdity of the thoughts they accompany. If absurd images meant absurd thought, then we should all be thinking nonsense all the time. And the Christians themselves make it clear that the images are not to be identified with the thing believed. They may picture the Father as a human form, but they also maintain that He has no body. They may picture Him older than the son, but they also maintain the one did not exist before the other, both having existed from all eternity. I am speaking, of course, about Christian adults. Christianity is not to be judged from the fancies of children any more than medicine from the ideas of the little girl who believed in horrid red things.

At this stage I must turn aside to deal with a rather simpleminded illusion. When we point out that what the Christians mean is not to be iden-tified with their mental pictures, some people say, 'In that case, would it not be better to get rid of the mental pictures, and of the language which suggests them, altogether?' But this is impossible. The people who rec-ommend it have not noticed that when they try to get rid of man-like, or as they are called, 'anthropomorphic', images they merely succeed in substituting images of some other kind. 'I don't believe in a personal God,' says one, 'but I do believe in a great spiritual force'. What he has not noticed is that the word 'force' has let in all sorts of images about winds and tides and electricity and gravitation. 'I don't believe in a per-sonal God,' says another, 'but I do believe we are all parts of one great Being which moves and works through us all'—not noticing that he has merely exchanged the image of a fatherly and royal-looking man for the image of some widely extended gas or fluid. A girl I knew was brought up by 'higher thinking' parents to regard God as a perfect 'substance';

in later life she realised that this had actually led her to think of Him as something like a vast tapioca pudding. (To make matters worse, she disliked tapioca). We may feel ourselves quite safe from this degree of absurdity, but we are mistaken. If a man watches his own mind, I believe he will find that what profess to be specially advanced or philosophic conceptions of God are, in his thinking, always accompanied by vague images which, if inspected, would turn out to be even more absurd than the man-like images aroused by Christian theology. For man, after all, is the highest of the things we meet in sensuous experience. He has, at least, conquered the globe, honoured (though not followed) virtue, achieved knowledge, made poetry, music and art. If God exists at all it is not unreasonable to suppose that we are less unlike Him than anything else we know. No doubt we are unspeakably different from Him; to that extent all man-like images are false. But those images of shapeless mists and irrational forces which, unacknowledged, haunt the mind when we think we are rising to the conception of impersonal and absolute Being, must be very much more so. For images, of the one kind or of the other, will come; we cannot jump off our own shadow.

As far, then, as the adult Christian of modern times is concerned, the absurdity of the images does not imply absurdity in the doctrines; but it may be asked whether the early Christian was in the same position. Perhaps he mistook the images for true ones, and really believed in the sky-palace or the decorated chair. But as we have seen from the example of the Horrid Red Things, even this would not necessarily invalidate everything that he thought on these subjects. The child in our example might know many truths about poison and even, in some particular cases, truths which a given adult might not know. We can suppose a Galilean peasant who thought that Christ had literally and physically 'sat down at the right hand of the Father'. If such a man had then gone to Alexandria and had a philosophical education he would have discovered that the Father had no right hand and did not sit on a throne. Is it conceivable that he would regard this as making any difference to what he had really intended and valued, in the doctrine during the days of his naïvety? For unless we suppose him to have been not only a peasant but a fool (two very different things) physical details about a supposed celestial throne-room would not have been what he cared about. What mattered must have been the belief that a person whom he had known as a man in Palestine had, as a person, survived death and was now operating as the supreme agent of the supernatural Being who governed and maintained the whole field of reality. And that belief would survive substantially unchanged after the falsity of the earlier images had been recognised.

Even if it could be shown, then, that the early Christians accepted their imagery literally, this would not mean that we are justified in relegating their doctrines as a whole to the lumber-room. Whether they actually did, is another matter. The difficulty here is that they were not writing as philosophers to satisfy speculative curiosity about the nature of God and of the universe. They *believed* in God; and once a man does that, philosophical definiteness can never be the *first* necessity. A drowning man does not analyse the rope that is flung at him, nor an impassioned lover consider the chemistry of his mistress's complexion. Hence the sort of question we are now considering is never raised by the New Testament writers. When once it is raised, Christianity decides quite clearly that the naïf images are false. The sect in the Egyptian desert which thought that God was like a man is condemned: the desert monk who felt he had lost something by its correction is recognised as 'muddle-headed'.[1] All three Persons of the Trinity are declared 'incomprehensible'.[2] God is pronounced 'inexpressible, unthinkable, invisible to all created beings'.[3] The Second Person is not only bodiless but so unlike man that if self-revelation had been His sole purpose He would not have chosen to be incarnate in a human form.[4] We do not find similar statements in the New Testament, because the issue has not yet been made explicit: but we do find statements which make it certain how that issue will be decided when once it becomes explicit. The title 'Son' may sound 'primitive' or 'naïf'. But already in the New Testament this 'Son' is identified with the Discourse or Reason or Word which was eternally 'with God' and yet also *was* God.[5] He is the all-pervasive principle of concretion or cohesion whereby the universe holds together.[6] All things, and specially Life, arose *within* Him,[7] and

---

[1] *Senex mente confusus* Cassian quoted in Gibbon, cap. xlvii.

[2] Athanasian Creed.

[3] St Chrysostom *De Incomprehensibili* quoted in Otto, *Idea of the Holy*, Appendix 1.

[4] Athanasius De Incarnatione viii.

[5] John 1:1.

[6] Colossians 1:17.

[7] Colossians 1 $\epsilon\nu$ αυ'τῳ ϵ'χτισθη. John 1:4.

within Him all things will reach their conclusion—the final statement of what they have been trying to express.[8]

It is, of course, always possible to imagine an earlier stratum of Christianity from which such ideas were absent; just as it is always possible to say that anything you dislike in Shakespeare was put in by an 'adapter' and the original play was free from it. But what have such assumptions to do with serious inquiry? And here the fabrication of them is specially perverse, since even if we go back beyond Christianity into Judaism itself, we shall not find the unambiguous anthropomorphism (or man-likeness) we are looking for. Neither, I admit, shall we find its denial. We shall find, on the one hand, God pictured as living above 'in the high and holy place': we shall find, on the other, 'Do not I fill heaven and earth? saith the Lord'.[9] We shall find that in Ezekiel's vision God appeared (notice the hesitating words) in 'the likeness as the appearance of a man'.[10] But we shall find also the warning, 'Take ye therefore good heed unto yourselves. For ye saw no manner of similitude on the day that the Lord spake unto you in Horeb out of the midst of the fire—lest ye corrupt yourselves and make a graven image'.[11] Most baffling of all to a modern literalist, the God who seems to live locally in the sky, also *made* it.[12]

The reason why the modern literalist is puzzled is that he is trying to get out of the old writers something which is not there. Starting from a clear modern distinction between material and immaterial he tries to find out on which side of that distinction the ancient Hebrew conception fell. He forgets that the distinction itself has been made clear only by later thought.

We are often told that primitive man could not conceive pure spirit; but then neither could he conceive mere matter. A throne and a local habitation are attributed to God only at that stage when it is still impossible to regard the throne, or palace even of an earthly king as merely physical objects. In earthly thrones and palaces it was the spiritual significance—as we should say, the 'atmosphere'—that mattered to the ancient mind. As soon as the contrast of 'spiritual' and 'material' was before their

---

[8] Ephesians 1:10.

[9] Jeremiah 23:24.

[10] Ezekiel 1:26.

[11] Deuteronomy 4:15.

[12] Genesis 1:1.

minds, they knew God to be 'spiritual' and realised that their religion had implied this all along. But at an earlier stage that contrast was not there. To regard that earlier stage as unspiritual because we find there no clear assertion of unembodied spirit, is a real misunderstanding. You might just as well call it spiritual because it contained no clear consciousness of mere matter. Mr Barfield has shown, as regards the history of language, that words did not start by referring merely to physical objects and then get extended by metaphor to refer to emotions, mental states and the like. On the contrary, what we now call the 'literal and metaphorical' meanings have both been disengaged by analysis from an ancient unity of meaning which was neither or both. In the same way it is quite erroneous to think that man started with a 'material' God or 'Heaven' and gradually spiritualised them. He could not have started with something 'material' for the 'material', as we understand it, comes to be realised only by contrast to the 'immaterial', and the two sides of the contrast grow at the same speed. He started with something which was neither and both. As long as we are trying to read back into that ancient unity either the one or the other of the two opposites which have since been analysed out of it, we shall misread all early literature and ignore many states of consciousness which we ourselves still from time to time experience. The point is crucial not only for the present discussion but for any sound literary criticism or philosophy.

The Christian doctrines, and even the Jewish doctrines which preceded them, have always been statements about spiritual reality, not specimens of primitive physical science. Whatever is positive in the conception of the spiritual has always been contained in them; it is only its negative aspect (immateriality) which has had to wait for recognition until abstract thought was fully developed. The material imagery has never been taken literally by anyone who had reached the stage when he could understand what 'taking it literally' meant. And now we come to the difference between 'explaining' and 'explaining away'. It shows itself in two ways. (1) Some people when they say that a thing is meant 'metaphorically' conclude from this that it is hardly meant at all. They rightly think that Christ spoke metaphorically when he told us to carry the cross: they wrongly conclude that carrying the cross means nothing more than leading a respectable life and subscribing moderately to charities. They reasonably think that hell 'fire' is a metaphor—and unwisely conclude that it means nothing more serious than remorse. They say that the story of the Fall in Genesis is not literal; and then go on to say (I have heard them myself) that it was really a fall upwards—which is like saying that because 'My heart is broken' contains a metaphor, it therefore means 'I feel very cheerful'. This mode of interpretation I regard, frankly, as nonsense. For me the Christian doctrines which are 'metaphorical'—or which have become metaphorical with the increase of abstract thought—mean something which is just as 'supernatural' or shocking after we have removed the ancient imagery as it was before. They mean that in addition to the physical or psycho-physical universe known to the sciences, there exists an uncreated and unconditioned reality which causes the universe to be; that this reality has a positive structure or constitution which is usefully, though doubtless not completely, described in the doctrine of the Trinity; and that this reality, at a definite point in time, entered the universe we know by becoming one of its own creatures and there produced effects on the historical level which the normal workings of the natural universe do not produce; and that this has brought about a change in our relations to the unconditioned reality. It will be noticed that our colourless 'entered the universe' is not a whit less metaphorical than the more picturesque 'came down from Heaven'. We have only substituted a picture of horizontal or unspecified movement for one of vertical movement. And every attempt to improve the ancient language will have the same result. These things not only cannot be asserted—they cannot even be presented for discussion—without metaphor. We can make our speech duller; we cannot make it more literal. (2) These statements concern two things—the supernatural, unconditioned reality, and those events on the historical level which its irruption into the natural universe is held to have produced. The first thing is indescribable in 'literal' speech, and therefore we rightly interpret all that is said about it metaphorically. But the second thing is in a wholly different position. Events on the historical level are the sort of things we can talk about literally. If they occurred, they were perceived by the senses of men. Legitimate 'explanation' degenerates into muddled or dishonest 'explaining away' as soon as we start applying to these events the metaphorical interpretation which we rightly apply to the statements about God. The assertion that God has a Son was never intended to mean that He is a being propagating His kind by sexual intercourse: and so we do not alter Christianity by rendering explicit the fact that 'sonship' is not used of Christ in exactly the same sense in which it is used of men. But the assertion that Jesus turned water into wine was meant perfectly literally, for this refers to something which, if it happened, was well within the reach of our senses and our language. When I say, 'My heart is broken,' you know perfectly well that I don't mean anything you could verify at a post-mortem. But when I say, 'My bootlace is broken,' then, if your own observation shows it to be intact, I am either lying or mistaken. The accounts of the 'miracles' in first-century Palestine are either lies, or legends, or history. And if all, or the most important, of them are lies or legends then the claim which Christianity has been making for the last two thousand years is simply false. No doubt it might even so contain noble sentiments and moral truths. So does Greek mythology; so does Norse. But that is quite a different affair.

Nothing in this chapter helps us to a decision about the probability or improbability of the Christian claim. We have merely removed a misunderstanding in order to secure for that question a fair hearing.

CHRISTIANITY AND 'RELIGION'

Those who make religion their god will not have God for their religion.

THOMAS ERSKINE OF LINLATHEN

HAVING ELIMINATED THE confusions which come from ignoring the relations of thought, imagination, and speech, we may now return to our question. The Christians say that God has done miracles. The modern world, even when it believes in God, and even when it has seen the defencelessness of Nature, does not. It thinks God would not do that sort of thing. Have we any reason for supposing that the modern world is right? I agree that the sort of God conceived by the popular 'religion' of our own times would almost certainly work no miracles. The question is whether that popular religion is at all likely to be true.

I call it 'religion' advisedly. We who defend Christianity find ourselves constantly opposed not by the irreligion of our hearers but by their real religion. Speak about beauty, truth and goodness, or about a God who is simply the indwelling principle of these three, speak about a great spiritual force pervading all things, a common mind of which we are all parts, a pool of generalised spirituality to which we can all flow, and you will command friendly interest. But the temperature drops as soon as you mention a God who has purposes and performs particular actions, who does one thing and not another, a concrete, choosing, commanding, prohibiting God with a determinate character. People become embarrassed or angry. Such a conception seems to them primitive and crude and even irreverent. The popular 'religion' excludes miracles because it excludes the 'living God' of Christianity and believes instead in a kind of God who obviously would not do miracles, or indeed anything else. This popular 'religion' may roughly be called Pantheism, and we must now examine its credentials.

In the first place it is usually based on a quite fanciful picture of the history of religion. According to this picture, Man starts by inventing 'spirits' to explain natural phenomena; and at first he imagines these spirits to be exactly like himself. As he gets more enlightened they become less man-like, less 'anthropomorphic' as the scholars call it. Their anthropomorphic attributes drop off one by one—first the human shape, the human passions, the personality, will, activity—in the end every concrete or positive attribute whatever. There is left in the end a pure abstraction—mind as such, spirituality as such. God, instead of being a particular entity with a real character of its own, becomes simply 'the whole show' looked at in a particular way or the theoretical point at which all the lines of human aspiration would meet if produced to infinity. And since, on the modern view, the final stage of anything is the most refined and civilised stage, this 'religion' is held to be a more profound, more spiritual, and more enlightened belief than Christianity.

Now this imagined history of religion is not true. Pantheism certainly is (as its advocates would say) congenial to the modern mind; but the fact that a shoe slips on easily does not prove that it is a new shoe—much less that it will keep your feet dry. Pantheism is congenial to our minds not because it is the final stage in a slow process of enlightenment, but because it is almost as old as we are. It may even be the most primitive of all religions, and the *orenda* of a savage tribe has been interpreted by some to be an 'all-pervasive spirit'. It is immemorial in India. The Greeks rose above it only at their peak, in the thought of Plato and Aristotle; their successors relapsed into the great Pantheistic system of the Stoics. Modern Europe escaped it only while she remained predominantly Christian; with Giordano Bruno and Spinoza it returned. With Hegel it became almost the agreed philosophy of highly educated people, while the more popular Pantheism of Wordsworth, Carlyle and Emerson conveyed the same doctrine to those on a slightly lower cultural level. So far from being the final religious refinement, Pantheism is in fact the permanent natural bent of the human mind; the permanent ordinary level below which man sometimes sinks, under the influence of priestcraft and superstition, but above which his own unaided efforts can never raise him for very long. Platonism and Judaism, and Christianity (which has incorporated both) have proved the only things capable of resisting it. It is the attitude into which the human mind automatically falls when left to itself. No wonder we find it congenial. If 'religion' means simply what man says about God, and not what God does about man, then Pantheism almost *is* religion. And 'religion' in that sense has, in the long run, only one really formidable opponent—namely Christianity.[1] Modern philosophy has rejected Hegel and modern science started out with no bias in favour of religion; but they have both proved quite powerless to curb the human impulse toward Pantheism. It is nearly as strong today as it was in ancient India or in ancient Rome. Theosophy and the worship of the life-force are both forms of it: even the German worship of a racial spirit is only Pantheism truncated or whittled down to suit barbarians. Yet, by a strange irony, each new relapse into this immemorial 'religion' is hailed as the last word in novelty and emancipation.

This native bent of the mind can be paralleled in quite a different field of thought. Men believed in atoms centuries before they had any experimental evidence of their existence. It was apparently natural to do so. And the sort of atoms we naturally believe in are little hard pellets—just like the hard substances we meet in experience, but too small to see. The mind reaches this conception by an easy analogy from grains of sand or of salt. It explains a number of phenomena; and we feel at home with atoms of that sort—we can picture them. The belief would have lasted forever if later science had not been so troublesome as to find out what atoms are *really* like. The moment it does that, all our mental comfort, all the immediate plausibility and obviousness of the old atomic theory, is destroyed. The real atoms turn out to be quite alien from our natural mode of thought. They are not even made of hard 'stuff' or 'matter' (as the imagination understands 'matter') at all: they are not simple, but have

---

[1] Hence, if a Minister of Education professes to value religion and at the same time takes steps to suppress Christianity, it does not necessarily follow that he is a hypocrite or even (in the ordinary this-wordly sense of the word) a fool. He may sincerely desire more 'religion' and rightly see that the suppression of Christianity is a necessary preliminary to his design.

a structure: they are not all the same: and they are unpicturable. The old atomic theory is in physics what Pantheism is in religion—the normal, instinctive guess of the human mind, not utterly wrong, but needing correction. Christian theology, and quantum physics, are both, by comparison with the first guess, hard, complex, dry and repellent. The first shock of the object's real nature, breaking in on our spontaneous dreams of what that object ought to be, always has these characteristics. You must not expect Schrödinger to be as plausible as Democritus; he knows too much. You must not expect St Athanasius to be as plausible as Mr Bernard Shaw: he also knows too much.

The true state of the question is often misunderstood because people compare an adult knowledge of Pantheism with a knowledge of Christianity which they acquired in their childhood. They thus get the impression that Christianity gives the 'obvious' account of God, the one that is too easy to be true, while Pantheism offers something sublime and mysterious. In reality, it is the other way round. The apparent profundity of Pantheism thinly veils a mass of spontaneous picture-thinking and owes its plausibility to that fact. Pantheists and Christians agree that God is present everywhere. Pantheists conclude that He is 'diffused' or 'concealed' in all things and therefore a universal medium rather that a concrete entity, because their minds are really dominated by the picture of a gas, or fluid, or space itself. The Christian, on the other hand, deliberately rules out such images by saying that God is totally present at every point of space and time, and *locally* present in none. Again the Pantheist and Christian agree that we are all dependent on God and intimately related to Him. But the Christian defines this relation in terms of Maker and made, whereas the Pantheist (at least of the popular kind) says, we are 'parts' of Him, or are contained in Him. Once more, the picture of a vast extended something which can be divided into areas has crept in. Because of this fatal picture Pantheism concludes that God must be equally present in what we call evil and what we call good and therefore indifferent to both (ether permeates the mud and the marble impartially). The Christian has to reply that this is far too simple; God is present in a great many different modes: not present in matter as He is present in man, not present in all men as in some, not present in any other man as in Jesus. Pantheist and Christian also agree that God is super-personal. The Christian means by this that God has a positive structure which we could never have guessed in advance, any more than a knowledge of squares would have enabled us to guess at a cube. He contains 'persons' (three of them) while remaining one God, as a cube contains six squares while remaining one solid body. We cannot comprehend such a structure any more than the Flatlanders could comprehend a cube. But we can at least comprehend our incomprehension, and see that if there is something beyond personality it *ought* to be incomprehensible in that sort of way. The Pantheist, on the other hand, though he may say 'super-personal' really conceives God in terms of what is sub-personal—as though the Flatlanders thought a cube existed in *fewer* dimensions than a square.

At every point Christianity has to correct the natural expectations of the Pantheist and offer something more difficult, just as Schrödinger has to correct Democritus. At every moment he has to multiply distinctions and rule out false analogies. He has to substitute the mappings of something that has a positive, concrete, and highly articulated character for the formless generalities in which Pantheism is at home. Indeed, after the discussion has been going on for some time, the Pantheist is apt to change his ground and where he before accused us of childish naïvety now to blame us for the pedantic complexity of our 'cold Christs and tangled Trinities'. And we may well sympathise with him. Christianity, faced with popular 'religion' is continuously troublesome. To the large well-meant statements of 'religion' it finds itself forced to reply again and again, 'Well, not quite like that,' or 'I should hardly put it that way'. This troublesomeness does not of course prove it to be true; but if it were true it would be bound to have this troublesomeness. The real musician is similarly troublesome to a man who wishes to indulge in untaught 'musical appreciation'; the real historian is similarly a nuisance when we want to romance about 'the old days' or 'the ancient Greeks and Romans'. The ascertained nature of any real thing is always at first a nuisance to our natural fantasies—a wretched, pedantic, logic-chopping intruder upon a conversation which was getting on famously without it.

But 'religion' also claims to base itself on experience. The experiences of the mystics (that ill-defined but popular class) are held to indicate that God is the God of 'religion' rather than of Christianity; that He—or It— is not a concrete Being but 'being in general' about which nothing can be truly asserted. To everything which we try to say about Him, the mystics tend to reply, 'Not thus'. What all these negatives of the mystics really mean I shall consider in a moment: but I must first point out why it seems to me impossible that they should be true in the sense popularly understood.

It will be agreed that, however they came there, concrete, individual, determinate things do now exist: things like flamingoes, German generals, lovers, sandwiches, pineapples, comets and kangaroos. These are not mere principles or generalities or theorems, but things—facts—real, resistant existences. One might even say *opaque* existences, in the sense that each contains something which our intelligence cannot completely digest. In so far as they illustrate general laws it can digest them: but then they are never mere illustrations. Above and beyond that there is in each of them the 'opaque' brute fact of existence, the fact that it is actually there and is itself. Now this opaque fact, this concreteness, is not in the least accounted for by the laws of Nature or even by the laws of thought. Every law can be reduced to the form 'If A, then B.' Laws give us only a universe of 'Ifs and Ands': not this universe which actually exists. What we know through laws and general principles is a series of connections. But in order for there to be a real universe the connections must be given something to connect; a torrent of opaque actualities must be fed into the pattern. If God created the world, then He is precisely the source of this torrent, and it alone gives our truest principles anything to be true *about*. But if God is the ultimate source of all concrete, individual things and events, then God Himself must be concrete, and individual in the highest degree. Unless the origin of all other things were itself concrete and individual, nothing else could be so; for there is no conceivable means whereby what is abstract or general could itself produce concrete reality. Bookkeeping, continued to all eternity, could never produce one farthing. Metre, of itself, could never produce a poem. Bookkeeping needs something else (namely, real money put into the account) and metre needs something else (real words, fed into it by a poet) before any income or any poem can exist. If anything is to exist at all, then the Original Thing must be, not a principle nor a generality, much less an 'ideal' or a 'value', but an utterly concrete fact.

Probably no thinking person would, in so many words, deny that God is concrete and individual. But not all thinking people, and certainly not all who believe in 'religion', keep this truth steadily before their minds. We must beware, as Professor Whitehead says, of paying God ill-judged 'metaphysical compliments'. We say that God is 'infinite'. In the sense that His knowledge and power extend not to some things but to all, this is true. But if by using the word 'infinite' we encourage ourselves to think of Him as a formless 'everything' about whom nothing in particular and everything in general is true, then it would be better to drop that word altogether. Let us dare to say that God is a particular Thing. Once He was the only Thing: but He is creative. He made other things to be. He is not those other things. He is not 'universal being': if He were there would be no creatures, for a generality can make nothing. He is 'absolute being'—or rather *the* Absolute Being—in the sense that He alone exists in His own right. But there are things which God is not. In that sense He has a determinate character. Thus He is righteous, not amoral; creative, not inert. The Hebrew writings here observe an admirable balance. Once God says simply I AM, proclaiming the mystery of self-existence. But times without number He says 'I am the Lord'—I, the ultimate Fact, have *this* determinate character, and not *that*. And men are exhorted to 'know the Lord', to discover and experience this particular character.

The error which I am here trying to correct is one of the most sincere and respectable errors in the world; I have sympathy enough with it to feel shocked at the language I have been driven to use in stating the opposite view, which I believe to be the true one. To say that God 'is a particular Thing' does seem to obliterate the immeasurable difference not only between what He is and what all other things are but between the very mode of His existence and theirs. I must at once restore the balance by insisting that derivative things, from atoms to archangels, hardly attain to existence at all in comparison with their Creator. Their principle of existence is not in themselves. You can distinguish *what* they are from the fact *that* they are. The definition of them can be understood and a clear idea of them formed without even knowing *whether* they are. Existence is an 'opaque' addition to the idea of them. But with God it is not so: if we fully understood *what* God is we should see that there is no question *whether* He is. It would always have been impossible that He should not exist. He is the opaque centre of all existences, the thing that simply and entirely *is,* the fountain of facthood. And yet, now that He has created, there is a sense in which we must say that He is a particular Thing and even one Thing among others. To say this is not to lessen the immeasurable difference between Him and them. On the contrary, it is to recognise in Him a positive perfection which Pantheism has obscured; the perfection of being creative. He is so brim-full of existence that He can give existence away, can cause things to be, and to be really other than Himself, can make it untrue to say that He is everything.

It is clear that there never was a time when nothing existed; otherwise nothing would exist now. But to exist means to be a positive Something, to have (metaphorically) a certain shape or structure, to be this and not that. The Thing which always existed, namely God, has therefore always had His own positive character. Throughout all eternity certain statements about Him would have been true and others false. And from the mere fact of our own existence and Nature's we already know to some extent which are which. We know that He invents, acts, creates. After that there can be no ground for assuming in advance that He does not do miracles.

Why, then, do the mystics talk of Him as they do, and why are many people prepared in advance to maintain that, whatever else God may be, He is not the concrete, living, willing, and acting God of Christian theology? I think the reason is as follows. Let us suppose a mystical limpet, a sage among limpets, who (rapt in vision) catches a glimpse of what Man is like. In reporting it to his disciples, who have some vision themselves (though less than he) he will have to use many negatives. He will have to tell them that Man has no shell, is not attached to a rock, is not surrounded by water. And his disciples, having a little vision of their own to help them, do get some idea of Man. But then there come erudite limpets, limpets who write histories of philosophy and give lectures on comparative religion, and who have never had any vision of their own. What they get out of the prophetic limpet's words is simply and solely the negatives. From these, uncorrected by any positive insight, they build up a picture of Man as a sort of amorphous jelly (he has no shell) existing nowhere in particular (he is not attached to a rock) and never taking nourishment (there is no water to drift it towards him). And having a traditional reverence for Man they conclude that to be a famished jelly in a dimensionless void is the supreme mode of existence, and reject as crude, materialistic superstition any doctrine which would attribute to Man a definite shape, a structure, and organs.

Our own situation is much like that of the erudite limpets. Great prophets and saints have an intuition of God which is positive and concrete in the highest degree. Because, just touching the fringes of His being, they have seen that He is plenitude of life and energy and joy, therefore (and for no other reason) they have to pronounce that He transcends those limitations which we call personality, passion, change, materiality, and the like. The positive quality in Him which repels these limitations is their only ground for all the negatives. But when we come limping after and try to construct an intellectual or 'enlightened' religion, we take over these negatives (infinite, immaterial, impassible, immutable, etc.) and use them unchecked by any positive intuition. At each step we have to strip off from our idea of God some human attribute. But the only real reason for stripping off the human attribute is to make room for putting in some positive divine attribute. In St Paul's language, the purpose of all this unclothing is not that our idea of God should reach nakedness but that it should be reclothed. But unhappily we have no means of doing the reclothing. When we have removed from our idea of God some puny human characteristic, we (as merely erudite or intelligent enquirers) have no resources from which to supply that blindingly real and concrete attribute of Deity which ought to replace it. Thus at each step in the process of refinement our idea of God contains less, and the fatal pictures come in (an endless, silent sea, an empty sky beyond all stars, a dome of white radiance) and we reach at last mere zero and worship a nonentity. And the understanding, left to itself, can hardly help following this path. That is why the Christian statement that only He who does the will of the Father will ever know the true doctrine is philosophically accurate. Imagination may help a little: but in the moral life, and (still more) in the devotional life we touch something concrete which will at once begin to correct the growing emptiness of our idea of God. One moment even of feeble contrition or blurred thankfulness will, at least in some degree, head us off from the abyss of abstraction. It is Reason herself which teaches us not to rely on Reason only in this matter. For Reason knows that she cannot work without materials. When it becomes clear that you cannot find out by reasoning whether the cat is in the linen-cupboard, it is Reason herself who whispers, 'Go and look. This is not my job: it is a matter for the senses'. So here. The materials for correcting our abstract conception of God cannot be supplied by Reason: she will be the first to tell you to go and try experience—'Oh, taste and see!' For of course she will have already pointed out that your present position is absurd. As long as we remain Erudite Limpets we are forgetting that if no one had ever seen more of God than we, we should have no reason even to believe Him immaterial, immutable, impassible and all the rest of it. Even that negative knowledge which seems to us so enlightened is only a relic left over from the positive knowledge of better men—only the pattern which that heavenly wave left on the sand when it retreated.

'A Spirit and a Vision,' said Blake, 'are not, as the modern philosophy supposes, a cloudy vapour, or a nothing. They are organised and minutely articulated beyond all that the mortal and perishing nature can produce'.[2] He is speaking only of how to draw pictures of apparitions which may well have been illusory, but his words suggest a truth on the metaphysical level also. God is basic Fact or Actuality, the source of all other facthood. At all costs therefore He must not be thought of as a featureless generality. If He exists at all, He is the most concrete thing there is, the most individual, 'organised and minutely articulated'. He is unspeakable not by being indefinite but by being too definite for the unavoidable vagueness of language. The words *incorporeal* and *impersonal* are misleading, because they suggest that He lacks some reality which we possess. It would be safer to call Him *trans-corporeal, trans-personal*. Body and personality as we know them are the real negatives—they are what is left of positive being when it is sufficiently diluted to appear in temporal or finite forms. Even our sexuality should be regarded as the transposition into a minor key of that creative joy which in Him is unceasing and irresistible. Grammatically the things we say of Him are 'metaphorical': but in a deeper sense it is our physical and psychic energies that are mere 'metaphors' of the real Life which is God. Divine Sonship is, so to speak, the solid of which biological sonship is merely a diagrammatic representation on the flat.

And here the subject of imagery, which crossed our path in the last chapter, can be seen in a new light. For it is just the recognition of God's positive and concrete reality which the religious imagery preserves. The crudest Old Testament picture of Jahweh thundering and lightning out of dense smoke, making mountains skip like rams, threatening, promising, pleading, even changing His mind, transmits that sense of *living* Deity which evaporates in abstract thought. Even sub-Christian images—even

---

[2] *A Descriptive Catalogue.* Number IV.

a Hindoo idol with a hundred hands—gets in *something* which mere 're-ligion' in our own days has left out. We rightly reject it, for by itself it would encourage the most blackguardly of superstitions, the adoration of mere power. Perhaps we may rightly reject much of the Old Testament imagery. But we must be clear why we are doing so: not because the images are too strong but because they are too weak. The ultimate spiritual reality is not vaguer, more inert, more transparent than the images, but more positive, more dynamic, more opaque. Confusion between Spirit and soul (or 'ghost') has here done much harm. Ghosts must be pictured, if we are to picture them at all, as shadowy and tenuous, for ghosts are half-men, one element abstracted from a creature that ought to have flesh. But Spirit, if pictured at all, must be pictured in the very opposite way. Neither God nor even the gods are 'shadowy' in traditional imagination: even the human dead, when glorified in Christ, cease to be 'ghosts' and become 'saints'. The difference of atmosphere which even now surrounds the words 'I saw a ghost' and the words 'I saw a saint'—all the pallor and insubstantiality of the one, all the gold and blue of the other—contains more wisdom than whole libraries of 'religion'. If we must have a mental picture to symbolise Spirit, we should represent it as something *heavier* than matter.

And if we say that we are rejecting the old images in order to do more justice to the moral attributes of God, we must again be careful of what we are really meaning. When we wish to learn of the love and goodness of God by *analogy*—by imagining parallels to them in the realm of human relations—we turn of course to the parables of Christ. But when we try to conceive the reality as it may be in itself, we must beware lest we interpret 'moral attributes' in terms of mere conscientiousness or abstract benevolence. The mistake is easily made because we (correctly) deny that God has passions; and with us a love that is not passionate means a love that is something less. But the reason why God has no passions is that passions imply passivity and intermission. The passion of love is something that happens to us, as 'getting wet' happens to a body: and God is exempt from that 'passion' in the same way that water is exempt from 'getting wet'. He cannot be affected with love, because He *is* love. To imagine that love as something less torrential or less sharp than our own temporary and derivative 'passions' is a most disastrous fantasy.

Again, we may find a violence in some of the traditional imagery which tends to obscure the changelessness of God, the peace, which nearly all who approach Him have reported—the 'still, small voice'. And it is here, I think, that the pre-Christian imagery is least suggestive. Yet even here, there is a danger lest the half conscious picture of some huge thing at rest—a clear, still ocean, a dome of 'white radiance'—should smuggle in ideas of inertia or vacuity. The stillness in which the mystics approach Him is intent and alert—at the opposite pole from sleep or reverie. They are becoming like Him. Silences in the physical world occur in empty places: but the ultimate Peace is silent through very density of life. Saying is swallowed up in being. There is no movement because His action (which is Himself) is timeless. You might, if you wished, call it movement at an infinite speed, which is the same thing as rest, but reached by a different—perhaps a less misleading—way of approach.

Men are reluctant to pass over from the notion of an abstract and negative deity to the living God. I do not wonder. Here lies the deepest tap-root of Pantheism and of the objection to traditional imagery. It was hated not, at bottom, because it pictured Him as man but because it pictured Him as king, or even as warrior. The Pantheist's God does nothing, demands nothing. He is there if you wish for Him, like a book on a shelf. He will not pursue you. There is no danger that at any time heaven and earth should flee away at His glance. If He were the truth, then we could really say that all the Christian images of kingship were a historical accident of which our religion ought to be cleansed. It is with a shock that we discover them to be indispensable. You have had a shock like that before, in connection with smaller matters—when the line pulls at your hand, when something breathes beside you in the darkness. So here; the shock comes at the precise moment when the thrill of *life* is communicated to us along the clue we have been following. It is always shocking to meet life where we thought we were alone. 'Look out!' we cry, 'it's *alive*'. And therefore this is the very point at which so many draw back—I would have done so myself if I could—and proceed no further with Christianity. An 'impersonal God'—well and good. A subjective God of beauty, truth and goodness, inside our own heads—better still. A formless life-force surging through us, a vast power which we can tap—best of all. But God Himself, alive, pulling at the other end of the cord, perhaps approaching at an infinite speed, the hunter, king, husband—that is quite another matter. There comes a moment when the children who have been playing at burglars hush suddenly: was that a *real* footstep in the hall? There comes a moment when people who have been dabbling in religion ('Man's search for God!') suddenly draw back. Supposing we really found Him? We never meant it to come to *that!* Worse still, supposing He had found us?

So it is a sort of Rubicon. One goes across; or not. But if one does, there is no manner of security against miracles. One may be in for *anything.*

12

THE PROPRIETY
OF MIRACLES

The Principle at the same moment that it explains the
Rules supersedes them.

SEELEY, *ECCE HOMO*, CHAP. XVI.

IF THE ULTIMATE Fact is not an abstraction but the living God, opaque
by the very fullness of His blinding actuality, then He might do things.
He might work miracles. But would He? Many people of sincere piety
feel that He would not. They think it unworthy of Him. It is petty and
capricious tyrants who break their own laws: good and wise kings obey
them. Only an incompetent workman will produce work which needs
to be interfered with. And people who think in this way are not satisfied by the assurance given them in Chapter VIII that miracles do not, in
fact, break the laws of Nature. That may be undeniable. But it will still
be felt (and justly) that miracles interrupt the orderly march of events,
the steady development of Nature according to her own inherent genius
or character. That regular march seems to such critics as I have in mind
more impressive than any miracle. Looking up (like Lucifer in Meredith's
sonnet) at the night sky, they feel it almost impious to suppose that God
should sometimes unsay what He has once said with such magnificence.
This feeling springs from deep and noble sources in the mind and must
always be treated with respect. Yet it is, I believe, founded on an error.

385

When schoolboys begin to be taught to make Latin verses at school they are very properly forbidden to have what is technically called 'a spondee in the fifth foot'. It is a good rule for boys because the normal hexameter does not have a spondee there: if boys were allowed to use this abnormal form they would be constantly doing it for convenience and might never get the typical music of the hexameter into their heads at all. But when the boys come to read Virgil they find that Virgil does the very thing they have been forbidden to do—not very often, but not so very rarely either. In the same way, young people who have just learned how to write English rhyming verse, may be shocked at finding 'bad' rhymes (i.e. half-rhymes) in the great poets. Even in carpentry or car-driving or surgery there are, I expect, 'licenses'—abnormal ways of doing things—which the master will use himself both safely and judiciously but which he would think it unwise to teach his pupils.

Now one often finds that the beginner, who has just mastered the strict formal rules, is over-punctilious and pedantic about them. And the mere critic, who is never going to begin himself, may be more pedantic still. The classical critics were shocked at the 'irregularity' or 'licenses' of Shakespeare. A stupid schoolboy might think that the abnormal hexameters in Virgil, or the half-rhymes in English poets, were due to incompetence. In reality, of course, every one of them is there for a purpose and breaks the superficial regularity of the metre in obedience to a higher and subtler law: just as the irregularities in *The Winter's Tale* do not impair, but embody and perfect, the inward unity of its spirit.

In other words, there are rules behind the rules, and a unity which is deeper than uniformity. A supreme workman will never break by one note or one syllable or one stroke of the brush the living and inward law of the work he is producing. But he will break without scruple any number of those superficial regularities and orthodoxies which little, unimaginative critics mistake for its laws. The extent to which one can distinguish a just 'license' from a mere botch or failure of unity depends on the extent to which one has grasped the real and inward significance of the work as a whole. If we had grasped as a whole the innermost spirit of that 'work which God worketh from the beginning to the end', and of which Nature is only a part and perhaps a small part, we should be in a position to decide whether miraculous interruptions of Nature's history were mere improprieties unworthy of the Great Workman or expressions of the truest and deepest unity in His total work. In fact, of course, we are in no such position. The gap between God's mind and ours must, on any view, be incalculably greater than the gap between Shakespeare's mind and that of the most peddling critics of the old French school.

For who can suppose that God's external act, seen from within, would be that same complexity of mathematical relations which Nature, scientifically studied, reveals? It is like thinking that a poet builds up his line out of those metrical feet into which we can analyse it, or that living speech takes grammar as its starting point. But the best illustration of all is Bergson's. Let us suppose a race of people whose peculiar mental limitation compels them to regard a painting as something made up of little coloured dots which have been put together like a mosaic. Studying the brushwork of a great painting, through their magnifying glasses, they discover more and more complicated relations between the dots, and sort these relations out, with great toil, into certain regularities. Their labour will not be in vain. These regularities will in fact 'work'; they will cover most of the facts. But if they go on to conclude that any departure from them would be unworthy of the painter, and an arbitrary breaking of his own rules, they will be far astray. For the regularities they have observed never were the rule the painter was following. What they painfully reconstruct from a million dots, arranged in an agonising complexity, he really produced with a single lightning-quick turn of the wrist, his eye meanwhile taking in the canvas as a whole and his mind obeying laws of composition which the observers, counting their dots, have not yet come within sight of, and perhaps never will. I do not say that the normalities of Nature are unreal. The living fountain of divine energy, solidified for purposes of this spatio-temporal Nature into bodies moving in space and time, and thence, by our abstract thought, turned into mathematical formulae, does in fact for us, commonly fall into such and such patterns. In finding out those patterns we are therefore gaining real, and often useful, knowledge. But to think that a disturbance of them would constitute a breach of the living rule and organic unity whereby God, from His own point of view, works, is a mistake. If miracles do occur then we may be sure that *not* to have wrought them would be the real inconsistency.

How a miracle can be no inconsistency, but the highest consistency, will be clear to those who have read Miss Dorothy Sayers' indispensable book, *The Mind of the Maker*. Miss Sayers' thesis is based on the analogy between God's relation to the world, on the one hand, and an author's relation to his book on the other. If you are writing a story, miracles or abnormal events may be bad art, or they may not. If, for example, you are writing an ordinary realistic novel and have got your characters into a hopeless muddle, it would be quite intolerable if you suddenly cut the knot and secured a happy ending by having a fortune left to the hero from an unexpected quarter. On the other hand there is nothing against taking as your subject from the outset the adventures of a man who inherits an unexpected fortune. The unusual event is perfectly permissible if it is what you are really writing *about:* it is an artistic crime if you simply drag it in by the heels to get yourself out of a hole. The ghost story is a legitimate form of art; but you must not bring a ghost into an ordinary novel to get over a difficulty in the plot. Now there is no doubt that a great deal of the modern objection to miracles is based on the suspicion that they are marvels of the wrong sort; that a story of a certain kind (Nature) is arbitrarily interfered with, to get the characters out of a difficulty, by events that do not really belong to that kind of story. Some people probably think of the Resurrection as a desperate last moment expedient to save the Hero from a situation which had got out of the Author's control.

The reader may set his mind at rest. If I thought miracles were like that, I should not believe in them. If they have occurred, they have occurred because they are the very thing this universal story is about. They are not exceptions (however rarely they occur) not irrelevancies. They are precisely those chapters in this great story on which the plot turns. Death and Resurrection are what the story is about; and had we but eyes to see it, this has been hinted on every page, met us, in some disguise, at every turn, and even been muttered in conversations between such minor characters (if they are minor characters) as the vegetables. If you have hitherto disbelieved in miracles, it is worth pausing a moment to consider whether this is not chiefly because you thought you had discovered what the story was really about?—that atoms, and time and space and economics and politics were the main plot? And is it certain you were right? It is easy to make mistakes in such matters. A friend of mine wrote a play in which the main idea was that the hero had a pathological horror of trees and a mania for cutting them down. But naturally other things came in as well; there was some sort of love story mixed up with it. And the

trees killed the man in the end. When my friend had written it, he sent it
an older man to criticise. It came back with the comment, 'Not bad. But
I'd cut out those bits of *padding* about the trees'. To be sure, God might
be expected to make a better story than my friend. But it is a very *long*
story, with a complicated plot; and we are not, perhaps, very attentive
readers.

13

ON PROBABILITY

Probability is founded on the presumption of a
resemblance between those objects of which we have had
experience and those of which we have had none; and
therefore it is impossible that this presumption can arise
from probability.

HUME, *TREATISE OF HUMAN NATURE*, I, III, VI.

THE ARGUMENT UP to date shows that miracles are possible and that
there is nothing antecedently ridiculous in the stories which say that God
has sometimes performed them. This does not mean, of course, that we
are committed to believing all stories of miracles. Most stories about miraculous events are probably false: if it comes to that, most stories about
natural events are false. Lies, exaggerations, misunderstandings and
hearsay make up perhaps more than half of all that is said and written in
the world. We must therefore find a criterion whereby to judge any particular story of the miraculous.

In one sense, of course, our criterion is plain. Those stories are to be
accepted for which the historical evidence is sufficiently good. But then,
as we saw at the outset, the answer to the question, 'How much evidence
should we require for this story?' depends on our answer to the question,
'How far is this story intrinsically probable?' We must therefore find a
criterion of probability.

The ordinary procedure of the modern historian, even if he admits the possibility of miracle, is to admit no particular instance of it until every possibility of 'natural' explanation has been tried and failed. That is, he will accept the most improbable 'natural' explanations rather than say that a miracle occurred. Collective hallucination, hypnotism of unconsenting spectators, widespread instantaneous conspiracy in lying by persons not otherwise known to be liars and not likely to gain by the lie—all these are known to be very improbable events: so improbable that, except for the special purpose of excluding a miracle, they are never suggested. But they are preferred to the admission of a miracle.

Such a procedure is, from the purely historical point of view, sheer midsummer madness *unless* we start by knowing that any Miracle whatever is more improbable than the most improbable natural event. Do we know this?

We must distinguish the different kinds of improbability. Since miracles are, by definition, rarer than other events, it is obviously improbable beforehand that one will occur at any given place and time. In that sense every miracle is improbable. But that sort of improbability does not make the story that a miracle *has* happened incredible; for in the same sense all events whatever were once improbable. It is immensely improbable beforehand that a pebble dropped from the stratosphere over London will hit any given spot or that any one particular person will win a large lottery. But the report that the pebble has landed outside such and such a shop or that Mr So-and-So has won the lottery is not at all incredible. When you consider the immense number of meetings and fertile unions between ancestors which were necessary in order that you should be born, you perceive that it was once immensely improbable that such a person as you should come to exist: but once you are here, the report of your existence is not in the least incredible. With probability of this kind—antecedent probability of chances—we are not here concerned. Our business is with historical probability.

Ever since Hume's famous *Essay* it has been believed that historical statements about miracles are the most intrinsically improbable of all historical statements. According to Hume, probability rests on what may be called the majority vote of our past experiences. The more often a thing has been known to happen, the more probable it is that it should happen again; and the less often the less probable. Now the regularity of Nature's course, says Hume, is supported by something better than the majority vote of past experiences: it is supported by their unanimous vote, or, as Hume says, by 'firm and unalterable experience'. There is, in fact, 'uniform experience' against Miracle; otherwise, says Hume, it would not be a Miracle. A miracle is therefore the most improbable of all events. It is always more probable that the witnesses were lying or mistaken than that a miracle occurred.

Now of course we must agree with Hume that if there is absolutely 'uniform experience' against miracles, if in other words they have never happened, why then they never have. Unfortunately we know the experience against them to be uniform only if we know that all the reports of them are false. And we can know all the reports to be false only if we know already that miracles have never occurred. In fact, we are arguing in a circle.

There is also an objection to Hume which leads us deeper into our problem. The whole idea of Probability (as Hume understands it) depends on the principle of the Uniformity of Nature. Unless Nature always goes on in the same way, the fact that a thing had happened ten million times would not make it a whit more probable that it would happen again. And how do we know the Uniformity of Nature? A moment's thought shows that we do not know it by experience. We observe many regularities in Nature. But of course all the observations that men have made or will make while the race lasts cover only a minute fraction of the events that actually go on. Our observations would therefore be of no use unless we felt sure that Nature when we are not watching her behaves in the same way as when we are: in other words, unless we believed in the Uniformity of Nature. Experience therefore cannot prove uniformity, because uniformity has to be assumed before experience proves anything. And mere length of experience does not help matters. It is no good saying, 'Each fresh experience confirms our belief in uniformity and therefore we reasonably expect that it will always be confirmed'; for that argument works only on the assumption that the future will resemble the past—which is simply the assumption of Uniformity under a new name. Can we say that Uniformity is at any rate very probable? Unfortunately not. We have just seen that all probabilities depend on *it*. Unless Nature is uniform, nothing is either probable or improbable. And clearly the assumption which you have to make before there is any such thing as probability cannot itself be probable.

The odd thing is that no man knew this better than Hume. His *Essay on Miracles* is quite inconsistent with the more radical, and honourable, scepticism of his main work.

The question, 'Do miracles occur?' and the question, 'Is the course of Nature absolutely uniform?' are the same question asked in two different ways. Hume, by sleight of hand, treats them as two different questions. He first answers 'Yes,' to the question whether Nature is absolutely uniform: and then uses this 'Yes' as a ground for answering, 'No,' to the question, 'Do miracles occur?' The single real question which he set out to answer is never discussed at all. He gets the answer to one form of the question by assuming the answer to another form of the same question.

Probabilities of the kind that Hume is concerned with hold inside the framework of an assumed Uniformity of Nature. When the question of miracles is raised we are asking about the validity or perfection of the frame itself. No study of probabilities inside a given frame can ever tell us how probable it is that the frame itself can be violated. Granted a school timetable with French on Tuesday morning at ten o'clock, it is really probable that Jones, who always skimps his French preparation, will be in trouble next Tuesday, and that he was in trouble on any previous Tuesday. But what does this tell us about the probability of the timetable's being altered? To find that out you must eavesdrop in the masters' common-room. It is no use studying the timetable.

If we stick to Hume's method, far from getting what he hoped (namely, the conclusion that all miracles are infinitely improbable) we get a complete deadlock. The only kind of probability he allows holds exclusively within the frame of uniformity. When uniformity is itself in question (and it is in question the moment we ask whether miracles occur) this kind of probability is suspended. And Hume knows no other. By his method, therefore, we cannot say that uniformity is either probable or improbable; and equally we cannot say that miracles are either probable or improbable. We have impounded *both* uniformity *and* miracles in a sort of limbo where probability and improbability can never come. This result is equally disastrous for the scientist and the theologian; but along Hume's lines there is nothing whatever to be done about it.

Our only hope, then, will be to cast about for some quite different kind of Probability. Let us for the moment cease to ask what right we have to believe in the Uniformity of Nature and ask why in fact men do believe in it. I think the belief has three causes, two of which are irrational. In the first place we are creatures of habit. We expect new situations to resemble old ones. It is a tendency which we share with animals; one can see it working, often to very comic results, in our dogs and cats. In the second place, when we plan our actions, we have to leave out of account the theoretical possibility that Nature might not behave as usual tomorrow, because we can do nothing about it. It is not worth bothering about because no action can be taken to meet it. And what we habitually put out of our minds we soon forget. The picture of uniformity thus comes to dominate our minds without rival and we believe it. Both these causes are irrational and would be just as effective in building up a false belief as in building up a true one.

But I am convinced that there is a third cause. 'In science,' said the late Sir Arthur Eddington, 'we sometimes have convictions which we cherish but cannot justify; we are influenced by some innate sense of the fitness of things'. This may sound a perilously subjective and aesthetic criterion; but can one doubt that it is a principal source of our belief in Uniformity? A universe in which unprecedented and unpredictable events were at every moment flung into Nature would not merely be inconvenient to us: it would be profoundly repugnant. We will not accept such a universe on any terms whatever. It is utterly detestable to us. It shocks our 'sense of the fitness of things'. In advance of experience, in the teeth of many experiences, we are already enlisted on the side of uniformity. For of course science actually proceeds by concentrating not on the regularities of Nature but on her apparent irregularities. It is the apparent irregularity that prompts each new hypothesis. It does so because we refuse to acquiesce in irregularities: we never rest till we have formed and verified a hypothesis which enables us to say that they were not really irregularities at all. Nature as it comes to us looks at first like a mass of irregularities. The stove which lit all right yesterday won't light today; the water which was wholesome last year is poisonous this year. The whole mass of seemingly irregular experience could never have been turned into scientific knowledge at all unless from the very start we had brought to it a faith in uniformity which almost no number of disappointments can shake.

This faith—the preference—is it a thing we can trust? Or is it only the way our minds happen to work? It is useless to say that it has hitherto always been confirmed by the event. That is no good unless you (at least silently) add, 'And therefore always will be': and you cannot add that unless you know already that our faith in uniformity is well grounded. And that is just what we are now asking. Does this sense of fitness of ours correspond to anything in external reality?

The answer depends on the Metaphysic one holds. If all that exists is Nature, the great mindless interlocking event, if our own deepest convictions are merely the by-products of an irrational process, then clearly there is not the slightest ground for supposing that our sense of fitness and our consequent faith in uniformity tell us anything about a reality external to ourselves. Our convictions are simply a fact *about us*—like the colour of our hair. If Naturalism is true we have no reason to trust our conviction that Nature is uniform. It can be trusted only if quite a different Metaphysic is true. If the deepest thing in reality, the Fact which is the source of all other facthood, is a thing in some degree like ourselves—if it is a Rational Spirit and we derive our rational spirituality from It—then indeed our conviction can be trusted. Our repugnance to disorder is derived from Nature's Creator and ours. The disorderly world which we cannot endure to believe in is the disorderly world He would not have endured to create. Our conviction that the timetable will not be perpetually or meaninglessly altered is sound because we have (in a sense) eavesdropped in the Masters' common-room.

The sciences logically require a metaphysic of this sort. Our greatest natural philosopher thinks it is also the metaphysic out of which they originally grew. Professor Whitehead points out[1] that centuries of belief in a God who combined 'the personal energy of Jehovah' with 'the rationality of a Greek philosopher' first produced that firm expectation of systematic order which rendered possible the birth of modern science. Men became scientific because they expected Law in Nature, and they expected Law in Nature because they believed in a Legislator. In most modern scientists this belief has died: it will be interesting to see how long their confidence in uniformity survives it. Two significant developments have already appeared—the hypothesis of a lawless sub-nature, and the surrender of the claim that science is true. We may be living nearer than we suppose to the end of the Scientific Age.

But if we admit God, must we admit Miracle? Indeed, indeed, you have no security against it. That is the bargain. Theology says to you in effect, 'Admit God and with Him the risk of a few miracles, and I in re-

[1] *Science and the Modern World*, Chapter II.

turn will ratify your faith in uniformity as regards the overwhelming majority of events'. The philosophy which forbids you to make uniformity absolute is also the philosophy which offers you solid grounds for believing it to be general, to be *almost* absolute. The Being who threatens Nature's claim to omnipotence confirms her in her lawful occasions. Give us this ha'porth of tar and we will save the ship. The alternative is really much worse. Try to make Nature absolute and you find that her uniformity is not even probable. By claiming too much, you get nothing. You get the deadlock, as in Hume. Theology offers you a working arrangement, which leaves the scientist free to continue his experiments and the Christian to continue his prayers.

We have also, I suggest, found what we were looking for—a criterion whereby to judge the intrinsic probability of an alleged miracle. We must judge it by our 'innate sense of the fitness of things', that same sense of fitness which led us to anticipate that the universe would be orderly. I do not mean, of course, that we are to use this sense in deciding whether miracles in general are possible: we know that they are on philosophical grounds. Nor do I mean that a sense of fitness will do instead of close inquiry into the historical evidence. As I have repeatedly pointed out, the historical evidence cannot be estimated unless we have first estimated the intrinsic probability of the recorded event. It is in making that estimate as regards each story of the miraculous that our sense of fitness comes into play.

If in giving such weight to the sense of fitness I were doing anything new, I should feel rather nervous. In reality I am merely giving formal acknowledgement to a principle which is always used. Whatever men may *say*, no one really thinks that the Christian doctrine of the Resurrection is exactly on the same level with some pious tittle-tattle about how Mother Egarée Louise miraculously found her second best thimble by the aid of St Anthony. The religious and the irreligious are really quite agreed on the point. The whoop of delight with which the sceptic would unearth the story of the thimble, and the 'rosy pudency' with which the Christian would keep it in the background, both tell the same tale. Even those who think all stories of miracles absurd think some very much more absurd than others: even those who believe them all (if anyone does) think that some require a specially robust faith. The criterion which both parties are actually using is that of fitness. More than half the disbelief in miracles that exists is based on a sense of their *unfitness:* a conviction (due, as I have argued, to false philosophy) that they are unsuitable to the dignity of God or Nature or else to the indignity and insignificance of man.

In the three following chapters I will try to present the central miracles of the Christian Faith in such a way as to exhibit their 'fitness'. I shall not, however, proceed by formally setting out the conditions which 'fitness' in the abstract ought to satisfy and then dovetailing the Miracles into that scheme. Our 'sense of fitness' is too delicate and elusive a thing to submit to such treatment. If I succeed, the fitness—and if I fail, the unfitness—of these miracles will of itself become apparent while we study them.

THE GRAND MIRACLE

A light that shone from behind the sun; the sun
Was not so fierce as to pierce where that light could.

CHARLES WILLIAMS

THE CENTRAL MIRACLE asserted by Christians is the Incarnation. They say that God became Man. Every other miracle prepares for this, or exhibits this, or results from this. Just as every natural event is the manifestation at a particular place and moment of Nature's total character, so every particular Christian miracle manifests at a particular place and moment the character and significance of the Incarnation. There is no question in Christianity of arbitrary interferences just scattered about. It relates not a series of disconnected raids on Nature but the various steps of a strategically coherent invasion—an invasion which intends complete conquest and 'occupation'. The fitness, and therefore credibility, of the particular miracles depends on their relation to the Grand Miracle; all discussion of them in isolation from it is futile.

The fitness or credibility of the Grand Miracle itself cannot, obviously, be judged by the same standard. And let us admit at once that it is very difficult to find a standard by which it can be judged. If the thing happened, it was the central event in the history of the Earth—the very thing that the whole story has been about. Since it happened only once, it is by Hume's standards infinitely improbable. But then the whole history of the Earth has also happened only once; is it therefore incredible? Hence the difficulty, which weighs upon Christian and atheist alike, of estimating the probability of the Incarnation. It is like asking whether the existence of Nature herself is intrinsically probable. That is why it is easier to argue, on historical grounds, that the Incarnation actually occurred than to show, on philosophical grounds, the probability of its occurrence. The historical difficulty of giving for the life, sayings and influence of Jesus any explanation that is not harder than the Christian explanation, is very great. The discrepancy between the depth and sanity and (let me add) *shrewdness* of His moral teaching and the rampant megalomania which must lie behind His theological teaching unless He is indeed God, has never been satisfactorily got over. Hence the non-Christian hypotheses succeed one another with the restless fertility of bewilderment. Today we are asked to regard all the theological elements as later accretions to the story of a 'historical' and merely human Jesus: yesterday we were asked to believe that the whole thing began with vegetation myths and mystery religions and that the pseudo-historical Man was only fadged up at a later date. But this historical inquiry is outside the scope of my book.

Since the Incarnation, if it is a fact, holds this central position, and since we are assuming that we do not yet know it to have happened on historical grounds, we are in a position which may be illustrated by the following analogy. Let us suppose we possess parts of a novel or a symphony. Someone now brings us a newly discovered piece of manuscript and says, 'This is the missing part of the work. This is the chapter on which the whole plot of the novel really turned. This is the main theme of the symphony'. Our business would be to see whether the new passage, if admitted to the central place which the discoverer claimed for it, did actually illuminate all the parts we had already seen and 'pull them together'. Nor should we be likely to go very far wrong. The new passage, if spurious, however attractive it looked at the first glance, would become harder and harder to reconcile with the rest of the work the longer we considered the matter. But if it were genuine then at every fresh hearing of the music or every fresh reading of the book, we should find it settling down, making itself more at home and eliciting significance from all sorts of details in the whole work which we had hitherto neglected. Even though the new central chapter or main theme contained great difficulties in itself, we should still think it genuine provided that it continually removed difficulties elsewhere. Something like this we must do with the doctrine of the Incarnation. Here, instead of a symphony or a novel, we have the whole mass of our knowledge. The credibility will depend on the extent to which the doctrine, if accepted, can illuminate and integrate that whole mass. It is much less important that the doctrine itself should be fully comprehensible. We believe that the sun is in the sky at midday in summer not because we can clearly see the sun (in fact, we cannot) but because we can see everything else.

The first difficulty that occurs to any critic of the doctrine lies in the very centre of it. What can be meant by 'God becoming man'? In what sense is it conceivable that eternal self-existent Spirit, basic Fact-hood, should be so combined with a natural human organism as to make one person? And this would be a fatal stumbling-block if we had not already discovered that in every human being a more than natural activity (the act of reasoning) and therefore presumably a more than natural agent is thus united with a part of Nature: so united that the composite creature calls itself 'I' and 'Me'. I am not, of course, suggesting that what happened when God became Man was simply another instance of this process. In other men a supernatural *creature* thus becomes, in union with the natural creature, one human being. In Jesus, it is held, the Supernatural Creator Himself did so. I do not think anything we do will enable us to imagine the mode of consciousness of the incarnate God. That is where the doctrine is not fully comprehensible. But the difficulty which we felt in the mere idea of the Supernatural descending into the Natural is apparently non-existent, or is at least overcome in the person of every man. If we did not know by experience what it feels like to be a rational animal—how all these natural facts, all this biochemistry and instinctive affection or repulsion and sensuous perception, can become the medium of rational thought and moral will which understand necessary relations and acknowledge modes of behaviour as universally binding, we could not conceive, much less imagine, the thing happening. The discrepancy between a movement of atoms in an astronomer's cortex and his understanding that there must be a still unobserved planet beyond Uranus, is already so immense that the Incarnation of God Himself is, in one sense, scarcely more startling. We cannot conceive how the Divine Spirit dwelled within the created and human spirit of Jesus: but neither can we conceive how His human spirit, or that of any man, dwells within his natural organism. What we can understand, if the Christian doctrine is true, is that our own composite existence is not the sheer anomaly it might seem to be, but a faint image of the Divine Incarnation itself—the same theme in a very minor key. We can understand that if God so descends into a human spirit, and human spirit so descends into Nature, and our thoughts into our senses and passions, and if adult minds (but only the best of them) can descend into sympathy with children, and men into sympathy with beasts, then everything hangs together and the total reality, both Natural and Supernatural, in which we are living is more multifariously and subtly harmonious than we had suspected. We catch sight of a new key principle—the power of the Higher, just in so far as it is truly Higher, to come down, the power of the greater to include the less. Thus solid bodies exemplify many truths of plane geometry, but plane figures no truths of solid geometry: many inorganic propositions are true of organisms but no organic propositions are true of minerals; Montaigne became kittenish with his kitten but she never talked philosophy to him.[1] Everywhere the great enters the little—its power to do so is almost the test of its greatness.

In the Christian story God descends to reascend. He comes down; down from the heights of absolute being into time and space, down into humanity; down further still, if embryologists are right, to recapitulate in the womb ancient and pre-human phases of life; down to the very roots and seabed of the Nature He has created. But He goes down to come up again and bring the whole ruined world up with Him. One has the picture of a strong man stooping lower and lower to get himself underneath some great complicated burden. He must stoop in order to lift, he must almost disappear under the load before he incredibly straightens his back and marches off with the whole mass swaying on his shoulders. Or one may think of a diver, first reducing himself to nakedness, then glancing in mid-air, then gone with a splash, vanished, rushing down through green and warm water into black and cold water, down through increasing pressure into the death-like region of ooze and slime and old decay; then up again, back to colour and light, his lungs almost bursting, till suddenly he breaks surface again, holding in his hand the dripping, precious thing that he went down to recover. He and it are both coloured now that they have come up into the light: down below, where it lay colourless in the dark, he lost his colour too.

---

[1] *Essays*, I, xii, Apology for Raimond de Sebonde.

In this descent and reascent everyone will recognise a familiar pattern: a thing written all over the world. It is the pattern of all vegetable life. It must belittle itself into something hard, small and deathlike, it must fall into the ground: thence the new life reascends. It is the pattern of all animal generation too. There is descent from the full and perfect organisms into the spermatozoon and ovum, and in the dark womb a life at first inferior in kind to that of the species which is being reproduced: then the slow ascent to the perfect embryo, to the living, conscious baby, and finally to the adult. So it is also in our moral and emotional life. The first innocent and spontaneous desires have to submit to the deathlike process of control or total denial: but from that there is a reascent to fully formed character in which the strength of the original material all operates but in a new way. Death and Rebirth—go down to go up—it is a key principle. Through this bottleneck, this belittlement, the highroad nearly always lies.

The doctrine of the Incarnation, if accepted, puts this principle even more emphatically at the centre. The pattern is there in Nature because it was first there in God. All the instances of it which I have mentioned turn out to be but transpositions of the Divine theme into a minor key. I am not now referring simply to the Crucifixion and Resurrection of Christ. The total pattern, of which they are only the turning point, is the real Death and Rebirth: for certainly no seed ever fell from so fair a tree into so dark and cold a soil as would furnish more than a faint analogy to this huge descent and reascension in which God dredged the salt and oozy bottom of Creation.

From this point of view the Christian doctrine makes itself so quickly at home amid the deepest apprehensions of reality which we have from other sources, that doubt may spring up in a new direction. Is it not fitting in too well? So well that it must have come into men's minds from seeing this pattern elsewhere, particularly in the annual death and resurrection of the corn? For there have, of course, been many religions in which that annual drama (so important for the life of the tribe) was almost admittedly the central theme, and the deity—Adonis, Osiris, or another—almost undisguisedly a personification of the corn, a 'corn-king' who died and rose again each year. Is not Christ simply another corn-king?

Now this brings us to the oddest thing about Christianity. In a sense the view which I have just described is actually true. From a certain point of view Christ is 'the same sort of thing' as Adonis or Osiris (always, of course, waiving the fact that they lived nobody knows where or when, while He was executed by a Roman magistrate we know in a year which can be roughly dated). And that is just the puzzle. If Christianity is a religion of that kind why is the analogy of the seed falling into the ground so seldom mentioned (twice only if I mistake not) in the New Testament? Corn-religions are popular and respectable: if that is what the first Christian teachers were putting across, what motive could they have for concealing the fact? The impression they make is that of men who simply don't know how close they are to the corn-religions: men who simply overlook the rich sources of relevant imagery and association which they must have been on the verge of tapping at every moment. If you say they suppressed it because they were Jews, that only raises the puzzle in a new form. Why should the only religion of a 'dying God' which has actually survived and risen to unexampled spiritual heights occur precisely among those people to whom, and to whom almost alone, the whole circle of ideas that belong to the 'dying God' was foreign? I myself, who first seriously read the New Testament when I was, imaginatively and poetically, all agog for the Death and Rebirth pattern and anxious to meet a corn-king, was chilled and puzzled by the almost total absence of such ideas in the Christian documents. One moment particularly stood out. A 'dying God'—the only dying God who might possibly be historical—holds bread, that is, corn, in His hand and says, 'This is my body'. Surely here, even if nowhere else—or surely if not here, at least in the earliest comments on this passage and through all later devotional usage in ever swelling volume—the truth must come out; the connection between this and the annual drama of the crops must be made. But it is not. It is there for me. There is no sign that it was there for the disciples or (humanly speaking) for Christ Himself. It is almost as if He didn't realise what He had said.

The records, in fact, show us a Person who *enacts* the part of the Dying God, but whose thoughts and words remain quite outside the circle of religious ideas to which the Dying God belongs. The very thing which the Nature-religions are all about seems to have really happened once; but it happened in a circle where no trace of Nature-religion was present. It is as if you met the sea-serpent and found that it disbelieved in sea-serpents: as if history recorded a man who had done all the things attributed to Sir Launcelot but who had himself never apparently heard of chivalry.

There is, however, one hypothesis which, if accepted, makes every-thing easy and coherent. The Christians are not claiming that simply 'God' was incarnate in Jesus. They are claiming that the one true God is He whom the Jews worshipped as Jahweh, and that it is He who has descended. Now the double character of Jahweh is this. On the one hand He is the God of Nature, her glad Creator. It is He who sends rain into the furrows till the valleys stand so thick with corn that they laugh and sing. The trees of the wood rejoice before Him and His voice causes the wild deer to bring forth their young. He is the God of wheat and wine and oil. In that respect He is constantly doing all the things that Nature-Gods do: He is Bacchus, Venus, Ceres all rolled into one. There is no trace in Judaism of the idea found in some pessimistic and Pantheistic religions that Nature is some kind of illusion or disaster, that finite exis-tence is in itself an evil and that the cure lies in the relapse of all things into God. Compared with such anti-natural conceptions Jahweh might almost be mistaken for a Nature-God.

On the other hand, Jahweh is clearly *not* a Nature-God. He does not die and come to life each year as a true Corn-king should. He may give wine and fertility, but must not be worshipped with Bacchanalian or aph-rodisiac rites. He is not the soul of Nature nor of any part of Nature. He inhabits eternity: He dwells in the high and holy place: heaven is His throne, not His vehicle, earth is His footstool, not His vesture. One day He will dismantle both and make a new heaven and earth. He is not to be identified even with the 'divine spark' in man. He is 'God and not man': His thoughts are not our thoughts: all our righteousness is filthy rags. His appearance to Ezekiel is attended with imagery that does not bor-row from Nature, but (it is a mystery too seldom noticed[2]) from those machines which men were to make centuries after Ezekiel's death. The prophet saw something suspiciously like a *dynamo*.

Jahweh is neither the soul of Nature nor her enemy. She is neither His body nor a declension and falling away from Him. She is His creature. He is not a nature-God, but the God of Nature—her inventor, maker, owner, and controller. To everyone who reads this book the conception has been familiar from childhood; we therefore easily think it is the most ordinary conception in the world. 'If people are going to believe in a God at all,' we ask, 'what other kind would they believe in?' But the answer

---

[2] I owe this point to Canon Adam Fox.

of history is, 'Almost any other kind'. We mistake our privileges for our instincts: just as one meets ladies who believe their own refined manners to be natural to them. They don't remember being taught.

Now if there is such a God and if He descends to rise again, then we can understand why Christ is at once so like the Corn-King and so silent about him. He is like the Corn-King because the Corn-King is a portrait of Him. The similarity is not in the least unreal or accidental. For the Corn-King is derived (through human imagination) from the facts of Nature, and the facts of Nature from her Creator; the Death and Rebirth pattern is in her because it was first in Him. On the other hand, elements of Nature-religion are strikingly absent from the teaching of Jesus and from the Judaic preparation which led up to it precisely because in them Nature's Original is manifesting Itself. In them you have from the very outset got in behind Nature-religion and behind Nature herself. Where the real God is present the shadows of that God do not appear; that which the shadows resembled does. The Hebrews throughout their history were being constantly headed off from the worship of Nature-gods; not because the Nature-gods were in all respects unlike the God of Nature but because, at best, they were merely like, and it was the destiny of that nation to be turned away from likenesses to the thing itself.

The mention of that nation turns our attention to one of those features in the Christian story which is repulsive to the modern mind. To be quite frank, we do not at all like the idea of a 'chosen people'. Democrats by birth and education, we should prefer to think that all nations and individuals start level in the search for God, or even that all religions are equally true. It must be admitted at once that Christianity makes no concessions to this point of view. It does not tell of a human search for God at all, but of something done by God for, to, and about, Man. And the way in which it is done is selective, undemocratic, to the highest degree. After the knowledge of God had been universally lost or obscured, one man from the whole earth (Abraham) is picked out. He is separated (miserably enough, we may suppose) from his natural surroundings, sent into a strange country, and made the ancestor of a nation who are to carry the knowledge of the true God. Within this nation there is further selection: some die in the desert, some remain behind in Babylon. There is further selection still. The process grows narrower and narrower, sharpens at last into one small bright point like the head of a spear. It is a Jewish girl at her prayers. All humanity (so far as concerns its redemption) has narrowed to that.

Such a process is very unlike what modern feeling demands: but it is startlingly like what Nature habitually does. Selectiveness, and with it (we must allow) enormous wastage, is her method. Out of enormous space a very small portion is occupied by matter at all. Of all the stars, perhaps very few, perhaps only one, have planets. Of the planets in our own system probably only one supports organic life. In the transmission of organic life, countless seeds and spermatozoa are emitted: some few are selected for the distinction of fertility. Among the species only one is rational. Within that species only a few attain excellence of beauty, strength or intelligence.

At this point we come perilously near the argument of Butler's famous *Analogy*. I say 'perilously' because the argument of that book very nearly admits parodying in the form 'You say that the behaviour attributed to the Christian God is both wicked and foolish: but it is no less likely to be true on that account for I can show that Nature (which He created) behaves just as badly.' To which the atheist will answer—and the nearer he is to Christ in his heart, the more certainly he will do so—'If there is a God like that I despise and defy Him.' But I am not saying that Nature, as we now know her, is good; that is a point we must return to in a moment. Nor am I saying that a God whose actions were no better than Nature's would be a proper object of worship for any honest man. The point is a little finer than that. This selective or undemocratic quality in Nature, at least in so far as it affects human life, is neither good nor evil. According as spirit exploits or fails to exploit this Natural situation, it gives rise to one or the other. It permits, on the one hand, ruthless competition, arrogance, and envy: it permits on the other, modesty and (one of our greatest pleasures) admiration. A world in which I was *really* (and not merely by a useful legal fiction) 'as good as everyone else', in which I never looked up to anyone wiser or cleverer or braver or more learned than I, would be insufferable. The very 'fans' of the cinema stars and the famous footballers know better than to desire that! What the Christian story does is not to instate on the Divine level a cruelty and wastefulness which have already disgusted us on the Natural, but to show us in God's act, working neither cruelly nor wastefully, the same principle which is in Nature also, though down there it works sometimes in one way and sometimes in the other. It illuminates the Natural scene by suggesting that a principle which at first looked meaningless may yet be derived from a principle which is good and fair, may indeed be a depraved and blurred copy of it—the pathological form which it would take in a *spoiled* Nature.

For when we look into the Selectiveness which the Christians attribute to God we find in it none of that 'favouritism' which we were afraid of. The 'chosen' people are chosen not for their own sake (certainly not for their own honour or pleasure) but for the sake of the unchosen. Abraham is told that 'in his seed' (the chosen nation) 'all nations shall be blest'. That nation has been chosen to bear a heavy burden. Their sufferings are great: but, as Isaiah recognised, their sufferings heal others. On the finally selected Woman falls the utmost depth of maternal anguish. Her Son, the incarnate God, is a 'man of sorrows'; the one Man into whom Deity descended, the one Man who can be lawfully adored, is pre-eminent for suffering.

But, you will ask, does this much mend matters? Is not this still injustice, though now the other way round? Where, at the first glance, we accused God of undue favour to His 'chosen', we are now tempted to accuse Him of undue disfavour. (The attempt to keep up both charges at the same time had better be dropped.) And certainly we have here come to a principle very deep-rooted in Christianity: what may be called the principle of *Vicariousness*. The Sinless Man suffers for the sinful, and, in their degree, all good men for all bad men. And this Vicariousness—no less than Death and Rebirth or Selectiveness—is also a characteristic of Nature. Self-sufficiency, living on one's own resources, is a thing impossible in her realm. Everything is indebted to everything else, sacrificed to everything else, dependent on everything else. And here too we must recognise that the principle is in itself neither good nor bad. The cat lives on the mouse in a way I think bad: the bees and the flowers live on one another in a more pleasing manner. The parasite lives on its 'host': but so also the unborn child on its mother. In social life without Vicariousness there would be no exploitation or oppression; but also no kindness or gratitude. It is a fountain both of love and hatred, both of misery and happiness. When we have understood this we shall no longer think that the depraved examples of Vicariousness in Nature forbid us to suppose that the principle itself is of divine origin.

At this point it may be well to take a backward glance and notice how the doctrine of Incarnation is already acting on the rest of our knowledge. We have already brought it into contact with four other principles:

the composite nature of man, the pattern of descent and reascension, Selectiveness, and Vicariousness. The first may be called a fact about the frontier between Nature and Supernature; the other three are characteristics of Nature herself. Now most religions, when brought face to face with the facts of Nature either simply reaffirm them, give them (just as they stand) a transcendent prestige, or else simply negate them, promise us release from such facts and from Nature altogether. The Nature-Religions take the first line. They sanctify our agricultural concerns and indeed our whole biological life. We get really drunk in the worship of Dionysus and lie with real women in the temple of the fertility goddess. In Life-force worship, which is the modern and western type of Nature-religion, we take over the existing trend towards 'development' of increasing complexity in organic, social, and industrial life, and make it a god. The anti-Natural or pessimistic religions, which are more civilised and sensitive, such as Buddhism or higher Hinduism, tell us that Nature is evil and illusory, that there is an escape from this incessant change, this furnace of striving and desire. Neither the one nor the other sets the facts of Nature in a new light. The Nature-religions merely reinforce that view of Nature which we spontaneously adopt in our moments of rude health and cheerful brutality; the anti-natural religions do the same for the view we take in moments of compassion, fastidiousness, or lassitude. The Christian doctrine does neither of these things. If any man approaches it with the idea that because Jahweh is the God of fertility our lasciviousness is going to be authorised or that the Selectiveness and Vicariousness of God's method will excuse us for imitating (as 'Heroes', 'Supermen' or social parasites) the lower Selectiveness and Vicariousness of Nature, he will be stunned and repelled by the inflexible Christian demand for chastity, humility, mercy and justice. On the other hand if we come to it regarding the death which precedes every rebirth, or the fact of inequality, or our dependence on others and their dependence on us, as the mere odious necessities of an evil cosmos, and hoping to be delivered into transparent and 'enlightened' spirituality where all these things just vanish, we shall be equally disappointed. We shall be told that, in one sense, and despite enormous differences, it is 'the same all the way up'; that hierarchical inequality, the need for self surrender, the willing sacrifice of self to others, and the thankful and loving (but unashamed) acceptance of others' sacrifice to us, hold sway in the realm beyond Nature. It is indeed only love that makes the difference: all those very same principles which are evil in the world of selfishness and necessity are good in the world of love and understanding. Thus, as we accept this doctrine of the higher world we make new discoveries about the lower world. It is from that hill that we first really understand the landscape of this valley. Here, at last, we find (as we do not find either in the Nature-religions or in the religions that deny Nature) a real illumination: Nature is being lit up by a light from beyond Nature. Someone is speaking who knows more about her than can be known from inside her.

Throughout this doctrine it is, of course, implied that Nature is infested with evil. Those great key-principles which exist as modes of goodness in the Divine Life, take on, in her operations, not merely a less perfect form (that we should, on any view, expect) but forms which I have been driven to describe as morbid or depraved. And this depravity could not be totally removed without the drastic remaking of Nature. Complete human virtue could indeed banish from human life all the evils that now arise in it from Vicariousness and Selectiveness and retain only the good: but the wastefulness and painfulness of non-human Nature would remain—and would, of course, continue to infect human life in the form of disease. And the destiny which Christianity promises to man clearly involves a 'redemption' or 'remaking' of Nature which could not stop at Man, or even at this planet. We are told that 'the whole creation' is in travail, and that Man's rebirth will be the signal for hers. This gives rise to several problems, the discussion of which puts the whole doctrine of the Incarnation in a clearer light.

In the first place, we ask how the Nature created by a good God comes to be in this condition? By which question we may mean either how she comes to be imperfect—to leave 'room for improvement' as the schoolmasters say in their reports—or else, how she comes to be positively depraved. If we ask the question in the first sense, the Christian answer (I think) is that God, from the first, created her such as to reach her perfection by a process in time. He made an Earth at first 'without form and void' and brought it by degrees to its perfection. In this, as elsewhere, we see the familiar pattern—descent from God to the formless Earth and reascent from the formless to the finished. In that sense a certain degree of 'evolutionism' or 'developmentalism' is inherent in Christianity. So much for Nature's imperfection; her positive depravity calls for a very different explanation. According to the Christians this is all due to sin: the sin both of men and of powerful, non-human beings, super-natural but created. The unpopularity of this doctrine arises from the widespread Naturalism of our age—the belief that nothing but Nature exists and that if anything else did she is protected from it by a Maginot Line—and will disappear as this error is corrected. To be sure, the morbid inquisitiveness about such beings which led our ancestors to a pseudo-science of Demonology, is to be sternly discouraged: our attitude should be that of the sensible citizen in wartime who believes that there are enemy spies in our midst but disbelieves nearly every particular spy story. We must limit ourselves to the general statement that beings in a different, and higher 'Nature' which is *partially* interlocked with ours have, like men, fallen and have tampered with things inside our frontier. The doctrine, besides proving itself fruitful of good in each man's spiritual life, helps to protect us from shallowly optimistic or pessimistic views of Nature. To call her either 'good' or 'evil' is boys' philosophy. We find ourselves in a world of transporting pleasures, ravishing beauties, and tantalising possibilities, but all constantly being destroyed, all coming to nothing. Nature has all the air of a good thing spoiled.

The sin, both of men and of angels, was rendered possible by the fact that God gave them free will: thus surrendering a portion of His omnipotence (it is again a deathlike or descending movement) because He saw that from a world of free creatures, even though they fell, He could work out (and this is the reascent) a deeper happiness and a fuller splendour than any world of automata would admit.

Another question that arises is this. If the redemption of Man is the beginning of Nature's redemption as a whole, must we then conclude after all that Man is the most important thing in Nature? If I had to answer 'Yes' to this question I should not be embarrassed. Supposing Man to be the only rational animal in the universe, then (as has been shown) his small size and the small size of the globe he inhabits would not make it ridiculous to regard him as the hero of the cosmic drama: Jack after all is the smallest character in *Jack the Giant-Killer*. Nor do I think it in the least improbable that Man is in fact the only rational creature in this spatio-temporal Nature. That is just the sort of lonely pre-eminence— just the disproportion between picture and frame—which all that I know of Nature's 'selectiveness' would lead me to anticipate. But I do not need to assume that it actually exists. Let Man be only one among a myriad of rational species, and let him be the only one that has fallen. Because he has fallen, for him God does the great deed; just as in the parable it is the one lost sheep for whom the shepherd hunts. Let Man's pre-eminence or solitude be one not of superiority but of misery and evil: then, all the more, Man will be the very species into which Mercy will descend. For this prodigal the fatted calf, or, to speak more suitably, the eternal Lamb, is killed. But once the Son of God, drawn hither not by our merits but by our unworthiness, has put on human nature, then our species (whatever it may have been before) does become in one sense the central fact in all Nature: our species, rising after its long descent, will drag all Nature up with it because in our species the Lord of Nature is now included. And it would be all of a piece with what we already know if ninety and nine righteous races inhabiting distant planets that circle distant suns, and needing no redemption on their own account, were remade and glorified by the glory which had descended into our race. For God is not merely mending, not simply restoring a *status quo*. Redeemed humanity is to be something more glorious than unfallen humanity would have been, more glorious than any unfallen race now is (if at this moment the night sky conceals any such). The greater the sin, the greater the mercy: the deeper the death the brighter the rebirth. And this super-added glory will, with true vicariousness, exalt all creatures and those who have never fallen will thus bless Adam's fall.

I write so far on the assumption that the Incarnation was occasioned only by the Fall. Another view has, of course, been sometimes held by Christians. According to it the descent of God into Nature was not in itself occasioned by sin. It would have occurred for Glorification and Perfection even if it had not been required for Redemption. Its attendant circumstances would have been very different: the divine humility would not have been a divine humiliation, the sorrows, the gall and vinegar, the crown of thorns and the cross, would have been absent. If this view is taken, then clearly the Incarnation, wherever and however it occurred, would always have been the beginning of Nature's rebirth. The fact that it has occurred in the human species, summoned thither by that strong incantation of misery and abjection which Love has made Himself unable to resist, would not deprive it of its universal significance.

This doctrine of a universal redemption spreading outwards from the redemption of Man, mythological as it will seem to modern minds, is in reality far more philosophical than any theory which holds that God, having once entered Nature, should leave her, and leave her substantially unchanged, or that the glorification of one creature could be realised without the glorification of the whole system. God never undoes anything but evil, never does good to undo it again. The union between God and Nature in the Person of Christ admits no divorce. He will not *go out* of Nature again and she must be glorified in all ways which this miraculous union demands. When spring comes it 'leaves no corner of the land untouched'; even a pebble dropped in a pond sends circles to the margin. The question we want to ask about Man's 'central' position in this drama is really on a level with the disciples' question, 'Which of them was the greatest?' It is the sort of question which God does not answer. If from Man's point of view the re-creation of non-human and even inanimate Nature appears a mere by-product of his own redemption, then equally from some remote, non-human point of view Man's redemption may seem merely the preliminary to this more widely diffused springtime, and the very permission of Man's fall may be supposed to have had that larger end in view. Both attitudes will be right if they will consent to drop the words *mere* and *merely*. Where a God who is totally purposive and totally foreseeing acts upon a Nature which is totally interlocked, there can be no accidents or loose ends, nothing whatever of which we can safely use the word *merely*. Nothing is 'merely a by-product' of anything else. All results are intended from the first. What is subservient from one point of view is the main purpose from another. No thing or event is first or highest in a sense which forbids it to be also last and lowest. The partner who bows to Man in one movement of the dance receives Man's reverences in another. To be high or central means to abdicate continually: to be low means to be raised: all good masters are servants: God washes the feet of men. The concepts we usually bring to the consideration of such matters are miserably political and prosaic. We think of flat repetitive equality and arbitrary privilege as the only two alternatives—thus missing all the overtones, the counterpoint, the vibrant sensitiveness, the inter-inanimations of reality.

For this reason I do not think it at all likely that there have been (as Alice Meynell suggested in an interesting poem) many Incarnations to redeem many different kinds of creature. One's sense of *style*—of the divine idiom—rejects it. The suggestion of mass-production and of waiting queues comes from a level of thought which is here hopelessly inadequate. If other natural creatures than Man have sinned we must believe that they are redeemed: but God's Incarnation as Man will be one unique act in the drama of total redemption and other species will have witnessed wholly different acts, each equally unique, equally necessary and differently necessary to the whole process, and each (from a certain point of view) justifiably regarded as 'the great scene' of the play. To those who live in Act II, Act III looks like an epilogue: to those who live in Act III, Act II looks like a prologue. And both are right until they add the fatal word *merely*, or else try to avoid it by the dullard's supposition that both acts are the same.

It ought to be noticed at this stage that the Christian doctrine, if accepted, involves a particular view of Death. There are two attitudes towards Death which the human mind naturally adopts. One is the lofty view, which reached its greatest intensity among the Stoics, that Death 'doesn't matter', that it is 'kind nature's signal for retreat', and that we ought to regard it with indifference. The other is the 'natural' point of view, implicit in nearly all private conversations on the subject, and in much modern thought about the survival of the human species, that Death is the greatest of all evils: Hobbes is perhaps the only philosopher who erected a system on this basis. The first idea simply negates, the second simply affirms, our instinct for self-preservation; neither throws any new light on Nature, and Christianity countenances neither. Its doctrine is subtler. On the one hand Death is the triumph of Satan, the punishment of the Fall, and the last enemy. Christ shed tears at the grave of Lazarus and sweated blood in Gethsemane: the Life of Lives that was in Him detested this penal obscenity not less than we do, but more. On the other hand, only he who loses his life will save it. We are baptised into the *death* of Christ, and it is the remedy for the Fall. Death is, in fact, what some modern people call 'ambivalent'. It is Satan's great weapon and also God's great weapon: it is holy and unholy; our supreme disgrace and our only hope; the thing Christ came to conquer and the means by which He conquered.

To penetrate the whole of this mystery is, of course, far beyond our power. If the pattern of Descent and Reascent is (as looks not unlikely) the very formula of reality, then in the mystery of Death the secret of secrets lies hid. But something must be said in order to put the Grand Miracle in its proper light. We need not discuss Death on the highest level of all: the mystical slaying of the Lamb 'before the foundation of the world' is above our speculations. Nor need we consider Death on the lowest level. The death of organisms which are nothing more than organisms, which have developed no personality, does not concern us. Of it we may truly say, as some spiritually minded people would have us say of human Death, that it 'doesn't matter'. But the startling Christian doctrine of human Death cannot be passed over.

Human Death, according to the Christians, is a result of human sin; Man, as originally created, was immune from it: Man, when redeemed, and recalled to a new life (which will, in some undefined sense, be a bodily life) in the midst of a more organic and more fully obedient Nature, will be immune from it again. This doctrine is of course simply nonsense if a man is nothing but a Natural organism. But if he were, then, as we have seen, all thoughts would be equally nonsensical, for all would have irrational causes. Man must therefore be a composite being—a natural organism tenanted by, or in a state of *symbiosis* with, a supernatural spirit. The Christian doctrine, startling as it must seem to those who have not fully cleared their minds of Naturalism, states that the relations which we now observe between that spirit and that organism, are abnormal or pathological ones. At present spirit can retain its foothold against the incessant counter-attacks of Nature (both physiological and psychological) only by perpetual vigilance, and physiological Nature always defeats it in the end. Sooner or later it becomes unable to resist the disintegrating processes at work in the body and death ensues. A little later the Natural organism (for it does not long enjoy its triumph) is similarly conquered by merely physical Nature and returns to the inorganic. But, on the Christian view, this was not always so. The spirit was once not a garrison, maintaining its post with difficulty in a hostile Nature, but was fully 'at home' with its organism, like a king in his own country or a rider on his own horse—or better still, as the human part of a Centaur was 'at home' with the equine part. Where spirit's power over the organism was complete and unresisted, death would never occur. No doubt, spirit's permanent triumph over natural forces which, if left to themselves, would kill the organism, would involve a continued miracle: but only the same sort of miracle which occurs every day—for whenever we think rationally we are, by direct spiritual power, forcing certain atoms in our brain and certain psychological tendencies in our natural soul to do what they would never have done if left to Nature. The Christian doctrine would be fantastic only if the present frontier-situation between spirit and Nature in each human being were so intelligible and self-explanatory that we just 'saw' it to be the only one that could ever have existed. But is it?

In reality the frontier situation is so odd that nothing but custom could make it seem natural, and nothing but the Christian doctrine can make it fully intelligible. There is certainly a state of war. But not a war of mutual destruction. Nature by dominating spirit wrecks all spiritual activities: spirit by dominating Nature confirms and improves natural activities. The brain does not become less a brain by being used for rational thought. The emotions do not become weak or jaded by being organised in the service of a moral will—indeed they grow richer and stronger as a beard is strengthened by being shaved or a river is deepened by being banked. The body of the reasonable and virtuous man, other things being equal, is a better body than that of the fool or the debauchee, and his sensuous pleasures better simply as sensuous pleasures: for the slaves of the senses, after the first bait, are starved by their masters. Everything happens as if what we saw was not war, but rebellion: that rebellion of the lower against the higher by which the lower destroys both the higher and itself. And if the present situation is one of rebellion, then reason cannot reject but will rather demand the belief that there was a time before the rebellion broke out and may be a time after it has been settled. And if we thus see grounds for believing that the supernatural spirit and the natural organism in Man have quarrelled, we shall immediately find it confirmed from two quite unexpected quarters.

Almost the whole of Christian theology could perhaps be deduced from the two facts (a) That men make coarse jokes, and (b) That they feel the dead to be uncanny. The coarse joke proclaims that we have here an animal which finds its own animality either objectionable or funny. Unless there had been a quarrel between the spirit and the organism I do not see how this could be: it is the very mark of the two not being 'at home' together. But is very difficult to imagine such a state of affairs as original—to suppose a creature which from the very first was half shocked and half tickled to death at the mere fact of being the creature it is. I do not perceive that dogs see anything funny about being dogs: I suspect that angels see nothing funny about being angels. Our feeling about the dead is equally odd. It is idle to say that we dislike corpses because we are afraid of ghosts. You might say with equal truth that we fear ghosts because we dislike corpses—for the ghost owes much of its horror to the associated ideas of pallor, decay, coffins, shrouds, and worms. In reality we hate the division which makes possible the conception of either corpse or ghost. Because the thing ought not to be divided, each of the halves into which it falls by division is detestable. The explanations which Naturalism gives both of bodily shame and of our feeling about the dead are not satisfactory. It refers us to primitive taboos and superstitions—as if these themselves were not obviously results of the thing to be explained. But once accept the Christian doctrine that man was originally a unity and that the present division is unnatural, and all the phenomena fall into place. It would be fantastic to suggest that the doctrine was devised to explain our enjoyment of a chapter in Rabelais, a good ghost story, or the *Tales* of Edgar Allan Poe. It does so none the less.

I ought, perhaps, to point out that the argument is not in the least affected by the value-judgements we make about ghost stories or coarse humour. You may hold that both are bad. You may hold that both, though they result (like clothes) from the Fall, are (like clothes) the proper way to deal with the Fall once it has occurred: that while perfected and recreated Man will no longer experience that kind of laughter or that kind of shudder, yet here and now not to feel the horror and not to see the joke is to be less than human. But either way the facts bear witness to our present maladjustment.

So much for the sense in which human Death is the result of sin and the triumph of Satan. But it is also the means of redemption from sin, God's medicine for Man and His weapon against Satan. In a general way it is not difficult to understand how the same thing can be a masterstroke on the part of one combatant and also the very means whereby the superior combatant defeats him. Every good general, every good chess-player, takes what is precisely the strong point of his opponent's plan and makes it the pivot of his own plan. Take that castle of mine if you insist. It was not my original intention that you should—indeed, I thought you would have had more sense. But take it by all means. For now I move thus . . . and thus . . . and it is mate in three moves. Something like this must be supposed to have happened about Death. Do not say that such metaphors are too trivial to illustrate so high a matter: the unnoticed mechanical and mineral metaphors which, in this age, will dominate our whole minds (without being recognised as metaphors at all) the moment we relax our vigilance against them, must be incomparably less adequate.

And one can see how it might have happened. The Enemy persuades Man to rebel against God: Man, by doing so, loses power to control that other rebellion which the Enemy now raises in Man's organism (both psychical and physical) against Man's spirit: just as that organism, in its turn, loses power to maintain itself against the rebellion of the inorganic. In that way, Satan produced human Death. But when God created Man he gave him such a constitution that, if the highest part of it rebelled against Himself, it would be bound to lose control over the lower parts: i.e. in the long run to suffer Death. This provision may be regarded equally as a punitive sentence ('In the day ye eat of that fruit ye shall die'), as a mercy, and as a safety device. It is punishment because Death—that Death of which Martha says to Christ 'But . . . Sir . . . it'll *smell*'—is horror and ignominy. ('I am not so much afraid of death as ashamed of it,' said Sir Thomas Browne). It is mercy because by willing and humble surrender to it Man undoes his act of rebellion and makes even this depraved and monstrous mode of Death an instance of that higher and mystical Death which is eternally good and a necessary ingredient in the highest life. 'The readiness is all'—not, of course, the merely heroic readiness but that of humility and self-renunciation. Our enemy, so welcomed, becomes our servant: bodily Death, the monster, becomes blessed spiritual Death to self, if the spirit so wills—or rather if it allows the Spirit of the willingly dying God so to will in it. It is a safety-device because, once Man has fallen, natural immortality would be the one utterly hopeless destiny for him. Aided to the surrender that he must make by no external necessity of Death, free (if you call it freedom) to rivet faster and faster about himself through unending centuries the chains of his own pride and lust and of the nightmare civilisations which these build up in ever-increasing power and complication, he would progress from being merely a fallen man to being a fiend, possibly beyond all modes of redemption. This danger was averted. The sentence that those who ate of the forbidden fruit would be driven away from the Tree of Life was implicit in the composite nature with which Man was created. But to convert this penal death into the means of eternal life—to add to its negative and preventive function a positive and saving function—it was further necessary that death should be *accepted*. Humanity must embrace death freely, submit to it with total humility, drink it to the dregs, and so convert it into that mystical death which is the secret of life. But only a Man who did not need to have been a Man at all unless He had chosen, only one who served in our sad regiment as a volunteer, yet also only one who was perfectly a Man, could perform this perfect dying; and thus (which way you put it is unimportant) either defeat death or redeem it. He tasted death on behalf of all others. He is the representative 'Die-er' of the universe: and for that very reason the Resurrection and the Life. Or conversely, because He truly lives, He truly dies, for that is the very pattern of reality. Because the higher can descend into the lower He who from all eternity has been incessantly plunging Himself in the blessed death of self-surrender to the Father can also most fully descend into the horrible and (for us) involuntary death of the body. Because Vicariousness is the very idiom of the reality He has created, His death can become ours. The whole Miracle, far from denying what we already know of reality, writes the comment which makes that crabbed text plain: or rather, proves itself to be the text on which Nature was only the commentary. In science we have been reading only the notes to a poem; in Christianity we find the poem itself.

With this our sketch of the Grand Miracle may end. Its credibility does not lie in Obviousness. Pessimism, Optimism, Pantheism, Materialism, all have this 'obvious' attraction. Each is confirmed at the first glance by multitudes of facts: later on, each meets insuperable obstacles. The doctrine of the Incarnation works into our minds quite differently. It digs beneath the surface, works through the rest of our knowledge by unexpected channels, harmonises best with our deepest apprehensions and our 'second thoughts', and in union with these undermines our superficial opinions. It has little to say to the man who is still certain that everything is going to the dogs, or that everything is getting better and better, or that everything is God, or that everything is electricity. Its hour comes when these wholesale creeds have begun to fail us. Whether the thing really happened is a historical question. But when you turn to history, you will not demand for it that kind and degree of evidence which you would rightly demand for something intrinsically improbable; only that kind and degree which you demand for something which, if accepted, illuminates and orders all other phenomena, explains both our laughter and our logic, our fear of the dead and our knowledge that it is somehow good to die, and which at one stroke covers what multitudes of separate theories will hardly cover for us if this is rejected.

15

MIRACLES
OF THE OLD CREATION

*The Son can do nothing of himself, but what he seeth
the Father do.*

JOHN 5:19

IF WE OPEN such books as Grimm's *Fairy Tales* or Ovid's *Metamorphoses* or the Italian epics we find ourselves in a world of miracles so diverse that they can hardly be classified. Beasts turn into men and men into beasts or trees, trees talk, ships become goddesses, and a magic ring can cause tables richly spread with food to appear in solitary places. Some people cannot stand this kind of story, others find it fun. But the least suspicion that it was true would turn the fun into nightmare. If such things really happened they would, I suppose, show that Nature was being invaded. But they would show that she was being invaded by an alien power. The fitness of the Christian miracles, and their difference from these mythological miracles, lies in the fact that they show invasion by a Power which is not alien. They are what might be expected to happen when she is invaded not simply by a god, but by the God of Nature: by a Power which is outside her jurisdiction not as a foreigner but as a sovereign. They proclaim that He who has come is not merely a king, but *the* King, her King and ours.

419

It is this which, to my mind, puts the Christian miracles in a different class from most other miracles. I do not think that it is the duty of a Christian apologist (as many sceptics suppose) to disprove all stories of the miraculous which fall outside the Christian records, nor of a Christian man to disbelieve them. I am in no way committed to the assertion that God has never worked miracles through and for Pagans or never permitted created supernatural beings to do so. If, as Tacitus, Suetonius, and Dion Cassius relate, Vespasian performed two cures, and if modern doctors tell me that they could not have been performed without miracle, I have no objection. But I claim that the Christian miracles have a much greater intrinsic probability in virtue of their organic connection with one another and with the whole structure of the religion they exhibit. If it can be shown that one particular Roman emperor—and, let us admit, a fairly good emperor as emperors go—once was empowered to do a miracle, we must of course put up with the fact. But it would remain a quite isolated and anomalous fact. Nothing comes of it, nothing leads up to it, it establishes no body of doctrine, explains nothing, is connected with nothing. And this, after all, is an unusually favourable instance of a non-Christian miracle. The immoral, and sometimes almost idiotic interferences attributed to gods in Pagan stories, even if they had a trace of historical evidence, could be accepted only on the condition of our accepting a wholly meaningless universe. What raises infinite difficulties and solves none will be believed by a rational man only under absolute compulsion. Sometimes the credibility of the miracles is in an inverse ratio to the credibility of the religion. Thus miracles are (in late documents, I believe) recorded of the Buddha. But what could be more absurd than that he who came to teach us that Nature is an illusion from which we must escape should occupy himself in producing effects on the Natural level—that he who comes to wake us from a nightmare should *add* to the nightmare? The more we respect his teaching the less we could accept his miracles. But in Christianity, the more we understand what God it is who is said to be present and the purpose for which He is said to have appeared, the more credible the miracles become. That is why we seldom find the Christian miracles denied except by those who have abandoned some part of the Christian doctrine. The mind which asks for a non-miraculous Christianity is a mind in process of relapsing from Christianity into mere 'religion'.[1]

The miracles of Christ can be classified in two ways. The first system yields the classes (1) Miracles of Fertility (2) Miracles of Healing (3) Miracles of Destruction (4) Miracles of Dominion over the Inorganic (5) Miracles of Reversal (6) Miracles of Perfecting or Glorification. The second system, which cuts across the first, yields two classes only: they are (1) Miracles of the Old Creation, and (2) Miracles of the New Creation.

I contend that in all these miracles alike the incarnate God does suddenly and locally something that God has done or will do in general. Each miracle writes for us in small letters something that God has already written, or will write, in letters almost too large to be noticed, across the whole canvas of Nature. They focus at a particular point either God's actual, or His future, operations on the universe. When they reproduce operations we have already seen on the large scale they are miracles of the Old Creation: when they focus those which are still to come they are miracles of the New. Not one of them is isolated or anomalous: each carries the signature of the God whom we know through conscience and from Nature. Their authenticity is attested by the *style*.

---

[1] A consideration of the Old Testament miracles is beyond the scope of this book and would require many kinds of knowledge which I do not possess. My present view—which is tentative and liable to any amount of correction—would be that just as, on the factual side, a long preparation culminates in God's becoming incarnate as Man, so, on the documentary side, the truth first appears in *mythical* form and then by a long process of condensing or focusing finally becomes incarnate as History. This involves the belief that Myth in general is not merely misunderstood history (as Euhemerus thought) nor diabolical illusion (as some of the Fathers thought) nor priestly lying (as the philosophers of the Enlightenment thought) but, at its best, a real though unfocused gleam of divine truth falling on human imagination. The Hebrews, like other people, had mythology: but as they were the chosen people so their mythology was the chosen mythology—the mythology chosen by God to be the vehicle of the earliest sacred truths, the first step in that process which ends in the New Testament where truth has become completely historical. Whether we can ever say with certainty where, in this process of crystallisation, any particular Old Testament story fails, is another matter. I take it that the Memoirs of David's court come at one end of the scale and are scarcely less historical than St Mark or Acts; and that the Book of Jonah is at the opposite end. It should be noted that on this view (a) Just as God, in becoming Man, is 'emptied' of His glory, so the truth, when it comes down from the 'heaven' of myth to the 'earth' of history, undergoes a certain humiliation. Hence the New Testament is, and ought to be, more prosaic, in some ways less *splendid*, than the Old; just as the Old Testament is and ought to be less rich in many kinds of imaginative beauty than the Pagan mythologies. (b) Just as God is none the less God by being Man, so the Myth remains Myth even when it becomes Fact. The story of Christ demands from us, and repays, not only a religious and historical but also an imaginative response. It is directed to the child, the poet, and the savage in us as well as to the conscience and to the intellect. One of its functions is to break down dividing walls.

Before going any further I should say that I do not propose to raise the question, which has before now been asked, whether Christ was able to do these things only because He was God or also because He was perfect man; for it is a possible view that if Man had never fallen all men would have been able to do the like. It is one of the glories of Christianity that we can say of this question. 'It doesn't matter.' Whatever may have been the powers of unfallen man, it appears that those of redeemed Man will be almost unlimited.[2] Christ, reascending from His great dive, is bringing up Human Nature with Him. Where He goes, it goes too. It will be made 'like Him'.[3] If in His miracles He is not acting as the Old Man might have done before his Fall, then He is acting as the New Man, every new man, will do after his redemption. When humanity, borne on His shoulders, passes with Him up from the cold dark water into the green warm water and out at last into the sunlight and the air, it also will be bright and coloured.

Another way of expressing the real character of the miracles would be to say that though isolated from other actions, they are not isolated in either of the two ways we are apt to suppose. They are not, on the one hand, isolated from other Divine acts: they do close and small and, as it were, in focus what God at other times does so large that men do not attend to it. Neither are they isolated exactly as we suppose from other human acts: they anticipate powers which all men will have when they also are 'sons' of God and enter into that 'glorious liberty'. Christ's isolation is not that of a prodigy but of a pioneer. He is the first of His kind; He will not be the last.

Let us return to our classification and firstly to Miracles of *Fertility*. The earliest of these was the conversion of water into wine at the wedding feast in Cana. This miracle proclaims that the God of all wine is present. The vine is one of the blessings sent by Jahweh: He is the reality behind the false god Bacchus. Every year, as part of the Natural order, God makes wine. He does so by creating a vegetable organism that can turn water, soil and sunlight into a juice which will, under proper conditions, become wine. Thus, in a certain sense, He constantly turns water into wine, for wine, like all drinks, is but water modified. Once, and in one year only, God, now incarnate, short circuits the process: makes wine

---

[2] Matthew 17:20, 21:21, Mark 11:23, Luke 10:19, John 14:12, 1 Corinthians 3:22, 2 Timothy 2:12.

[3] Philippians 3:21, 1 John 3:1, 2.

in a moment: uses earthenware jars instead of vegetable fibres to hold the water. But uses them to do what He is always doing. The miracle consists in the short cut; but the event to which it leads is the usual one. If the thing happened, then we know that what has come into Nature is no anti-Natural spirit, no God who loves tragedy and tears and fasting *for their own sake* (however He may permit or demand them for special purposes) but the God of Israel who has through all these centuries given us wine to gladden the heart of man.

Other miracles that fall in this class are the two instances of miraculous feeding. They involve the multiplication of a little bread and a little fish into much bread and much fish. Once in the desert Satan had tempted Him to make bread of stones: He refused the suggestion. 'The Son does nothing except what He sees the Father do': perhaps one may without boldness surmise that the direct change from stone to bread appeared to the Son to be not quite in the hereditary style. Little bread into much bread is quite a different matter. Every year God makes a little corn into much corn: the seed is sown and there is an increase. And men say, according to their several fashions, 'It is the laws of Nature,' or 'It is Ceres, it is Adonis, it is the Corn-King'. But the laws of Nature are only a pattern: nothing will come of them unless they can, so to speak, take over the universe as a going concern. And as for Adonis, no man can tell us where he died or when he rose again. Here, at the feeding of the five thousand, is He whom we have ignorantly worshipped: the *real* Corn-King who will die once and rise once at Jerusalem during the term of office of Pontius Pilate.

That same day He also multiplied fish. Look down into every bay and almost every river. This swarming, undulating fecundity shows He is still at work 'thronging the seas with spawn innumerable'. The ancients had a god called Genius; the god of animal and human fertility, the patron of gynaecology, embryology, and the marriage bed—the 'genial' bed as they called it after its god Genius. But Genius is only another mask for the God of Israel, for it was He who at the beginning commanded all species 'to be fruitful and multiply and replenish the earth'. And now, that day, at the feeding of the thousands, incarnate God does the same: does close and small, under His human hands, a workman's hands, what He has always been doing in the seas, the lakes and the little brooks.

With this we stand on the threshold of that miracle which for some reason proves hardest of all for the modern mind to accept. I can understand the man who denies miracles altogether: but what is one to make of people who will believe other miracles and 'draw the line' at the Virgin Birth? Is it that for all their lip service to the laws of Nature there is only one natural process in which they really believe? Or is it that they think they see in this miracle a slur upon sexual intercourse (though they might just as well see in the feeding of the five thousand an insult to bakers) and that sexual intercourse is the one thing still venerated in this unvenerating age? In reality the miracle is no less, and no more, surprising than any others.

Perhaps the best way to approach it is from the remark I saw in one of the most archaic of our anti-god papers. The remark was that Christians believed in a God who had 'committed adultery with the wife of a Jewish carpenter'. The writer was probably merely 'letting off steam' and did not really think that God, in the Christian story, had assumed human form and lain with a mortal woman, as Zeus lay with Alcmena. But if one had to answer this person, one would have to say that if you called the miraculous conception divine adultery you would by driven to find a similar divine adultery in the conception of every child—nay, of every animal too. I am sorry to use expressions which will offend pious ears, but I do not know how else to make my point.

In a normal act of generation the father has no creative function. A microscopic particle of matter from his body, and a microscopic particle from the woman's body, meet. And with that there passes the colour of his hair and the hanging lower lip of her grandfather and the form of humanity in all its complexity of bones, sinews, nerves, liver and heart, and the form of those pre-human organisms which the embryo will recapitulate in the womb. Behind every spermatozoon lies the whole history of the universe: locked within it lies no inconsiderable part of the world's future. The weight or drive behind it is the momentum of the whole interlocked event which we call Nature up-to-date. And we know now that the 'laws of Nature' cannot supply that momentum. If we believe that God created Nature that momentum comes from Him. The human father is merely an instrument, a carrier, often an unwilling carrier, always simply the last in a long line of carriers—a line that stretches back far beyond his ancestors into pre-human and pre-organic deserts of time, back to the creation of matter itself. That line is in God's hand. It is the instrument by which He normally creates a man. For He is the reality behind both Genius and Venus; no woman ever conceived a child, no mare a foal, without Him. But once, and for a special purpose, He dispensed with that long line which is His instrument: once His life-giving finger touched a woman without passing through the ages of interlocked events. Once the great glove of Nature was taken off His hand. His naked hand touched her. There was of course a unique reason for it. That time He was creating not simply a man but the Man who was to be Himself: was creating Man anew: was beginning, at this divine and human point, the New Creation of all things. The whole soiled and weary universe quivered at this direct injection of essential life—direct, uncontaminated, not drained through all the crowded history of Nature. But it would be out of place here to explore the religious significance of the miracle. We are here concerned with it simply as Miracle—that and nothing more. As far as concerns the creation of Christ's human nature (the Grand Miracle whereby His divine begotten nature enters into it is another matter) the miraculous conception is one more witness that here is Nature's Lord. He is doing now, small and close, what He does in a different fashion for every woman who conceives. He does it this time without a line of human ancestors: but even where He uses human ancestors it is not the less He who gives life.[4] The bed is barren where that great third party, Genius, is not present.

The miracles of *Healing*, to which I turn next, are now in a peculiar position. Men are ready to admit that many of them happened, but are inclined to deny that they were miraculous. The symptoms of very many diseases can be aped by hysteria, and hysteria can often be cured by 'suggestion'. It could, no doubt, be argued that such suggestion is a spiritual power, and therefore (if you like) a supernatural power, and that all instances of 'faith healing' are therefore miracles. But in our terminology they would be miraculous only in the same sense in which every instance of human reason is miraculous: and what we are now looking for is miracles other than that. My own view is that it would be unreasonable to ask a person who has not yet embraced Christianity in its entirety to allow that all the healings mentioned in the Gospels were miracles—that is, that they go beyond the possibilities of human 'suggestions'. It is for the doctors to decide as regards each particular case—supposing that the narratives are sufficiently detailed to allow even probable diagnosis. We have here a good example to what was said in an earlier chapter. So far

---

[4] Cf. Matthew 23:9.

from belief in miracles depending upon ignorance of natural law, we are here finding for ourselves that ignorance of law makes miracle unascertainable.

Without deciding in detail which of the healings must (apart from acceptance of the Christian faith) be regarded as miraculous, we can however indicate the kind of miracle involved. Its character can easily be obscured by the somewhat magical view which many people still take of ordinary and medical healing. There is a sense in which no doctor ever heals. The doctors themselves would be the first to admit this. The magic is not in the medicine but in the patient's body—in the *vis medicatrix naturae*, the recuperative or self-corrective energy of Nature. What the treatment does is to simulate Natural functions or to remove what hinders them. We speak for convenience of the doctor, or the dressing, healing a cut. But in another sense every cut heals itself: no cut can be healed in a corpse. That same mysterious force which we call gravitational when it steers the planets and biochemical when it heals a live body, is the efficient cause of all recoveries. And that energy proceeds from God in the first instance. All who are cured are cured by Him, not merely in the sense that His providence provides them with medical assistance and wholesome environments, but also in the sense that their very tissues are repaired by the far-descended energy which, flowing from Him, energises the whole system of Nature. But once He did it visibly to the sick in Palestine, a Man meeting with men. What in its general operations we refer to laws of Nature or once referred to Apollo or Aesculapius thus reveals itself. The Power that always was behind all healings puts on a face and hands. Hence, of course, the apparent chanciness of the miracles. It is idle to complain that He heals those whom He happens to meet, not those whom He doesn't. To be a man means to be in one place and not in another. The world which would not know Him as present everywhere was saved by His becoming *local*.

Christ's single miracle of Destruction, the withering of the fig-tree, has proved troublesome to some people, but I think its significance is plain enough. The miracle is an acted parable, a symbol of God's sentence on all that is 'fruitless' and specially, no doubt, on the official Judaism of that age. That is its moral significance. As a miracle, it again does in focus, repeats small and close, what God does constantly and throughout Nature. We have seen in the previous chapter how God, twisting Satan's weapon out of his hand, had become, since the Fall, the God even of human death. But much more, and perhaps ever since the creation, He has been the God of the death of organisms. In both cases, though in somewhat different ways, He is the God of death because He is the God of Life: the God of human death because through it increase of life now comes—the God of merely organic death because death is part of the very mode by which organic life spreads itself out in Time and yet remains new. A forest a thousand years deep is still collectively alive because some trees are dying and others are growing up. His human face, turned with negation in its eyes upon that one fig-tree, did once what His unincarnate action does to all trees. No tree died that year in Palestine, or any year anywhere, except because God did—or rather ceased to do—something to it.

All the miracles which we have considered so far are Miracles of the Old Creation. In all of them we see the Divine Man focusing for us what the God of Nature has already done on a larger scale. In our next class, the Miracles of Dominion over the Inorganic, we find some that are of the Old Creation and some that are of the New. When Christ stills the storm He does what God has often done before. God made Nature such that there would be both storms and calms: in that way all storms (except those that are still going on at this moment) have been stilled by God. It is unphilosophical, if you have once accepted the Grand Miracle, to reject the stilling of the storm. There is really no difficulty about adapting the weather conditions of the rest of the world to this one miraculous calm. I myself can still a storm in a room by shutting the window. Nature must make the best she can of it. And to do her justice she makes no trouble at all. The whole system, far from being thrown out of gear (which is what some nervous people seem to think a miracle would do) digests the new situation as easily as an elephant digests a drop of water. She is, as I have said before, an accomplished hostess. But when Christ walks on the water we have a miracle of the New Creation. God had not made the Old Nature, the world before the Incarnation, of such a kind that water would support a human body. This miracle is the foretaste of a Nature that is still in the future. The New creation is just breaking in. For a moment it looks as if it were going to spread. For a moment two men are living in that new world. St Peter also walks on the water—a pace or two: then his trust fails him and he sinks. He is back in Old Nature. That momentary glimpse was a snowdrop of a miracle. The snowdrops show that we have turned the corner of the year. Summer is coming. But it is a long way off and the snowdrops do not last long.

The Miracles of Reversal all belong to the New Creation. It is a Miracle of Reversal when the dead are raised. Old Nature knows nothing of this process: it involves playing backwards a film that we have always seen played forwards. The one or two instances of it in the Gospels are early flowers—what we call spring flowers, because they are prophetic, although they really bloom while it is still winter. And the Miracles of Perfecting or of Glory, the Transfiguration, the Resurrection, and the Ascension, are even more emphatically of the New Creation. These are the true spring, or even the summer, of the world's new year. The Captain, the forerunner, is already in May or June, though His followers on earth are still living in the frosts and east winds of Old Nature—for 'spring comes slowly up this way'.

None of the Miracles of the New Creation can be considered apart from the Resurrection and Ascension: and that will require another chapter.

16

MIRACLES OF THE NEW CREATION

Beware, for fiends in triumph laugh
O'er him who learns the truth by half!
Beware; for God will not endure
For men to make their hope more pure
Than His good promise, or require
Another than the five-stringed lyre[1]
Which He has vowed again to the hands
Devout of him who understands
To tune it justly here!

C. PATMORE, *THE VICTORIES OF LOVE*

IN THE EARLIEST days of Christianity an 'apostle' was first and fore-most a man who claimed to be an eyewitness of the Resurrection. Only a few days after the Crucifixion when two candidates were nominated for the vacancy created by the treachery of Judas, their qualification was that they had known Jesus personally both before and after His death and could offer first-hand evidence of the Resurrection in addressing the outer world (Acts 1:22). A few days later St Peter, preaching the first Christian sermon, makes the same claim—'God raised Jesus, of which

---

[1] i.e. the Body with its five senses.

429

we all (we Christians) are witnesses (Acts 2:32). In the first Letter to the Corinthians, St Paul bases his claim to apostleship on the same ground— 'Am I not an apostle? Have I not seen the Lord Jesus?' (1:9).

As this qualification suggests, to preach Christianity meant primarily to preach the Resurrection. Thus people who had heard only fragments of St Paul's teaching at Athens got the impression that he was talking about two new gods, Jesus and Anastasis (i.e. Resurrection) (Acts 17:18). The Resurrection is the central theme in every Christian sermon reported in the Acts. The Resurrection, and its consequences, were the 'gospel' or good news which the Christians brought: what we call the 'gospels', the narratives of Our Lord's life and death, were composed later for the benefit of those who had already accepted the *gospel*. They were in no sense the basis of Christianity: they were written for those already converted. The miracle of the Resurrection, and the theology of that miracle, comes first: the biography comes later as a comment on it. Nothing could be more unhistorical than to pick out selected sayings of Christ from the gospels and to regard those as the datum and the rest of the New Testament as a construction upon it. The first fact in the history of Christendom is a number of people who say they have seen the Resurrection. If they had died without making anyone else believe this 'gospel' no gospels would ever have been written.

It is very important to be clear about what these people meant. When modern writers talk of the Resurrection they usually mean one particular moment—the discovery of the Empty Tomb and the appearance of Jesus a few yards away from it. The story of that moment is what Christian apologists now chiefly try to support and sceptics chiefly try to impugn. But this almost exclusive concentration on the first five minutes or so of the Resurrection would have astonished the earliest Christian teachers. In claiming to have seen the Resurrection they were not necessarily claiming to have seen *that*. Some of them had, some of them had not. It had no more importance than any of the other appearances of the risen Jesus— apart from the poetic and dramatic importance which the beginnings of things must always have. What they were claiming was that they had all, at one time or another, met Jesus during the six or seven weeks that followed His death. Sometimes they seem to have been alone when they did so, but on one occasion twelve of them saw Him together, and on another occasion about five hundred of them. St Paul says that the majority of the five hundred were still alive when he wrote the First Letter to the Corinthians, i.e. in about 55 AD.

The 'Resurrection' to which they bore witness was, in fact, not the action of rising from the dead but the state of having risen; a state, as they held, attested by intermittent meetings during a limited period (except for the special, and in some ways different, meeting vouchsafed to St Paul). This termination of the period is important, for, as we shall see, there is no possibility of isolating the doctrine of the Resurrection from that of the Ascension.

The next point to notice is that the Resurrection was not regarded simply or chiefly as evidence for the immortality of the soul. It is, of course, often so regarded today: I have heard a man maintain that 'the importance of the Resurrection is that it proves *survival*'. Such a view cannot at any point be reconciled with the language of the New Testament. On such a view Christ would simply have done what all men do when they die: the only novelty would have been that in His case we were allowed to see it happening. But there is not in Scripture the faintest suggestion that the Resurrection was new evidence for something that had *in fact* been always happening. The New Testament writers speak as if Christ's achievement in rising from the dead was the first event of its kind in the whole history of the universe. He is the 'first fruits', the 'pioneer of life'. He has forced open a door that has been locked since the death of the first man. He has met, fought, and beaten the King of Death. Everything is different because He has done so. This is the beginning of the New Creation: a new chapter in cosmic history has opened.

I do not mean, of course, that the writers of the New Testament disbelieved in 'survival'. On the contrary they believed in it so readily that Jesus on more than one occasion had to assure them that He was not a ghost. From the earliest times the Jews, like many other nations, had believed that man possessed a 'soul' or *Nephesh* separable from the body, which went at death into the shadowy world called *Sheol*: a land of forgetfulness and imbecility where none called upon Jehovah any more, a land half unreal and melancholy like the Hades of the Greeks or the Niflheim of the Norsemen. From it shades could return and appear to the living, as Samuel's shade had done at the command of the Witch of Endor. In much more recent times there had arisen a more cheerful belief that the righteous passed at death to 'heaven'. Both doctrines are doctrines of 'the immortality of the soul' as a Greek or modern Englishman understands it: and both are quite irrelevant to the story of the Resurrection. The writers look upon this event as an absolute novelty. Quite clearly they do not think they have been haunted by a ghost from Sheol, nor even that they have had a vision of a 'soul' in 'heaven'. It must be clearly understood that if the Psychical Researchers succeeded in proving 'survival' and showed that the Resurrection was an instance of it, they would not be supporting the Christian faith but refuting it. If that were all that had happened the original 'gospel' would have been untrue. What the apostles claimed to have seen did not corroborate, nor exclude, and had indeed nothing to do with, either the doctrine of 'heaven' or the doctrine of Sheol. Insofar as it corroborated anything it corroborated a third Jewish belief which is quite distinct from both these. This third doctrine taught that in 'the day of Jahweh' peace would be restored and world dominion given to Israel under a righteous King: and that when this happened the righteous dead, or some of them, would come back to earth—not as floating wraiths but as solid men who cast shadows in the sunlight and made a noise when they tramped the floors. 'Awake and sing, ye that dwell in the dust', said Isaiah, 'And the earth shall cast out the dead' (26:19). What the apostles thought they had seen was, if not that, at any rate a lonely first instance of that: the first movement of a great wheel beginning to turn in the direction opposite to that which all men hitherto had observed. Of all the ideas entertained by man about death it is this one, and this one only, which the story of the Resurrection tends to confirm. If the story is false then it is this Hebrew myth of resurrection which begot it. If the story is true then the hint and anticipation of the truth is to be found not in popular ideas about ghosts nor in eastern doctrines of reincarnation nor in philosophical speculations about the immortality of the soul, but exclusively in the Hebrew prophecies of the return, the restoration, the great reversal. Immortality simply as immortality is irrelevant to the Christian claim.

There are, I allow, certain respects in which the risen Christ resembles the 'ghost' of popular tradition. Like a ghost He 'appears' and 'disappears': locked doors are no obstacle to Him. On the other hand He Himself vigorously asserts that He is corporeal (Luke 24: 39–40) and eats broiled fish. It is at this point that the modern reader becomes uncomfortable. He becomes more uncomfortable still at the word, 'Don't touch me; I have not yet gone up to the Father' (John 20:17). For voices and apparitions we are, in some measure, prepared. But what is this that must not be touched? What is all this about going 'up' to the Father? Is He not already 'with the Father' in the only sense that matters? What can 'going up' be except a metaphor for *that?* And if so, why has He 'not yet' gone? These discomforts arise because the story the 'apostles' actually had to tell begins at this point to conflict with the story we expect and are determined beforehand to read into their narrative.

We expect them to tell of a risen life which is purely 'spiritual' in the negative sense of that word: that is, we use the word 'spiritual' to mean not what it is but what it is not. We mean a life without space, without history, without environment, with no sensuous elements in it. We also, in our heart of hearts, tend to slur over the risen *manhood* of Jesus, to conceive Him, after death, simply returning into Deity, so that the Resurrection would be no more than the reversal or undoing of the Incarnation. That being so, all references to the risen *body* make us uneasy: they raise awkward questions. For as long as we hold the negatively spiritual view, we have not really been believing in that body at all. We have thought (whether we acknowledged it or not) that the body was not objective: that it was an appearance sent by God to assure the disciples of truths otherwise incommunicable. But what truths? If the truth is that after death there comes a negatively spiritual life, an eternity of mystical experience, what more misleading way of communicating it could possibly be found than the appearance of a human form which eats broiled fish? Again, on such a view, the body would really be a hallucination. And any theory of hallucination breaks down on the fact (and if it is invention it is the oddest invention that ever entered the mind of man) that on three separate occasions this hallucination was not immediately recognised as Jesus (Luke 24:13–31; John 20:15, 21:4). Even granting that God sent a holy hallucination to teach truths already widely believed without it, and far more easily taught by other methods, and certain to be completely obscured by this, might we not at least hope that He would get the face of the hallucination *right?* Is He who made all faces such a bungler that He cannot even work up a recognisable likeness of the Man who was Himself?

It is at this point that awe and trembling fall upon us as we read the records. If the story is false, it is at least a much stranger story than we expected, something for which philosophical 'religion', psychical research, and popular superstition have all alike failed to prepare us. If the story is true, then a wholly new mode of being has arisen in the universe.

The body which lives in that new mode is like, and yet unlike, the body His friends knew before the execution. It is differently related to space and probably to time, but by no means cut off from all relation to them. It can perform the animal act of eating. It is so related to matter, as we know it, that it can be touched, though at first it had better not be touched. It has also a history before it which is in view from the first moment of the Resurrection; it is presently going to become different or go somewhere else. That is why the story of the Ascension cannot be separated from that of the Resurrection. All the accounts suggest that the appearances of the Risen Body came to an end; some describe an abrupt end about six weeks after the death. And they describe this abrupt end in a way which presents greater difficulties to the modern mind than any other part of Scripture. For here, surely, we get the implication of all those primitive crudities to which I have said that Christians are not committed: the vertical ascent like a balloon, the local Heaven, the decorated chair to the right of the Father's throne. 'He was caught up into the sky (*ouranos*)', says St Mark's Gospel 'and sat down at the right hand of God'. 'He was lifted up', says the author of Acts 'and a cloud cut Him off from their sight'.

It is true that if we wish to get rid of these embarrassing passages we have the means to do so. The Marcan one probably formed no part of the earliest text of St Mark's Gospel: and you may add that the Ascension, though constantly implied throughout the New Testament, is described only in these two places. Can we then simply drop the Ascension story? The answer is that we can do so only if we regard the Resurrection appearances as those of a ghost or hallucination. For a phantom can just fade away; but an objective entity must go somewhere—something must happen to it. And if the Risen Body were not objective, then all of us (Christian or not) must invent some explanation for the disappearance of the corpse. And all Christians must explain why God sent or permitted a 'vision' or 'ghost' whose behaviour seems almost exclusively directed to convincing the disciples that it was not a vision or a ghost but a really corporeal being. If it were a vision then it was the most systematically deceptive and lying vision on record. But if it were real, then something happened to it after it ceased to appear. You cannot take away the Ascension without putting something else in its place.

The records represent Christ as passing after death (as no man had passed before) neither into a purely, that is, negatively, 'spiritual' mode of existence nor into a 'natural' life such as we know, but into a life which has its own, new Nature. It represents Him as withdrawing six weeks later, into some different mode of existence. It says—He says—that He goes 'to prepare a place for us'. This presumably means that He is about to create that whole new Nature which will provide the environment or conditions for His glorified humanity and, in Him, for ours. The picture is not what we expected—though whether it is less or more probable and philosophical on that account is another question. It is not the picture of an escape from any and every kind of Nature into some unconditioned and utterly transcendent life. It is the picture of a new human nature, and a new Nature in general, being brought into existence. We must, indeed, believe the risen body to be extremely different from the mortal body: but the existence, in that new state, of anything that could in any sense be described as 'body' at all, involves some sort of spatial relations and in the long run a whole new universe. That is the picture—not of unmaking but of remaking. The old field of space, time, matter, and the senses is to be weeded, dug, and sown for a new crop. We may be tired of that old field: God is not.

And yet the very way in which this New Nature begins to shine in has a certain affinity with the habits of Old Nature. In Nature as we know her, things tend to be anticipated. Nature is fond of 'false dawns', of precursors: thus, as I said before, some flowers come before true spring: submen (the evolutionists would have it) before the true men. So, here also, we get Law before Gospel, animal sacrifices foreshadowing the great sacrifice of God to God, the Baptist before the Messiah, and those 'miracles of the New Creation' which come before the Resurrection. Christ's walking on the water, and His raising of Lazarus fall in this class. Both give us hints of what the New Nature will be like.

In the Walking on the Water we see the relations of spirit and Nature so altered that Nature can be made to do whatever spirit pleases. This new obedience of Nature is, of course, not to be separated even in thought from spirit's own obedience to the Father of Spirits. Apart from that proviso such obedience by Nature, if it were possible, would result in chaos: the evil dream of Magic arises from finite spirit's longing to get that power without paying that price. The evil reality of lawless applied science (which is Magic's son and heir) is actually reducing large tracts of Nature to disorder and sterility at this very moment. I do not know how radically Nature herself would need to be altered to make her thus obedient to spirits, when spirits have become wholly obedient to their source. One thing at least we must observe. If we are in fact spirits, not Nature's offspring, then there must be some point (probably the brain) at which created spirit even now can produce effects on matter not by manipulation or technics but simply by the wish to do so. If that is what you mean by Magic then Magic is a reality manifested every time you move your hand or think a thought. And Nature, as we have seen, is not destroyed but rather perfected by her servitude.

The raising of Lazarus differs from the Resurrection of Christ Himself because Lazarus, so far as we know, was not raised to a new and more glorious mode of existence but merely restored to the sort of life he had had before. The fitness of the miracle lies in the fact that He who will raise all men at the general resurrection here does it small and close, and in an inferior—a merely anticipatory—fashion. For the mere restoration of Lazarus is as inferior in splendour to the *glorious* resurrection of the New Humanity as stone jars are to the green and growing vine or five little barley loaves to all the waving bronze and gold of a fat valley ripe for harvest. The resuscitation of Lazarus, so far as we can see, is simple reversal: a series of changes working in the direction opposite to that we have always experienced. At death, matter which has been organic, begins to flow away into the inorganic, to be finally scattered and used (some of it) by other organisms. The resurrection of Lazarus involves the reverse process. The general resurrection involves the reverse process universalised—a rush of matter toward organisation at the call of spirits which require it. It is presumably a foolish fancy (not justified by the words of Scripture) that each spirit should recover those particular units of matter which he ruled before. For one thing, they would not be enough to go round: we all live in second-hand suits and there are doubtless atoms in my chin which have served many another man, many a dog, many an eel, many a dinosaur. Nor does the unity of our bodies, even in this present life, consist in retaining the same particles. My form remains one, though the matter in it changes continually. I am, in that respect, like a curve in a waterfall.

But the miracle of Lazarus, though only anticipatory in one sense, belongs emphatically to the New Creation, for nothing is more definitely excluded by Old Nature than any return to a *status quo*. The pattern of Death and Rebirth never restores the previous individual organism. And similarly, on the inorganic level, we are told that Nature never restores order where disorder has once occurred. 'Shuffling,' said Professor Eddington, 'is the thing Nature never undoes'. Hence we live in a universe where organisms are always getting more disordered. These laws between them—irreversible death and irreversible entropy—cover almost the whole of what St Paul calls the 'vanity' of Nature: her futility, her ruinousness. And the film is never reversed. The movement from more order to less almost serves to determine the direction in which Time is flowing. You could almost define the future as the period in which what is now living will be dead and in which what order still remains will be diminished.

But entropy by its very character assures us that though it may be the universal rule in the Nature we know, it cannot be universal absolutely. If a man says 'Humpty Dumpty is falling,' you see at once that this is not a complete story. The bit you have been told implies both a later chapter in which Humpty Dumpty will have reached the ground, and an earlier chapter in which he was still seated on the wall. A Nature which is 'running down' cannot be the whole story. A clock can't run down unless it has been wound up. Humpty Dumpty can't fall off a wall which never existed. If a Nature which disintegrates order were the whole of reality, where would she find any order to disintegrate? Thus on any view there must have been a time when processes the reverse of those we now see were going on: a time of winding up. The Christian claim is that those days are not gone for ever. Humpty Dumpty is going to be replaced on the wall—at least in the sense that what has died is going to recover life, probably in the sense that the inorganic universe is going to be reordered. Either Humpty Dumpty will never reach the ground (being caught in mid-fall by the everlasting arms) or else when he reaches it he will be put together again and replaced on a new and better wall. Admittedly, science discerns no 'king's horses and men' who can 'put Humpty Dumpty together again'. But you would not expect her to. She is based on observation: and all our observations are observations of Humpty Dumpty in mid-air. They do not reach either the wall above or the ground below—much less the King with his horses and men hastening towards the spot.

The Transfiguration or 'Metamorphosis' of Jesus is also, no doubt, an anticipatory glimpse of something to come. He is seen conversing with two of the ancient dead. The change which His own human form had undergone is described as one to luminosity, to 'shining whiteness'. A similar whiteness characterises His appearance at the beginning of the book of Revelation. One rather curious detail is that this shining or white-ness affected His clothes as much as His body. St Mark indeed mentions the clothes more explicitly than the face, and adds, with his inimitable naïvety, that 'no laundry could do anything like it'. Taken by itself this episode bears all the marks of a 'vision': that is, of an experience which, though it may be divinely sent and may reveal great truth, yet is not, objectively speaking, the experience it seems to be. But if the theory of 'vision' (or holy hallucination) will not cover the Resurrection appear-ances, it would be only a multiplying of hypotheses to introduce it here. We do not know to what phase or feature of the New Creation this epi-sode points. It may reveal some special glorifying of Christ's manhood at some phase of its history (since history it apparently has) or it may reveal the glory which that manhood always has in its New Creation: it may even reveal a glory which all risen men will inherit. We do not know.

It must indeed be emphasised throughout that we know and can know very little about the New Nature. The task of the imagination here is not to forecast it but simply, by brooding on many possibilities, to make room for a more complete and circumspect agnosticism. It is useful to remember that even now senses responsive to different vibrations would admit us to quite new worlds of experience: that a multi-dimensional space would be different, almost beyond recognition, from the space we are now aware of, yet not discontinuous from it: that time may not al-ways be for us, as it now is, unilinear and irreversible: that others parts of Nature might some day obey us as our cortex now does. It is useful not because we can trust these fancies to give us any positive truths about the New Creation but because they teach us not to limit, in our rashness, the vigour and variety of the new crops which this old field might yet produce. We are therefore compelled to believe that nearly all we are told about the New Creation is metaphorical. But not quite all. That is just where the story of the Resurrection suddenly jerks us back like a tether. The local appearances, the eating, the touching, the claim to be corpo-real, must be either reality or sheer illusion. The New Nature is, in the most troublesome way, interlocked at some points with the Old. Because of its novelty we have to think of it, for the most part, metaphorically: but because of the partial interlocking, some facts about it come through into our present experience in all their literal facthood—just as some facts about an organism are inorganic facts, and some facts about a solid body are facts of linear geometry.

Even apart from that, the mere idea of a New Nature, a Nature beyond Nature, a systematic and diversified reality which is 'supernatural' in relation to the world of our five present senses but 'natural' from its own point of view, is profoundly shocking to a certain philosophical preconception from which we all suffer. I think Kant is at the root of it. It may be expressed by saying that we are prepared to believe either in a reality with one floor or in a reality with two floors, but not in a reality like a skyscraper with several floors. We are prepared, on the one hand, for the sort of reality that Naturalists believe in. That is a one-floor reality: this present Nature is all that there is. We are also prepared for reality as 'religion' conceives it: a reality with a ground floor (Nature) and then above that one other floor and one only—an eternal, spaceless, timeless, spiritual Something of which we can have no images and which, if it presents itself to human consciousness at all, does so in a mystical experience which shatters all our categories of thought. What we are not prepared for is anything in between. We feel quite sure that the first step beyond the world of our present experience must lead either nowhere at all or else into the blinding abyss of undifferentiated spirituality, the unconditioned, the absolute. That is why many believe in God who cannot believe in angels and an angelic world. That is why many believe in immortality who cannot believe in the resurrection of the body. That is why Pantheism is more popular than Christianity, and why many desire a Christianity stripped of its miracles. I cannot now understand, but I well remember, the passionate conviction with which I myself once defended this prejudice. Any rumour of floors or levels intermediate between the Unconditioned and the world revealed by our present senses I rejected without trial as 'mythology'.

Yet it is very difficult to see any rational grounds for the dogma that reality must have no more than two levels. There cannot, from the nature of the case, be evidence that God never created and never will create, more than one system. Each of them would be at least extra-natural in relation to all the others: and if any of them is more concrete, more permanent, more excellent, and richer than another it will be to that other super-natural. Nor will a partial contact between any two obliterate their distinctness. In that way there might be Natures piled upon Natures to any height God pleased, each Supernatural to that below it and Subnatural to that which surpassed it. But the tenor of Christian teaching is that we are actually living in a situation even more complex than that. A new Nature is being not merely made but made out of an old one. We live amid all the anomalies, inconveniences, hopes, and excitements of a house that is being rebuilt. Something is being pulled down and something going up in its place.

To accept the idea of intermediate floors—which the Christian story will, quite simply, force us to do if it is not a falsehood—does not of course involve losing our spiritual apprehension of the top floor of all. Most certainly, beyond all worlds, unconditioned and unimaginable, transcending discursive thought, there yawns for ever the ultimate Fact, the fountain of all other facthood, the burning and undimensioned depth of the Divine Life. Most certainly also, to be united with that Life in the eternal Sonship of Christ is, strictly speaking, the only thing worth a moment's consideration. And in so far as *that* is what you mean by *Heaven*, Christ's divine Nature never left it, and therefore never returned to it: and His human nature ascended thither not at the moment of the Ascension but at every moment. In that sense not one word that the spiritualisers have uttered will, please God, ever be unsaid by me. But it by no means follows that there are not other truths as well. I allow, indeed I insist, that Christ cannot be at 'the right hand of God' except in a metaphorical sense. I allow and insist that the Eternal Word, the Second Person of the Trinity, can never be, nor have been, confined to any place at all: it is rather in Him that all places exist. But the records say that the glorified, but still in some sense corporeal, Christ withdrew into some different mode of being about six weeks after the Crucifixion: and that He is 'preparing a place' for us. The statement in St Mark that He sat down at the right hand of God we must take as a metaphor: it was indeed, even for the writer, a poetical quotation, from Psalm 110. But the statement that the holy Shape went up and vanished does not permit the same treatment.

What troubles us here is not simply the statement itself but what (we feel sure) the author meant by it. Granted that there are different Natures, different levels of being, distinct but not always discontinuous—granted that Christ withdrew from one of these to another, that His withdrawal from one was indeed the first step in His creation of the other—what precisely should we expect the onlookers to see? Perhaps mere instantaneous vanishing would make us most comfortable. A sudden break between the perceptible and the imperceptible would worry us less than any kind of joint. But if the spectators say they saw first a short vertical movement and then a vague luminosity (that is what 'cloud' presumably means here as it certainly does in the account of the Transfiguration) and then nothing—have we any reason to object? We are well aware that increased distance from the centre of this planet could not *in itself* be equated with increase of power or beatitude. But this is only saying that *if* the movement had no connection with such spiritual events, why then it had no connection with them.

Movement (in any direction but one) away from the position momentarily occupied by our moving Earth will certainly be to us movement 'upwards'. To say that Christ's passage to a new 'Nature' could involve no such movement, or no movement at all, within the 'Nature' he was leaving, is very arbitrary. Where there is passage, there is departure; and departure is an event in the region from which the traveller is departing. All this, even on the assumption that the Ascending Christ is in a three-dimensional space. If it is not that kind of body, and space is not that kind of space, then we are even less qualified to say what the spectators of this entirely new event might or might not see or feel as if they had seen. There is, of course, no question of a human body as we know it existing in interstellar space as we know it. The Ascension belongs to a New Nature. We are discussing only what the 'joint' between the Old Nature and the new, the precise moment of transition, would look like.

But what really worries us is the conviction that, whatever we say, the New Testament writers meant something quite different. We feel sure that they thought they had seen their Master setting off on a journey for a local 'Heaven' where God sat in a throne and where there was another throne waiting for Him. And I believe that in a sense that is just what they did think. And I believe that, for this reason, whatever they had actually seen (sense perception, almost by hypothesis, would be confused at such a moment) they would almost certainly have remembered it as a vertical movement. What we must not say is that they 'mistook' local 'Heavens' and celestial throne-rooms and the like for the 'spiritual' Heaven of union with God and supreme power and beatitude. You and I have been gradually disentangling different senses of the word *Heaven* throughout this chapter. It may be convenient here to make a list. *Heaven* can mean (1) The unconditioned Divine Life beyond all worlds. (2) Blessed participation in that Life by a created spirit. (3) The whole Nature or system of conditions in which redeemed human spirits, still remaining human, can enjoy such participation fully and for ever. This is the Heaven Christ goes to 'prepare' for us. (4) The physical Heaven, the sky, the space in which Earth moves. What enables us to distinguish these senses and hold them clearly apart is not any special spiritual purity but the fact that we are the heirs to centuries of logical analysis: not that we are sons to Abraham but that we are sons to Aristotle. We are not to suppose that the writers of the New Testament mistook Heaven in sense four or three for Heaven in sense two or one. You cannot mistake a half sovereign for a sixpence until you know the English system of coinage—that is, until you know the difference between them. In their idea of Heaven all these meanings were latent, ready to be brought out by later analysis. They never thought merely of the blue sky or merely of a 'spiritual' heaven. When they looked up at the blue sky they never doubted that there, whence light and heat and the precious rain descended, was the home of God: but on the other hand, when they thought of one ascending to that Heaven they never doubted He was 'ascending' in what we should call a 'spiritual' sense. The real and pernicious period of literalism comes far later, in the Middle Ages and the seventeenth century, when the distinctions have been made and heavy-handed people try to force the separated concepts together again in wrong ways. The fact that Galilean shepherds could not distinguish what they saw at the Ascension from that kind of ascent which, by its very nature, could never be seen at all, does not prove on the one hand that they were unspiritual, nor on the other that they saw nothing. A man who really believes that 'Heaven' is in the sky may well, in his heart, have a far truer and more spiritual conception of it than many a modern logician who could expose that fallacy with a few strokes of his pen. For he who does the will of the Father shall know the doctrine. Irrelevant material splendours in such a man's idea of the vision of God will do no harm, for they are not there for their own sakes. Purity from such images in a merely theoretical Christian's idea will do no good if they have been banished only by logical criticism.

But we must go a little further than this. It is not an accident that simple-minded people, however spiritual, should blend the ideas of God and Heaven and the blue sky. It is a fact, not a fiction, that light and life-giving heat do come down from the sky to Earth. The analogy of the sky's role to begetting and of the Earth's role to bearing is sound as far as it goes. The huge dome of the sky is of all things sensuously perceived the most like infinity. And when God made space and worlds that move in space, and clothed our world with air, and gave us such eyes and such imaginations as those we have, He knew what the sky would mean to us. And since nothing in His work is accidental, if He knew, He intended. We cannot be certain that this was not indeed one of the chief purposes for which Nature was created; still less that it was not one of the chief reasons why the withdrawal was allowed to affect human senses as a movement upwards. (A disappearance into the Earth would beget a wholly different religion.) The ancients in letting the spiritual symbolism of the sky flow straight into their minds without stopping to discover by analysis that it was a symbol, were not entirely mistaken. In one way they were perhaps less mistaken than we.

For we have fallen into an opposite difficulty. Let us confess that probably every Christian now alive finds a difficulty in reconciling the two things he has been told about 'heaven'—that it is, on the one hand, a life in Christ, a vision of God, a ceaseless adoration, and that it is, on the other hand, a bodily life. When we seem nearest to the vision of God in this life, the body seems almost an irrelevance. And if we try to conceive our eternal life as one in a body (any kind of body) we tend to find that some vague dream of Platonic paradises and gardens of the Hesperides has substituted itself for that mystical approach which we feel (and I think rightly) to be more important. But if that discrepancy were final then it would follow—which is absurd—that God was originally mistaken when He introduced our spirits into the Natural order at all. We must conclude that the discrepancy itself is precisely one of the disorders which the New Creation comes to heal. The fact that the body, and locality and locomotion and time, now feel irrelevant to the highest reaches of the spiritual life is (like the fact that we can think of our bodies as 'coarse') a *symptom*. Spirit and Nature have quarrelled in us; that is our disease. Nothing we can yet do enables us to imagine its complete healing. Some glimpses and faint hints we have: in the Sacraments, in the use made of sensuous imagery by the great poets, in the best instances of sexual love, in our experiences of the earth's beauty. But the full healing is utterly beyond our present conceptions. Mystics have got as far in contemplation of God as the point at which the senses are banished: the further point, at which they will be put back again, has (to the best of my knowledge) been reached by no one. The destiny of redeemed man is not less but more unimaginable than mysticism would lead us to suppose—because it is full of semi-imaginables which we cannot at present admit without destroying its essential character.

One point must be touched on because, though I kept silence, it would none the less be present in most readers' minds. The letter and spirit of scripture, and of all Christianity, forbid us to suppose that life in the New Creation will be a sexual life; and this reduces our imagination to the withering alternative either of bodies which are hardly recognisable as human bodies at all or else of a perpetual fast. As regards the fast, I think our present outlook might be like that of a small boy who, on being told that the sexual act was the highest bodily pleasure should immediately ask whether you ate chocolates at the same time. On receiving the answer 'No,' he might regard absence of chocolates as the chief characteristic of sexuality. In vain would you tell him that the reason why lovers in their carnal raptures don't bother about chocolates is that they have something better to think of. The boy knows chocolate: he does not know the positive thing that excludes it. We are in the same position. We know the sexual life; we do not know, except in glimpses, the other thing which, in Heaven, will leave no room for it. Hence where fullness awaits us we anticipate fasting. In denying that sexual life, as we now understand it, makes any part of the final beatitude, it is not of course necessary to suppose that the distinction of sexes will disappear. What is no longer needed for biological purposes may be expected to survive for splendour. Sexuality is the instrument both of virginity and of conjugal virtue; neither men nor women will be asked to throw away weapons they have used victoriously. It is the beaten and the fugitives who throw away their swords. The conquerors sheathe theirs and retain them. 'Trans-sexual' would be a better word than 'sexless' for the heavenly life.

I am well aware that this last paragraph may seem to many readers unfortunate and to some comic. But that very comedy, as I must repeatedly insist, is the symptom of our estrangement, as spirits, from Nature and our estrangement, as animals, from Spirit. The whole conception of the New Creation involves the belief that this estrangement will be healed. A curious consequence will follow. The archaic type of thought which could not clearly distinguish spiritual 'Heaven' from the sky, is from our point of view a confused type of thought. But it also resembles and anticipates a type of thought which will one day be true. That archaic sort of thinking will become simply the correct sort when Nature and Spirit are fully harmonised—when Spirit rides Nature so perfectly that the two together make rather a *Centaur* than a mounted knight. I do not mean necessarily that the blending of Heaven and sky, in particular, will turn out to be specially true, but that that kind of blending will accurately mirror the reality which will then exist. There will be no room to get the finest razor-blade of thought in between Spirit and Nature. Every state of affairs in the New Nature will be the perfect expression of a spiritual state and every spiritual state the perfect informing of, and bloom upon, a state of affairs; one with it as the perfume with a flower or the 'spirit' of great poetry with its form. There is thus in the history of human thought, as elsewhere, a pattern of death and rebirth. The old, richly imaginative thought which still survives in Plato has to submit to the deathlike, but indispensable, process of logical analysis: nature and spirit, matter and mind, fact and myth, the literal and the metaphorical, have to be more and more sharply separated, till at last a purely mathematical universe and a purely subjective mind confront one another across an unbridgeable chasm. But from this descent also, if thought itself is to survive, there must be reascent and the Christian conception provides for it. Those who attain the glorious resurrection will see the dry bones clothed again with flesh, the fact and the myth remarried, the literal and the metaphorical rushing together.

The remark so often made that 'Heaven is a state of mind' bears witness to the wintry and deathlike phase of this process in which we are now living. The implication is that if Heaven is a state of mind—or, more correctly, of the spirit—then it must be only a state of the spirit, or at least that anything else, if added to that state of spirit, would be irrelevant. That is what every great religion *except* Christianity would say. But Christian teaching by saying that God made the world and called it good teaches that Nature or environment cannot be simply irrelevant to spiritual beatitude in general, however far in one particular Nature, during the days of her bondage, they may have drawn apart. By teaching the resurrection of the body it teaches that Heaven is not merely a state of the spirit but a state of the body as well: and therefore a state of Nature as a whole. Christ, it is true, told His hearers that the Kingdom of Heaven was 'within' or 'among' them. But His hearers were not *merely* in 'a state of mind'. The planet He had created was beneath their feet, His sun above their heads; blood and lungs and guts were working in the bodies He had invented, photons and sound waves of His devising were blessing them with the sight of His human face and the sound of His voice. We are never *merely* in a state of mind. The prayer and the meditation made in howling wind or quiet sunshine, in morning alacrity or evening resignation, in youth or age, good health or ill, may be equally, but are differently, blessed. Already in this present life we have all seen how God can take up all these seeming irrelevances into the spiritual fact and cause them to bear no small part in making the blessing of that moment to be the particular blessing it was—as fire can burn coal and wood equally but a wood fire is different from a coal one. From this factor of environment Christianity does not teach us to desire a total release. We desire, like St Paul, not to be un-clothed but to be re-clothed: to find not the formless Everywhere-and-Nowhere but the promised land, that Nature which will be always and perfectly—as present Nature is partially and intermittently—the instrument for that music which will then arise between Christ and us.

And what, you ask, does it matter? Do not such ideas only excite us and distract us from the more immediate and more certain things, the love of God and our neighbours, the bearing of the daily cross? If you find that they so distract you, think of them no more. I most fully allow that it is of more importance for you or me today to refrain from one sneer or to extend one charitable thought to an enemy than to know all that angels and archangels know about the mysteries of the New Creation. I write of these things not because they are the most important but because this book is about miracles. From the title you cannot have expected a book of devotion or of ascetic theology. Yet I will not admit that the things we have been discussing for the last few pages are of no importance for the practice of the Christian life. For I suspect that our conception of Heaven as *merely* a state of mind is not unconnected with the fact that the specifically Christian virtue of Hope has in our time grown so languid. Where our fathers, peering into the future, saw gleams of gold, we see only the mist, white, featureless, cold and never moving.

The thought at the back of all this negative spirituality is really one forbidden to Christians. They, of all men, must not conceive spiritual joy and worth as things that need to be rescued or tenderly protected from time and place and matter and the senses. Their God is the God of corn and oil and wine. He is the glad Creator. He has become Himself incarnate. The sacraments have been instituted. Certain spiritual gifts are offered us only on condition that we perform certain bodily acts. After that we cannot really be in doubt of His intention. To shrink back from all that can be called Nature into negative spirituality is as if we ran away from horses instead of learning to ride. There is in our present pilgrim condition plenty of room (more room than most of us like) for abstinence and renunciation and mortifying our natural desires. But behind all asceticism the thought should be, 'Who will trust us with the true wealth if we cannot be trusted even with the wealth that perishes?' Who will trust me with a spiritual body if I cannot control even an earthly body? These small and perishable bodies we now have were given to us as ponies are given to schoolboys. We must learn to manage: not that we may some day be free of horses altogether but that some day we may ride bareback, confident and rejoicing, those greater mounts, those winged, shining and world-shaking horses which perhaps even now expect us with impatience, pawing and snorting in the King's stables. Not that the gallop would be of any value unless it were a gallop with the King; but how else—since He has retained His own charger—should we accompany Him?

17

EPILOGUE

*If you leave a thing alone you leave it to a torrent of
change. If you leave a white post alone it will soon be a
black post.*

G. K. CHESTERTON, *ORTHODOXY*

MY WORK ENDS here. If, after reading it, you now turn to study the historical evidence for yourself, begin with the New Testament and not with
the books about it. If you do not know Greek get it in a modern translation. Moffat's is probably the best: Monsignor Knox is also good. I do
not advise the *Basic English* version. And when you turn from the New
Testament to modern scholars, remember that you go among them as a
sheep among wolves. Naturalistic assumptions, beggings of the question
such as that which I noted on the first page of this book, will meet you on
every side—even from the pens of clergymen. This does not mean (as I
was once tempted to suspect) that these clergymen are disguised apos-
tates who deliberately exploit the position and the livelihood given them
by the Christian Church to undermine Christianity. It comes partly from
what we may call a 'hangover'. We all have Naturalism in our bones and
even conversion does not at once work the infection out of our system.
Its assumptions rush back upon the mind the moment vigilance is re-
laxed. And in part the procedure of these scholars arises from the feeling

which is greatly to their credit—which indeed is honourable to the point of being Quixotic. They are anxious to allow to the enemy every advantage he can with any show of fairness claim. They thus make it part of their method to eliminate the supernatural wherever it is even remotely possible to do so, to strain natural explanation even to the breaking point before they admit the least suggestion of miracle. Just in the same spirit some examiners tend to overmark any candidate whose opinions and character, as revealed by his work, are revolting to them. We are so afraid of being led into unfairness by our instant dislike of the man that we are liable to overshoot the mark and treat him too kindly. Many modern Christian scholars overshoot the mark for a similar reason.

In using the books of such people you must therefore be continually on guard. You must develop a nose like a bloodhound for those steps in the argument which depend not on historical and linguistic knowledge but on the concealed assumption that miracles are impossible, improbable or improper. And this means that you must really re-educate yourself: must work hard and consistently to eradicate from your mind the whole type of thought in which we have all been brought up. It is the type of thought which, under various disguises, has been our adversary throughout this book. It is technically called *Monism*; but perhaps the unlearned reader will understand me best if I call it *Everythingism*. I mean by this the belief that 'everything', or 'the whole show', must be self-existent, must be more important than every particular thing, and must contain all particular things in such a way that they cannot be really very different from one another—that they must be not merely 'at one', but one. Thus the Everythingist, if he starts from God, becomes a Pantheist; there must be nothing that is not God. If he starts from Nature he becomes a Naturalist; there must be nothing that is not Nature. He thinks that everything is in the long run 'merely' a precursor or a development or a relic or an instance or a disguise, of everything else. This philosophy I believe to be profoundly untrue. One of the moderns has said that reality is 'incorrigibly plural'. I think he is right. All things come from One. All things are related—related in different and complicated ways. But all things are not one. The word 'everything' should mean simply the total (a total to be reached, if we knew enough, by enumeration) of all the things that exist at a given moment. It must not be given a mental capital letter; must not (under the influence of picture thinking) be turned into a sort of pool in which particular things sink or even a cake in which they are the currants. Real things are sharp and knobbly and complicated and different. Everythingism is congenial to our minds because it is the natural philosophy of a totalitarian, mass-producing, conscripted age. That is why we must be perpetually on our guard against it.

And yet . . . and yet . . . It is that *and yet* which I fear more than any positive argument against miracles: that soft, tidal return of your habitual outlook as you close the book and the familiar four walls about you and the familiar noises from the street reassert themselves. Perhaps (if I dare suppose so much) you have been led on at times while you were reading, have felt ancient hopes and fears astir in your heart, have perhaps come almost to the threshold of belief—but now? No. It just won't do. Here is the ordinary, here is the 'real' world, round you again. The dream is ending; as all other similar dreams have always ended. For of course this is not the first time such a thing has happened. More than once in your life before this you have heard a strange story, read some odd book, seen something queer or imagined you have seen it, entertained some wild hope or terror: but always it ended in the same way. And always you wondered how you could, even for a moment, have expected it not to. For that 'real world' when you came back to it is so unanswerable. *Of course* the strange story was false, of course the voice was really subjective, of course the apparent portent was a coincidence. You are ashamed of yourself for having ever thought otherwise: ashamed, relieved, amused, disappointed, and angry all at once. You ought to have known that, as Arnold says, 'Miracles don't happen'.

About this state of mind I have just two things to say. First, that it is precisely one of those counterattacks by Nature which, on my theory, you ought to have anticipated. Your rational thinking has no foothold in your merely natural consciousness except what it wins and maintains by conquest. The moment rational thought ceases, imagination, mental habit, temperament, and the 'spirit of the age' take charge of you again. New thoughts, until they have themselves become habitual, will affect your consciousness as a whole only while you are actually thinking them. Reason has but to nod at his post, and instantly Nature's patrols are infiltrating. Therefore, while counter-arguments against Miracle are to be given full attention (for if I am wrong, then the sooner I am refuted the better not only for you but for me) the mere gravitation of the mind back to its habitual outlook must be discounted. Not only in this enquiry but in every enquiry. That same familiar room, reasserting itself as one closes the book, can make other things *feel* incredible besides miracles. Whether the book has been telling you that the end of civilisation is at hand, that you are kept in your chair by the curvature of space, or even that you are upside down in relation to Australia, it may still seem a little unreal as you yawn and think of going to bed. I have found even a simple truth (e.g. that my hand, this hand now resting on the book, will one day be a skeleton's hand) singularly unconvincing at such a moment. 'Belief-feelings', as Dr Richards calls them, do not follow reason except by long training: they follow Nature, follow the grooves and ruts which already exist in the mind. The firmest theoretical conviction in favour of materialism will not prevent a particular kind of man, under certain conditions, from being afraid of ghosts. The firmest theoretical conviction in favour of miracles will not prevent another kind of man, in other conditions, from *feeling* a heavy, inescapable certainty that no miracle can ever occur. But the feelings of a tired and nervous man, unexpectedly reduced to passing a night in a large empty country house at the end of a journey on which he has been reading a ghost-story, are no evidence that ghosts exist. Your feelings at this moment are no evidence that miracles do not occur.

The second thing is this. You are probably quite right in thinking that you will never see a miracle done: you are probably equally right in thinking that there was a natural explanation of anything in your past life which seemed, at the first glance, to be 'rum' or odd'. God does not shake miracles into Nature at random as if from a pepper-caster. They come on great occasions: they are found at the great ganglions of history—not of political or social history, but of that spiritual history which cannot be fully known by men. If your own life does not happen to be near one of those great ganglions, how should you expect to see one? If we were heroic missionaries, apostles, or martyrs, it would be a different matter. But why you or I? Unless you live near a railway, you will not see trains go past your windows. How likely is it that you or I will be present when a peace-treaty is signed, when a great scientific discovery is made, when a dictator commits suicide? That we should see a miracle is even less likely. Nor, if we understand, shall we be anxious to do so. 'Nothing almost sees miracles but misery'. Miracles and martyrdoms tend to bunch about the same areas of history—areas we have naturally no wish to frequent. Do not, I earnestly advise you, demand an ocular proof unless you are already perfectly certain that it is not forthcoming.

ON THE WORDS 'SPIRIT' AND 'SPIRITUAL'

THE READER SHOULD be warned that the angle from which Man is approached in Chapter IV is quite different from that which would be proper in a devotional or practical treatise on the spiritual life. The kind of analysis which you make of any complex thing depends on the purpose you have in view. Thus in a society the important distinctions, from one point of view, would be those of male and female, children and adults, and the like. From another point of view the important distinctions would be those of rulers and ruled. From a third point of view distinctions of class or occupation might be the most important. All these different analyses might be equally correct, but they would be useful for different purposes. When we are considering Man as evidence for the fact that this spatio-temporal Nature is not the only thing in existence, the important distinction is between that part of Man which belongs to this spatio-temporal Nature and that part which does not: or, if you prefer, between those phenomena of humanity which are rigidly interlocked with all other events in this space and time and those which have a certain independence. These two parts of a man may rightly be called Natural and Supernatural: in calling the second 'Super-Natural' we mean that it is something which invades, or is added to, the great interlocked event in space and time, instead of merely arising from it. On the other hand this 'Supernatural' part is itself a created being—a thing called into existence by the Absolute Being and given by Him a certain character or 'nature'.

We could therefore say that while 'supernatural' in relation to *this* Nature (this complex event in space and time) it is, in another sense, 'natural'— i.e. it is a specimen of a class of things which God normally creates after a stable pattern.

There is, however, a sense in which the life of this part can become *absolutely* Supernatural, i.e. not beyond *this* Nature but beyond any and every Nature, in the sense that it can achieve a kind of life which could never have been *given* to any created being in its mere creation. The distinction will, perhaps, become clearer if we consider it in relation not to men but to angels. (It does not matter, here, whether the reader believes in angels or not. I am using them only to make the point clearer.) All angels, both the 'good' ones and the bad or 'fallen' ones which we call devils, are equally 'Super-natural' in relation to *this* spatio-temporal Nature: i.e. they are outside it and have powers and a mode of existence which it could not provide. But the good angels lead a life which is Supernatural in another sense as well. That is to say, they have, of their own free will, offered back to God in love the 'natures' He gave them at their creation. All creatures of course live from God in the sense that He made them and at every moment maintains them in existence. But there is a further and higher kind of 'life from God' which can be given only to a creature who voluntarily surrenders himself to it. This life the good angels have and the bad angels have not: and it is absolutely Supernatural because no creature in any world can have it by the mere fact of being the sort of creature it is.

As with angels, so with us. The rational part of every man is supernatural in the relative sense—the same sense in which *both* angels and devils are supernatural. But if it is, as the theologians say, 'born again', if it surrenders itself back to God in Christ, it will then have a life which is absolutely Supernatural, which is not created at all but begotten, for the creature is then sharing the begotten life of the Second Person of the Deity.

When devotional writers talk of the 'spiritual life'—and often when they talk of the 'supernatural life' or when I myself, in another book, talked of *Zoë*—they mean this *absolutely* Supernatural life which no creature can be given simply by being created but which every rational creature can have by voluntarily surrendering itself to the life of Christ. But much confusion arises from the fact that in many books the words 'Spirit' or 'Spiritual' are also used to mean the *relatively* supernatural element in Man, the element external to *this* Nature which is (so to speak) 'issued' or handed out to him by the mere fact of being created as a Man at all.

It will perhaps be helpful to make a list of the sense in which the words 'spirit', 'spirits' and 'spiritual' are, or have been, used in English.

1. The chemical sense, e.g. 'Spirits evaporate very quickly.'

2. The (now obsolete) medical sense. The older doctors believed in certain extremely fine fluids in the human body which were called 'the spirits'. As medical science this view has long been abandoned, but it is the origin of some expressions we still use; as when we speak of being 'in high spirits' or 'in low spirits' or say that a horse is 'spirited' or that a boy is 'full of animal spirits'.

3. 'Spiritual' is often used to mean simply the opposite of 'bodily' or 'material'. Thus all that is immaterial in man (emotions, passions, memory, etc.) is often called 'spiritual'. It is very important to remember that what is 'spiritual' in this sense is not necessarily good. There is nothing specially fine about the mere fact of immateriality. Immaterial things may, like material things, be good or bad or indifferent.

4. Some people use 'spirit' to mean that relatively supernatural element which is given to every man at his creation—the rational element. This is, I think, the most useful way of employing the word. Here again it is important to realise that what is 'spiritual' is not necessarily good. A Spirit (in this sense) can be either the best or the worst of created things. It is because Man is (in this sense) a spiritual animal that he can become either a son of God or a devil.

5. Finally, Christian writers use 'spirit' and 'spiritual' to mean the life which arises in such rational beings when they voluntarily surrender to Divine grace and become sons of the Heavenly Father in Christ. It is in this sense, and in this sense alone, that the 'spiritual' is always good.

It is idle to complain that words have more than one sense. Language is a living thing and words are bound to throw out new senses as a tree throws out new branches. It is not wholly a disadvantage, since in the act of disentangling these senses we learn a great deal about the things involved which we might otherwise have overlooked. What is disastrous is that any word should change its sense during a discussion without our being aware of the change. Hence, for the present discussion, it might be useful to give different names to the three things which are meant by the word 'Spirit' in senses three, four, and five. Thus for sense three a good word would be 'soul': and the adjective to go with it would be 'psychological'. For sense four we might keep the words 'spirit' and 'spiritual'. For sense five the best adjective would be 'regenerate', but there is no very suitable noun.[1] And this is perhaps significant: for what we are talking about is not (as *soul* and *spirit* are) a part or element in Man but a redirection and revitalising of all the parts or elements. Thus in one sense there is nothing more in a regenerate man than in an unregenerate man, just as there is nothing more in a man who is walking in the right direction than in one who is walking in the wrong direction. In another sense, however, it might be said that the regenerate man is *totally* different from the unregenerate, for the regenerate life, the Christ that is formed in him, transforms every part of him: in it his spirit, soul and body will all be reborn. Thus if the regenerate life is not a *part* of the man, this is largely because where it arises at all it cannot rest till it becomes the whole man. It is not divided from any of the parts as they are divided from each other. The life of the 'spirit' (in sense four) is in a sense cut off from the life of the soul: the purely rational and moral man who tries to live entirely by his created spirit finds himself forced to treat the passions and imaginations of his soul as mere enemies to be destroyed or imprisoned. But the regenerate man will find his soul eventually harmonised with his spirit by the life of Christ that is in him. Hence Christians believe in the resurrection of the body, whereas the ancient philosophers regard the body as a mere encumbrance. And this perhaps is a universal law, that the higher you rise the lower you can descend. Man is a tower in which the different floors can hardly be reached from one another but all can be reached from the top floor.

N.B. In the Authorised Version the 'spiritual' man means what I am calling the 'regenerate' man: the 'natural' man means, I think, both what I call the 'spirit man' and the 'soul man'.

---

[1] Because the 'spirit' in this sense is identical with the New Man (the Christ formed in each perfected Christian) some Latin theologians call it simply our *Novitas* i.e. our 'newness'.

APPENDIX B

ON 'SPECIAL PROVIDENCES'

IN THIS BOOK the reader has heard of two classes of events and two only—miracles and natural events. The former are not interlocked with the history of Nature in the backward direction—i.e. in the time before their occurrence. The latter are. Many pious people, however, speak of certain events as being 'providential' or 'special providences' without meaning that they are miraculous. This generally implies a belief that, quite apart from miracles, some events are providential in a sense in which some others are not. Thus some people thought that the weather which enabled us to bring off so much of our army at Dunkirk was 'providential' in some way in which weather as a whole is not providential. The Christian doctrine that some events, though not miracles, are yet answers to prayer, would seem at first to imply this.

I find it very difficult to conceive an intermediate class of events which are neither miraculous nor merely 'ordinary'. Either the weather at Dunkirk was or was not that which the previous physical history of the universe, by its own character, would inevitably produce. If it was, then how is it 'specially' providential? If it was not, then it was a miracle.

It seems to me, therefore, that we must abandon the idea that there is any special class of events (apart from miracles) which can be distinguished as 'specially providential'. Unless we are to abandon the conception of Providence altogether, and with it the belief in efficacious prayer, it follows that all events are equally providential. If God directs the course of events at all then he directs the movement of every atom at every moment; 'not one sparrow falls to the ground' without that direction. The 'naturalness' of natural events does not consist in being somehow outside God's providence. It consists in their being interlocked with one another inside a common space-time in accordance with the fixed pattern of the 'laws'.

In order to get any picture at all of a thing, it is sometimes necessary to begin with a false picture and then correct it. The false picture of Providence (false because it represents God and Nature as being both contained in a common Time) would be as follows. Every event in Nature results from some previous event, not from the laws of Nature. In the long run the first natural event, whatever it was, has dictated every other event. That is, when God at the moment of creation fed the first event into the framework of the 'laws'—first set the ball rolling—He determined the whole history of Nature. Foreseeing every part of that history, He intended every part of it. If He had wished for different weather at Dunkirk He would have made the first event slightly different.

The weather we actually had is therefore in the strictest sense providential; it was decreed, and decreed for a purpose, when the world was made—but no more so (though more interestingly to us) than the precise position at this moment of every atom in the ring of Saturn.

It follows (still retaining our false picture) that every physical event was determined so as to serve a great number of purposes.

Thus God must be supposed in predetermining the weather at Dunkirk to have taken fully into account the effect it would have not only on the destiny of two nations but (what is incomparably more important) on all the individuals involved on both sides, on all animals, vegetables and minerals within range, and finally on every atom in the universe. This may sound excessive, but in reality we are attributing to the Omniscient only an infinitely superior degree of the same kind of skill which a mere human novelist exercises daily in constructing his plot.

Suppose I am writing a novel. I have the following problems on my hands: (1) Old Mr A. has got to be dead before Chapter 15. (2) And he'd better die suddenly because I have to prevent him from altering his will. (3) His daughter (my heroine) has got to be kept out of London for three chapters at least. (4) My hero has somehow got to recover the heroine's good opinion which he lost in Chapter 7. (5) That young prig B. who has to improve before the end of the book, needs a bad moral shock to take the conceit out of him. (6) We haven't decided on B.'s job yet; but the whole development of his character will involve giving him a job and showing him actually at work. How on earth am I to get in all these six things? . . . I have it. What about a railway accident? Old A. can be killed in it, and that settles him. In fact the accident can occur while he is actually going up to London to see his solicitor with the very purpose of getting his will altered. What more natural than that his daughter should run up with him? We'll have her slightly injured in the accident: that'll prevent her reaching London for as many chapters as we need. And the hero can be on the same train. He can behave with great coolness and heroism during the accident—probably he'll rescue the heroine from a burning carriage. That settles my fourth point. And the young prig B.? We'll make him the signalman whose negligence caused the accident. That gives him his moral shock and also links him up with the main plot. In fact, once we have thought of the railway accident, that single event will solve six apparently separate problems.

No doubt this is in some ways an intolerably misleading image: firstly because (except as regards the prig B.) I have been thinking not of the ultimate good of my characters but of the entertainment of my readers: secondly because we are simply ignoring the effect of the railway accident on all the other passengers in that train: and finally because it is I who make B. give the wrong signal. That is, though I pretend that he has free will, he really hasn't. In spite of these objections, however, the example may perhaps suggest how Divine ingenuity could so contrive the physical 'plot' of the universe as to provide a 'providential' answer to the needs of innumerable creatures.

But some of these creatures have free will. It is at this point that we must begin to correct the admittedly false picture of Providence which we have hitherto been using. That picture, you will remember, was false because it represented God and Nature as inhabiting a common Time. But it is probable that Nature is not really in Time and almost certain that God is not. Time is probably (like perspective) the mode of our perception. There is therefore in reality no question of God's at one point in time (the moment of creation) adapting the material history of the universe in advance to free acts which you or I are to perform at a later point in Time. To Him all the physical events and all the human acts are present in an eternal Now. The liberation of finite wills and the creation of the whole material history of the universe (related to the acts of those wills in all the necessary complexity) is to Him a single operation. In this sense God did not create the universe long ago but creates it at this minute—at every minute.

Suppose I find a piece of paper on which a black wavy line is already drawn, I can now sit down and draw other lines (say in red) so shaped as to combine with the black line into a pattern. Let us now suppose that the original black line is conscious. But it is not conscious along the whole length at once—only on each point on that length in turn.

Its consciousness in fact is travelling along that line from left to right retaining point A only as a memory when it reaches B and unable until it has left B to become conscious of C. Let us also give this black line free will. It chooses the direction it goes in. The particular wavy shape of it is the shape it wills to have. But whereas it is aware of its own chosen shape only moment by moment and does not know at point D which way it will decide to turn at point F, I can see its shape as a whole and all at once. At every moment it will find my red lines waiting for it and adapted to it. Of course: because I, in composing the total red-and-black design have the whole course of the black line in view and take it into account. It is a matter not of impossibility but merely of designer's skill for me to devise red lines which at every point have a right relation not only to the black line but to one another so as to fill the whole paper with a satisfactory design.

In this model the black line represents a creature with free will, the red lines represent material events, and I represent God. The model would of course be more accurate if I were making the paper as well as the pattern and if there were hundreds of millions of black lines instead of one—but for the sake of simplicity we must keep it as it is.[1]

It will be seen that if the black line addressed prayers to me I might (if I chose) grant them. It prays that when it reaches point N it may find the red lines arranged around it in a certain shape. That shape may by the laws of design require to be balanced by other arrangements of red lines on quite different parts of the paper—some at the top or bottom so far away from the black line that it knows nothing about them: some so far to

---

[1] Admittedly all I have done is to turn the tables by making human volitions the constant and physical destiny the variable. This is as false as the opposite view; the point is that it is no falser. A subtler image of creation and freedom (or rather, creation of the free and the unfree in a single timeless act) would be the *almost* simultaneous mutual adaptation in the movement of two expert dancing partners.

the left that they come before the beginning of the black line, some so far to the right that they come after its end. (The black line would call these parts of the paper, 'The time before I was born,' and, 'The time after I'm dead.') But these other parts of the pattern demanded by that red shape which Black Line wants at N, do not prevent my granting its prayer. For his whole course has been visible to me from the moment I looked at the paper and his requirements at point N are among the things I took into account in deciding the total pattern.

Most of our prayers if fully analysed, ask either for a miracle or for events whose foundation will have to have been laid before I was born, indeed, laid when the universe began. But then to God (though not to me) I and the prayer I make in 1945 were just as much present at the creation of the world as they are now and will be a million years hence. God's creative act is timeless and timelessly adapted to the 'free' elements within it: but this timeless adaptation meets our consciousness as a sequence and prayer and answer.

Two corollaries follow:

1. People often ask whether a given event (not a miracle) was really an answer to prayer or not. I think that if they analyse their thought they will find they are asking, 'Did God bring it about for a special purpose or would it have happened anyway as part of the natural course of events?' But this (like the old question, 'Have you left off beating your wife?') makes either answer impossible. In the play, *Hamlet*, Ophelia climbs out on a branch overhanging a river: the branch breaks, she falls in and drowns. What would you reply if anyone asked, 'Did Ophelia die because Shakespeare for poetic reasons wanted her to die at that moment—or because the branch broke?' I think one would have to say, 'For both reasons.' Every event in the play happens as a result of other events in the play, but also every event happens because the poet wants it to happen. All events in the play are Shakespearian events; similarly all events in the real world are providential events. All events in the play, however, come about (or ought to come about) by the dramatic logic of events. Similarly all events in the real world (except miracles) come about by natural causes. 'Providence' and Natural causation are not alternatives; both determine every event because both are one.

2. When we are praying about the result, say, of a battle or a medical consultation the thought will often cross our minds that (if only we

knew it) the event is already decided one way or the other. I believe this to be no good reason for ceasing our prayers. The event certainly has been decided—in a sense it was decided 'before all worlds'. But one of the things taken into account in deciding it, and therefore one of the things that really cause it to happen, may be this very prayer that we are now offering. Thus, shocking as it may sound, I conclude that we can at noon become part causes of an event occurring at ten a.m. (Some scientists would find this easier than popular thought does.) The imagination will, no doubt, try to play all sorts of tricks on us at this point. It will ask, 'Then if I stop praying can God go back and alter what has already happened?' No. The event has already happened and one of its causes has been the fact that you are asking such questions instead of praying. It will ask, 'Then if I begin to pray can God go back and alter what has already happened?' No. The event has already happened and one of its causes is your present prayer. Thus something does really depend on my choice. My free act contributes to the cosmic shape. That contribution is made in eternity or 'before all worlds'; but my consciousness of contributing reaches me at a particular point in the time-series.

The following question may be asked: If we can reasonably pray for an event which must in fact have happened or failed to happen several hours ago, why can we not pray for an event which we know *not* to have happened? e.g. pray for the safety of someone who, as we know, was killed yesterday. What makes the difference is precisely our knowledge. The known event states God's will. It is psychologically impossible to pray for what we know to be unobtainable; and if it were possible the prayer would sin against the duty of submission to God's known will.

One more consequence remains to be drawn. It is never possible to prove empirically that a given, nonmiraculous event was or was not an answer to prayer. Since it was non-miraculous the sceptic can always point to its natural causes and say, 'Because of these it would have happened anyway,' and the believer can always reply, 'But because these were only links in a chain of events, hanging on other links, and the whole chain hanging upon God's will, they may have occurred because someone prayed.' The efficacy of prayer, therefore, cannot be either asserted or denied without an exercise of the will—the will choosing or rejecting faith in the light of a whole philosophy. Experimental evidence there can be none on either side. In the sequence M.N.O. event N, unless it is a miracle, is always caused by M and causes O; but the real question is whether the total series (say A–Z) does or does not originate in a will that can take human prayers into account.

This impossibility of empirical proof is a spiritual necessity. A man who knew empirically that an event had been caused by his prayer would feel like a magician. His head would turn and his heart would be corrupted. The Christian is not to ask whether this or that event happened because of a prayer. He is rather to believe that all events without exception are *answers* to prayer in the sense that whether they are grantings or refusals the prayers of all concerned and their needs have all been taken into account. All prayers are heard, though not all prayers are granted. We must not picture destiny as a film unrolling for the most part on its own, but in which our prayers are sometimes allowed to insert additional items. On the contrary; what the film displays to us as it unrolls already contains the results of our prayers and of all our other acts. There is no question *whether* an event has happened because of your prayer. When the event you prayed for occurs your prayer has always contributed to it. When the opposite event occurs your prayer has never been ignored; it has been considered and refused, for your ultimate good and the good of the whole universe. (For example, because it is better for you and for everyone else in the long run that other people, including wicked ones, should exercise free will than that you should be protected from cruelty or treachery by turning the human race into automata.) But this is, and must remain, a matter of faith. You will, I think, only deceive yourself by trying to find special evidence for it in some cases more than in others.

THE GREAT DIVORCE

a dream

'No, there is no escape. There is no heaven with a little
of hell in it—no plan to retain this or that of the devil
in our hearts or our pockets. Out Satan must go, every
hair and feather.'

GEORGE MACDONALD

To Barbara Wall
Best and most long-suffering of scribes

PREFACE

BLAKE WROTE THE Marriage of Heaven and Hell. If I have written of their Divorce, this is not because I think myself a fit antagonist for so great a genius, nor even because I feel at all sure that I know what he meant. But in some sense or other the attempt to make that marriage is perennial. The attempt is based on the belief that reality never presents us with an absolutely unavoidable 'either-or'; that, granted skill and patience and (above all) time enough, some way of embracing both alternatives can always be found; that mere development or adjustment or refinement will somehow turn evil into good without our being called on for a final and total rejection of anything we should like to retain. This belief I take to be a disastrous error. You cannot take all luggage with you on all journeys; on one journey even your right hand and your right eye may be among the things you have to leave behind. We are not living in a world where all roads are radii of a circle and where all, if followed long enough, will therefore draw gradually nearer and finally meet at the centre: rather in a world where every road, after a few miles, forks into two, and each of those into two again, and at each fork you must make a decision. Even on the biological level life is not like a river but like a tree. It does not move towards unity but away from it and the creatures grow further apart as they increase in perfection. Good, as it ripens, becomes continually more different not only from evil but from other good.

I do not think that all who choose wrong roads perish; but their rescue consists in being put back on the right road. A sum can be put right: but only by going back till you find the error and working it afresh from that

465

point, never by simply *going on*. Evil can be undone, but it cannot 'develop' into good. Time does not heal it. The spell must be unwound, bit by bit, 'with backward mutters of dissevering power'—or else not. It is still 'either-or'. If we insist on keeping Hell (or even Earth) we shall not see Heaven: if we accept Heaven we shall not be able to retain even the smallest and most intimate souvenirs of Hell. I believe, to be sure, that any man who reaches Heaven will find that what he abandoned (even in plucking out his right eye) has not been lost: that the kernel of what he was really seeking even in his most depraved wishes will be there, beyond expectation, waiting for him in 'the High Countries'. In that sense it will be true for those who have completed the journey (and for no others) to say that good is everything and Heaven everywhere. But we, at this end of the road, must not try to anticipate that retrospective vision. If we do, we are likely to embrace the false and disastrous converse and fancy that everything is good and everywhere is Heaven.

But what, you ask, of earth? Earth, I think, will not be found by anyone to be in the end a very distinct place. I think earth, if chosen instead of Heaven, will turn out to have been, all along, only a region in Hell: and earth, if put second to Heaven, to have been from the beginning a part of Heaven itself.

There are only two things more to be said about this small book. Firstly, I must acknowledge my debt to a writer whose name I have forgotten and whom I read several years ago in a highly coloured American magazine of what they call 'Scientifiction'. The unbendable and unbreakable quality of my heavenly matter was suggested to me by him, though he used the fancy for a different and most ingenious purpose. His hero travelled into the *past:* and there, very properly, found raindrops that would pierce him like bullets and sandwiches that no strength could bite—because, of course, nothing in the past can be altered. I, with less originality but (I hope) equal propriety; have transferred this to the eternal. If the writer of that story ever reads these lines I ask him to accept my grateful acknowledgement. The second thing is this. I beg readers to remember that this is a fantasy. It has of course—or I intended it to have—a moral. But the transmortal conditions are solely an imaginative supposal: they are not even a guess or a speculation at what may actually await us. The last thing I wish is to arouse factual curiosity about the details of the after-world.

C. S. LEWIS

APRIL, 1945

I

I SEEMED TO be standing in a busy queue by the side of a long, mean street. Evening was just closing in and it was raining. I had been wandering for hours in similar mean streets, always in the rain and always in evening twilight. Time seemed to have paused on that dismal moment when only a few shops have lit up and it is not yet dark enough for their windows to look cheering. And just as the evening never advanced to night, so my walking had never brought me to the better parts of the town. However far I went I found only dingy lodging houses, small tobacconists, hoardings from which posters hung in rags, windowless warehouses, goods stations without trains, and bookshops of the sort that sell *The Works of Aristotle*. I never met anyone. But for the little crowd at the bus stop, the whole town seemed to be empty. I think that was why I attached myself to the queue.

I had a stroke of luck right away, for just as I took my stand a little waspish woman who would have been ahead of me snapped out at a man who seemed to be with her, 'Very well, then. I won't go at all. So there,' and left the queue. 'Pray don't imagine,' said the man, in a very dignified voice, 'that I care about going in the least. I have only been trying to please *you,* for peace sake. My own feelings are of course a matter of no importance, I quite understand *that*'—and suiting the action to the word he also walked away. 'Come,' thought I, 'that's two places gained.' I was now next to a very short man with a scowl who glanced at me with an expression of extreme disfavour and observed, rather unnecessarily loudly, to the man beyond him, 'This sort of thing really makes one think twice about going at all.' 'What sort of thing?' growled the other, a big beefy person. 'Well,' said the Short Man, 'this is hardly the sort of society I'm used to as a matter of fact.' 'Huh!' said the Big Man: and then added with a glance at me, 'Don't you stand any sauce from *him*, Mister. You're not *afraid* of him, are you?' Then, seeing I made no move, he rounded suddenly on the Short Man and said, 'Not good enough for you, aren't we? Like your lip.' Next moment he had fetched the Short Man one on the side of the face that sent him sprawling into the gutter. 'Let him lay, let him lay,' said the Big Man to no one in particular. 'I'm a plain man that's what I am and I got to have my rights same as anyone else, see?' As the Short Man showed no disposition to rejoin the queue and soon began limping away, I closed up, rather cautiously, behind the Big Man and congratulated myself on having gained yet another step. A moment later two young people in front of him also left us arm in arm. They were both so trousered, slender, giggly and falsetto that I could be sure of the sex of neither, but it was clear that each for the moment preferred the other to the chance of a place in the bus. 'We shall never all get in,' said a female voice with a whine in it from some four places ahead of me. 'Change places with you for five bob, lady,' said someone else. I heard the clink of money and then a scream in the female voice, mixed with roars of laughter from the rest of the crowd. The cheated woman leaped out of her place to fly at the man who had bilked her, but the others immediately closed up and flung her out . . . So what with one thing and another the queue had reduced itself to manageable proportions long before the bus appeared.

It was a wonderful vehicle, blazing with golden light, heraldically coloured. The Driver himself seemed full of light and he used only one hand to drive with. The other he waved before his face as if to fan away the greasy steam of the rain. A growl went up from the queue as he came in sight. 'Looks as if *he* had a good time of it, eh? . . . Bloody pleased with himself, I bet . . . My dear, why can't he behave *naturally?*—Thinks himself too good to look at us . . . Who does he imagine he is? . . . All that gilding and purple, I call it a wicked waste. Why don't they spend some of the money on their house property down here?—God! I'd like to give him one in the ear-'ole.' I could see nothing in the countenance of the Driver to justify all this, unless it were that he had a look of authority and seemed intent on carrying out his job.

My fellow passengers fought like hens to get on board the bus though there was plenty of room for us all. I was the last to get in. The bus was only half full and I selected a seat at the back, well away from the others. But a tousle-haired youth at once came and sat down beside me. As he did so we moved off.

'I thought you wouldn't mind my tacking on to you,' he said, 'for I've noticed that you feel just as I do about the present company. Why on earth they insist on coming I can't imagine. They won't like it at all when we get there, and they'd really be much more comfortable at home. It's different for you and me.'

'Do they *like* this place?' I asked.

'As much as they'd like anything,' he answered. 'They've got cinemas and fish and chip shops and advertisements and all the sorts of things they want. The appalling lack of any intellectual life doesn't worry *them*. I realised as soon as I got here that there'd been some mistake. I ought to have taken the first bus but I've fooled about trying to wake people up here. I found a few fellows I'd known before and tried to form a little circle, but they all seem to have sunk to the level of their surroundings. Even before we came here I'd had some doubts about a man like Cyril Blellow. I always thought he was working in a false idiom. But he was at least intelligent: one could get some criticism worth hearing from him, even if he was a failure on the creative side. But now he seems to have nothing left but his self-conceit. The last time I tried to read him some of my own stuff . . . but wait a minute, I'd just like you to look at it.'

Realising with a shudder that what he was producing from his pocket was a thick wad of type-written paper, I muttered something about not having my spectacles and exclaimed, 'Hullo! We've left the ground.'

It was true. Several hundred feet below us, already half hidden in the rain and mist, the wet roofs of the town appeared, spreading without a break as far as the eye could reach.

I WAS NOt left very long at the mercy of the Tousle-Headed Poet, because another passenger interrupted our conversation: but before that
happened I had learned a good deal about him. He appeared to be a singularly ill-used man. His parents had never appreciated him and none
of the five schools at which he had been educated seemed to have made
any provision for a talent and temperament such as his. To make matters worse he had been exactly the sort of boy in whose case the examination system works out with the maximum unfairness and absurdity. It
was not until he reached the university that he began to recognise that all
these injustices did not come by chance but were the inevitable results of
our economic system. Capitalism did not merely enslave the workers, it
also vitiated taste and vulgarised intellect: hence our educational system
and hence the lack of 'Recognition' for new genius. This discovery had
made him a Communist. But when the war came along and he saw Russia in alliance with the capitalist governments, he had found himself once
more isolated and had to become a conscientious objector. The indigni-
ties he suffered at this stage of his career had, he confessed, embittered
him. He decided he could serve the cause best by going to America: but
then America came into the war too. It was at this point that he suddenly
saw Sweden as the home of a really new and radical art, but the various
oppressors had given him no facilities for going to Sweden. There were
money troubles. His father, who had never progressed beyond the most
atrocious mental complacency and smugness of the Victorian epoch, was

giving him a ludicrously inadequate allowance. And he had been very badly treated by a girl too. He had thought her a really civilised and adult personality, and then she had unexpectedly revealed that she was a mass of bourgeois prejudices and monogamic instincts. Jealousy, possessiveness, was a quality he particularly disliked. She had even shown herself, at the end, to be mean about money. That was the last straw. He had jumped under a train . . .

I gave a start, but he took no notice.

Even then, he continued, ill luck had continued to dog him. He'd been sent to the grey town. But of course it was a mistake. I would find, he assured me, that all the other passengers would be with me on the return journey. But he would not. He was going to stay 'there'. He felt quite certain that he was going where, at last, his finely critical spirit would no longer be outraged by an uncongenial environment—where he would find 'Recognition' and 'Appreciation'. Meanwhile, since I hadn't got my glasses, he would read me the passage about which Cyril Blellow had been so insensitive . . .

It was just then that we were interrupted. One of the quarrels which were perpetually simmering in the bus had boiled over and for a moment there was a stampede. Knives were drawn: pistols were fired: but it all seemed strangely innocuous and when it was over I found myself unharmed, though in a different seat and with a new companion. He was an intelligent-looking man with a rather bulbous nose and a bowler hat. I looked out of the windows. We were now so high that all below us had become featureless. But fields, rivers, or mountains I did not see, and I got the impression that the grey town still filled the whole field of vision.

'It seems the deuce of a town,' I volunteered, 'and that's what I can't understand. The parts of it that I saw were so empty. Was there once a much larger population?'

'Not at all,' said my neighbour. 'The trouble is that they're so quarrelsome. As soon as anyone arrives he settles in some street. Before he's been there twenty-four hours he quarrels with his neighbour. Before the week is over he's quarrelled so badly that he decides to move. Very likely he finds the next street empty because all the people there have quarrelled with *their* neighbours—and moved. If so he settles in. If by any chance the street is full, he goes further. But even if he stays, it makes no odds. He's sure to have another quarrel pretty soon and then he'll move on again. Finally he'll move right out to the edge of the town and build a new house. You see, it's easy here. You've only got to *think* a house and there it is. That's how the town keeps on growing.'

'Leaving more and more empty streets?'

'That's right. And time's sort of odd here. That place where we caught the bus is thousands of miles from the Civic Centre where all the newcomers arrive from earth. All the people you've met were living near the bus stop: but they'd taken centuries—of our time—to get there, by gradual removals.'

'And what about the earlier arrivals? I mean—there must be people who came from Earth to your town even longer ago.'

'That's right. There are. They've been moving on and on. Getting further apart. They're so far off by now that they could never think of coming to the bus stop at all. Astronomical distances. There's a bit of rising ground near where I live and a chap has a telescope. You can see the lights of the inhabited houses, where those old ones live, millions of miles away. Millions of miles from us and from one another. Every now and then they move further still. That's one of the disappointments. I thought you'd meet interesting historical characters. But you don't: they're too far away.'

'Would they get to the bus stop in time, if they ever set out?'

'Well—theoretically. But it'd be a distance of light-years. And they wouldn't want to by now: not those old chaps like Tamberlaine and Genghis Khan, or Julius Caesar, or Henry the Fifth.'

'Wouldn't want to?'

'That's right. The nearest of those old ones is Napoleon. We know that because two chaps made the journey to see him. They'd started long before I came, of course, but I was there when they came back. About fifteen thousand years of our time it took them. We've picked out the house by now. Just a little pin prick of light and nothing else near it for millions of miles.'

'But they got there?'

'That's right. He'd built himself a huge house all in the Empire style— rows of windows flaming with light, though it only shows as a pin prick from where I live.'

'Did they see Napoleon?'

'That's right. They went up and looked through one of the windows. Napoleon was there all right.'

'What was he doing?'

'Walking up and down—up and down all the time—left-right, left-right—never stopping for a moment. The two chaps watched him for about a year and he never rested. And muttering to himself all the time. "It was Soult's fault. It was Ney's fault. It was Josephine's fault. It was the fault of the Russians. It was the fault of the English." Like that all the time. Never stopped for a moment. A little, fat man and he looked kind of tired. But he didn't seem able to stop it.'

From the vibrations I gathered that the bus was still moving, but there was now nothing to be seen from the windows which confirmed this—nothing but grey void above and below.

'Then the town will go on spreading indefinitely?' I said.

'That's right,' said the Intelligent Man. 'Unless someone can do something about it.'

'How do you mean?'

'Well, as a matter of fact, between you and me and the wall, that's my job at the moment. What's the trouble about this place? Not that people are quarrelsome—that's only human nature and was always the same even on Earth. The trouble is they have no Needs. You get everything you want (not very good quality, of course) by just imagining it. That's why it never costs any trouble to move to another street or build another house. In other words, there's no proper economic basis for any community life. If they needed real shops, chaps would have to stay near where the real shops were. If they needed real houses they'd have to stay near where builders were. It's scarcity that enables a society to exist. Well, that's where I come in. I'm not going on this trip for my health. As far as that goes I don't think it would suit me up there. But if I can come back with some *real* commodities—anything at all that you could really bite or drink or sit on—why, at once you'd get a demand down in our town. I'd start a little business. I'd have something to sell. You'd soon get people coming to live near—centralisation. Two fully-inhabited streets would accommodate the people that are now spread over a million square miles of empty streets. I'd make a nice little profit and be a public benefactor as well.'

'You mean, if they *had* to live together they'd gradually learn to quarrel less?'

'Well, I don't know about that. I daresay they could be kept a bit quieter. You'd have a chance to build up a police force. Knock some kind of discipline into them. Anyway' (here he dropped his voice) 'it'd be *better*, you know. Everyone admits that. Safety in numbers.'

'Safety from what?' I began, but my companion nudged me to be silent. I changed my question.

'But look here,' said I, 'if they can get everything just by imagining it, why would they want any *real* things, as you call them?'

'Eh? Oh well, they'd like houses that really kept out the rain.'

'Their present houses don't?'

'Well, of course not. How could they?'

'What the devil is the use of building them, then?' The Intelligent Man put his head closer to mine. 'Safety again,' he muttered. 'At least, the feeling of safety. It's all right *now:* but later on . . . you understand.'

'What?' said I, almost involuntarily sinking my own voice to a whisper.

He articulated noiselessly as if expecting that I understood lipreading. I put my ear up close to his mouth. 'Speak up,' I said. 'It will be dark presently,' he mouthed.

'You mean the evening *is* really going to turn into a night in the end?'

He nodded.

'What's that got to do with it?' said I.

'Well . . . no one wants to be out of doors when that happens.'

'Why?'

His reply was so furtive that I had to ask him several times to repeat it. When he had done so, being a little annoyed (as one so often is with whisperers), I replied without remembering to lower my voice.

'Who are "They"?' I asked. 'And what are you afraid they'll do to you? And why should they come out when it's dark? And what protection could an imaginary house give if there was any danger?'

'Here!' shouted the Big Man. 'Who's talking all that stuff? You stop your whispering, you two, if you don't want a hiding, see? Spreading rumours, that's what I call it. You shut your face, Ikey, see?'

'Quite right. Scandalous. Ought to be prosecuted. How did they get on the bus?' growled the passengers.

A fat clean-shaven man who sat on the seat in front of me leaned back and addressed me in a cultured voice.

'Excuse me,' he said, 'but I couldn't help overhearing parts of your conversation. It is astonishing how these primitive superstitions linger on. I beg your pardon? Oh, God bless my soul, that's all it is. There is not a shred of evidence that this twilight is ever going to turn into a night. There has been a revolution of opinion on that in educated circles. I am surprised that you haven't heard of it. All the nightmare fantasies of our ancestors are being swept away. What we now see in this subdued and delicate half-light is the promise of the dawn: the slow turning of a whole nation towards the light. Slow and imperceptible, of course. "And not through Eastern windows only, When daylight comes, comes in the light." And that passion for "real" commodities which our friend speaks of is only materialism, you know. It's retrogressive. Earth-bound! A hankering for matter. But *we* look on this spiritual city—for with all its faults it *is* spiritual—as a nursery in which the creative functions of man, now freed from the clogs of matter, begin to try their wings. A sublime thought.'

Hours later there came a change. It began to grow light in the bus. The greyness outside the windows turned from mud-colour to mother of pearl, then to faintest blue, then to a bright blueness that stung the eyes. We seemed to be floating in a pure vacancy. There were no lands, no sun, no stars in sight: only the radiant abyss. I let down the window beside me. Delicious freshness came in for a second, and then—

'What the hell are you doing?' shouted the Intelligent Man, leaning roughly across me and pulling the window sharply up. 'Want us all to catch our death of cold?'

'Hit him a biff,' said the Big Man.

I glanced round the bus. Though the windows were closed, and soon muffed, the bus was full of light. It was cruel light. I shrank from the faces and forms by which I was surrounded. They were all fixed faces, full not of possibilities but impossibilities, some gaunt, some bloated, some glaring with idiotic ferocity, some drowned beyond recovery in dreams; but all, in one way or another, distorted and faded. One had a feeling that they might fall to pieces at any moment if the light grew much stronger. Then—there was a mirror on the end wall of the bus—I caught sight of my own.

And still the light grew.

3

A CLIFF HAD loomed up ahead. It sank vertically beneath us so far that I could not see the bottom, and it was dark and smooth. We were mounting all the time. At last the top of the cliff became visible like a thin line of emerald green stretched tight as a fiddle-string. Presently we glided over that top: we were flying above a level, grassy country through which there ran a wide river. We were losing height now: some of the tallest tree tops were only twenty feet below us. Then, suddenly we were at rest. Everyone had jumped up. Curses, taunts, blows, a filth of vituperation, came to my ears as my fellow-passengers struggled to get out. A moment later, and they had all succeeded. I was alone in the bus, and through the open door there came to me in the fresh stillness the singing of a lark.

I got out. The light and coolness that drenched me were like those of summer morning, early morning a minute or two before the sunrise, only that there was a certain difference. I had the sense of being in a larger space, perhaps even a larger *sort* of space, than I had ever known before: as if the sky were further off and the extent of the green plain wider that they could be on this little ball of earth. I had got 'out' in some sense which made the Solar System itself seem an indoor affair. It gave me a feeling of freedom, but also of exposure, possibly of danger, which continued to accompany me through all that followed. It is the impossibility of communicating that feeling, or even of inducing you to remember it as I proceed, which makes me despair of conveying the real quality of what I saw and heard.

At first, of course, my attention was caught by my fellow-passengers, who were still grouped about in the neighbourhood of the omnibus, though beginning, some of them, to walk forward into the landscape with hesitating steps. I gasped when I saw them. Now that they were in the light, they were transparent—fully transparent when they stood between me and it, smudgy and imperfectly opaque when they stood in the shadow of some tree. They were in fact ghosts: man-shaped stains on the brightness of that air. One could attend to them or ignore them at will as you do with the dirt on a window pane. I noticed that the grass did not bend under their feet: even the dew drops were not disturbed.

Then some re-adjustment of the mind or some focussing of my eyes took place, and I saw the whole phenomenon the other way round. The men were as they had always been; as all the men I had known had been perhaps. It was the light, the grass, the trees that were different; made of some different substance, so much solider than things in our country that men were ghosts by comparison. Moved by a sudden thought, I bent down and tried to pluck a daisy which was growing at my feet. The stalk wouldn't break. I tried to twist it, but it wouldn't twist. I tugged till the sweat stood out on my forehead and I had lost most of the skin off my hands. The little flower was hard, not like wood or even like iron, but like diamond. There was a leaf—a young tender beech-leaf, lying in the grass beside it. I tried to pick the leaf up: my heart almost cracked with the effort, and I believe I did just raise it. But I had to let it go at once; it was heavier than a sack of coal. As I stood, recovering my breath with great gasps and looking down at the daisy, I noticed that I could see the grass not only between my feet but *through* them. I also was a phantom. Who will give me words to express the terror of that discovery? 'Golly!' thought I, 'I'm in for it this time.'

'I don't like it! I don't like it,' screamed a voice. 'It gives me the pip!' One of the ghosts had darted past me, back into the bus. She never came out of it again as far as I know.

The others remained, uncertain.

'Hi, Mister,' said the Big Man, addressing the Driver, 'when have we got to be back?'

'You need never come back unless you want to,' he replied. 'Stay as long as you please.' There was an awkward pause.

'This is simply ridiculous,' said a voice in my ear. One of the quieter and more respectable ghosts had sidled up to me. 'There must be some mismanagement,' he continued. 'What's the sense of allowing all that riff-raff to float about here all day? Look at them. They're not enjoying it. They'd be far happier at home. They don't even know what to do.'

'I don't know very well myself,' said I. 'What does one do?'

'Oh me? I shall be met in a moment or two. I'm expected. I'm not bothering about that. But it's rather unpleasant on one's first day to have the whole place crowded out with trippers. Damn it, one's chief object in coming here at all was to avoid them!'

He drifted away from me. And I began to look about. In spite of his reference to a 'crowd', the solitude was so vast that I could hardly notice the knot of phantoms in the foreground. Greenness and light had almost swallowed them up. But very far away I could see what might be either a great bank of cloud or a range of mountains. Sometimes I could make out in it steep forests, far-withdrawing valleys, and even mountain cities perched on inaccessible summits. At other times it became indistinct. The height was so enormous that my waking sight could not have taken in such an object at all. Light brooded on the top of it: slanting down thence it made long shadows behind every tree on the plain. There was no change and no progression as the hours passed. The promise—or the threat—of sunrise rested immovably up there.

Long after that I saw people coming to meet us. Because they were bright I saw them while they were still very distant, and at first I did not know that they were people at all. Mile after mile they drew nearer. The earth shook under their tread as their strong feet sank into the wet turf. A tiny haze and a sweet smell went up where they had crushed the grass and scattered the dew. Some were naked, some robed. But the naked ones did not seem less adorned, and the robes did not disguise in those who wore them the massive grandeur of muscle and the radiant smoothness of flesh. Some were bearded but no one in that company struck me as being of any particular age. One gets glimpses, even in our country, of that which is ageless—heavy thought in the face of an infant, and frolic childhood in that of a very old man. Here it was all like that. They came on steadily. I did not entirely like it. Two of the ghosts screamed and ran for the bus. The rest of us huddled closer to one another.

4

AS THE SOLID people came nearer still I noticed that they were moving with order and determination as though each of them had marked his man in our shadowy company. 'There are going to be affecting scenes,' I said to myself. 'Perhaps it would not be right to look on.' With that, I sidled away on some vague pretext of doing a little exploring. A grove of huge cedars to my right seemed attractive and I entered it. Walking proved difficult. The grass, hard as diamonds to my unsubstantial feet, made me feel as if I were walking on wrinkled rock, and I suffered pains like those of the mermaid in Hans Andersen. A bird ran across in front of me and I envied it. It belonged to that country and was as real as the grass. It could bend the stalks and spatter itself with the dew.

Almost at once I was followed by what I have called the Big Man—to speak more accurately, the Big Ghost. He in his turn was followed by one of the bright people. 'Don't you know me?' he shouted to the Ghost: and I found it impossible not to turn and attend. The face of the solid spirit— he was one of those that wore a robe—made me want to dance, it was so jocund, so established in its youthfulness.

'Well, I'm damned,' said the Ghost. 'I wouldn't have believed it. It's a fair knock-out. It isn't right, Len, you know. What about poor Jack, eh? You look pretty pleased with yourself, but what I say is, What about poor Jack?'

'He is here,' said the other. 'You will meet him soon, if you stay.'

'But you murdered him.'

'Of course I did. It is all right now.'

'All right, is it? All right for you, you mean. But what about the poor chap himself, laying cold and dead?'

'But he isn't. I have told you, you will meet him soon. He sent you his love.'

'What I'd like to understand,' said the Ghost, 'is what you're here for, as pleased as Punch, you, a bloody murderer, while I've been walking the streets down there and living in a place like a pigsty all these years.'

'That is a little hard to understand at first. But it is all over now. You will be pleased about it presently. Till then there is no need to bother about it.'

'No need to bother about it? Aren't you ashamed of yourself?'

'No. Not as you mean. I do not look at myself. I have given up myself. I had to, you know, after the murder. That was what it did for me. And that was how everything began.'

'Personally,' said the Big Ghost with an emphasis which contradicted the ordinary meaning of the word, 'Personally, I'd have thought you and I ought to be the other way round. That's my personal opinion.'

'Very likely we soon shall be,' said the other. 'If you'll stop thinking about it.'

'Look at me, now,' said the Ghost, slapping its chest (but the slap made no noise). 'I gone straight all my life. I don't say I was a religious man and I don't say I had no faults, far from it. But I done my best all my life, see? I done my best by everyone, that's the sort of chap I was. I never asked for anything that wasn't mine by rights. If I wanted a drink I paid for it and if I took my wages I done my job, see? That's the sort I was and I don't care who knows it.'

'It would be much better not to go on about that now.'

'Who's going on? I'm not arguing. I'm just telling you the sort of chap I was, see? I'm asking for nothing but my rights. You may think you can put me down because you're dressed up like that (which you weren't when you worked under me) and I'm only a poor man. But I got to have my rights same as you, see?'

'Oh no. It's not so bad as that. I haven't got my rights, or I should not be here. You will not get yours either. You'll get something far better. Never fear.'

'That's just what I say. I haven't got my rights. I always done my best and I never done nothing wrong. And what I don't see is why I should be put below a bloody murderer like you.'

'Who knows whether you will be? Only be happy and come with me.'

'What do you keep on arguing for? I'm only telling you the sort of chap I am. I only want my rights. I'm not asking for anybody's bleeding charity.'

'Then do. At once. Ask for the Bleeding Charity. Everything is here for the asking and nothing can be bought.'

'That may do very well for you, I daresay. If they choose to let in a bloody murderer all because he makes a poor mouth at the last moment, that's their look out. But I don't see myself going in the same boat as you, see? Why should I? I don't want charity. I'm a decent man and if I had my rights I'd have been here long ago and you can tell them I said so.'

The other shook his head. 'You can never do it like that,' he said. 'Your feet will never grow hard enough to walk on our grass that way. You'd be tired out before we got to the mountains. And it isn't exactly true, you know.' Mirth danced in his eyes as he said it.

'What isn't true?' asked the Ghost sulkily.

'You weren't a decent man and you didn't do your best. We none of us were and none of us did. Lord bless you, it doesn't matter. There is no need to go into it all now.'

'You!' gasped the Ghost. '*You* have the face to tell *me* I wasn't a decent chap?'

'Of course. Must I go into all that? I will tell you one thing to begin with. Murdering old Jack wasn't the worst thing I did. That was the work of a moment and I was half mad when I did it. But I murdered you in my heart, deliberately, for years. I used to lie awake at nights thinking what I'd do to you if I ever got the chance. That is why I have been sent to you now: to ask your forgiveness and to be your servant as long as you need one, and longer if it pleases you. I was the worst. But all the men who worked under you felt the same. You made it hard for us, you know. And you made it hard for your wife too and for your children.'

'You mind your own business, young man,' said the Ghost. 'None of your lip, see? Because I'm not taking any impudence from you about my private affairs.'

'There are no private affairs,' said the other.

'And I'll tell you another thing,' said the Ghost. 'You can clear off, see? You're not wanted. I may be only a poor man but I'm not making pals with a murderer, let alone taking lessons from him. Made it hard for you and your like, did I? If I had you back there I'd show you what work is.'

'Come and show me now,' said the other with laughter in his voice, 'It will be joy going to the mountains, but there will be plenty of work.'

'You don't suppose I'd go with you?'

'Don't refuse. You will never get there alone. And I am the one who was sent to you.'

'So that's the trick, is it?' shouted the Ghost, outwardly bitter, and yet I thought there was a kind of triumph in its voice. It had been entreated: it could make a refusal: and this seemed to it a kind of advantage. 'I thought there'd be some damned nonsense. It's all a clique, all a bloody clique. Tell them I'm not coming, see? I'd rather be damned than go along with you. I came here to get my rights, see? Not to go snivelling along on charity tied onto your apron-strings. If they're too fine to have me without me, I'll go home.' It was almost happy now that it could, in a sense, threaten. 'That's what I'll do,' it repeated, 'I'll go home. I didn't come here to be treated like a dog. I'll go home. That's what I'll do. Damn and blast the whole pack of you . . .' In the end, still grumbling, but whimpering also a little as it picked its way over the sharp grasses, it made off.

5

FOR A MOMENT there was silence under the cedar trees and then—
pad, pad, pad—it was broken. Two velvet-footed lions came bouncing
into the open space, their eyes fixed upon each other, and started playing
some solemn romp. Their manes looked as if they had been just dipped
in the river whose noise I could hear close at hand, though the tree hid
it. Not greatly liking my company, I moved away to find that river, and
after passing some thick flowering bushes, I succeeded. The bushes came
almost down to the brink. It was as smooth as the Thames but flowed
swiftly like a mountain stream: pale green where trees overhung it but so
clear that I could count the pebbles at the bottom. Close beside me I saw
another of the Bright People in conversation with a ghost. It was that fat
ghost with the cultured voice who had addressed me in the bus, and it
seemed to be wearing gaiters.

'My dear boy, I'm delighted to see you,' it was saying to the Spirit,
who was naked and almost blindingly white. 'I was talking to your poor
father the other day and wondering where you were.'

'You didn't bring him?' said the other.

'Well, no. He lives a long way from the bus, and, to be quite frank,
he's been getting a little eccentric lately. A little difficult. Losing his grip.
He never was prepared to make any great efforts, you know. If you remember, he used to go to sleep when you and I got talking seriously! Ah,
Dick, I shall never forget some of our talks. I expect you've changed your
views a bit since then. You became rather narrow-minded towards the
end of your life: but no doubt you've broadened out again.'

'How do you mean?'

'Well, it's obvious by now, isn't it, that you weren't quite right. Why, my dear boy, you were coming to believe in a literal Heaven and Hell!'

'But wasn't I right?'

'Oh, in a spiritual sense, to be sure. I still believe in them in that way. I am still, my dear boy, looking for the Kingdom. But nothing superstitious or mythological . . .'

'Excuse me. Where do you imagine you've been?'

'Ah, I see. You mean that the grey town with its continual hope of morning (we must all live by hope, must we not?), with its field for indefinite progress, is, in a sense, Heaven, if only we have eyes to see it? That is a beautiful idea.'

'I didn't mean that at all. Is it possible you don't know where you've been?'

'Now that you mention it, I don't think we ever do give it a name. What do you call it?'

'We call it Hell.'

'There is no need to be profane, my dear boy. I may not be very orthodox, in your sense of that word, but I do feel that these matters ought to be discussed simply, and seriously, and reverently.'

'Discuss Hell *reverently?* I meant what I said. You have been in Hell: though if you don't go back you may call it Purgatory.'

'Go on, my dear boy, go on. That is *so* like you. No doubt you'll tell me why, on your view, I was sent there. I'm not angry.'

'But don't you know? You went there because you are an apostate.'

'Are you serious, Dick?'

'Perfectly.'

'This is worse than I expected. Do you really think people are penalised for their honest opinions? Even assuming, for the sake of argument, that those opinions were mistaken.'

'Do you really think there are no sins of intellect?'

'There are indeed, Dick. There is hide-bound prejudice, and intellectual dishonesty, and timidity, and stagnation. But honest opinions fearlessly followed—they are not sins.'

'I know we used to talk that way. I did it too until the end of my life when I became what you call narrow. It all turns on what are honest opinions.'

'Mine certainly were. They were not only honest but heroic. I asserted them fearlessly. When the doctrine of the Resurrection ceased to commend itself to the critical faculties which God had given me, I openly rejected it. I preached my famous sermon. I defied the whole chapter. I took every risk.'

'What risk? What was at all likely to come of it except what actually came—popularity, sales for your books, invitations, and finally a bishopric?'

'Dick, this is unworthy of you. What are you suggesting?'

'Friend, I am not suggesting at all. You see, I *know* now. Let us be frank. Our opinions were not honestly come by. We simply found ourselves in contact with a certain current of ideas and plunged into it because it seemed modern and successful. At College, you know, we just started automatically writing the kind of essays that got good marks and saying the kind of things that won applause. When, in our whole lives, did we honestly face, in solitude, the one question on which all turned: whether after all the Supernatural might not in fact occur? When did we put up one moment's real resistance to the loss of our faith?'

'If this is meant to be a sketch of the genesis of liberal theology in general, I reply that it is a mere libel. Do you suggest that men like . . .'

'I have nothing to do with any generality. Nor with any man but you and me. Oh, as you love your own soul, remember. You know that you and I were playing with loaded dice. We didn't *want* the other to be true. We were afraid of crude salvationism, afraid of a breach with the spirit of the age, afraid of ridicule, afraid (above all) of real spiritual fears and hopes.'

'I'm far from denying that young men may make mistakes. They may well be influenced by current fashions of thought. But it's not a question of how the opinions are formed. The point is that they were my honest opinions, sincerely expressed.'

'Of course. Having allowed oneself to drift, unresisting, unpraying, accepting every half-conscious solicitation from our desires, we reached a point where we no longer believed the Faith. Just in the same way, a jealous man, drifting and unresisting, reaches a point at which he believes lies about his best friend: a drunkard reaches a point at which (for the moment) he actually believes that another glass will do him no harm. The beliefs are sincere in the sense that they do occur as psychological events in the man's mind. If that's what you mean by sincerity they are sincere, and so were ours. But errors which are sincere in that sense are not innocent.'

'You'll be justifying the Inquisition in a moment!'

'Why? Because the Middle Ages erred in one direction, does it follow that there is no error in the opposite direction?'

'Well, this is extremely interesting,' said the Episcopal Ghost. 'It's a point of view. Certainly, it's a point of view. In the meantime . . .'

'There is no meantime,' replied the other. 'All that is over. We are not playing now. I have been talking of the past (your past and mine) only in order that you may turn from it forever. One wrench and the tooth will be out. You can begin as if nothing had ever gone wrong. White as snow. It's all true, you know. He is in me, for you, with that power. And—I have come a long journey to meet you. You have seen Hell: you are in sight of Heaven. Will you, even now, repent and believe?'

'I'm not sure that I've got the exact point you are trying to make,' said the Ghost.

'I am not trying to make any point,' said the Spirit. 'I am telling you to repent and believe.'

'But my dear boy, I believe already. We may not be perfectly agreed, but you have completely misjudged me if you do not realise that my religion is a very real and a very precious thing to me.'

'Very well,' said the other, as if changing his plan. 'Will you believe in *me*?'

'In what sense?'

'Will you come with me to the mountains? It will hurt at first, until your feet are hardened. Reality is harsh to the feet of shadows. But will you come?'

'Well, that is a plan. I am perfectly ready to consider it. Of course I should require some assurances . . . I should want a guarantee that you are taking me to a place where I shall find a wider sphere of usefulness—and scope for the talents that God has given me—and an atmosphere of free inquiry—in short, all that one means by civilisation and—er—the spiritual life.'

'No,' said the other. 'I can promise you none of these things. No sphere of usefulness: you are not needed there at all. No scope for your talents:

only forgiveness for having perverted them. No atmosphere of inquiry, for I will bring you to the land not of questions but of answers, and you shall see the face of God.'

'Ah, but we must all interpret those beautiful words in our own way! For me there is no such thing as a final answer. The free wind of inquiry must *always* continue to blow through the mind, must it not? "Prove all things" . . . to travel hopefully is better than to arrive.'

'If that were true, and known to be true, how could anyone travel hopefully? There would be nothing to hope for.'

'But you must feel yourself that there is something stifling about the idea of finality? Stagnation, my dear boy, what is more soul-destroying than stagnation?'

'You think that, because hitherto you have experienced truth only with the abstract intellect. I will bring you where you can taste it like honey and be embraced by it as by a bridegroom. Your thirst shall be quenched.'

'Well, really, you know, I am not aware of a thirst for some ready-made truth which puts an end to intellectual activity in the way you seem to be describing. Will it leave me the free play of Mind, Dick? I must insist on that, you know.'

'Free, as a man is free to drink while he is drinking. He is not free still to be dry.' The Ghost seemed to think for a moment. 'I can make nothing of that idea,' it said.

'Listen!' said the White Spirit. 'Once you were a child. Once you knew what inquiry was for. There was a time when you asked questions because you wanted answers, and were glad when you had found them. Become that child again: even now.'

'Ah, but when I became a man I put away childish things.'

'You have gone far wrong. Thirst was made for water; inquiry for truth. What you now call the free play of inquiry has neither more nor less to do with the ends for which intelligence was given you than masturbation has to do with marriage.'

'If we cannot be reverent, there is at least no need to be obscene. The suggestion that I should return at my age to the mere factual inquisitiveness of boyhood strikes me as preposterous. In any case, that question-and-answer conception of thought only applies to matters of fact. Religious and speculative questions are surely on a different level.'

'We know nothing of religion here: we think only of Christ. We know nothing of speculation. Come and see. I will bring you to Eternal Fact, the Father of all other facthood.'

'I should object very strongly to describing God as a "fact". The Supreme Value would surely be a less inadequate description. It is hardly . . .'

'Do you not even believe that He exists?'

'Exists? What does Existence mean? You *will* keep on implying some sort of static, ready-made reality which is, so to speak, "there", and to which our minds have simply to conform. These great mysteries cannot be approached in that way. If there were such a thing (there is no need to interrupt, my dear boy) quite frankly, I should not be interested in it. It would be of no *religious* significance. God, for me, is something purely spiritual. The spirit of sweetness and light and tolerance—and, er, service, Dick, service. We mustn't forget that, you know.'

'If the thirst of the Reason is really dead . . . ,' said the Spirit, and then stopped as though pondering. Then suddenly he said, 'Can you, at least, still desire happiness?'

'Happiness, my dear Dick,' said the Ghost placidly, 'happiness, as you will come to see when you are older, lies in the path of duty. Which reminds me . . . Bless my soul, I'd nearly forgotten. Of course I can't come with you. I have to be back next Friday to read a paper. We have a little Theological Society down there. Oh yes! there is plenty of intellectual life. Not of a very high quality, perhaps. One notices a certain lack of grip—a certain confusion of mind. That is where I can be of some use to them. There are even regrettable jealousies . . . I don't know why, but tempers seem less controlled than they used to be. Still, one mustn't expect too much of human nature. I feel I can do a great work among them. But you've never asked me what my paper is about! I'm taking the text about growing up to the measure of the stature of Christ and working out an idea which I feel sure you'll be interested in. I'm going to point out how people always forget that Jesus (here the Ghost bowed) was a comparatively young man when he died. He would have outgrown some of his earlier views, you know, if he'd lived. As he might have done, with a little more tact and patience. I am going to ask my audience to consider what his mature views would have been. A profoundly interesting question. What a different Christianity we might have had if only the Founder had reached his full stature! I shall end up by pointing out how this deepens the significance of the Crucifixion. One feels for the first time what a disaster it was: what a tragic waste . . . so much promise cut short. Oh, must you be going? Well, so must I. Goodbye, my dear boy. It has been a great pleasure. Most stimulating and provocative. Goodbye, goodbye, goodbye.'

The Ghost nodded its head and beamed on the Spirit with a bright clerical smile—or with the best approach to it which such unsubstantial lips could manage—and then turned away humming softly to itself 'City of God, how broad and far.'

But I did not watch him for long, for a new idea had just occurred to me. If the grass were hard as rock, I thought, would not the water be hard enough to walk on? I tried it with one foot, and my foot did not go in. Next moment I stepped boldly out on the surface. I fell on my face at once and got some nasty bruises. I had forgotten that though it was, to me, solid, it was not the less in rapid motion. When I had picked myself up I was about thirty yards further down-stream than the point where I had left the bank. But this did not prevent me from walking up-stream: it only meant that by walking very fast indeed I made very little progress.

6

THE COOL SMOOTH skin of the bright water was delicious to my feet
and I walked on it for about an hour, making perhaps a couple of hundred yards. Then the going became difficult. The current grew swifter.
Great flakes or islands of foam came swirling down towards me, bruis-
ing my shins like stones if I did not get out of their way. The surface
became uneven, rounded itself into lovely hollows and elbows of water
which distorted the appearance of the pebbles on the bottom and threw
me off my balance, so that I had to scramble to shore. But as the banks
hereabouts consisted of great flat stones, I continued my journey without
much hurt to my feet. An immense yet lovely noise vibrated through the
forest. Hours later I rounded a bend and saw the explanation.

Before me green slopes made a wide amphitheatre, enclosing a frothy
and pulsating lake into which, over many-coloured rocks, a waterfall was
pouring. Here once again I realised that something had happened to my
senses so that they were now receiving impressions which would normally exceed their capacity. On Earth, such a waterfall could not have
been perceived at all as a whole; it was too big. Its sound would have been
a terror in the woods for twenty miles. Here, after the first shock, my
sensibility 'took' both as a well-built ship takes a huge wave. I exulted.
The noise, though gigantic, was like giants' laughter: like the revelry of
a whole college of giants together laughing, dancing, singing, roaring at
their high works.

Near the place where the fall plunged into the lake there grew a tree.
Wet with the spray, half-veiled in foam-bows, flashing with the bright,

innumerable birds that flew among its branches, it rose in many shapes of billowy foliage, huge as a fen-land cloud. From every point apples of gold gleamed through the leaves.

Suddenly my attention was diverted by a curious appearance in the foreground. A hawthorn bush not twenty yards away seemed to be behaving oddly. Then I saw that it was not the bush but something standing close to the bush and on this side of it. Finally I realised that it was one of the Ghosts. It was crouching as if to conceal itself from something beyond the bush, and it was looking back at me and making signals. It kept on signing to me to duck down. As I could not see what the danger was, I stood fast.

Presently the Ghost, after peering around in every direction, ventured beyond the hawthorn bush. It could not get on very fast because of the torturing grasses beneath its feet, but it was obviously going as fast as it possibly could, straight for another tree. There it stopped again, standing straight upright against the trunk as though it were taking cover. Because the shadow of the branches now covered it, I could see it better: it was my bowler-hatted companion, the one whom the Big Ghost had called Ikey. After it had stood panting at the tree for about ten minutes and carefully reconnoitred the ground ahead, it made a dash for another tree—such a dash as was possible to it. In this way, with infinite labour and caution, it had reached the great Tree in about an hour. That is, it had come within ten yards of it.

Here it was checked. Round the Tree grew a belt of lilies: to the Ghost an insuperable obstacle. It might as well have tried to tread down an anti-tank trap as to walk *on* them. It lay down and tried to crawl between them but they grew too close and they would not bend. And all the time it was apparently haunted by the terror of discovery. At every whisper of the wind it stopped and cowered: once, at the cry of a bird, it struggled back to its last place of cover: but then desire hounded it out again and it crawled once more to the Tree. I saw it clasp its hands and writhe in the agony of its frustration.

The wind seemed to be rising. I saw the Ghost wring its hand and put its thumb into its mouth—cruelly pinched, I doubt not, between two stems of the lilies when the breeze swayed them. Then came a real gust. The branches of the Tree began to toss. A moment later and half a dozen apples had fallen round the Ghost and on it. He gave a sharp cry, but suddenly checked it. I thought the weight of the golden fruit where it had fallen on him would have disabled him: and certainly, for a few minutes, he was unable to rise. He lay whimpering, nursing his wounds. But soon he was at work again. I could see him feverishly trying to fill his pockets with the apples. Of course it was useless. One could see how his ambitions were gradually forced down. He gave up the idea of a pocketful: two would have to do. He gave up the idea of two, he would take one, the largest one. He gave up that hope. He was now looking for the smallest one. He was trying to find if there was one small enough to carry.

The amazing thing was that he succeeded. When I remembered what the leaf had felt like when I tried to lift it, I could hardly help admiring this unhappy creature when I saw him rise staggering to his feet actually holding the smallest of the apples in his hands. He was lame from his hurts, and the weight bent him double. Yet even so, inch by inch, still availing himself of every scrap of cover, he set out on his *via dolorosa* to the bus, carrying his torture.

'Fool. Put it down,' said a great voice suddenly. It was quite unlike any other voice I had heard so far. It was a thunderous yet liquid voice. With an appalling certainty I knew that the waterfall itself was speaking: and I saw now (though it did not cease to look like a waterfall) that it was also a bright angel who stood, like one crucified, against the rocks and poured himself perpetually down towards the forest with loud joy.

'Fool', he said, 'put it down. You cannot take it back. There is not room for it in Hell. Stay here and learn to eat such apples. The very leaves and the blades of grass in the wood will delight to teach you.'

Whether the Ghost heard or not, I don't know. At any rate, after pausing for a few minutes, it braced itself anew for its agonies and continued with even greater caution till I lost sight of it.

7

ALTHOUGH I WATCHED the misfortunes of the Ghost in the Bowler with some complacency, I found, when we were left alone, that I could not bear the presence of the Water-Giant. It did not appear to take any notice of me, but I became self-conscious; and I rather think there was some assumed nonchalance in my movements as I walked away over the flat rocks, down-stream again. I was beginning to be tired. Looking at the silver fish which darted over the river-bed, I wished greatly that to me also that water were permeable. I should have liked a dip.

'Thinking of going back?' said a voice close at hand. I turned and saw a tall ghost standing with its back against a tree, chewing a ghostly cheroot. It was that of a lean hard-bitten man with grey hair and a gruff, but not uneducated voice: the kind of man I have always instinctively felt to be reliable.

'I don't know,' said I. 'Are you?'

'Yes,' it replied. 'I guess I've seen about all there is to see.'

'You don't think of staying?'

'That's all propaganda,' it said. 'Of course there never was any question of our staying. You can't eat the fruit and you can't drink the water and it takes you all your time to walk on the grass. A human being couldn't live here. All that idea of staying is only an advertisement stunt.'

'Then why did you come?'

'Oh, I don't know. Just to have a look round. I'm the sort of chap who likes to see things for himself. Wherever I've been I've always had a look at anything that was being cracked up. When I was out East, I went to see Pekin. When . . .'

'What was Pekin like?'

'Nothing to it. Just one darn wall inside another. Just a trap for tourists. I've been pretty well everywhere. Niagara Falls, the Pyramids, Salt Lake City, the Taj Mahal . . .'

'What was *it* like?'

'Not worth looking at. They're all advertisement stunts. All run by the same people. There's a combine, you know, a World Combine, that just takes an Atlas and decides where they'll have a Sight. Doesn't matter what they choose: anything'll do as long as the publicity's properly managed.'

'And you've lived—er—*down there*—in the Town—for some time?'

'In what they call Hell? Yes. It's a flop too. They lead you to expect red fire and devils and all sorts of interesting people sizzling on grids— Henry VIII and all that—but when you get there it's just like any other town.'

'I prefer it up here,' said I.

'Well, I don't see what all the talk is about,' said the Hard-Bitten Ghost. 'It's as good as any other park to look at, and darned uncomfortable.'

'There seems to be some idea that if one stays here one would get— well, solider—grow acclimatised.'

'I know all about that,' said the Ghost. 'Same old lie. People have been telling me that sort of thing all my life. They told me in the nursery that if I were good I'd be happy. And they told me at school that Latin would get easier as I went on. After I'd been married a month some fool was telling me that there were always difficulties at first, but with Tact and Patience I'd soon "settle down" and like it! And all through two wars what didn't they say about the good time coming if only I'd be a brave boy and go on being shot at? Of course they'll play the old game here if anyone's fool enough to listen.'

'But who are "They"? This might be run by someone different?'

'Entirely new management, eh? Don't you believe it! It's *never* a new management. You'll always find the same old Ring. I know all about dear, kind Mummie coming up to your bedroom and getting all she wants to know out of you: but you always found she and Father were the same firm really. Didn't we find that both sides in all the wars were run by the same Armament Firms? or the same Firm, which is behind the Jews and the Vatican and the Dictators and the Democracies and all the rest of it. All this stuff up here is run by the same people as the Town. They're just laughing at us.'

'I thought they were at war?'

'Of course you did. That's the official version. But who's ever seen any signs of it? Oh, I know that's how they *talk*. But if there's a real war why don't they do anything? Don't you see that if the official version were true these chaps up here would attack and sweep the Town out of existence? They've got the strength. If they wanted to rescue *us* they could do it. But obviously the last thing they want is to end their so-called "war". The whole game depends on keeping it going.'

This account of the matter struck me as uncomfortably plausible. I said nothing.

'Anyway,' said the Ghost, 'who wants to be rescued? What the hell would there be to *do* here?'

'Or there?' said I.

'Quite,' said the Ghost. 'They've got you either way.'

'What would you like to do if you had your choice?' I asked.

'There you go!' said the Ghost with a certain triumph. 'Asking *me* to make a plan. It's up to the Management to find something that doesn't bore us, isn't it? It's their job. Why should we do it for them? That's just where all the parsons and moralists have got the thing upside down. They keep on asking *us* to alter ourselves. But if the people who run the show are so clever and so powerful, why don't they find something to suit their public? All this poppycock about growing harder so that the grass doesn't hurt our feet, now! There's an example. What would you say if you went to a hotel where the eggs were all bad and when you complained to the Boss, instead of apologising and changing his dairyman, he just told you that if you tried you'd get to like bad eggs in time?'

'Well, I'll be getting along,' said the Ghost after a short silence. 'You coming my way?'

'There doesn't seem to be much point in going anywhere on your showing,' I replied. A great depression had come over me. 'And at least it's not raining here.'

'Not at the moment,' said the Hard-Bitten Ghost. 'But I never saw one of those bright mornings that didn't turn to rain later on. And, by gum, when it does rain here! Ah, you hadn't thought of that? It hadn't occurred to you that with the sort of water they have here every raindrop will make a hole in you, like a machine-gun bullet. That's their little joke, you see. First of all tantalise you with ground you can't walk on and water you can't drink and then drill you full of holes. But they won't catch *me* that way.'

A few minutes later he moved off.

8

I SAT STILL on a stone by the river's side feeling as miserable as I ever felt in my life. Hitherto it had not occurred to me to doubt the intentions of the Solid People, nor to question the essential goodness of their country even if it were a country which I could not long inhabit. It had indeed once crossed my mind that if these Solid People were as benevolent as I had heard one or two of them claim to be, they might have done something to help the inhabitants of the Town—something more than meeting them on the plain. Now a terrible explanation came into my mind. How if this whole trip were allowed the Ghosts merely to mock them? Horrible myths and doctrines stirred in my memory. I thought how the Gods had punished Tantalus. I thought of the place in the Book of Revelation where it says that the smoke of Hell goes up forever in the sight of the blessed spirits. I remembered how poor Cowper, dreaming that he was not after all doomed to perdition, at once knew the dream to be false and said, 'These are the sharpest arrows in His quiver.' And what the Hard-Bitten Ghost had said about the rain was clearly true. Even a shower of dew-drops from a branch might tear me in pieces. I had not thought of this before. And how easily I might have ventured into the spray of the waterfall!

The sense of danger, which had never been entirely absent since I left the bus, awoke with sharp urgency. I gazed around on the trees, the flowers, and the talking cataract: they had begun to look unbearably sinister. Bright insects darted to and fro. If one of those were to fly into my face, would it not go right through me? If it settled on my head, would it crush me to earth? Terror whispered, 'This is no place for you.' I remembered also the lions.

With no very clear plan in my mind, I rose and began walking away from the river in the direction where the trees grew closest together. I had not fully made up my mind to go back to the bus, but I wanted to avoid open places. If only I could find a trace of evidence that it was really possible for a Ghost to stay—that the choice was not only a cruel comedy—I would not go back. In the meantime I went on, gingerly, and keeping a sharp look-out. In about half an hour I came to a little clearing with some bushes in the centre. As I stopped, wondering if I dared cross it, I realised that I was not alone.

A Ghost hobbled across the clearing—as quickly as it could on that uneasy soil—looking over its shoulder as if it were pursued. I saw that it had been a woman: a well-dressed woman, I thought, but its shadows of finery looked ghastly in the morning light. It was making for the bushes. It could not really get in among them—the twigs and leaves were too hard—but it pressed as close up against them as it could. It seemed to believe it was hiding.

A moment later I heard the sound of feet, and one of the Bright People came in sight: one always noticed that sound there, for we Ghosts made no noise when we walked.

'Go away!' squealed the Ghost. 'Go away! Can't you see I want to be alone?'

'But you need help,' said the Solid One.

'If you have the least trace of decent feeling left,' said the Ghost, 'you'll keep away. I don't want help. I want to be left alone. Do go away. You know I can't walk fast enough on those horrible spikes to get away from you. It's abominable of you to take advantage.'

'Oh, that!' said the Spirit. 'That'll soon come right. But you're going in the wrong direction. It's back there—to the mountains—you need to go. You can lean on me all the way. I can't absolutely *carry* you, but you need have almost no weight on your own feet: and it will hurt less at every step.'

'I'm not afraid of being hurt. You know that.'

'Then what is the matter?'

'Can't you understand *anything?* Do you really suppose I'm going out there among all those people, like *this?*'

'But why not?'

'I'd never have come at all if I'd known you were all going to be dressed like that.'

'Friend, you see I'm not dressed at all.'

'I didn't mean that. Do go away.'

'But can't you even tell me?'

'If you can't understand, there'd be no good trying to explain it. How *can* I go out like this among a lot of people with real solid bodies? It's far worse than going out with nothing on would have been on Earth. Have everyone staring *through* me.'

'Oh, I see. But we were all a bit ghostly when we first arrived, you know. That'll wear off. Just come out and try.'

'But they'll see me.'

'What does it matter if they do?'

'I'd rather die.'

'But you've died already. There's no good trying to go back to that.'

The Ghost made a sound something between a sob and a snarl. 'I wish I'd never been born,' it said. 'What *are* we born for?'

'For infinite happiness,' said the Spirit. 'You can step out into it at any moment . . .'

'But, I tell you, they'll *see* me.'

'An hour hence and you will not care. A day hence and you will laugh at it. Don't you remember on earth—there were things too hot to touch with your finger but you could drink them all right? Shame is like that. If you will accept it—if you will drink the cup to the bottom—you will find it very nourishing: but try to do anything else with it and it scalds.'

'You really mean? . . .' said the Ghost, and then paused. My suspense was strained up to the height. I felt that my own destiny hung on her reply. I could have fallen at her feet and begged her to yield.

'Yes,' said the Spirit. 'Come and try.'

Almost, I thought the Ghost had obeyed. Certainly it had moved: but suddenly it cried out, 'No, I can't. I tell you I can't. For a moment, while you were talking, I almost thought . . . but when it comes to the point . . . You've no right to ask me to do a thing like that. It's disgusting. I should never forgive myself if I did. Never, never. And it's not fair. They ought to have warned us. I'd never have come. And now—please, please go away!"

'Friend,' said the Spirit. 'Could you, only for a moment, fix your mind on something not yourself?'

'I've already given you my answer,' said the Ghost, coldly but still tearful.

'Then only one expedient remains,' said the Spirit, and to my great surprise he set a horn to his lips and blew. I put my hands over my ears. The earth seemed to shake: the whole wood trembled and dindled at the sound. I suppose there must have been a pause after that (though there seemed to be none) before I heard the thudding of hoofs—far off at first, but already nearer before I had well identified it, and soon so near that I began to look about for some place of safety. Before I had found one the danger was all about us. A herd of unicorns came thundering through the glades: twenty-seven hands high the smallest of them and white as swans but for the red gleam in eyes and nostrils and the flashing indigo of their horns. I can still remember the squelching noise of the soft wet turf under their hoofs, the breaking of the undergrowth, the snorting and the whinneyings; how their hind legs went up and their horned heads down in mimic battle. Even then I wondered for what real battle it might be the rehearsal. I heard the Ghost scream, and I think it made a bolt away from the bushes . . . perhaps towards the Spirit, but I don't know. For my own nerve failed and I fled, not heeding, for the moment, the horrible going underfoot, and not once daring to pause. So I never saw the end of that interview.

9

'WHERE ARE YE going?' said a voice with a strong Scotch accent. I stopped and looked. The sound of the unicorns had long since died away and my flight had brought me to open country. I saw the mountains where the unchanging sunrise lay, and in the foreground two or three pines on a little knoll, with some large smooth rocks, and heather. On one of the rocks sat a very tall man, almost a giant, with a flowing beard. I had not yet looked one of the Solid People in the face. Now, when I did so, I discovered that one sees them with a kind of double vision. Here was an enthroned and shining god, whose ageless spirit weighed upon mine like a burden of solid gold: and yet, at the very same moment, here was an old weather-beaten man, one who might have been a shepherd—such a man as tourists think simple because he is honest and neighbours think 'deep' for the same reason. His eyes had the far-seeing look of one who has lived long in open, solitary places; and somehow I divined the network of wrinkles which must have surrounded them before re-birth had washed him in immortality.

'I—I don't quite know,' said I.

'Ye can sit and talk to me then,' he said, making room for me on the stone.

'I don't know you, Sir,' said I, taking my seat beside him.

'My name is George,' he answered. 'George MacDonald.'

'Oh!' I cried. 'Then you can tell me! You at least will not deceive me.' Then, supposing that these expressions of confidence needed some explanation, I tried, trembling to tell this man all that his writings had done for me. I tried to tell how a certain frosty afternoon at Leatherhead Station when I first bought a copy of *Phantastes* (being then about sixteen years old) had been to me what the first sight of Beatrice had been to Dante: *Here begins the New Life*. I started to confess how long that Life had delayed in the region of imagination merely: how slowly and reluctantly I had come to admit that his Christendom had more than an accidental connexion with it, how hard I had tried not to see that the true name of the quality which first met me in his books is Holiness. He laid his hand on mine and stopped me.

'Son,' he said, 'Your love—all love—is of inexpressible value to me. But it may save precious time' (here he suddenly looked very Scotch) 'if I inform ye that I am already well acquainted with these biographical details. In fact, I have noticed that your memory misleads you in one or two particulars.'

'Oh!' said I, and became still.

'Ye had started,' said my Teacher, 'to talk of something more profitable.'

'Sir,' said I, 'I had almost forgotten it, and I have no anxiety about the answer now, though I have still a curiosity. It is about these Ghosts. *Do* any of them stay? *Can* they stay? Is any real choice offered to them? How do they come to be here?'

'Did ye never hear of the *Refrigerium?* A man with your advantages might have read of it in Prudentius, not to mention Jeremy Taylor.'

'The name is familiar, Sir, but I'm afraid I've forgotten what it means.'

'It means that the damned have holidays—excursions, ye understand.'

'Excursions to *this* country?'

'For those that will take them. Of course most of the silly creatures don't. They prefer taking trips back to Earth. They go and play tricks on the poor daft women ye call mediums. They go and try to assert their ownership of some house that once belonged to them: and then ye get what's called a Haunting. Or they go to spy on their children. Or literary ghosts hang about public libraries to see if anyone's still reading their books.'

'But if they come here they can really stay?'

'Aye. Ye'll have heard that the emperor Trajan did.'

'But I don't understand. Is judgement not final? Is there really a way out of Hell into Heaven?'

'It depends on the way ye're using the words. If they leave that grey town behind it will not have been Hell. To any that leaves it, it is Purgatory. And perhaps ye had better not call this country Heaven. *Not Deep Heaven*, ye understand.' (Here he smiled at me.) 'Ye can call it the Valley of the Shadow of Life. And yet to those who stay here it will have been Heaven from the first. And ye can call those sad streets in the town yonder the Valley of the Shadow of Death: but to those who remain there they will have been Hell even from the beginning.'

I suppose he saw that I looked puzzled, for presently he spoke again.

'Son,' he said, 'ye cannot in your present state understand eternity: when Anodos looked through the door of the Timeless he brought no message back. But ye can get some likeness of it if ye say that both good and evil, when they are full grown, become retrospective. Not only this valley but all their earthly past will have been Heaven to those who are saved. Not only the twilight in that town, but all their life on Earth too, will then be seen by the damned to have been Hell. That is what mortals misunderstand. They say of some temporal suffering, "No future bliss can make up for it," not knowing that Heaven, once attained, will work backwards and turn even that agony into a glory. And of some sinful pleasure they say "Let me have but *this* and I'll take the consequences": little dreaming how damnation will spread back and back into their past and contaminate the pleasure of the sin. Both processes begin even before death. The good man's past begins to change so that his forgiven sins and remembered sorrows take on the quality of Heaven: the bad man's past already conforms to his badness and is filled only with dreariness. And that is why, at the end of all things, when the sun rises here and the twilight turns to blackness down there, the Blessed will say "We have never lived anywhere except in Heaven," and the Lost, "We were always in Hell." And both will speak truly.'

'Is that not very hard, Sir?'

'I mean, that is the real sense of what they will say. In the actual language of the Lost, the words will be different, no doubt. One will say he has always served his country right or wrong; and another that he has sacrificed everything to his Art; and some that they've never been taken in, and some that, thank God, they've always looked after Number One, and nearly all, that, at least they've been true to themselves.'

'And the Saved?'

'Ah, the Saved . . . what happens to them is best described as the opposite of a mirage. What seemed, when they entered it, to be the vale of misery turns out, when they look back, to have been a well; and where present experience saw only salt deserts, memory truthfully records that the pools were full of water.'

'Then those people are right who say that Heaven and Hell are only states of mind?'

'Hush,' he said sternly. 'Do not blaspheme. Hell is a state of mind—ye never said a truer word. And every state of mind, left to itself, every shutting up of the creature within the dungeon of its own mind—is, in the end, Hell. But Heaven is not a state of mind. Heaven is reality itself. All that is fully real is Heavenly. For all that can be shaken will be shaken and only the unshakeable remains.'

'But there is a real choice after death? My Roman Catholic friends would be surprised, for to them souls in Purgatory are already saved. And my Protestant friends would like it no better, for they'd say that the tree lies as it falls.'

'They're both right, maybe. Do not fash yourself with such questions. Ye cannot fully understand the relations of choice and Time till you are beyond both. And ye were not brought here to study such curiosities. What concerns you is the nature of the choice itself: and that ye can watch them making.'

'Well, Sir,' I said, 'That also needs explaining. What do they choose, these souls who go back (I have yet seen no others)? And how can they choose it?'

'Milton was right,' said my Teacher. 'The choice of every lost soul can be expressed in the words "Better to reign in Hell than serve in Heaven." There is always something they insist on keeping even at the price of misery. There is always something they prefer to joy—that is, to reality. Ye see it easily enough in a spoiled child that would sooner miss its play and its supper than say it was sorry and be friends. Ye call it the Sulks. But in adult life it has a hundred fine names—Achilles' wrath and Coriolanus' grandeur, Revenge and Injured Merit and Self-Respect and Tragic Greatness and Proper Pride.'

'Then is no one lost through the undignified vices, Sir? Through mere sensuality?'

'Some are, no doubt. The sensualist, I'll allow ye, begins by pursuing a real pleasure, though a small one. His sin is the less. But the time comes on when, though the pleasure becomes less and less and the craving fiercer and fiercer, and though he knows that joy can never come that way, yet he prefers to joy the mere fondling of unappeasable lust and would not have it taken from him. He'd fight to the death to keep it. He'd like well to be able to scratch; but even when he can scratch no more he'd rather itch than not.'

He was silent for a few minutes, and then began again.

'Ye'll understand, there are innumerable forms of this choice. Sometimes forms that one hardly thought of at all on Earth. There was a creature came here not long ago and went back—Sir Archibald they called him. In his earthly life he'd been interested in nothing but Survival. He'd written a whole shelf-full of books about it. He began by being philosophical, but in the end he took up Psychical Research. It grew to be his only occupation—experimenting, lecturing, running a magazine. And travelling too: digging out queer stories among Tibetan lamas and being initiated into brotherhoods in Central Africa. Proofs—and more proofs—and then more proofs again—were what he wanted. It drove him mad if ever he saw anyone taking an interest in anything else. He got into trouble during one of your wars for running up and down the country telling them not to fight because it wasted a lot of money that ought to be spent on Research. Well, in good time, the poor creature died and came here: and there was no power in the universe would have prevented him staying and going on to the mountains. But do ye think that did him any good? This country was no use to him at all. Everyone here had "survived" already. Nobody took the least interest in the question. There was nothing more to prove. His occupation was clean gone. Of course if he would only have admitted that he'd mistaken the means for the end and had a good laugh at himself he could have begun all over again like a little child and entered into joy. But he would not do that. He cared nothing about joy. In the end he went away.'

'How fantastic!' said I.

'Do ye think so?' said the Teacher with a piercing glance. 'It is nearer to such as you than ye think. There have been men before now who got so interested in proving the existence of God that they came to care nothing for God Himself . . . as if the good Lord had nothing to do but *exist!* There have been some who were so occupied in spreading Christianity that they never gave a thought to Christ. Man! Ye see it in smaller matters. Did ye never know a lover of books that with all his first editions and signed copies had lost the power to read them? Or an organiser of charities that had lost all love for the poor? It is the subtlest of all the snares.'

Moved by a desire to change the subject, I asked why the Solid People, since they were full of love, did not go down into Hell to rescue the Ghosts. Why were they content simply to meet them on the plain? One would have expected a more militant charity.

'Ye will understand that better, perhaps before ye go,' said he. 'In the meantime, I must tell ye they have come further for the sake of the Ghosts than ye can understand. Every one of us lives only to journey further and further into the mountains. Every one of us has interrupted that journey and retraced immeasurable distances to come down today on the mere chance of saving some Ghost. Of course it is also joy to do so, but ye cannot blame us for that! And it would be no use to come further even if it were possible. The sane would do no good if they made themselves mad to help madmen.'

'But what of the poor Ghosts who never get into the omnibus at all?'

'Everyone who wishes it does. Never fear. There are only two kinds of people in the end: those who say to God, "Thy will be done," and those to whom God says, in the end, *"Thy* will be done." All that are in Hell, choose it. Without that self-choice there could be no Hell. No soul that seriously and constantly desires joy will ever miss it. Those who seek find. To those who knock it is opened.'

At this moment we were suddenly interrupted by the thin voice of a Ghost talking at an enormous speed. Looking behind us we saw the creature. It was addressing one of the Solid People and was doing so too busily to notice us. Every now and then the Solid Spirit tried to get in a word but without success. The Ghost's talk was like this:

'Oh, my dear, I've had such a dreadful time, I don't know how I ever got here at all, I was coming with Elinor Stone and we'd arranged the whole thing and we were to meet at the corner of Sink Street; I made it perfectly plain because I knew what she was like and if I told her once I told her a hundred times I would *not* meet her outside that dreadful Marjoribanks woman's house, not after the way she'd treated me . . . that was one of the most dreadful things that happened to me; I've been dying to tell you because I felt sure you'd tell me I acted rightly; no, wait a moment, dear, till I've told you—I tried living with her when I first came and it was all fixed up, she was to do the cooking and I was to look after the house and I *did* think I was going to be comfortable after all I'd been through but she turned out to be so changed, absolutely selfish, and not a particle of sympathy for anyone but herself—and as I once said to her, "I *do* think I'm entitled to a little consideration because you at least lived out your time, but I oughtn't to have been here for years and years yet"—oh but of course I'm forgetting you don't know—I was murdered, simply murdered, dear, that man should never have operated, I ought to be alive today and they simply *starved* me in that dreadful nursing home and no one ever came near me and . . .'

The shrill monotonous whine died away as the speaker, still accompanied by the bright patience at her side, moved out of hearing.

'What troubles ye, son?' asked my Teacher.

'I am troubled, Sir,' said I, 'because that unhappy creature doesn't seem to me to be the sort of soul that ought to be even in danger of damnation. She isn't wicked: she's only a silly, garrulous old woman who has got into a habit of grumbling, and feels that a little kindness, and rest, and change would do her all right.'

'That is what she once was. That is maybe what she still is. If so, she certainly will be cured. But the whole question is whether she is now a grumbler.'

'I should have thought there was no doubt about that!'

'Aye, but ye misunderstand me. The question is whether she is a grumbler, or only a grumble. If there is a real woman—even the least trace of one—still there inside the grumbling, it can be brought to life again. If there's one wee spark under all those ashes, we'll blow it till the whole pile is red and clear. But if there's nothing but ashes we'll not go on blowing them in our own eyes forever. They must be swept up.'

'But how can there be a grumble without a grumbler?'

'The whole difficulty of understanding Hell is that the thing to be understood is so nearly Nothing. But ye'll have had experiences . . . it begins with a grumbling mood, and yourself still distinct from it: perhaps criticising it. And yourself, in a dark hour, may will that mood, embrace it. Ye can repent and come out of it again. But there may come a day when you can do that no longer. Then there will be no *you* left to criticise the mood, nor even to enjoy it, but just the grumble itself going on forever like a machine. But come! Ye are here to watch and listen. Lean on my arm and we will go for a little walk.'

I obeyed. To lean on the arm of someone older than myself was an experience that carried me back to childhood, and with this support I found the going tolerable: so much so, indeed, that I flattered myself my feet were already growing more solid, until a glance at the poor transparent shapes convinced me that I owed all this ease to the strong arm of the Teacher. Perhaps it was because of his presence that my other senses also appeared to be quickened. I noticed scents in the air which had hitherto escaped me, and the country put on new beauties. There was water everywhere and tiny flowers quivering in the early breeze. Far off in the woods we saw the deer glancing past, and, once, a sleek panther came purring to my companion's side. We also saw many of the Ghosts.

I think the most pitiable was a female Ghost. Her trouble was the very opposite of that which afflicted the other, the lady frightened by the Unicorns. This one seemed quite unaware of her phantasmal appearance. More than one of the Solid People tried to talk to her, and at first I was quite at a loss to understand her behaviour to them. She appeared to be contorting her all but invisible face and writhing her smokelike body in a quite meaningless fashion. At last I came to the conclusion—incredible as it seemed—that she supposed herself still capable of attracting them and was trying to do so. She was a thing that had become incapable of conceiving conversation save as a means to that end. If a corpse already liquid with decay had arisen from the coffin, smeared its gums with lipstick, and attempted a flirtation, the result could not have been more appalling. In the end she muttered, 'Stupid creatures,' and turned back to the bus.

This put me in mind to ask my Teacher what he thought of the affair with the Unicorns. 'It will maybe have succeeded,' he said. 'Ye will have divined that he meant to frighten her, not that fear itself could make her less a Ghost, but if it took her mind a moment off herself, there might, in that moment, be a chance. I have seen them saved so.'

We met several Ghosts that had come so near to Heaven only in order to tell the Celestials about Hell. Indeed this is one of the commonest types. Others, who had perhaps been (like myself) teachers of some kind actually wanted to give lectures about it: they brought fat notebooks full of statistics, and maps, and (one of them) a magic lantern. Some wanted to tell anecdotes of the notorious sinners of all ages whom they had met below. But the most part seemed to think that the mere fact of having contrived for themselves so much misery gave them a kind of superiority. 'You have led a sheltered life!' they bawled. 'You don't know the seamy side. We'll tell you. We'll give you some hard facts'—as if to tinge

Heaven with infernal images and colours had been the only purpose for which they came. All alike, so far as I could judge from my own exploration of the lower world, were wholly unreliable, and all equally incurious about the country in which they had arrived. They repelled every attempt to teach them, and when they found that nobody listened to them they went back, one by one, to the bus.

This curious wish to describe Hell turned out, however, to be only the mildest form of a desire very common among the Ghosts—the desire to *extend* Hell, to bring it bodily, if they could, into Heaven. There were tub-thumping Ghosts who in thin, bat-like voices urged the blessed spirits to shake off their fetters, to escape from their imprisonment in happiness, to tear down the mountains with their hands, to seize Heaven 'for their own': Hell offered her co-operation. There were planning Ghosts who implored them to dam the river, cut down the trees, kill the animals, build a mountain railway, smooth out the horrible grass and moss and heather with asphalt. There were materialistic Ghosts who informed the immortals that they were deluded: there was no life after death, and this whole country was a hallucination. There were Ghosts, plain and simple: mere bogies, fully conscious of their own decay, who had accepted the traditional role of the spectre, and seemed to hope they could frighten someone. I had had no idea that this desire was possible. But my Teacher reminded me that the pleasure of frightening is by no means unknown on Earth, and also of Tacitus' saying: 'They terrify lest they should fear.' When the debris of a decayed human soul finds itself crumbled into ghosthood and realises 'I myself am now that which all humanity has feared, I am just that cold churchyard shadow, that horrible thing which cannot be, yet somehow is', then to terrify others appears to it an escape from the doom of being a Ghost yet still fearing Ghosts—fearing even the Ghost it is. For to be afraid of oneself is the last horror.

But, beyond all these, I saw other grotesque phantoms in which hardly a trace of the human form remained; monsters who had faced the journey to the bus stop—perhaps for them it was thousands of miles—and come up to the country of the Shadow of Life and limped far into it over the torturing grass, only to Spit and gibber out in one ecstasy of hatred their envy and (what is harder to understand) their contempt, of joy. The voyage seemed to them a small price to pay if once, only once, within sight of that eternal dawn, they could tell the prigs, the toffs, the sanctimonious humbugs, the snobs, the 'haves', what they thought of them.

'How do they come to be here at all?' I asked my Teacher.

'I have seen that kind converted,' said he, 'when those ye would think less deeply damned have gone back. Those that hate goodness are sometimes nearer than those that know nothing at all about it and think they have it already.'

'Whisht, now!' said my Teacher suddenly. We were standing close to some bushes and beyond them I saw one of the Solid People and a Ghost who had apparently just that moment met. The outlines of the Ghost looked vaguely familiar, but I soon realized that what I had seen on Earth was not the man himself but photographs of him in the papers. He had been a famous artist.

'God' said the Ghost, glancing round the landscape.

'God what?' asked the Spirit.

'What do you mean, "God what"?' asked the Ghost.

'In our grammar God is a noun.'

'Oh—I see. I only meant "By Gum" or something of the sort. I meant . . . well, all *this*. It's . . . it's . . . I should like to paint this.'

'I shouldn't bother about that just at present if I were you.'

'Look here; isn't one going to be allowed to go on painting?'

'Looking comes first.'

'But I've had my look. I've seen just what I want to do. God!—I wish I'd thought of bringing my things with me!'

The Spirit shook his head, scattering light from his hair as he did so. 'That sort of thing's no good here,' he said.

'What do you mean?' said the Ghost.

'When you painted on earth—at least in your earlier days—it was because you caught glimpses of Heaven in the earthly landscape. The success of your painting was that it enabled others to see the glimpses too. But here you are having the thing itself. It is from here that the messages came. There is no good *telling* us about this country, for we see it already. In fact we see it better than you do.'

'Then there's never going to be any point in painting here?'

'I don't say that. When you've grown into a Person (it's all right, we all had to do it) there'll be some things which you'll see better than anyone else. One of the things you'll want to do will be to tell us about them. But not yet. At present your business is to see. Come and see. He is endless. Come and feed.'

There was a little pause. 'That will be delightful,' said the Ghost presently in a rather dull voice.

'Come, then,' said the Spirit, offering it his arm.

'How soon do you think I *could* begin painting?' it asked.

The Spirit broke into laughter. 'Don't you see you'll never paint at all if that's what you're thinking about?' he said.

'What do you mean?' asked the Ghost.

'Why, if you are interested in the country only for the sake of painting it, you'll never learn to see the country.'

'But that's just how a real artist is interested in the country.'

'No. You're forgetting,' said the Spirit. 'That was not how you began. Light itself was your first love: you loved paint only as a means of telling about light.'

'Oh, that's ages ago,' said the Ghost. 'One grows out of that. Of course, you haven't seen my later works. One becomes more and more interested in paint for its own sake.'

'One does, indeed. I also have had to recover from that. It was all a snare. Ink and catgut and paint were necessary down there, but they are also dangerous stimulants. Every poet and musician and artist, but for Grace, is drawn away from love of the thing he tells, to love of the telling till, down in Deep Hell, they cannot be interested in God at all but only in what they say about Him. For it doesn't stop at being interested in paint, you know. They sink lower—become interested in their own personalities and then in nothing but their own reputations.'

'I don't think I'm much troubled in *that* way,' said the Ghost stiffly.

'That's excellent,' said the Spirit. 'Not many of us had quite got over it when we first arrived. But if there is any of that inflammation left it will be cured when you come to the fountain.'

'What fountain's that?'

'It is up there in the mountains,' said the Spirit. 'Very cold and clear, between two green hills. A little like Lethe. When you have drunk of it you forget forever all proprietorship in your own works. You enjoy them just as if they were someone else's: without pride and without modesty.'

'That'll be grand,' said the Ghost without enthusiasm.

'Well, come,' said the Spirit: and for a few paces he supported the hobbling shadow forward to the East.

'Of course,' said the Ghost, as if speaking to itself, 'there'll always be interesting people to meet . . .'

'Everyone will be interesting.'

'Oh—ah—yes, to be sure. I was thinking of people in our own line. Shall I meet Claude? Or Cézanne? Or—.'

'Sooner or later—if they're here.'

'But don't you know?'

'Well, of course not. I've only been here a few years. All the chances are against my having run across them . . . there are a good many of us, you know.'

'But surely in the case of distinguished people, you'd hear?'

'But they aren't distinguished—no more than anyone else. Don't you understand? The Glory flows into everyone, and back from everyone: like light and mirrors. But the light's the thing.'

'Do you mean there are no famous men?'

'They are all famous. They are all known, remembered, recognised by the only Mind that can give a perfect judgement.'

'Oh, of course, in *that* sense . . .' said the Ghost.

'Don't stop,' said the Spirit, making to lead him still forward.

'One must be content with one's reputation among posterity, then,' said the Ghost.

'My friend,' said the Spirit. 'Don't you know?'

'Know what?'

'That you and I are already completely forgotten on the Earth?'

'Eh? What's that?' exclaimed the Ghost, disengaging its arm. 'Do you mean those damned Neo-Regionalists have won after all?'

'Lord love you, yes!' said the Spirit, once more shaking and shining with laughter. 'You couldn't get five pounds for any picture of mine or even of yours in Europe or America to-day. We're dead out of fashion.'

'I must be off at once,' said the Ghost. 'Let me go! Damn it all, one has one's duty to the future of Art. I must go back to my friends. I must write an article. There must be a manifesto. We must start a periodical. We must have publicity. Let me go. This is beyond a joke!'

And without listening to the Spirit's reply, the spectre vanished.

10

THIS CONVERSATION ALSO we overheard.

'That is quite, *quite* out of the question,' said a female Ghost to one of the bright Women, 'I should not dream of staying if I'm expected to meet Robert. I am ready to forgive him, of course. But anything more is quite impossible. How he comes to be here . . . but that is your affair.'

'But if you have forgiven him,' said the other, 'surely —.'

'I forgive him as a Christian,' said the Ghost. 'But there are some things one can never forget.'

'But I don't understand . . .' began the She-Spirit.

'Exactly,' said the Ghost with a little laugh. 'You never did. You always thought Robert could do no wrong. *I* know. Please don't interrupt for *one* moment. You haven't the faintest conception of what I went through with your dear Robert. The ingratitude! It was I who made a man of him! Sacrificed my whole life to him! And what was my reward? Absolute, utter selfishness. No, but listen. He was pottering along on about six hundred a year when I married him. And mark my words, Hilda, he'd have been in that position to the day of his death if it hadn't been for me. It was I who had to drive him every step of the way. He hadn't a spark of ambition. It was like trying to lift a sack of coal. I had to positively nag him to take on that extra work in the other department, though it was really the beginning of everything for him. The laziness of men! He said, if you please, he couldn't work more than thirteen hours a day! As if I weren't working far longer. For *my* day's work wasn't over when his was. I had to keep him going all evening, if you understand what I mean. If he'd had his way he'd have just sat in an armchair and sulked when dinner was over. It was I who had to draw him out of himself and brighten him up and make conversation. With no help from him, of course. Sometimes he didn't even listen. As I said to him, I should have thought good manners, if nothing else . . . he seemed to have forgotten that I was a lady even if I *had* married him, and all the time I was working my fingers to the bone for him: and without the slightest appreciation. I used to spend simply *hours* arranging flowers to make that poky little house nice, and instead of thanking me, what do you think he said? He said he wished I wouldn't fill up the writing desk with them when he wanted to use it: and there was a perfectly frightful fuss one evening because I'd spilled one of the vases over some papers of his. If was all nonsense really, because they weren't anything to do with his work. He had some silly idea of writing a book in those days . . . as if he could. I cured him of that in the end.

'No, Hilda, you *must* listen to me. The trouble I went to, entertaining! Robert's idea was that he'd just slink off by himself every now and then to see what he called his old friends . . . and leave me to amuse myself! But I knew from the first that those friends were doing him no good. "No, Robert," said I, "your friends are now mine. It is my duty to have them *here*, however tired I am and however little we can afford it." You'd have thought that would have been enough. But they did come for a bit. That is where I had to use a certain amount of tact. A woman who has her wits about her can always drop in a word here and there. I wanted Robert to see them against a different background. They weren't quite at their ease, somehow, in my drawing-room: not at their best. I couldn't help laughing sometimes. Of course Robert was uncomfortable while the treatment was going on, but it was all for his own good in the end. None of that set were friends of his any longer by the end of the first year.

'And then, he got the new job. A great step up. But what *do* you think? Instead of realising that we now had a chance to spread out a bit, all he said was "Well *now*, for God's sake let's have some peace." That nearly finished me. I nearly gave him up altogether: but I knew my duty. I have always done my duty. You can't believe the work I had getting him to agree to a bigger house, and then finding a house. I wouldn't have grudged it one scrap if only he'd taken it in the right spirit—if only he'd seen the *fun* of it all. If he'd been a different sort of man it *would* have been fun meeting him on the doorstep as he came back from the office and saying, "Come along, Bobs, no time for dinner to-night. I've just heard of a house near Watford and I've got the keys and we can get there and back by one o'clock." But with *him!* It was perfect misery, Hilda. For by this time your wonderful Robert was turning into the sort of man who cares about nothing but food.

'Well, I got him into the new house at last. Yes, I know. It was a little more than we could really afford at the moment, but all sorts of things were opening out before him. And, of course, I began to entertain properly. No more of his sort of friends, thank you. I was doing it all for his sake. Every useful friend he ever made was due to me. Naturally, I had to dress well. They ought to have been the happiest years of both our lives. If they weren't, he had no one but himself to thank. Oh, he was a maddening man, simply maddening! He just set himself to get old and silent and grumpy. Just sank into himself. He could have looked years younger if he'd taken the trouble. He needn't have walked with a stoop—I'm sure I warned him about that often enough. He was the most miserable host. Whenever we gave a party everything rested on my shoulders: Robert was simply a wet blanket. As I said to him (and if I said it once, I said it a hundred times) he hadn't always been like that. There had been a time when he took an interest in all sorts of things and had been quite ready to make friends. "What on earth is coming over you?" I used to say. But now he just didn't answer at all. He would sit staring at me with his great big eyes (I came to hate a man with dark eyes) and—I know it now—just hating me. That was my reward. After all I'd done. Sheer wicked, senseless hatred: at the very moment when he was a richer man that he'd ever dreamed of being! As I used to say to him, "Robert, you're simply letting yourself go to seed." The younger men who came to the house—it wasn't my fault if they liked me better than my old bear of a husband—used to laugh at him.

'I did my duty to the very end. I *forced* him to take exercise—that was really my chief reason for keeping a great Dane. I kept on giving parties. I took him for the most wonderful holidays. I saw that he didn't drink too much. Even, when things became desperate, I encouraged him to take up his writing again. It couldn't do any harm by then. How could I help it if he *did* have a nervous breakdown in the end? My conscience is clear. I've done my duty by him, if ever a woman has. So you see why it would be impossible to . . .

'And yet . . . I don't know. I believe I have changed my mind. I'll make them a fair offer, Hilda. I will *not* meet him, if it means just meeting him and no more. But if I'm given a free hand I'll take charge of him again. I will take up my burden once more. But I must have a free hand. With all the time one would have here, I believe I could still make something of him. Somewhere quiet to ourselves. Wouldn't that be a good plan? He's not fit to be on his own. Put me in charge of him. He wants firm handling. I know him better than you do. What's that? No, give him to me, do you hear? Don't consult *him:* just give him to me. I'm his wife, aren't I? I was only beginning. There's lots, lots, lots of things I still want to do with him. No, listen, Hilda. Please, please! I'm so miserable. I must have someone to—to do things to. It's simply frightful down there. No one minds about me at all. I can't alter them. It's dreadful to see them all sitting about and not be able to do anything with them. Give him back to me. Why should he have everything his own way? It's not good for him. It isn't right, it's not fair. I want Robert. What right have you to keep him from me? I hate you. How can I pay him out if you won't let me have him?'

The Ghost which had towered up like a dying candle-flame snapped suddenly. A sour, dry smell lingered in the air for a moment and then there was no Ghost to be seen.

11

ONE OF THE most painful meetings we witnessed was between a woman's Ghost and a Bright Spirit who had apparently been her brother. They must have met only a moment before we ran across them, for the Ghost was just saying in a tone of unconcealed disappointment, 'Oh . . . Reginald! It's *you*, is it?'

'Yes, dear,' said the Spirit. 'I know you expected someone else. Can you . . . I hope you can be a little glad to see even me; for the present.'

'I did think Michael would have come,' said the Ghost; and then, almost fiercely, 'He is *here*, of course?'

'He's there—far up in the mountains.'

'Why hasn't he come to meet me? Didn't he know?'

'My dear (don't worry, it will all come right presently) it wouldn't have done. Not yet. He wouldn't be able to see or hear you as you are at present. You'd be totally invisible to Michael. But we'll soon build you up.'

'I should have thought if *you* can see me, my own son could!'

'It doesn't always happen like that. You see, I have specialised in this sort of work.'

'Oh, it's work, is it?' snapped the Ghost. Then, after a pause, 'Well. When *am* I going to be allowed to see him?'

'There's no question of being *allowed*, Pam. As soon as it's possible for him to see you, of course he will. You need to be thickened up a bit.'

'How?' said the Ghost. The monosyllable was hard and a little threatening.

'I'm afraid the first step is a hard one,' said the Spirit. 'But after that you'll go on like a house on fire. You will become solid enough for Michael to perceive you when you learn to want Someone Else besides Michael. I don't say "more than Michael", not as a beginning. That will come later. It's only the little germ of a desire for God that we need to start the process.'

'Oh, you mean religion and all that sort of thing? This is hardly the moment . . . and from *you*, of all people. Well, never mind. I'll do whatever's necessary. What do you want me to do? Come on. The sooner I begin it, the sooner they'll let me see my boy. I'm quite ready.'

'But, Pam, do think! Don't you see you are not beginning at all as long as you are in that state of mind? You're treating God only as a means to Michael. But the whole thickening treatment consists in learning to want God for His own sake.'

'You wouldn't talk like that if you were a mother.'

'You mean, if I were *only* a mother. But there is no such thing as being only a mother. You exist as Michael's mother only because you first exist as God's creature. That relation is older and closer. No, listen, Pam! He also loves. He also has suffered. He also has waited a long time.'

'If He loved me He'd let me see my boy. If He loved me why did He take Michael away from me? I wasn't going to say anything about that. But it's pretty hard to forgive, you know.'

'But He had to take Michael away. Partly for Michael's sake . . .'

'I'm sure I did my best to make Michael happy. I gave up my whole life . . .'

'Human beings can't make one another really happy for long. And secondly, for your sake. He wanted your merely instinctive love for your child (tigresses share *that*, you know!) to turn into something better. He wanted you to love Michael as He understands love. You cannot love a fellow-creature fully till you love God. Sometimes this conversion can be done while the instinctive love is still gratified. But there was, it seems, no chance of that in your case. The instinct was uncontrolled and fierce and monomaniac. (Ask your daughter, or your husband. Ask our own mother. You haven't once thought of *her*.) The only remedy was to take away its object. It was a case for surgery. When that first kind of love was thwarted, then there was just a chance that in the loneliness, in the silence, something else might begin to grow.'

'This is all nonsense—cruel and wicked nonsense. What *right* have you to say things like that about Mother-love? It is the highest and holiest feeling in human nature.'

'Pam, Pam—no natural feelings are high or low, holy or unholy, in themselves. They are all holy when God's hand is on the rein. They all go bad when they set up on their own and make themselves into false gods.'

'My love for Michael would never have gone bad. Not if we'd lived together for millions of years.'

'You are mistaken. And you must know. Haven't you met—down there—mothers who have their sons with them, in Hell? Does *their* love make them happy?'

'If you mean people like the Guthrie woman and her dreadful Bobby, of course not. I hope you're not suggesting . . . If I had Michael I'd be perfectly happy, even in that town. I wouldn't be always talking about him till everyone hated the sound of his name, which is what Winifred Guthrie does about *her* brat. I wouldn't quarrel with people for not taking enough notice of him and then be furiously jealous if they did. I wouldn't go about whining and complaining that he wasn't nice to me. Because, of course, he would be nice. Don't you dare to suggest that Michael could ever become like the Guthrie boy. There are some things I won't stand.'

'What you have seen in the Guthries is what natural affection turns to in the end if it will not be converted.'

'It's a lie. A wicked, cruel lie. How could anyone love their son more than I did? Haven't I lived only for his memory all these years?'

'That was rather a mistake, Pam. In your heart of hearts you know it was.'

'What was a mistake?'

'All that ten years' ritual of grief. Keeping his room exactly as he'd left it; keeping anniversaries; refusing to leave that house though Dick and Muriel were both wretched there.'

'Of course they didn't care. I know that. I soon learned to expect no real sympathy from them.'

'You're wrong. No man ever felt his son's death more than Dick. Not many girls loved their brothers better than Muriel. It wasn't against Michael they revolted: it was against you—against having their whole life dominated by the tyranny of the past: and not really even Michael's past, but your past.'

'You are heartless. Everyone is heartless. The past was all I had.'

'It was all you chose to have. It was the wrong way to deal with a sorrow. It was Egyptian—like embalming a dead body.'

'Oh, of course. I'm wrong. Everything I say or do is wrong, according to you.'

'But of course!' said the Spirit, shining with love and mirth so that my eyes were dazzled. 'That's what we all find when we reach this country. We've all been wrong! That's the great joke. There's no need to go on pretending one was right! After that we begin living.'

'How dare you laugh about it? Give me my boy. Do you hear? I don't care about all your rules and regulations. I don't believe in a God who keeps mother and son apart. I believe in a God of love. No one had a right to come between me and my son. Not even God. Tell Him that to His face. I want my boy, and I mean to have him. He is mine, do you understand? Mine, mine, mine, for ever and ever.'

'He will be, Pam. Everything will be yours. God Himself will be yours. But not that way. Nothing can be yours by nature.'

'What? Not my own son, born out of my own body?'

'And where is your own body now? Didn't you know that Nature draws to an end? Look! The sun is coming, over the mountains there: it will be up any moment now.'

'Michael is mine.'

'How yours? You didn't make him. Nature made him to grow in your body without your will. Even against your will . . . you sometimes forget that you didn't intend to have a baby then at all. Michael was originally an Accident.'

'Who told you that?' said the Ghost: and then, recovering itself, 'It's a lie. It's not true. And it's no business of yours. I hate your religion and I hate and despise your God. I believe in a God of Love.'

'And yet, Pam, you have no love at this moment for your own mother or for me.'

'Oh, I see! *That's* the trouble, is it? *Really,* Reginald! The idea of your being hurt because . . .'

'Lord love you!' said the Spirit with a great laugh. 'You needn't bother about that! Don't you know that you *can't* hurt anyone in this country?'

The Ghost was silent and open-mouthed for a moment; more wilted, I thought, by this reassurance than by anything else that had been said.

'Come. We will go a bit further,' said my Teacher, laying his hand on my arm.

'Why did you bring me away, Sir?' said I when we had passed out of earshot of this unhappy Ghost.

'It might take a long while, that conversation,' said my Teacher. 'And ye have heard enough to see what the choice is.'

'Is there any hope for her, Sir?'

'Aye, there's some. What she calls her love for her son has turned into a poor, prickly, astringent sort of thing. But there's still a wee spark of something that's not just herself in it. That might be blown into a flame.'

'Then some natural feelings are really better than others—I mean, are a better starting-point for the real thing?'

'Better *and* worse. There's something in natural affection which will lead it on to eternal love more easily than natural appetite could be led on. But there's also something in it which makes it easier to stop at the natural level and mistake it for the heavenly. Brass is mistaken for gold more easily than clay is. And if it finally refuses conversion its corruption will be worse than the corruption of what ye call the lower passions. It is a stronger angel, and therefore, when it falls, a fiercer devil.'

'I don't know that I dare repeat this on Earth, Sir,' said I. 'They'd say I was inhuman: they'd say I believed in total depravity: they'd say I was attacking the best and the holiest things. They'd call me . . .'

'It might do you no harm if they did,' said he with (I really thought) a twinkle in his eye.

'But could one dare—could one have the face—to go to a bereaved mother, in her misery—when one's not bereaved oneself? . . .'

'No, no, Son, that's no office of yours. You're not a good enough man for that. When your own heart's been broken it will be time for you to think of talking. But someone must say in general what's been unsaid among you this many a year: that love, as mortals understand the word, isn't enough. Every natural love will rise again and live forever in this country: but none will rise again until it has been buried.'

'The saying is almost too hard for us.'

'Ah, but it's cruel not to say it. They that know have grown afraid to speak. That is why sorrows that used to purify now only fester.'

'Keats was wrong, then, when he said he was certain of the holiness of the heart's affections.'

'I doubt if he knew clearly what he meant. But you and I must be clear. There is but one good; that is God. Everything else is good when it looks to Him and bad when it turns from Him. And the higher and mightier it is in the natural order, the more demoniac it will be if it rebels. It's not out of bad mice or bad fleas you make demons, but out of bad archangels. The false religion of lust is baser than the false religion of mother-love or patriotism or art: but lust is less likely to be made into a religion. But look!'

I saw coming towards us a Ghost who carried something on his shoulder. Like all the Ghosts, he was unsubstantial, but they differed from one another as smokes differ. Some had been whitish; this one was dark and oily. What sat on his shoulder was a little red lizard, and it was twitching its tail like a whip and whispering things in his ear. As we caught sight of him he turned his head to the reptile with a snarl of impatience. 'Shut up, I tell you!' he said. It wagged its tail and continued to whisper to him. He ceased snarling, and presently began to smile. Then he turned and started to limp westward, away from the mountains.

'Off so soon?' said a voice.

The speaker was more or less human in shape but larger than a man, and so bright that I could hardly look at him. His presence smote on my eyes and on my body too (for there was heat coming from him as well as light) like the morning sun at the beginning of a tyrannous summer day.

'Yes. I'm off,' said the Ghost. 'Thanks for all your hospitality. But it's no good, you see. I told this little chap' (here he indicated the Lizard) 'that he'd have to be quiet if he came—which he insisted on doing. Of course his stuff won't do here: I realise that. But he won't stop. I shall just have to go home.'

'Would you like me to make him quiet?' said the flaming Spirit—an angel, as I now understood.

'Of course I would,' said the Ghost.

'Then I will kill him,' said the Angel, taking a step forward.

'Oh—ah—look out! You're burning me. Keep away,' said the Ghost, retreating.

'Don't you *want* him killed?'

'You didn't say anything about *killing* him at first. I hardly meant to bother you with anything so drastic as that.'

'It's the only way,' said the Angel, whose burning hands were now very close to the Lizard. 'Shall I kill it?'

'Well, that's a further question. I'm quite open to consider it, but it's a new point, isn't it? I mean, for the moment I was only thinking about silencing it because up here—well, it's so damned embarrassing.'

'May I kill it?'

'Well, there's time to discuss that later.'

'There is no time. May I kill it?'

'Please, I never meant to be such a nuisance. Please—really—don't bother. Look! It's gone to sleep of its own accord. I'm sure it'll be all right now. Thanks ever so much.'

'May I kill it?'

'Honestly, I don't think there's the slightest necessity for that. I'm sure I shall be able to keep it in order now. I think the gradual process would be far better than killing it.'

'The gradual process is of no use at all.'

'Don't you think so? Well, I'll think over what you've said very carefully. I honestly will. In fact I'd let you kill it now, but as a matter of fact I'm not feeling frightfully well to-day. It would be most silly to do it *now*. I'd need to be in good health for the operation. Some other day, perhaps.'

'There is no other day. All days are present now.'

'Get back! You're burning me. How can I tell you to kill it? You'd kill *me* if you did.'

'It is not so.'

'Why, you're hurting me now.'

'I never said it wouldn't hurt you. I said it wouldn't kill you.'

'Oh, I know. You think I'm a coward. But it isn't that. Really it isn't. I say! Let me run back by to-night's bus and get an opinion from my own doctor. I'll come again the first moment I can.'

'This moment contains all moments.'

'Why are you torturing me? You are jeering at me. How *can* I let you tear me in pieces? If you wanted to help me, why didn't you kill the damned thing without asking me—before I knew? It would be all over by now if you had.'

'I cannot kill it against your will. It is impossible. Have I your permission?'

The Angel's hands were almost closed on the Lizard, but not quite. Then the Lizard began chattering to the Ghost so loud that even I could hear what it was saying.

'Be careful,' it said. 'He can do what he says. He can kill me. One fatal word from you and he *will!* Then you'll be without me for ever and ever. It's not natural. How could you live? You'd be only a sort of ghost, not a real man as you are now. He doesn't understand. He's only a cold, bloodless abstract thing. It may be natural for him, but it isn't for us. Yes, yes. I know there are no real pleasures now, only dreams. But aren't they better than nothing? And I'll be so good. I admit I've sometimes gone too far in the past, but I promise I won't do it again. I'll give you nothing but really nice dreams—all sweet and fresh and almost innocent. You might say, quite innocent . . .'

'Have I your permission?' said the Angel to the Ghost.

'I know it will kill me.'

'It won't. But supposing it did?'

'You're right. It would be better to be dead than to live with this creature.'

'Then I may?'

'Damn and blast you! Go on, can't you? Get it over. Do what you like,' bellowed the Ghost: but ended, whimpering, 'God help me. God help me.'

Next moment the Ghost gave a scream of agony such as I never heard on Earth. The Burning One closed his crimson grip on the reptile: twisted it, while it bit and writhed, and then flung it, broken-backed, on the turf.

'Ow! That's done for me,' gasped the Ghost, reeling backwards.

For a moment I could make out nothing distinctly. Then I saw, between me and the nearest bush, unmistakably solid but growing every moment solider, the upper arm and the shoulder of a man. Then, brighter still and stronger, the legs and hands. The neck and golden head materialised while I watched, and if my attention had not wavered I should have seen the actual completing of a man—an immense man, naked, not much smaller than the Angel. What distracted me was the fact that at the same moment something seemed to be happening to the Lizard. At first I thought the operation had failed. So far from dying, the creature was still struggling and even growing bigger as it struggled. And as it grew it changed. Its hinder parts grew rounder. The tail, still flickering, became a tail of hair that flickered between huge and glossy buttocks. Suddenly I started back, rubbing my eyes. What stood before me was the greatest stallion I have ever seen, silvery white but with mane and tail of gold. It was smooth and shining, rippled with swells of flesh and muscle, whinneying and stamping with its hoofs. At each stamp the land shook and the trees dindled.

The new-made man turned and clapped the new horse's neck. It nosed his bright body. Horse and master breathed each into the other's nostrils. The man turned from it, flung himself at the feet of the Burning One, and embraced them. When he rose I thought his face shone with tears, but it may have been only the liquid love and brightness (one cannot distinguish them in that country) which flowed from him. I had not long to think about it. In joyous haste the young man leaped upon the horse's back. Turning in his seat he waved a farewell, then nudged the stallion with his heels. They were off before I knew well what was happening. There was riding if you like! I came out as quickly as I could from among the bushes to follow them with my eyes; but already they were only like a shooting star far off on the green plain, and soon among the foothills of the mountains. Then, still like a star, I saw them winding up, scaling what seemed impossible steeps, and quicker every moment, till near the dim brow of the landscape, so high that I must strain my neck to see them, they vanished, bright themselves, into the rose-brightness of that everlasting morning.

While I still watched, I noticed that the whole plain and forest were shaking with a sound which in our world would be too large to hear, but there I could take it with joy. I knew it was not the Solid People who were singing. It was the voice of that earth, those woods and those waters. A strange archaic, inorganic noise, that came from all directions at once. The Nature or Arch-Nature of that land rejoiced to have been once more ridden, and therefore consummated, in the person of the horse. It sang,

'The Master says to our master, Come up. Share my rest and splendour till all natures that were your enemies become slaves to dance before you and backs for you to ride, and firmness for your feet to rest on.

'From beyond all place and time, out of the very Place, authority will be given you: the strengths that once opposed your will shall be obedient fire in your blood and heavenly thunder in your voice.

'Overcome us that, so overcome, we may be ourselves: we desire the beginning of your reign as we desire dawn and dew, wetness at the birth of light.

'Master, your Master has appointed you for ever: to be our King of Justice and our high Priest.'

'Do ye understand all this, my Son?' said the Teacher.

'I don't know about *all*, Sir,' said I. 'Am I right in thinking the Lizard really turned into the Horse?'

'Aye. But it was killed first. Ye'll not forget that part of the story?'

'I'll try not to, Sir. But does it mean that everything—everything— that is in us can go on to the Mountains?'

'Nothing, not even the best and noblest, can go on as it now is. Nothing, not even what is lowest and most bestial, will not be raised again if it submits to death. It is sown a natural body, it is raised a spiritual body. Flesh and blood cannot come to the Mountains. Not because they are too rank, but because they are too weak. What is a lizard compared with a stallion? Lust is a poor, weak, whimpering, whispering thing compared with that richness and energy of desire which will arise when lust has been killed.'

'But am I to tell them at home that this man's sensuality proved less of an obstacle than that poor woman's love for her son? For that was, at any rate, an excess of *love*.'

'Ye'll tell them no such thing,' he replied sternly. 'Excess of love, did ye say? There was no excess, there was defect. She loved her son too little, not too much. If she had loved him more there'd be no difficulty. I do not know how her affair will end. But it may well be that at this moment she's demanding to have him down with her in Hell. That kind is sometimes perfectly ready to plunge the soul they say they love in endless misery if only they can still in some fashion possess it. No, no. Ye must draw another lesson. Ye must ask, if the risen body even of appetite is as grand a horse as ye saw, what would the risen body of maternal love or friendship be?'

But once more my attention was diverted. 'Is there *another* river, Sir?' I asked.

12

THE REASON WHY I asked if there were another river was this. All down one long aisle of the forest the under-sides of the leafy branches had begun to tremble with dancing light; and on Earth I knew nothing so likely to produce this appearance as the reflected lights cast upward by moving water. A few moments later I realised my mistake. Some kind of procession was approaching us, and the light came from the persons who composed it.

First came bright Spirits, not the Spirits of men, who danced and scattered flowers—soundlessly falling, lightly drifting flowers, though by the standards of the ghost-world each petal would have weighed a hundred-weight and their fall would have been like the crashing of boulders. Then, on the left and right, at each side of the forest avenue, came youthful shapes, boys upon one hand, and girls upon the other. If I could remember their singing and write down the notes, no man who read that score would ever grow sick or old. Between them went musicians: and after these a lady in whose honour all this was being done.

I cannot now remember whether she was naked or clothed. If she were naked, then it must have been the almost visible penumbra of her courtesy and joy which produces in my memory the illusion of a great and shining train that followed her across the happy grass. If she were clothed, then the illusion of nakedness is doubtless due to the clarity with which her innermost spirit shone through the clothes. For clothes in that country are not a disguise: the spiritual body lives along each thread and turns them into living organs. A robe or a crown is there as much one of the wearer's features as a lip or an eye.

But I have forgotten. And only partly do I remember the unbearable beauty of her face.

'Is it? . . . is it?' I whispered to my guide.

'Not at all,' said he. 'It's someone ye'll never have heard of. Her name on Earth was Sarah Smith and she lived at Golders Green.'

'She seems to be . . . well, a person of particular importance?'

'Aye. She is one of the great ones. Ye have heard that fame in this country and fame on Earth are two quite different things.'

'And who are these gigantic people . . . look! They're like emeralds . . . who are dancing and throwing flowers before her?'

'Haven't ye read your Milton? *A thousand liveried angels lackey her.*'

'And who are all these young men and women on each side?'

'They are her sons and daughters.'

'She must have had a very large family, Sir.'

'Every young man or boy that met her became her son—even if it was only the boy that brought the meat to her back door. Every girl that met her was her daughter.'

'Isn't that a bit hard on their own parents?'

'No. There *are* those that steal other people's children. But her motherhood was of a different kind. Those on whom it fell went back to their natural parents loving them more. Few men looked on her without becoming, in a certain fashion, her lovers. But it was the kind of love that made them not less true, but truer, to their own wives.'

'And how . . . but hullo! What are all these animals? A cat—two cats—dozens of cats. And all these dogs . . . why, I can't count them. And the birds. And the horses.'

'They are her beasts.'

'Did she keep a sort of zoo? I mean, this is a bit too much.'

'Every beast and bird that came near her had its place in her love. In her they became themselves. And now the abundance of life she has in Christ from the Father flows over into them.'

I looked at my Teacher in amazement.

'Yes,' he said. 'It is like when you throw a stone into a pool, and the concentric waves spread out further and further. Who knows where it will end? Redeemed humanity is still young, it has hardly come to its full strength. But already there is joy enough in the little finger of a great saint such as yonder lady to waken all the dead things of the universe into life.'

While we spoke the Lady was steadily advancing towards us, but it was not at us she looked. Following the direction of her eyes, I turned and saw an oddly-shaped phantom approaching. Or rather two phantoms: a great tall Ghost, horribly thin and shaky, who seemed to be leading on a chain another Ghost no bigger than an organ-grinder's monkey. The taller Ghost wore a soft black hat, and he reminded me of something that my memory could not quite recover. Then, when he had come within a few feet of the Lady he spread out his lean, shaky hand flat on his chest with the fingers wide apart, and exclaimed in a hollow voice, 'At last!' All at once I realised what it was that he had put me in mind of. He was like a seedy actor of the old school.

'Darling! At last!' said the Lady. 'Good Heavens!' thought I. 'Surely she can't —', and then I noticed two things. In the first place, I noticed that the little Ghost was not being led by the big one. It was the dwarf-ish figure that held the chain in its hand and the theatrical figure that wore the collar round its neck. In the second place, I noticed that the Lady was looking solely at the dwarf Ghost. She seemed to think it was the Dwarf who had addressed her, or else she was deliberately ignoring the other. On the poor dwarf she turned her eyes. Love shone not from her face only, but from all her limbs, as if it were some liquid in which she had just been bathing. Then, to my dismay, she came nearer. She stooped down and kissed the Dwarf. It made one shudder to see her in such close contact with that cold, damp, shrunken thing. But she did not shudder.

'Frank,' she said, 'before anything else, forgive me. For all I ever did wrong and for all I did not do right since the first day we met, I ask your pardon.'

I looked properly at the Dwarf for the first time now: or perhaps, when he received her kiss he became a little more visible. One could just make out the sort of face he must have had when he was a man: a little, oval, freckled face with a weak chin and a tiny wisp of unsuccessful moustache. He gave her a glance, not a full look. He was watching the Tragedian out of the corner of his eyes. Then he gave a jerk to the chain: and it was the Tragedian, not he, who answered the Lady.

'There, there,' said the Tragedian. 'We'll say no more about it. We all make mistakes.' With the words there came over his features a ghastly contortion which, I think, was meant for an indulgently playful smile. 'We'll say no more,' he continued. 'It's not myself I'm thinking about. It is you. That is what has been continually on my mind—all these years. The thought of you—you here alone, breaking your heart about me.'

'But now,' said the Lady to the Dwarf, 'you can set all that aside. Never think like that again. It is all over.'

Her beauty brightened so that I could hardly see anything else, and under that sweet compulsion the Dwarf really looked at her for the first time. For a second I thought he was growing more like a man. He opened his mouth. He himself was going to speak this time. But oh, the disappointment when the words came!

'You missed me?' he croaked in a small, bleating voice.

Yet even then she was not taken aback. Still the love and courtesy flowed from her.

'Dear, you will understand about that very soon,' she said. 'But to-day —.'

What happened next gave me a shock. The Dwarf and Tragedian spoke in unison, not to her but to one another. 'You'll notice,' they warned one another, 'she hasn't answered our question.' I realised then that they were one person, or rather that both were the remains of what had once been a person. The Dwarf again rattled the chain.

'You missed me?' said the Tragedian to the Lady, throwing a dreadful theatrical tremor into his voice.

'Dear friend,' said the Lady, still attending exclusively to the Dwarf, 'you may be happy about that and about everything else. Forget all about it for ever.'

And really, for a moment, I thought the Dwarf was going to obey: partly because the outlines of his face became a little clearer, and partly because the invitation to all joy, singing out of her whole being like a bird's song on an April evening, seemed to me such that no creature could resist it. Then he hesitated. And then—once more he and his accomplice spoke in unison.

'Of course it would be rather fine and magnanimous not to press the point,' they said to one another. 'But can we be sure she'd notice? We've done these sort of things before. There was the time we let her have the last stamp in the house to write to her mother and said nothing although she *had* known we wanted to write a letter ourself. We'd thought she'd remember and see how unselfish we'd been. But she never did. And there was the time . . . oh, lots and lots of times!' So the Dwarf gave a shake to the chain and —

'I can't forget it,' cried the Tragedian. 'And I won't forget it, either. I could forgive them all they've done to me. But for your miseries —.'

'Oh, don't you understand?' said the Lady. 'There *are* no miseries here.'

'Do you mean to say,' answered the Dwarf, as if this new idea had made him quite forget the Tragedian for a moment, 'do you mean to say you've been *happy?*'

'Didn't you want me to be? But no matter. Want it now. Or don't think about it at all.'

The Dwarf blinked at her. One could see an unheard-of idea trying to enter his little mind: one could see even that there was for him some sweetness in it. For a second he had almost let the chain go: then, as if it were his life-line, he clutched it once more.

'Look here,' said the Tragedian. 'We've got to face this.' He was using his 'manly' bullying tone this time: the one for bringing women to their senses.

'Darling,' said the Lady to the Dwarf, 'there's nothing to face. You don't want me to have been miserable for misery's sake. You only think I must have been if I loved you. But if you'll only wait you'll see that isn't so.'

'Love!' said the Tragedian striking his forehead with his hand: then, a few notes deeper, 'Love! Do you know the meaning of the word?'

'How should I not?' said the Lady. 'I am in love. *In* love, do you understand? Yes, now I love truly.'

'You mean,' said the Tragedian, 'you mean—you did *not* love me truly in the old days.'

'Only in a poor sort of way,' she answered. 'I have asked you to forgive me. There was a little real love in it. But what we called love down there was mostly the craving to be loved. In the main I loved you for my own sake: because I needed you.'

'And now!' said the Tragedian with a hackneyed gesture of despair. 'Now, you need me no more?'

'But of course not!' said the Lady; and her smile made me wonder how both the phantoms could refrain from crying out with joy.

'What needs could I have,' she said, 'now that I have all? I am full now, not empty. I am in Love Himself, not lonely. Strong, not weak. You shall be the same. Come and see. We shall have no *need* for one another now: we can begin to love truly.'

But the Tragedian was still striking attitudes. 'She needs me no more—no more. No more,' he said in a choking voice to no one in particular. 'Would to God,' he continued, but he was now pronouncing it *Gud*—'would to Gud I had seen her lying dead at my feet before I heard those words. Lying dead at my feet. Lying dead at my feet.'

I do not know how long the creature intended to go on repeating the phrase, for the Lady put an end to that. 'Frank! Frank!' she cried in a voice that made the whole wood ring. 'Look at me. *Look* at me. What are you doing with that great, ugly doll? Let go of the chain. Send it away. It is *you* I want. Don't you see what nonsense it's talking.' Merriment danced in her eyes. She was sharing a joke with the Dwarf, right over the head of the Tragedian. Something not at all unlike a smile struggled to appear on the Dwarf's face. For he *was* looking at her now. Her laughter was past his first defences. He was struggling hard to keep it out, but already with imperfect success. Against his will, he was even growing a little bigger. 'Oh, you great goose,' said she. 'What is the good of talking like that here? You know as well as I do that you *did* see me lying dead years and years ago. Not "at your feet", of course, but on a bed in a nursing home. A very good nursing home it was too. Matron would never have dreamed of leaving bodies lying about the floor! It's ridiculous for that doll to try to be impressive about death *here*. It just won't work.'

13

I DO NOT know that I ever saw anything more terrible than the struggle of that Dwarf Ghost against joy. For he had almost been overcome. Somewhere, incalculable ages ago, there must have been gleams of humour and reason in him. For one moment, while she looked at him in her love and mirth, he saw the absurdity of the Tragedian. For one moment he did not at all misunderstand her laughter: he too must once have known that no people find each other more absurd than lovers. But the light that reached him, reached him against his will. This was not the meeting he had pictured; he would not accept it. Once more he clutched at his death-line, and at once the Tragedian spoke.

'You dare to laugh at it!' it stormed. 'To my face? And this is my reward. Very well. It is fortunate that you give yourself no concern about my fate. Otherwise you might be sorry afterwards to think that you had driven me back to Hell. What? Do you think I'd stay *now?* Thank you. I believe I'm fairly quick at recognising where I'm not wanted. "Not needed" was the exact expression, if I remember rightly.'

From this time on the Dwarf never spoke again: but still the Lady addressed it.

'Dear, no one sends you back. Here is all joy. Everything bids you stay.' But the Dwarf was growing smaller even while she spoke.

'Yes,' said the Tragedian. 'On terms you might offer to a dog. I happen to have some self-respect left, and I see that my going will make no difference to you. It is nothing to you that I go back to the cold and the gloom, the lonely, lonely streets —.'

'Don't, don't, Frank,' said the Lady. 'Don't let it talk like that.' But the Dwarf was now so small that she had dropped on her knees to speak to it. The Tragedian caught her words greedily as a dog catches a bone.

'Ah, you can't bear to hear it!' he shouted with miserable triumph. 'That was always the way. *You* must be sheltered. Grim realities must be kept out of *your* sight. You who can be happy without me, forgetting me! You don't want even to hear of my sufferings. You say, *don't*. Don't tell you. Don't make you unhappy. Don't break in on your sheltered, self-centred little heaven. And this is the reward —.'

She stooped still lower to speak to the Dwarf which was now a figure no bigger than a kitten, hanging on the end of the chain with his feet off the ground.

'That wasn't why I said, Don't,' she answered. 'I meant, stop acting. It's no good. He is killing you. Let go of that chain. Even now.'

'Acting,' screamed the Tragedian. 'What do you mean?'

The Dwarf was now so small that I could not distinguish him from the chain to which he was clinging. And now for the first time I could not be certain whether the Lady was addressing him or the Tragedian.

'Quick,' she said. 'There is still time. Stop it. Stop it at once.'

'Stop what?'

'Using pity, other people's pity, in the wrong way. We have all done it a bit on earth, you know. Pity was meant to be a spur that drives joy to help misery. But it can be used the wrong way round. It can be used for a kind of blackmailing. Those who choose misery can hold joy up to ransom, by pity. You see, I know now. Even as a child you did it. Instead of saying you were sorry, you went and sulked in the attic . . . because you knew that sooner or later one of your sisters would say, "I can't bear to think of him sitting up there alone, crying." You used their pity to blackmail them, and they gave in in the end. And afterwards, when we were married . . . oh, it doesn't matter, if only you will *stop* it.'

'And *that*,' said the Tragedian, 'that is all you have understood of me, after all these years.' I don't know what had become of the Dwarf Ghost by now. Perhaps it was climbing up the chain like an insect: perhaps it was somehow absorbed into the chain.

'No, Frank, not *here*,' said the Lady. 'Listen to reason. Did you think joy was created to live always under that threat? Always defenceless against those who would rather be miserable than have their self-will crossed? For it was real misery. I know that now. You made yourself really wretched. That you can still do. But you can no longer communicate your wretchedness. Everything becomes more and more itself. Here is joy that cannot be shaken. Our light can swallow up your darkness: but your darkness cannot now infect our light. No, no, no. Come to us. We will not go to you. Can you really have thought that love and joy would always be at the mercy of frowns and sighs? Did you not know they were stronger than their opposites?'

'Love? How dare *you* use that sacred word?' said the Tragedian. At the same moment he gathered up the chain which had now for some time been swinging uselessly at his side, and somehow disposed of it. I am not quite sure, but I think he swallowed it. Then for the first time it became clear that the Lady saw and addressed him only.

'Where is Frank?' she said. 'And who are you, Sir? I never knew you. Perhaps you had better leave me. Or stay, if you prefer. If it would help you and if it were possible I would go down with you into Hell: but you cannot bring Hell into me.'

'You do not love me,' said the Tragedian in a thin bat-like voice: and he was now very difficult to see.

'I cannot love a lie,' said the Lady. 'I cannot love the thing which is not. I am in Love, and out of it I will not go.'

There was no answer. The Tragedian had vanished. The Lady was alone in that woodland place, and a brown bird went hopping past her, bending with its light feet the grasses I could not bend.

Presently the lady got up and began to walk away. The other Bright Spirits came forward to receive her, singing as they came:

'The Happy Trinity is her home: nothing can trouble her joy.
She is the bird that evades every net: the wild deer that leaps every pitfall.
Like the mother bird to its chickens or a shield to the arm'd knight: so is
    the Lord to her mind, in His unchanging lucidity.
Bogies will not scare her in the dark: bullets will not frighten her in the day.
Falsehoods tricked out as truths assail her in vain: she sees through the lie
    as if it were glass.
The invisible germ will not harm her: nor yet the glittering sun-stroke.
A thousand fail to solve the problem, ten thousand choose the wrong
    turning: but she passes safely through.
He details immortal gods to attend her: upon every road where she must
    travel.

They take her hand at hard places: she will not stub her toes in the dark.
She may walk among Lions and rattlesnakes: among dinosaurs and
  nurseries of lionets.
He fills her brim-full with immensity of life: he leads her to see the world's
  desire.'

'And yet . . . and yet . . . ,' said I to my Teacher, when all the shapes and the singing had passed some distance away into the forest, 'even now I am not quite sure. Is it really tolerable that she should be untouched by his misery, even his self-made misery?'

'Would ye rather he still had the power of tormenting her? He did it many a day and many a year in their earthly life.'

'Well, no. I suppose I don't want that.'

'What then?'

'I hardly know, Sir. What some people say on Earth is that the final loss of one soul gives the lie to all the joy of those who are saved.'

'Ye see it does not.'

'I feel in a way that it ought to.'

'That sounds very merciful: but see what lurks behind it.'

'What?'

'The demand of the loveless and the self-imprisoned that they should be allowed to blackmail the universe: that till they consent to be happy (on their own terms) no one else shall taste joy: that theirs should be the final power; that Hell should be able to *veto* Heaven.'

'I don't know what I want, Sir.'

'Son, son, it must be one way or the other. Either the day must come when joy prevails and all the makers of misery are no longer able to infect it: or else for ever and ever the makers of misery can destroy in others the happiness they reject for themselves. I know it has a grand sound to say ye'll accept no salvation which leaves even one creature in the dark outside. But watch that sophistry or ye'll make a Dog in a Manger the tyrant of the universe.'

'But dare one say—it is horrible to say—that Pity must ever die?'

'Ye must distinguish. The action of Pity will live for ever: but the passion of Pity will not. The passion of Pity, the Pity we merely suffer, the ache that draws men to concede what should not be conceded and to flatter when they should speak truth, the pity that has cheated many a woman out of her virginity and many a statesman out of his honesty—

that will die. It was used as a weapon by bad men against good ones: their weapon will be broken.'

'And what is the other kind—the action?'

'It's a weapon on the other side. It leaps quicker than light from the highest place to the lowest to bring healing and joy, whatever the cost to itself. It changes darkness into light and evil into good. But it will not, at the cunning tears of Hell, impose on good the tyranny of evil. Every disease that submits to a cure shall be cured: but we will not call blue yellow to please those who insist on still having jaundice, nor make a midden of the world's garden for the sake of some who cannot abide the smell of roses.'

'You say it will go down to the lowest, Sir. But she didn't go down with him to Hell. She didn't even see him off by the bus.'

'Where would ye have had her go?'

'Why, where we all came from by that bus. The big gulf, beyond the edge of the cliff. Over there. You can't see it from here, but you must know the place I mean.'

My Teacher gave a curious smile. 'Look,' he said, and with the word he went down on his hands and knees. I did the same (how it hurt my knees!) and presently saw that he had plucked a blade of grass. Using its thin end as a pointer, he made me see, after I had looked very closely, a crack in the soil so small that I could not have identified it without this aid.

'I cannot be certain,' he said, 'that this *is* the crack ye came up through. But through a crack no bigger than that ye certainly came.'

'But—but,' I gasped with a feeling of bewilderment not unlike terror. 'I saw an infinite abyss. And cliffs towering up and up. And then *this* country on top of the cliffs.'

'Aye. But the voyage was not mere locomotion. That bus, and all you inside it, were increasing *in size*.'[1]

'Do you mean then that Hell—all that infinite empty town—is down in some little crack like this?'

'Yes. All Hell is smaller than one pebble of your earthly world: but it is smaller than one atom of *this* world, the Real World. Look at yon butterfly. If it swallowed all Hell, Hell would not be big enough to do it any harm or to have any taste.'

---

[1] This method of travel also I learned from the 'scientifictionists'.

'It seems big enough when you're in it, Sir.'

'And yet all loneliness, angers, hatreds, envies and itchings that it contains, if rolled into one single experience and put into the scale against the least moment of the joy that is felt by the least in Heaven, would have no weight that could be registered at all. Bad cannot succeed even in being bad as truly as good is good. If all Hell's miseries together entered the consciousness of yon wee yellow bird on the bough there, they would be swallowed up without trace, as if one drop of ink had been dropped into that Great Ocean to which your terrestrial Pacific itself is only a molecule.'

'I see,' said I at last. 'She couldn't *fit* into Hell.'

He nodded. 'There's not room for her,' he said. 'Hell could not open its mouth wide enough.'

'And she couldn't make herself smaller?—like Alice, you know.'

'Nothing like small enough. For a damned soul is nearly nothing: it is shrunk, shut up in itself. Good beats upon the damned incessantly as sound waves beat on the ears of the deaf, but they cannot receive it. Their fists are clenched, their teeth are clenched, their eyes fast shut. First they will not, in the end they cannot, open their hands for gifts, or their mouth for food, or their eyes to see.'

'Then no one can ever reach them?'

'Only the Greatest of all can make Himself small enough to enter Hell. For the higher a thing is, the lower it can descend—a man can sympathise with a horse but a horse cannot sympathise with a rat. Only One has descended into Hell.'

'And will He ever do so again?'

'It was not once long ago that He did it. Time does not work that way when once ye have left the Earth. All moments that have been or shall be were, or are, present in the moment of His descending. There is no spirit in prison to Whom He did not preach.'

'And some hear him?'

'Aye.'

'In your own books, Sir,' said I, 'you were a Universalist. You talked as if all men would be saved. And St. Paul too.'

'Ye can know nothing of the end of all things, or nothing expressible in those terms. It may be, as the Lord said to the Lady Julian, that all will be well, and all will be well, and all manner of things will be well. But it's ill talking of such questions.'

'Because they are too terrible, Sir?'

'No. Because all answers deceive. If ye put the question from within Time and are asking about possibilities, the answer is certain. The choice of ways is before you. Neither is closed. Any man may choose eternal death. Those who choose it will have it. But if ye are trying to leap on into eternity, if ye are trying to see the final state of all things as it *will* be (for so ye must speak) when there are no more possibilities left but only the Real, then ye ask what cannot be answered to mortal ears. Time is the very lens through which ye see—small and clear, as men see through the wrong end of a telescope—something that would otherwise be too big for ye to see at all. That thing is Freedom: the gift whereby ye most resemble your Maker and are yourselves parts of eternal reality. But ye can see it only through the lens of Time, in a little clear picture, through the inverted telescope. It is a picture of moments following one another and yourself in each moment making some choice that might have been otherwise. Neither the temporal succession nor the phantom of what ye might have chosen and didn't is itself Freedom. They are a lens. The picture is a symbol: but it's truer than any philosophical theorem (or, perhaps, than any mystic's vision) that claims to go behind it. For every attempt to see the shape of eternity except through the lens of Time destroys your knowledge of Freedom. Witness the doctrine of Predestination which shows (truly enough) that eternal reality is not waiting for a future in which to be real; but at the price of removing Freedom which is the deeper truth of the two. And wouldn't Universalism do the same? Ye *cannot* know eternal reality by a definition. Time itself, and all acts and events that fill Time, are the definition, and it must be lived. The Lord said we were gods. How long could ye bear to look (without Time's lens) on the greatness of your own soul and the eternal reality of her choice?'

14

AND SUDDENLY ALL was changed. I saw a great assembly of gigantic forms all motionless, all in deepest silence, standing forever about a little silver table and looking upon it. And on the table there were little figures like chessmen who went to and fro doing this and that. And I knew that each chessman was the idolum or puppet representative of some of the great presences that stood by. And the acts and motions of each chessman were a moving portrait, a mimicry or pantomime, which delineated the inmost nature of his giant master. And these chessmen are men and women as they appear to themselves and to one another in this world. And the silver table is Time. And those who stand and watch are the immortal souls of those same men and women. Then vertigo and terror seized me and, clutching at my Teacher, I said, 'Is *that* the truth? Then is all that I have been seeing in this country false? These conversations between the Spirits and the Ghosts—were they only the mimicry of choices that had really been made long ago?'

'Or might ye not as well say, anticipations of a choice to be made at the end of all things? But ye'd do better to say neither. Ye saw the choices a bit more clearly than ye could see them on Earth: the lens was clearer. But it was still seen through the lens. Do not ask of a vision in a dream more than a vision in a dream can give.'

'A dream? Then—then—am I not really here, Sir?'

'No, Son,' said he kindly, taking my hand in his. 'It is not so good as that. The bitter drink of death is still before you. Ye are only dreaming. And if ye come to tell of what ye have seen, make it plain that it was but a dream. See ye make it very plain. Give no poor fool the pretext to think ye are claiming knowledge of what no mortal knows. I'll have no Swedenborgs and no Vale Owens among my children.'

'God forbid, Sir,' said I, trying to look very wise.

'He *has* forbidden it. That's what I'm telling ye.' As he said this he looked more Scotch than ever. I was gazing steadfastly on his face. The vision of the chessmen had faded, and once more the quiet woods in the cool light before sunrise were about us. Then, still looking at his face, I saw there something that sent a quiver through my whole body. I stood at that moment with my back to the East and the mountains, and he, facing me, looked towards them. His face flushed with a new light. A fern, thirty yards behind him, turned golden. The eastern side of every tree-trunk grew bright. Shadows deepened. All the time there had been bird noises, trillings, chatterings, and the like; but now suddenly the full chorus was poured from every branch; cocks were crowing, there was music of hounds, and horns; above all this ten thousand tongues of men and woodland angels and the wood itself sang. 'It comes, it comes!' they sang. 'Sleepers awake! It comes, it comes, it comes.' One dreadful glance over my shoulder I essayed—not long enough to see (or did I see?) the rim of the sunrise that shoots Time dead with golden arrows and puts to flight all phantasmal shapes. Screaming, I buried my face in the fold of my Teacher's robe. 'The morning! The morning!' I cried, 'I am caught by the morning and I am a ghost.' But it was too late. The light, like solid blocks, intolerable of edge and weight, came thundering upon my head. Next moment the folds of my Teacher's garment were only the folds of the old ink-stained cloth on my study table which I had pulled down with me as I fell from my chair. The blocks of light were only the books which I had pulled off with it, falling about my head. I awoke in a cold room, hunched on the floor beside a black and empty grate, the clock striking three, and the siren howling overhead.

THE PROBLEM OF PAIN

To The Inklings

The Son of God suffered unto the death, not that men might not suffer, but that their sufferings might be like His.

GEORGE MACDONALD,
UNSPOKEN SERMONS, FIRST SERIES

THE PROBLEM OF PAIN
CONTENTS

PREFACE

WHEN MR ASHLEY Sampson suggested to me the writing of this book, I asked leave to be allowed to write it anonymously, since, if I were to say what I really thought about pain, I should be forced to make statements of such apparent fortitude that they would become ridiculous if anyone knew who made them. Anonymity was rejected as inconsistent with the series; but Mr Sampson pointed out that I could write a preface explaining that I did not live up to my own principles! This exhilarating programme I am now carrying out. Let me confess at once, in the words of good Walter Hilton, that throughout this book 'I feel myself so far from true feeling of that I speak, that I can naught else but cry mercy and desire after it as I may'.[1] Yet for that very reason there is one criticism which cannot be brought against me. No one can say 'He jests at scars who never felt a wound', for I have never for one moment been in a state of mind to which even the imagination of serious pain was less than intolerable. If any man is safe from the danger of underestimating this adversary, I am that man. I must add, too, that the only purpose of the book is to solve the intellectual problem raised by suffering; for the far higher task of teaching fortitude and patience I was never fool enough to suppose myself qualified, nor have I anything to offer my readers except my conviction that when pain is to be borne, a little courage helps more than much knowledge, a little human sympathy more than much courage, and the least tincture of the love of God more than all.

---

[1] *Scale of Perfection*, I, xvi.

If any real theologian reads these pages he will very easily see that they are the work of a layman and an amateur. Except in the last two chapters, parts of which are admittedly speculative, I have believed myself to be restating ancient and orthodox doctrines. If any parts of the book are 'original', in the sense of being novel or unorthodox, they are so against my will and as a result of my ignorance. I write, of course, as a layman of the Church of England: but I have tried to assume nothing that is not professed by all baptised and communicating Christians.

As this is not a work of erudition I have taken little pains to trace ideas or quotations to their sources when they were not easily recoverable. Any theologian will see easily enough what, and how little, I have read.

C. S. LEWIS

MAGDALEN COLLEGE,

OXFORD, 1940

I

INTRODUCTORY

*I wonder at the hardihood with which such persons
undertake to talk about God. In a treatise addressed to
infidels they begin with a chapter proving the existence
of God from the works of Nature . . . this only gives
their readers grounds for thinking that the proofs of our
religion are very weak. . . . It is a remarkable fact that
no canonical writer has ever used Nature to prove God.*

PASCAL, PENSÉES, IV, 242, 243

NOT MANY YEARS ago when I was an atheist, if anyone had asked me,
'Why do you not believe in God?' my reply would have run something
like this: 'Look at the universe we live in. By far the greatest part of it consists of empty space, completely dark and unimaginably cold. The bodies
which move in this space are so few and so small in comparison with the
space itself that even if every one of them were known to be crowded as
full as it could hold with perfectly happy creatures, it would still be difficult to believe that life and happiness were more than a by-product to
the power that made the universe. As it is, however, the scientists think it
likely that very few of the suns of space—perhaps none of them except
our own—have any planets; and in our own system it is improbable that
any planet except the Earth sustains life. And Earth herself existed with-

out life for millions of years and may exist for millions more when life has left her. And what is it like while it lasts? It is so arranged that all the forms of it can live only by preying upon one another. In the lower forms this process entails only death, but in the higher there appears a new quality called consciousness which enables it to be attended with pain. The creatures cause pain by being born, and live by inflicting pain, and in pain they mostly die. In the most complex of all the creatures, Man, yet another quality appears, which we call reason, whereby he is enabled to foresee his own pain which henceforth is preceded with acute mental suffering, and to foresee his own death while keenly desiring permanence. It also enables men by a hundred ingenious contrivances to inflict a great deal more pain than they otherwise could have done on one another and on the irrational creatures. This power they have exploited to the full. Their history is largely a record of crime, war, disease, and terror, with just sufficient happiness interposed to give them, while it lasts, an agonised apprehension of losing it, and, when it is lost, the poignant misery of remembering. Every now and then they improve their condition a little and what we call a civilisation appears. But all civilisations pass away and, even while they remain, inflict peculiar sufferings of their own probably sufficient to outweigh what alleviations they may have brought to the normal pains of man. That our own civilisation has done so, no one will dispute; that it will pass away like all its predecessors is surely probable. Even if it should not, what then? The race is doomed. Every race that comes into being in any part of the universe is doomed; for the universe, they tell us, is running down, and will sometime be a uniform infinity of homogeneous matter at a low temperature. All stories will come to nothing: all life will turn out in the end to have been a transitory and senseless contortion upon the idiotic face of infinite matter. If you ask me to believe that this is the work of a benevolent and omnipotent spirit, I reply that all the evidence points in the opposite direction. Either there is no spirit behind the universe, or else a spirit indifferent to good and evil, or else an evil spirit.'

There was one question which I never dreamed of raising. I never noticed that the very strength and facility of the pessimists' case at once poses us a problem. If the universe is so bad, or even half so bad, how on earth did human beings ever come to attribute it to the activity of a wise and good Creator? Men are fools, perhaps; but hardly so foolish as that. The direct inference from black to white, from evil flower to virtuous root, from senseless work to a workman infinitely wise, staggers belief. The spectacle of the universe as revealed by experience can never have been the ground of religion: it must always have been something in spite of which religion, acquired from a different source, was held.

It would be an error to reply that our ancestors were ignorant and therefore entertained pleasing illusions about nature which the progress of science has since dispelled. For centuries, during which all men believed, the nightmare size and emptiness of the universe was already known. You will read in some books that the men of the Middle Ages thought the Earth flat and the stars near, but that is a lie. Ptolemy had told them that the Earth was a mathematical point without size in relation to the distance of the fixed stars—a distance which one medieval popular text estimates as a hundred and seventeen million miles. And in times yet earlier, even from the beginnings, men must have got the same sense of hostile immensity from a more obvious source. To prehistoric man the neighbouring forest must have been infinite enough, and the utterly alien and infest which we have to fetch from the thought of cosmic rays and cooling suns, came snuffing and howling nightly to his very doors. Certainly at all periods the pain and waste of human life was equally obvious. Our own religion begins among the Jews, a people squeezed between great warlike empires, continually defeated and led captive, familiar as Poland or Armenia with the tragic story of the conquered. It is mere nonsense to put pain among the discoveries of science. Lay down this book and reflect for five minutes on the fact that all the great religions were first preached, and long practised, in a world without chloroform.

At all times, then, an inference from the course of events in this world to the goodness and wisdom of the Creator would have been equally preposterous; and it was never made.[1] Religion has a different origin. In what follows it must be understood that I am not *primarily* arguing the truth of Christianity but describing its origin—a task, in my view, necessary if we are to put the problem of pain in its right setting.

In all developed religion we find three strands or elements, and in Christianity one more. The first of these is what Professor Otto calls the experience of the *Numinous*. Those who have not met this term may be introduced to it by the following device. Suppose you were told there was

---

[1] i.e., never made at the beginnings of a religion. *After* belief in God has been accepted, 'theodicies' explaining, or explaining away, the miseries of life, will naturally appear often enough.

a tiger in the next room: you would know that you were in danger and would probably feel fear. But if you were told 'There is a ghost in the next room', and believed it, you would feel, indeed, what is often called fear, but of a different kind. It would not be based on the knowledge of danger, for no one is primarily afraid of what a ghost may do to him, but of the mere fact that it is a ghost. It is 'uncanny' rather than dangerous, and the special kind of fear it excites may be called Dread. With the Uncanny one has reached the fringes of the Numinous. Now suppose that you were told simply 'There is a mighty spirit in the room', and believed it. Your feelings would then be even less like the mere fear of danger: but the disturbance would be profound. You would feel wonder and a certain shrinking—a sense of inadequacy to cope with such a visitant and of prostration before it—an emotion which might be expressed in Shakespeare's words 'Under it my genius is rebuked'. This feeling may be described as awe, and the object which excites it as the *Numinous*.

Now nothing is more certain than that man, from a very early period, began to believe that the universe was haunted by spirits. Professor Otto perhaps assumes too easily that from the very first such spirits were regarded with numinous awe. This is impossible to prove for the very good reason that utterances expressing awe of the Numinous and utterances expressing mere fear of danger may use identical language—as we can still say that we are 'afraid' of a ghost or 'afraid' of a rise in prices. It is therefore theoretically possible that there was a time when men regarded these spirits simply as dangerous and felt towards them just as they felt towards tigers. What is certain is that now, at any rate, the numinous experience exists and that if we start from ourselves we can trace it a long way back.

A modern example may be found (if we are not too proud to seek it there) in *The Wind in the Willows* where Rat and Mole approach Pan on the island.

'"Rat," he found breath to whisper, shaking, "Are you afraid?" "Afraid?" murmured the Rat, his eyes shining with unutterable love. "Afraid? of Him? O, never, never. And yet—and yet—O Mole, I am afraid."'

Going back about a century we find copious examples in Wordsworth—perhaps the finest being that passage in the first book of the *Prelude* where he describes his experience while rowing on the lake in the stolen boat. Going back further we get a very pure and strong example in Malory,[2] when Galahad 'began to tremble right hard when the deadly (= mortal) flesh began to behold the spiritual things'. At the beginning of our era it finds expression in the Apocalypse where the writer fell at the feet of the risen Christ 'as one dead'. In Pagan literature we find Ovid's picture of the dark grove on the Aventine of which you would say at a glance *numen inest*[3]—the place is haunted, or there is a Presence here; and Virgil gives us the palace of Latinus 'awful (*horrendum*) with woods and sanctity (*religione*) of elder days'.[4] A Greek fragment attributed, but improbably, to Aeschylus, tells us of earth, sea, and mountain shaking beneath the 'dread eye of their Master'.[5] And far further back Ezekiel tells us of the 'rings' in his Theophany that 'they were so high that they were dreadful':[6] and Jacob, rising from sleep, says 'How dreadful is this place!'[7]

We do not know how far back in human history this feeling goes. The earliest men almost certainly believed in things which would excite the feeling in us if *we* believed in them, and it seems therefore probable that numinous awe is as old as humanity itself. But our main concern is not with its dates. The important thing is that somehow or other it has come into existence, and is widespread, and does not disappear from the mind with the growth of knowledge and civilisation.

Now this awe is not the result of an inference from the visible universe. There is no possibility of arguing from mere danger to the uncanny, still less to the fully Numinous. You may say that it seems to you very natural that early man, being surrounded by real dangers, and therefore frightened, should invent the uncanny and the Numinous. In a sense it is, but let us understand what we mean. You feel it to be natural because, sharing human nature with your remote ancestors, you can imagine yourself reacting to perilous solitudes in the same way; and this reaction is indeed 'natural' in the sense of being in accord with human nature. But it is not in the least 'natural' in the sense that the idea of the uncanny or the Numinous is already contained in the idea of the dangerous, or that

---

[2] xvii, xxii.

[3] *Fasti*, iii, 296.

[4] *Aen.* vii, 172.

[5] Fragm. 464. Sidgwick's edition.

[6] Ezekiel 1:18.

[7] Genesis 28:17.

any perception of danger or any dislike of the wounds and death which it may entail could give the slightest conception of ghostly dread or numinous awe to an intelligence which did not already understand them. When man passes from physical fear to dread and awe, he makes a sheer jump, and apprehends something which could never be *given*, as danger is, by the physical facts and logical deductions from them. Most attempts to explain the Numinous presuppose the thing to be explained—as when anthropologists derive it from fear of the dead, without explaining why dead men (assuredly the least dangerous kind of men) should have attracted this peculiar feeling. Against all such attempts we must insist that dread and awe are in a different dimension from fear. They are in the nature of an interpretation man gives to the universe, or an impression he gets from it; and just as no enumeration of the physical qualities of a beautiful object could ever include its beauty, or give the faintest hint of what we mean by beauty to a creature without aesthetic experience, so no factual description of any human environment could include the uncanny and the Numinous or even hint at them. There seem, in fact, to be only two views we can hold about awe. Either it is a mere twist in the human mind, corresponding to nothing objective and serving no biological function, yet showing no tendency to disappear from that mind at its fullest development in poet, philosopher, or saint: or else it is a direct experience of the really supernatural, to which the name Revelation might properly be given.

The Numinous is not the same as the morally good, and a man overwhelmed with awe is likely, if left to himself, to think the numinous object 'beyond good and evil'. This brings us to the second strand or element in religion. All the human beings that history has heard of acknowledge some kind of morality; that is, they feel towards certain proposed actions the experiences expressed by the words 'I ought' or 'I ought not'. These experiences resemble awe in one respect, namely that they cannot be logically deduced from the environment and physical experiences of the man who undergoes them. You can shuffle 'I want' and 'I am forced' and 'I shall be well advised' and 'I dare not' as long as you please without getting out of them the slightest hint of 'ought' and 'ought not'. And, once again, attempts to resolve the moral experience into something else always presuppose the very thing they are trying to explain—as when a famous psychoanalyst deduces it from prehistoric parricide. If the parricide produced a sense of guilt, that was because men felt that they ought not to have committed it: if they did not so feel, it could produce no sense of guilt. Morality, like numinous awe, is a jump; in it, man goes beyond anything that can be 'given' in the facts of experience. And it has one characteristic too remarkable to be ignored. The moralities accepted among men may differ—though not, at bottom, so widely as is often claimed—but they all agree in prescribing a behaviour which their adherents fail to practise. All men alike stand condemned, not by alien codes of ethics, but by their own, and all men therefore are conscious of guilt. The second element in religion is the consciousness not merely of a moral law, but of a moral law at once approved and disobeyed. This consciousness is neither a logical, nor an illogical, inference from the facts of experience; if we did not bring it to our experience we could not find it there. It is either inexplicable illusion, or else revelation.

The moral experience and the numinous experience are so far from being the same that they may exist for quite long periods without establishing a mutual contact. In many forms of Paganism the worship of the gods and the ethical discussions of the philosophers have very little to do with each other. The third stage in religious development arises when men identify them—when the Numinous Power to which they feel awe is made the guardian of the morality to which they feel obligation. Once again, this may seem to you very 'natural'. What can be more natural than for a savage haunted at once by awe and by guilt to think that the power which awes him is also the authority which condemns his guilt? And it is, indeed, natural to humanity. But it is not in the least obvious. The actual behaviour of that universe which the Numinous haunts bears no resemblance to the behaviour which morality demands of us. The one seems wasteful, ruthless, and unjust; the other enjoins upon us the opposite qualities. Nor can the identification of the two be explained as a wish-fulfilment, for it fulfils no one's wishes. We desire nothing less than to see that Law whose naked authority is already unsupportable armed with the incalculable claims of the Numinous. Of all the jumps that humanity takes in its religious history this is certainly the most surprising. It is not unnatural that many sections of the human race refused it; non-moral religion, and non-religious morality, existed and still exist. Perhaps only a single people, as a people, took the new step with perfect decision—I mean the Jews: but great individuals in all times and places have taken it also, and only those who take it are safe from the obscenities and barbarities of the unmoralised worship or the cold, sad self-righteousness of sheer moralism. Judged by its fruits, this step is a step towards increased health. And though logic does not compel us to take it, it is very hard to resist—even on Paganism and Pantheism morality is always breaking in, and even Stoicism finds itself willy-nilly bowing the knee to God. Once more, it may be madness—a madness congenital to man and oddly fortunate in its results—or it may be revelation. And if revelation, then it is most really and truly in Abraham that all people shall be blessed, for it was the Jews who fully and unambiguously identified the awful Presence haunting black mountain-tops and thunderclouds with 'the *righteous* Lord' who 'loveth righteousness'.[8]

The fourth strand or element is a historical event. There was a man born among these Jews who claimed to be, or to be the son of, or to be 'one with', the Something which is at once the awful haunter of nature and the giver of the moral law. The claim is so shocking—a paradox, and even a horror, which we may easily be lulled into taking too lightly—that only two views of this man are possible. Either he was a raving lunatic of an unusually abominable type, or else He was, and is, precisely what He said. There is no middle way. If the records make the first hypothesis unacceptable, you must submit to the second. And if you do that, all else that is claimed by Christians becomes credible—that this Man, having been killed, was yet alive, and that His death, in some manner incomprehensible to human thought, has effected a real change in our relations to the 'awful' and 'righteous' Lord, and a change in our favour.

To ask whether the universe as we see it looks more like the work of a wise and good Creator or the work of chance, indifference, or malevolence, is to omit from the outset all the relevant factors in the religious problem. Christianity is not the conclusion of a philosophical debate on the origins of the universe: it is a catastrophic historical event following on the long spiritual preparation of humanity which I have described. It is not a system into which we have to fit the awkward fact of pain: it is itself one of the awkward facts which have to be fitted into any system we make. In a sense, it creates, rather than solves, the problem of pain, for pain would be no problem unless, side by side with our daily experience of this painful world, we had received what we think a good assurance that ultimate reality is righteous and loving.

---

[8] Psalm 11:8.

Why this assurance seems to me good, I have more or less indicated. It does not amount to logical compulsion. At every stage of religious development man may rebel, if not without violence to his own nature, yet without absurdity. He can close his spiritual eyes against the Numinous, if he is prepared to part company with half the great poets and prophets of his race, with his own childhood, with the richness and depth of uninhibited experience. He can regard the moral law as an illusion, and so cut himself off from the common ground of humanity. He can refuse to identify the Numinous with the righteous, and remain a barbarian, worshipping sexuality, or the dead, or the lifeforce, or the future. But the cost is heavy. And when we come to the last step of all, the historical Incarnation, the assurance is strongest of all. The story is strangely like many myths which have haunted religion from the first, and yet it is not like them. It is not transparent to the reason: we could not have invented it ourselves. It has not the suspicious *a priori* lucidity of Pantheism or of Newtonian physics. It has the seemingly arbitrary and idiosyncratic character which modern science is slowly teaching us to put up with in this wilful universe, where energy is made up in little parcels of a quantity no one could predict, where speed is not unlimited, where irreversible entropy gives time a real direction and the cosmos, no longer static or cyclic, moves like a drama from a real beginning to a real end. If any message from the core of reality ever were to reach us, we should expect to find in it just that unexpectedness, that wilful, dramatic anfractuosity which we find in the Christian faith. It has the master touch—the rough, male taste of reality, not made by us, or, indeed, for us, but hitting us in the face.

If, on such grounds, or on better ones, we follow the course on which humanity has been led, and become Christians, we then have the 'problem' of pain.

2

DIVINE OMNIPOTENCE

*Nothing which implies contradiction falls under the
omnipotence of God.*

THOMAS AQUINAS, *SUMM. THEOL.*,
IA Q XXV, ART 4

IF GOD WERE good, He would wish to make His creatures perfectly
happy, and if God were almighty He would be able to do what He wished.
But the creatures are not happy. Therefore God lacks either goodness, or
power, or both.' This is the problem of pain, in its simplest form. The
possibility of answering it depends on showing that the terms 'good' and
'almighty', and perhaps also the term 'happy', are equivocal: for it must
be admitted from the outset that if the popular meanings attached to these
words are the best, or the only possible, meanings, then the argument is
unanswerable. In this chapter I shall make some comments on the idea of
Omnipotence, and, in the following, some on the idea of Goodness.

Omnipotence means 'power to do all, or everything'.' And we are told
in Scripture that 'with God all things are possible'. It is common enough,
in argument with an unbeliever, to be told that God, if He existed and
were good, would do this or that; and then, if we point out that the pro-

---

' The original meaning in Latin may have been 'power *over* or *in* all'. I give what I take to be
the current sense.

posed action is impossible, to be met with the retort 'But I thought God was supposed to be able to do anything'. This raises the whole question of impossibility.

In ordinary usage the word *impossible* generally implies a suppressed clause beginning with the word *unless*. Thus it is impossible for me to see the street from where I sit writing at this moment; that is, it is impossible to see the street *unless* I go up to the top floor where I shall be high enough to overlook the intervening building. If I had broken my leg I should say 'But it is impossible to go up to the top floor'—meaning, however, that it is impossible *unless* some friends turn up who will carry me. Now let us advance to a different plane of impossibility, by saying 'It is, at any rate, impossible to see the street *so long as* I remain where I am and the intervening building remains where it is.' Someone might add 'unless the nature of space, or of vision, were different from what it is'. I do not know what the best philosophers and scientists would say to this, but I should have to reply 'I don't know whether space and vision *could possibly* have been of such a nature as you suggest.' Now it is clear that the words *could possibly* here refer to some absolute kind of possibility or impossibility which is different from the relative possibilities and impossibilities we have been considering. I cannot say whether seeing round corners is, in this new sense, possible or not, because I do not know whether it is self-contradictory or not. But I know very well that if it is self-contradictory it is absolutely impossible. The absolutely impossible may also be called the intrinsically impossible because it carries its impossibility within itself, instead of borrowing it from other impossibilities which in their turn depend upon others. It has no *unless* clause attached to it. It is impossible under all conditions and in all worlds and for all agents.

'All agents' here includes God Himself. His Om-nipotence means power to do all that is intrinsically possible, not to do the intrinsically impossible. You may attribute miracles to Him, but not nonsense. This is no limit to His power. If you choose to say 'God can give a creature free will and at the same time withhold free will from it', you have not succeeded in saying *anything* about God: meaningless combinations of words do not suddenly acquire meaning simply because we prefix to them the two other words 'God can'. It remains true that all *things* are possible with God: the intrinsic impossibilities are not things but nonentities. It is no more possible for God than for the weakest of His creatures to carry out both of two mutually exclusive alternatives; not because His power meets an obstacle, but because nonsense remains nonsense even when we talk it about God.

It should, however, be remembered that human reasoners often make mistakes, either by arguing from false data or by inadvertence in the argument itself. We may thus come to think things possible which are really impossible, and *vice versa*.[2] We ought, therefore, to use great caution in defining those intrinsic impossibilities which even Omnipotence cannot perform. What follows is to be regarded less as an assertion of what they are than a sample of what they might be like.

The inexorable 'laws of Nature' which operate in defiance of human suffering or desert, which are not turned aside by prayer, seem, at first sight, to furnish a strong argument against the goodness and power of God. I am going to submit that not even Omnipotence could create a society of free souls without at the same time creating a relatively independent and 'inexorable' Nature.

There is no reason to suppose that self-consciousness, the recognition of a creature by itself as a 'self', can exist except in contrast with an 'other', a something which is not the self. It is against an environment and preferably a social environment, an environment of other selves, that the awareness of Myself stands out. This would raise a difficulty about the consciousness of God if we were mere theists: being Christians, we learn from the doctrine of the Blessed Trinity that something analogous to 'society' exists within the Divine being from all eternity—that God is Love, not merely in the sense of being the Platonic form of love, but because, within Him, the concrete reciprocities of love exist before all worlds and are thence derived to the creatures.

Again, the freedom of a creature must mean freedom to choose: and choice implies the existence of things to choose between. A creature with no environment would have no choices to make: so that freedom, like self-consciousness (if they are not, indeed, the same thing), again demands the presence to the self of something other than the self.

The minimum condition of self-consciousness and freedom, then, would be that the creature should apprehend God and, therefore, itself as distinct from God. It is possible that such creatures exist, aware of God

---

[2] e.g., every good conjuring trick does something which to the audience, with their data and their power of reasoning, seems self-contradictory.

and themselves, but of no fellow-creatures. If so, their freedom is simply that of making a single naked choice—of loving God more than the self or the self more than God. But a life so reduced to essentials is not imaginable to us. As soon as we attempt to introduce the mutual knowledge of fellow-creatures we run up against the necessity of 'Nature'.

People often talk as if nothing were easier than for two naked minds to 'meet' or become aware of each other. But I see no possibility of their doing so except in a common medium which forms their 'external world' or environment. Even our vague attempt to imagine such a meeting between disembodied spirits usually slips in surreptitiously the idea of, at least, a common space and common time, to give the *co-* in *co-existence* a meaning: and space and time are already an environment. But more than this is required. If your thoughts and passions were directly present to me, like my own, without any mark of externality or otherness, how should I distinguish them from mine? And what thoughts or passions could we begin to have without objects to think and feel about? Nay, could I even begin to have the conception of 'external' and 'other' unless I had experience of an 'external world'? You may reply, as a Christian, that God (and Satan) do, in fact, affect my consciousness in this direct way without signs of 'externality'. Yes: and the result is that most people remain ignorant of the existence of both. We may therefore suppose that if human souls affected one another directly and immaterially, it would be a rare triumph of faith and insight for any one of them to believe in the existence of the others. It would be harder for me to know my neighbour under such conditions than it now is for me to know God: for in recognising the impact of God upon me I am now helped by things that reach me through the external world, such as the tradition of the Church, Holy Scripture, and the conversation of religious friends. What we need for human society is exactly what we have—a neutral something, neither you nor I, which we can both manipulate so as to make signs to each other. I can talk to you because we can both set up sound-waves in the common air between us. Matter, which keeps souls apart, also brings them together. It enables each of us to have an 'outside' as well as an 'inside', so that what are acts of will and thought for you are noises and glances for me; you are enabled not only to *be*, but to *appear:* and hence I have the pleasure of making your acquaintance.

Society, then, implies a common field or 'world' in which its members meet. If there is an angelic society, as Christians have usually believed, then the angels also must have such a world or field; something which is to them as 'matter' (in the modern, not the scholastic, sense) is to us.

But if matter is to serve as a neutral field it must have a fixed nature of its own. If a 'world' or material system had only a single inhabitant it might conform at every moment to his wishes—'trees for his sake would crowd into a shade'. But if you were introduced into a world which thus varied at my every whim, you would be quite unable to act in it and would thus lose the exercise of your free will. Nor is it clear that you could make your presence known to me—all the matter by which you attempted to make signs to me being already in my control and therefore not capable of being manipulated by you.

Again, if matter has a fixed nature and obeys constant laws, not all states of matter will be equally agreeable to the wishes of a given soul, nor all equally beneficial for that particular aggregate of matter which he calls his body. If fire comforts that body at a certain distance, it will destroy it when the distance is reduced. Hence, even in a perfect world, the necessity for those danger signals which the pain-fibres in our nerves are apparently designed to transmit. Does this mean an inevitable element of evil (in the form of pain) in any possible world? I think not: for while it may be true that the least sin is an incalculable evil, the evil of pain depends on degree, and pains below a certain intensity are not feared or resented at all. No one minds the process 'warm—beautifully hot—too hot—it stings' which warns him to withdraw his hand from exposure to the fire: and, if I may trust my own feeling, a slight aching in the legs as we climb into bed after a good day's walking is, in fact, pleasurable.

Yet again, if the fixed nature of matter prevents it from being always, and in all its dispositions, equally agreeable even to a single soul, much less is it possible for the matter of the universe at any moment to be distributed so that it is equally convenient and pleasurable to each member of a society. If a man travelling in one direction is having a journey down hill, a man going in the opposite direction must be going up hill. If even a pebble lies where I want it to lie, it cannot, except by a coincidence, be where you want it to lie. And this is very far from being an evil: on the contrary, it furnishes occasion for all those acts of courtesy, respect, and unselfishness by which love and good humour and modesty express themselves. But it certainly leaves the way open to a great evil, that of competition and hostility. And if souls are free, they cannot be prevented from dealing with the problem by competition instead of courtesy. And once they have advanced to actual hostility, they can then exploit the fixed nature of matter to hurt one another. The permanent nature of wood which enables us to use it as a beam also enables us to use it for hitting our neighbour on the head. The permanent nature of matter in general means that when human beings fight, the victory ordinarily goes to those who have superior weapons, skill, and numbers, even if their cause is unjust.

We can, perhaps, conceive of a world in which God corrected the results of this abuse of free will by His creatures at every moment: so that a wooden beam became soft as grass when it was used as a weapon, and the air refused to obey me if I attempted to set up in it the sound-waves that carry lies or insults. But such a world would be one in which wrong actions were impossible, and in which, therefore, freedom of the will would be void; nay, if the principle were carried out to its logical conclusion, evil thoughts would be impossible, for the cerebral matter which we use in thinking would refuse its task when we attempted to frame them. All matter in the neighbourhood of a wicked man would be liable to undergo unpredictable alterations. That God can and does, on occasions, modify the behaviour of matter and produce what we call miracles, is part of Christian faith; but the very conception of a common, and therefore stable, world, demands that these occasions should be extremely rare. In a game of chess you can make certain arbitrary concessions to your opponent, which stand to the ordinary rules of the game as miracles stand to the laws of nature. You can deprive yourself of a castle, or allow the other man sometimes to take back a move made inadvertently. But if you conceded everything that at any moment happened to suit him—if all his moves were revocable and if all your pieces disappeared whenever their position on the board was not to his liking—then you could not have a game at all. So it is with the life of souls in a world: fixed laws, consequences unfolding by causal necessity, the whole natural order, are at once limits within which their common life is confined and also the sole condition under which any such life is possible. Try to exclude the possibility of suffering which the order of nature and the existence of free wills involve, and you find that you have excluded life itself.

As I said before, this account of the intrinsic necessities of a world is meant merely as a specimen of what they might be. What they really are, only Omniscience has the data and the wisdom to see: but they are not likely to be *less* complicated than I have suggested. Needless to say, 'complicated' here refers solely to the human understanding of them; we are not to think of God arguing, as we do, from an end (co-existence of free spirits) to the conditions involved in it, but rather of a single, utterly self-consistent act of creation which to us appears, at first sight, as the creation of many independent things, and then, as the creation of things mutually necessary. Even we can rise a little beyond the conception of mutual necessities as I have outlined it—can reduce matter as that which separates souls and matter as that which brings them together under the single concept of Plurality, whereof 'separation' and 'togetherness' are only two aspects. With every advance in our thought the unity of the creative act, and the impossibility of tinkering with the creation as though this or that element of it could have been removed, will become more apparent. Perhaps this is not the 'best of all possible' universes, but the only possible one. Possible worlds can mean only 'worlds that God could have made, but didn't'. The idea of that which God 'could have' done involves a too anthropomorphic conception of God's freedom. Whatever human freedom means, Divine freedom cannot mean indeterminacy between alternatives and choice of one of them. Perfect goodness can never debate about the end to be attained, and perfect wisdom cannot debate about the means most suited to achieve it. The freedom of God consists in the fact that no cause other than Himself produces His acts and no external obstacle impedes them—that His own goodness is the root from which they all grow and His own omnipotence the air in which they all flower.

And that brings us to our next subject—the Divine goodness. Nothing so far has been said of this, and no answer attempted to the objection that if the universe must, from the outset, admit the possibility of suffering, then absolute goodness would have left the universe uncreated. And I must warn the reader that I shall not attempt to prove that to create was better than not to create: I am aware of no human scales in which such a portentous question can be weighed. Some comparison between one state of being and another can be made, but the attempt to compare being and not being ends in mere words. 'It would be better for me not to exist'—in what sense 'for me'? How should I, if I did not exist, profit by not existing? Our design is a less formidable one: it is only to discover how, perceiving a suffering world, and being assured, on quite different grounds, that God is good, we are to conceive that goodness and that suffering without contradiction.

3

DIVINE GOODNESS

Love can forbear, and Love can forgive . . . but Love
can never be reconciled to an unlovely object. . . . He
can never therefore be reconciled to your sin, because
sin itself is incapable of being altered; but He may be
reconciled to your person, because that may be restored.

TRAHERNE, *CENTURIES OF MEDITATION,*
II, 30

ANY CONSIDERATION OF the goodness of God at once threatens us with the following dilemma.

On the one hand, if God is wiser than we His judgement must differ from ours on many things, and not least on good and evil. What seems to us good may therefore not be good in His eyes, and what seems to us evil may not be evil.

On the other hand, if God's moral judgement differs from ours so that our 'black' may be His 'white', we can mean nothing by calling Him good; for to say 'God is good', while asserting that His goodness is wholly other than ours, is really only to say 'God is we know not what'. And an utterly unknown quality in God cannot give us moral grounds for loving or obeying Him. If He is not (in our sense) 'good' we shall obey, if at all, only through fear—and should be equally ready to obey an omnipotent Fiend. The doctrine of Total Depravity—when the consequence is drawn that, since we are totally depraved, our idea of good is worth simply nothing—may thus turn Christianity into a form of devil-worship.

The escape from this dilemma depends on observing what happens, in human relations, when the man of inferior moral standards enters the society of those who are better and wiser than he and gradually learns to accept *their* standards—a process which, as it happens, I can describe fairly accurately, since I have undergone it. When I came first to the University I was as nearly without a moral conscience as a boy could be. Some faint distaste for cruelty and for meanness about money was my utmost reach—of chastity, truthfulness, and self-sacrifice I thought as a baboon thinks of classical music. By the mercy of God I fell among a set of young men (none of them, by the way, Christians) who were sufficiently close to me in intellect and imagination to secure immediate intimacy, but who knew, and tried to obey, the moral law. Thus their judgement of good and evil was very different from mine. Now what happens in such a case is not in the least like being asked to treat as 'white' what was hitherto called black. The new moral judgements never enter the mind as mere reversals (though they do reverse them) of previous judgements but 'as lords that are certainly expected'. You can have no doubt in which direction you are moving: they are more like good than the little shreds of good you already had, but are, in a sense, continuous with them. But the great test is that the recognition of the new standards is accompanied with the sense of shame and guilt: one is conscious of having blundered into society that one is unfit for. It is in the light of such experiences that we must consider the goodness of God. Beyond all doubt, His idea of 'goodness' differs from ours; but you need have no fear that, as you approach it, you will be asked simply to reverse your moral standards. When the relevant difference between the Divine ethics and your own appears to you, you will not, in fact, be in any doubt that the change demanded of you is in the direction you already call 'better'. The Divine 'goodness' differs from ours, but it is not sheerly different: it differs from ours not as white from black but as a perfect circle from a child's first attempt to draw a wheel. But when the child has learned to draw, it will know that the circle it then makes is what it was trying to make from the very beginning.

This doctrine is presupposed in Scripture. Christ calls men to repent— a call which would be meaningless if God's standards were sheerly different from that which they already knew and failed to practise. He appeals to our existing moral judgement—'Why even of yourselves judge ye not what is right?'[1] God in the Old Testament expostulates with men on the basis of their own conceptions of gratitude, fidelity, and fair play: and puts Himself, as it were, at the bar before His own creatures—'What iniquity have your fathers found in me, that they are gone far from me?'[2]

After these preliminaries it will, I hope, be safe to suggest that some conceptions of the Divine goodness which tend to dominate our thought, though seldom expressed in so many words, are open to criticism.

By the goodness of God we mean nowadays almost exclusively His lovingness; and in this we may be right. And by Love, in this context, most of us mean kindness—the desire to see others than the self happy; not happy in this way or in that, but just happy. What would really satisfy us would be a God who said of anything we happened to like doing, 'What does it matter so long as they are contented?' We want, in fact, not so much a Father in Heaven as a grandfather in heaven—a senile benevolence who, as they say, 'liked to see young people enjoying themselves', and whose plan for the universe was simply that it might be truly said at the end of each day, 'a good time was had by all'. Not many people, I admit, would formulate a theology in precisely those terms: but a conception not very different lurks at the back of many minds. I do not claim to be an exception: I should very much like to live in a universe which was governed on such lines. But since it is abundantly clear that I don't, and since I have reason to believe, nevertheless, that God is Love, I conclude that my conception of love needs correction.

I might, indeed, have learned, even from the poets, that Love is something more stern and splendid than mere kindness: that even the love between the sexes is, as in Dante, 'a lord of terrible aspect'. There is kindness in Love: but Love and kindness are not coterminous, and when kindness (in the sense given above) is separated from the other elements of Love, it involves a certain fundamental indifference to its object, and even something like contempt of it. Kindness consents very readily to the removal of its object—we have all met people whose kindness to animals is constantly leading them to kill animals lest they should suffer. Kindness, merely as such, cares not whether its object becomes good or bad, provided only that it escapes suffering. As Scripture points out,

---

[1] Luke 12:57.

[2] Jeremiah 2:5.

it is bastards who are spoiled: the legitimate sons, who are to carry on the family tradition, are punished.[3] It is for people whom we care nothing about that we demand happiness on any terms: with our friends, our lovers, our children, we are exacting and would rather see them suffer much than be happy in contemptible and estranging modes. If God is Love, He is, by definition, something more than mere kindness. And it appears, from all the records, that though He has often rebuked us and condemned us, He has never regarded us with contempt. He has paid us the intolerable compliment of loving us, in the deepest, most tragic, most inexorable sense.

The relation between Creator and creature is, of course, unique, and cannot be paralleled by any relations between one creature and another. God is both further from us, and nearer to us, than any other being. He is further from us because the sheer difference between that which has Its principle of being in Itself and that to which being is communicated, is one compared with which the difference between an archangel and a worm is quite insignificant. He makes, we are made: He is original, we derivative. But at the same time, and for the same reason, the intimacy between God and even the meanest creature is closer than any that creatures can attain with one another. Our life is, at every moment, supplied by Him: our tiny, miraculous power of free will only operates on bodies which His continual energy keeps in existence—our very power to think is His power communicated to us. Such a unique relation can be apprehended only by analogies: from the various types of love known among creatures we reach an inadequate, but useful, conception of God's love for man.

The lowest type, and one which is 'love' at all only by an extension of the word, is that which an artist feels for an artefact. God's relation to man is pictured thus in Jeremiah's vision of the potter and the clay,[4] or when St Peter speaks of the whole Church as a building on which God is at work, and of the individual members as stones.[5] The limitation of such an analogy is, of course, that in the symbol the patient is not sentient, and that certain questions of justice and mercy which arise when the 'stones' are really 'living' therefore remain unrepresented. But it is an important

---

[3] Hebrews 12:8.

[4] Jeremiah 18.

[5] 1 Peter 2:5.

analogy so far as it goes. We are, not metaphorically but in very truth, a Divine work of art, something that God is making, and therefore something with which He will not be satisfied until it has a certain character. Here again we come up against what I have called the 'intolerable compliment'. Over a sketch made idly to amuse a child, an artist may not take much trouble: he may be content to let it go even though it is not exactly as he meant it to be. But over the great picture of his life—the work which he loves, though in a different fashion, as intensely as a man loves a woman or a mother a child—he will take endless trouble—and would, doubtless, thereby *give* endless trouble to the picture if it were sentient. One can imagine a sentient picture, after being rubbed and scraped and recommenced for the tenth time, wishing that it were only a thumbnail sketch whose making was over in a minute. In the same way, it is natural for us to wish that God had designed for us a less glorious and less arduous destiny; but then we are wishing not for more love but for less.

Another type is the love of a man for a beast—a relation constantly used in Scripture to symbolise the relation between God and men; 'we are his people and the sheep of his pasture'. This is in some ways a better analogy than the preceding, because the inferior party is sentient, and yet unmistakably inferior: but it is less good in so far as man has not made the beast and does not fully understand it. Its great merit lies in the fact that the association of (say) man and dog is primarily for the man's sake: he tames the dog primarily that he may love it, not that it may love him, and that it may serve him, not that he may serve it. Yet at the same time, the dog's interests are not sacrificed to the man's. The one end (that he may love it) cannot be fully attained unless it also, in its fashion, loves him, nor can it serve him unless he, in a different fashion, serves it. Now just because the dog is by human standards one of the 'best' of irrational creatures, and a proper object for a man to love—of course, with that degree and kind of love which is proper to such an object, and not with silly anthropomorphic exaggerations—man interferes with the dog and makes it more lovable than it was in mere nature. In its state of nature it has a smell, and habits, which frustrate man's love: he washes it, housetrains it, teaches it not to steal, and is so enabled to love it completely. To the puppy the whole proceeding would seem, if it were a theologian, to cast grave doubts on the 'goodness' of man: but the full-grown and full-trained dog, larger, healthier, and longer-lived than the wild dog, and admitted, as it were by Grace, to a whole world of affections, loyalties, interests, and comforts entirely beyond its animal destiny, would have no such doubts. It will be noted that the man (I am speaking throughout of the good man) takes all these pains with the dog, and gives all these pains to the dog, only because it is an animal high in the scale—because it is so nearly lovable that it is worth his while to make it fully lovable. He does not house-train the earwig or give baths to centipedes. We may wish, indeed, that we were of so little account to God that He left us alone to follow our natural impulses—that He would give over trying to train us into something so unlike our natural selves: but once again, we are asking not for more love, but for less.

A nobler analogy, sanctioned by the constant tenor of Our Lord's teaching, is that between God's love for man and a father's love for a son. Whenever this is used, however (that is, whenever we pray the Lord's Prayer), it must be remembered that the Saviour used it in a time and place where paternal authority stood much higher than it does in modern England. A father half apologetic for having brought his son into the world, afraid to restrain him lest he should create inhibitions or even to instruct him lest he should interfere with his independence of mind, is a most misleading symbol of the Divine Fatherhood. I am not here discussing whether the authority of fathers, in its ancient extent, was a good thing or a bad thing: I am only explaining what conception of Fatherhood would have meant to Our Lord's first hearers, and indeed to their successors for many centuries. And it will become even plainer if we consider how Our Lord (though, in our belief, one with His Father and co-eternal with Him as no earthly son is with an earthly father) regards His own Sonship, surrendering His will wholly to the paternal will and not even allowing Himself to be called 'good' because Good is the name of the Father. Love between father and son, in this symbol, means essentially authoritative love on the one side, and obedient love on the other. The father uses his authority to make the son into the sort of human being he, rightly, and in his superior wisdom, wants him to be. Even in our own days, though a man might say it, he could mean nothing by saying, 'I love my son but don't care how great a blackguard he is provided he has a good time.'

Finally we come to an analogy full of danger, and of much more limited application, which happens, nevertheless, to be the most useful for our special purpose at the moment—I mean, the analogy between God's love for man and a man's love for a woman. It is freely used in Scripture. Israel is a false wife, but her heavenly Husband cannot forget the happier days; 'I remember thee, the kindness of thy youth, the love of thy espousals, when thou wentest after Me in the wilderness.'[6] Israel is the pauper bride, the waif whom her Lover found abandoned by the wayside, and clothed and adorned and made lovely and yet she betrayed Him.[7] 'Adulteresses' St James calls us, because we turn aside to the 'friendship of the world', while God 'jealously longs for the spirit He has implanted in us'.[8] The Church is the Lord's bride whom He so loves that in her no spot or wrinkle is endurable.[9] For the truth which this analogy serves to emphasise is that Love, in its own nature, demands the perfecting of the beloved; that the mere 'kindness' which tolerates anything except suffering in its object is, in that respect, at the opposite pole from Love. When we fall in love with a woman, do we cease to care whether she is clean or dirty, fair or foul? Do we not rather then first begin to care? Does any woman regard it as a sign of love in a man that he neither knows nor cares how she is looking? Love may, indeed, love the beloved when her beauty is lost: but not because it is lost. Love may forgive all infirmities and love still in spite of them: but Love cannot cease to will their removal. Love is more sensitive than hatred itself to every blemish in the beloved; his 'feeling is more soft and sensible than are the tender horns of cockled snails'. Of all powers he forgives most, but he condones least: he is pleased with little, but demands all.

When Christianity says that God loves man, it means that God *loves* man: not that He has some 'disinterested', because really indifferent, concern for our welfare, but that, in awful and surprising truth, we are the objects of His love. You asked for a loving God: you have one. The great spirit you so lightly invoked, the 'lord of terrible aspect', is present: not a senile benevolence that drowsily wishes you to be happy in your own way, not the cold philanthropy of a conscientious magistrate, nor the care of a host who feels responsible for the comfort of his guests, but the consuming fire Himself, the Love that made the worlds, persistent as the art-

---

[6] Jeremiah 2:2.

[7] Ezekiel 16:6–15.

[8] James 4:4, 5. Authorised Version mistranslates.

[9] Ephesians 5:27.

ist's love for his work and despotic as a man's love for a dog, provident and venerable as a father's love for a child, jealous, inexorable, exacting as love between the sexes. How this should be, I do not know: it passes reason to explain why any creatures, not to say creatures such as we, should have a value so prodigious in their Creator's eyes. It is certainly a burden of glory not only beyond our deserts but also, except in rare moments of grace, beyond our desiring; we are inclined, like the maidens in the old play, to deprecate the love of Zeus.[10] But the fact seems unquestionable. The Impassible speaks as if it suffered passion, and that which contains in Itself the cause of its own and all other bliss talks as though it could be in want and yearning. 'Is Ephraim my dear son? is he a pleasant child? for since I spake against him I do earnestly remember him still: therefore my bowels are troubled for him.'[11] 'How shall I give thee up, Ephraim? How shall I abandon thee, Israel? Mine heart is turned within me.'[12] 'Oh Jerusalem, how often would I have gathered thy children together, even as a hen gathereth her chickens under her wings, and ye would not.'[13]

The problem of reconciling human suffering with the existence of a God who loves, is only insoluble so long as we attach a trivial meaning to the word 'love', and look on things as if man were the centre of them. Man is not the centre. God does not exist for the sake of man. Man does not exist for his own sake. 'Thou hast created all things, and for thy pleasure they are and were created.'[14] We were made not primarily that we may love God (though we were made for that too) but that God may love us, that we may become objects in which the Divine love may rest 'well pleased'. To ask that God's love should be content with us as we are is to ask that God should cease to be God: because He is what He is, His love must, in the nature of things, be impeded and repelled by certain stains in our present character, and because He already loves us He must labour to make us lovable. We cannot even wish, in our better moments, that He could reconcile Himself to our present impurities—no more than the beggar maid could wish that King Cophetua should be content with her rags and dirt, or a dog, once having learned to love man, could wish that

---

[10] *Prometheus Vinctus*, 887–900.

[11] Jeremiah 31:20.

[12] Hosea 11:8.

[13] Matthew 23:37.

[14] Revelation 4:11.

man were such as to tolerate in his house the snapping, verminous, polluting creature of the wild pack. What we would here and now call our 'happiness' is not the end God chiefly has in view: but when we are such as He can love without impediment, we shall in fact be happy.

I plainly foresee that the course of my argument may provoke a protest. I had promised that in coming to understand the Divine goodness we should not be asked to accept a mere reversal of our own ethics. But it may be objected that a reversal is precisely what we have been asked to accept. The kind of love which I attribute to God, it may be said, is just the kind which in human beings we describe as 'selfish' or 'possessive', and contrast unfavourably with another kind which seeks first the happiness of the beloved and not the contentment of the lover. I am not sure that this is quite how I feel even about human love. I do not think I should value much the love of a friend who cared only for my happiness and did not object to my becoming dishonest. Nevertheless, the protest is welcome, and the answer to it will put the subject in a new light, and correct what has been one-sided in our discussion.

The truth is that this antithesis between egoistic and altruistic love cannot be unambiguously applied to the love of God for His creatures. Clashes of interest, and therefore opportunities either of selfishness or unselfishness, occur only between beings inhabiting a common world: God can no more be in competition with a creature than Shakespeare can be in competition with Viola. When God becomes a Man and lives as a creature among His own creatures in Palestine, then indeed His life is one of supreme self-sacrifice and leads to Calvary. A modern pantheistic philosopher has said, 'When the Absolute falls into the sea it becomes a fish'; in the same way, we Christians can point to the Incarnation and say that when God empties Himself of His glory and submits to those conditions under which alone egoism and altruism have a clear meaning, He is seen to be wholly altruistic. But God in His transcendence—God as the unconditioned ground of all conditions—cannot easily be thought of in the same way. We call human love selfish when it satisfies its own needs at the expense of the object's needs—as when a father keeps at home, because he cannot bear to relinquish their society, children who ought, in their own interests, to be put out into the world. The situation implies a need or passion on the part of the lover, an incompatible need on the part of the beloved, and the lover's disregard or culpable ignorance of the beloved's need. None of these conditions is present in the relation of God to man. God has no needs. Human love, as Plato teaches us, is the child of Poverty—of a want or lack; it is caused by a real or supposed good in its beloved which the lover needs and desires. But God's love, far from being caused by goodness in the object, causes all the goodness which the object has, loving it first into existence and then into real, though derivative, lovability. God is Goodness. He can give good, but cannot need or get it. In that sense all His love is, as it were, bottomlessly selfless by very definition; it has everything to give and nothing to receive. Hence, if God sometimes speaks as though the Impassible could suffer passion and eternal fullness could be in want, and in want of those beings on whom it bestows all from their bare existence upwards, this can mean only, if it means anything intelligible by us, that God of mere miracle has made Himself able so to hunger and created in Himself that which we can satisfy. If He requires us, the requirement is of His own choosing. If the immutable heart can be grieved by the puppets of its own making, it is Divine Omnipotence, no other, that has so subjected it, freely, and in a humility that passes understanding. If the world exists not chiefly that we may love God but that God may love us, yet that very fact, on a deeper level, is so for our sakes. If He who in Himself can lack nothing chooses to need us, it is because we need to be needed. Before and behind all the relations of God to man, as we now learn them from Christianity, yawns the abyss of a Divine act of pure giving—the election of man, from nonentity, to be the beloved of God, and therefore (in some sense) the needed and desired of God, who but for that act needs and desires nothing, since He eternally has, and is, all goodness. And that act is for our sakes. It is good for us to know love; and best for us to know the love of the best object, God. But to know it as a love in which we were primarily the wooers and God the wooed, in which we sought and He was found, in which His conformity to our needs, not ours to His, came first, would be to know it in a form false to the very nature of things. For we are only creatures: our role must always be that of patient to agent, female to male, mirror to light, echo to voice. Our highest activity must be response, not initiative. To experience the love of God in a true, and not an illusory form, is therefore to experience it as our surrender to His demand, our conformity to His desire: to experience it in the opposite way is, as it were, a solecism against the grammar of being. I do not deny, of course, that on a certain level we may rightly speak of the soul's search for God, and of God as receptive of the soul's love: but in the long run the soul's search for God can only be a mode, or appearance (*Erscheinung*) of His search for her, since all comes from Him, since the very possibility of our loving is His gift to us, and since our freedom is only a freedom of better or worse response. Hence I think that nothing marks off Pagan theism from Christianity so sharply as Aristotle's doctrine that God moves the universe, Himself unmoving, as the Beloved moves a lover.[15] But for Christendom 'Herein is love, not that we loved God but that He loved us'.[16]

The first condition, then, of what is called a selfish love among men is lacking with God. He has no natural necessities, no passion, to compete with His wish for the beloved's welfare: or if there is in Him something which we have to imagine after the analogy of a passion, a want, it is there by His own will and for our sakes. And the second condition is lacking too. The real interests of a child may differ from that which his father's affection instinctively demands, because the child is a separate being from the father with a nature which has its own needs and does not exist solely for the father nor find its whole perfection in being loved by him, and which the father does not fully understand. But creatures are not thus separate from their Creator, nor can He misunderstand them. The place for which He designs them in His scheme of things is the place they are made for. When they reach it their nature is fulfilled and their happiness attained: a broken bone in the universe has been set, the anguish is over. When we want to be something other than the thing God wants us to be, we must be wanting what, in fact, will not make us happy. Those Divine demands which sound to our natural ears most like those of a despot and least like those of a lover, in fact marshal us where we should want to go if we knew what we wanted. He demands our worship, our obedience, our prostration. Do we suppose that they can do Him any good, or fear, like the chorus in Milton, that human irreverence can bring about 'His glory's diminution'? A man can no more diminish God's glory by refusing to worship Him than a lunatic can put out the sun by scribbling the word 'darkness' on the walls of his cell. But God wills our good, and our good is to love Him (with that responsive love proper to creatures) and to love Him we must know Him: and if we know Him, we shall in fact fall on our faces. If we do not, that only shows that what we are trying to love is not

---

[15] *Met.*, xii, 7.

[16] 1 John 4:10.

yet God—though it may be the nearest approximation to God which our thought and fantasy can attain. Yet the call is not only to prostration and awe; it is to a reflection of the Divine life, a creaturely participation in the Divine attributes which is far beyond our present desires. We are bidden to 'put on Christ', to become like God. That is, whether we like it or not, God intends to give us what we need, not what we now think we want. Once more, we are embarrassed by the intolerable compliment, by too much love, not too little.

Yet perhaps even this view falls short of the truth. It is not simply that God has arbitrarily made us such that He is our only good. Rather God is the only good of all creatures: and by necessity, each must find its good in that kind and degree of the fruition of God which is proper to its nature. The kind and degree may vary with the creature's nature: but that there ever could be any other good, is an atheistic dream. George Macdonald, in a passage I cannot now find, represents God as saying to men, 'You must be strong with my strength and blessed with my blessedness, *for I have no other to give you.*' That is the conclusion of the whole matter. God gives what He has, not what He has not: He gives the happiness that there is, not the happiness that is not. To be God—to be like God and to share His goodness in creaturely response—to be miserable—these are the only three alternatives. If we will not learn to eat the only food that the universe grows—the only food that any possible universe ever can grow—then we must starve eternally.

4

HUMAN WICKEDNESS

*You can have no greater sign of confirmed pride than
when you think you are humble enough.*

LAW, *SERIOUS CALL*, CAP. XVI

THE EXAMPLES GIVEN in the last chapter went to show that love may
cause pain to its object, but only on the supposition that that object needs
alteration to become fully lovable. Now why do we men need so much
alteration? The Christian answer—that we have used our free will to become very bad—is so well known that it hardly needs to be stated. But to
bring this doctrine into real life in the minds of modern men, and even of
modern Christians, is very hard. When the apostles preached, they could
assume even in their Pagan hearers a real consciousness of deserving the
Divine anger. The Pagan mysteries existed to allay this consciousness,
and the Epicurean philosophy claimed to deliver men from the fear of
eternal punishment. It was against this background that the Gospel appeared as good news. It brought news of possible healing to men who
knew that they were mortally ill. But all this has changed. Christianity
now has to preach the diagnosis—in itself very bad news—before it can
win a hearing for the cure.

There are two principal causes. One is the fact that for about a hundred years we have so concentrated on one of the virtues—'kindness' or
mercy—that most of us do not feel anything except kindness to be re-

ally good or anything but cruelty to be really bad. Such lopsided ethical developments are not uncommon, and other ages too have had their pet virtues and curious insensibilities. And if one virtue must be cultivated at the expense of all the rest, none has a higher claim than mercy—for every Christian must reject with detestation that covert propaganda for cruelty which tries to drive mercy out of the world by calling it names such as 'Humanitarianism' and 'Sentimentality'. The real trouble is that 'kindness' is a quality fatally easy to attribute to ourselves on quite inadequate grounds. Everyone *feels* benevolent if nothing happens to be annoying him at the moment. Thus a man easily comes to console himself for all his other vices by a conviction that 'his heart's in the right place' and 'he wouldn't hurt a fly', though in fact he has never made the slightest sacrifice for a fellow creature. We think we are kind when we are only happy: it is not so easy, on the same grounds, to imagine oneself temperate, chaste, or humble.

The second cause is the effect of Psychoanalysis on the public mind, and, in particular, the doctrine of repressions and inhibitions. Whatever these doctrines really mean, the impression they have actually left on most people is that the sense of Shame is a dangerous and mischievous thing. We have laboured to overcome that sense of shrinking, that desire to conceal, which either Nature herself or the tradition of almost all mankind has attached to cowardice, unchastity, falsehood, and envy. We are told to 'get things out into the open', not for the sake of self-humiliation, but on the grounds that these 'things' are very natural and we need not be ashamed of them. But unless Christianity is wholly false, the perception of ourselves which we have in moments of shame must be the only true one; and even Pagan society has usually recognised 'shamelessness' as the nadir of the soul. In trying to extirpate shame we have broken down one of the ramparts of the human spirit, madly exulting in the work as the Trojans exulted when they broke their walls and pulled the Horse into Troy. I do not know that there is anything to be done but to set about the rebuilding as soon as we can. It is mad work to remove hypocrisy by removing the *temptation* to hypocrisy: the 'frankness' of people sunk below shame is a very cheap frankness.

A recovery of the old sense of sin is essential to Christianity. Christ takes it for granted that men are bad. Until we really feel this assumption of His to be true, though we are part of the world He came to save, we are not part of the audience to whom His words are addressed. We lack the first condition for understanding what He is talking about. And when men attempt to be Christians without this preliminary consciousness of sin, the result is almost bound to be a certain resentment against God as to one always inexplicably angry. Most of us have at times felt a secret sympathy with the dying farmer who replied to the Vicar's dissertation on repentance by asking 'What harm have I ever done *Him?*' There is the real rub. The worst we have done to God is to leave Him alone—why can't He return the compliment? Why not live and let live? What call has He, of all beings, to be 'angry'? It's easy for Him to be good!

Now at the moment when a man feels real guilt—moments too rare in our lives—all these blasphemies vanish away. Much, we may feel, can be excused to human infirmities: but not *this*—this incredibly mean and ugly action which none of our friends would have done, which even such a thorough-going little rotter as X would have been ashamed of, which we would not for the world allow to be published. At such a moment we really do know that our character, as revealed in this action, is, and ought to be, hateful to all good men, and, if there are powers above man, to them. A God who did not regard this with unappeasable distaste would not be a good being. We cannot even wish for such a God—it is like wishing that every nose in the universe were abolished, that smell of hay or roses or the sea should never again delight any creature, because our own breath happens to stink.

When we merely *say* that we are bad, the 'wrath' of God seems a barbarous doctrine; as soon as we *perceive* our badness, it appears inevitable, a mere corollary from God's goodness. To keep ever before us the insight derived from such a moment as I have been describing, to learn to detect the same real inexcusable corruption under more and more of its complex disguises, is therefore indispensable to a real understanding of the Christian faith. This is not, of course, a new doctrine. I am attempting nothing very splendid in this chapter. I am merely trying to get my reader (and, still more, myself) over a *pons asinorum*—to take the first step out of fools' paradise and utter illusion. But the illusion has grown, in modern times, so strong, that I must add a few considerations tending to make the reality less incredible.

1. We are deceived by looking on the outside of things. We suppose ourselves to be roughly not much worse than Y, whom all acknowledge for a decent sort of person, and certainly (though we should not claim it out loud) better than the abominable X. Even on the superficial level

we are probably deceived about this. Don't be too sure that your friends think you as good as Y. The very fact that you selected him for the comparison is suspicious: he is probably head and shoulders above you and your circle. But let us suppose that Y and yourself both appear 'not bad'. How far Y's appearance is deceptive, is between Y and God. His may not be deceptive: you know that yours is. Does this seem to you a mere trick, because I could say the same to Y and so to every man in turn? But that is just the point. Every man, not very holy or very arrogant, has to 'live up to' the outward appearance of other men: he knows there is that within him which falls far below even his most careless public behaviour, even his loosest talk. In an instant of time—while your friend hesitates for a word—what things pass through your mind? We have never told the whole truth. We may confess ugly *facts*—the meanest cowardice or the shabbiest and most prosaic impurity—but the *tone* is false. The very act of confessing—an infinitesimally hypocritical glance—a dash of humour—all this contrives to dissociate the facts from your very self. No one could guess how familiar and, in a sense, congenial to your soul these things were, how much of a piece with all the rest: down there, in the dreaming inner warmth, they struck no such discordant note, were not nearly so odd and detachable from the rest of you, as they seem when they are turned into words. We imply, and often believe, that habitual vices are exceptional single acts, and make the opposite mistake about our virtues—like the bad tennis player who calls his normal form his 'bad days' and mistakes his rare successes for his normal. I do not think it is our fault that we cannot tell the real truth about ourselves; the persistent, life-long, inner murmur of spite, jealousy, prurience, greed and self-complacence, simply will not go into words. But the important thing is that we should not mistake our inevitably limited utterances for a full account of the worst that is inside.

2. A reaction—in itself wholesome—is now going on against purely private or domestic conceptions of morality, a reawakening of the *social* conscience. We feel ourselves to be involved in an iniquitous social system and to share a corporate guilt. This is very true: but the enemy can exploit even truths to our deception. Beware lest you are making use of the idea of corporate guilt to distract your attention from those humdrum, old-fashioned guilts of your own which have nothing to do with 'the system' and which can be dealt with without waiting for the millennium. For corporate guilt perhaps cannot be, and certainly is not,

felt with the same force as personal guilt. For most of us, as we now are, this conception is a mere excuse for evading the real issue. When we have really learned to know our individual corruption, then indeed we can go on to think of the corporate guilt and can hardly think of it too much. But we must learn to walk before we run.

3. We have a strange illusion that mere time cancels sin. I have heard others, and I have heard myself, recounting cruelties and falsehoods committed in boyhood as if they were no concern of the present speaker's, and even with laughter. But mere time does nothing either to the fact or to the guilt of a sin. The guilt is washed out not by time but by repentance and the blood of Christ: if we have repented these early sins we should remember the price of our forgiveness and be humble. As for the fact of a sin, is it probable that anything cancels it? All times are eternally present to God. Is it not at least possible that along some one line of His multi-dimensional eternity He sees you forever in the nursery pulling the wings off a fly, forever toadying, lying, and lusting as a schoolboy, forever in that moment of cowardice or insolence as a subaltern? It may be that salvation consists not in the cancelling of these eternal moments but in the perfected humanity that bears the shame forever, rejoicing in the occasion which it furnished to God's compassion and glad that it should be common knowledge to the universe. Perhaps in that eternal moment St Peter—he will forgive me if I am wrong—forever denies his Master. If so, it would indeed be true that the joys of Heaven are for most of us, in our present condition, 'an acquired taste'—and certain ways of life may render the taste impossible of acquisition. Perhaps the lost are those who dare not go to such a *public* place. Of course I do not know that this is true; but I think the possibility is worth keeping in mind.

4. We must guard against the feeling that there is 'safety in numbers'. It is natural to feel that if *all* men are as bad as the Christians say, then badness must be very excusable. If all the boys plough in the examination, surely the papers must have been too hard? And so the masters at that school feel till they learn that there are other schools where ninety per cent of the boys passed on the same papers. Then they begin to suspect that the fault did not lie with the examiners. Again, many of us have had the experience of living in some local pocket of human society— some particular school, college, regiment or profession where the tone was bad. And inside that pocket certain actions were regarded as merely normal ('Everyone does it') and certain others as impracticably virtu-

ous and Quixotic. But when we emerged from that bad society we made the horrible discovery that in the outer world our 'normal' was the kind of thing that no decent person ever dreamed of doing, and our 'Quixotic' was taken for granted as the minimum standard of decency. What had seemed to us morbid and fantastic scruples so long as we were in the 'pocket' now turned out to be the only moments of sanity we there enjoyed. It is wise to face the possibility that the whole human race (being a small thing in the universe) is, in fact, just such a local pocket of evil—an isolated bad school or regiment inside which minimum decency passes for heroic virtue and utter corruption for pardonable imperfection. But is there any evidence—except Christian doctrine itself—that this is so? I am afraid there is. In the first place, there are those odd people among us who do not accept the local standard, who demonstrate the alarming truth that a quite different behaviour is, in fact, possible. Worse still, there is the fact that these people, even when separated widely in space and time, have a suspicious knack of agreeing with one another in the main—almost as if they were in touch with some larger public opinion outside the pocket. What is common to Zarathustra, Jeremiah, Socrates, Gautama, Christ[1] and Marcus Aurelius, is something pretty substantial. Thirdly, we find in ourselves even now a theoretical approval of this behaviour which no one practises. Even inside the pocket we do not say that justice, mercy, fortitude, and temperance are of no value, but only that the local custom is as just, brave, temperate and merciful as can reasonably be expected. It begins to look as if the neglected school rules even inside this bad school were connected with some larger world—and that when the term ends we might find ourselves facing the public opinion of that larger world. But the worst of all is this: we cannot help seeing that only the degree of virtue which we now regard as impracticable can possibly save our race from disaster even on this planet. The standard which seems to have come into the 'pocket' from outside, turns out to be terribly relevant to conditions inside the pocket—so relevant that a consistent practice of virtue by the human race even for ten years would fill the earth from pole to pole with peace, plenty, health, merriment, and heartsease, and that nothing else will. It may be the custom, down here,

---

[1] I mention the Incarnate God among human teachers to emphasise the fact that the *principal* difference between Him and them lies not in ethical teaching (which is here my concern) but in Person and Office.

to treat the regimental rules as a dead letter or a counsel of perfection: but even now, everyone who stops to think can see that when we meet the enemy this neglect is going to cost every man of us his life. It is then that we shall envy the 'morbid' person, the 'pedant' or 'enthusiast' who really *has* taught his company to shoot and dig in aond spare their water bottles.

5. The larger society to which I here contrast the human 'pocket' may not exist according to some people, and at any rate we have no experience of it. We do not meet angels, or unfallen races. But we can get some inkling of the truth even inside our own race. Different ages and cultures can be regarded as 'pockets' in relation to one another. I said, a few pages back, that different ages excelled in different virtues. If, then, you are ever tempted to think that we modern Western Europeans cannot really be so very bad because we are, comparatively speaking, humane—if, in other words, you think God might be content with us on that ground— ask yourself whether you think God ought to have been content with the cruelty of cruel ages because they excelled in courage or chastity. You will see at once that this is an impossibility. From considering how the cruelty of our ancestors looks to us, you may get some inkling how our softness, worldliness, and timidity would have looked to them, and hence how both must look to God.

6. Perhaps my harping on the word 'kindness' has already aroused a protest in some readers' minds. Are we not really an increasingly cruel age? Perhaps we are: but I think we have become so in the attempt to reduce all virtues to kindness. For Plato rightly taught that virtue is one. You cannot be kind unless you have all the other virtues. If, being cowardly, conceited and slothful, you have never yet done a fellow creature great mischief, that is only because your neighbour's welfare has not yet happened to conflict with your safety, self-approval, or ease. Every vice leads to cruelty. Even a good emotion, pity, if not controlled by charity and justice, leads through anger to cruelty. Most atrocities are stimulated by accounts of the enemy's atrocities; and pity for the oppressed classes, when separated from the moral law as a whole, leads by a very natural process to the unremitting brutalities of a reign of terror.

7. Some modern theologians have, quite rightly, protested against an excessively moralistic interpretation of Christianity. The Holiness of God is something more and other than moral perfection: His claim upon us is something more and other than the claim of moral duty. I do not deny it: but this conception, like that of corporate guilt, is very easily

used as an evasion of the real issue. God may be more than moral goodness: He is not less. The road to the promised land runs past Sinai. The moral law may exist to be transcended: but there is no transcending it for those who have not first admitted its claims upon them, and then tried with all their strength to meet that claim, and fairly and squarely faced the fact of their failure.

8. 'Let no man say when he is tempted, I am tempted of God.'[2] Many schools of thought encourage us to shift the responsibility for our behaviour from our own shoulders to some inherent necessity in the nature of human life, and thus, indirectly, to the Creator. Popular forms of this view are the evolutionary doctrine that what we call badness is an unavoidable legacy from our animal ancestors, or the idealistic doctrine that it is merely a result of our being finite. Now Christianity, if I have understood the Pauline epistles, does admit that perfect obedience to the moral law, which we find written in our hearts and perceive to be necessary even on the biological level, is not in fact possible to men. This would raise a real difficulty about our responsibility if perfect obedience had any practical relation at all to the lives of most of us. Some degree of obedience which you and I have failed to attain in the last twenty-four hours is certainly possible. The ultimate problem must not be used as one more means of evasion. Most of us are less urgently concerned with the Pauline question than with William Law's simple statement: 'If you will here stop and ask yourselves why you are not as pious as the primitive Christians were, your own heart will tell you, that it is neither through ignorance nor inability, but purely because you never thoroughly intended it.'[3]

This chapter will have been misunderstood if anyone describes it as a reinstatement of the doctrine of Total Depravity. I disbelieve that doctrine, partly on the logical ground that if our depravity were total we should not know ourselves to be depraved, and partly because experience shows us much goodness in human nature. Nor am I recommending universal gloom. The emotion of shame has been valued not as an emotion but because of the insight to which it leads. I think that insight should be permanent in each man's mind: but whether the painful emotions that

---

[2] James 1:13.

[3] *Serious Call*, cap 2.

attend it should also be encouraged, is a technical problem of spiritual direction on which, as a layman, I have little call to speak. My own idea, for what it is worth, is that all sadness which is not either arising from the repentance of a concrete sin and hastening towards concrete amendment or restitution, or else arising from pity and hastening to active assistance, is simply bad; and I think we all sin by needlessly disobeying the apostolic injunction to 'rejoice' as much as by anything else. Humility, after the first shock, is a cheerful virtue: it is the high-minded unbeliever, desperately trying in the teeth of repeated disillusions to retain his 'faith in human nature', who is really sad. I have been aiming at an intellectual, not an emotional, effect: I have been trying to make the reader believe that we actually are, at present, creatures whose character must be, in some respects, a horror to God, as it is, when we really see it, a horror to ourselves. This I believe to be a fact: and I notice that the holier a man is, the more fully he is aware of that fact. Perhaps you have imagined that this humility in the saints is a pious illusion at which God smiles. That is a most dangerous error. It is theoretically dangerous, because it makes you identify a virtue (i.e., a perfection) with an illusion (i.e., an imperfection), which must be nonsense. It is practically dangerous because it encourages a man to mistake his first insights into his own corruption for the first beginnings of a halo round his own silly head. No, depend upon it; when the saints say that they—even they—are vile, they are recording truth with scientific accuracy.

How did this state of affairs come about? In the next chapter I shall give as much as I can understand of the Christian answer to that question.

5

THE FALL OF MAN

To obey is the proper office of a rational soul.

MONTAIGNE II, XII

THE CHRISTIAN ANSWER to the question proposed in the last chapter is contained in the doctrine of the Fall. According to that doctrine, man is now a horror to God and to himself and a creature ill-adapted to the universe not because God made him so but because he has made himself so by the abuse of his free will. To my mind this is the sole function of the doctrine. It exists to guard against two sub-Christian theories of the origin of evil—Monism, according to which God Himself, being 'above good and evil', produces impartially the effects to which we give those two names, and Dualism, according to which God produces good, while some equal and independent Power produces evil. Against both these views Christianity asserts that God is good; that He made all things good and for the sake of their goodness; that one of the good things He made, namely, the free will of rational creatures, by its very nature included the possibility of evil; and that creatures, availing themselves of this possibility, have become evil. Now this function—which is the only one I allow to the doctrine of the Fall—must be distinguished from two other functions which it is sometimes, perhaps, represented as performing, but which I reject. In the first place, I do not think the doctrine answers the question 'Was it better for God to create than not to create?' That is a question I have already declined. Since I believe God to be good, I am sure that, if the question has a meaning, the answer must be Yes. But I doubt whether the question has any meaning: and even if it has, I am sure that the answer cannot be attained by the sort of value-judgement which men can significantly make. In the second place, I do not think the doctrine of the Fall can be used to show that it is 'just', in terms of retributive justice, to punish individuals for the faults of their remote ancestors. Some forms of doctrine seem to involve this; but I question whether any of them, as understood by its exponents, really meant it. The Fathers may sometimes say that we are punished for Adam's sin: but they much more often say that *we* sinned 'in Adam'. It may be impossible to find out what they meant by this, or we may decide that what they meant was erroneous. But I do not think we can dismiss their way of talking as a mere 'idiom'. Wisely, or foolishly, they believed that we were *really*— and not simply by legal fiction—involved in Adam's action. The attempt to formulate this belief by saying that we were 'in' Adam in a physical sense—Adam being the first vehicle of the 'immortal germ plasm'—may be unacceptable: but it is, of course, a further question whether the belief itself is merely a confusion or a real insight into spiritual realities beyond our normal grasp. At the moment, however, this question does not arise; for, as I have said, I have no intention of arguing that the descent to modern man of inabilities contracted by his remote ancestors is a specimen of retributive justice. For me it is rather a specimen of those things necessarily involved in the creation of a stable world which we considered in Chapter 2. It would, no doubt, have been possible for God to remove by miracle the results of the first sin ever committed by a human being; but this would not have been much good unless He was prepared to remove the results of the second sin, and of the third, and so on forever. If the miracles ceased, then sooner or later we might have reached our present lamentable situation: if they did not, then a world thus continually underpropped and corrected by Divine interference, would have been a world in which nothing important ever depended on human choice, and in which choice itself would soon cease from the certainty that one of the apparent alternatives before you would lead to no results and was therefore not really an alternative. As we saw, the chess player's freedom to play chess depends on the rigidity of the squares and the moves.

Having isolated what I conceive to be the true import of the doctrine that Man is fallen, let us now consider the doctrine in itself. The story in

Genesis is a story (full of the deepest suggestion) about a magic apple of knowledge; but in the developed doctrine the inherent magic of the apple has quite dropped out of sight, and the story is simply one of disobedience. I have the deepest respect even for Pagan myths, still more for myths in Holy Scripture. I therefore do not doubt that the version which emphasises the magic apple, and brings together the trees of life and knowledge, contains a deeper and subtler truth than the version which makes the apple simply and solely a pledge of obedience. But I assume that the Holy Spirit would not have allowed the latter to grow up in the Church and win the assent of great doctors unless it also was true and useful as far as it went. It is this version which I am going to discuss, because, though I suspect the primitive version to be far more profound, I know that I, at any rate, cannot penetrate its profundities. I am to give my readers not the best absolutely but the best I have.

In the developed doctrine, then, it is claimed that Man, as God made him, was completely good and completely happy, but that he disobeyed God and became what we now see. Many people think that this proposition has been proved false by modern science. 'We now know,' it is said, 'that so far from having fallen out of a primeval state of virtue and happiness, men have slowly risen from brutality and savagery.' There seems to me to be a complete confusion here. *Brute* and *savage* both belong to that unfortunate class of words which are sometimes used rhetorically, as terms of reproach, and sometimes scientifically, as terms of description; and the pseudo-scientific argument against the Fall depends on a confusion between the usages. If by saying that man rose from brutality you mean simply that man is physically descended from animals, I have no objection. But it does not follow that the further back you go the more *brutal*—in the sense of wicked or wretched—you will find man to be. No animal has moral virtue: but it is not true that all animal behaviour is of the kind one should call 'wicked' if it were practised by men. On the contrary, not all animals treat other creatures of their own species as badly as men treat men. Not all are as gluttonous or lecherous as we, and no animal is ambitious. Similarly if you say that the first men were 'savages', meaning by this that their artefacts were few and clumsy like those of modern 'savages', you may well be right; but if you mean that they were 'savage' in the sense of being lewd, ferocious, cruel, and treacherous, you will be going beyond your evidence, and that for two reasons. In the first place, modern anthropologists and missionaries are less inclined than their fathers to endorse your unfavourable picture even of the modern savage. In the second place you cannot argue from the artefacts of the earliest men that they were in all respects like the contemporary people who make similar artefacts. We must be on our guard here against an illusion which the study of prehistoric man seems naturally to beget. Prehistoric man, because he is prehistoric, is known to us only by the material things he made—or rather by a chance selection from among the more durable things he made. It is not the fault of archaeologists that they have no better evidence: but this penury constitutes a continual temptation to infer more than we have any right to infer, to assume that the community which made the superior artefacts was superior in all respects. Everyone can see that the assumption is false; it would lead to the conclusion that the leisured classes of our own time were in all respects superior to those of the Victorian age. Clearly the prehistoric men who made the worst pottery might have made the best poetry and we should never know it. And the assumption becomes even more absurd when we are comparing prehistoric men with modern savages. The equal crudity of artefacts here tells you nothing about the intelligence or virtue of the makers. What is learned by trial and error must begin by being crude, whatever the character of the beginner. The very same pot which would prove its maker a genius if it were the first pot ever made in the world, would prove its maker a dunce if it came after millenniums of pot-making. The whole modern estimate of primitive man is based upon that idolatry of artefacts which is a great corporate sin of our own civilisation. We forget that our prehistoric ancestors made all the useful discoveries, except that of chloroform, which have ever been made. To them we owe language, the family, clothing, the use of fire, the domestication of animals, the wheel, the ship, poetry and agriculture.

Science, then, has nothing to say for or against the doctrine of the Fall. A more philosophical difficulty has been raised by the modern theologian to whom all students of the subject are most indebted.[1] This writer points out that the idea of sin presupposes a law to sin against: and since it would take centuries for the 'herd-instinct' to crystallise into custom and for custom to harden into law, the first man—if there ever was a being who could be so described—could not commit the first sin. This argument assumes that virtue and the herd-instinct commonly coincide, and that the

[1] N. P. Williams, *The Ideas of the Fall and of Original Sin*, p. 516.

'first sin' was essentially a *social* sin. But the traditional doctrine points to a sin against God, an act of disobedience, not a sin against the neighbour. And certainly, if we are to hold the doctrine of the Fall in any real sense, we must look for the great sin on a deeper and more timeless level than that of social morality.

This sin has been described by Saint Augustine as the result of Pride, of the movement whereby a creature (that is, an essentially dependent being whose principle of existence lies not in itself but in another) tries to set up on its own, to exist for itself.[2] Such a sin requires no complex social conditions, no extended experience, no great intellectual development. From the moment a creature becomes aware of God as God and of itself as self, the terrible alternative of choosing God or self for the centre is opened to it. This sin is committed daily by young children and ignorant peasants as well as by sophisticated persons, by solitaries no less than by those who live in society: it is the fall in every individual life, and in each day of each individual life, the basic sin behind all particular sins: at this very moment you and I are either committing it, or about to commit it, or repenting it. We try, when we wake, to lay the new day at God's feet; before we have finished shaving, it becomes *our* day and God's share in it is felt as a tribute which we must pay out of 'our own' pocket, a deduction from the time which ought, we feel, to be 'our own'. A man starts a new job with a sense of vocation and, perhaps, for the first week still keeps the discharge of the vocation as his end, taking the pleasures and pains from God's hand, as they come, as 'accidents'. But in the second week he is beginning to 'know the ropes': by the third, he has quarried out of the total job his own plan for himself within that job, and when he can pursue this he feels that he is getting no more than his rights, and, when he cannot, that he is being interfered with. A lover, in obedience to a quite uncalculating impulse, which may be full of good will as well as of desire and need not be forgetful of God, embraces his beloved, and then, quite innocently, experiences a thrill of sexual pleasure; but the second embrace may have that pleasure in view, may be a means to an end, may be the first downward step towards the state of regarding a fellow creature as a thing, as a machine to be used for his pleasure. Thus the bloom of innocence, the element of obedience and the readiness to take what comes is rubbed off every activity. Thoughts undertaken for God's sake—like

_____

[2] *De Civitate Dei*, xiv, xiii.

that on which we are engaged at the moment—are continued as if they were an end in themselves, and then as if our pleasure in thinking were the end, and finally as if our pride or celebrity were the end. Thus all day long, and all the days of our life, we are sliding, slipping, falling away—as if God were, to our present consciousness, a smooth inclined plane on which there is no resting. And indeed we are now of such a nature that we must slip off, and the sin, because it is unavoidable, may be venial. But God cannot have made us so. The gravitation away from God, 'the journey homeward to habitual self', must, we think, be a product of the Fall. What exactly happened when Man fell, we do not know; but if it is legitimate to guess, I offer the following picture—a 'myth' in the Socratic sense,[3] a not unlikely tale.

For long centuries God perfected the animal form which was to become the vehicle of humanity and the image of Himself. He gave it hands whose thumb could be applied to each of the fingers, and jaws and teeth and throat capable of articulation, and a brain sufficiently complex to execute all the material motions whereby rational thought is incarnated. The creature may have existed for ages in this state before it became man: it may even have been clever enough to make things which a modern archaeologist would accept as proof of its humanity. But it was only an animal because all its physical and psychical processes were directed to purely material and natural ends. Then, in the fullness of time, God caused to descend upon this organism, both on its psychology and physiology, a new kind of consciousness which could say 'I' and 'me', which could look upon itself as an object, which knew God, which could make judgements of truth, beauty, and goodness, and which was so far above time that it could perceive time flowing past. This new consciousness ruled and illuminated the whole organism, flooding every part of it with light, and was not, like ours, limited to a selection of the movements going on in one part of the organism, namely the brain. Man was then all consciousness. The modern Yogi claims—whether falsely or truly—to have under control those functions which to us are almost part of the external world, such as digestion and circulation. This power the first man had in eminence. His organic processes obeyed the law of his own will, not the law of nature. His organs sent up appetites to the judgement seat of will

---

[3] i.e., an account of what may have been the historical fact. Not to be confused with 'myth' in Dr Niebuhr's sense (i.e., a symbolical representation of non-historical truth).

not because they had to, but because he chose. Sleep meant to him not the stupor which we undergo, but willed and conscious repose—he remained awake to enjoy the pleasure and duty of sleep. Since the processes of decay and repair in his tissues were similarly conscious and obedient, it may not be fanciful to suppose that the length of his life was largely at his own discretion. Wholly commanding himself, he commanded all lower lives with which he came into contact. Even now we meet rare individuals who have a mysterious power of taming beasts. This power the Paradisal man enjoyed in eminence. The old picture of the brutes sporting before Adam and fawning upon him may not be wholly symbolical. Even now more animals than you might expect are ready to adore man if they are given a reasonable opportunity: for man was made to be the priest and even, in one sense, the Christ, of the animals—the mediator through whom they apprehend so much of the Divine splendour as their irrational nature allows. And God was to such a man no slippery, inclined plane. The new consciousness had been made to repose on its Creator, and repose it did. However rich and varied man's experience of his fellows (or fellow) in charity and friendship and sexual love, or of the beasts, or of the surrounding world then first recognised as beautiful and awful, God came first in his love and in his thought, and that without painful effort. In perfect cyclic movement, being, power and joy descended from God to man in the form of gift and returned from man to God in the form of obedient love and ecstatic adoration: and in this sense, though not in all, man was then truly the son of God, the prototype of Christ, perfectly enacting in joy and ease of all the faculties and all the senses that filial self-surrender which Our Lord enacted in the agonies of the crucifixion.

Judged by his artefacts, or perhaps even by his language, this blessed creature was, no doubt, a savage. All that experience and practice can teach he had still to learn: if he chipped flints, he doubtless chipped them clumsily enough. He may have been utterly incapable of expressing in conceptual form his Paradisal experience. All that is quite irrelevant. From our own childhood we remember that before our elders thought us capable of 'understanding' anything, we already had spiritual experience as pure and as momentous as any we have undergone since, though not, of course, as rich in factual context. From Christianity itself we learn that there is a level—in the long run the only level of importance—on which the learned and the adult have no advantage at all over the simple and the child. I do not doubt that if the Paradisal man could now appear among us, we should regard him as an utter savage, a creature to be exploited or, at best, patronised. Only one or two, and those the holiest among us, would glance a second time at the naked, shaggy-bearded, slow-spoken creature: but they, after a few minutes, would fall at his feet.

We do not know how many of these creatures God made, nor how long they continued in the Paradisal state. But sooner or later they fell. Someone or something whispered that they could become as gods—that they could cease directing their lives to their Creator and taking all their delights as uncovenanted mercies, as 'accidents' (in the logical sense) which arose in the course of a life directed not to those delights but to the adoration of God. As a young man wants a regular allowance from his father which he can count on as his own, within which he makes his own plans (and rightly, for his father is after all a fellow creature), so they desired to be on their own, to take care for their own future, to plan for pleasure and for security, to have a *meum* from which, no doubt, they would pay some reasonable tribute to God in the way of time, attention, and love, but which, nevertheless, was theirs not His. They wanted, as we say, to 'call their souls their own'. But that means to live a lie, for our souls are not, in fact, our own. They wanted some corner in the universe of which they could say to God, 'This is our business, not yours.' But there is no such corner. They wanted to be nouns, but they were, and eternally must be, mere adjectives. We have no idea in what particular act, or series of acts, the self-contradictory, impossible wish found expression. For all I can see, it might have concerned the literal eating of a fruit, but the question is of no consequence.

This act of self-will on the part of the creature, which constitutes an utter falseness to its true creaturely position, is the only sin that can be conceived as the Fall. For the difficulty about the first sin is that it must be very heinous, or its consequences would not be so terrible, and yet it must be something which a being free from the temptations of fallen man could conceivably have committed. The turning from God to self fulfils both conditions. It is a sin possible even to Paradisal man, because the mere existence of a self—the mere fact that we call it 'me'—includes, from the first, the danger of self-idolatry. Since I am I, I must make an act of self-surrender, however small or however easy, in living to God rather than to myself. This is, if you like, the 'weak spot' in the very nature of creation, the risk which God apparently thinks worth taking. But the sin was very heinous, because the self which Paradisal man had to surrender contained no natural recalcitrancy to being surrendered. His *data*, so to speak, were a psycho- physical organism wholly subject to the will and a will wholly disposed, though not compelled, to turn to God. The self-surrender which he practised before the Fall meant no struggle but only the delicious overcoming of an infinitesimal self-adherence which delighted to be overcome—of which we see a dim analogy in the rapturous mutual self-surrenders of lovers even now. He had, therefore, no *temptation* (in our sense) to choose the self—no passion or inclination obstinately inclining that way—nothing but the bare fact that the self was *him*self.

Up to that moment the human spirit had been in full control of the human organism. It doubtless expected that it would retain this control when it had ceased to obey God. But its authority over the organism was a delegated authority which it lost when it ceased to be God's delegate. Having cut itself off, as far as it could, from the source of its being, it had cut itself off from the source of power. For when we say of created things that A rules B this must mean that God rules B through A. I doubt whether it would have been intrinsically possible for God to continue to rule the organism *through* the human spirit when the human spirit was in revolt against Him. At any rate He did not. He began to rule the organism in a more external way, not by the laws of spirit, but by those of nature.[4] Thus the organs, no longer governed by man's will, fell under the control of ordinary biochemical laws and suffered whatever the interworkings of those laws might bring about in the way of pain, senility and death. And desires began to come up into the mind of man, not as his reason chose, but just as the biochemical and environmental facts happened to cause them. And the mind itself fell under the psychological laws of association and the like which God had made to rule the psychology of the higher anthropoids. And the will, caught in the tidal wave of mere nature, had no resource but to force back some of the new thoughts and desires by main strength, and these uneasy rebels became the subconscious as we now know it. The process was not, I conceive, comparable to mere deterioration as it may now occur in a human individual; it was a loss of

---

[4] This is a development of Hooker's conception of Law. To disobey your *proper* law (i.e., the law God makes for a being such as you) means to find yourself obeying one of God's lower laws: e.g., if, when walking on a slippery pavement, you neglect the law of Prudence, you suddenly find yourself obeying the law of gravitation.

status as a *species*. What man lost by the Fall was his original specific nature. 'Dust thou art, and unto dust shalt thou return.' The total organism which had been taken up into his spiritual life was allowed to fall back into the merely natural condition from which, at his making, it had been raised—just as, far earlier in the story of creation, God had raised vegetable life to become the vehicle of animality, and chemical process to be the vehicle of vegetation, and physical process to be the vehicle of chemical. Thus human spirit from being the master of human nature became a mere lodger in its own house, or even a prisoner; rational consciousness became what it now is—a fitful spotlight resting on a small part of the cerebral motions. But this limitation of the spirit's powers was a lesser evil than the corruption of the spirit itself. It had turned from God and become its own idol, so that though it could still turn back to God,[5] it could do so only by painful effort, and its inclination was self-ward. Hence pride and ambition, the desire to be lovely in its own eyes and to depress and humiliate all rivals, envy, and restless search for more, and still more, security, were now the attitudes that came easiest to it. It was not only a weak king over its own nature, but a bad one: it sent down into the psycho-physical organism desires far worse than the organism sent up into it. This condition was transmitted by heredity to all later generations, for it was not simply what biologists call an acquired variation; it was the emergence of a new kind of man—a new species, never made by God, had sinned itself into existence. The change which man had undergone was not parallel to the development of a new habit; it was a radical alteration of his constitution, a disturbance of the relation between his component parts, and an internal perversion of one of them.

God might have arrested this process by miracle: but this—to speak in somewhat irreverent metaphor—would have been to decline the problem which God had set Himself when He created the world, the problem of expressing His goodness through the total drama of a world containing free agents, in spite of, and by means of, their rebellion against Him. The symbol of a drama, a symphony, or a dance, is here useful to correct a certain absurdity which may arise if we talk too much of God planning

---

[5] Theologians will note that I am not here intending to make any contribution to the Pelagian-Augustinian controversy. I mean only that such return to God was not, even now, an impossibility. Where the initiative lies in any instance of such return is a question on which I am saying nothing.

and creating the world process for good and of that good being frustrated by the free will of the creatures. This may raise the ridiculous idea that the Fall took God by surprise and upset His plan, or else—more ridiculously still—that God planned the whole thing for conditions which, He well knew, were never going to be realised. In fact, of course, God saw the crucifixion in the act of creating the first nebula. The world is a dance in which good, descending from God, is disturbed by evil arising from the creatures, and the resulting conflict is resolved by God's own assumption of the suffering nature which evil produces. The doctrine of the free Fall asserts that the evil which thus makes the fuel or raw material for the second and more complex kind of good is not God's contribution but man's. This does not mean that if man had remained innocent God could not then have contrived an equally splendid symphonic whole—supposing that we insist on asking such questions. But it must always be remembered that when we talk of what might have happened, of contingencies outside the whole actuality, we do not really know what we are talking about. There are no times or places outside the existing universe in which all this 'could happen' or 'could have happened'. I think the most significant way of stating the real freedom of man is to say that if there are other rational species than man, existing in some other part of the actual universe, then it is not necessary to suppose that they also have fallen.

Our present condition, then, is explained by the fact that we are members of a spoiled species. I do not mean that our sufferings are a punishment for being what we cannot now help being nor that we are morally responsible for the rebellion of a remote ancestor. If, none the less, I call our present condition one of original Sin, and not merely one of original misfortune, that is because our actual religious experience does not allow us to regard it in any other way. Theoretically, I suppose, we might say 'Yes: we behave like vermin, but then that is because we *are* vermin. And that, at any rate, is not our fault.' But the fact that we are vermin, so far from being felt as an excuse, is a greater shame and grief to us than any of the particular acts which it leads us to commit. The situation is not nearly so hard to understand as some people make out. It arises among human beings whenever a very badly brought up boy is introduced into a decent family. They rightly remind themselves that it is 'not his own fault' that he is a bully, a coward, a tale-bearer and a liar. But none the less, however it came there, his present character is detestable. They not only hate it, but ought to hate it. They cannot love him for what he is, they can only try to turn him into what he is not. In the meantime, though the boy is most unfortunate in having been so brought up, you cannot quite call his character a 'misfortune' as if he were one thing and his character another. It is he—he himself—who bullies and sneaks and likes doing it. And if he begins to mend he will inevitably feel shame and guilt at what he is just beginning to cease to be.

With this I have said all that can be said on the level at which alone I feel able to treat the subject of the Fall. But I warn my readers once more that this level is a shallow one. We have said nothing about the trees of life and of knowledge which doubtless conceal some great mystery: and we have said nothing about the Pauline statement that 'as in Adam all die, so in Christ shall all be made alive'.[6] It is this passage which lies behind the Patristic doctrine of our physical presence in Adam's loins and Anselm's doctrine of our inclusion, by legal fiction, in the suffering Christ. These theories may have done good in their day but they do no good to me, and I am not going to invent others. We have recently been told by the scientists that we have no right to expect that the real universe should be picturable, and that if we make mental pictures to illustrate quantum physics we are moving further away from reality, not nearer to it.[7] We have clearly even less right to demand that the highest spiritual realities should be picturable, or even explicable in terms of our abstract thought. I observe that the difficulty of the Pauline formula turns on the word *in,* and that this word, again and again in the New Testament, is used in senses we cannot fully understand. That we can die 'in' Adam and live 'in' Christ seems to me to imply that man, as he really is, differs a good deal from man as our categories of thought and our three-dimensional imaginations represent him; that the separateness—modified only by causal relations—which we discern between individuals, is balanced, in absolute reality, by some kind of 'inter-inanimation' of which we have no conception at all. It may be that the acts and sufferings of great archetypal individuals such as Adam and Christ are ours, not by legal fiction, metaphor, or causality, but in some much deeper fashion. There is no question, of course, of individuals melting down into a kind of spiritual continuum such as Pantheistic systems believe in; that is excluded by the whole tenor of our faith. But there may be a tension between individual-

---

[6] 1 Corinthians 15:22.

[7] Sir James Jeans' *The Mysterious Universe,* cap. 5.

ity and some other principle. We believe that the Holy Spirit can be really present and operative in the human spirit, but we do not, like Pantheists, take this to mean that we are 'parts' or 'modifications' or 'appearances' of God. We may have to suppose, in the long run, that something of the same kind is true, in its appropriate degree, even of created spirits, that each, though distinct, is really present in all, or in some, others—just as we may have to admit 'action at a distance' into our conception of matter. Everyone will have noticed how the Old Testament seems at times to ignore our conception of the individual. When God promises Jacob that 'He will go down with him into Egypt and will also surely bring him up again',[8] this is fulfilled either by the burial of Jacob's body in Palestine or by the exodus of Jacob's descendants from Egypt. It is quite right to connect this notion with the social structure of early communities in which the individual is constantly overlooked in favour of the tribe or family: but we ought to express this connection by two propositions of equal importance—firstly that their social experience blinded the ancients to some truths which we perceive, and secondly that it made them sensible of some truths to which we are blind. Legal fiction, adoption, and transference or imputation of merit and guilt, could never have played the part they did play in theology if they had always been felt to be so artificial as we now feel them to be.

I have thought it right to allow this one glance at what is for me an impenetrable curtain, but, as I have said, it makes no part of my present argument. Clearly it would be futile to attempt to solve the problem of pain by producing another problem. The thesis of this chapter is simply that man, as a species, spoiled himself, and that good, to us in our present state, must therefore mean primarily remedial or corrective good. What part pain actually plays in such remedy or correction, is now to be considered.

---

[8] Genesis 46:4.

6

HUMAN PAIN

Since the life of Christ is every way most bitter to nature
and the Self and the Me (for in the true life of Christ,
the Self and the Me and nature must be forsaken and
lost and die altogether), therefore in each of us, nature
hath a horror of it.

THEOLOGIA GERMANICA, XX

I HAVE TRIED to show in a previous chapter that the possibility of pain is inherent in the very existence of a world where souls can meet. When souls become wicked they will certainly use this possibility to hurt one another; and this, perhaps, accounts for four-fifths of the sufferings of men. It is men, not God, who have produced racks, whips, prisons, slavery, guns, bayonets, and bombs; it is by human avarice or human stupidity, not by the churlishness of nature, that we have poverty and overwork. But there remains, none the less, much suffering which cannot thus be traced to ourselves. Even if all suffering were man-made, we should like to know the reason for the enormous permission to torture their fellows which God gives to the worst of men.[1] To say, as was said in the last chapter, that good, for such creatures as we now are, means primarily corrective or remedial good, is an incomplete answer. Not all medicine tastes nasty: or if it did, that is itself one of the unpleasant facts for which we should like to know the reason.

Before proceeding I must pick up a point made in Chapter 2. I there said that pain, below a certain level of intensity, was not resented and might even be rather liked. Perhaps you then wanted to reply 'In that case I should not call it Pain,' and you may have been right. But the truth is that the word Pain has two senses which must now be distinguished. A.) A particular kind of sensation, probably conveyed by specialised nerve fibres, and recognisable by the patient as that kind of sensation whether he dislikes it or not (e.g., the faint ache in my limbs would be recognised as an ache even if I didn't object to it). B.) Any experience, whether physical or mental, which the patient dislikes. It will be noticed that all Pains in sense A become Pains in sense B if they are raised above a certain very low level of intensity, but that Pains in the B sense need not be Pains in the A sense. Pain in the B sense, in fact, is synonymous with 'suffering', 'anguish', 'tribulation', 'adversity', or 'trouble', and it is about it that the problem of pain arises. For the rest of this book Pain will be used in the B sense and will include all types of suffering: with the A sense we have no further concern.

Now the proper good of a creature is to surrender itself to its Creator—to enact intellectually, volitionally, and emotionally, that relationship which is given in the mere fact of its being a creature. When it does so, it is good and happy. Lest we should think this a hardship, this kind of good begins on a level far above the creatures, for God Himself, as Son, from all eternity renders back to God as Father by filial obedience the being which the Father by paternal love eternally generates in the Son. This is the pattern which man was made to imitate—which Paradisal man did imitate—and wherever the will conferred by the Creator is thus perfectly offered back in delighted and delighting obedience by the creature, there, most undoubtedly, is Heaven, and there the Holy Ghost proceeds. In the world as we now know it, the problem is how to recover this self-surrender. We are not merely imperfect creatures who must be improved: we are, as Newman said, rebels who must lay down our arms. The first answer, then, to the question why our cure should be painful, is that to render back the will which we have so long claimed for our

---

[1] Or perhaps it would be safer to say 'of creatures'. I by no means reject the view that the 'efficient cause' of disease, or some disease, may be a created being other than man (see Chapter 9). In Scripture Satan is specially associated with disease in Job, in Luke 13:16, 1 Corinthians 5:5, and (probably) in 1 Timothy 1:20. It is, at the present stage of the argument, indifferent whether all the created wills to which God allows a power of tormenting other creatures are human or not.

own, is in itself, wherever and however it is done, a grievous pain. Even in Paradise I have supposed a minimal self-adherence to be overcome, though the overcoming, and the yielding, would there be rapturous. But to surrender a self-will inflamed and swollen with years of usurpation is a kind of death. We all remember this self-will as it was in childhood: the bitter, prolonged rage at every thwarting, the burst of passionate tears, the black, Satanic wish to kill or die rather than to give in. Hence the older type of nurse or parent was quite right in thinking that the first step in education is 'to break the child's will'. Their methods were often wrong: but not to see the necessity is, I think, to cut oneself off from all understanding of spiritual laws. And if, now that we are grown up, we do not howl and stamp quite so much, that is partly because our elders began the process of breaking or killing our self-will in the nursery, and partly because the same passions now take more subtle forms and have grown clever at avoiding death by various 'compensations'. Hence the necessity to die daily: however often we think we have broken the rebellious self we shall still find it alive. That this process cannot be without pain is sufficiently witnessed by the very history of the word 'Mortification'.

But this intrinsic pain, or death, in mortifying the usurped self, is not the whole story. Paradoxically, mortification, though itself a pain, is made easier by the presence of pain in its context. This happens, I think, principally in three ways.

The human spirit will not even begin to try to surrender self-will as long as all seems to be well with it. Now error and sin both have this property, that the deeper they are the less their victim suspects their existence; they are masked evil. Pain is unmasked, unmistakable evil; every man knows that something is wrong when he is being hurt. The Masochist is no real exception. Sadism and Masochism respectively isolate, and then exaggerate, a 'moment' or 'aspect' in normal sexual passion. Sadism[2] exaggerates the aspect of capture and domination to a point at which only ill-treatment of the beloved will satisfy the pervert—as though he said 'I am so much master that I even torment you.' Masochism exaggerates the complementary and opposite aspect, and says 'I am so enthralled that I welcome even pain at your hands.' Unless the pain were felt as evil—as an outrage underlining the complete mastery of the other party—it

---

[2] The modern tendency to mean by 'sadistic cruelty' simply 'great cruelty', or cruelty specially condemned by the writer, is not useful

would cease, for the Masochist, to be an erotic stimulus. And pain is not only immediately recognisable evil, but evil impossible to ignore. We can rest contentedly in our sins and in our stupidities; and anyone who has watched gluttons shovelling down the most exquisite foods as if they did not know what they were eating, will admit that we can ignore even pleasure. But pain insists upon being attended to. God whispers to us in our pleasures, speaks in our conscience, but shouts in our pain: it is His megaphone to rouse a deaf world. A bad man, happy, is a man without the least inkling that his actions do not 'answer', that they are not in accord with the laws of the universe.

A perception of this truth lies at the back of the universal human feeling that bad men ought to suffer. It is no use turning up our noses at this feeling, as if it were wholly base. On its mildest level it appeals to everyone's sense of justice. Once when my brother and I, as very small boys, were drawing pictures at the same table, I jerked his elbow and caused him to make an irrelevant line across the middle of his work; the matter was amicably settled by my allowing him to draw a line of equal length across mine. That is, I was 'put in his place', made to see my negligence from the other end. On a sterner level the same idea appears as 'retributive punishment', or 'giving a man what he deserves'. Some enlightened people would like to banish all conceptions of retribution or desert from their theory of punishment and place its value wholly in the deterrence of others or the reform of the criminal himself. They do not see that by so doing they render all punishment unjust. What can be more immoral than to inflict suffering on me for the sake of deterring others if I do not *deserve* it? And if I do deserve it, you are admitting the claims of 'retribution'. And what can be more outrageous than to catch me and submit me to a disagreeable process of moral improvement without my consent, unless (once more) I *deserve* it? On yet a third level we get vindictive passion—the thirst for revenge. This, of course, is evil and expressly forbidden to Christians. But it has perhaps appeared already from our discussion of Sadism and Masochism that the ugliest things in human nature are perversions of good or innocent things. The good thing of which vindictive passion is the perversion comes out with startling clarity in Hobbes's definition of Revengefulness, 'desire by doing hurt to another to make him condemn some fact of his own'.[3] Revenge loses sight

---

[3] *Leviathan*, Pt. I, cap. 6.

of the end in the means, but its end is not wholly bad—it wants the evil of the bad man to be to him what it is to everyone else. This is proved by the fact that the avenger wants the guilty party not merely to suffer, but to suffer at his hands, and to know it, and to know why. Hence the impulse to taunt the guilty man with his crime at the moment of taking vengeance: hence, too, such natural expressions as 'I wonder how he'd like it if the same thing were done to him' or 'I'll teach him'. For the same reason when we are going to abuse a man in words we say we are going to 'let him know what we think of him'.

When our ancestors referred to pains and sorrows as God's 'vengeance' upon sin they were not necessarily attributing evil passions to God; they may have been recognising the good element in the idea of retribution. Until the evil man finds evil unmistakably present in his existence, in the form of pain, he is enclosed in illusion. Once pain has roused him, he knows that he is in some way or other 'up against' the real universe: he either rebels (with the possibility of a clearer issue and deeper repentance at some later stage) or else makes some attempt at an adjustment, which, if pursued, will lead him to religion. It is true that neither effect is so certain now as it was in ages when the existence of God (or even of the gods) was more widely known, but even in our own days we see it operating. Even atheists rebel and express, like Hardy and Housman, their rage against God although (or because) He does not, in their view, exist: and other atheists, like Mr Huxley, are driven by suffering to raise the whole problem of existence and to find some way of coming to terms with it which, if not Christian, is almost infinitely superior to fatuous contentment with a profane life. No doubt Pain as God's megaphone is a terrible instrument; it may lead to final and unrepented rebellion. But it gives the only opportunity the bad man can have for amendment. It removes the veil; it plants the flag of truth within the fortress of a rebel soul.

If the first and lowest operation of pain shatters the illusion that all is well, the second shatters the illusion that what we have, whether good or bad in itself, is our own and enough for us. Everyone has noticed how hard it is to turn our thoughts to God when everything is going well with us. We 'have all we want' is a terrible saying when 'all' does not include God. We find God an interruption. As St Augustine says somewhere, 'God wants to give us something, but cannot, because our hands are full—there's nowhere for Him to put it.' Or as a friend of mine said,

'We regard God as an airman regards his parachute; it's there for emergencies but he hopes he'll never have to use it.' Now God, who has made us, knows what we are and that our happiness lies in Him. Yet we will not seek it in Him as long as He leaves us any other resort where it can even plausibly be looked for. While what we call 'our own life' remains agreeable we will not surrender it to Him. What then can God do in our interests but make 'our own life' less agreeable to us, and take away the plausible source of false happiness? It is just here, where God's providence seems at first to be most cruel, that the Divine humility, the stooping down of the Highest, most deserves praise. We are perplexed to see misfortune falling upon decent, inoffensive, worthy people—on capable, hard-working mothers of families or diligent, thrifty little tradespeople, on those who have worked so hard, and so honestly, for their modest stock of happiness and now seem to be entering on the enjoyment of it with the fullest right. How can I say with sufficient tenderness what here needs to be said? It does not matter that I know I must become, in the eyes of every hostile reader, as it were, personally responsible for all the sufferings I try to explain—just as, to this day, everyone talks as if St Augustine *wanted* unbaptised infants to go to Hell. But it matters enormously if I alienate anyone from the truth. Let me implore the reader to try to believe, if only for the moment, that God, who made these deserving people, may really be right when He thinks that their modest prosperity and the happiness of their children are not enough to make them blessed: that all this must fall from them in the end, and that if they have not learned to know Him they will be wretched. And therefore He troubles them, warning them in advance of an insufficiency that one day they will have to discover. The life to themselves and their families stands between them and the recognition of their need; He makes that life less sweet to them. I call this a Divine humility because it is a poor thing to strike our colours to God when the ship is going down under us; a poor thing to come to Him as a last resort, to offer up 'our own' when it is no longer worth keeping. If God were proud He would hardly have us on such terms: but He is not proud, He stoops to conquer, He will have us even though we have shown that we prefer everything else to Him, and come to Him because there is 'nothing better' now to be had. The same humility is shown by all those Divine appeals to our fears which trouble high-minded readers of Scripture. It is hardly complimentary to God that we should choose Him as an alternative to Hell: yet even this He accepts.

The creature's illusion of self-sufficiency must, for the creature's sake, be shattered; and by trouble or fear of trouble on earth, by crude fear of the eternal flames, God shatters it 'unmindful of His glory's diminution'. Those who would like the God of Scripture to be more purely ethical, do not know what they ask. If God were a Kantian, who would not have us till we came to Him from the purest and best motives, who could be saved? And this illusion of self-sufficiency may be at its strongest in some very honest, kindly, and temperate people, and on such people, therefore, misfortune must fall.

The dangers of apparent self-sufficiency explain why Our Lord regards the vices of the feckless and dissipated so much more leniently than the vices that lead to worldly success. Prostitutes are in no danger of finding their present life so satisfactory that they cannot turn to God: the proud, the avaricious, the self-righteous, are in that danger.

The third operation of suffering is a little harder to grasp. Everyone will admit that choice is essentially conscious; to choose involves knowing that you choose. Now Paradisal man always chose to follow God's will. In following it he also gratified his own desire, both because all the actions demanded of him were, in fact, agreeable to his blameless inclination, and also because the service of God was itself his keenest pleasure, without which as their razor edge all joys would have been insipid to him. The question 'Am I doing this for God's sake or only because I happen to like it?' did not then arise, since doing things for God's sake was what he chiefly 'happened to like'. His God-ward will rode his happiness like a well-managed horse, whereas our will, when we are happy, is carried away in the happiness as in a ship racing down a swift stream. Pleasure was then an acceptable offering to God because offering was a pleasure. But we inherit a whole system of desires which do not necessarily contradict God's will but which, after centuries of usurped autonomy, steadfastly ignore it. If the thing we like doing is, in fact, the thing God wants us to do, yet that is not our reason for doing it; it remains a mere happy coincidence. We cannot therefore know that we are acting at all, or primarily, for God's sake, unless the material of the action is contrary to our inclinations, or (in other words) painful, and what we cannot know that we are choosing, we cannot choose. The full acting out of the self's surrender to God therefore demands pain: this action, to be perfect, must be done from the pure will to obey, in the absence, or in the teeth, of inclination. How impossible it is to enact the surrender of the self by doing what we like, I know very well from my own experience at the moment. When I undertook to write this book I hoped that the will to obey what might be a 'leading' had at least some place in my motives. But now that I am thoroughly immersed in it, it has become a temptation rather than a duty. I may still hope that the writing of the book is, in fact, in conformity with God's will: but to contend that I am learning to surrender myself by doing what is so attractive to me would be ridiculous.

Here we tread on very difficult ground. Kant thought that no action had moral value unless it were done out of pure reverence for the moral law, that is, without inclination, and he has been accused of a 'morbid frame of mind' which measures the value of an act by its unpleasantness. All popular opinion is, indeed, on Kant's side. The people never admire a man for doing something he likes: the very words 'But he *likes* it' imply the corollary 'And therefore it has no merit'. Yet against Kant stands the obvious truth, noted by Aristotle, that the more virtuous a man becomes the more he enjoys virtuous actions. What an atheist ought to do about this conflict between the ethics of duty and the ethics of virtue, I do not know: but as a Christian I suggest the following solution.

It has sometimes been asked whether God commands certain things because they are right, or whether certain things are right because God commands them. With Hooker, and against Dr Johnson, I emphatically embrace the first alternative. The second might lead to the abominable conclusion (reached, I think, by Paley) that charity is good only because God arbitrarily commanded it—that He might equally well have commanded us to hate Him and one another and that hatred would then have been right. I believe, on the contrary, that 'they err who think that of the will of God to do this or that there is no reason besides His will'.[4] God's will is determined by His wisdom which always perceives, and His goodness which always embraces, the intrinsically good. But when we have said that God commands things only because they are good, we must add that one of the things intrinsically good is that rational creatures should freely surrender themselves to their Creator in obedience. The content of our obedience—the thing we are commanded to do—will always be something intrinsically good, something we ought to do even if (by an impossible supposition) God had not commanded it. But in addition to the content, the mere obeying is also intrinsically good, for, in obeying, a

---

[4] Hooker, *Laws of Eccl. Polity*, I, i, 5.

rational creature consciously enacts its creaturely *rôle*, reverses the act by which we fell, treads Adam's dance backward, and returns.

We therefore agree with Aristotle that what is intrinsically right may well be agreeable, and that the better a man is the more he will like it; but we agree with Kant so far as to say that there is one right act—that of self-surrender—which cannot be willed to the height by fallen creatures unless it is unpleasant. And we must add that this one right act includes all other righteousness, and that the supreme cancelling of Adam's fall, the movement 'full speed astern' by which we retrace our long journey from Paradise, the untying of the old, hard knot, must be when the creature, with no desire to aid it, stripped naked to the bare willing of obedience, embraces what is contrary to its nature, and does that for which only one motive is possible. Such an act may be described as a 'test' of the creature's return to God: hence our fathers said that troubles were 'sent to try us'. A familiar example is Abraham's 'trial' when he was ordered to sacrifice Isaac. With the historicity or the morality of that story I am not now concerned, but with the obvious question, 'If God is omniscient He must have known what Abraham would do, without any experiment; why, then, this needless torture?' But as St Augustine points out,[5] whatever God knew, Abraham at any rate did not know that his obedience could endure such a command until the event taught him: and the obedience which he did not know that he would choose, he cannot be said to have chosen. The reality of Abraham's obedience was the act itself; and what God knew in knowing that Abraham 'would obey' was Abraham's actual obedience on that mountain top at that moment. To say that God 'need not have tried the experiment' is to say that because God knows, the thing known by God need not exist.

If pain sometimes shatters the creature's false self-sufficiency, yet in supreme 'Trial' or 'Sacrifice' it teaches him the self-sufficiency which really ought to be his—the 'strength, which, if Heaven gave it, may be called his own': for then, in the absence of all merely natural motives and supports, he acts in that strength, and that alone, which God confers upon him through his subjected will. Human will becomes truly creative and truly our own when it is wholly God's, and this is one of the many senses in which he that loses his soul shall find it. In all other acts our will is fed through nature, that is, through created things other than the

---

[5] *De Civitate Dei*, XVI, xxxii.

self—through the desires which our physical organism and our heredity supply to us. When we act from ourselves alone—that is, from God *in* ourselves—we are collaborators in, or live instruments of, creation: and that is why such an act undoes with 'backward mutters of dissevering power' the uncreative spell which Adam laid upon his species. Hence as suicide is the typical expression of the stoic spirit, and battle of the warrior spirit, martyrdom always remains the supreme enacting and perfection of Christianity. This great action has been initiated for us, done on our behalf, exemplified for our imitation, and inconceivably communicated to all believers, by Christ on Calvary. There the degree of accepted Death reaches the utmost bounds of the imaginable and perhaps goes beyond them; not only all natural supports, but the presence of the very Father to whom the sacrifice is made deserts the victim, and surrender to God does not falter though God 'forsakes' it.

The doctrine of death which I describe is not peculiar to Christianity. Nature herself has written it large across the world in the repeated drama of the buried seed and the re-arising corn. From nature, perhaps, the oldest agricultural communities learned it and with animal, or human, sacrifices showed forth for centuries the truth that 'without shedding of blood is no remission';[6] and though at first such conceptions may have concerned only the crops and offspring of the tribe, they came later, in the Mysteries, to concern the spiritual death and resurrection of the individual. The Indian ascetic, mortifying his body on a bed of spikes, preaches the same lesson; the Greek philosopher tells us that the life of wisdom is 'a practice of death'.[7] The sensitive and noble heathen of modern times makes his imagined gods 'die into life'.[8] Mr Huxley expounds 'non-attachment'. We cannot escape the doctrine by ceasing to be Christians. It is an 'eternal gospel' revealed to men wherever men have sought, or endured, the truth: it is the very nerve of redemption, which anatomising wisdom at all times and in all places lays bare; the unescapable knowledge which the Light that lighteneth every man presses down upon the minds of all who seriously question what the universe is 'about'. The peculiarity of the Christian faith is not to teach this doctrine but to render it, in vari-

---

[6] Hebrews 9:22.

[7] Plato. *Phaed.*, 81, A (cf. 64, A).

[8] Keats. *Hyperion*, III, 130.

ous ways, more tolerable. Christianity teaches us that the terrible task has already in some sense been accomplished for us—that a master's hand is holding ours as we attempt to trace the difficult letters and that our script need only be a 'copy', not an original. Again, where other systems expose our total nature to death (as in Buddhist renunciation) Christianity demands only that we set right a *misdirection* of our nature, and has no quarrel, like Plato, with the body as such, nor with the psychical elements in our make-up. And sacrifice in its supreme realisation is not exacted of all. Confessors as well as martyrs are saved, and some old people whose state of grace we can hardly doubt seem to have got through their seventy years surprisingly easily. The sacrifice of Christ is repeated, or re-echoed, among His followers in very varying degrees, from the cruellest martyrdom down to a self-submission of intention whose outward signs have nothing to distinguish them from the ordinary fruits of temperance and 'sweet reasonableness'. The causes of this distribution I do not know; but from our present point of view it ought to be clear that the real problem is not why some humble, pious, believing people suffer, but why some do *not*. Our Lord Himself, it will be remembered, explained the salvation of those who are fortunate in this world only by referring to the unsearchable omnipotence of God.[9]

All arguments in justification of suffering provoke bitter resentment against the author. You would like to know how I behave when I am experiencing pain, not writing books about it. You need not guess, for I will tell you; I am a great coward. But what is that to the purpose? When I think of pain—of anxiety that gnaws like fire and loneliness that spreads out like a desert, and the heartbreaking routine of monotonous misery, or again of dull aches that blacken our whole landscape or sudden nauseating pains that knock a man's heart out at one blow, of pains that seem already intolerable and then are suddenly increased, of infuriating scorpion-stinging pains that startle into maniacal movement a man who seemed half dead with his previous tortures—it 'quite o'ercrows my spirit'. If I knew any way of escape I would crawl through sewers to find it. But what is the good of telling you about my feelings? You know them already: they are the same as yours. I am not arguing that pain is not painful. Pain hurts. That is what the word means. I am only trying

---

[9] Mark 10:27.

to show that the old Christian doctrine of being made 'perfect through suffering'[10] is not incredible. To prove it palatable is beyond my design.

In estimating the credibility of the doctrine two principles ought to be observed. In the first place we must remember that the actual moment of present pain is only the centre of what may be called the whole tribulational system which extends itself by fear and pity. Whatever good effects these experiences have are dependent upon the centre; so that even if pain itself was of no spiritual value, yet, if fear and pity were, pain would have to exist in order that there should be something to be feared and pitied. And that fear and pity help us in our return to obedience and charity is not to be doubted. Everyone has experienced the effect of pity in making it easier for us to love the unlovely—that is, to love men not because they are in any way naturally agreeable to us but because they are our brethren. The beneficence of fear most of us have learned during the period of 'crises' that led up to the present war. My own experience is something like this. I am progressing along the path of life in my ordinary contentedly fallen and godless condition, absorbed in a merry meeting with my friends for the morrow or a bit of work that tickles my vanity today, a holiday or a new book, when suddenly a stab of abdominal pain that threatens serious disease, or a headline in the newspapers that threatens us all with destruction, sends this whole pack of cards tumbling down. At first I am overwhelmed, and all my little happinesses look like broken toys. Then, slowly and reluctantly, bit by bit, I try to bring myself into the frame of mind that I should be in at all times. I remind myself that all these toys were never intended to possess my heart, that my true good is in another world and my only real treasure is Christ. And perhaps, by God's grace, I succeed, and for a day or two become a creature consciously dependent on God and drawing its strength from the right sources. But the moment the threat is withdrawn, my whole nature leaps back to the toys: I am even anxious, God forgive me, to banish from my mind the only thing that supported me under the threat because it is now associated with the misery of those few days. Thus the terrible necessity of tribulation is only too clear. God has had me for but forty-eight hours and then only by dint of taking everything else away from me. Let Him but sheathe that sword for a moment and I behave like a puppy when the hated bath is over—I shake myself as dry as I can and race off to reac-

[10] Hebrews 2:10.

quire my comfortable dirtiness, if not in the nearest manure heap, at least in the nearest flower bed. And that is why tribulations cannot cease until God either sees us remade or sees that our remaking is now hopeless.

In the second place, when we are considering pain itself—the centre of the whole tribulational system—we must be careful to attend to what we know and not to what we imagine. That is one of the reasons why the whole central part of this book is devoted to human pain, and animal pain is relegated to a special chapter. About human pain we know, about animal pain we only speculate. But even within the human race we must draw our evidence from instances that have come under our own observation. The tendency of this or that novelist or poet may represent suffering as wholly bad in its effects, as producing, and justifying, every kind of malice and brutality in the sufferer. And, of course, pain, like pleasure, can be so received: all that is given to a creature with free will must be two-edged, not by the nature of the giver or of the gift, but by the nature of the recipient.[11] And, again, the evil results of pain can be multiplied if sufferers are persistently taught by the bystanders that such results are the proper and manly results for them to exhibit. Indignation at others' sufferings, though a generous passion, needs to be well managed lest it steal away patience and humanity from those who suffer and plant anger and cynicism in their stead. But I am not convinced that suffering, if spared such officious vicarious indignation, has any natural tendency to produce such evils. I did not find the front-line trenches or the C.C.S. more full than any other place of hatred, selfishness, rebellion, and dishonesty. I have seen great beauty of spirit in some who were great sufferers. I have seen men, for the most part, grow better not worse with advancing years, and I have seen the last illness produce treasures of fortitude and meekness from most unpromising subjects. I see in loved and revered historical figures, such as Johnson and Cowper, traits which might scarcely have been tolerable if the men had been happier. If the world is indeed a 'vale of soul making' it seems on the whole to be doing its work. Of poverty— the affliction which actually or potentially includes all other afflictions—I would not dare to speak as from myself; and those who reject Christianity will not be moved by Christ's statement that poverty is blessed. But here a rather remarkable fact comes to my aid. Those who would most scornfully repudiate Christianity as a mere 'opiate of the people' have a

---

[11] On the two-edged nature of pain, see Appendix.

contempt for the rich, that is, for all mankind *except* the poor. They regard the poor as the only people worth preserving from 'liquidation', and place in them the only hope of the human race. But this is not compatible with a belief that the effects of poverty on those who suffer it are wholly evil; it even implies that they are good. The Marxist thus finds himself in real agreement with the Christian in those two beliefs which Christianity paradoxically demands—that poverty is blessed and yet ought to be removed.

7

HUMAN PAIN, *CONTINUED*

All things which are as they ought to be are conformed
unto this second law eternal; and even those things which
to this eternal law are not conformable are notwith-
standing in some sort ordered by the first eternal law.

HOOKER, *LAWS OF ECCLES*. POL., I, III, I

IN THIS CHAPTER I advance six propositions necessary to complete
our account of human suffering which do not arise out of one another
and must therefore be given in an arbitrary order.

1. There is a paradox about tribulation in Christianity. Blessed are
the poor, but by 'judgement' (i.e., social justice) and alms we are to remove poverty wherever possible. Blessed are we when persecuted, but
we may avoid persecution by flying from city to city, and may pray to be
spared it, as Our Lord prayed in Gethsemane. But if suffering is good,
ought it not to be pursued rather than avoided? I answer that suffering
is not good in itself. What is good in any painful experience is, for the
sufferer, his submission to the will of God, and, for the spectators, the
compassion aroused and the acts of mercy to which it leads. In the fallen
and partially redeemed universe we may distinguish (1) the simple good
descending from God, (2) the simple evil produced by rebellious creatures, and (3) the exploitation of that evil by God for His redemptive
purpose, which produces (4) the complex good to which accepted suffer-

ing and repented sin contribute. Now the fact that God can make complex good out of simple evil does not excuse—though by mercy it may save—those who do the simple evil. And this distinction is central. Offences must come, but woe to those by whom they come; sins *do* cause grace to abound, but we must not make that an excuse for continuing to sin. The crucifixion itself is the best, as well as the worst, of all historical events, but the role of Judas remains simply evil. We may apply this first to the problem of other people's suffering. A merciful man aims at his neighbour's good and so does 'God's will', consciously co-operating with 'the simple good'. A cruel man oppresses his neighbour, and so does simple evil. But in doing such evil, he is used by God, without his own knowledge or consent, to produce the complex good—so that the first man serves God as a son, and the second as a tool. For you will certainly carry out God's purpose, however you act, but it makes a difference to you whether you serve like Judas or like John. The whole system is, so to speak, calculated for the clash between good men and bad men, and the good fruits of fortitude, patience, pity and forgiveness for which the cruel man is permitted to be cruel, presuppose that the good man ordinarily continues to seek simple good. I say 'ordinarily' because a man is sometimes entitled to hurt (or even, in my opinion, to kill) his fellow, but only where the necessity is urgent and the good to be attained obvious, and usually (though not always) when he who inflicts the pain has a definite authority to do so—a parent's authority derived from nature, a magistrate's or soldier's derived from civil society, or a surgeon's derived, most often, from the patient. To turn this into a general charter for afflicting humanity 'because affliction is good for them' (as Marlowe's lunatic Tamberlaine boasted himself the 'scourge of God') is not indeed to break the Divine scheme but to volunteer for the post of Satan within that scheme. If you do his work, you must be prepared for his wages.

The problem about avoiding our own pain admits a similar solution. Some ascetics have used self-torture. As a layman, I offer no opinion on the prudence of such a regimen; but I insist that, whatever its merits, self-torture is quite a different thing from tribulation sent by God. Everyone knows that fasting is a different experience from missing your dinner by accident or through poverty. Fasting asserts the will against the appetite—the reward being self-mastery and the danger pride: involuntary hunger subjects appetite and will together to the Divine will, furnishing an occasion for submission and exposing us to the danger of rebellion.

But the redemptive effect of suffering lies chiefly in its tendency to re-duce the rebel will. Ascetic practices, which in themselves strengthen the will, are only useful in so far as they enable the will to put its own house (the passions) in order, as a preparation for offering the whole man to God. They are necessary as a means; as an end, they would be abomina-ble, for in substituting will for appetite and there stopping, they would merely exchange the animal self for the diabolical self. It was, therefore, truly said that 'only God can mortify'. Tribulation does its work in a world where human beings are ordinarily seeking, by lawful means, to avoid their own natural evil and to attain their natural good, and presup-poses such a world. In order to submit the will to God, we must have a will and that will must have objects. Christian renunciation does not mean stoic 'Apathy', but a readiness to prefer God to inferior ends which are in themselves lawful. Hence the Perfect Man brought to Gethsemane a will, and a strong will, to escape suffering and death if such escape were compatible with the Father's will, combined with a perfect readiness for obedience if it were not. Some of the saints recommend a 'total renuncia-tion' at the very threshold of our discipleship; but I think this can mean only a total readiness for every particular renunciation[1] that may be de-manded, for it would not be possible to live from moment to moment willing nothing but submission to God as such. What would be the *mate-rial* for the submission? It would seem self-contradictory to say 'What I will is to subject what I will to God's will,' for the second *what* has no content. Doubtless we all spend too much care in the avoidance of our own pain: but a duly subordinated intention to avoid it, using lawful means, is in accordance with 'nature'—that is, with the whole working system of creaturely life for which the redemptive work of tribulation is calculated.

It would be quite false, therefore, to suppose that the Christian view of suffering is incompatible with the strongest emphasis on our duty to leave the world, even in a temporal sense, 'better' than we found it. In the full-est parabolic picture which He gave of the Judgement, Our Lord seems to reduce all virtue to active beneficence: and though it would be mislead-ing to take that one picture in isolation from the Gospel as a whole, it is

---

[1] Cf. Brother Lawrence, *Practice of the Presence of God*, ivth conversation, 25 November 1667. The 'one hearty renunciation' there is 'of everything which we are sensible does not lead us to God'.

sufficient to place beyond doubt the basic principles of the social ethics of Christianity.

2. If tribulation is a necessary element in redemption, we must anticipate that it will never cease till God sees the world to be either redeemed or no further redeemable. A Christian cannot, therefore, believe any of those who promise that if only some reform in our economic, political, or hygienic system were made, a heaven on earth would follow. This might seem to have a discouraging effect on the social worker, but it is not found in practice to discourage him. On the contrary, a strong sense of our common miseries, simply as men, is at least as good a spur to the removal of all the miseries we can, as any of those wild hopes which tempt men to seek their realisation by breaking the moral law and prove such dust and ashes when they are realised. If applied to individual life, the doctrine that an imagined heaven on earth is necessary for vigorous attempts to remove present evil, would at once reveal its absurdity. Hungry men seek food and sick men healing none the less because they know that after the meal or the cure the ordinary ups and downs of life still await them. I am not, of course, discussing whether very drastic changes in our social system are, or are not, desirable; I am only reminding the reader that a particular medicine is not to be mistaken for the elixir of life.

3. Since political issues have here crossed our path, I must make it clear that the Christian doctrine of self-surrender and obedience is a purely theological, and not in the least a political, doctrine. Of forms of government, of civil authority and civil obedience, I have nothing to say. The kind and degree of obedience which a creature owes to its Creator is unique because the relation between creature and Creator is unique: no inference can be drawn from it to any political proposition whatsoever.

4. The Christian doctrine of suffering explains, I believe, a very curious fact about the world we live in. The settled happiness and security which we all desire, God withholds from us by the very nature of the world: but joy, pleasure, and merriment, He has scattered broadcast. We are never safe, but we have plenty of fun, and some ecstasy. It is not hard to see why. The security we crave would teach us to rest our hearts in this world and oppose an obstacle to our return to God: a few moments of happy love, a landscape, a symphony, a merry meeting with our friends, a bathe or a football match, have no such tendency. Our Father refreshes us on the journey with some pleasant inns, but will not encourage us to mistake them for home.

5. We must never make the problem of pain worse than it is by vague talk about the 'unimaginable sum of human misery'. Suppose that I have a toothache of intensity x: and suppose that you, who are seated beside me, also begin to have a toothache of intensity x. You may, if you choose, say that the total amount of pain in the room is now $2x$. But you must remember that no one is suffering $2x$: search all time and all space and you will not find that composite pain in anyone's consciousness. There is no such thing as a sum of suffering, for no one suffers it. When we have reached the maximum that a single person can suffer, we have, no doubt, reached something very horrible, but we have reached all the suffering there ever can be in the universe. The addition of a million fellow-sufferers adds no more pain.

6. Of all evils, pain only is sterilised or disinfected evil. Intellectual evil, or error, may recur because the cause of the first error (such as fatigue or bad handwriting) continues to operate; but quite apart from that, error in its own right breeds error—if the first step in an argument is wrong, everything that follows will be wrong. Sin may recur because the original temptation continues; but quite apart from that, sin of its very nature breeds sin by strengthening sinful habit and weakening the conscience. Now pain, like the other evils, may of course recur because the cause of the first pain (disease, or an enemy) is still operative: but pain has no tendency, in its own right, to proliferate. When it is over, it is over, and the natural sequel is joy. This distinction may be put the other way round. After an error you need not only to remove the causes (the fatigue or bad writing) but also to correct the error itself: after a sin you must not only, if possible, remove the temptation, you must also go back and repent the sin itself. In each case an 'undoing' is required. Pain requires no such undoing. You may need to heal the disease which caused it, but the pain, once over, is sterile—whereas every uncorrected error and unrepented sin is, in its own right, a fountain of fresh error and fresh sin flowing on to the end of time. Again, when I err, my error infects every one who believes me. When I sin publicly, every spectator either condones it, thus sharing my guilt, or condemns it with imminent danger to his charity and humility. But suffering naturally produces in the spectators (unless they are unusually depraved) no bad effect, but a good one—pity. Thus that evil which God chiefly uses to produce the 'complex good' is most markedly disinfected, or deprived of that proliferous tendency which is the worst characteristic of evil in general.

8

HELL

What is the world, O soldiers?
It is I:
I, this incessant snow,
This northern sky;
Soldiers, this solitude
Through which we go
Is I.

W. DE LA MARE, *NAPOLEON*

Richard loves Richard; that is, I am I.

SHAKESPEARE

IN AN EARLIER chapter it was admitted that the pain which alone could rouse the bad man to a knowledge that all was not well, might also lead to a final and unrepented rebellion. And it has been admitted throughout that man has free will and that all gifts to him are therefore two-edged. From these premises it follows directly that the Divine labour to redeem the world cannot be certain of succeeding as regards every individual soul. Some will not be redeemed. There is no doctrine which I would more willingly remove from Christianity than this, if it lay in my power. But it has the full support of Scripture and, specially, of Our Lord's own words; it has always been held by Christendom; and it has the support of reason. If a game is played, it must be possible to lose it. If the happiness of a creature lies in self-surrender, no one can make that surrender but himself (though many can help him to make it) and he may refuse. I would pay any price to be able to say truthfully 'All will be saved.' But my reason retorts 'Without their will, or with it?' If I say 'Without their will' I at once perceive a contradiction; how can the supreme voluntary act of self-surrender be involuntary? If I say 'With their will,' my reason replies 'How if they *will not* give in?'

The Dominical utterances about Hell, like all Dominical sayings, are addressed to the conscience and the will, not to our intellectual curiosity. When they have roused us into action by convincing us of a terrible possibility, they have done, probably, all they were intended to do; and if all the world were convinced Christians it would be unnecessary to say a word more on the subject. As things are, however, this doctrine is one of the chief grounds on which Christianity is attacked as barbarous, and the goodness of God impugned. We are told that it is a detestable doctrine—and indeed, I too detest it from the bottom of my heart—and are reminded of the tragedies in human life which have come from believing it. Of the other tragedies which come from not believing it we are told less. For these reasons, and these alone, it becomes necessary to discuss the matter.

The problem is not simply that of a God who consigns some of His creatures to final ruin. That would be the problem if we were Mahometans. Christianity, true, as always, to the complexity of the real, presents us with something knottier and more ambiguous—a God so full of mercy that He becomes man and dies by torture to avert that final ruin from His creatures, and who yet, where that heroic remedy fails, seems unwilling, or even unable, to arrest the ruin by an act of mere power. I said glibly a moment ago that I would pay 'any price' to remove this *doctrine*. I lied. I could not pay one-thousandth part of the price that God has already paid to remove the *fact*. And here is the real problem: so much mercy, yet still there is Hell.

I am not going to try to prove the doctrine tolerable. Let us make no mistake; it is *not* tolerable. But I think the doctrine can be shown to be moral, by a critique of the objections ordinarily made, or felt, against it.

First, there is an objection, in many minds, to the idea of retributive punishment as such. This has been partly dealt with in a previous chapter.

It was there maintained that all punishment became unjust if the ideas of ill-desert and retribution were removed from it; and a core of righteousness was discovered within the vindictive passion itself, in the demand that the evil man must not be left perfectly satisfied with his own evil, that it must be made to appear to him what it rightly appears to others—evil. I said that Pain plants the flag of truth within a rebel fortress. We were then discussing pain which might still lead to repentance. How if it does not—if no further conquest than the planting of the flag ever takes place? Let us try to be honest with ourselves. Picture to yourself a man who has risen to wealth or power by a continued course of treachery and cruelty, by exploiting for purely selfish ends the noble motions of his victims, laughing the while at their simplicity; who, having thus attained success, uses it for the gratification of lust and hatred and finally parts with the last rag of honour among thieves by betraying his own accomplices and jeering at their last moments of bewildered disillusionment. Suppose, further, that he does all this, not (as we like to imagine) tormented by remorse or even misgiving, but eating like a schoolboy and sleeping like a healthy infant—a jolly, ruddy-cheeked man, without a care in the world, unshakably confident to the very end that he alone has found the answer to the riddle of life, that God and man are fools whom he has got the better of, that his way of life is utterly successful, satisfactory, unassailable. We must be careful at this point. The least indulgence of the passion for revenge is very deadly sin. Christian charity counsels us to make every effort for the conversion of such a man: to prefer his conversion, at the peril of our own lives, perhaps of our own souls, to his punishment; to prefer it infinitely. But that is not the question. Supposing he *will* not be converted, what destiny in the eternal world can you regard as proper for him? Can you really desire that such a man, *remaining what he is* (and he must be able to do that if he has free will) should be confirmed forever in his present happiness—should continue, for all eternity, to be perfectly convinced that the laugh is on his side? And if you cannot regard this as tolerable, is it only your wickedness—only spite—that prevents you from doing so? Or do you find that conflict between Justice and Mercy, which has sometimes seemed to you such an outmoded piece of theology, now actually at work in your own mind, and feeling very much as if it came to you from above, not from below? You are moved not by a desire for the wretched creature's pain as such, but by a truly ethical demand that, soon or late, the right should be asserted, the flag planted in this horribly rebellious soul, even if no fuller and better conquest is to follow. In a sense, it is better for the creature itself, even if it never becomes good, that it should know itself a failure, a mistake. Even mercy can hardly wish to such a man his eternal, contented continuance in such ghastly illusion. Thomas Aquinas said of suffering, as Aristotle had said of shame, that it was a thing not good in itself; but a thing which might have a certain goodness in particular circumstances. That is to say, if evil is present, pain at recognition of the evil, being a kind of knowledge, is relatively good; for the alternative is that the soul should be ignorant of the evil, or ignorant that the evil is contrary to its nature, 'either of which', says the philosopher, 'is *manifestly* bad'.[1] And I think, though we tremble, we agree.

The demand that God should forgive such a man while he remains what he is, is based on a confusion between condoning and forgiving. To condone an evil is simply to ignore it, to treat it as if it were good. But forgiveness needs to be accepted as well as offered if it is to be complete: and a man who admits no guilt can accept no forgiveness.

I have begun with the conception of Hell as a positive retributive punishment inflicted by God because that is the form in which the doctrine is most repellent, and I wished to tackle the strongest objection. But, of course, though Our Lord often speaks of Hell as a sentence inflicted by a tribunal, He also says elsewhere that the judgement consists in the very fact that men prefer darkness to light, and that not He, but His 'word', judges men.[2] We are therefore at liberty—since the two conceptions, in the long run, mean the same thing—to think of this bad man's perdition not as a sentence imposed on him but as the mere fact of being what he is. The characteristic of lost souls is 'their rejection of everything that is not simply themselves'.[3] Our imaginary egoist has tried to turn everything he meets into a province or appendage of the self. The taste for the *other*, that is, the very capacity for enjoying good, is quenched in him except in so far as his body still draws him into some rudimentary contact with an outer world. Death removes this last contact. He has his wish—to lie wholly in the self and to make the best of what he finds there. And what he finds there is Hell.

---

[1] *Summa Theol.*, I, II[ae], Q. xxxix, Art. 1.

[2] John 3:19; 12:48.

[3] See von Hügel, Essays and Addresses, 1st series, *What do we mean by Heaven and Hell?*

Another objection turns on the apparent disproportion between eternal damnation and transitory sin. And if we think of eternity as a mere prolongation of time, it is disproportionate. But many would reject this idea of eternity. If we think of time as a line—which is a good image, because the parts of time are successive and no two of them can co-exist; i.e., there is no *width* in time, only length—we probably ought to think of eternity as a plane or even a solid. Thus the whole reality of a human being would be represented by a solid figure. That solid would be mainly the work of God, acting through grace and nature, but human free will would have contributed the base-line which we call earthly life: and if you draw your base-line askew, the whole solid will be in the wrong place. The fact that life is short, or, in the symbol, that we contribute only one little line to the whole complex figure, might be regarded as a Divine mercy. For if even the drawing of that little line, left to our free will, is sometimes so badly done as to spoil the whole, how much worse a mess might we have made of the figure if more had been entrusted to us? A simpler form of the same objection consists in saying that death ought not to be final, that there ought to be a second chance.[4] I believe that if a million chances were likely to do good, they would be given. But a master often knows, when boys and parents do not, that it is really useless to send a boy in for a certain examination again. Finality must come some time, and it does not require a very robust faith to believe that omniscience knows when.

A third objection turns on the frightful intensity of the pains of Hell as suggested by medieval art and, indeed, by certain passages in Scripture. Von Hügel here warns us not to confuse the doctrine itself with the *imagery* by which it may be conveyed. Our Lord speaks of Hell under three symbols: first, that of punishment ('everlasting punishment', Matthew 25:46); second, that of destruction ('fear Him who is able to destroy both body and soul in Hell', Matthew 10:28); and thirdly, that of privation, exclusion, or banishment into 'the darkness outside', as in the parables of the man without a wedding garment or of the wise and foolish virgins. The prevalent image of fire is significant because it combines the ideas of torment and destruction. Now it is quite certain that all these expressions are intended to suggest something unspeakably horrible, and any inter-

---

[4] The conception of a 'second chance' must not be confused either with that of Purgatory (for souls already saved) or of Limbo (for souls already lost).

pretation which does not face that fact is, I am afraid, out of court from the beginning. But it is not necessary to concentrate on the images of torture to the exclusion of those suggesting destruction and privation. What can that be whereof all three images are equally proper symbols? Destruction, we should naturally assume, means the unmaking, or cessation, of the destroyed. And people often talk as if the 'annihilation' of a soul were intrinsically possible. In all our experience, however, the destruction of one thing means the emergence of something else. Burn a log, and you have gases, heat and ash. To *have been* a log means now being those three things. If souls can be destroyed, must there not be a state of *having been* a human soul? And is not that, perhaps, the state which is equally well described as torment, destruction, and privation? You will remember that in the parable, the saved go to a place prepared for *them,* while the damned go to a place never made for men at all.[5] To enter heaven is to become more human than you ever succeeded in being on earth; to enter hell, is to be banished from humanity. What is cast (or casts itself) into hell is not a man: it is 'remains'. To be a complete man means to have the passions obedient to the will and the will offered to God: to *have been* a man—to be an ex-man or 'damned ghost'—would presumably mean to consist of a will utterly centred in its self and passions utterly uncontrolled by the will. It is, of course, impossible to imagine what the consciousness of such a creature—already a loose congeries of mutually antagonistic sins rather than a sinner—would be like. There may be a truth in the saying that 'hell is hell, not from its own point of view, but from the heavenly point of view'. I do not think this belies the severity of Our Lord's words. It is only to the damned that their fate could ever seem less than unendurable. And it must be admitted that as, in these last chapters, we think of eternity, the categories of pain and pleasure, which have engaged us so long, begin to recede, as vaster good and evil loom in sight. Neither pain nor pleasure as such has the last word. Even if it were possible that the experience (if it can be called experience) of the lost contained no pain and much pleasure, still, that black pleasure would be such as to send any soul, not already damned, flying to its prayers in nightmare terror: even if there were pains in heaven, all who understand would desire them.

---

[5] Matthew 25:34, 41.

A fourth objection is that no charitable man could himself be blessed in heaven while he knew that even one human soul was still in hell; and if so, are we more merciful than God? At the back of this objection lies a mental picture of heaven and hell co-existing in unilinear time as the histories of England and America co-exist: so that at each moment the blessed could say 'The miseries of hell are *now* going on.' But I notice that Our Lord, while stressing the terror of hell with unsparing severity, usually emphasises the idea not of duration but of *finality*. Consignment to the destroying fire is usually treated as the end of the story—not as the beginning of a new story. That the lost soul is eternally fixed in its diabolical attitude we cannot doubt: but whether this eternal fixity implies endless duration—or duration at all—we cannot say. Dr Edwyn Bevan has some interesting speculations on this point.[6] We know much more about heaven than hell, for heaven is the home of humanity and therefore contains all that is implied in a glorified human life: but hell was not made for men. It is in no sense *parallel* to heaven: it is 'the darkness outside', the outer rim where being fades away into nonentity.

Finally, it is objected that the ultimate loss of a single soul means the defeat of omnipotence. And so it does. In creating beings with free will, omnipotence from the outset submits to the possibility of such defeat. What you call defeat, I call miracle: for to make things which are not Itself, and thus to become, in a sense, capable of being resisted by its own handiwork, is the most astonishing and unimaginable of all the feats we attribute to the Deity. I willingly believe that the damned are, in one sense, successful, rebels to the end; that the doors of hell are locked on the *inside*. I do not mean that the ghosts may not *wish* to come out of hell, in the vague fashion wherein an envious man 'wishes' to be happy: but they certainly do not will even the first preliminary stages of that self-abandonment through which alone the soul can reach any good. They enjoy forever the horrible freedom they have demanded, and are therefore self-enslaved: just as the blessed, forever submitting to obedience, become through all eternity more and more free.

In the long run the answer to all those who object to the doctrine of hell, is itself a question: 'What are you asking God to do?' To wipe out their past sins and, at all costs, to give them a fresh start, smoothing every difficulty and offering every miraculous help? But He has done so, on

---

[6] *Symbolism and Belief*, 101.

Calvary. To forgive them? They will not be forgiven. To leave them alone? Alas, I am afraid that is what He does.

One caution, and I have done. In order to rouse modern minds to an understanding of the issues, I ventured to introduce in this chapter a picture of the sort of bad man whom we most easily perceive to be truly bad. But when the picture has done that work, the sooner it is forgotten the better. In all discussions of Hell we should keep steadily before our eyes the possible damnation, not of our enemies nor our friends (since both these disturb the reason) but of ourselves. This chapter is not about your wife or son, nor about Nero or Judas Iscariot; it is about you and me.

9

ANIMAL PAIN

And whatsoever Adam called every living creature, that was the name thereof.

GENESIS 2:19

To find out what is natural, we must study specimens which retain their nature and not those which have been corrupted.

ARISTOTLE, *POLITICS*, I, V, 5

THUS FAR OF human suffering; but all this time 'a plaint of guiltless hurt doth pierce the sky'. The problem of animal suffering is appalling; not because the animals are so numerous (for, as we have seen, no more pain is felt when a million suffer than when one suffers) but because the Christian explanation of human pain cannot be extended to animal pain. So far as we know beasts are incapable either of sin or virtue: therefore they can neither deserve pain nor be improved by it. At the same time we must never allow the problem of animal suffering to become the centre of the problem of pain; not because it is unimportant—whatever furnishes plausible grounds for questioning the goodness of God is very important indeed—but because it is outside the range of our knowledge. God has given us data which enable us, in some degree, to understand our own suffering: He has given us no such data about beasts. We know neither why they were made nor what they are, and everything we say about them is speculative. From the doctrine that God is good we may confidently deduce that the *appearance* of reckless Divine cruelty in the animal kingdom is an illusion—and the fact that the only suffering we know at first hand (our own) turns out not to be a cruelty will make it easier to believe this. After that, everything is guesswork.

We may begin by ruling out some of the pessimistic bluff put up in the first chapter. The fact that vegetable lives 'prey upon' one another and are in a state of 'ruthless' competition is of no moral importance at all. 'Life' in the biological sense has nothing to do with good and evil until sentience appears. The very words 'prey' and 'ruthless' are mere metaphors. Wordsworth believed that every flower 'enjoyed the air it breathes', but there is no reason to suppose he was right. No doubt, living plants react to injuries differently from inorganic matter; but an anaesthetised human body reacts more differently still and such reactions do not prove sentience. We are, of course, justified in speaking of the death or thwarting of a plant as if it were a tragedy, provided that we know we are using a metaphor. To furnish symbols for spiritual experiences may be one of the functions of the mineral and vegetable worlds. But we must not become the victims of our metaphor. A forest in which half the trees are killing the other half may be a perfectly 'good' forest: for its goodness consists in its utility and beauty and it does not feel.

When we turn to the beasts, three questions arise. There is, first, the question of fact; what do animals suffer? There is, secondly, the question of origin; how did disease and pain enter the animal world? And, thirdly, there is the question of justice; how can animal suffering be reconciled with the justice of God?

1. In the long run the answer to the first question is, We don't know; but some speculations may be worth setting down. We must begin by distinguishing among animals: for if the ape could understand us he would take it very ill to be lumped along with the oyster and the earthworm in a single class of 'animals' and contrasted to men. Clearly in some ways the ape and man are much more like each other than either is like the worm. At the lower end of the animal realm we need not assume anything we could recognise as sentience. Biologists in distinguishing animal from vegetable do not make use of sentience or locomotion or other such characteristics as a layman would naturally fix upon. At some point, however (though

where, we cannot say), sentience almost certainly comes in, for the higher animals have nervous systems very like our own. But at this level we must still distinguish sentience from consciousness. If you happen never to have heard of this distinction before, I am afraid you will find it rather startling, but it has great authority and you would be ill-advised to dismiss it out of hand. Suppose that three sensations follow one another—first A, then B, then C. When this happens to you, you have the experience of passing through the process ABC. But note what this implies. It implies that there is something in you which stands sufficiently outside A to notice A passing away, and sufficiently outside B to notice B now beginning and coming to fill the place which A has vacated; and something which recognises itself as the same through the transition from A to B and B to C, so it can say 'I have had the experience ABC'. Now this something is what I call Consciousness or Soul and the process I have just described is one of the proofs that the soul, though experiencing time, is not itself completely 'timeful'. The simplest experience of ABC as a succession demands a soul which is not itself a mere succession of states, but rather a permanent bed along which these different portions of the stream of sensation roll, and which recognises itself as the same beneath them all. Now it is almost certain that the nervous system of one of the higher animals presents it with successive sensations. It does not follow that it has any 'soul', anything which recognises itself as having had A, and now having B, and now marking how B glides away to make room for C. If it had no such 'soul', what we call the experience ABC would never occur. There would, in philosophic language, be 'a succession of perceptions'; that is, the sensations would, in fact, occur in that order, and God would know that they were so occurring, but the animal would not know. There would not be 'a perception of succession'. This would mean that if you give such a creature two blows with a whip, there are, indeed, two pains: but there is no co-ordinating self which can recognise that 'I have had two pains'. Even in the single pain, there is no self to say 'I am in pain'—for if it could distinguish itself from the sensation—the bed from the stream—sufficiently to say 'I am in pain', it would also be able to connect the two sensations as *its* experience. The correct description would be 'Pain is taking place in this animal'; not, as we commonly say, 'This animal feels pain', for the words 'this' and 'feels' really smuggle in the assumption that it is a 'self' or 'soul' or 'consciousness' standing above the sensations and organising them into an 'experience' as we do. Such sentience without consciousness, I admit, we cannot imagine: not because it never occurs in us, but because, when it does, we describe ourselves as being 'unconscious'. And rightly. The fact that animals react to pain much as we do is, of course, no proof that they are conscious; for we may also so react under chloroform, and even answer questions while asleep.

How far up the scale such unconscious sentience may extend, I will not even guess. It is certainly difficult to suppose that the apes, the elephant, and the higher domestic animals, have not, in some degree, a self or soul which connects experiences and gives rise to rudimentary individuality. But at least a great deal of what appears to be animal suffering need not be suffering in any real sense. It may be we who have invented the 'sufferers' by the 'pathetic fallacy' of reading into the beasts a self for which there is no real evidence.

2. The origin of animal suffering could be traced, by earlier generations, to the Fall of man—the whole world was infected by the uncreating rebellion of Adam. This is now impossible, for we have good reason to believe that animals existed long before men. Carnivorousness, with all that it entails, is older than humanity. Now it is impossible at this point not to remember a certain sacred story which, though never included in the creeds, has been widely believed in the Church and seems to be implied in several Dominical, Pauline, and Johannine utterances—I mean the story that man was not the first creature to rebel against the Creator, but that some older and mightier being long since became apostate and is now the emperor of darkness and (significantly) the Lord of this world. Some people would like to reject all such elements from Our Lord's teaching: and it might be argued that when He emptied Himself of His glory He also humbled Himself to share, as man, the current superstitions of His time. And I certainly think that Christ, in the flesh, was not omniscient—if only because a human brain could not, presumably, be the vehicle of omniscient consciousness, and to say that Our Lord's thinking was not really conditioned by the size and shape of His brain might be to deny the real incarnation and become a Docetist. Thus, if Our Lord had committed Himself to any scientific or historical statement which we knew to be untrue, this would not disturb my faith in His deity. But the doctrine of Satan's existence and fall is not among the things we know to be untrue: it contradicts not the facts discovered by scientists but the mere, vague 'climate of opinion' that we happen to be living in. Now I take a very low view of 'climates of opinion'. In his own subject every

man knows that all discoveries are made and all errors corrected by those who ignore the 'climate of opinion'.

It seems to me, therefore, a reasonable supposition, that some mighty created power had already been at work for ill on the material universe, or the solar system, or, at least, the planet Earth, before ever man came on the scene: and that when man fell, someone had, indeed, tempted him. This hypothesis is not introduced as a general 'explanation of evil': it only gives a wider application to the principle that evil comes from the abuse of free will. If there is such a power, as I myself believe, it may well have corrupted the animal creation before man appeared. The intrinsic evil of the animal world lies in the fact that animals, or some animals, live by destroying each other. That plants do the same I will not admit to be an evil. The Satanic corruption of the beasts would therefore be analogous, in one respect, with the Satanic corruption of man. For one result of man's fall was that his animality fell back from the humanity into which it had been taken up but which could no longer rule it. In the same way, animality may have been encouraged to slip back into behaviour proper to vegetables. It is, of course, true that the immense mortality occasioned by the fact that many beasts live on beasts is balanced, in nature, by an immense birthrate, and it might seem, that if all animals had been herbivorous and healthy, they would mostly starve as a result of their own multiplication. But I take the fecundity and the death rate to be correlative phenomena. There was, perhaps, no necessity for such an excess of the sexual impulse: the Lord of this world thought of it as a response to carnivorousness—a double scheme for securing the maximum amount of torture. If it offends less, you may say that the 'life-force' is corrupted where I say that living creatures were corrupted by an evil angelic being. We mean the same thing: but I find it easier to believe in a myth of gods and demons than in one of hypostatised abstract nouns. And after all, our mythology may be much nearer to literal truth than we suppose. Let us not forget that Our Lord, on one occasion, attributes human disease not to God's wrath, not to nature, but quite explicitly to Satan.[1]

If this hypothesis is worth considering, it is also worth considering whether man, at his first coming into the world, had not already a redemptive function to perform. Man, even now, can do wonders to animals: my cat and dog live together in my house and seem to like it. It may

---

[1] Luke 13:16.

have been one of man's functions to restore peace to the animal world, and if he had not joined the enemy he might have succeeded in doing so to an extent now hardly imaginable.

3. Finally, there is the question of justice. We have seen reason to believe that not all animals suffer as we think they do: but some, at least, look as if they had selves, and what shall be done for these innocents? And we have seen that it is possible to believe that animal pain is not God's handiwork but begun by Satan's malice and perpetuated by man's desertion of his post: still, if God has not caused it, He has permitted it, and, once again, what shall be done for these innocents? I have been warned not even to raise the question of animal immortality, lest I find myself 'in company with all the old maids'.[2] I have no objection to the company. I do not think either virginity or old age contemptible, and some of the shrewdest minds I have met inhabited the bodies of old maids. Nor am I greatly moved by jocular inquiries such as 'Where will you put all the mosquitoes?'—a question to be answered on its own level by pointing out that, if the worst came to the worst, a heaven for mosquitoes and a hell for men could very conveniently be combined. The complete silence of Scripture and Christian tradition on animal immortality is a more serious objection; but it would be fatal only if Christian revelation showed any signs of being intended as a *système de la nature* answering all questions. But it is nothing of the sort: the curtain has been rent at one point, and at one point only, to reveal our immediate practical necessities and not to satisfy our intellectual curiosity. If animals were, in fact, immortal, it is unlikely, from what we discern of God's method in the revelation, that He would have revealed this truth. Even our own immortality is a doctrine that comes late in the history of Judaism. The argument from silence is therefore very weak.

The real difficulty about supposing most animals to be immortal is that immortality has almost no meaning for a creature which is not 'conscious' in the sense explained above. If the life of a newt is merely a succession of sensations, what should we mean by saying that God may recall to life the newt that died today? It would not recognise itself as the same newt; the pleasant sensations of any other newt that lived after its death would be just as much, or just as little, a recompense for its earthly sufferings (if any) as those of its resurrected—I was going to say 'self', but the

---

[2] But also with J. Wesley, Sermon LXV. *The Great Deliverance.*

whole point is that the newt probably has no self. The thing we have to try to say, on this hypothesis, will not even be said. There is, therefore, I take it, no question of immortality for creatures that are merely sentient. Nor do justice and mercy demand that there should be, for such creatures have no painful experience. Their nervous system delivers all the *letters* A, P, N, I, but since they cannot read they never build it up into the word PAIN. And all animals *may* be in that condition.

If, nevertheless, the strong conviction which we have of a real, though doubtless rudimentary, selfhood in the higher animals, and specially in those we tame, is not an illusion, their destiny demands a somewhat deeper consideration. The error we must avoid is that of considering them in themselves. Man is to be understood only in his relation to God. The beasts are to be understood only in their relation to man and, through man, to God. Let us here guard against one of those untransmuted lumps of atheistical thought which often survive in the minds of modern believers. Atheists naturally regard the co-existence of man and the animals as a mere contingent result of interacting biological facts; and the taming of an animal by a man as a purely arbitrary interference of one species with another. The 'real' or 'natural' animal to them is the wild one, and the tame animal is an artificial or unnatural thing. But a Christian must not think so. Man was appointed by God to have dominion over the beasts, and everything a man does to an animal is either a lawful exercise, or a sacrilegious abuse, of an authority by Divine right. The tame animal is therefore, in the deepest sense, the only 'natural' animal—the only one we see occupying the place it was made to occupy, and it is on the tame animal that we must base all our doctrine of beasts. Now it will be seen that, in so far as the tame animal has a real self or personality, it owes this almost entirely to its master. If a good sheepdog seems 'almost human' that is because a good shepherd has made it so. I have already noted the mysterious force of the word 'in'. I do not take all the senses of it in the New Testament to be identical, so that man is *in* Christ and Christ *in* God and the Holy Spirit *in* the Church and also *in* the individual believer in exactly the same sense. They may be senses that rhyme or correspond rather than a single sense. I am now going to suggest— though with great readiness to be set right by real theologians—that there may be a sense, corresponding, though not identical, with these, in which those beasts that attain a real self are *in* their masters. That is to say, you must not think of a beast by itself, and call that a personality and then inquire whether God will raise and bless *that*. You must take the whole context *in* which the beast acquires its selfhood—namely 'The–good-man–and–the–goodwife– ruling–their–children–and–their–beasts–in–the–good–homestead'. That whole context may be regarded as a 'body' in the Pauline (or a closely sub-Pauline) sense; and how much of that 'body' may be raised along with the goodman and the goodwife, who can predict? So much, presumably, as is necessary not only for the glory of God and the beatitude of the human pair, but for that particular glory and that particular beatitude which is eternally coloured by that particular terrestrial experience. And in this way it seems to me possible that certain animals may have an immortality, not in themselves, but in the immortality of their masters. And the difficulty about personal identity in a creature barely personal disappears when the creature is thus kept in its proper context. If you ask, concerning an animal thus raised as a member of the whole Body of the homestead, where its personal identity resides, I answer 'Where its identity always did reside even in the earthly life—in its relation to the Body and, specially, to the master who *is* the head of that Body.' In other words, the man will know his dog: the dog will know its master and, in knowing him, will *be* itself. To ask that it should, in any other way, *know* itself, is probably to ask for what has no meaning. Animals aren't like that, and don't want to be.

My picture of the good sheepdog in the good homestead does not, of course, cover wild animals nor (a matter even more urgent) ill-treated domestic animals. But it is intended only as an illustration drawn from one privileged instance—which is, also, in my view the only normal and unperverted instance—of the general principles to be observed in framing a theory of animal resurrection. I think Christians may justly hesitate to suppose any beasts immortal, for two reasons. Firstly because they fear, by attributing to beasts a 'soul' in the full sense, to obscure that difference between beast and man which is as sharp in the spiritual dimension as it is hazy and problematical in the biological. And secondly, a future happiness connected with the beast's present life simply as a compensation for suffering—so many millenniums in the happy pastures paid down as 'damages' for so many years of pulling carts—seems a clumsy assertion of Divine goodness. We, because we are fallible, often hurt a child or an animal unintentionally, and then the best we can do is to 'make up for it' by some caress or tidbit. But it is hardly pious to imagine omniscience acting in that way—as though God trod on the animals' tails in the dark and then did the best He could about it! In such a botched adjustment I cannot recognise the master-touch; whatever the answer is, it must be something better than that. The theory I am suggesting tries to avoid both objections. It makes God the centre of the universe and man the subordinate centre of terrestrial nature: the beasts are not co-ordinate with man, but subordinate to him, and their destiny is through and through related to his. And the derivative immortality suggested for them is not a mere *amende* or compensation: it is part and parcel of the new heaven and new earth, organically related to the whole suffering process of the world's fall and redemption.

Supposing, as I do, that the personality of the tame animals is largely the gift of man—that their mere sentience is reborn to soulhood in us as our mere soulhood is reborn to spirituality in Christ—I naturally suppose that very few animals indeed, in their wild state, attain to a 'self' or *ego*. But if any do, and if it is agreeable to the goodness of God that they should live again, their immortality would also be related to man—not, this time, to individual masters, but to humanity. That is to say, if in any instance the quasi-spiritual and emotional value which human tradition attributes to a beast (such as the 'innocence' of the lamb or the heraldic royalty of the lion) has a real ground in the beast's nature, and is not merely arbitrary or accidental, then it is in *that* capacity, or principally in that, that the beast may be expected to attend on risen man and make part of his 'train'. Or if the traditional character is quite erroneous, then the beast's heavenly life[3] would be in virtue of the real, but unknown, effect it has actually had on man during his whole history: for if Christian cosmology is in *any* sense (I do not say, in a literal sense) true, then all that exists on our planet is related to man, and even the creatures that were extinct before men existed are then only seen in their true light when they are seen as the unconscious harbingers of man.

When we are speaking of creatures so remote from us as wild beasts, and prehistoric beasts, we hardly know what we are talking about. It may well be that they have no selves and no sufferings. It may even be that each species has a corporate self—that Lionhood, not lions, has shared in the travail of creation and will enter into the restoration of all things.

---

[3] That is, its participation in the heavenly life of men *in* Christ *to* God; to suggest a 'heavenly life' for the beast *as such* is probably nonsense.

And if we cannot imagine even our own eternal life, much less can we imagine the life the beasts may have as our 'members'. If the earthly lion could read the prophecy of that day when he shall eat hay like an ox, he would regard it as a description not of heaven, but of hell. And if there is nothing in the lion but carnivorous sentience, then he is unconscious and his 'survival' would have no meaning. But if there is a rudimentary Leonine self, to that also God can give a 'body' as it pleases Him—a body no longer living by the destruction of the lamb, yet richly Leonine in the sense that it also expresses whatever energy and splendour and exulting power dwelled within the visible lion on this earth. I think, under correction, that the prophet used an eastern hyperbole when he spoke of the lion and the lamb *lying down* together. That would be rather impertinent of the lamb. To have lions and lambs that so consorted (except on some rare celestial Saturnalia of topsy-turvydom) would be the same as having neither lambs nor lions. I think the lion, when he has ceased to be dangerous, will still be awful: indeed, that we shall then first see that of which the present fangs and claws are a clumsy, and satanically perverted, imitation. There will still be something like the shaking of a golden mane: and often the good Duke will say, 'Let him roar again'.

10

HEAVEN

It is required
You do awake your faith. Then all stand still;
Or those that think it is unlawful business
I am about, let them depart.

SHAKESPEARE, *WINTER'S TALE*

Plunged in thy depth of mercy let me die
The death that every soul that lives desires.

COWPER OUT OF *MADAME GUION*

'I RECKON,' SAID St Paul, 'that the sufferings of this present time are not worthy to be compared with the glory that shall be revealed in us.'[1] If this is so, a book on suffering which says nothing of heaven, is leaving out almost the whole of one side of the account. Scripture and tradition habitually put the joys of heaven into the scale against the sufferings of earth, and no solution of the problem of pain which does not do so can be called a Christian one. We are very shy nowadays of even mentioning heaven. We are afraid of the jeer about 'pie in the sky', and of being told that we are trying to 'escape' from the duty of making a happy world

---

[1] Romans 8:18.

638

here and now into dreams of a happy world elsewhere. But either there is 'pie in the sky' or there is not. If there is not, then Christianity is false, for this doctrine is woven into its whole fabric. If there is, then this truth, like any other, must be faced, whether it is useful at political meetings or no. Again, we are afraid that heaven is a bribe, and that if we make it our goal we shall no longer be disinterested. It is not so. Heaven offers nothing that a mercenary soul can desire. It is safe to tell the pure in heart that they shall see God, for only the pure in heart want to. There are rewards that do not sully motives. A man's love for a woman is not mercenary because he wants to marry her, nor his love for poetry mercenary because he wants to read it, nor his love of exercise less disinterested because he wants to run and leap and walk. Love, by definition, seeks to enjoy its object.

You may think that there is another reason for our silence about heaven—namely, that we do not really desire it. But that may be an illusion. What I am now going to say is merely an opinion of my own without the slightest authority, which I submit to the judgement of better Christians and better scholars than myself. There have been times when I think we do not desire heaven; but more often I find myself wondering whether, in our heart of hearts, we have ever desired anything else. You may have noticed that the books you really love are bound together by a secret thread. You know very well what is the common quality that makes you love them, though you cannot put it into words: but most of your friends do not see it at all, and often wonder why, liking this, you should also like that. Again, you have stood before some landscape, which seems to embody what you have been looking for all your life; and then turned to the friend at your side who appears to be seeing what you saw—but at the first words a gulf yawns between you, and you realise that this landscape means something totally different to him, that he is pursuing an alien vision and cares nothing for the ineffable suggestion by which you are transported. Even in your hobbies, has there not always been some secret attraction which the others are curiously ignorant of—something, not to be identified with, but always on the verge of breaking through, the smell of cut wood in the workshop or the clap-clap of water against the boat's side? Are not all lifelong friendships born at the moment when at last you meet another human being who has some inkling (but faint and uncertain even in the best) of that something which you were born desiring, and which, beneath the flux of other desires and in all the momentary silences between the louder passions, night and day, year by year, from childhood to old age, you are looking for, watching for, listening for? You have never *had* it. All the things that have ever deeply possessed your soul have been but hints of it—tantalising glimpses, promises never quite fulfilled, echoes that died away just as they caught your ear. But if it should really become manifest—if there ever came an echo that did not die away but swelled into the sound itself—you would know it. Beyond all possibility of doubt you would say 'Here at last is the thing I was made for.' We cannot tell each other about it. It is the secret signature of each soul, the incommunicable and unappeasable want, the thing we desired before we met our wives or made our friends or chose our work, and which we shall still desire on our deathbeds, when the mind no longer knows wife or friend or work. While we are, this is. If we lose this, we lose all.[2]

This signature on each soul may be a product of heredity and environment, but that only means that heredity and environment are among the instruments whereby God creates a soul. I am considering not how, but why, He makes each soul unique. If He had no use for all these differences, I do not see why He should have created more souls than one. Be sure that the ins and outs of your individuality are no mystery to Him; and one day they will no longer be a mystery to you. The mould in which a key is made would be a strange thing, if you had never seen a key: and the key itself a strange thing if you had never seen a lock. Your soul has a curious shape because it is a hollow made to fit a particular swelling in the infinite contours of the Divine substance, or a key to unlock one of the doors in the house with many mansions. For it is not humanity in the abstract that is to be saved, but you—you, the individual reader, John Stubbs or Janet Smith. Blessed and fortunate creature, your eyes shall behold Him and not another's. All that you are, sins apart, is destined, if you will let God have His good way, to utter satisfaction. The Brocken spectre 'looked to every man like his first love', because she was a cheat. But God will look to every soul like its first love because He is its first love. Your place in heaven will seem to be made for you and you alone, because you were made for it—made for it stitch by stitch as a glove is made for a hand.

---

[2] I am not, of course, suggesting that these immortal longings which we have from the Creator because we are men, should be confused with the gifts of the Holy Spirit to those who are in Christ. We must not fancy we are holy because we are human.

It is from this point of view that we can understand hell in its aspect of privation. All your life an unattainable ecstasy has hovered just beyond the grasp of your consciousness. The day is coming when you will wake to find, beyond all hope, that you have attained it, or else, that it was within your reach and you have lost it forever.

This may seem a perilously private and subjective notion of the pearl of great price, but it is not. The thing I am speaking of is not an experience. You have experienced only the *want* of it. The thing itself has never actually been embodied in any thought, or image, or emotion. Always it has summoned you out of yourself. And if you will not go out of yourself to follow it, if you sit down to brood on the desire and attempt to cherish it, the desire itself will evade you. 'The door into life generally opens behind us' and 'the only wisdom' for one 'haunted with the scent of unseen roses, is work.'³ This secret fire goes out when you use the bellows: bank it down with what seems unlikely fuel of dogma and ethics, turn your back on it and attend to your duties, and then it will blaze. The world is like a picture with a golden background, and we the figures in that picture. Until you step off the plane of the picture into the large dimensions of death you cannot see the gold. But we have reminders of it. To change our metaphor, the blackout is not quite complete. There are chinks. At times the daily scene looks big with its secret.

Such is my opinion; and it may be erroneous. Perhaps this secret desire also is part of the Old Man and must be crucified before the end. But this opinion has a curious trick of evading denial. The desire—much more the satisfaction—has always refused to be fully present in any experience. Whatever you try to identify with it, turns out to be not it but something else: so that hardly any degree of crucifixion or transformation could go beyond what the desire itself leads us to anticipate. Again, if this opinion is not true, something better is. But 'something better'— not this or that experience, but beyond it—is almost the definition of the thing I am trying to describe.

The thing you long for summons you away from the self. Even the desire for the thing lives only if you abandon it. This is the ultimate law— the seed dies to live, the bread must be cast upon the waters, he that loses his soul will save it. But the life of the seed, the finding of the bread, the recovery of the soul, are as real as the preliminary sacrifice. Hence it is

---

³ George MacDonald, *Alec Forbes*, cap. XXXIII.

truly said of heaven 'in heaven there is no ownership. If any there took upon him to call anything his own, he would straightway be thrust out into hell and become an evil spirit.'[4] But it is also said 'To him that overcometh I will give a white stone, and in the stone a new name written, which no man knoweth saving he that receiveth it.'[5] What can be more a man's own than this new name which even in eternity remains a secret between God and him? And what shall we take this secrecy to mean? Surely, that each of the redeemed shall forever know and praise some one aspect of the Divine beauty better than any other creature can. Why else were individuals created, but that God, loving all infinitely, should love each differently? And this difference, so far from impairing, floods with meaning the love of all blessed creatures for one another, the communion of the saints. If all experienced God in the same way and returned Him an identical worship, the song of the Church triumphant would have no symphony, it would be like an orchestra in which all the instruments played the same note. Aristotle has told us that a city is a unity of unlikes,[6] and St Paul that a body is a unity of different members.[7] Heaven is a city, and a Body, because the blessed remain eternally different: a society, because each has something to tell all the others—fresh and ever fresh news of the 'My God' whom each finds in Him whom all praise as 'Our God'. For doubtless the continually successful, yet never complete, attempt by each soul to communicate its unique vision to all others (and that by means whereof earthly art and philosophy are but clumsy imitations) is also among the ends for which the individual was created.

For union exists only between distincts; and, perhaps, from this point of view, we catch a momentary glimpse of the meaning of all things. Pantheism is a creed not so much false as hopelessly behind the times. Once, before creation, it would have been true to say that everything was God. But God created: He caused things to be other than Himself that, being distinct, they might learn to love Him, and achieve union instead of mere sameness. Thus He also cast His bread upon the waters. Even within the creation we might say that inanimate matter, which has no will, is one with God in a sense in which men are not. But it is not God's purpose

---

[4] *Theologia Germanica*, li.

[5] Revelation 2:17.

[6] *Politics*, ii, 2, 4.

[7] 1 Corinthians 12:12–30.

that we should go back into that old identity (as, perhaps, some Pagan mystics would have us do) but that we should go on to the maximum distinctness there to be reunited with Him in a higher fashion. Even within the Holy One Himself, it is not sufficient that the Word should *be* God, it must also be *with* God. The Father eternally begets the Son and the Holy Ghost proceeds: deity introduces distinction within itself so that the union of reciprocal loves may transcend mere arithmetical unity or self-identity.

But the eternal distinctness of each soul—the secret which makes of the union between each soul and God a species in itself—will never abrogate the law that forbids ownership in heaven. As to its fellow-creatures, each soul, we suppose, will be eternally engaged in giving away to all the rest that which it receives. And as to God, we must remember that the soul is but a hollow which God fills. Its union with God is, almost by definition, a continual self-abandonment—an opening, an unveiling, a surrender, of itself. A blessed spirit is a mould ever more and more patient of the bright metal poured into it, a body ever more completely uncovered to the meridian blaze of the spiritual sun. We need not suppose that the necessity for something analogous to self-conquest will ever be ended, or that eternal life will not also be eternal dying. It is in this sense that, as there may be pleasures in hell (God shield us from them), there may be something not all unlike pains in heaven (God grant us soon to taste them).

For in self-giving, if anywhere, we touch a rhythm not only of all creation but of all being. For the Eternal Word also gives Himself in sacrifice; and that not only on Calvary. For when He was crucified He 'did that in the wild weather of His outlying provinces which He had done at home in glory and gladness'.[8] From before the foundation of the world He surrenders begotten Deity back to begetting Deity in obedience. And as the Son glorifies the Father, so also the Father glorifies the Son.[9] And, with submission, as becomes a layman, I think it was truly said 'God loveth not Himself as Himself but as Goodness; and if there were aught better than God, He would love that and not Himself'.[10] From the highest to the lowest, self exists to be abdicated and, by that abdication, becomes the more truly self, to be thereupon yet the more abdicated, and so forever. This

---

[8] George MacDonald, *Unspoken Sermons:* 3rd Series, pp. 11, 12.

[9] John 17:1, 4, 5.

[10] *Theol. Germ.*, xxxii.

is not a heavenly law which we can escape by remaining earthly, nor an earthly law which we can escape by being saved. What is outside the system of self-giving is not earth, nor nature, nor 'ordinary life', but simply and solely hell. Yet even hell derives from this law such reality as it has. That fierce imprisonment in the self is but the obverse of the self-giving which is absolute reality; the negative shape which the outer darkness takes by surrounding and defining the shape of the real, or which the real imposes on the darkness by having a shape and positive nature of its own.

The golden apple of selfhood, thrown among the false gods, became an apple of discord because they scrambled for it. They did not know the first rule of the holy game, which is that every player must by all means touch the ball and then immediately pass it on. To be found with it in your hands is a fault: to cling to it, death. But when it flies to and fro among the players too swift for eye to follow, and the great master Himself leads the revelry, giving Himself eternally to His creatures in the generation, and back to Himself in the sacrifice, of the Word, then indeed the eternal dance 'makes heaven drowsy with the harmony'. All pains and pleasures we have known on earth are early initiations in the movements of that dance: but the dance itself is strictly incomparable with the sufferings of this present time. As we draw nearer to its uncreated rhythm, pain and pleasure sink almost out of sight. There is joy in the dance, but it does not exist for the sake of joy. It does not even exist for the sake of good, or of love. It is Love Himself, and Good Himself, and therefore happy. It does not exist for us, but we for it. The size and emptiness of the universe which frightened us at the outset of this book, should awe us still, for though they may be no more than a subjective by-product of our three-dimensional imagining, yet they symbolise great truth. As our Earth is to all the stars, so doubtless are we men and our concerns to all creation; as all the stars are to space itself, so are all creatures, all thrones and powers and mightiest of the created gods, to the abyss of the self-existing Being, who is to us Father and Redeemer and indwelling Comforter, but of whom no man nor angel can say nor conceive what He is in and for Himself, or what is the work that he 'maketh from the beginning to the end'. For they are all derived and unsubstantial things. Their vision fails them and they cover their eyes from the intolerable light of utter actuality, which was and is and shall be, which never could have been otherwise, which has no opposite.

APPENDIX

THIS NOTE ON the observed effects of pain has been kindly supplied by R. Havard, MD, from clinical experience:

Pain is a common and definite event which can easily be recognised: but the observation of character or behaviour is less easy, less complete, and less exact, especially in the transient, if intimate, relation of doctor and patient. In spite of this difficulty certain impressions gradually take form in the course of medical practice which are confirmed as experience grows. A short attack of severe physical pain is overwhelming while it lasts. The sufferer is not usually loud in his complaints. He will beg for relief but does not waste his breath on elaborating his troubles. It is unusual for him to lose self-control and to become wild and irrational. It is rare for the severest physical pain to become in this sense unbearable. When short, severe, physical pain passes it leaves no obvious alteration in behaviour. Long-continued pain has more noticeable effects. It is often accepted with little or no complaint and great strength and resignation are developed. Pride is humbled or, at times, results in a determination to conceal suffering. Women with rheumatoid arthritis show a cheerfulness which is so characteristic that it can be compared to the *spes phthisica* of the consumptive: and is perhaps due more to a slight intoxication of the patient by the infection than to an increased strength of character. Some victims of chronic pain deteriorate. They become querulous and exploit their privileged position as invalids to practise domestic tyranny. But the wonder is that the failures are so few and the heroes so many; there is a challenge in physical pain which most can recognise and answer. On the other hand, a long illness, even without pain, exhausts the mind as well as the body. The invalid gives up the struggle and drifts helplessly and plaintively into a self-pitying despair. Even so, some, in a similar physical state, will preserve their serenity and selflessness to the end. To see it is a rare but moving experience.

Mental pain is less dramatic than physical pain, but it is more common and also more hard to bear. The frequent attempt to conceal mental pain increases the burden: it is easier to say 'My tooth is aching' than to say 'My heart is broken'. Yet if the cause is accepted and faced, the conflict will strengthen and purify the character and in time the pain will usually pass. Sometimes, however, it persists and the effect is devastating; if the cause is not faced or not recognised, it produces the dreary state of the chronic neurotic. But some by heroism overcome even chronic mental pain. They often produce brilliant work and strengthen, harden, and sharpen their characters till they become like tempered steel.

In actual insanity the picture is darker. In the whole realm of medicine there is nothing so terrible to contemplate as a man with chronic melancholia. But most of the insane are not unhappy or, indeed, conscious of their condition. In either case, if they recover, they are surprisingly little changed. Often they remember nothing of their illness.

Pain provides an opportunity for heroism; the opportunity is seized with surprising frequency.

A GRIEF OBSERVED

A GRIEF OBSERVED
CONTENTS

INTRODUCTION

A GRIEF OBSERVED is not an ordinary book. In a sense it is not a book at all; it is, rather, the passionate result of a brave man turning to face his agony and examine it in order that he might further understand what is required of us in living this life in which we have to expect the pain and sorrow of the loss of those whom we love. It is true to say that very few men could have written this book, and even truer to say that even fewer men would have written this book even if they could, fewer still would have published it even if they had written it.

My stepfather, C. S. Lewis, had written before on the topic of pain (*The Problem of Pain*, 1940), and pain was not an experience with which he was unfamiliar. He had met grief as a child: he lost his mother when he was nine years old. He had grieved for friends lost to him over the years, some lost in battle during the First World War, others to sickness.

He had written also about the great poets and their songs of love, but somehow neither his learning nor his experiences had ever prepared him for the combination of both the great love and the great loss which is its counterpoint; the soaring joy which is the finding and winning of the mate whom God has prepared for us; and the crushing blow, the loss, which is Satan's corruption of that great gift of loving and being loved.

In referring to this book in conversation, one often tends to leave out, either inadvertently or from laziness, the indefinite article at the beginning of the title. This we must not do, for the title completely and thoroughly describes what this book is, and thus expresses very accurately its real value. Anything entitled "Grief Observed" would have to be so general and nonspecific as to be academic in its approach and thus of little use to anyone approaching or experiencing bereavement.

This book, on the other hand, is a stark recounting of one man's studied attempts to come to grips with and in the end defeat the emotional paralysis of the most shattering grief of his life.

What makes *A Grief Observed* even more remarkable is that the author was an exceptional man, and the woman whom he mourns, an exceptional woman. Both of them were writers, both of them were academically talented, both were committed Christians, but here the similarities end. It fascinates me how God sometimes brings people together who are so far apart, in so many ways, and merges them into that spiritual homogeneity which is marriage.

Jack (C. S. Lewis) was a man whose extraordinary scholarship and intellectual ability isolated him from much of mankind. There were few people among his peers who could match him in debate or discussion, and those who could almost inevitably found themselves drawn to one another in a small, tight-knit group which became known as "The Inklings," and which has left us with a legacy of literature. J.R.R. Tolkien, John Wain, Roger Lancelyn-Green, and Neville Coghill were among those who frequented these informal gatherings.

Helen Joy Gresham (née Davidman), the "H." referred to in this book, was perhaps the only woman whom Jack ever met who was his intellectual equal and also as well-read and widely educated as he was himself. They shared another common factor: they were both possessed of total recall. Jack never forgot anything he had read, and neither did she.

Jack's upbringing was a mixture of middle-class Irish (he came from Belfast, where his father was a police-court solicitor) and English, set in the very beginnings of the twentieth century—a time when the concepts of personal honour, total commitment to one's given word, and the general principles of chivalry and good manners were still drummed into the young British male with rather more intensity than was any other form of religious observance. The writing of E. Nesbit, Sir Walter Scott, and perhaps Rudyard Kipling were the exemplars of the standards with which Jack was indoctrinated as a young man.

My mother, on the other hand, could not have come from a background more divergent from his. The daughter of two lower-middle-class Jewish second-generation immigrants, her father of Ukrainian, her mother of Polish origins, she was born and brought up in the Bronx in

New York City. The only striking similarities to be found in the comparison of their early developments were that they were both possessed of truly amazing intelligence combined with academic talent and eidetic memory. They both came to Christ via the long and difficult road which leads from Atheism, to Agnosticism, and thence by way of Theism finally to Christianity, and they both enjoyed remarkable success in their university student careers. Jack's was interrupted by his duty to his country in the First World War, and Mother's by political activism and marriage.

Much has been written, both fictional and factual (sometimes one masquerading as the other) concerning their lives and their meeting and marriage, but the most important part of the story pertaining to this book is simply a recognition of the great love that grew between them until it was an almost visible incandescence. They seemed to walk together within a glow of their own making.

To understand even a little of the agony which this book contains, and the courage it demonstrates, we must first acknowledge that love between them. As a child, I watched these two remarkable people come together, first as friends, then, in an unusual progression, as husband and wife, and finally as lovers. I was part of the friendship; I was an adjunct to the marriage, but I stood aside from the love. By that I do not mean that I was in any way deliberately excluded, but rather that their love was something of which I could not, and should not, be a part.

Even then in my early teen years I stood aside and watched the love grow between these two, and was able to be happy for them. It was a happiness tinged with both sadness and fear, for I knew, as did both Mother and Jack, that this, the best of times, was to be brief and was to end in sorrow.

I had yet to learn that all human relationships end in pain—it is the price that our imperfection has allowed Satan to exact from us for the privilege of love. I had the resilience of youth upon which to fall when Mother died; for me there would be other loves to find and no doubt in time to lose or be lost by. But for Jack this was the end of so much which life had for so long denied him and then briefly held out to him like a barren promise. For Jack there were none of the hopes (however dimly I might see them) of bright sunlit meadows and life-light and laughter. I had Jack to lean upon, poor Jack only had me.

I have always wanted the opportunity to explain one small thing that is in this book and which displays a misunderstanding. Jack refers to the fact that if he mentioned Mother, I would always seem to be embarrassed as if he had said something obscene. He did not understand, which was very unusual for him. I was fourteen when Mother died and the product of almost seven years of British Preparatory School indoctrination. The lesson I was most strongly taught throughout that time was that the most shameful thing that could happen to me would be to be reduced to tears in public. British boys don't cry. But I knew that if Jack talked to me about Mother, I would weep uncontrollably and, worse still, so would he. This was the source of my embarrassment. It took me almost thirty years to learn how to cry without feeling ashamed.

This book is a man emotionally naked in his own Gethsemane. It tells of the agony and the emptiness of a grief such as few of us have to bear, for the greater the love the greater the grief, and the stronger the faith the more savagely will Satan storm its fortress.

When Jack was racked with the emotional pain of his bereavement, he also suffered the mental anguish resulting from three years of living in constant fear, the physical agony of osteoporosis and other ailments, and the sheer exhaustion of spending those last few weeks in constant caring for his dying wife. His mind stretched to some unimaginable tension far beyond anything a lesser man could bear; he turned to writing down his thoughts and his reactions to them, in order to try to make some sense of the whirling chaos that was assaulting his mind. At the time that he was writing them, he did not intend that these effusions were to be published, but on reading through them some time later, he felt that they might well be of some help to others who were similarly afflicted with the turmoil of thought and feeling which grief forces upon us. This book was first published under the pseudonym of N. W. Clerk. In its stark honesty and unadorned simplicity the book has a power which is rare: it is the power of unabashed truth.

To fully appreciate the depths of his grief I think it is important to understand a little more of the circumstances of Jack and Mother's initial meeting and relationship. My mother and father (novelist W. L. Gresham) were both highly intelligent and talented people and in their marriage there were many conflicts and difficulties. Mother was brought up an atheist, and became a communist. Her native intelligence did not allow her to be deceived for long by that hollow philosophy, and (by this time, married to my father) she found herself searching for something less posturing and more real.

Encountering amid her reading of a wide variety of authors the work of the British writer C. S. Lewis, she became aware that beneath the fragile and very human veneer of the organized churches of the world, there lies a truth so real and so pristine that all of man's concocted philosophical posings tumble into ruin beside it. She became aware also that here was a mind of hitherto unparalleled clarity. As all new believers do, she had questions, and so she wrote to him. Jack noticed her letters at once, for they too signalled a remarkable mind, and a pen-friendship soon developed.

In 1952 Mother was working on a book about the Ten Commandments (*Smoke on the Mountain:* Westminster Press, 1953), and while convalescing from a serious illness journeyed to England determined to discuss the book with C. S. Lewis. His friendship and advice were unstinting as were those of his brother, W. H. Lewis, an historian and himself a writer of no mean ability.

On her return to America, Mother (now a complete Anglophile), discovered that her marriage to my father was over, and following the divorce she fled to England with myself and my brother. We lived for a while in London, and although letters were exchanged, Jack was not a visitor to our home, he rarely came to London, which was a city he was not fond of, and Mother and he were merely intellectual friends at this time, though in common with many other people we were the recipients of considerable financial assistance from his special charity fund.

Mother found London a depressing place to live and wanted to be near her circle of friends in Oxford, which included Jack, his brother "Warnie," and such people as Kay and Austin Farrer. I think it is too simple and too supposititious to say that her only motive for moving was to be near Jack, but it was certainly a contributory factor.

Our short time in Headington, just outside Oxford, seemed to be the beginning of so much that could have been wonderful. Our home was visited frequently by good friends and was the scene of many lively intellectual debates. It was also during this time that the relationship between Jack and Mother began to redefine itself.

I think that Jack resisted the deep emotional attachment to my mother which he began to be aware of, largely because it was something which he mistakenly thought was alien to his nature. Their friendship on a platonic level was convenient and caused no ripples on the placid surface of his existence. However, he was forced not merely to inward awareness of his love for her, but also to public acknowledgement of it by the sudden realisation that he was about to lose her.

It almost seems cruel that her death was delayed long enough for him to grow to love her so completely that she filled his world as the greatest gift that God had ever given him, and then she died and left him alone in a place that her presence in his life had created for him.

What many of us discover in this outpouring of anguish is that we know exactly what he is talking about. Those of us who have walked this same path, or are walking it as we read this book, find that we are not, after all, as alone as we thought.

C. S. Lewis, the writer of so much that is so clear and so right, the thinker whose acuity of mind and clarity of expression enabled us to understand so much, this strong and determined Christian, he too fell headlong into the vortex of whirling thoughts and feelings and dizzily groped for support and guidance deep in the dark chasm of grief. How I wish that he had been blessed with just such a book as this. If we find no comfort in the world around us, and no solace when we cry to God, if it does nothing else for us, at least this book will help us to face our grief, and to "misunderstand a little less completely."

For further reading, I recommend *Jack: C. S. Lewis and His Times* by George Sayer (Harper & Row, 1988; Crossway Books) as the best available biography of C. S. Lewis; Lyle Dorsett's biography of my mother, *And God Came In* (Macmillan, 1983); and also, somewhat immodestly perhaps, for an inside viewpoint of our family life, my own book, *Lenten Lands* (Macmillan, 1988; HarperSanFrancisco, 1994).

DOUGLAS H. GRESHAM

CHAPTER ONE

NO ONE EVER told me that grief felt so like fear. I am not afraid, but the sensation is like being afraid. The same fluttering in the stomach, the same restlessness, the yawning. I keep on swallowing.

At other times it feels like being mildly drunk, or concussed. There is a sort of invisible blanket between the world and me. I find it hard to take in what anyone says. Or perhaps, hard to want to take it in. It is so uninteresting. Yet I want the others to be about me. I dread the moments when the house is empty. If only they would talk to one another and not to me.

There are moments, most unexpectedly, when something inside me tries to assure me that I don't really mind so much, not so very much, after all. Love is not the whole of a man's life. I was happy before I ever met H. I've plenty of what are called 'resources.' People get over these things. Come, I shan't do so badly. One is ashamed to listen to this voice but it seems for a little to be making out a good case. Then comes a sudden jab of red-hot memory and all this 'commonsense' vanishes like an ant in the mouth of a furnace.

On the rebound one passes into tears and pathos. Maudlin tears. I almost prefer the moments of agony. These are at least clean and honest. But the bath of self-pity, the wallow, the loathsome sticky-sweet pleasure of indulging it—that disgusts me. And even while I'm doing it I know it leads me to misrepresent H. herself. Give that mood its head and in a few minutes I shall have substituted for the real woman a mere doll to be blubbered over. Thank God the memory of her is still too strong (will it always be too strong?) to let me get away with it.

For H. wasn't like that at all. Her mind was lithe and quick and muscular as a leopard. Passion, tenderness, and pain were all equally unable to disarm it. It scented the first whiff of cant or slush; then sprang, and knocked you over before you knew what was happening. How many bubbles of mine she pricked! I soon learned not to talk rot to her unless I did it for the sheer pleasure—and there's another red-hot jab—of being exposed and laughed at. I was never less silly than as H.'s lover.

And no one ever told me about the laziness of grief. Except at my job—where the machine seems to run on much as usual—I loathe the slightest effort. Not only writing but even reading a letter is too much. Even shaving. What does it matter now whether my cheek is rough or smooth? They say an unhappy man wants distractions—something to take him out of himself. Only as a dog-tired man wants an extra blanket on a cold night; he'd rather lie there shivering than get up and find one. It's easy to see why the lonely become untidy, finally, dirty and disgusting.

Meanwhile, where is God? This is one of the most disquieting symptoms. When you are happy, so happy that you have no sense of needing Him, so happy that you are tempted to feel His claims upon you as an interruption, if you remember yourself and turn to Him with gratitude and praise, you will be—or so it feels—welcomed with open arms. But go to Him when your need is desperate, when all other help is vain, and what do you find? A door slammed in your face, and a sound of bolting and double bolting on the inside. After that, silence. You may as well turn away. The longer you wait, the more emphatic the silence will become. There are no lights in the windows. It might be an empty house. Was it ever inhabited? It seemed so once. And that seeming was as strong as this. What can this mean? Why is He so present a commander in our time of prosperity and so very absent a help in time of trouble?

I tried to put some of these thoughts to C. this afternoon. He reminded me that the same thing seems to have happened to Christ: 'Why hast thou forsaken me?' I know. Does that make it easier to understand?

Not that I am (I think) in much danger of ceasing to believe in God. The real danger is of coming to believe such dreadful things about Him. The conclusion I dread is not 'So there's no God after all,' but 'So this is what God's really like. Deceive yourself no longer.'

Our elders submitted and said, 'Thy will be done.' How often had bitter resentment been stifled through sheer terror and an act of love—yes, in every sense, an act—put on to hide the operation?

Of course it's easy enough to say that God seems absent at our greatest need because He *is* absent—non-existent. But then why does He seem so present when, to put it quite frankly, we don't ask for Him?

One thing, however, marriage has done for me. I can never again believe that religion is manufactured out of our unconscious, starved desires and is a substitute for sex. For those few years H. and I feasted on love, every mode of it—solemn and merry, romantic and realistic, sometimes as dramatic as a thunderstorm, sometimes as comfortable and unemphatic as putting on your soft slippers. No cranny of heart or body remained unsatisfied. If God were a substitute for love we ought to have lost all interest in Him. Who'd bother about substitutes when he has the thing itself? But that isn't what happens. We both knew we wanted something besides one another—quite a different kind of something, a quite different kind of want. You might as well say that when lovers have one another they will never want to read, or eat—or breathe.

After the death of a friend, years ago, I had for some time a most vivid feeling of certainty about his continued life; even his enhanced life. I have begged to be given even one hundredth part of the same assurance about H. There is no answer. Only the locked door, the iron curtain, the vacuum, absolute zero. 'Them as asks don't get.' I was a fool to ask. For now, even if that assurance came I should distrust it. I should think it a self-hypnosis induced by my own prayers.

At any rate I must keep clear of the spiritualists. I promised H. I would. She knew something of those circles.

Keeping promises to the dead, or to anyone else, is very well. But I begin to see that 'respect for the wishes of the dead' is a trap. Yesterday I stopped myself only in time from saying about some trifle 'H. wouldn't have liked that.' This is unfair to the others. I should soon be using 'what H. would have liked' as an instrument of domestic tyranny, with her supposed likings becoming a thinner and thinner disguise for my own.

I cannot talk to the children about her. The moment I try, there appears on their faces neither grief, nor love, nor fear, nor pity, but the most fatal of all non-conductors, embarrassment. They look as if I were committing an indecency. They are longing for me to stop. I felt just the same after my own mother's death when my father mentioned her. I can't blame them. It's the way boys are.

I sometimes think that shame, mere awkward, senseless shame, does as much towards preventing good acts and straightforward happiness as any of our vices can do. And not only in boyhood.

Or are the boys right? What would H. herself think of this terrible little notebook to which I come back and back? Are these jottings morbid? I once read the sentence 'I lay awake all night with toothache, thinking about toothache and about lying awake.' That's true to life. Part of every misery is, so to speak, the misery's shadow or reflection: the fact that you don't merely suffer but have to keep on thinking about the fact that you suffer. I not only live each endless day in grief, but live each day thinking about living each day in grief. Do these notes merely aggravate that side of it? Merely confirm the monotonous, tread-mill march of the mind round one subject? But what am I to do? I must have some drug, and reading isn't a strong enough drug now. By writing it all down (all?—no: one thought in a hundred) I believe I get a little outside it. That's how I'd defend it to H. But ten to one she'd see a hole in the defence.

It isn't only the boys either. An odd byproduct of my loss is that I'm aware of being an embarrassment to everyone I meet. At work, at the club, in the street, I see people, as they approach me, trying to make up their minds whether they'll 'say something about it' or not. I hate it if they do, and if they don't. Some funk it altogether. R. has been avoiding me for a week. I like best the well brought-up young men, almost boys, who walk up to me as if I were a dentist, turn very red, get it over, and then edge away to the bar as quickly as they decently can. Perhaps the bereaved ought to be isolated in special settlements like lepers.

To some I'm worse than an embarrassment. I am a death's head. Whenever I meet a happily married pair I can feel them both thinking, 'One or other of us must some day be as he is now.'

At first I was very afraid of going to places where H. and I had been happy—our favourite pub, our favourite wood. But I decided to do it at once—like sending a pilot up again as soon as possible after he's had a crash. Unexpectedly, it makes no difference. Her absence is no more emphatic in those places than anywhere else. It's not local at all. I suppose that if one were forbidden all salt one wouldn't notice it much more in any one food than in another. Eating in general would be different, every day, at every meal. It is like that. The act of living is different all through. Her absence is like the sky, spread over everything.

But no, that is not quite accurate. There is one place where her absence comes locally home to me, and it is a place I can't avoid. I mean my own body. It had such a different importance while it was the body of H.'s lover. Now it's like an empty house. But don't let me deceive myself. This body would become important to me again, and pretty quickly, if I thought there was anything wrong with it.

Cancer, and cancer, and cancer. My mother, my father, my wife. I wonder who is next in the queue.

Yet H. herself, dying of it, and well knowing the fact, said that she had lost a great deal of her old horror at it. When the reality came, the name and the idea were in some degree disarmed. And up to a point I very nearly understood. This is important. One never meets just Cancer, or War, or Unhappiness (or Happiness). One only meets each hour or moment that comes. All manner of ups and downs. Many bad spots in our best times, many good ones in our worst. One never gets the total impact of what we call 'the thing itself.' But we call it wrongly. The thing itself is simply all these ups and downs: the rest is a name or an idea.

It is incredible how much happiness, even how much gaiety, we sometimes had together after all hope was gone. How long, how tranquilly, how nourishingly, we talked together that last night!

And yet, not quite together. There's a limit to the 'one flesh.' You can't really share someone else's weakness, or fear or pain. What you feel may be bad. It might conceivably be as bad as what the other felt, though I should distrust anyone who claimed that it was. But it would still be quite different. When I speak of fear, I mean the merely animal fear, the recoil of the organism from its destruction; the smothery feeling; the sense of being a rat in a trap. It can't be transferred. The mind can sympathize; the body, less. In one way the bodies of lovers can do it least. All their love passages have trained them to have, not identical, but complementary, correlative, even opposite, feelings about one another.

We both knew this. I had my miseries, not hers; she had hers, not mine. The end of hers would be the coming-of-age of mine. We were setting out on different roads. This cold truth, this terrible traffic-regulation ('You, Madam, to the right—you, Sir, to the left') is just the beginning of the separation which is death itself.

And this separation, I suppose, waits for all. I have been thinking of H. and myself as peculiarly unfortunate in being torn apart. But presumably all lovers are. She once said to me, 'Even if we both died at exactly the same moment, as we lie here side by side, it would be just as much a separation as the one you're so afraid of.' Of course she didn't *know*, any more than I do. But she was near death; near enough to make a good shot. She used to quote 'Alone into the Alone.' She said it felt like that. And how immensely improbable that it should be otherwise! Time and space and body were the very things that brought us together; the telephone wires by which we communicated. Cut one off, or cut both off simultaneously. Either way, mustn't the conversation stop?

Unless you assume that some other means of communication—utterly different, yet doing the same work—would be immediately substituted. But then, what conceivable point could there be in severing the old ones? Is God a clown who whips away your bowl of soup one moment in order, next moment, to replace it with another bowl of the same soup? Even nature isn't such a clown as that. She never plays exactly the same tune twice.

It is hard to have patience with people who say, 'There is no death' or 'Death doesn't matter.' There is death. And whatever is matters. And whatever happens has consequences, and it and they are irrevocable and irreversible. You might as well say that birth doesn't matter. I look up at the night sky. Is anything more certain than that in all those vast times and spaces, if I were allowed to search them, I should nowhere find her face, her voice, her touch? She died. She is dead. Is the word so difficult to learn?

I have no photograph of her that's any good. I cannot even see her face distinctly in my imagination. Yet the odd face of some stranger seen in a crowd this morning may come before me in vivid perfection the moment I close my eyes tonight. No doubt, the explanation is simple enough. We have seen the faces of those we know best so variously, from so many angles, in so many lights, with so many expressions—waking, sleeping, laughing, crying, eating, talking, thinking—that all the impressions crowd into our memory together and cancel out into a mere blur. But her voice is still vivid. The remembered voice—that can turn me at any moment to a whimpering child.

CHAPTER TWO

FOR THE FIRST time I have looked back and read these notes. They appall me. From the way I've been talking anyone would think that H.'s death mattered chiefly for its effect on myself. Her point of view seems to have dropped out of sight. Have I forgotten the moment of bitterness when she cried out, 'And there was so much to live for'? Happiness had not come to her early in life. A thousand years of it would not have made her *blasée*. Her palate for all the joys of sense and intellect and spirit was fresh and unspoiled. Nothing would have been wasted on her. She liked more things and liked them more than anyone I have known. A noble hunger, long unsatisfied, met at last its proper food, and almost instantly the food was snatched away. Fate (or whatever it is) delights to produce a great capacity and then frustrate it. Beethoven went deaf. By our standards a mean joke; the monkey trick of a spiteful imbecile.

I must think more about H. and less about myself.

Yes, that sounds very well. But there's a snag. I am thinking about her nearly always. Thinking of the H. facts—real words, looks, laughs, and actions of hers. But it is my own mind that selects and groups them. Already, less than a month after her death, I can feel the slow, insidious beginning of a process that will make the H. I think of into a more and more imaginary woman. Founded on fact, no doubt. I shall put in nothing fictitious (or I hope I shan't). But won't the composition inevitably become more and more my own? The reality is no longer there to check me, to pull me up short, as the real H. so often did, so unexpectedly, by being so thoroughly herself and not me.

The most precious gift that marriage gave me was this constant impact of something very close and intimate yet all the time unmistakably other, resistant—in a word, real. Is all that work to be undone? Is what I shall still call H. to sink back horribly into being not much more than one of my old bachelor pipe-dreams? Oh my dear, my dear, come back for one moment and drive that miserable phantom away. Oh God, God, why did you take such trouble to force this creature out of its shell if it is now doomed to crawl back—to be sucked back—into it?

Today I had to meet a man I haven't seen for ten years. And all that time I had thought I was remembering him well—how he looked and spoke and the sort of things he said. The first five minutes of the real man shattered the image completely. Not that he had changed. On the contrary. I kept on thinking, 'Yes, of course, of course. I'd forgotten that he thought that—or disliked this, or knew so-and-so—or jerked his head back that way.' I had known all these things once and I recognized them the moment I met them again. But they had all faded out of my mental picture of him, and when they were all replaced by his actual presence the total effect was quite astonishingly different from the image I had carried about with me for those ten years. How can I hope that this will not happen to my memory of H.? That it is not happening already? Slowly, quietly, like snow-flakes—like the small flakes that come when it is going to snow all night—little flakes of me, my impressions, my selections, are settling down on the image of her. The real shape will be quite hidden in the end. Ten minutes—ten seconds—of the real H. would correct all this. And yet, even if those ten seconds were allowed me, one second later the little flakes would begin to fall again. The rough, sharp, cleansing tang of her otherness is gone.

What pitiable cant to say, 'She will live forever in my memory!' *Live?* That is exactly what she won't do. You might as well think like the old Egyptians that you can keep the dead by embalming them. Will nothing persuade us that they are gone? What's left? A corpse, a memory, and (in some versions) a ghost. All mockeries or horrors. Three more ways of spelling the word *dead*. It was H. I loved. As if I wanted to fall in love with my memory of her, an image in my own mind! It would be a sort of incest.

I remember being rather horrified one summer morning long ago when a burly, cheerful labouring man, carrying a hoe and a watering pot came into our churchyard and, as he pulled the gate behind him, shouted over his shoulder to two friends, 'See you later, I'm just going to visit Mum.' He meant he was going to weed and water and generally tidy up her grave. It horrified me because this mode of sentiment, all this churchyard stuff, was and is simply hateful, even inconceivable, to me. But in the light of my recent thoughts I am beginning to wonder whether, if one could take that man's line (I can't), there isn't a good deal to be said for it. A six-by-three-foot flower-bed had become Mum. That was his symbol for her, his link with her. Caring for it was visiting her. May this not be in one way better than preserving and caressing an image in one's own memory? The grave and the image are equally links with the irrecoverable and symbols for the unimaginable. But the image has the added disadvantage that it will do whatever you want. It will smile or frown, be tender, gay, ribald, or argumentative just as your mood demands. It is a puppet of which you hold the strings. Not yet of course. The reality is still too fresh; genuine and wholly involuntary memories can still, thank God, at any moment rush in and tear the strings out of my hands. But the fatal obedience of the image, its insipid dependence on me, is bound to increase. The flower-bed on the other hand is an obstinate, resistant, often intractable bit of reality, just as Mum in her lifetime doubtless was. As H. was.

Or as H. is. Can I honestly say that I believe she now is anything? The vast majority of the people I meet, say, at work, would certainly think she is not. Though naturally they wouldn't press the point on me. Not just now anyway. What do I really think? I have always been able to pray for the other dead, and I still do, with some confidence. But when I try to pray for H., I halt. Bewilderment and amazement come over me. I have a ghastly sense of unreality, of speaking into a vacuum about a nonentity.

The reason for the difference is only too plain. You never know how much you really believe anything until its truth or falsehood becomes a matter of life and death to you. It is easy to say you believe a rope to be strong and sound as long as you are merely using it to cord a box. But suppose you had to hang by that rope over a precipice. Wouldn't you then first discover how much you really trusted it? The same with people. For years I would have said that I had perfect confidence in B.R. Then came the moment when I had to decide whether I would or would not trust him with a really important secret. That threw quite a new light on what I called my 'confidence' in him. I discovered that there was no such thing. Only a real risk tests the reality of a belief. Apparently the faith—I thought it faith—which enables me to pray for the other dead has seemed strong only because I have never really cared, not desperately, whether they existed or not. Yet I thought I did.

But there are other difficulties. 'Where is she now?' That is, *in what place* is she *at the present time?* But if H. is not a body—and the body I loved is certainly no longer she—she is in no place at all. And 'the present time' is a date or point in our time series. It is as if she were on a journey without me and I said, looking at my watch, 'I wonder is she at Euston now.' But unless she is proceeding at sixty seconds a minute along this same timeline that all we living people travel by, what does *now* mean? If the dead are not in time, or not in our sort of time, is there any clear difference, when we speak of them, between *was* and *is* and *will be?*

Kind people have said to me, 'She is with God.' In one sense that is most certain. She is, like God, incomprehensible and unimaginable.

But I find that this question, however important it may be in itself, is not after all very important in relation to grief. Suppose that the earthly lives she and I shared for a few years are in reality only the basis for, or prelude to, or earthly appearance of, two unimaginable, supercosmic, eternal somethings. Those somethings could be pictured as spheres or globes. Where the plane of Nature cuts through them—that is, in earthly life—they appear as two circles (circles are slices of spheres). Two circles that touched. But those two circles, above all the point at which they touched, are the very thing I am mourning for, homesick for, famished for. You tell me, 'she goes on.' But my heart and body are crying out, come back, come back. Be a circle, touching my circle on the plane of Nature. But I know this is impossible. I know that the thing I want is exactly the thing I can never get. The old life, the jokes, the drinks, the arguments, the lovemaking, the tiny, heartbreaking commonplace. On any view whatever, to say, 'H. is dead,' is to say, 'All that is gone.' It is a part of the past. And the past is the past and that is what time means, and time itself is one more name for death, and Heaven itself is a state where 'the former things have passed away.'

Talk to me about the truth of religion and I'll listen gladly. Talk to me about the duty of religion and I'll listen submissively. But don't come talking to me about the consolations of religion or I shall suspect that you don't understand.

Unless, of course, you can literally believe all that stuff about family reunions 'on the further shore,' pictured in entirely earthly terms. But that is all unscriptural, all out of bad hymns and lithographs. There's not a word of it in the Bible. And it rings false. We *know* it couldn't be like that. Reality never repeats. The exact same thing is never taken away and given back. How well the spiritualists bait their hook! 'Things on this side are not so different after all.' There are cigars in Heaven. For that is what we should all like. The happy past restored.

And that, just that, is what I cry out for, with mad, midnight endearments and entreaties spoken into the empty air.

And poor C. quotes to me, 'Do not mourn like those that have no hope.' It astonishes me, the way we are invited to apply to ourselves words so obviously addressed to our betters. What St. Paul says can comfort only those who love God better than the dead, and the dead better than themselves. If a mother is mourning not for what she has lost but for what her dead child has lost, it is a comfort to believe that the child has not lost the end for which it was created. And it is a comfort to believe that she herself, in losing her chief or only natural happiness, has not lost a greater thing, that she may still hope to 'glorify God and enjoy Him forever.' A comfort to the God-aimed, eternal spirit within her. But not to her motherhood. The specifically maternal happiness must be written off. Never, in any place or time, will she have her son on her knees, or bathe him, or tell him a story, or plan for his future, or see her grandchild.

They tell me H. is happy now, they tell me she is at peace. What makes them so sure of this? I don't mean that I fear the worst of all. Nearly her last words were, 'I am at peace with God.' She had not always been. And she never lied. And she wasn't easily deceived, least of all, in her own favour. I don't mean that. But why are they so sure that all anguish ends with death? More than half the Christian world, and millions in the East, believe otherwise. How do they know she is 'at rest?' Why should the separation (if nothing else) which so agonizes the lover who is left behind be painless to the lover who departs?

'Because she is in God's hands.' But if so, she was in God's hands all the time, and I have seen what they did to her here. Do they suddenly become gentler to us the moment we are out of the body? And if so, why? If God's goodness is inconsistent with hurting us, then either God is not good or there is no God: for in the only life we know He hurts us beyond our worst fears and beyond all we can imagine. If it is consistent with hurting us, then He may hurt us after death as unendurably as before it.

Sometimes it is hard not to say, 'God forgive God.' Sometimes it is hard to say so much. But if our faith is true, He didn't. He crucified Him.

Come, what do we gain by evasions? We are under the harrow and can't escape. Reality, looked at steadily, is unbearable. And how or why did such a reality blossom (or fester) here and there into the terrible phenomenon called consciousness? Why did it produce things like us who can see it and, seeing it, recoil in loathing? Who (stranger still) want to see it and take pains to find it out, even when no need compels them and even though the sight of it makes an incurable ulcer in their hearts? People like H. herself, who would have truth at any price.

If H. 'is not,' then she never was. I mistook a cloud of atoms for a person. There aren't, and never were, any people. Death only reveals the vacuity that was always there. What we call the living are simply those who have not yet been unmasked. All equally bankrupt, but some not yet declared.

But this must be nonsense; vacuity revealed to whom? Bankruptcy declared to whom? To other boxes of fireworks or clouds of atoms. I will never believe—more strictly I can't believe—that one set of physical events could be, or make, a mistake about other sets.

No, my real fear is not of materialism. If it were true, we—or what we mistake for 'we'—could get out, get from under the harrow. An overdose of sleeping pills would do it. I am more afraid that we are really rats in a trap. Or, worse still, rats in a laboratory. Someone said, I believe, 'God always geometrizes.' Supposing the truth were 'God always vivisects'?

Sooner or later I must face the question in plain language. What reason have we, except our own desperate wishes, to believe that God is, by any standard we can conceive, 'good'? Doesn't all the *prima facie* evidence suggest exactly the opposite? What have we to set against it?

We set Christ against it. But how if He were mistaken? Almost His last words may have a perfectly clear meaning. He had found that the Being He called Father was horribly and infinitely different from what He had supposed. The trap, so long and carefully prepared and so subtly baited, was at last sprung, on the cross. The vile practical joke had succeeded.

What chokes every prayer and every hope is the memory of all the prayers H. and I offered and all the false hopes we had. Not hopes raised merely by our own wishful thinking, hopes encouraged, even forced upon us, by false diagnoses, by X-ray photographs, by strange remissions, by one temporary recovery that might have ranked as a miracle. Step by step we were 'led up the garden path.' Time after time, when He seemed most gracious He was really preparing the next torture.

I wrote that last night. It was a yell rather than a thought. Let me try it over again. Is it rational to believe in a bad God? Anyway, in a God so bad as all that? The Cosmic Sadist, the spiteful imbecile?

I think it is, if nothing else, too anthropomorphic. When you come to think of it, it is far more anthropomorphic than picturing Him as a grave old king with a long beard. That image is a Jungian archetype. It links God with all the wise old kings in the fairy-tales, with prophets, sages, magicians. Though it is (formally) the picture of a man, it suggests something more than humanity. At the very least it gets in the idea of something older than yourself, something that knows more, something you can't fathom. It preserves mystery. Therefore room for hope. Therefore room for a dread or awe that needn't be mere fear of mischief from a spiteful potentate. But the picture I was building up last night is simply the picture of a man like S.C.—who used to sit next to me at dinner and tell me what he'd been doing to the cats that afternoon. Now a being like S.C., however magnified, couldn't invent or create or govern anything. He would set traps and try to bait them. But he'd never have thought of baits like love, or laughter, or daffodils, or a frosty sunset. *He* make a universe? He couldn't make a joke, or a bow, or an apology, or a friend.

Or could one seriously introduce the idea of a bad God, as it were by the back door, through a sort of extreme Calvinism? You could say we are fallen and depraved. We are so depraved that our ideas of goodness count for nothing; or worse than nothing—the very fact that we think something good is presumptive evidence that it is really bad. Now God has in fact—our worst fears are true—all the characteristics we regard as bad: unreasonableness, vanity, vindictiveness, injustice, cruelty. But all these blacks (as they seem to us) are really whites. It's only our depravity that makes them look black to us.

And so what? This, for all practical (and speculative) purposes, sponges God off the slate. The word *good*, applied to Him, becomes meaningless: like abracadabra. We have no motive for obeying Him. Not even fear. It is true we have His threats and promises. But why should we believe them? If cruelty is from His point of view 'good,' telling lies may be 'good' too. Even if they are true, what then? If His ideas of good are so very different from ours, what He calls Heaven might well be what we should call Hell, and vice-versa. Finally, if reality at its very root is so meaningless to us—or, putting it the other way round, if we are such total imbeciles—what is the point of trying to think either about God or about anything else? This knot comes undone when you try to pull it tight.

Why do I make room in my mind for such filth and nonsense? Do I hope that if feeling disguises itself as thought I shall feel less? Aren't all these notes the senseless writhings of a man who won't accept the fact that there is nothing we can do with suffering except to suffer it? Who still thinks there is some device (if only he could find it) which will make pain not to be pain. It doesn't really matter whether you grip the arms of the dentist's chair or let your hands lie in your lap. The drill drills on.

And grief still feels like fear. Perhaps, more strictly, like suspense. Or like waiting; just hanging about waiting for something to happen. It gives life a permanently provisional feeling. It doesn't seem worth starting anything. I can't settle down. I yawn, I fidget, I smoke too much. Up till this I always had too little time. Now there is nothing but time. Almost pure time, empty successiveness.

One flesh. Or, if you prefer, one ship. The starboard engine has gone. I, the port engine, must chug along somehow till we make harbour. Or rather, till the journey ends. How can I assume a harbour? A lee shore, more likely, a black night, a deafening gale, breakers ahead—and any lights shown from the land probably being waved by wreckers. Such was H.'s landfall. Such was my mother's. I say their landfalls; not their arrivals.

CHAPTER THREE

IT'S NOT TRUE that I'm always thinking of H. Work and conversation make that impossible. But the times when I'm not are perhaps my worst. For then, though I have forgotten the reason, there is spread over everything a vague sense of wrongness, of something amiss. Like in those dreams where nothing terrible occurs—nothing that would sound even remarkable if you told it at breakfast-time—but the atmosphere, the taste, of the whole thing is deadly. So with this. I see the rowan berries reddening and don't know for a moment why they, of all things, should be depressing. I hear a clock strike and some quality it always had before has gone out of the sound. What's wrong with the world to make it so flat, shabby, worn-out looking? Then I remember.

This is one of the things I'm afraid of. The agonies, the mad midnight moments, must, in the course of nature, die away. But what will follow? Just this apathy, this dead flatness? Will there come a time when I no longer ask why the world is like a mean street, because I shall take the squalor as normal? Does grief finally subside into boredom tinged by faint nausea?

Feelings, and feelings, and feelings. Let me try thinking instead. From the rational point of view, what new factor has H.'s death introduced into the problem of the universe? What grounds has it given me for doubting all that I believe? I knew already that these things, and worse, happened daily. I would have said that I had taken them into account. I had been warned—I had warned myself—not to reckon on worldly happiness. We were even promised sufferings. They were part of the programme. We were even told, 'Blessed are they that mourn,' and I accepted it. I've got nothing that I hadn't bargained for. Of course it is different when the thing happens to oneself, not to others, and in reality, not in imagination. Yes; but should it, for a sane man, make quite such a difference as this? No. And it wouldn't for a man whose faith had been real faith and whose concern for other people's sorrows had been real concern. The case is too plain. If my house has collapsed at one blow, that is because it was a house of cards. The faith which 'took these things into account' was not faith but imagination. The taking them into account was not real sympathy. If I had really cared, as I thought I did, about the sorrows of the world, I should not have been so overwhelmed when my own sorrow came. It has been an imaginary faith playing with innocuous counters labelled 'Illness,' 'Pain,' 'Death,' and 'Loneliness.' I thought I trusted the rope until it mattered to me whether it would bear me. Now it matters, and I find I didn't.

Bridge-players tell me that there must be some money on the game 'or else people won't take it seriously.' Apparently it's like that. Your bid—for God or no God, for a good God or the Cosmic Sadist, for eternal life or nonentity—will not be serious if nothing much is staked on it. And you will never discover how serious it was until the stakes are raised horribly high, until you find that you are playing not for counters or for sixpences but for every penny you have in the world. Nothing less will shake a man—or at any rate a man like me—out of his merely verbal thinking and his merely notional beliefs. He has to be knocked silly before he comes to his senses. Only torture will bring out the truth. Only under torture does he discover it himself.

And I must surely admit—H. would have forced me to admit in a few passes—that, if my house was a house of cards, the sooner it was knocked down the better. And only suffering could do it. But then the Cosmic Sadist and Eternal Vivisector becomes an unnecessary hypothesis.

Is this last note a sign that I'm incurable, that when reality smashes my dream to bits, I mope and snarl while the first shock lasts, and then patiently, idiotically, start putting it together again? And so always? However often the house of cards falls, shall I set about rebuilding it? Is that what I'm doing now?

Indeed it's likely enough that what I shall call, if it happens, a 'restoration of faith' will turn out to be only one more house of cards. And I shan't know whether it is or not until the next blow comes—when, say, fatal disease is diagnosed in my body too, or war breaks out, or I have ruined myself by some ghastly mistake in my work. But there are two questions here. In which sense may it be a house of cards? Because the things I am believing are only a dream, or because I only dream that I believe them?

As for the things themselves, why should the thoughts I had a week ago be any more trustworthy than the better thoughts I have now? I am surely, in general, a saner man than I was then. Why should the desperate imaginings of a man dazed—I said it was like being concussed—be especially reliable?

Because there was no wishful thinking in them? Because, being so horrible, they were therefore all the more likely to be true? But there are fear-fulfilment as well as wish-fulfilment dreams. And were they wholly distasteful? No. In a way I liked them. I am even aware of a slight reluctance to accept the opposite thoughts. All that stuff about the Cosmic Sadist was not so much the expression of thought as of hatred. I was getting from it the only pleasure a man in anguish can get; the pleasure of hitting back. It was really just Billingsgate—mere abuse; 'telling God what I thought of Him.' And of course, as in all abusive language, 'what I thought' didn't mean what I thought true. Only what I thought would offend Him (and His worshippers) most. That sort of thing is never said without some pleasure. Gets it 'off your chest.' You feel better for a moment.

But the mood is no evidence. Of course the cat will growl and spit at the operator and bite him if she can. But the real question is whether he is a vet or a vivisector. Her bad language throws no light on it one way or the other.

And I can believe He is a vet when I think of my own suffering. It is harder when I think of hers. What is grief compared with physical pain? Whatever fools may say, the body can suffer twenty times more than the mind. The mind has always some power of evasion. At worst, the unbearable thought only comes back and back, but the physical pain can be absolutely continuous. Grief is like a bomber circling round and dropping its bombs each time the circle brings it overhead; physical pain is like the steady barrage on a trench in World War One, hours of it with no let-up for a moment. Thought is never static; pain often is.

What sort of a lover am I to think so much about my affliction and so much less about hers? Even the insane call, 'Come back,' is all for my own sake. I never even raised the question whether such a return, if it were possible, would be good for her. I want her back as an ingredient in the restoration of *my* past. Could I have wished her anything worse? Having got once through death, to come back and then, at some later date, have all her dying to do over again? They call Stephen the first martyr. Hadn't Lazarus the rawer deal?

I begin to see. My love for H. was of much the same quality as my faith in God. I won't exaggerate, though. Whether there was anything but imagination in the faith, or anything but egoism in the love, God knows. I don't. There may have been a little more; especially in my love for H. But neither was the thing I thought it was. A good deal of the card-castle about both.

What does it matter how this grief of mine evolves or what I do with it? What does it matter how I remember her or whether I remember her at all? None of these alternatives will either ease or aggravate her past anguish.

Her past anguish. How do I know that all her anguish is past? I never believed before—I thought it immensely improbable—that the faithfulest soul could leap straight into perfection and peace the moment death has rattled in the throat. It would be wishful thinking with a vengeance to take up that belief now. H. was a splendid thing; a soul straight, bright, and tempered like a sword. But not a perfected saint. A sinful woman married to a sinful man; two of God's patients, not yet cured. I know there are not only tears to be dried but stains to be scoured. The sword will be made even brighter.

But oh God, tenderly, tenderly. Already, month by month and week by week you broke her body on the wheel whilst she still wore it. Is it not yet enough?

The terrible thing is that a perfectly good God is in this matter hardly less formidable than a Cosmic Sadist. The more we believe that God hurts only to heal, the less we can believe that there is any use in begging for tenderness. A cruel man might be bribed—might grow tired of his vile sport—might have a temporary fit of mercy, as alcoholics have fits of sobriety. But suppose that what you are up against is a surgeon whose intentions are wholly good. The kinder and more conscientious he is, the more inexorably he will go on cutting. If he yielded to your entreaties, if he stopped before the operation was complete, all the pain up to that point would have been useless. But is it credible that such extremities of torture should be necessary for us? Well, take your choice. The tortures occur. If they are unnecessary, then there is no God or a bad one. If there is a good God, then these tortures are necessary. For no even moderately good Being could possibly inflict or permit them if they weren't.

Either way, we're for it.

What do people mean when they say, 'I am not afraid of God because I know He is good'? Have they never even been to a dentist?

Yet this is unendurable. And then one babbles—'If only I could bear it, or the worst of it, or any of it, instead of her.' But one can't tell how serious that bid is, for nothing is staked on it. If it suddenly became a real possibility, then, for the first time, we should discover how seriously we had meant it. But is it ever allowed?

It was allowed to One, we are told, and I find I can now believe again, that He has done vicariously whatever can be so done. He replies to our babble, 'You cannot and you dare not. I could and dared.'

Something quite unexpected has happened. It came this morning early. For various reasons, not in themselves at all mysterious, my heart was lighter than it had been for many weeks. For one thing, I suppose I am recovering physically from a good deal of mere exhaustion. And I'd had a very tiring but very healthy twelve hours the day before, and a sounder night's sleep; and after ten days of low-hung grey skies and motionless warm dampness, the sun was shining and there was a light breeze. And suddenly at the very moment when, so far, I mourned H. least, I remembered her best. Indeed it was something (almost) better than memory; an instantaneous, unanswerable impression. To say it was like a meeting would be going too far. Yet there was that in it which tempts one to use those words. It was as if the lifting of the sorrow removed a barrier.

Why has no one told me these things? How easily I might have misjudged another man in the same situation? I might have said, 'He's got over it. He's forgotten his wife,' when the truth was, 'He remembers her better *because* he has partly got over it.'

Such was the fact. And I believe I can make sense out of it. You can't see anything properly while your eyes are blurred with tears. You can't, in most things, get what you want if you want it too desperately: anyway, you can't get the best out of it. 'Now! Let's have a real good talk' reduces everyone to silence. 'I *must* get a good sleep tonight' ushers in hours of wakefulness. Delicious drinks are wasted on a really ravenous thirst. Is it similarly the very intensity of the longing that draws the iron curtain, that makes us feel we are staring into a vacuum when we think about our dead? 'Them as asks' (at any rate 'as asks too importunately') don't get. Perhaps can't.

And so, perhaps, with God. I have gradually been coming to feel that the door is no longer shut and bolted. Was it my own frantic need that slammed it in my face? The time when there is nothing at all in your soul except a cry for help may be just the time when God can't give it: you are like the drowning man who can't be helped because he clutches and grabs. Perhaps your own reiterated cries deafen you to the voice you hoped to hear.

On the other hand, 'Knock and it shall be opened.' But does knocking mean hammering and kicking the door like a maniac? And there's also 'To him that hath shall be given.' After all, you must have a capacity to receive, or even omnipotence can't give. Perhaps your own passion temporarily destroys the capacity.

For all sorts of mistakes are possible when you are dealing with Him. Long ago, before we were married, H. was haunted all one morning as she went about her work with the obscure sense of God (so to speak) 'at her elbow,' demanding her attention. And of course, not being a perfected saint, she had the feeling that it would be a question, as it usually is, of some unrepented sin or tedious duty. At last she gave in—I know how one puts it off—and faced Him. But the message was, 'I want to *give* you something' and instantly she entered into joy.

I think I am beginning to understand why grief feels like suspense. It comes from the frustration of so many impulses that had become habitual. Thought after thought, feeling after feeling, action after action, had H. for their object. Now their target is gone. I keep on through habit fitting an arrow to the string, then I remember and have to lay the bow down. So many roads lead thought to H. I set out on one of them. But now there's an impassable frontierpost across it. So many roads once; now so many *culs de sac*.

For a good wife contains so many persons in herself. What was H. not to me? She was my daughter and my mother, my pupil and my teacher, my subject and my sovereign; and always, holding all these in solution, my trusty comrade, friend, shipmate, fellow-soldier. My mistress; but at the same time all that any man friend (and I have good ones) has ever been to me. Perhaps more. If we had never fallen in love we should have none the less been always together, and created a scandal. That's what I meant when I once praised her for her 'masculine virtues.' But she soon put a stop to that by asking how I'd like to be praised for my feminine ones. It was a good *riposte*, dear. Yet there was something of the Amazon, something of Penthesileia and Camilla. And you, as well as I, were glad it should be there. You were glad I should recognize it.

Solomon calls his bride Sister. Could a woman be a complete wife unless, for a moment, in one particular mood, a man felt almost inclined to call her Brother?

'It was too perfect to last,' so I am tempted to say of our marriage. But it can be meant in two ways. It may be grimly pessimistic—as if God no sooner saw two of His creatures happy than He stopped it ('None of that here!'). As if He were like the Hostess at the sherry-party who separates two guests the moment they show signs of having got into a real conversation. But it could also mean 'This had reached its proper perfection. This had become what it had in it to be. Therefore of course it would not be prolonged.' As if God said, 'Good; you have mastered that exercise. I am very pleased with it. And now you are ready to go on to the next.' When you have learned to do quadratics and enjoy doing them you will not be set them much longer. The teacher moves you on.

For we did learn and achieve something. There is, hidden or flaunted, a sword between the sexes till an entire marriage reconciles them. It is arrogance in us to call frankness, fairness, and chivalry 'masculine' when we see them in a woman; it is arrogance in them to describe a man's sensitiveness or tact or tenderness as 'feminine.' But also what poor, warped fragments of humanity most mere men and mere women must be to make the implications of that arrogance plausible. Marriage heals this. Jointly the two become fully human. 'In the image of God created He *them*.' Thus, by a paradox, this carnival of sexuality leads us out beyond our sexes.

And then one or other dies. And we think of this as love cut short; like a dance stopped in mid-career or a flower with its head unluckily snapped off—something truncated and therefore, lacking its due shape. I wonder. If, as I can't help suspecting, the dead also feel the pains of separation (and this may be one of their purgatorial sufferings), then for both lovers, and for all pairs of lovers without exception, bereavement is a universal and integral part of our experience of love. It follows marriage as normally as marriage follows courtship or as autumn follows summer. It is not a truncation of the process but one of its phases; not the interruption of the dance, but the next figure. We are 'taken out of ourselves' by the loved one while she is here. Then comes the tragic figure of the dance in which we must learn to be still taken out of ourselves though the bodily presence is withdrawn, to love the very Her, and not fall back to loving our past, or our memory, or our sorrow, or our relief from sorrow, or our own love.

Looking back, I see that only a very little time ago I was greatly concerned about my memory of H. and how false it might become. For some reason—the merciful good sense of God is the only one I can think of—I have stopped bothering about that. And the remarkable thing is that since I stopped bothering about it, she seems to meet me everywhere. *Meet* is far too strong a word. I don't mean anything remotely like an apparition or a voice. I don't mean even any strikingly emotional experience at any particular moment. Rather, a sort of unobtrusive but massive sense that she is, just as much as ever, a fact to be taken into account.

'To be taken into account' is perhaps an unfortunate way of putting it. It sounds as if she were rather a battle-axe. How can I put it better? Would 'momentously real' or 'obstinately real' do? It is as if the experience said to me, 'You are, as it happens, extremely glad that H. is still a fact. But remember she would be equally a fact whether you liked it or not. Your preferences have not been considered.'

How far have I got? Just as far, I think, as a widower of another sort who would stop, leaning on his spade, and say in answer to our inquiry, 'Thank'ee. Mustn't grumble. I do miss her something dreadful. But they say these things are sent to try us.' We have come to the same point; he with his spade, and I, who am not now much good at digging, with my own instrument. But of course one must take 'sent to try us' the right way. God has not been trying an experiment on my faith or love in order to find out their quality. He knew it already. It was I who didn't. In this trial He makes us occupy the dock, the witness box, and the bench all at once. He always knew that my temple was a house of cards. His only way of making me realize the fact was to knock it down.

Getting over it so soon? But the words are ambiguous. To say the patient is getting over it after an operation for appendicitis is one thing; after he's had his leg off it is quite another. After that operation either the wounded stump heals or the man dies. If it heals, the fierce, continuous pain will stop. Presently he'll get back his strength and be able to stump about on his wooden leg. He has 'got over it.' But he will probably have recurrent pains in the stump all his life, and perhaps pretty bad ones; and he will always be a one-legged man. There will be hardly any moment when he forgets it. Bathing, dressing, sitting down and getting up again, even lying in bed, will all be different. His whole way of life will be changed. All sorts of pleasures and activities that he once took for granted will have to be simply written off. Duties too. At present I am learning to get about on crutches. Perhaps I shall presently be given a wooden leg. But I shall never be a biped again.

Still, there's no denying that in some sense I 'feel better,' and with that comes at once a sort of shame, and a feeling that one is under a sort of obligation to cherish and foment and prolong one's unhappiness. I've read about that in books, but I never dreamed I should feel it myself. I am sure H. wouldn't approve of it. She'd tell me not to be a fool. So I'm pretty certain, would God. What is behind it?

Partly, no doubt, vanity. We want to prove to ourselves that we are lovers on the grand scale, tragic heroes; not just ordinary privates in the huge army of the bereaved, slogging along and making the best of a bad job. But that's not the whole of the explanation.

I think there is also a confusion. We don't really want grief, in its first agonies, to be prolonged: nobody could. But we want something else of which grief is a frequent symptom, and then we confuse the symptom with the thing itself. I wrote the other night that bereavement is not the truncation of married love but one of its regular phases—like the honeymoon. What we want is to live our marriage well and faithfully through that phase too. If it hurts (and it certainly will) we accept the pains as a necessary part of this phase. We don't want to escape them at the price of desertion or divorce. Killing the dead a second time. We were one flesh. Now that it has been cut in two, we don't want to pretend that it is whole and complete. We will be still married, still in love. Therefore we shall still ache. But we are not at all—if we understand ourselves—seeking the aches for their own sake. The less of them the better, so long as the marriage is preserved. And the more joy there can be in the marriage between dead and living, the better.

The better in every way. For, as I have discovered, passionate grief does not link us with the dead but cuts us off from them. This become clearer and clearer. It is just at those moments when I feel least sorrow—getting into my morning bath is usually one of them—that H. rushes upon my mind in her full reality, her otherness. Not, as in my worst moments, all foreshortened and patheticized and solemnized by my miseries, but as she is in her own right. This is good and tonic.

I seem to remember—though I couldn't quote one at the moment—all sorts of ballads and folk-tales in which the dead tell us that our mourning does them some kind of wrong. They beg us to stop it. There may be far more depth in this than I thought. If so, our grandfathers' generation went very far astray. All that (sometimes lifelong) ritual of sorrow—visiting graves, keeping anniversaries, leaving the empty bedroom exactly as 'the departed' used to keep it, mentioning the dead either not at all or always in a special voice, or even (like Queen Victoria) having the dead man's clothes put out for dinner every evening—this was like mummification. It made the dead far more dead.

Or was that (unconsciously) its purpose? Something very primitive may be at work here. To keep the dead thoroughly dead, to make sure that they won't come sidling back among the living, is a main preoccupation of the savage mind. At all costs make them 'stay put.' Certainly these rituals do in fact emphasize their deadness. Perhaps this result was not really so unwelcome, not always, as the ritualists believed.

But I've no business to judge them. All guess-work; I'd better keep my breath to cool my own porridge. For me at any rate the programme is plain. I will turn to her as often as possible in gladness. I will even salute her with a laugh. The less I mourn her the nearer I seem to her.

An admirable programme. Unfortunately it can't be carried out. Tonight all the hells of young grief have opened again; the mad words, the bitter resentment, the fluttering in the stomach, the nightmare unreality, the wallowed-in tears. For in grief nothing 'stays put.' One keeps on emerging from a phase, but it always recurs. Round and round. Everything repeats. Am I going in circles, or dare I hope I am on a spiral?

But if a spiral, am I going up or down it?

How often—will it be for always?—how often will the vast emptiness astonish me like a complete novelty and make me say, 'I never realized my loss till this moment'? The same leg is cut off time after time. The first plunge of the knife into the flesh is felt again and again.

They say, 'The coward dies many times'; so does the beloved. Didn't the eagle find a fresh liver to tear in Prometheus every time it dined?

CHAPTER FOUR

THIS IS THE fourth—and the last—empty MS. book I can find in the house; at least nearly empty, for there are some pages of very ancient arithmetic at the end by J. I resolve to let this limit my jottings. I *will not* start buying books for the purpose. In so far as this record was a defence against total collapse, a safety-valve, it has done some good. The other end I had in view turns out to have been based on a misunderstanding. I thought I could describe a *state;* make a map of sorrow. Sorrow, however, turns out to be not a state but a process. It needs not a map but a history, and if I don't stop writing that history at some quite arbitrary point, there's no reason why I should ever stop. There is something new to be chronicled every day. Grief is like a long valley, a winding valley where any bend may reveal a totally new landscape. As I've already noted, not every bend does. Sometimes the surprise is the opposite one; you are presented with exactly the same sort of country you thought you had left behind miles ago. That is when you wonder whether the valley isn't a circular trench. But it isn't. There are partial recurrences, but the sequence doesn't repeat.

Here, for instance, is a new phase, a new loss. I do all the walking I can, for I'd be a fool to go to bed not tired. Today I have been revisiting old haunts, taking one of the long rambles that made me so happy in my bachelor days. And this time the face of nature was not emptied of its beauty and the world didn't look (as I complained some days ago) like a mean street. On the contrary, every horizon, every stile or clump of trees, summoned me into a past kind of happiness, my pre-H. happiness. But the invitation seemed to me horrible. The happiness into which it invited me was insipid. I find that I don't want to go back again and be happy in *that* way. It frightens me to think that a mere going back should even be possible. For this fate would seem to me the worst of all, to reach a state in which my years of love and marriage should appear in retrospect a charming episode—like a holiday—that had briefly interrupted my interminable life and returned me to normal, unchanged. And then it would come to seem unreal—something so foreign to the usual texture of my history that I could almost believe it had happened to someone else. Thus H. would die to me a second time; a worse bereavement than the first. Anything but that.

Did you ever know, dear, how much you took away with you when you left? You have stripped me even of my past, even of the things we never shared. I was wrong to say the stump was recovering from the pain of the amputation. I was deceived because it has so many ways to hurt me that I discover them only one by one.

Still, there are the two enormous gains—I know myself too well now to call them 'lasting.' Turned to God, my mind no longer meets that locked door; turned to H., it no longer meets that vacuum—nor all that fuss about my mental image of her. My jottings show something of the process, but not so much as I'd hoped. Perhaps both changes were really not observable. There was no sudden, striking, and emotional transition. Like the warming of a room or the coming of daylight. When you first notice them they have already been going on for some time.

The notes have been about myself, and about H., and about God. In that order. The order and the proportions exactly what they ought not to have been. And I see that I have nowhere fallen into that mode of thinking about either which we call praising them. Yet that would have been best for me. Praise is the mode of love which always has some element of joy in it. Praise in due order; of Him as the giver, of her as the gift. Don't we in praise somehow enjoy what we praise, however far we are from it? I must do more of this. I have lost the fruition I once had of H. And I am far, far away in the valley of my unlikeness, from the fruition which, if His mercies are infinite, I may some time have of God. But by praising I can still, in some degree, enjoy her, and already, in some degree, enjoy Him. Better than nothing.

But perhaps I lack the gift. I see I've described H. as being like a sword. That's true as far as it goes. But utterly inadequate by itself, and misleading. I ought to have balanced it. I ought to have said, 'But also like a garden. Like a nest of gardens, wall within wall, hedge within hedge, more secret, more full of fragrant and fertile life, the further you entered.'

And then, of her, and of every created thing I praise, I should say, 'In some way, in its unique way, like Him who made it.'

Thus up from the garden to the Gardener, from the sword to the Smith. To the life-giving Life and the Beauty that makes beautiful.

'She is in God's hands.' That gains a new energy when I think of her as a sword. Perhaps the earthly life I shared with her was only part of the tempering. Now perhaps He grasps the hilt; weighs the new weapon; makes lightnings with it in the air. 'A right Jerusalem blade.'

One moment last night can be described in similes; otherwise it won't go into language at all. Imagine a man in total darkness. He thinks he is in a cellar or dungeon. Then there comes a sound. He thinks it might be a sound from far off—waves or wind-blown trees or cattle half a mile away. And if so, it proves he's not in a cellar, but free, in the open air. Or it may be a much smaller sound close at hand—a chuckle of laughter. And if so, there is a friend just beside him in the dark. Either way, a good, good sound. I'm not mad enough to take such an experience as evidence for anything. It is simply the leaping into imaginative activity of an idea which I would always have theoretically admitted—the idea that I, or any mortal at any time, may be utterly mistaken as to the situation he is really in.

Five senses; an incurably abstract intellect; a haphazardly selective memory; a set of preconceptions and assumptions so numerous that I can never examine more than a minority of them—never become even conscious of them all. How much of total reality can such an apparatus let through?

I will not, if I can help it, shin up either the feathery or the prickly tree. Two widely different convictions press more and more on my mind. One is that the Eternal Vet is even more inexorable and the possible operations even more painful than our severest imaginings can forbode. But the other, that 'all shall be well, and all shall be well, and all manner of thing shall be well.'

It doesn't matter that all the photographs of H. are bad. It doesn't matter—not much—if my memory of her is imperfect. Images, whether on paper or in the mind, are not important for themselves. Merely links. Take a parallel from an infinitely higher sphere. Tomorrow morning a priest will give me a little round, thin, cold, tasteless wafer. Is it a disadvantage—is it not in some ways an advantage—that it can't pretend the least *resemblance* to that with which it unites me?

I need Christ, not something that resembles Him. I want H., not something that is like her. A really good photograph might become in the end a snare, a horror, and an obstacle.

Images, I must suppose, have their use or they would not have been so popular. (It makes little difference whether they are pictures and statues outside the mind or imaginative constructions within it.) To me, however, their danger is more obvious. Images of the Holy easily become holy images—sacrosanct. My idea of God is not a divine idea. It has to be shattered time after time. He shatters it Himself. He is the great iconoclast. Could we not almost say that this shattering is one of the marks of His presence? The Incarnation is the supreme example; it leaves all previous ideas of the Messiah in ruins. And most are 'offended' by the iconoclasm; and blessed are those who are not. But the same thing happens in our private prayers.

All reality is iconoclastic. The earthly beloved, even in this life, incessantly triumphs over your mere idea of her. And you want her to; you want her with all her resistances, all her faults, all her unexpectedness. That is, in her foursquare and independent reality. And this, not any image or memory, is what we are to love still, after she is dead.

But 'this' is not now imaginable. In that respect H. and all the dead are like God. In that respect loving her has become, in its measure, like loving Him. In both cases I must stretch out the arms and hands of love—its eyes cannot here be used—to the reality, through—across—all the changeful phantasmagoria of my thoughts, passions, and imaginings. I mustn't sit down content with the phantasmagoria itself and worship that for Him, or love that for her.

Not my idea of God, but God. Not my idea of H., but H. Yes, and also not my idea of my neighbour, but my neighbour. For don't we often make this mistake as regards people who are still alive—who are with us in the same room? Talking and acting not to the man himself but to the picture—almost the *précis*—we've made of him in our own minds? And he has to depart from it pretty widely before we even notice the fact. In real life—that's one way it differs from novels—his words and acts are, if we observe closely, hardly ever quite 'in character,' that is, in what we call his character. There's always a card in his hand we didn't know about.

My reason for assuming that I do this to other people is the fact that so often I find them obviously doing it to me. We all think we've got one another taped.

And all this time I may, once more, be building with cards. And if I am He will once more knock the building flat. He will knock it down as often as proves necessary. Unless I have to be finally given up as hopeless, and left building pasteboard palaces in Hell forever; 'free among the dead.'

Am I, for instance, just sidling back to God because I know that if there's any road to H., it runs through Him? But then of course I know perfectly well that He can't be used as a road. If you're approaching Him not as the goal but as a road, not as the end but as a means, you're not really approaching Him at all. That's what was really wrong with all those popular pictures of happy reunions 'on the further shore'; not the simple-minded and very earthly images, but the fact that they make an End of what we can get only as a by-product of the true End.

Lord, are these your real terms? Can I meet H. again only if I learn to love you so much that I don't care whether I meet her or not? Consider, Lord, how it looks to us. What would anyone think of me if I said to the boys, 'No toffee now. But when you've grown up and don't really want toffee you shall have as much of it as you choose'?

If I knew that to be eternally divided from H. and eternally forgotten by her would add a greater joy and splendour to her being, of course I'd say, 'Fire ahead.' Just as if, on earth, I could have cured her cancer by never seeing her again, I'd have arranged never to see her again. I'd have had to. Any decent person would. But that's quite different. That's not the situation I'm in.

When I lay these questions before God I get no answer. But a rather special sort of 'No answer.' It is not the locked door. It is more like a silent, certainly not uncompassionate, gaze. As though He shook His head not in refusal but waiving the question. Like, 'Peace, child; you don't understand.'

Can a mortal ask questions which God finds unanswerable? Quite easily, I should think. All nonsense questions are unanswerable. How many hours are there in a mile? Is yellow square or round? Probably half the questions we ask—half our great theological and metaphysical problems—are like that.

And now that I come to think of it, there's no practical problem before me at all. I know the two great commandments, and I'd better get on with them. Indeed, H.'s death has ended the practical problem. While she was alive I could, in practice, have put her before God; that is, could have done what she wanted instead of what He wanted; if there'd been a conflict. What's left is not a problem about anything I could *do*. It's all about weights of feelings and motives and that sort of thing. It's a problem I'm setting myself. I don't believe God set it me at all.

The fruition of God. Reunion with the dead. These can't figure in my thinking except as counters. Blank cheques. My idea—if you can call it an idea—of the first is a huge, risky extrapolation from a very few and short experiences here on earth. Probably not such valuable experiences as I think. Perhaps even of less value than others that I take no account of. My idea of the second is also an extrapolation. The reality of either—the cashing of either cheque—would probably blow all one's ideas about both (how much more one's ideas about their relations to each other) into smithereens.

The mystical union on the one hand. The resurrection of the body, on the other. I can't reach the ghost of an image, a formula, or even a feeling, that combines them. But the reality, we are given to understand, does. Reality the iconoclast once more. Heaven will solve our problems, but not, I think, by showing us subtle reconciliations between all our apparently contradictory notions. The notions will all be knocked from under our feet. We shall see that there never was any problem.

And, more than once, that impression which I can't describe except by saying that it's like the sound of a chuckle in the darkness. The sense that some shattering and disarming simplicity is the real answer.

It is often thought that the dead see us. And we assume, whether reasonably or not, that if they see us at all they see us more clearly than before. Does H. now see exactly how much froth or tinsel there was in what she called, and I call, my love? So be it. Look your hardest, dear. I wouldn't hide if I could. We didn't idealize each other. We tried to keep no secrets. You knew most of the rotten places in me already. If you now see anything worse, I can take it. So can you. Rebuke, explain, mock, forgive. For this is one of the miracles of love; it gives—to both, but perhaps especially to the woman—a power of seeing through its own enchantments and yet not being disenchanted.

To see, in some measure, like God. His love and His knowledge are not distinct from one another, nor from Him. We could almost say He sees because He loves, and therefore loves although He sees.

Sometimes, Lord, one is tempted to say that if you wanted us to behave like the lilies of the field you might have given us an organization more like theirs. But that, I suppose, is just your grand experiment. Or no; not an experiment, for you have no need to find things out. Rather your grand enterprise. To make an organism which is also a spirit; to make that terrible oxymoron, a 'spiritual animal.' To take a poor primate, a beast with nerve-endings all over it, a creature with a stomach that wants to be filled, a breeding animal that wants its mate, and say, 'Now get on with it. Become a god.'

I said, several notebooks ago, that even if I got what seemed like an assurance of H.'s presence, I wouldn't believe it. Easier said than done. Even now, though, I won't treat anything of that sort as evidence. It's the *quality* of last night's experience—not what it proves but what it was— that makes it worth putting down. It was quite incredibly unemotional. Just the impression of her *mind* momentarily facing my own. Mind, not 'soul' as we tend to think of soul. Certainly the reverse of what is called 'soulful.' Not at all like a rapturous reunion of lovers. Much more like getting a telephone call or a wire from her about some practical arrangement. Not that there was any 'message'—just intelligence and attention. No sense of joy or sorrow. No love even, in our ordinary sense. No un-love. I had never in any mood imagined the dead as being so—well, so business-like. Yet there was an extreme and cheerful intimacy. An intimacy that had not passed through the senses or the emotions at all.

If this was a throw-up from my unconscious, then my unconscious must be a far more interesting region than the depth psychologists have led me to expect. For one thing, it is apparently much less primitive than my consciousness.

Wherever it came from, it has made a sort of spring cleaning in my mind. The dead could be like that; sheer intellects. A Greek philosopher wouldn't have been surprised at an experience like mine. He would have expected that if anything of us remained after death it would be just that. Up to now this always seemed to me a most arid and chilling idea. The absence of emotion repelled me. But in this contact (whether real or apparent) it didn't do anything of the sort. One didn't need emotion. The intimacy was complete—sharply bracing and restorative too—without it. Can that intimacy be love itself—always in this life attended with emotion, not because it is itself an emotion, or needs an attendant emotion, but because our animal souls, our nervous systems, our imaginations, have to respond to it in that way? If so, how many preconceptions I must scrap! A society, a communion, of pure intelligences would not be cold, drab, and comfortless. On the other hand it wouldn't be very like what people usually mean when they use such words as *spiritual*, or *mystical*, or *holy*. It would, if I have had a glimpse, be—well, I'm almost scared at the adjectives I'd have to use. Brisk? cheerful? keen? alert? intense? wide-awake? Above all, solid. Utterly reliable. Firm. There is no nonsense about the dead.

When I say 'intellect' I include will. Attention is an act of will. Intelligence in action is will *par excellence*. What seemed to meet me was full of resolution.

Once very near the end I said, 'If you can—if it is allowed—come to me when I too am on my death bed.' 'Allowed!' she said. 'Heaven would have a job to hold me; and as for Hell, I'd break it into bits.' She knew she was speaking a kind of mythological language, with even an element of comedy in it. There was a twinkle as well as a tear in her eye. But there was no myth and no joke about the will, deeper than any feeling, that flashed through her.

But I mustn't, because I have come to misunderstand a little less completely what a pure intelligence might be, lean over too far. There is also, whatever it means, the resurrection of the body. We cannot understand. The best is perhaps what we understand least.

Didn't people dispute once whether the final vision of God was more an act of intelligence or of love? That is probably another of the nonsense questions.

How wicked it would be, if we could, to call the dead back! She said not to me but to the chaplain, 'I am at peace with God.' She smiled, but not at me. *Poi si tornò all' eterna fontana.*

THE ABOLITION
OF MAN

or

REFLECTIONS ON EDUCATION
WITH SPECIAL REFERENCE
TO THE TEACHING OF ENGLISH
IN THE UPPER FORMS OF SCHOOLS

The Master said, He who sets to work on a
different strand destroys the whole fabric

CONFUCIUS, ANALECTS II. 16

THE ABOLITION OF MAN
CONTENTS

MEN WITHOUT CHESTS

So he sent the word to slay
And slew the little childer.

TRADITIONAL CAROL

I DOUBT WHETHER we are sufficiently attentive to the importance of elementary text books. That is why I have chosen as the starting-point for these lectures a little book on English intended for 'boys and girls in the upper forms of schools'. I do not think the authors of this book (there were two of them) intended any harm, and I owe them, or their publisher, good language for sending me a complimentary copy. At the same time I shall have nothing good to say of them. Here is a pretty predicament. I do not want to pillory two modest practising schoolmasters who were doing the best they knew: but I cannot be silent about what I think the actual tendency of their work. I therefore propose to conceal their names. I shall refer to these gentlemen as Gaius and Titius and to their book as *The Green Book*. But I promise you there is such a book and I have it on my shelves.

In their second chapter Gaius and Titius quote the well-known story of Coleridge at the waterfall. You remember that there were two tourists present: that one called it 'sublime' and the other 'pretty'; and that

Coleridge mentally endorsed the first judgement and rejected the second with disgust. Gaius and Titius comment as follows: 'When the man said *This is sublime,* he appeared to be making a remark about the waterfall . . . Actually . . . he was not making a remark about the waterfall, but a remark about his own feelings. What he was saying was really *I have feelings associated in my mind with the word "Sublime",* or shortly, *I have sublime feelings.*' Here are a good many deep questions settled in a pretty summary fashion. But the authors are not yet finished. They add: 'This confusion is continually present in language as we use it. We appear to be saying something very important about something: and actually we are only saying something about our own feelings.'[1]

Before considering the issues really raised by this momentous little paragraph (designed, you will remember, for 'the upper forms of schools') we must eliminate one mere confusion into which Gaius and Titius have fallen. Even on their own view—on any conceivable view—the man who says *This is sublime* cannot mean *I have sublime feelings.* Even if it were granted that such qualities as sublimity were simply and solely projected into things from our own emotions, yet the emotions which prompt the projection are the correlatives, and therefore almost the opposites, of the qualities projected. The feelings which make a man call an object sublime are not sublime feelings but feelings of veneration. If *This is sublime* is to be reduced at all to a statement about the speaker's feelings, the proper translation would be *I have humble feelings.* If the view held by Gaius and Titius were consistently applied it would lead to obvious absurdities. It would force them to maintain that *You are contemptible* means *I have contemptible feelings*: in fact that *Your feelings are contemptible* means *My feelings are contemptible.* But we need not delay over this which is the very *pons asinorum* of our subject. It would be unjust to Gaius and Titius themselves to emphasize what was doubtless a mere inadvertence.

The schoolboy who reads this passage in *The Green Book* will believe two propositions: firstly, that all sentences containing a predicate of value are statements about the emotional state of the speaker, and secondly, that all such statements are unimportant. It is true that Gaius and Titius have said neither of these things in so many words. They have treated only one particular predicate of value (*sublime*) as a word descriptive of the speaker's emotions. The pupils are left to do for themselves the work of

---

[1] *The Green Book,* pp. 19, 20.

extending the same treatment to all predicates of value: and no slightest obstacle to such extension is placed in their way. The authors may or may not desire the extension: they may never have given the question five minutes' serious thought in their lives. I am not concerned with what they desired but with the effect their book will certainly have on the schoolboy's mind. In the same way, they have not said that judgements of value are unimportant. Their words are that we '*appear* to be saying something very important' when in reality we are '*only* saying something about our own feelings'. No schoolboy will be able to resist the suggestion brought to bear upon him by that word *only*. I do not mean, of course, that he will make any conscious inference from what he reads to a general philosophical theory that all values are subjective and trivial. The very power of Gaius and Titius depends on the fact that they are dealing with a boy: a boy who thinks he is 'doing' his 'English prep' and has no notion that ethics, theology, and politics are all at stake. It is not a theory they put into his mind, but an assumption, which ten years hence, its origin forgotten and its presence unconscious, will condition him to take one side in a controversy which he has never recognized as a controversy at all. The authors themselves, I suspect, hardly know what they are doing to the boy, and he cannot know what is being done to him.

Before considering the philosophical credentials of the position which Gaius and Titius have adopted about value, I should like to show its practical results on the educational procedure. In their fourth chapter they quote a silly advertisement of a pleasure cruise and proceed to inoculate their pupils against the sort of writing it exhibits.[2] The advertisement tells us that those who buy tickets for this cruise will go 'across the Western Ocean where Drake of Devon sailed', 'adventuring after the treasures of the Indies', and bringing home themselves also a 'treasure' of 'golden hours' and 'glowing colours'. It is a bad bit of writing, of course: a venal and bathetic exploitation of those emotions of awe and pleasure which men feel in visiting places that have striking associations with history or legend. If Gaius and Titius were to stick to their last and teach their readers (as they promised to do) the art of English composition, it was their business to put this advertisement side by side with passages from great writers in which the very emotion is well expressed, and then show where the difference lies.

---

[2] *The Green Book*, p 53.

They might have used Johnson's famous passage from the *Western Islands*, which concludes: 'That man is little to be envied, whose patriotism would not gain force upon the plain of Marathon, or whose piety would not grow warmer among the ruins of Iona.'[3] They might have taken that place in *The Prelude* where Wordsworth describes how the antiquity of London first descended on his mind with 'Weight and power, Power growing under weight'.[4] A lesson which had laid such literature beside the advertisement and really discriminated the good from the bad would have been a lesson worth teaching. There would have been some blood and sap in it—the trees of knowledge and of life growing together. It would also have had the merit of being a lesson in literature: a subject of which Gaius and Titius, despite their professed purpose, are uncommonly shy.

What they actually do is to point out that the luxurious motor-vessel won't really sail where Drake did, that the tourists will not have any adventures, that the treasures they bring home will be of a purely metaphorical nature, and that a trip to Margate might provide 'all the pleasure and rest' they required.[5] All this is very true: talents inferior to those of Gaius and Titius would have sufficed to discover it. What they have not noticed, or not cared about, is that a very similar treatment could be applied to much good literature which treats the same emotion. What, after all, can the history of early British Christianity, in pure reason, add to the motives for piety as they exist in the eighteenth century? Why should Mr Wordsworth's inn be more comfortable or the air of London more healthy because London has existed for a long time? Or, if there is indeed any obstacle which will prevent a critic from 'debunking' Johnson and Wordsworth (and Lamb, and Virgil, and Thomas Browne, and Mr de la Mare) as *The Green Book* debunks the advertisement, Gaius and Titius have given their schoolboy readers no faintest help to its discovery.

From this passage the schoolboy will learn about literature precisely nothing. What he will learn quickly enough, and perhaps indelibly, is the belief that all emotions aroused by local association are in themselves contrary to reason and contemptible. He will have no notion that there are two ways of being immune to such an advertisement—that it falls

---

[3] *Journey to the Western Islands* (Samuel Johnson).

[4] *The Prelude*, viii, ll. 549–59.

[5] *The Green Book*, pp. 53–5.

equally flat on those who are above it and those who are below it, on the man of real sensibility and on the mere trousered ape who has never been able to conceive the Atlantic as anything more than so many million tons of cold salt water. There are two men to whom we offer in vain a false leading article on patriotism and honour: one is the coward, the other is the honourable and patriotic man. None of this is brought before the schoolboy's mind. On the contrary, he is encouraged to reject the lure of the 'Western Ocean' on the very dangerous ground that in so doing he will prove himself a knowing fellow who can't be bubbled out of his cash. Gaius and Titius, while teaching him nothing about letters, have cut out of his soul, long before he is old enough to choose, the possibility of having certain experiences which thinkers of more authority than they have held to be generous, fruitful, and humane.

But it is not only Gaius and Titius. In another little book, whose author I will call Orbilius, I find that the same operation, under the same general anaesthetic, is being carried out. Orbilius chooses for 'debunking' a silly bit of writing on horses, where these animals are praised as the 'willing servants' of the early colonists in Australia.[6] And he falls into the same trap as Gaius and Titius. Of Ruksh and Sleipnir and the weeping horses of Achilles and the war-horse in the Book of Job—nay even of Brer Rabbit and of Peter Rabbit—of man's prehistoric piety to 'our brother the ox'—of all that this semi-anthropomorphic treatment of beasts has meant in human history and of the literature where it finds noble or piquant expression—he has not a word to say.[7] Even of the problems of animal psychology as they exist for science he says nothing. He contents himself with explaining that horses are not, *secundum litteram*, interested in colonial expansion.[8] This piece of information is really all that his pupils get from him. Why the composition before them is bad, when others that lie open to the same charge are good, they do not hear. Much less do they

---

[6] Orbilius' book, p 5.

[7] Orbilius is so far superior to Gaius and Titius that he does (pp. 19–22) contrast a piece of good writing to animals with the piece condemned. Unfortunately, however, the only superiority he really demonstrates in the second extract is its superiority in factual truth. The specifically literary problem (the use and abuse of expressions which are false *secundum litteram*) is not tackled. Orbilius indeed tells us (p. 97) that we must 'learn to distinguish between legitimate and illegitimate figurative statement', but he gives us very little help in doing so. At the same time it is fair to record my opinion that his work is on quite a different level from *The Green Book*.

[8] Orbilius' book, p 9.

learn of the two classes of men who are, respectively, above and below the danger of such writing—the man who really knows horses and really loves them, not with anthropomorphic illusions, but with ordinate love, and the irredeemable urban blockhead to whom a horse is merely an old-fashioned means of transport. Some pleasure in their own ponies and dogs they will have lost; some incentive to cruelty or neglect they will have received; some pleasure in their own knowingness will have entered their minds. That is their day's lesson in English, though of English they have learned nothing. Another little portion of the human heritage has been quietly taken from them before they were old enough to understand.

I have hitherto been assuming that such teachers as Gaius and Titius do not fully realize what they are doing and do not intend the far-reaching consequences it will actually have. There is, of course, another possibility. What I have called (presuming on their concurrence in a certain traditional system of values) the 'trousered ape' and the 'urban blockhead' may be precisely the kind of man they really wish to produce. The differences between us may go all the way down. They may really hold that the ordinary human feelings about the past or animals or large waterfalls are contrary to reason and contemptible and ought to be eradicated. They may be intending to make a clean sweep of traditional values and start with a new set. That position will be discussed later. If it is the position which Gaius and Titius are holding, I must, for the moment, content myself with pointing out that it is a philosophical and not a literary position. In filling their book with it they have been unjust to the parent or headmaster who buys it and who has got the work of amateur philosophers where he expected the work of professional grammarians. A man would be annoyed if his son returned from the dentist with his teeth untouched and his head crammed with the dentist's *obiter dicta* on bimetallism or the Baconian theory.

But I doubt whether Gaius and Titius have really planned, under cover of teaching English, to propagate their philosophy. I think they have slipped into it for the following reasons. In the first place, literary criticism is difficult, and what they actually do is very much easier. To explain why a bad treatment of some basic human emotion is bad literature is, if we exclude all question-begging attacks on the emotion itself, a very hard thing to do. Even Dr Richards, who first seriously tackled the problem of badness in literature, failed, I think, to do it. To 'debunk' the emotion, on the basis of a commonplace rationalism, is within almost anyone's capacity. In the second place, I think Gaius and Titius may have honestly misunderstood the pressing educational need of the moment. They see the world around them swayed by emotional propaganda—they have learned from tradition that youth is sentimental—and they conclude that the best thing they can do is to fortify the minds of young people against emotion. My own experience as a teacher tells an opposite tale. For every one pupil who needs to be guarded from a weak excess of sensibility there are three who need to be awakened from the slumber of cold vulgarity. The task of the modern educator is not to cut down jungles but to irrigate deserts. The right defence against false sentiments is to inculcate just sentiments. By starving the sensibility of our pupils we only make them easier prey to the propagandist when he comes. For famished nature will be avenged and a hard heart is no infallible protection against a soft head.

But there is a third, and a profounder, reason for the procedure which Gaius and Titius adopt. They may be perfectly ready to admit that a good education should build some sentiments while destroying others. They may endeavour to do so. But it is impossible that they should succeed. Do what they will, it is the 'debunking' side of their work, and this side alone, which will really tell. In order to grasp this necessity clearly I must digress for a moment to show that what may be called the educational predicament of Gaius and Titius is different from that of all their predecessors.

Until quite modern times all teachers and even all men believed the universe to be such that certain emotional reactions on our part could be either congruous or incongruous to it—believed, in fact, that objects did not merely receive, but could *merit*, our approval or disapproval, our reverence or our contempt. The reason why Coleridge agreed with the tourist who called the cataract sublime and disagreed with the one who called it pretty was of course that he believed inanimate nature to be such that certain responses could be more 'just' or 'ordinate' or 'appropriate' to it than others. And he believed (correctly) that the tourists thought the same. The man who called the cataract sublime was not intending simply to describe his own emotions about it: he was also claiming that the object was one which *merited* those emotions. But for this claim there would be nothing to agree or disagree about. To disagree with *This is pretty* if those words simply described the lady's feelings, would be absurd: if she had said *I feel sick* Coleridge would hardly have replied *No; I feel quite well*. When Shelley, having compared the human sensibility to an Aeolian lyre, goes on to add that it differs from a lyre in having a power of 'internal adjustment' whereby it can 'accommodate its chords to the motions of that which strikes them',[9] he is assuming the same belief. 'Can you be righteous', asks Traherne, 'unless you be just in rendering to things their due esteem? All things were made to be yours and you were made to prize them according to their value.'[10]

St Augustine defines virtue as *ordo amoris*, the ordinate condition of the affections in which every object is accorded that kind of degree of love which is appropriate to it.[11] Aristotle says that the aim of education is to make the pupil like and dislike what he ought.[12] When the age for reflective thought comes, the pupil who has been thus trained in 'ordinate affections' or 'just sentiments' will easily find the first principles in Ethics; but to the corrupt man they will never be visible at all and he can make no progress in that science.[13] Plato before him had said the same. The little human animal will not at first have the right responses. It must be trained to feel pleasure, liking, disgust, and hatred at those things which really are pleasant, likeable, disgusting and hateful.[14] In the *Republic*, the well-nurtured youth is one 'who would see most clearly whatever was amiss in ill-made works of man or ill-grown works of nature, and with a just distaste would blame and hate the ugly even from his earliest years and would give delighted praise to beauty, receiving it into his soul and being nourished by it, so that he becomes a man of gentle heart. All this before he is of an age to reason; so that when Reason at length comes to him, then, bred as he has been, he will hold out his hands in welcome and recognize her because of the affinity he bears to her.'[15] In early Hinduism that conduct in men which can be called good consists in conformity to, or almost participation in, the *Rta*—that great ritual or pattern of nature and supernature which is revealed alike in the cosmic order, the moral virtues, and the ceremonial of the temple. Righteousness, correctness,

---

[9] *Defence of Poetry.*

[10] *Centuries of Meditations*, i, 12.

[11] *De Civ. Dei*, xv. 22. Cf. ix. 5, xi. 28.

[12] *Eth. Nic.* 1104 B.

[13] *Eth. Nic.* 1095 B.

[14] *Laws*, 653.

[15] *Republic*, 402 A.

order, the *Rta*, is constantly identified with *satya* or truth, correspondence to reality. As Plato said that the Good was 'beyond existence' and Wordsworth that through virtue the stars were strong, so the Indian masters say that the gods themselves are born of the *Rta* and obey it.[16]

The Chinese also speak of a great thing (the greatest thing) called the *Tao*. It is the reality beyond all predicates, the abyss that was before the Creator Himself. It is Nature, it is the Way, the Road. It is the Way in which the universe goes on, the Way in which things everlastingly emerge, stilly and tranquilly, into space and time. It is also the Way which every man should tread in imitation of that cosmic and supercosmic progression, conforming all activities to that great exemplar.[17] 'In ritual', say the *Analects*, 'it is harmony with Nature that is prized.'[18] The ancient Jews likewise praise the Law as being 'true'.[19]

This conception in all its forms, Platonic, Aristotelian, Stoic, Christian, and Oriental alike, I shall henceforth refer to for brevity simply as 'the *Tao*'. Some of the accounts of it which I have quoted will seem, perhaps, to many of you merely quaint or even magical. But what is common to them all is something we cannot neglect. It is the doctrine of objective value, the belief that certain attitudes are really true, and others really false, to the kind of thing the universe is and the kind of things we are. Those who know the *Tao* can hold that to call children delightful or old men venerable is not simply to record a psychological fact about our own parental or filial emotions at the moment, but to recognize a quality which *demands* a certain response from us whether we make it or not. I myself do not enjoy the society of small children: because I speak from within the *Tao* I recognize this as a defect in myself—just as a man may have to recognize that he is tone deaf or colour blind. And because our approvals and disapprovals are thus recognitions of objective value or responses to an objective order, therefore emotional states can be in harmony with

---

[16] A. B. Keith, s.v. 'Righteousness (Hindu)' *Enc. Religion and Ethics*, vol. x.

[17] *Enc. Religion and Ethics*, vol. ii, p. 454 B; iv. 12 B; ix. 87 A.

[18] *The Analects of Confucius*, trans. Arthur Waley, London, 1938, i. 12

[19] Psalm 119:151. The word is *emeth*, 'truth'. Where the *Satya* of the Indian sources emphasizes truth as 'correspondence', *emeth* (connected with a verb that means 'to be firm') emphasizes rather the reliability or trustworthiness of truth. *Faithfulness* and *permanence* are suggested by Hebraists as alternative renderings. *Emeth* is that which does not deceive, does not 'give', does not change, that which holds water. (See T. K. Cheyne in *Encyclopedia Biblica*, 1914, s.v. 'Truth'.)

reason (when we feel liking for what ought to be approved) or out of harmony with reason (when we perceive that liking is due but cannot feel it). No emotion is, in itself, a judgement; in that sense all emotions and sentiments are alogical. But they can be reasonable or unreasonable as they conform to Reason or fail to conform. The heart never takes the place of the head: but it can, and should, obey it.

Over against this stands the world of *The Green Book*. In it the very possibility of a sentiment being reasonable—or even unreasonable—has been excluded from the outset. It can be reasonable or unreasonable only if it conforms or fails to conform to something else. To say that the cataract is sublime means saying that our emotion of humility is appropriate or ordinate to the reality, and thus to speak of something else besides the emotion; just as to say that a shoe fits is to speak not only of shoes but of feet. But this reference to something beyond the emotion is what Gaius and Titius exclude from every sentence containing a predicate of value. Such statements, for them, refer solely to the emotion. Now the emotion, thus considered by itself, cannot be either in agreement or disagreement with Reason. It is irrational not as a paralogism is irrational, but as a physical event is irrational: it does not rise even to the dignity of error. On this view, the world of facts, without one trace of value, and the world of feelings, without one trace of truth or falsehood, justice or injustice, confront one another, and no *rapprochement* is possible.

Hence the educational problem is wholly different according as you stand within or without the *Tao*. For those within, the task is to train in the pupil those responses which are in themselves appropriate, whether anyone is making them or not, and in making which the very nature of man consists. Those without, if they are logical, must regard all sentiments as equally non-rational, as mere mists between us and the real objects. As a result, they must either decide to remove all sentiments, as far as possible, from the pupil's mind; or else to encourage some sentiments for reasons that have nothing to do with their intrinsic 'justness' or 'ordinacy'. The latter course involves them in the questionable process of creating in others by 'suggestion' or incantation a mirage which their own reason has successfully dissipated.

Perhaps this will become clearer if we take a concrete instance. When a Roman father told his son that it was a sweet and seemly thing to die for his country, he believed what he said. He was communicating to the son an emotion which he himself shared and which he believed to be in accord with the value which his judgement discerned in noble death. He was giving the boy the best he had, giving of his spirit to humanize him as he had given of his body to beget him. But Gaius and Titius cannot believe that in calling such a death sweet and seemly they would be saying 'something important about something'. Their own method of debunking would cry out against them if they attempted to do so. For death is not something to eat and therefore cannot be *dulce* in the literal sense, and it is unlikely that the real sensations preceding it will be *dulce* even by analogy. And as for *decorum*—that is only a word describing how some other people will feel about your death when they happen to think of it, which won't be often, and will certainly do you no good. There are only two courses open to Gaius and Titius. Either they must go the whole way and debunk this sentiment like any other, or must set themselves to work to produce, from outside, a sentiment which they believe to be of no value to the pupil and which may cost him his life, because it is useful to us (the survivors) that our young men should feel it. If they embark on this course the difference between the old and the new education will be an important one. Where the old initiated, the new merely 'conditions'. The old dealt with its pupils as grown birds deal with young birds when they teach them to fly; the new deals with them more as the poultry-keeper deals with young birds—making them thus or thus for purposes of which the birds know nothing. In a word, the old was a kind of propagation—men transmitting manhood to men; the new is merely propaganda.

It is to their credit that Gaius and Titius embrace the first alternative. Propaganda is their abomination: not because their own philosophy gives a ground for condemning it (or anything else) but because they are better than their principles. They probably have some vague notion (I will examine it in my next lecture) that valour and good faith and justice could be sufficiently commended to the pupil on what they would call 'rational' or 'biological' or 'modern' grounds, if it should ever become necessary. In the meantime, they leave the matter alone and get on with the business of debunking.

But this course, though less inhuman, is not less disastrous than the opposite alternative of cynical propaganda. Let us suppose for a moment that the harder virtues could really be theoretically justifed with no appeal to objective value. It still remains true that no justification of virtue will enable a man to be virtuous. Without the aid of trained emotions the intellect is powerless against the animal organism. I had sooner play cards against a man who was quite sceptical about ethics, but bred to believe that 'a gentleman does not cheat', than against an irreproachable moral philosopher who had been brought up among sharpers. In battle it is not syllogisms that will keep the reluctant nerves and muscles to their post in the third hour of the bombardment. The crudest sentimentalism (such as Gaius and Titius would wince at) about a flag or a country or a regiment will be of more use. We were told it all long ago by Plato. As the king governs by his executive, so Reason in man must rule the mere appetites by means of the 'spirited element'.[20] The head rules the belly through the chest—the seat, as Alanus tells us, of Magnanimity,[21] of emotions organized by trained habit into stable sentiments. The Chest–Magnanimity–Sentiment—these are the indispensable liaison officers between cerebral man and visceral man. It may even be said that it is by this middle element that man is man: for by his intellect he is mere spirit and by his appetite mere animal.

The operation of *The Green Book* and its kind is to produce what may be called Men without Chests. It is an outrage that they should be commonly spoken of as Intellectuals. This gives them the chance to say that he who attacks them attacks Intelligence. It is not so. They are not distinguished from other men by any unusual skill in finding truth nor any virginal ardour to pursue her. Indeed it would be strange if they were: a persevering devotion to truth, a nice sense of intellectual honour, cannot be long maintained without the aid of a sentiment which Gaius and Titius could debunk as easily as any other. It is not excess of thought but defect of fertile and generous emotion that marks them out. Their heads are no bigger than the ordinary: it is the atrophy of the chest beneath that makes them seem so.

And all the time—such is the tragi-comedy of our situation—we continue to clamour for those very qualities we are rendering impossible. You can hardly open a periodical without coming across the statement that what our civilization needs is more 'drive', or dynamism, or self-sacrifice, or 'creativity'. In a sort of ghastly simplicity we remove the organ and demand the function. We make men without chests and expect of them virtue and enterprise. We laugh at honour and are shocked to find traitors in our midst. We castrate and bid the geldings be fruitful.

---

[20] *Republic*, 442 B, C.

[21] Alanus ab Insulis. *De Planctu Naturae Prosa*, iii.

2

THE WAY

It is upon the Trunk that a gentleman works.

ANALECTS OF CONFUCIUS, I.2

THE PRACTICAL RESULT of education in the spirit of *The Green Book* must be the destruction of the society which accepts it. But this is not necessarily a refutation of subjectivism about values as a theory. The true doctrine might be a doctrine which if we accept we die. No one who speaks from within the *Tao* could reject it on that account: ἐν δὲ φάει καὶ 'δλεσσου. But it has not yet come to that. There are theoretical difficulties in the philosophy of Gaius and Titius.

However subjective they may be about some traditional values, Gaius and Titius have shown by the very act of writing *The Green Book* that there must be some other values about which they are not subjective at all. They write in order to produce certain states of mind in the rising generation, if not because they think those states of mind intrinsically just or good, yet certainly because they think them to be the means to some state of society which they regard as desirable. It would not be difficult to collect from various passages in *The Green Book* what their ideal is. But we need not. The important point is not the precise nature of their end, but the fact that they have an end at all. They must have, or their book (being purely practical in intention) is written to no purpose. And this end must have real value in their eyes. To abstain from calling it good and to use, instead, such predicates as 'necessary' or 'progressive' or 'efficient' would be a subterfuge. They could be forced by argument to answer the questions 'necessary for what?', 'progressing towards what?', 'effecting what?'; in the last resort they would have to admit that some state of affairs was in their opinion good for its own sake. And this time they could not maintain that 'good' simply described their own emotion about it. For the whole purpose of their book is so to condition the young reader that he will share their approval, and this would be either a fool's or a villain's undertaking unless they held that their approval was in some way valid or correct.

In actual fact Gaius and Titius will be found to hold, with complete uncritical dogmatism, the whole system of values which happened to be in vogue among moderately educated young men of the professional classes during the period between the two wars.[1] Their scepticism about values is on the surface: it is for use on other people's values; about the values current in their own set they are not nearly sceptical enough. And this phenomenon is very usual. A great many of those who 'debunk' traditional or (as they would say) 'sentimental' values have in the background values of their own which they believe to be immune from the debunking process. They claim to be cutting away the parasitic growth of emotion, religious sanction, and inherited taboos, in order that 'real' or 'basic' values may emerge. I will now try to find out what happens if this is seriously attempted.

Let us continue to use the previous example—that of death for a good cause—not, of course, because virtue is the only value or martyrdom the

---

[1] The real (perhaps unconscious) philosophy of Gaius and Titius becomes clear if we contrast the two following lists of disapprovals and approvals.

A. Disapprovals: A mother's appeal to a child to be 'brave' is 'nonsense' (*Green Book*, p. 62). The reference of the word 'gentleman' is 'extremely vague' (ibid.) 'To call a man a coward tells us really nothing about what he does' (p. 64). Feelings about a country or empire are feelings 'about nothing in particular' (p. 77).

B. Approvals: Those who prefer the arts of peace to the arts of war (it is not said in what circumstances) are such that 'we may want to call them wise men' (p. 65). The pupil is expected 'to believe in a democractic community life' (p. 67). 'Contact with the ideas of other people is, as we know, healthy' (p. 86). The reason for bathrooms ('that people are healthier and pleasanter to meet when they are clean') is 'too obvious to need mentioning' (p. 142). It will be seen that comfort and security, as known to a suburban street in peace-time, are the ultimate values: those things which can alone produce or spiritualize comfort and security are mocked. Man lives by bread alone, and the ultimate source of bread is the baker's van: peace matters more than honour and can be preserved by jeering at colonels and reading newspapers.

only virtue, but because this is the *experimentum crucis* which shows different systems of thought in the clearest light. Let us suppose that an Innovator in values regards *dulce et decorum* and *greater love hath no man* as mere irrational sentiments which are to be stripped off in order that we may get down to the 'realistic' or 'basic' ground of this value. Where will he find such a ground?

First of all, he might say that the real value lay in the utility of such sacrifice to the community. 'Good', he might say, '*means* what is useful to the community.' But of course the death of the community is not useful to the community—only the death of some of its members. What is really meant is that the death of some men is useful to other men. That is very true. But on what ground are some men being asked to die for the benefit of others? Every appeal to pride, honour, shame, or love is excluded by hypothesis. To use these would be to return to sentiment and the Innovator's task is, having cut all that away, to explain to men, in terms of pure reasoning, why they will be well advised to die that others may live. He may say 'Unless some of us *risk* death all of us are *certain* to die.' But that will be true only in a limited number of cases; and even when it is true it provokes the very reasonable counter question 'Why should I be one of those who take the risk?'

At this point the Innovator may ask why, after all, selfishness should be more 'rational' or 'intelligent' than altruism. The question is welcome. If by Reason we mean the process actually employed by Gaius and Titius when engaged in debunking (that is, the connecting by inference of propositions, ultimately derived from sense data, with further propositions), then the answer must be that a refusal to sacrifice oneself is no more rational than a consent to do so. And no less rational. Neither choice is rational—or irrational—at all. From propositions about fact alone no *practical* conclusion can ever be drawn. *This will preserve society* cannot lead to *do this* except by the mediation of *society ought to be preserved*. *This will cost you your life* cannot lead directly to *do not do this:* it can lead to it only through a felt desire or an acknowledged duty of self-preservation. The Innovator is trying to get a conclusion in the imperative mood out of premises in the indicative mood: and though he continues trying to all eternity he cannot succeed, for the thing is impossible. We must therefore either extend the word Reason to include what our ancestors called Practical Reason and confess that judgements such as *society ought to be preserved* (though they can support themselves by no reason of the sort that Gaius and Titius demand) are not mere sentiments but are rationality itself; or else we must give up at once, and for ever, the attempt to find a core of 'rational' value behind all the sentiments we have debunked. The Innovator will not take the first alternative, for practical principles known to all men by Reason are simply the *Tao* which he has set out to supersede. He is more likely to give up the quest for a 'rational' core and to hunt for some other ground even more 'basic' and 'realistic'.

This he will probably feel that he has found in Instinct. The preservation of society, and of the species itself, are ends that do not hang on the precarious thread of Reason: they are given by Instinct. That is why there is no need to argue against the man who does not acknowledge them. We have an instinctive urge to preserve our own species. That is why men ought to work for posterity. We have no instinctive urge to keep promises or to respect individual life: that is why scruples of justice and humanity—in fact the *Tao*—can be properly swept away when they conflict with our real end, the preservation of the species. That, again, is why the modern situation permits and demands a new sexual morality: the old taboos served some real purpose in helping to preserve the species, but contraceptives have modified this and we can now abandon many of the taboos. For of course sexual desire, being instinctive, is to be gratified whenever it does not conflict with the preservation of the species. It looks, in fact, as if an ethics based on instinct will give the Innovator all he wants and nothing that he does not want.

In reality we have not advanced one step. I will not insist on the point that Instinct is a name for we know not what (to say that migratory birds find their way by instinct is only to say that we do not know how migratory birds find their way), for I think it is here being used in a fairly definite sense, to mean an unreflective or spontaneous impulse widely felt by the members of a given species. In what way does Instinct, thus conceived, help us to find 'real' values? Is it maintained that we *must* obey Instinct, that we cannot do otherwise? But if so, why are *Green Books* and the like written? Why this stream of exhortation to drive us where we cannot help going? Why such praise for those who have submitted to the inevitable? Or is it maintained that if we do obey Instinct we shall be happy and satisfied? But the very question we are considering was that of facing death which (so far as the Innovator knows) cuts off every possible satisfaction: and if we have an instinctive desire for the good of posterity then this desire, by the very nature of the case, can never be satisfied, since its aim is achieved, if at all, when we are dead. It looks very much as if the Innovator would have to say not that we must obey Instinct, nor that it will satisfy us to do so, but that we *ought* to obey it.[2]

But why ought we to obey Instinct? Is there another instinct of a higher order directing us to do so, and a third of a still higher order directing us to obey *it?*—an infinite regress of instincts? This is presumably impossible, but nothing else will serve. From the statement about psychological fact 'I have an impulse to do so and so' we cannot by any ingenuity derive the practical principle 'I ought to obey this impulse'. Even if it were true that men had a spontaneous, unreflective impulse to sacrifice their own lives for the preservation of their fellows, it remains a quite separate question whether this is an impulse they should control or one they should indulge. For even the Innovator admits that many impulses (those which conflict with the preservation of the species) have to be controlled. And this admission surely introduces us to a yet more fundamental difficulty.

---

[2] The most determined effort which I know to construct a theory of value on the basis of 'satisfaction of impulses' is that of Dr I. A. Richards (*Principles of Literary Criticism*, 1924). The old objection to defining Value as Satisfaction is the universal value judgement that 'it is better to be Socrates dissatisfied than a pig satisfied'. To meet this Dr Richards endeavours to show that our impulses can be arranged in a hierarchy and some satisfactions preferred to others without an appeal to any criterion other than satisfaction. He does this by the doctrine that some impulses are more 'important' than others—an *important* impulse being one whose frustration involves the frustration of other impulses. A good systematization (i.e. the good life) consists in satisfying as many impulses as possible; which entails satisfying the 'important' at the expense of the 'unimportant'. The objections to this scheme seem to me to be two:

(1) Without a theory of immortality it leaves no room for the value of noble death. It may, of course, be said that a man who has saved his life by treachery will suffer for the rest of that life from frustration. But not, surely, frustration of *all* his impulses? Whereas the dead man will have *no* satisfaction. Or is it maintained that since he had no unsatisfied impulses he is better off than the disgraced and living man? This at once raises the second objection.

(2) Is the value of a systematization to be judged by the presence of satisfactions or the absence of dissatisfactions? The extreme case is that of the dead man in whom satisfactions and dissatisfactions (on the modern view) both equal zero, as against the successful traitor who can still eat, drink, sleep, scratch and copulate, even if he cannot have friendship or love or self-respect. But it arises at other levels. Suppose *A* has only 500 impulses and all are satisfied, and that *B* has 1200 impulses whereof 700 are satisfied and 500 not: which has the better systematization? There is no doubt which Dr Richards actually prefers—he even praises art on the ground that it makes us 'discontented' with ordinary crudities! (op. cit., p. 230). The only trace I find of a philosophical basis for this preference is the statement that 'the more complex an activity the more conscious it is' (p. 109). But if satisfaction is the only value, why should increase of consciousness be good? For consciousness is the condition of all dissatisfactions as well as of all satisfactions. Dr Richards's system gives no support to his (and our) actual preference for civil life over savage and human over animal—or even for life over death.

Telling us to obey Instinct is like telling us to obey 'people'. People say different things: so do instincts. Our instincts are at war. If it is held that the instinct for preserving the species should always be obeyed at the expense of other instincts, whence do we derive this rule of precedence? To listen to that instinct speaking in its own cause and deciding it in its own favour would be rather simple-minded. Each instinct, if you listen to it, will claim to be gratified at the expense of all the rest. By the very act of listening to one rather than to others we have already prejudged the case. If we did not bring to the examination of our instincts a knowledge of their comparative dignity we could never learn it from them. And that knowledge cannot itself be instinctive: the judge cannot be one of the parties judged; or, if he is, the decision is worthless and there is no ground for placing the preservation of the species above self-preservation or sexual appetite.

The idea that, without appealing to any court higher than the instincts themselves, we can yet find grounds for preferring one instinct above its fellows dies very hard. We grasp at useless words: we call it the 'basic', or 'fundamental', or 'primal', or 'deepest' instinct. It is of no avail. Either these words conceal a value judgement passed *upon* the instinct and therefore not derivable *from* it, or else they merely record its felt intensity, the frequency of its operation and its wide distribution. If the former, the whole attempt to base value upon instinct has been abandoned: if the latter, these observations about the quantitative aspects of a psychological event lead to no practical conclusion. It is the old dilemma. Either the premisses already concealed an imperative or the conclusion remains merely in the indicative.[3]

---

[3] The desperate expedients to which a man can be driven if he attempts to base value on fact are well illustrated by Dr C. H. Waddington's fate in *Science and Ethics*. Dr Waddington here explains that 'existence is its own justification' (p. 14), and writes: 'An existence which is essentially evolutionary is itself the justification for an evolution towards a more comprehensive existence' (p. 17). I do not think Dr Waddington is himself at ease in this view, for he does endeavour to recommend the course of evolution to us on three grounds other than its mere occurrence. (*a*) That the later stages include or 'comprehend' the earlier. (*b*) That T. H. Huxley's picture of Evolution will not revolt you if you regard it from an 'actuarial' point of view. (*c*) That, any way, after all, it isn't half so bad as people make out ('not so morally offensive that we cannot accept it', p. 18). These three palliatives are more creditable to Dr Waddington's heart than his head and seem to me to give up the main position. If Evolution is praised (or, at least, apologized for) on the ground of *any* properties it exhibits, then we are using an external standard and the attempt to make existence its own justification has been abandoned. If that attempt is maintained, why does

Finally, it is worth inquiry whether there *is* any instinct to care for posterity or preserve the species. I do not discover it in myself: and yet I am a man rather prone to think of remote futurity—a man who can read Mr Olaf Stapledon with delight. Much less do I find it easy to believe that the majority of people who have sat opposite me in buses or stood with me in queues feel an unreflective impulse to do anything at all about the species, or posterity. Only people educated in a particular way have ever had the idea 'posterity' before their minds at all. It is difficult to assign to instinct our attitude towards an object which exists only for reflective men. What we have by nature is an impulse to preserve our own children and grandchildren; an impulse which grows progressively feebler as the imagination looks forward and finally dies out in the 'deserts of vast futurity'. No parents who were guided by this instinct would dream for a moment of setting up the claims of their hypothetical descendants against those of the baby actually crowing and kicking in the room. Those of us who accept the *Tao* may, perhaps, say that they ought to do so: but that is not open to those who treat instinct as the source of value. As we pass from mother love to rational planning for the future we are passing away from the realm of instinct into that of choice and reflection: and if instinct is the source of value, planning for the future ought to be less respectable and less obligatory than the baby language and cuddling of the fondest mother or the most fatuous nursery anecdotes of a doting father. If we are to base ourselves upon instinct, these things are the substance, and care for posterity the shadow—the huge, flickering shadow of the nursery happiness cast upon the screen of the unknown future. I do not say this projection is a bad thing: but then I do not believe that instinct is the

---

Dr Waddington concentrate on Evolution: i.e., on a temporary phase of organic existence in one planet? This is 'geocentric'. If Good = 'whatever Nature happens to be doing', then surely we should notice what Nature is doing as a whole; and Nature as a whole, I understand, is working steadily and irreversibly towards the final extinction of all life in every part of the universe, so that Dr Waddington's ethics, stripped of their unaccountable bias towards such a parochial affair as tellurian biology, would leave murder and suicide our only duties. Even this, I confess, seems to me a lesser objection than the discrepancy between Dr Waddington's first principle and the value judgements men actually make. To value anything simply because it occurs is in fact to worship success, like Quislings or men of Vichy. Other philosophies more wicked have been devised: none more vulgar. I am far from suggesting that Dr Waddington practises in real life such grovelling prostration before the *fait accompli*. Let us hope that *Rasselas*, chap. 22, gives the right picture of what his philosophy amounts to in action. ('The philosopher, supposing the rest vanquished, rose up and departed with the air of a man that had co-operated with the present system.')

ground of value judgements. What is absurd is to claim that your care for posterity finds its justification in instinct and then flout at every turn the only instinct on which it could be supposed to rest, tearing the child almost from the breast to crèche and kindergarten in the interests of progress and the coming race.

The truth finally becomes apparent that neither in any operation with factual propositions nor in any appeal to instinct can the Innovator find the basis for a system of values. None of the principles he requires are to be found there: but they are all to be found somewhere else. 'All within the four seas are his brothers' (xii. 5) says Confucius of the *Chün-tzu*, the *cuor gentil* or gentleman. *Humani nihil a me alienum puto* says the Stoic. 'Do as you would be done by,' says Jesus. 'Humanity is to be preserved,' says Locke.[4] All the practical principles behind the Innovator's case for posterity, or society, or the species, are there from time immemorial in the *Tao*. But they are nowhere else. Unless you accept these without question as being to the world of action what axioms are to the world of theory, you can have no practical principles whatever. You cannot reach them as conclusions: they are premises. You may, since they can give no 'reason' for themselves of a kind to silence Gaius and Titius, regard them as sentiments: but then you must give up contrasting 'real' or 'rational' value with sentimental value. All value will be sentimental; and you must confess (on pain of abandoning every value) that all sentiment is not 'merely' subjective. You may, on the other hand, regard them as rational—nay as rationality itself—as things so obviously reasonable that they neither demand nor admit proof. But then you must allow that Reason can be practical, that an *ought* must not be dismissed because it cannot produce some *is* as its credential. If nothing is self-evident, nothing can be proved. Similarly if nothing is obligatory for its own sake, nothing is obligatory at all.

To some it will appear that I have merely restored under another name what they always meant by basic or fundamental instinct. But much more than a choice of words is involved. The Innovator attacks traditional values (the *Tao*) in defence of what he at first supposes to be (in some special sense) 'rational' or 'biological' values. But as we have seen, all the values which he uses in attacking the *Tao*, and even claims to be substituting for it, are themselves derived from the *Tao*. If he had really started

---

[4] See Appendix.

from scratch, from right outside the human tradition of value, no jug-glery could have advanced him an inch towards the conception that a man should die for the community or work for posterity. If the *Tao* falls, all his own conceptions of value fall with it. Not one of them can claim any authority other than that of the *Tao*. Only by such shreds of the *Tao* as he has inherited is he enabled even to attack it. The question therefore arises what title he has to select bits of it for acceptance and to reject others. For if the bits he rejects have no authority, neither have those he retains: if what he retains is valid, what he rejects is equally valid too.

The Innovator, for example, rates high the claims of posterity. He cannot get any valid claim for posterity out of instinct or (in the modern sense) reason. He is really deriving our duty to posterity from the *Tao*; our duty to do good to all men is an axiom of Practical Reason, and our duty to do good to our descendants is a clear deduction from it. But then, in every form of the *Tao* which has come down to us, side by side with the duty to children and descendants lies the duty to parents and ancestors. By what right do we reject one and accept the other? Again, the Innovator may place economic value first. To get people fed and clothed is the great end, and in pursuit of its scruples about justice and good faith may be set aside. The *Tao* of course agrees with him about the importance of getting the people fed and clothed. Unless the Innovator were himself using the *Tao* he could never have learned of such a duty. But side by side with it in the *Tao* lie those duties of justice and good faith which he is ready to debunk. What is his warrant? He may be a Jingoist, a Racialist, an extreme nationalist, who maintains that the advancement of his own people is the object to which all else ought to yield. But no kind of factual observation and no appeal to instinct will give him a ground for this option. Once more, he is in fact deriving it from the *Tao*: a duty to our own kin, because they are our own kin, is a part of traditional morality. But side by side with it in the *Tao*, and limiting it, lie the inflexible demands of justice, and the rule that, in the long run, all men are our brothers. Whence comes the Innovator's authority to pick and choose?

Since I can see no answer to these questions, I draw the following conclusions. This thing which I have called for convenience the *Tao*, and which others may call Natural Law or Traditional Morality or the First Principles of Practical Reason or the First Platitudes, is not one among a series of possible systems of value. It is the sole source of all value judgements. If it is rejected, all value is rejected. If any value is retained, it is retained. The effort to refute it and raise a new system of value in its place is self-contradictory. There has never been, and never will be, a radically new judgement of value in the history of the world. What purport to be new systems or (as they now call them) 'ideologies', all consist of fragments from the *Tao* itself, arbitrarily wrenched from their context in the whole and then swollen to madness in their isolation, yet still owing to the *Tao* and to it alone such validity as they possess. If my duty to my parents is a superstition, then so is my duty to posterity. If justice is a superstition, then so is my duty to my country or my race. If the pursuit of scientific knowledge is a real value, then so is conjugal fidelity. The rebellion of new ideologies against the *Tao* is a rebellion of the branches against the tree: if the rebels could succeed they would find that they had destroyed themselves. The human mind has no more power of inventing a new value than of imagining a new primary colour, or, indeed, of creating a new sun and a new sky for it to move in.

Does this mean, then, that no progress in our perceptions of value can ever take place? That we are bound down for ever to an unchanging code given once for all? And is it, in any event, possible to talk of obeying what I call the *Tao*? If we lump together, as I have done, the traditional moralities of East and West, the Christian, the Pagan, and the Jew, shall we not find many contradictions and some absurdities? I admit all this. Some criticism, some removal of contradictions, even some real development, is required. But there are two very different kinds of criticism.

A theorist about language may approach his native tongue, as it were from outside, regarding its genius as a thing that has no claim on him and advocating wholesale alterations of its idiom and spelling in the interests of commercial convenience or scientific accuracy. That is one thing. A great poet, who has 'loved, and been well nurtured in, his mother tongue', may also make great alterations in it, but his changes of the language are made in the spirit of the language itself: he works from within. The language which suffers, has also inspired the changes. That is a different thing—as different as the works of Shakespeare are from Basic English. It is the difference between alteration from within and alteration from without: between the organic and the surgical.

In the same way, the *Tao* admits development from within. There is a difference between a real moral advance and a mere innovation. From the Confucian 'Do not do to others what you would not like them to do to you' to the Christian 'Do as you would be done by' is a real advance. The morality of Nietzsche is a mere innovation. The first is an advance because no one who did not admit the validity of the old maxim could see reason for accepting the new one, and anyone who accepted the old would at once recognize the new as an extension of the same principle. If he rejected it, he would have to reject it as a superfluity, something that went too far, not as something simply heterogeneous from his own ideas of value. But the Nietzschean ethic can be accepted only if we are ready to scrap traditional morals as a mere error and then to put ourselves in a position where we can find no ground for any value judgements at all. It is the difference between a man who says to us: 'You like your vegetables moderately fresh; why not grow your own and have them perfectly fresh?' and a man who says, 'Throw away that loaf and try eating bricks and centipedes instead.'

Those who understand the spirit of the *Tao* and who have been led by that spirit can modify it in directions which that spirit itself demands. Only they can know what those directions are. The outsider knows nothing about the matter. His attempts at alteration, as we have seen, contradict themselves. So far from being able to harmonize discrepancies in its letter by penetration to its spirit, he merely snatches at some one precept, on which the accidents of time and place happen to have riveted his attention, and then rides it to death—for no reason that he can give. From within the *Tao* itself comes the only authority to modify the *Tao*. This is what Confucius meant when he said 'With those who follow a different Way it is useless to take counsel'.[5] This is why Aristotle said that only those who have been well brought up can usefully study ethics: to the corrupted man, the man who stands outside the *Tao*, the very starting point of this science is invisible.[6] He may be hostile, but he cannot be critical: he does not know what is being discussed. This is why it was also said 'This people that knoweth not the Law is accursed'[7] and 'He that believeth not shall be damned'.[8] An open mind, in questions that are not ultimate, is useful. But an open mind about the ultimate

---

[5] *Analects of Confucius,* XV. 39.

[6] *Eth. Nic.* 1095 B, 1140 B, 1151 A.

[7] John 7:49. The speaker said it in malice, but with more truth than he meant. Cf. John 13:51.

[8] Mark 16:6.

foundations either of Theoretical or of Practical Reason is idiocy. If a man's mind is open on these things, let his mouth at least be shut. He can say nothing to the purpose. Outside the *Tao* there is no ground for criticizing either the *Tao* or anything else.

In particular instances it may, no doubt, be a matter of some delicacy to decide where the legitimate internal criticism ends and the fatal external kind begins. But wherever any precept of traditional morality is simply challenged to produce its credentials, as though the burden of proof lay on it, we have taken the wrong position. The legitimate reformer endeavours to show that the precept in question conflicts with some precept which its defenders allow to be more fundamental, or that it does not really embody the judgement of value it professes to embody. The direct frontal attack 'Why?'—'What good does it do?'—'Who said so?' is never permissible; not because it is harsh or offensive but because no values at all can justify themselves on that level. If you persist in *that* kind of trial you will destroy all values, and so destroy the bases of your own criticism as well as the thing criticized. You must not hold a pistol to the head of the *Tao*. Nor must we postpone obedience to a precept until its credentials have been examined. Only those who are practising the *Tao* will understand it. It is the well-nurtured man, the *cuor gentil*, and he alone, who can recognize Reason when it comes.[9] It is Paul, the Pharisee, the man 'perfect as touching the Law' who learns where and how that Law was deficient.[10]

In order to avoid misunderstanding, I may add that though I myself am a Theist, and indeed a Christian, I am not here attempting any indirect argument for Theism. I am simply arguing that if we are to have values at all we must accept the ultimate platitudes of Practical Reason as having absolute validity: that any attempt, having become sceptical about these, to reintroduce value lower down on some supposedly more 'realistic' basis, is doomed. Whether this position implies a supernatural origin for the *Tao* is a question I am not here concerned with.

Yet how can the modern mind be expected to embrace the conclusion we have reached? This *Tao* which, it seems, we must treat as an absolute is simply a phenomenon like any other—the reflection upon the minds of our ancestors of the agricultural rhythm in which they lived or even

---

[9] *Republic,* 402 A

[10] Philippians 3:6.

of their physiology. We know already in principle how such things are produced: soon we shall know in detail: eventually we shall be able to produce them at will. Of course, while we did not know how minds were made, we accepted this mental furniture as a datum, even as a master. But many things in nature which were once our masters have become our servants. Why not this? Why must our conquest of nature stop short, in stupid reverence, before this final and toughest bit of 'nature' which has hitherto been called the conscience of man? You threaten us with some obscure disaster if we step outside it: but we have been threatened in that way by obscurantists at every step in our advance, and each time the threat has proved false. You say we shall have no values at all if we step outside the *Tao*. Very well: we shall probably find that we can get on quite comfortably without them. Let us regard all ideas of what we *ought* to do simply as an interesting psychological survival: let us step right out of all that and start doing what we like. Let us decide for ourselves what man is to be and make him into that: not on any ground of imagined value, but because we want him to be such. Having mastered our environment, let us now master ourselves and choose our own destiny.

This is a very possible position: and those who hold it cannot be accused of self-contradiction like the half-hearted sceptics who still hope to find 'real' values when they have debunked the traditional ones. This is the rejection of the concept of value altogether. I shall need another lecture to consider it.

3

THE ABOLITION OF MAN

It came burning hot into my mind, whatever he said and however he flattered, when he got me home to his house, he would sell me for a slave.

JOHN BUNYAN

'MAN'S CONQUEST OF NATURE' is an expression often used to describe the progress of applied science. 'Man has Nature whacked,' said someone to a friend of mine not long ago. In their context the words had a certain tragic beauty, for the speaker was dying of tuberculosis. 'No matter,' he said, 'I know I'm one of the casualties. Of course there are casualties on the winning as well as on the losing side. But that doesn't alter the fact that it is winning.' I have chosen this story as my point of departure in order to make it clear that I do not wish to disparage all that is really beneficial in the process described as 'Man's conquest', much less all the real devotion and self-sacrifice that has gone to make it possible. But having done so I must proceed to analyse this conception a little more closely. In what sense is Man the possessor of increasing power over Nature?

Let us consider three typical examples: the aeroplane, the wireless, and the contraceptive. In a civilized community, in peace-time, anyone who can pay for them may use these things. But it cannot strictly be said that when he does so he is exercising his own proper or individual power over Nature. If I pay you to carry me, I am not therefore myself a strong man. Any or all of the three things I have mentioned can be withheld from some men by other men—by those who sell, or those who allow the sale, or those who own the sources of production, or those who make the goods. What we call Man's power is, in reality, a power possessed by some men which they may, or may not, allow other men to profit by. Again, as regards the powers manifested in the aeroplane or the wireless, Man is as much the patient or subject as the possessor, since he is the target both for bombs and for propaganda. And as regards contraceptives, there is a paradoxical, negative sense in which all possible future generations are the patients or subjects of a power wielded by those already alive. By contraception simply, they are denied existence; by contraception used as a means of selective breeding, they are, without their concurring voice, made to be what one generation, for its own reasons, may choose to prefer. From this point of view, what we call Man's power over Nature turns out to be a power exercised by some men over other men with Nature as its instrument.

It is, of course, a commonplace to complain that men have hitherto used badly, and against their fellows, the powers that science has given them. But that is not the point I am trying to make. I am not speaking of particular corruptions and abuses which an increase of moral virtue would cure: I am considering what the thing called 'Man's power over Nature' must always and essentially be. No doubt, the picture could be modified by public ownership of raw materials and factories and public control of scientific research. But unless we have a world state this will still mean the power of one nation over others. And even within the world state or the nation it will mean (in principle) the power of majorities over minorities, and (in the concrete) of a government over the people. And all long-term exercises of power, especially in breeding, must mean the power of earlier generations over later ones.

The latter point is not always sufficiently emphasized, because those who write on social matters have not yet learned to imitate the physicists by always including Time among the dimensions. In order to understand fully what Man's power over Nature, and therefore the power of some men over other men, really means, we must picture the race extended in time from the date of its emergence to that of its extinction. Each generation exercises power over its successors: and each, in so far as it modifies the environment bequeathed to it and rebels against tradition, resists and limits the power of its predecessors. This modifies the picture which is sometimes painted of a progressive emancipation from tradition and a progressive control of natural processes resulting in a continual increase of human power. In reality, of course, if any one age really attains, by eugenics and scientific education, the power to make its descendants what it pleases, all men who live after it are the patients of that power. They are weaker, not stronger: for though we may have put wonderful machines in their hands we have pre-ordained how they are to use them. And if, as is almost certain, the age which had thus attained maximum power over posterity were also the age most emancipated from tradition, it would be engaged in reducing the power of its predecessors almost as drastically as that of its successors. And we must also remember that, quite apart from this, the later a generation comes—the nearer it lives to that date at which the species becomes extinct—the less power it will have in the forward direction, because its subjects will be so few. There is therefore no question of a power vested in the race as a whole steadily growing as long as the race survives. The last men, far from being the heirs of power, will be of all men most subject to the dead hand of the great planners and conditioners and will themselves exercise least power upon the future.

The real picture is that of one dominant age—let us suppose the hundredth century A.D.—which resists all previous ages most successfully and dominates all subsequent ages most irresistibly, and thus is the real master of the human species. But then within this master generation (itself an infinitesimal minority of the species) the power will be exercised by a minority smaller still. Man's conquest of Nature, if the dreams of some scientific planners are realized, means the rule of a few hundreds of men over billions upon billions of men. There neither is nor can be any simple increase of power on Man's side. Each new power won *by* man is a power *over* man as well. Each advance leaves him weaker as well as stronger. In every victory, besides being the general who triumphs, he is also the prisoner who follows the triumphal car.

I am not yet considering whether the total result of such ambivalent victories is a good thing or a bad. I am only making clear what Man's conquest of Nature really means and especially that final stage in the conquest, which, perhaps, is not far off. The final stage is come when Man by eugenics, by pre-natal conditioning, and by an education and propaganda based on a perfect applied psychology, has obtained full control over himself. *Human* nature will be the last part of Nature to surrender to Man. The battle will then be won. We shall have 'taken the thread of life out of the hand of Clotho' and be henceforth free to make our species whatever we wish it to be. The battle will indeed be won. But who, precisely, will have won it?

For the power of Man to make himself what he pleases means, as we have seen, the power of some men to make other men what *they* please. In all ages, no doubt, nurture and instruction have, in some sense, attempted to exercise this power. But the situation to which we must look forward will be novel in two respects. In the first place, the power will be enormously increased. Hitherto the plans of educationalists have achieved very little of what they attempted and indeed, when we read them—how Plato would have every infant 'a bastard nursed in a bureau', and Elyot would have the boy see no men before the age of seven and, after that, no women,[1] and how Locke wants children to have leaky shoes and no turn for poetry [2]—we may well thank the beneficent obstinacy of real mothers, real nurses, and (above all) real children for preserving the human race in such sanity as it still possesses. But the man-moulders of the new age will be armed with the powers of an omnicompetent state and an irresistible scientific technique: we shall get at last a race of conditioners who really can cut out all posterity in what shape they please.

The second difference is even more important. In the older systems both the kind of man the teachers wished to produce and their motives for producing him were prescribed by the *Tao*—a norm to which the teachers themselves were subject and from which they claimed no liberty to depart. They did not cut men to some pattern they had chosen. They handed on what they had received: they initiated the young neophyte into the mystery of humanity which over-arched him and them alike. It was but old birds teaching young birds to fly. This will be changed. Values are now mere natural phenomena. Judgements of value are to be produced in the pupil as part of the conditioning. Whatever *Tao* there is

---

[1] *The Boke Named the Governour*, 1. iv: 'Al men except physitions only shulde be excluded and kepte out of the norisery.' 1. vi: 'After that a childe is come to seuen yeres of age . . . the most sure counsaile is to withdrawe him from all company of women.'

[2] *Some Thoughts concerning Education*, §7: 'I will also advise his *Feet to be wash'd* every Day in cold Water, and to have his Shoes so thin that they might leak and *let in Water*, whenever he comes near it.' § 174: 'If he have a poetick vein, 'tis to me the strangest thing in the World that the Father should desire or suffer it to be cherished or improved. Methinks the Parents should labour to have it stifled and suppressed as much as may be.' Yet Locke is one of our most sensible writers on education.

will be the product, not the motive, of education. The conditioners have been emancipated from all that. It is one more part of Nature which they have conquered. The ultimate springs of human action are no longer, for them, something given. They have surrendered—like electricity: it is the function of the Conditioners to control, not to obey them. They know how to *produce* conscience and decide what kind of conscience they will produce. They themselves are outside, above. For we are assuming the last stage of Man's struggle with Nature. The final victory has been won. Human nature has been conquered—and, of course, has conquered, in whatever sense those words may now bear.

The Conditioners, then, are to choose what kind of artificial *Tao* they will, for their own good reasons, produce in the Human race. They are the motivators, the creators of motives. But how are they going to be motivated themselves?

For a time, perhaps, by survivals, within their own minds, of the old 'natural' *Tao*. Thus at first they may look upon themselves as servants and guardians of humanity and conceive that they have a 'duty' to do it 'good'. But it is only by confusion that they can remain in this state. They recognize the concept of duty as the result of certain processes which they can now control. Their victory has consisted precisely in emerging from the state in which they were acted upon by those processes to the state in which they use them as tools. One of the things they now have to decide is whether they will, or will not, so condition the rest of us that we can go on having the old idea of duty and the old reactions to it. How can duty help them to decide that? Duty itself is up for trial: it cannot also be the judge. And 'good' fares no better. They know quite well how to produce a dozen different conceptions of good in us. The question is which, if any, they should produce. No conception of good can help them to decide. It is absurd to fix on one of the things they are comparing and make it the standard of comparison.

To some it will appear that I am inventing a factitious difficulty for my Conditioners. Other, more simple-minded, critics may ask, 'Why should you suppose they will be such bad men?' But I am not supposing them to be bad men. They are, rather, not men (in the old sense) at all. They are, if you like, men who have sacrificed their own share in traditional humanity in order to devote themselves to the task of deciding what 'Humanity' shall henceforth mean. 'Good' and 'bad', applied to them, are words without content: for it is from them that the content of these words is henceforward to be derived. Nor is their difficulty factitious. We might suppose that it was possible to say 'After all, most of us want more or less the same things—food and drink and sexual intercourse, amusement, art, science, and the longest possible life for individuals and for the species. Let them simply say, This is what we happen to like, and go on to condition men in the way most likely to produce it. Where's the trouble?' But this will not answer. In the first place, it is false that we all really like the same things. But even if we did, what motive is to impel the Conditioners to scorn delights and live laborious days in order that we, and posterity, may have what we like? Their duty? But that is only the *Tao*, which they may decide to impose on us, but which cannot be valid for them. If they accept it, then they are no longer the makers of conscience but still its subjects, and their final conquest over Nature has not really happened. The preservation of the species? But why should the species be preserved? One of the questions before them is whether this feeling for posterity (they know well how it is produced) shall be continued or not. However far they go back, or down, they can find no ground to stand on. Every motive they try to act on becomes at once a *petitio*. It is not that they are bad men. They are not men at all. Stepping outside the *Tao*, they have stepped into the void. Nor are their subjects necessarily unhappy men. They are not men at all: they are artefacts. Man's final conquest has proved to be the abolition of Man.

Yet the Conditioners will act. When I said just now that all motives fail them, I should have said all motives except one. All motives that claim any validity other than that of their felt emotional weight at a given moment have failed them. Everything except the *sic volo, sic jubeo* has been explained away. But what never claimed objectivity cannot be destroyed by subjectivism. The impulse to scratch when I itch or to pull to pieces when I am inquisitive is immune from the solvent which is fatal to my justice, or honour, or care for posterity. When all that says 'it is good' has been debunked, what says 'I want' remains. It cannot be exploded or 'seen through' because it never had any pretentions. The Conditioners, therefore, must come to be motivated simply by their own pleasure. I am not here speaking of the corrupting influence of power nor expressing the fear that under it our Conditioners will degenerate. The very words *corrupt* and *degenerate* imply a doctrine of value and are therefore meaningless in this context. My point is that those who stand outside all judgements of value cannot have any ground for preferring one of their own impulses to another except the emotional strength of that impulse.

We may legitimately hope that among the impulses which arise in minds thus emptied of all 'rational' or 'spiritual' motives, some will be benevolent. I am very doubtful myself whether the benevolent impulses, stripped of that preference and encouragement which the *Tao* teaches us to give them and left to their merely natural strength and frequency as psychological events, will have much influence. I am very doubtful whether history shows us one example of a man who, having stepped outside traditional morality and attained power, has used that power benevolently. I am inclined to think that the Conditioners will hate the conditioned. Though regarding as an illusion the artificial conscience which they produce in us their subjects, they will yet perceive that it creates in us an illusion of meaning for our lives which compares favourably with the futility of their own: and they will envy us as eunuchs envy men. But I do not insist on this, for it is a mere conjecture. What is not conjecture is that our hope even of a 'conditioned' happiness rests on what is ordinarily called 'chance'—the chance that benevolent impulses may on the whole predominate in our Conditioners. For without the judgement 'Benevolence is good'—that is, without re-entering the *Tao*—they can have no ground for promoting or stabilizing these impulses rather than any others. By the logic of their position they must just take their impulses as they come, from chance. And Chance here means Nature. It is from heredity, digestion, the weather, and the association of ideas, that the motives of the Conditioners will spring. Their extreme rationalism, by 'seeing through' all 'rational' motives, leaves them creatures of wholly irrational behaviour. If you will not obey the *Tao*, or else commit suicide, obedience to impulse (and therefore, in the long run, to mere 'nature') is the only course left open.

At the moment, then, of Man's victory over Nature, we find the whole human race subjected to some individual men, and those individuals subjected to that in themselves which is purely 'natural'—to their irrational impulses. Nature, untrammelled by values, rules the Conditioners and, through them, all humanity. Man's conquest of Nature turns out, in the moment of its consummation, to be Nature's conquest of Man. Every victory we seemed to win has led us, step by step, to this conclusion. All Nature's apparent reverses have been but tactical withdrawals. We thought we were beating her back when she was luring us on. What looked to us like hands held up in surrender was really the opening of arms to enfold us for ever. If the fully planned and conditioned world (with its *Tao* a mere product of the planning) comes into existence, Nature will be troubled no more by the restive species that rose in revolt against her so many millions of years ago, will be vexed no longer by its chatter of truth and mercy and beauty and happiness. *Ferum victorem cepit*: and if the eugenics are efficient enough there will be no second revolt, but all snug beneath the Conditioners, and the Conditioners beneath her, till the moon falls or the sun grows cold.

My point may be clearer to some if it is put in a different form. Nature is a word of varying meanings, which can best be understood if we consider its various opposites. The Natural is the opposite of the Artificial, the Civil, the Human, the Spiritual, and the Supernatural. The Artificial does not now concern us. If we take the rest of the list of opposites, however, I think we can get a rough idea of what men have meant by Nature and what it is they oppose to her. Nature seems to be the spatial and temporal, as distinct from what is less fully so or not so at all. She seems to be the world of quantity, as against the world of quality; of objects as against consciousness; of the bound, as against the wholly or partially autonomous; of that which knows no values as against that which both has and perceives value; of efficient causes (or, in some modern systems, of no causality at all) as against final causes. Now I take it that when we understand a thing analytically and then dominate and use it for our own convenience, we reduce it to the level of 'Nature' in the sense that we suspend our judgements of value about it, ignore its final cause (if any), and treat it in terms of quantity. This repression of elements in what would otherwise be our total reaction to it is sometimes very noticeable and even painful: something has to be overcome before we can cut up a dead man or a live animal in a dissecting room. These objects *resist* the movement of the mind whereby we thrust them into the world of mere Nature. But in other instances too, a similar price is exacted for our analytical knowledge and manipulative power, even if we have ceased to count it. We do not look at trees either as Dryads or as beautiful objects while we cut them into beams: the first man who did so may have felt the price keenly, and the bleeding trees in Virgil and Spenser may be far-off echoes of that primeval sense of impiety. The stars lost their divinity as astronomy developed, and the Dying God has no place in chemical agriculture. To many, no doubt, this process is simply the gradual discovery that the real world is different from what we expected, and the old opposition to Galileo or to 'body-snatchers' is simply obscurantism. But that is not the whole story. It is not the greatest of modern scientists who feel most sure that the object, stripped of its qualitative properties and reduced to mere quantity, is wholly real. Little scientists, and little unscientific followers of science, may think so. The great minds know very well that the object, so treated, is an artificial abstraction, that something of its reality has been lost.

From this point of view the conquest of Nature appears in a new light. We reduce things to mere Nature *in order that* we may 'conquer' them. We are always conquering Nature, *because* 'Nature' is the name for what we have, to some extent, conquered. The price of conquest is to treat a thing as mere Nature. Every conquest over Nature increases her domain. The stars do not become Nature till we can weigh and measure them: the soul does not become Nature till we can psychoanalyse her. The wresting of powers *from* Nature is also the surrendering of things *to* Nature. As long as this process stops short of the final stage we may well hold that the gain outweighs the loss. But as soon as we take the final step of reducing our own species to the level of mere Nature, the whole process is stultified, for this time the being who stood to gain and the being who has been sacrificed are one and the same. This is one of the many instances where to carry a principle to what seems its logical conclusion produces absurdity. It is like the famous Irishman who found that a certain kind of stove reduced his fuel bill by half and thence concluded that two stoves of the same kind would enable him to warm his house with no fuel at all. It is the magician's bargain: give up our soul, get power in return. But once our souls, that is, ourselves, have been given up, the power thus conferred will not belong to us. We shall in fact be the slaves and puppets of that to which we have given our souls. It is in Man's power to treat himself as a mere 'natural object' and his own judgements of value as raw material for scientific manipulation to alter at will. The objection to his doing so does not lie in the fact that this point of view (like one's first day in a dissecting room) is painful and shocking till we grow used to it. The pain and the shock are at most a warning and a symptom. The real objection is that if man chooses to treat himself as raw material, raw material he will be: not raw material to be manipulated, as he fondly imagined, by himself, but by mere appetite, that is, mere Nature, in the person of his de-humanized Conditioners.

We have been trying, like Lear, to have it both ways: to lay down our human prerogative and yet at the same time to retain it. It is impossible. Either we are rational spirit obliged for ever to obey the absolute values of the *Tao*, or else we are mere nature to be kneaded and cut into new shapes for the pleasures of masters who must, by hypothesis, have no motive but their own 'natural' impulses. Only the *Tao* provides a common human law of action which can over-arch rulers and ruled alike. A dogmatic belief in objective value is necessary to the very idea of a rule which is not tyranny or an obedience which is not slavery.

I am not here thinking solely, perhaps not even chiefly, of those who are our public enemies at the moment. The process which, if not checked, will abolish Man goes on apace among Communists and Democrats no less than among Fascists. The methods may (at first) differ in brutality. But many a mild-eyed scientist in pince-nez, many a popular dramatist, many an amateur philosopher in our midst, means in the long run just the same as the Nazi rulers of Germany. Traditional values are to be 'debunked' and mankind to be cut out into some fresh shape at the will (which must, by hypothesis, be an arbitrary will) of some few lucky people in one lucky generation which has learned how to do it. The belief that we can invent 'ideologies' at pleasure, and the consequent treatment of mankind as mere ΰλη, specimens, preparations, begins to affect our very language. Once we killed bad men: now we liquidate unsocial elements. Virtue has become *integration* and diligence *dynamism*, and boys likely to be worthy of a commission are 'potential officer material'. Most wonderful of all, the virtues of thrift and temperance, and even of ordinary intelligence, are *sales-resistance*.

The true significance of what is going on has been concealed by the use of the abstraction Man. Not that the word Man is necessarily a pure abstraction. In the *Tao* itself, as long as we remain within it, we find the concrete reality in which to participate is to be truly human: the real common will and common reason of humanity, alive, and growing like a tree, and branching out, as the situation varies, into ever new beauties and dignities of application. While we speak from within the *Tao* we can speak of Man having power over himself in a sense truly analogous to an individual's self-control. But the moment we step outside and regard the *Tao* as a mere subjective product, this possibility has disappeared. What is now common to all men is a mere abstract universal, an H.C.F., and Man's conquest of himself means simply the rule of the Conditioners over the conditioned human material, the world of post-humanity which, some knowingly and some unknowingly, nearly all men in all nations are at present labouring to produce.

Nothing I can say will prevent some people from describing this lecture as an attack on science. I deny the charge, of course: and real Natural Philosophers (there are some now alive) will perceive that in defending value I defend *inter alia* the value of knowledge, which must die like every other when its roots in the *Tao* are cut. But I can go further than that. I even suggest that from Science herself the cure might come.

I have described as a 'magician's bargain' that process whereby man surrenders object after object, and finally himself, to Nature in return for power. And I meant what I said. The fact that the scientist has succeeded where the magician failed has put such a wide contrast between them in popular thought that the real story of the birth of Science is misunderstood. You will even find people who write about the sixteenth century as if Magic were a medieval survival and Science the new thing that came in to sweep it away. Those who have studied the period know better. There was very little magic in the Middle Ages: the sixteenth and seventeenth centuries are the high noon of magic. The serious magical endeavour and the serious scientific endeavour are twins: one was sickly and died, the other strong and throve. But they were twins. They were born of the same impulse. I allow that some (certainly not all) of the early scientists were actuated by a pure love of knowledge. But if we consider the temper of that age as a whole we can discern the impulse of which I speak.

There is something which unites magic and applied science while separating both from the 'wisdom' of earlier ages. For the wise men of old the cardinal problem had been how to conform the soul to reality, and the solution had been knowledge, self-discipline, and virtue. For magic and applied science alike the problem is how to subdue reality to the wishes of men: the solution is a technique; and both, in the practice of this technique, are ready to do things hitherto regarded as disgusting and impious—such as digging up and mutilating the dead.

If we compare the chief trumpeter of the new era (Bacon) with Marlowe's Faustus, the similarity is striking. You will read in some critics that Faustus has a thirst for knowledge. In reality, he hardly mentions it. It is not truth he wants from the devils, but gold and guns and girls. 'All things that move between the quiet poles shall be at his command' and 'a sound magician is a mighty god'.[3] In the same spirit Bacon condemns those who value knowledge as an end in itself: this, for him, is to use as a mistress for pleasure what ought to be a spouse for fruit.[4] The true object is to extend Man's power to the performance of all things possible. He rejects magic because it does not work;[5] but his goal is that of the magician. In Paracelsus the characters of magician and scientist are combined. No doubt those who really founded modern science were usually those whose love of truth exceeded their love of power; in every mixed movement the efficacy comes from the good elements not from the bad. But the presence of the bad elements is not irrelevant to the direction the efficacy takes. It might be going too far to say that the modern scientific movement was tainted from its birth: but I think it would be true to say that it was born in an unhealthy neighbourhood and at an inauspicious hour. Its triumphs may have been too rapid and purchased at too high a price: reconsideration, and something like repentance, may be required.

Is it, then, possible to imagine a new Natural Philosophy, continually conscious that the 'natural object' produced by analysis and abstraction is not reality but only a view, and always correcting the abstraction? I hardly know what I am asking for. I hear rumours that Goethe's approach to nature deserves fuller consideration—that even Dr Steiner may have seen something that orthodox researchers have missed. The regenerate science which I have in mind would not do even to minerals and vegetables what modern science threatens to do to man himself. When it explained it would not explain away. When it spoke of the parts it would remember the whole. While studying the *It* it would not lose what Martin Buber calls the *Thou*-situation. The analogy between the *Tao* of Man and the instincts of an animal species would mean for it new light cast on the unknown thing, Instinct, by the inly known reality of conscience and not a reduction of conscience to the category of Instinct. Its followers would not be free with the words *only* and *merely*. In a word, it would conquer Nature without being at the same time conquered by her and buy knowledge at a lower cost than that of life.

---

[3] *Dr Faustus*, 77–90.

[4] *Advancement of Learning*, Bk 1 (p. 60 in Ellis and Spedding, 1905; p. 35 in Everyman Edition).

[5] *Filum Labyrinthi*, i.

Perhaps I am asking impossibilities. Perhaps, in the nature of things, analytical understanding must always be a basilisk which kills what it sees and only sees by killing. But if the scientists themselves cannot arrest this process before it reaches the common Reason and kills that too, then someone else must arrest it. What I most fear is the reply that I am 'only one more' obscurantist, that this barrier, like all previous barriers set up against the advance of science, can be safely passed. Such a reply springs from the fatal serialism of the modern imagination—the image of infinite unilinear progression which so haunts our minds. Because we have to use numbers so much we tend to think of every process as if it must be like the numeral series, where every step, to all eternity, is the same kind of step as the one before. I implore you to remember the Irishman and his two stoves. There are progressions in which the last step is *sui generis*—incommensurable with the others—and in which to go the whole way is to undo all the labour of your previous journey. To reduce the *Tao* to a mere natural product is a step of that kind. Up to that point, the kind of explanation which explains things away may give us something, though at a heavy cost. But you cannot go on 'explaining away' for ever: you will find that you have explained explanation itself away. You cannot go on 'seeing through' things for ever. The whole point of seeing through something is to see something through it. It is good that the window should be transparent, because the street or garden beyond it is opaque. How if you saw through the garden too? It is no use trying to 'see through' first principles. If you see through everything, then everything is transparent. But a wholly transparent world is an invisible world. To 'see through' all things is the same as not to see.

APPENDIX

ILLUSTRATIONS OF THE *TAO*

THE FOLLOWING ILLUSTRATIONS of the Natural Law are collected from such sources as come readily to the hand of one who is not a professional historian. The list makes no pretence of completeness. It will be noticed that writers such as Locke and Hooker, who wrote within the Christian tradition, are quoted side by side with the New Testament. This would, of course, be absurd if I were trying to collect independent testimonies to the *Tao*. But (1) I am not trying to *prove* its validity by the argument from common consent. Its validity cannot be deduced. For those who do not perceive its rationality, even universal consent could not prove it. (2) The idea of collecting *independent* testimonies presupposes that 'civilizations' have arisen in the world independently of one another; or even that humanity has had several independent emergences on this planet. The biology and anthropology involved in such an assumption are extremely doubtful. It is by no means certain that there has ever (in the sense required) been more than one civilization in all history. It is at least arguable that every civilization we find has been derived from another civilization and, in the last resort, from a single centre—'carried' like an infectious disease or like the Apostolical succession.

1. THE LAW OF GENERAL BENEFICENCE

(a) Negative

'I have not slain men.' (Ancient Egyptian. From the Confession of the Righteous Soul, 'Book of the Dead'. v. *Encyclopedia of Religion and Ethics* [= *ERE*], vol. v, p. 478)
'Do not murder.' (Ancient Jewish. Exodus 20:13)

'Terrify not men or God will terrify thee.' (Ancient Egyptian. Precepts of Ptahhetep. H. R. Hall, *Ancient History of the Near East*, p. 133n)

'In Nástrond (= Hell) I saw . . . murderers.' (Old Norse. *Volospá* 38, 39)

'I have not brought misery upon my fellows. I have not made the beginning of every day laborious in the sight of him who worked for me.' (Ancient Egyptian. Confession of the Righteous Soul. *ERE* v. 478)

'I have not been grasping.' (Ancient Egyptian. Ibid.)

'Who meditates oppression, his dwelling is overturned.' (Babylonian. *Hymn to Samas. ERE* v. 445)

'He who is cruel and calumnious has the character of a cat.' (Hindu. Laws of Manu. Janet, *Histoire de la Science Politique*, vol. i, p. 6)

'Slander not.' (Babylonian. *Hymn to Samas.* ERE v. 445)

'Thou shalt not bear false witness against thy neighbour.' (Ancient Jewish. Exodus 20:16)

'Utter not a word by which anyone could be wounded.' (Hindu. Janet, p. 7)

'Has he . . . driven an honest man from his family? broken up a well cemented clan?' (Babylonian. List of Sins from incantation tablets. *ERE* v. 446)

'I have not caused hunger. I have not caused weeping.' (Ancient Egyptian. *ERE* v. 478)

'Never do to others what you would not like them to do to you.' (Ancient Chinese. *Analects of Confucius*, trans. A. Waley, xv. 23; cf. xii. 2)

'Thou shalt not hate thy brother in thy heart.' (Ancient Jewish. Leviticus 19:17)

'He whose heart is in the smallest degree set upon goodness will dislike no one.' (Ancient Chinese. *Analects*, iv. 4)

(b) Positive

'Nature urges that a man should wish human society to exist and should wish to enter it.' (Roman. Cicero, *De Officiis*, I. iv)

'By the fundamental Law of Nature Man [is] to be preserved as much as possible.' (Locke, *Treatises of Civil Govt.* ii. 3)

'When the people have multiplied, what next should be done for them? The Master said, Enrich them. Jan Ch'iu said, When one has enriched them, what next should be done for them? The Master said, Instruct them.' (Ancient Chinese. *Analects*, xiii. 9)

'Speak kindness . . . show good will.' (Babylonian. *Hymn to Samas. ERE* v. 445)

'Men were brought into existence for the sake of men that they might do one another good.' (Roman. Cicero. *De Off.* i. vii)

'Man is man's delight.' (Old Norse. *Hávamál* 47)

'He who is asked for alms should always give.' (Hindu. Janet, i. 7)

'What good man regards any misfortune as no concern of his?' (Roman. Juvenal xv. 140)

'I am a man: nothing human is alien to me.' (Roman. Terence, *Heaut. Tim.*)

'Love thy neighbour as thyself.' (Ancient Jewish. Leviticus 19:18)

'Love the stranger as thyself.' (Ancient Jewish. Ibid. 33, 34)

'Do to men what you wish men to do to you.' (Christian. Matthew 7:12)

2. THE LAW OF SPECIAL BENEFICENCE

'It is upon the trunk that a gentleman works. When that is firmly set up, the Way grows. And surely proper behaviour to parents and elder brothers is the trunk of goodness.' (Ancient Chinese. *Analects*, i. 2)

'Brothers shall fight and be each others' bane.' (Old Norse. Account of the Evil Age before the World's end, *Volospá* 45)

'Has he insulted his elder sister?' (Babylonian. List of Sins. *ERE* v. 446)

'You will see them take care of their kindred [and] the children of their friends . . . never reproaching them in the least.' (Redskin. Le Jeune, quoted *ERE* v. 437)

'Love thy wife studiously. Gladden her heart all thy life long.' (Ancient Egyptian. *ERE* v. 481)

'Nothing can ever change the claims of kinship for a right thinking man.' (Anglo-Saxon. *Beowulf*, 2600)

'Did not Socrates love his own children, though he did so as a free man and as one not forgetting that the gods have the first claim on our friendship?' (Greek, Epictetus, iii. 24)

'Natural affection is a thing right and according to Nature.' (Greek. Ibid. 1. xi)

'I ought not to be unfeeling like a statue but should fulfil both my natural and artificial relations, as a worshipper, a son, a brother, a father, and a citizen.' (Greek. Ibid. III. ii)

'This first I rede thee: be blameless to thy kindred. Take no vengeance even though they do thee wrong.' (Old Norse. *Sigdrifumál*, 22)

'Is it only the sons of Atreus who love their wives? For every good man, who is right-minded, loves and cherishes his own.' (Greek. Homer, *Iliad*, ix. 340)

'The union and fellowship of men will be best preserved if each receives from us the more kindness in proportion as he is more closely connected with us.' (Roman. Cicero. *De Off.* 1. xvi)

'Part of us is claimed by our country, part by our parents, part by our friends.' (Roman. Ibid. 1. vii)

'If a ruler . . . compassed the salvation of the whole state, surely you would call him Good? The Master said, It would no longer be a matter of "Good". He would without doubt be a Divine Sage.' (Ancient Chinese. *Analects*, vi. 28)

'Has it escaped you that, in the eyes of gods and good men, your native land deserves from you more honour, worship, and reverence than your mother and father and all your ancestors? That you should give a softer answer to its anger than to a father's anger? That if you cannot persuade it to alter its mind you must obey it in all quietness, whether it binds you or beats you or sends you to a war where you may get wounds or death?' (Greek. Plato, *Crito*, 51, a, b)

'If any provide not for his own, and specially for those of his own house, he hath denied the faith.' (Christian. 1 Timothy 5:8)

'Put them in mind to obey magistrates.' . . . 'I exhort that prayers be made for kings and all that are in authority.' (Christian. Titus 3:1 and 1 Timothy 2:1, 2)

3. DUTIES TO PARENTS, ELDERS, ANCESTORS

'Your father is an image of the Lord of Creation, your mother an image of the Earth. For him who fails to honour them, every work of piety is in vain. This is the first duty.' (Hindu. Janet, i. 9)

'Has he despised Father and Mother?' (Babylonian. List of Sins. *ERE* v. 446)

'I was a staff by my Father's side . . . I went in and out at his command.' (Ancient Egyptian. Confession of the Righteous Soul. *ERE* v. 481)

'Honour thy Father and thy Mother.' (Ancient Jewish. Exodus 20:12)

'To care for parents.' (Greek. List of duties in Epictetus, III. vii)

'Children, old men, the poor, and the sick, should be considered as the lords of the atmosphere.' (Hindu. Janet, i. 8)

'Rise up before the hoary head and honour the old man.' (Ancient Jewish. Leviticus 19:32)

'I tended the old man, I gave him my staff.' (Ancient Egyptian. *ERE* v. 481)

'You will see them take care . . . of old men.' (Redskin. Le Jeune, quoted *ERE* v. 437)

'I have not taken away the oblations of the blessed dead.' (Ancient Egyptian. Confession of the Righteous Soul. *ERE* v. 478)

'When proper respect towards the dead is shown at the end and continued after they are far away, the moral force *(tê)* of a people has reached its highest point.' (Ancient Chinese. *Analects*, i. 9)

4. DUTIES TO CHILDREN AND POSTERITY

'Children, the old, the poor, etc. should be considered as lords of the atmosphere.' (Hindu. Janet, i. 8)

'To marry and to beget children.' (Greek. List of duties. Epictetus, III. vii)

'Can you conceive an Epicurean commonwealth? . . . What will happen? Whence is the population to be kept up? Who will educate them? Who will be Director of Adolescents? Who will be Director of Physical Training? What will be taught?' (Greek. Ibid.)

'Nature produces a special love of offspring' and 'To live according to Nature is the supreme good.' (Roman. Cicero, *De Off.* 1. iv, and *De Legibus,* 1. xxi)

'The second of these achievements is no less glorious than the first; for while the first did good on one occasion, the second will continue to benefit the state for ever.' (Roman. Cicero. *De Off.* 1. xxii)

'Great reverence is owed to a child.' (Roman. Juvenal, xiv. 47)

'The Master said, Respect the young.' (Ancient Chinese. *Analects,* ix. 22)

'The killing of the women and more especially of the young boys and girls who are to go to make up the future strength of the people, is the saddest part . . . and we feel it very sorely.' (Redskin. Account of the Battle of Wounded Knee. *ERE* v. 432)

5. THE LAW OF JUSTICE

(a) Sexual Justice

'Has he approached his neighbour's wife?' (Babylonian. List of Sins. *ERE* v. 446)

'Thou shalt not commit adultery.' (Ancient Jewish. Exodus 20:14)

'I saw in Nástrond (= Hell) . . . beguilers of others' wives.' (Old Norse. *Volospá* 38, 39)

(b) Honesty

'Has he drawn false boundaries?' (Babylonian. List of Sins. *ERE* v. 446)

'To wrong, to rob, to cause to be robbed.' (Babylonian. Ibid.)

'I have not stolen.' (Ancient Egyptian. Confession of the Righteous Soul. *ERE* v. 478)

'Thou shalt not steal.' (Ancient Jewish. Exodus 20:15)

'Choose loss rather than shameful gains.' (Greek. Chilon Fr. 10. Diels)

'Justice is the settled and permanent intention of rendering to each man his rights.' (Roman. Justinian, *Institutions,* 1. i)

'If the native made a "find" of any kind (e.g., a honey tree) and marked it, it was thereafter safe for him, as far as his own tribesmen were concerned, no matter how long he left it.' (Australian Aborigines. *ERE* v. 441)

'The first point of justice is that none should do any mischief to another unless he has first been attacked by the other's wrongdoing. The second is that a man should treat common property as common property, and private property as his own. There is no such thing as private property by nature, but things have become private either through prior occupation (as when men of old came into empty territory) or by conquest, or law, or agreement, or stipulation, or casting lots.' (Roman. Cicero, *De Off.* 1. vii)

(c) Justice in Court, &c.

'Whoso takes no bribe . . . well pleasing is this to Samas.' (Babylonian. *ERE* v. 445)

'I have not traduced the slave to him who is set over him.' (Ancient Egyptian. Confession of the Righteous Soul. *ERE* v. 478)

'Thou shalt not bear false witness against thy neighbour.' (Ancient Jewish. Exodus 20:16)

'Regard him whom thou knowest like him whom thou knowest not.' (Ancient Egyptian. *ERE* v. 482)

'Do no unrighteousness in judgement. You must not consider the fact that one party is poor nor the fact that the other is a great man.' (Ancient Jewish. Leviticus 19:15)

6. THE LAW OF GOOD FAITH AND VERACITY

'A sacrifice is obliterated by a lie and the merit of alms by an act of fraud.' (Hindu. Janet, i. 6)

'Whose mouth, full of lying, avails not before thee: thou burnest their utterance.' (Babylonian. *Hymn to Samas. ERE* v. 445)

'With his mouth was he full of *Yea*, in his heart full of *Nay*?' (Babylonian. *ERE* v. 446)

'I have not spoken falsehood.' (Ancient Egyptian. Confession of the Righteous Soul. *ERE* v. 478)

'I sought no trickery, nor swore false oaths.' (Anglo-Saxon. *Beowulf*, 2738)

'The Master said, Be of unwavering good faith.' (Ancient Chinese. *Analects*, viii. 13)

'In Nástrond (= Hell) I saw the perjurers.' (Old Norse. *Volospá* 39)

'Hateful to me as are the gates of Hades is that man who says one thing, and hides another in his heart.' (Greek. Homer. *Iliad*, ix. 312)

'The foundation of justice is good faith.' (Roman. Cicero, *De Off.* i. vii)

'[The gentleman] must learn to be faithful to his superiors and to keep promises.' (Ancient Chinese. *Analects*, i. 8)

'Anything is better than treachery.' (Old Norse. *Hávamál* 124)

7. THE LAW OF MERCY

'The poor and the sick should be regarded as lords of the atmosphere.' (Hindu. Janet, i. 8)

'Whoso makes intercession for the weak, well pleasing is this to Samas.' (Babylonian. *ERE* v. 445)

'Has he failed to set a prisoner free?' (Babylonian. List of Sins. *ERE* v. 446)

'I have given bread to the hungry, water to the thirsty, clothes to the naked, a ferry boat to the boatless.' (Ancient Egyptian. *ERE* v. 446)

'One should never strike a woman; not even with a flower.' (Hindu. Janet, i. 8)

'There, Thor, you got disgrace, when you beat women.' (Old Norse. *Hárbarthsljóth* 38)

'In the Dalebura tribe a woman, a cripple from birth, was carried about by the tribespeople in turn until her death at the age of sixty-six.' . . . 'They never desert the sick.' (Australian Aborigines. *ERE* v. 443)

'You will see them take care of . . . widows, orphans, and old men, never reproaching them.' (Redskin. *ERE* v. 439)

'Nature confesses that she has given to the human race the tenderest hearts, by giving us the power to weep. This is the best part of us.' (Roman. Juvenal, xv. 131)

'They said that he had been the mildest and gentlest of the kings of the world.' (Anglo-Saxon. Praise of the hero in *Beowulf*, 3180)

'When thou cuttest down thine harvest . . . and hast forgot a sheaf . . . thou shalt not go again to fetch it: it shall be for the stranger, for the fatherless, and for the widow.' (Ancient Jewish. Deuteronomy 24:19)

8. THE LAW OF MAGNANIMITY

(a)

'There are two kinds of injustice: the first is found in those who do an injury, the second in those who fail to protect another from injury when they can.' (Roman. Cicero, *De Off.* 1. vii)

'Men always knew that when force and injury was offered they might be defenders of themselves; they knew that howsoever men may seek their own commodity, yet if this were done with injury unto others it was not to be suffered, but by all men and by all good means to be withstood.' (English. Hooker, *Laws of Eccl. Polity*, 1. ix. 4)

'To take no notice of a violent attack is to strengthen the heart of the enemy. Vigour is valiant, but cowardice is vile.' (Ancient Egyptian. The Pharaoh Senusert III, cit. H. R. Hall, *Ancient History of the Near East*, p. 161)

'They came to the fields of joy, the fresh turf of the Fortunate Woods and the dwellings of the Blessed . . . here was the company of those who had suffered wounds fighting for their fatherland.' (Roman. Virgil, *Aeneid*, vi. 638–9, 660)

'Courage has got to be harder, heart the stouter, spirit the sterner, as our strength weakens. Here lies our lord, cut to pieces, out best man in the dust. If anyone thinks of leaving this battle, he can howl forever.' (Anglo-Saxon. *Maldon*, 312)

'Praise and imitate that man to whom, while life is pleasing, death is not grievous.' (Stoic. Seneca, *Ep.* liv)

'The Master said, Love learning and if attacked be ready to die for the Good Way.' (Ancient Chinese. *Analects*, viii. 13)

(b)

'Death is to be chosen before slavery and base deeds.' (Roman. Cicero, *De Off.* 1, xxiii)

'Death is better for every man than life with shame.' (Anglo-Saxon. *Beowulf*, 2890)

'Nature and Reason command that nothing uncomely, nothing effeminate, nothing lascivious be done or thought.' (Roman. Cicero, *De Off.* 1. iv)

'We must not listen to those who advise us "being men to think human thoughts, and being mortal to think mortal thoughts," but must put on immortality as much as is possible and strain every nerve to live according to that best part of us, which, being small in bulk, yet much more in its power and honour surpasses all else.' (Ancient Greek. Aristotle, *Eth. Nic.* 1177 B)

'The soul then ought to conduct the body, and the spirit of our minds the soul. This is therefore the first Law, whereby the highest power of the mind requireth obedience at the hands of all the rest.' (Hooker, op. cit. I. viii. 6)

'Let him not desire to die, let him not desire to live, let him wait for his time . . . let him patiently bear hard words, entirely abstaining from bodily pleasures.' (Ancient Indian. Laws of Manu. *ERE* ii. 98)

'He who is unmoved, who has restrained his senses . . . is said to be devoted. As a flame in a windless place that flickers not, so is the devoted.' (Ancient Indian. *Bhagavad gita. ERE* ii 90)

(c)

'Is not the love of Wisdom a practice of death?' (Ancient Greek. Plato, *Phadeo,* 81 A)

'I know that I hung on the gallows for nine nights, wounded with the spear as a sacrifice to Odin, myself offered to Myself.' (Old Norse. *Hávamál,* 1. 10 in *Corpus Poeticum Boreale;* stanza 139 in Hildebrand's *Lieder der Älteren Edda.* 1922)

'Verily, verily I say to you unless a grain of wheat falls into the earth and dies, it remains alone, but if it dies it bears much fruit. He who loves his life loses it.' (Christian. John 12:24, 25)

THE FOUR LOVES

To Chad Walsh

THE FOUR LOVES
CONTENTS

I

INTRODUCTION

"GOD IS LOVE," says St John. When I first tried to write this book I thought that his maxim would provide me with a very plain highroad through the whole subject. I thought I should be able to say that human loves deserved to be called loves at all just in so far as they resembled that Love which is God. The first distinction I made was therefore between what I called Gift-love and Need-love. The typical example of Gift-love would be that love which moves a man to work and plan and save for the future well-being of his family which he will die without sharing or seeing; of the second, that which sends a lonely or frightened child to its mother's arms.

There was no doubt which was more like Love Himself. Divine Love is Gift-love. The Father gives all He is and has to the Son. The Son gives Himself back to the Father, and gives Himself to the world, and for the world to the Father, and thus gives the world (in Himself) back to the Father too.

And what, on the other hand, can be less like anything we believe of God's life than Need-love? He lacks nothing, but our Need-love, as Plato saw, is "the son of Poverty". It is the accurate reflection in consciousness of our actual nature. We are born helpless. As soon as we are fully conscious we discover loneliness. We need others physically, emotionally, intellectually; we need them if we are to know anything, even ourselves. I was looking forward to writing some fairly easy panegyrics on the first sort of love and disparagements of the second. And much of what I was going to say still seems to me to be true. I still think that if all we mean by our love is a craving to be loved, we are in a very deplorable state. But I would not now say (with my master, MacDonald) that if we mean only this craving we are mistaking for love something that is not love at all. I cannot now deny the name love to Need-love. Every time I have tried to think the thing out along those lines I have ended in puzzles and contradictions. The reality is more complicated than I supposed.

First of all, we do violence to most languages, including our own, if we do not call Need-love "love". Of course language is not an infallible guide, but it contains, with all its defects, a good deal of stored insight and experience. If you begin by flouting it, it has a way of avenging itself later on. We had better not follow Humpty Dumpty in making words mean whatever we please.

Secondly, we must be cautious about calling Need-love "mere selfishness". *Mere* is always a dangerous word. No doubt Need-love, like all our impulses, can be selfishly indulged. A tyrannous and gluttonous demand for affection can be a horrible thing. But in ordinary life no one calls a child selfish because it turns for comfort to its mother; nor an adult who turns to his fellow "for company". Those, whether children or adults, who do so least are not usually the most selfless. Where Need-love is felt there may be reasons for denying or totally mortifying it; but not to feel it is in general the mark of the cold egoist. Since we do in reality need one another ("it is not good for man to be alone"), then the failure of this need to appear as Need-love in consciousness—in other words, the illusory feeling that it *is* good for us to be alone—is a bad spiritual symptom; just as lack of appetite is a bad medical symptom because men do really need food.

But thirdly, we come to something far more important. Every Christian would agree that a man's spiritual health is exactly proportional to his love for God. But man's love for God, from the very nature of the case, must always be very largely, and must often be entirely, a Need-love. This is obvious when we implore forgiveness for our sins or support in our tribulations. But in the long run it is perhaps even more apparent in our growing—for it ought to be growing—awareness that our whole being by its very nature is one vast need; incomplete, preparatory, empty yet cluttered, crying out for Him who can untie things that are now knotted together and tie up things that are still dangling loose. I do not say that man can never bring to God anything at all but sheer Need-love. Exalted souls may tell us of a reach beyond that. But they would also,

I think, be the first to tell us that those heights would cease to be true Graces, would become Neo-Platonic or finally diabolical illusions, the moment a man dared to think that he could live on them and henceforth drop out the element of need. "The highest," says the *Imitation*, "does not stand without the lowest." It would be a bold and silly creature that came before its Creator with the boast "I'm no beggar. I love you disinterestedly." Those who come nearest to a Gift-love for God will next moment, even at the very same moment, be beating their breasts with the publican and laying their indigence before the only real Giver. And God will have it so. He addresses our Need-love: "Come unto me all ye that travail and are heavy-laden," or, in the Old Testament, "Open your mouth wide and I will fill it." Thus one Need-love, the greatest of all, either coincides with or at least makes a main ingredient in man's highest, healthiest, and most realistic spiritual condition. A very strange corollary follows. Man approaches God most nearly when he is in one sense least like God. For what can be more unlike than fullness and need, sovereignty and humility, righteousness and penitence, limitless power and a cry for help? This paradox staggered me when I first ran into it; it also wrecked all my previous attempts to write about love. When we face it, something like this seems to result.

We must distinguish two things which might both possibly be called "nearness to God". One is likeness to God. God has impressed some sort of likeness to Himself, I suppose, in all that He has made. Space and time, in their own fashion, mirror His greatness; all life, His fecundity; animal life, His activity. Man has a more important likeness than these by being rational. Angels, we believe, have likenesses which Man lacks: immortality and intuitive knowledge. In that way all men, whether good or bad, all angels including those that fell, are more like God than the animals are. Their natures are in this sense "nearer" to the Divine Nature. But, secondly, there is what we may call nearness of approach. If this is what we mean, the states in which a man is "nearest" to God are those in which he is most surely and swiftly approaching his final union with God, vision of God, and enjoyment of God. And as soon as we distinguish nearness-by-likeness and nearness-of-approach, we see that they do not necessarily coincide. They may or may not.

Perhaps an analogy may help. Let us suppose that we are doing a mountain walk to the village which is our home. At mid-day we come to the top of a cliff where we are, in space, very near it because it is just below us. We could drop a stone into it. But as we are no cragsmen we can't get down. We must go a long way round; five miles, maybe. At many points during that *détour* we shall, statically, be far further from the village than we were when we sat above the cliff. But only statically. In terms of progress we shall be far "nearer" our baths and teas.

Since God is blessed, omnipotent, sovereign, and creative, there is obviously a sense in which happiness, strength, freedom, and fertility (whether of mind or body), wherever they appear in human life, constitute likenesses, and in that way proximities, to God. But no one supposes that the possession of these gifts has any necessary connection with our sanctification. No kind of riches is a passport to the Kingdom of Heaven.

At the cliff's top we are near the village, but however long we sit there we shall never be any nearer to our bath and our tea. So here the likeness, and in that sense nearness, to Himself which God has conferred upon certain creatures and certain states of those creatures is something finished, built in. What is near Him by likeness is never, by that fact alone, going to be any nearer. But nearness of approach is, by definition, increasing nearness. And whereas the likeness is given to us—and can be received with or without thanks, can be used or abused—the approach, however initiated and supported by Grace, is something we must do. Creatures are made in their varying ways images of God without their own collaboration or even consent. It is not so that they become sons of God. And the likeness they receive by sonship is not that of images or portraits. It is in one way more than likeness, for it is unison or unity with God in will; but this is consistent with all the differences we have been considering. Hence, as a better writer has said, our imitation of God in this life—that is, our willed imitation as distinct from any of the likenesses which He has impressed upon our natures or states—must be an imitation of God incarnate: our model is the Jesus, not only of Calvary, but of the workshop, the roads, the crowds, the clamorous demands and surly oppositions, the lack of all peace and privacy, the interruptions. For this, so strangely unlike anything we can attribute to the Divine life in itself, is apparently not only like, but is, the Divine life operating under human conditions.

I must now explain why I have found this distinction necessary to any treatment of our loves. St John's saying that God is love has long been balanced in my mind against the remark of a modern author (M. Denis de Rougemont) that "love ceases to be a demon only when he ceases to be a god"; which of course can be re-stated in the form "begins to be a demon the moment he begins to be a god". This balance seems to me an indispensable safeguard. If we ignore it the truth that God is love may slyly come to mean for us the converse, that love is God.

I suppose that everyone who has thought about the matter will see what M. de Rougemont meant. Every human love, at its height, has a tendency to claim for itself a divine authority. Its voice tends to sound as if it were the will of God Himself. It tells us not to count the cost, it demands of us a total commitment, it attempts to over-ride all other claims and insinuates that any action which is sincerely done "for love's sake" is thereby lawful and even meritorious. That erotic love and love of one's country may thus attempt to "become gods" is generally recognised. But family affection may do the same. So, in a different way, may friendship. I shall not here elaborate the point, for it will meet us again and again in later chapters. Now it must be noticed that the natural loves make this blasphemous claim not when they are in their worst, but when they are in their best, natural condition; when they are what our grandfathers called "pure" or "noble". This is especially obvious in the erotic sphere. A faithful and genuinely self-sacrificing passion will speak to us with what seems the voice of God. Merely animal or frivolous lust will not. It will corrupt its addict in a dozen ways, but not in that way; a man may act upon such feelings but he cannot revere them any more than a man who scratches reveres the itch. A silly woman's temporary indulgence, which is really self-indulgence, to a spoiled child—her living doll while the fit lasts—is much less likely to "become a god" than the deep, narrow devotion of a woman who (quite really) "lives for her son". And I am inclined to think that the sort of love for a man's country which is worked up by beer and brass bands will not lead him to do much harm (or much good) for her sake. It will probably be fully discharged by ordering another drink and joining in the chorus.

And this of course is what we ought to expect. Our loves do not make their claim to divinity until the claim becomes plausible. It does not become plausible until there is in them a real resemblance to God, to Love Himself. Let us here make no mistake. Our Gift-loves are really God-like; and among our Gift-loves those are most God-like which are most boundless and unwearied in giving. All the things the poets say about them are true. Their joy, their energy, their patience, their readiness to forgive, their desire for the good of the beloved—all this is a real and all but adorable image of the Divine life. In its presence we are right to thank

God "who has given such power to men". We may say, quite truly and in an intelligible sense, that those who love greatly are "near" to God. But of course it is "nearness by likeness". It will not of itself produce "nearness of approach". The likeness has been given us. It has no necessary connection with that slow and painful approach which must be our own (though by no means our unaided) task. Meanwhile, however, the likeness is a splendour. That is why we may mistake Like for Same. We may give our human loves the unconditional allegiance which we owe only to God. Then they become gods: then they become demons. Then they will destroy us, and also destroy themselves. For natural loves that are allowed to become gods do not remain loves. They are still called so, but can become in fact complicated forms of hatred.

Our Need-loves may be greedy and exacting but they do not set up to be gods. They are not near enough (by likeness) to God to attempt that.

It follows from what has been said that we must join neither the idolaters nor the "debunkers" of human love. Idolatry both of erotic love and of "the domestic affections" was the great error of nineteenth-century literature. Browning, Kingsley, and Patmore sometimes talk as if they thought that falling in love was the same thing as sanctification; the novelists habitually oppose to "the World" not the Kingdom of Heaven but the home. We live in the reaction against this. The debunkers stigmatise as slush and sentimentality a very great deal of what their fathers said in praise of love. They are always pulling up and exposing the grubby roots of our natural loves. But I take it we must listen neither "to the over-wise nor to the over-foolish giant". The highest does not stand without the lowest. A plant must have roots below as well as sunlight above and roots must be grubby. Much of the grubbiness is clean dirt if only you will leave it in the garden and not keep on sprinkling it over the library table. The human loves can be glorious images of Divine love. No less than that: but also no more—proximities of likeness which in one instance may help, and in another may hinder, proximity of approach. Sometimes perhaps they have not very much to do with it either way.

II

LIKINGS AND LOVES FOR
THE SUB-HUMAN

MOST OF MY generation were reproved as children for saying that we "loved" strawberries, and some people take a pride in the fact that English has the two verbs *love* and *like* while French has to get on with *aimer* for both. But French has a good many other languages on its side. Indeed it very often has actual English usage on its side too. Nearly all speakers, however pedantic or however pious, talk every day about "loving" a food, a game, or a pursuit. And in fact there is a continuity between our elementary likings for things and our loves for people. Since "the highest does not stand without the lowest" we had better begin at the bottom, with mere likings; and since to "like" anything means to take some sort of pleasure in it, we must begin with pleasure.

Now it is a very old discovery that pleasures can be divided into two classes; those which would not be pleasures at all unless they were preceded by desire, and those which are pleasures in their own right and need no such preparation. An example of the first would be a drink of water. This is a pleasure if you are thirsty and a great one if you are very thirsty. But probably no one in the world, except in obedience to thirst or to a doctor's orders, ever poured himself out a glass of water and drank it just for the fun of the thing. An example of the other class would be the unsought and unexpected pleasures of smell—the breath from a bean-field or a row of sweet-peas meeting you on your morning walk. You were in want of nothing, completely contented, before it; the pleasure, which may be very great, is an unsolicited, super-added gift. I am taking very simple instances for clarity's sake, and of course there are many complications. If you are given coffee or beer where you expected (and would have been satisfied with) water, then of course you get a pleasure of the first kind (allaying of thirst) and one of the second (a nice taste) at the same time. Again, an addiction may turn what was once a pleasure of the second kind into one of the first. For the temperate man an occasional glass of wine is a treat—like the smell of the bean-field. But to the alcoholic, whose palate and digestion have long since been destroyed, no liquor gives any pleasure except that of relief from an unbearable craving. So far as he can still discern tastes at all, he rather dislikes it; but it is better than the misery of remaining sober. Yet through all their permutations and combinations the distinction between the two classes remains tolerably clear. We may call them Need-pleasures and Pleasures of Appreciation.

The resemblance between these Need-pleasures and the "Need-loves" in my first chapter will occur to everyone. But there, you remember, I confessed that I had had to resist a tendency to disparage the Need-loves or even to say they were not loves at all. Here, for most people, there may be an opposite inclination. It would be very easy to spread ourselves in laudation of the Need-pleasures and to frown upon those that are Appreciatives: the one so natural (a word to conjure with), so necessary, so shielded from excess by their very naturalness, the other unnecessary and opening the door to every kind of luxury and vice. If we were short of matter on this theme we could turn on the tap by opening the works of the Stoics and it would run till we had a bathful. But throughout this inquiry we must be careful never to adopt prematurely a moral or evaluating attitude. The human mind is generally far more eager to praise and dispraise than to describe and define. It wants to make every distinction a distinction of value; hence those fatal critics who can never point out the differing quality of two poets without putting them in an order of preference as if they were candidates for a prize. We must do nothing of the sort about the pleasures. The reality is too complicated. We are already warned of this by the fact that Need-pleasure is the state in which Appreciative pleasures end up when they go bad (by addiction).

For us at any rate the importance of the two sorts of pleasure lies in the extent to which they foreshadow characteristics in our "loves" (properly so called).

The thirsty man who has just drunk off a tumbler of water may say, "By Jove, I *wanted* that." So may the alcoholic who has just had his "nip". The man who passes the sweet-peas in his morning walk is more likely to say, "How lovely the smell *is*." The connoisseur after his first sip of the famous claret, may similarly say, "This *is* a great wine." When Need-pleasures are in question we tend to make statements about ourselves in the past tense; when Appreciative pleasures are in question we tend to make statements about the object in the present tense. It is easy to see why.

Shakespeare has described the satisfaction of a tyrannous lust as something

> Past reason hunted and, no sooner had,
> Past reason hated.

But the most innocent and necessary of Need-pleasures have about them something of the same character—only something, of course. They are not hated once we have had them, but they certainly "die on us" with extraordinary abruptness, and completely. The scullery tap and the tumbler are very attractive indeed when we come in parched from mowing the grass; six seconds later they are emptied of all interest. The smell of frying food is very different before and after breakfast. And, if you will forgive me for citing the most extreme instance of all, have there not for most of us been moments (in a strange town) when the sight of the word GENTLEMEN over a door has roused a joy almost worthy of celebration in verse?

Pleasures of Appreciation are very different. They make us feel that something has not merely gratified our senses in fact but claimed our appreciation by right. The connoisseur does not merely enjoy his claret as he might enjoy warming his feet when they were cold. He feels that here is a wine that deserves his full attention; that justifies all the tradition and skill that have gone to its making and all the years of training that have made his own palate fit to judge it. There is even a glimmering of unselfishness in his attitude. He wants the wine to be preserved and kept in good condition, not entirely for his own sake. Even if he were on his deathbed and was never going to drink wine again, he would be horrified at the thought of this vintage being spilled or spoiled or even drunk by clods (like myself) who can't tell a good claret from a bad. And so with the man who passes the sweet-peas. He does not simply enjoy, he feels that this fragrance somehow deserves to be enjoyed. He would blame himself if he went past inattentive and undelighted. It would be blockish, insensitive. It would be a shame that so fine a thing should have been wasted on him. He will remember the delicious moment years hence. He will be sorry when he hears that the garden past which his walk led him that day has now been swallowed up by cinemas, garages, and the new by-pass.

Scientifically both sorts of pleasure are, no doubt, relative to our organisms. But the Need-pleasures loudly proclaim their relativity not only to the human frame but to its momentary condition, and outside that relation have no meaning or interest for us at all. The objects which afford pleasures of appreciation give us the feeling—whether irrational or not—that we somehow owe it to them to savour, to attend to and praise it. "It would be a sin to set a wine like that before Lewis," says the expert in claret. "How can you walk past this garden taking no notice of the smell?" we ask. But we should never feel this about a Need-pleasure: never blame ourselves or others for not having been thirsty and therefore walking past a well without taking a drink of water.

How the Need-pleasures foreshadow our Need-loves is obvious enough. In the latter the beloved is seen in relation to our own needs, just as the scullery tap is seen by the thirsty man or the glass of gin by the alcoholic. And the Need-love, like the Need-pleasure, will not last longer than the need. This does not, fortunately, mean that all affections which begin in Need-love are transitory. The need itself may be permanent or recurrent. Another kind of love may be grafted on the Need-love. Moral principles (conjugal fidelity, filial piety, gratitude, and the like) may preserve the relationship for a lifetime. But where Need-love is left unaided we can hardly expect it not to "die on us" once the need is no more. That is why the world rings with the complaints of mothers whose grown-up children neglect them and of forsaken mistresses whose lovers' love was pure need—which they have satisfied. Our Need-love for God is in a different position because our need of Him can never end either in this world or in any other. But our awareness of it can, and then the Need-love dies too. "The Devil was sick, the Devil a monk would be." There seems no reason for describing as hypocritical the short-lived piety of those whose religion fades away once they have emerged from "danger, necessity, or tribulation". Why should they not have been sincere? They were desperate and they howled for help. Who wouldn't?

What Appreciative pleasure foreshadows is not so quickly described.

First of all, it is the starting point for our whole experience of beauty. It is impossible to draw a line below which such pleasures are "sensual" and above which they are "aesthetic". The experiences of the expert in claret already contain elements of concentration, judgment, and disciplined perceptiveness, which are not sensual; those of the musician still contain elements which are. There is no frontier—there is seamless continuity—between the sensuous pleasure of garden smells and an enjoyment of the countryside (or "beauty") as a whole, or even our enjoyment of the painters and poets who treat it.

And, as we have seen, there is in these pleasures from the very beginning a shadow or dawn of, or an invitation to, disinterestedness. Of course in one way we can be disinterested or unselfish, and far more heroically so, about the Need-pleasures: it is a cup of water that the wounded Sidney sacrifices to the dying soldier. But that is not the sort of disinterestedness I now mean. Sidney loves his neighbour. But in the Appreciative pleasures, even at their lowest, and more and more as they grow up into the full appreciation of all beauty, we get something that we can hardly help calling *love* and hardly help calling *disinterested,* towards the object itself. It is the feeling which would make a man unwilling to deface a great picture even if he were the last man left alive and himself about to die; which makes us glad of unspoiled forests that we shall never see; which makes us anxious that the garden or bean-field should continue to exist. We do not merely like the things; we pronounce them, in a momentarily God-like sense, "very good."

And now our principle of starting at the lowest—without which "the highest does not stand"—begins to pay a dividend. It has revealed to me a deficiency in our previous classification of the loves into those of Need and those of Gift. There is a third element in love, no less important than these, which is foreshadowed by our appreciative pleasures. This judgment that the object is very good, this attention (almost homage) offered to it as a kind of debt, this wish that it should be and should continue being what it is even if we were never to enjoy it, can go out not only to things but to persons. When it is offered to a woman we call it admiration; when to a man, hero-worship; when to God, worship simply.

Need-love cries to God from our poverty; Gift-love longs to serve, or even to suffer for, God; Appreciative love says: "We give thanks to thee for thy great glory." Need-love says of a woman "I cannot live without her"; Gift-love longs to give her happiness, comfort, protection—if possible, wealth; Appreciative love gazes and holds its breath and is silent, rejoices that such a wonder should exist even if not for him, will not be wholly dejected by losing her, would rather have it so than never to have seen her at all.

We murder to dissect. In actual life, thank God, the three elements of love mix and succeed on another, moment by moment. Perhaps none of them except Need-love ever exists alone, in "chemical" purity, for more than a few seconds. And perhaps that is because nothing about us except our neediness is, in this life, permanent.

Two forms of love for what is not personal demand special treatment.

For some people, perhaps especially for Englishmen and Russians, what we call "the love of nature" is a permanent and serious sentiment. I mean here that love of nature which cannot be adequately classified simply as an instance of our love for beauty. Of course many natural objects—trees, flowers, and animals—are beautiful. But the nature-lovers whom I have in mind are not very much concerned with individual beautiful objects of that sort. The man who is distracts them. An enthusiastic botanist is for them a dreadful companion on a ramble. He is always stopping to draw their attention to particulars. Nor are they looking for "views" or landscapes. Wordsworth, their spokesman, strongly deprecates this. It leads to "a comparison of scene with scene", makes you "pamper" yourself with "meagre novelties of colour and proportion". While you are busying yourself with this critical and discriminating activity you lose what really matters—the "moods of time and season", the "spirit" of the place. And of course Wordsworth is right. That is why, if you love nature in his fashion, a landscape painter is (out of doors) an even worse companion than a botanist.

It is the "moods" or the "spirit" that matter. Nature-lovers want to receive as fully as possible whatever nature, at each particular time and place, is, so to speak, saying. The obvious richness, grace, and harmony of some scenes are no more precious to them than the grimness, bleakness, terror, monotony, or "visionary dreariness" of others. The featureless itself gets from them a willing response. It is one more word uttered by nature. They lay themselves bare to the sheer quality of every countryside every hour of the day. They want to absorb it into themselves, to be coloured through and through by it.

This experience, like so many others, after being lauded to the skies in the nineteenth century, has been debunked by the moderns. And one must certainly concede to the debunkers that Wordsworth, not when he was communicating it as a poet, but when he was merely talking about it as a philosopher (or philosophaster), said some very silly things. It is silly, unless you have found any evidence, to believe that flowers enjoy the air they breathe, and sillier not to add that, if this were true, flowers would undoubtedly have pains as well as pleasures. Nor have many people been taught moral philosophy by an "impulse from a vernal wood".

If they were, it would not necessarily be the sort of moral philosophy Wordsworth would have approved. It might be that of ruthless competition. For some moderns I think it is. They love nature in so far as, for them, she calls to "the dark gods in the blood"; not although, but because, sex and hunger and sheer power there operate without pity or shame. If you take nature as a teacher she will teach you exactly the lessons you had already decided to learn; this is only another way of saying that nature does not teach. The tendency to take her as a teacher is obviously very easily grafted on to the experience we call "love of nature". But it is only a graft. While we are actually subjected to them, the "moods" and "spirits" of nature point no morals. Overwhelming gaiety, insupportable grandeur, sombre desolation are flung at you. Make what you can of them, if you must make at all. The only imperative that nature utters is, "Look. Listen. Attend."

The fact that this imperative is so often misinterpreted and sets people making theologies and pantheologies and antitheologies—all of which can be debunked—does not really touch the central experience itself. What nature-lovers—whether they are Wordsworthians or people with "dark gods in their blood"—get from nature is an iconography, a language of images. I do not mean simply visual images; it is the "moods" or "spirits" themselves—the powerful expositions of terror, gloom, jocundity, cruelty, lust, innocence, purity—that are the images. In them each man can clothe his own belief. We must learn our theology or philosophy elsewhere (not surprisingly, we often learn them from theologians and philosophers).

But when I speak of "clothing" our belief in such images I do not mean anything like using nature for similes or metaphors in the manner of the poets. Indeed I might have said "filling" or "incarnating" rather than "clothing". Many people—I am one myself—would never, but for what nature does to us, have had any content to put into the words we must use in confessing our faith. Nature never taught me that there exists a God of glory and of infinite majesty. I had to learn that in other ways. But nature gave the word *glory* a meaning for me. I still do not know where else I could have found one. I do not see how the "fear" of God could have ever meant to me anything but the lowest prudential efforts to be safe, if I had never seen certain ominous ravines and unapproachable crags. And if nature had never awakened certain longings in me, huge areas of what I can now mean by the "love" of God would never, so far as I can see, have existed.

Of course the fact that a Christian can so use nature is not even the beginning of a proof that Christianity is true. Those suffering from Dark Gods can equally use her (I suppose) for their creed. That is precisely the point. Nature does not teach. A true philosophy may sometimes validate an experience of nature; an experience of nature cannot validate a philosophy. Nature will not verify any theological or metaphysical proposition (or not in the manner we are now considering); she will help to show what it means.

And not, on the Christian premises, by accident. The created glory may be expected to give us hints of the uncreated; for the one is derived from the other and in some fashion reflects it.

In some fashion. But not perhaps in so direct and simple a fashion as we at first might suppose. For of course all the facts stressed by nature-lovers of the other school are facts too; there are worms in the belly as well as primroses in the wood. Try to reconcile them, or to show that they don't really need reconciliation, and you are turning from direct experience of nature—our present subject—to metaphysics or theodicy or something of that sort. That may be a sensible thing to do; but I think it should be kept distinct from the love of nature. While we are on that level, while we are still claiming to speak of what nature has directly "said" to us, we must stick to it. We have seen an image of glory. We must not try to find a direct path through it and beyond it to an increasing knowledge of God. The path peters out almost at once. Terrors and mysteries, the whole depth of God's counsels and the whole tangle of the history of the universe, choke it. We can't get through; not that way. We must make a *détour*—leave the hills and woods and go back to our studies, to church, to our Bibles, to our knees. Otherwise the love of nature is beginning to turn into a nature religion. And then, even if it does not lead us to the Dark Gods, it will lead us to a great deal of nonsense.

But we need not surrender the love of nature—chastened and limited as I have suggested—to the debunkers. Nature cannot satisfy the desires she arouses nor answer theological questions nor sanctify us. Our real journey to God involves constantly turning our backs on her; passing from the dawn-lit fields into some poky little church, or (it might be) going to work in an East End parish. But the love of her has been a valuable and, for some people, an indispensable initiation.

I need not say "has been". For in fact those who allow no more than this to the love of nature seem to be those who retain it. This is what one should expect. This love, when it sets up as a religion, is beginning to be a god—therefore to be a demon. And demons never keep their promises. Nature "dies" on those who try to live for a love of nature. Coleridge ended by being insensible to her; Wordsworth, by lamenting that the glory had passed away. Say your prayers in a garden early, ignoring steadfastly the dew, the birds, and the flowers, and you will come away overwhelmed by its freshness and joy; go there in order to be overwhelmed and, after a certain age, nine times out of ten nothing will happen to you.

I turn now to the love of one's country. Here there is no need to labour M. de Rougemont's maxim; we all know now that this love becomes a demon when it becomes a god. Some begin to suspect that it is never anything but a demon. But then they have to reject half the high poetry and half the heroic action our race has achieved. We cannot keep even Christ's lament over Jerusalem. He too exhibits love for His country.

Let us limit our field. There is no need here for an essay on international ethics. When this love becomes demoniac it will of course produce wicked acts. But others, more skilled, may say what acts between nations are wicked. We are only considering the sentiment itself in the hope of being able to distinguish its innocent from its demoniac condition. Neither of these is the efficient cause of national behaviour. For strictly speaking it is rulers, not nations, who behave internationally. Demoniac patriotism in their subjects—I write only for subjects—will make it easier for them to act wickedly; healthy patriotism may make it harder: when they are wicked they may by propaganda encourage a demoniac condition of our sentiments in order to secure our acquiescence in their wickedness. If they are good, they could do the opposite. That is one reason why we private persons should keep a wary eye on the health or disease of our own love for our country. And that is what I am writing about.

How ambivalent patriotism is may be gauged by the fact that no two writers have expressed it more vigorously than Kipling and Chesterton. If it were one element two such men could not both have praised it. In reality it contains many ingredients, of which many different blends are possible.

First, there is love of home, of the place we grew up in or the places, perhaps many, which have been our homes; and of all places fairly near these and fairly like them; love of old acquaintances, of familiar sights, sounds, and smells. Note that at its largest this is, for us, a love of England, Wales, Scotland, or Ulster. Only foreigners and politicians talk about "Britain". Kipling's "I do not love my empire's foes" strikes a ludicrously false note. *My* empire! With this love for the place there goes a love for the way of life; for beer and tea and open fires, trains with compartments in them and an unarmed police force and all the rest of it; for the local dialect and (a shade less) for our native language. As Chesterton says, a man's reasons for not wanting his country to be ruled by foreigners are very like his reasons for not wanting his house to be burned down; because he "could not even begin" to enumerate all the things he would miss.

It would be hard to find any legitimate point of view from which this feeling could be condemned. As the family offers us the first step beyond self-love, so this offers us the first step beyond family selfishness. Of course it is not pure charity; it involves love of our neighbours in the local, not of our Neighbour, in the Dominical, sense. But those who do not love the fellow-villagers or fellow-townsmen whom they have seen are not likely to have got very far towards loving "Man" whom they have not. All natural affections, including this, can become rivals to spiritual love: but they can also be preparatory imitations of it, training (so to speak) of the spiritual muscles which Grace may later put to a higher service; as women nurse dolls in childhood and later nurse children. There may come an occasion for renouncing this love; pluck out your right eye. But you need to have an eye first: a creature which had none—which had only got so far as a "photo-sensitive" spot—would be very ill employed in meditation on that severe text.

Of course patriotism of this kind is not in the least aggressive. It asks only to be let alone. It becomes militant only to protect what it loves. In any mind which has a pennyworth of imagination it produces a good attitude towards foreigners. How can I love my home without coming to realise that other men, no less rightly, love theirs? Once you have realised that the Frenchmen like *café complet* just as we like bacon and eggs—why, good luck to them and let them have it. The last thing we want is to make everywhere else just like our own home. It would not be home unless it were different.

The second ingredient is a particular attitude to our country's past. I mean to that past as it lives in popular imagination; the great deeds of our ancestors. Remember Marathon. Remember Waterloo. "We must be free or die who speak the tongue that Shakespeare spoke." This past is felt both to impose an obligation and to hold out an assurance; we must not fall below the standard our fathers set us, and because we are their sons there is good hope we shall not.

This feeling has not quite such good credentials as the sheer love of home. The actual history of every country is full of shabby and even shameful doings. The heroic stories, if taken to be typical, give a false impression of it and are often themselves open to serious historical criticism. Hence a patriotism based on our glorious past is fair game for the debunker. As knowledge increases it may snap and be converted into disillusioned cynicism, or may be maintained by a voluntary shutting of the eyes. But who can condemn what clearly makes many people, at many important moments, behave so much better than they could have done without its help?

I think it is possible to be strengthened by the image of the past without being either deceived or puffed up. The image becomes dangerous in the precise degree to which it is mistaken, or substituted, for serious and systematic historical study. The stories are best when they are handed on and accepted as stories. I do not mean by this that they should be handed on as mere fictions (some of them are after all true). But the emphasis should be on the tale as such, on the picture which fires the imagination, the example that strengthens the will. The schoolboy who hears them should dimly feel—though of course he cannot put it into words—that he is hearing *saga*. Let him be thrilled—preferably "out of school"—by the "Deeds that won the Empire"; but the less we mix this up with his "history lessons" or mistake it for a serious analysis—worse still, a justification—of imperial policy, the better. When I was a child I had a book full of coloured pictures called *Our Island Story*. That title has always seemed to me to strike exactly the right note. The book did not look at all like a text-book either. What does seem to me poisonous, what breeds a type of patriotism that is pernicious if it lasts but not likely to last long in an educated adult, is the perfectly serious indoctrination of the young in knowably false or biased history—the heroic legend drably disguised as text-book fact. With this creeps in the tacit assumption that other nations have not equally their heroes; perhaps even the belief—surely it is very bad biology—that we can literally "inherit" a tradition. And these almost inevitably lead on to a third thing that is sometimes called patriotism.

This third thing is not a sentiment but a belief: a firm, even prosaic belief that our own nation, in sober fact, has long been, and still is markedly superior to all others. I once ventured to say to an old clergyman who was voicing this sort of patriotism, "But, sir, aren't we told that *every* people thinks its own men the bravest and its own women the fairest in the world?" He replied with total gravity—he could not have been graver if he had been saying the Creed at the altar—"Yes, but in England it's true." To be sure, this conviction had not made my friend (God rest his soul) a villain; only an extremely lovable old ass. It can however produce asses that kick and bite. On the lunatic fringe it may shade off into that popular Racialism which Christianity and science equally forbid.

This brings us to the fourth ingredient. If our nation is really so much better than others it may be held to have either the duties or the rights of a superior being towards them. In the nineteenth century the English became very conscious of such duties: the "white man's burden". What we called *natives* were our wards and we their self-appointed guardians. This was not all hypocrisy. We did do them some good. But our habit of talking as if England's motives for acquiring an empire (or any youngster's motives for seeking a job in the Indian Civil Service) had been mainly altruistic nauseated the world. And yet this showed the sense of superiority working at its best. Some nations who have also felt it have stressed the rights not the duties. To them, some foreigners were so bad that one had the right to exterminate them. Others, fitted only to be hewers of wood and drawers of water to the chosen people, had better be made to get on with their hewing and drawing. Dogs, know your betters! I am far from suggesting that the two attitudes are on the same level. But both are fatal. Both demand that the area in which they operate should grow "wider still and wider". And both have about them this sure mark of evil: only by being terrible do they avoid being comic. If there were no broken treaties with Redskins, no extermination of the Tasmanians, no gas-chambers and no Belsen, no Amritsar, Black and Tans or Apartheid, the pomposity of both would be roaring farce.

Finally we reach the stage where patriotism in its demoniac form unconsciously denies itself. Chesterton picked on two lines from Kipling as the perfect example. It was unfair to Kipling, who knew—wonderfully, for so homeless a man—what the love of home can mean. But the lines, in isolation, can be taken to sum up the thing. They run:

If England was what England seems
　'Ow quick we'd drop 'er. But she ain't!

Love never spoke that way. It is like loving your children only "if they're good", your wife only while she keeps her looks, your husband only so long as he is famous and successful. "No man," said one of the Greeks, "loves his city because it is great, but because it is his." A man who really loves his country will love her in her ruin and degeneration—"England, with all thy faults, I love thee still." She will be to him "a poor thing but mine own". He may think her good and great, when she is not, because he loves her; the delusion is up to a point pardonable. But Kipling's soldier reverses it; he loves her because he thinks her good and great—loves her on her merits. She is a fine going concern and it gratifies his pride to be in it. How if she ceased to be such? The answer is plainly given: "'Ow quick we'd drop 'er." When the ship begins to sink he will leave her. Thus that kind of patriotism which sets off with the greatest swagger of drums and banners actually sets off on the road that can lead to Vichy. And this is a phenomenon which will meet us again. When the natural loves become lawless they do not merely do harm to other loves; they themselves cease to be the loves they were—to be loves at all.

Patriotism has then, many faces. Those who would reject it entirely do not seem to have considered what will certainly step—has already begun to step—into its place. For a long time yet, or perhaps forever, nations will live in danger. Rulers must somehow nerve their subjects to defend them or at least to prepare for their defence. Where the sentiment of patriotism has been destroyed this can be done only by presenting every international conflict in a purely ethical light. If people will spend neither sweat nor blood for "their country" they must be made to feel that they are spending them for justice, or civilisation, or humanity. This is a step down, not up. Patriotic sentiment did not of course need to disregard ethics. Good men needed to be convinced that their country's cause was just; but it was still their country's cause, not the cause of justice as such. The difference seems to me important. I may without self-righteousness or hypocrisy think it just to defend my house by force against a burglar; but if I start pretending that I blacked his eye purely on moral grounds—wholly indifferent to the fact that the house in question was mine—I become insufferable. The pretence that when England's cause is just we are on England's side—as some neutral Don Quixote might be—for that reason alone, is equally spurious. And nonsense draws evil after it. If our country's cause is the cause of God, wars must be wars of annihilation. A false transcendence is given to things which are very much of this world.

The glory of the old sentiment was that while it could steel men to the utmost endeavour, it still knew itself to be a sentiment. Wars could be heroic without pretending to be Holy Wars. The hero's death was not confused with the martyr's. And (delightfully) the same sentiment which could be so serious in a rearguard action, could also in peacetime, take itself as lightly as all happy loves often do. It could laugh at itself. Our older patriotic songs cannot be sung without a twinkle in the eye; later ones sound more like hymns. Give me "The British Grenadiers" (*with a tow-row-row-row*) any day rather than "Land of Hope and Glory".

It will be noticed that the sort of love I have been describing, and all its ingredients, can be for something other than a country: for a school, a regiment, a great family, or a class. All the same criticisms will still apply. It can also be felt for bodies that claim more than a natural affection: for a Church or (alas) a party in a Church, or for a religious order. This terrible subject would require a book to itself. Here it will be enough to say that the Heavenly Society is also an earthly society. Our (merely natural) patriotism towards the latter can very easily borrow the transcendent claims of the former and use them to justify the most abominable actions. If ever the book which I am not going to write is written it must be the full confession by Christendom of Christendom's specific contribution to the sum of human cruelty and treachery. Large areas of "the World" will not hear us till we have publicly disowned much of our past. Why should they? We have shouted the name of Christ and enacted the service of Moloch. It may be thought that I should not end this chapter without a word about our love for animals. But that will fit in better in the next. Whether animals are in fact sub-personal or not, they are never loved as if they were. The fact or the illusion of personality is always present, so that love for them is really an instance of that Affection which is the subject of the following chapter.

III

AFFECTION

I BEGIN WITH the humblest and most widely diffused of loves, the love in which our experience seems to differ least from that of the animals. Let me add at once that I do not on that account give it a lower value. Nothing in Man is either worse or better for being shared with the beasts. When we blame a man for being "a mere animal", we mean not that he displays animal characteristics (we all do) but that he displays these, and only these, on occasions where the specifically human was demanded. (When we call him "brutal" we usually mean that he commits cruelties impossible to most real brutes; they're not clever enough.)

The Greeks called this love *storge* (two syllables and the *g* is "hard"). I shall here call it simply Affection. My Greek Lexicon defines *storge* as "affection, especially of parents to offspring"; but also of offspring to parents. And that, I have no doubt, is the original form of the thing as well as the central meaning of the word. The image we must start with is that of a mother nursing a baby, a bitch or a cat with a basketful of puppies or kittens; all in a squeaking, nuzzling heap together; purrings, lickings, baby-talk, milk, warmth, the smell of young life.

The importance of this image is that it presents us at the very outset with a certain paradox. The Need and Need-love of the young is obvious; so is the Gift-love of the mother. She gives birth, gives suck, gives protection. On the other hand, she must give birth or die. She must give suck or suffer. That way, her Affection too is a Need-love. There is the paradox. It is a Need-love but what it needs is to give. It is a Gift-love but it needs to be needed. We shall have to return to this point.

But even in animal life, and still more in our own, Affection extends far beyond the relation of mother and young. This warm comfortableness, this satisfaction in being together, takes in all sorts of objects. It is indeed the least discriminating of loves. There are women for whom we can predict few wooers and men who are likely to have few friends. They have nothing to offer. But almost anyone can become an object of Affection; the ugly, the stupid, even the exasperating. There need be no apparent fitness between those whom it unites. I have seen it felt for an imbecile not only by his parents but by his brothers. It ignores the barriers of age, sex, class, and education. It can exist between a clever young man from the university and an old nurse, though their minds inhabit different worlds. It ignores even the barriers of species. We see it not only between dog and man but, more surprisingly, between dog and cat. Gilbert White claims to have discovered it between a horse and a hen.

Some of the novelists have seized this well. In *Tristram Shandy* "My Father" and Uncle Toby are so far from being united by any community of interests or ideas that they cannot converse for ten minutes without cross-purposes; but we are made to feel their deep mutual affection. So with Don Quixote and Sancho Panza, Pickwick and Sam Weller, Dick Swiveller and the Marchioness. So too, though probably without the author's conscious intention, in *The Wind in the Willows;* the quaternion of Mole, Rat, Badger, and Toad suggests the amazing heterogeneity possible between those who are bound by Affection.

But Affection has its own criteria. Its objects have to be familiar. We can sometimes point to the very day and hour when we fell in love or began a new friendship. I doubt if we ever catch Affection beginning. To become aware of it is to become aware that it has already been going on for some time. The use of *old* or *vieux* as a term of Affection is significant. The dog barks at strangers who have never done it any harm and wags its tail for old acquaintances even if they never did it a good turn. The child will love a crusty old gardener who has hardly ever taken any notice of it and shrink from the visitor who is making every attempt to win its regard. But it must be an *old* gardener, one who has "always" been there—the short but seemingly immemorial "always" of childhood.

Affection, as I have said, is the humblest love. It gives itself no airs. People can be proud of being "in love", or of friendship. Affection is modest—even furtive and shame-faced. Once when I had remarked on the affection quite often found between cat and dog, my friend replied,

"Yes. But I bet no dog would ever confess it to the other dogs." That is at least a good caricature of much human Affection. "Let homely faces stay at home," says Comus. Now Affection has a very homely face. So have many of those for whom we feel it. It is no proof of our refinement or perceptiveness that we love them; nor that they love us. What I have called Appreciative Love is no basic element in Affection. It usually needs absence or bereavement to set us praising those to whom only Affection binds us. We take them for granted: and this taking for granted, which is an outrage in erotic love, is here right and proper up to a point. It fits the comfortable, quiet nature of the feeling. Affection would not be affection if it was loudly and frequently expressed; to produce it in public is like getting your household furniture out for a move. It did very well in its place, but it looks shabby or tawdry or grotesque in the sunshine. Affection almost slinks or seeps through our lives. It lives with humble, un-dress, private things; soft slippers, old clothes, old jokes, the thump of a sleepy dog's tail on the kitchen floor, the sound of a sewing-machine, a gollywog left on the lawn.

But I must at once correct myself. I am talking of Affection as it is when it exists apart from the other loves. It often does so exist; often not. As gin is not only a drink in itself but also a base for many mixed drinks, so Affection, besides being a love itself, can enter into the other loves and colour them all through and become the very medium in which from day to day they operate. They would not perhaps wear very well without it. To make a friend is not the same as to become affectionate. But when your friend has become an old friend, all those things about him which had originally nothing to do with the friendship become familiar and dear with familiarity. As for erotic love, I can imagine nothing more disagreeable than to experience it for more than a very short time without this homespun clothing of affection. That would be a most uneasy condition, either too angelic or too animal or each by turn; never quite great enough or little enough for man. There is indeed a peculiar charm, both in friendship and in Eros, about those moments when Appreciative Love lies, as it were, curled up asleep, and the mere ease and ordinariness of the relationship (free as solitude, yet neither is alone) wraps us round. No need to talk. No need to make love. No needs at all except perhaps to stir the fire.

This blending and overlapping of the loves is well kept before us by the fact that at most times and places all three of them had in common, as their expression, the kiss. In modern England friendship no longer uses it, but Affection and Eros do. It belongs so fully to both that we cannot now tell which borrowed it from the other or whether there were borrowing at all. To be sure, you may say that the kiss of Affection differs from the kiss of Eros. Yes; but not all kisses between lovers are lovers' kisses. Again, both these loves tend—and it embarrasses many moderns—to use a "little language" or "baby talk". And this is not peculiar to the human species. Professor Lorenz has told us that when jackdaws are amorous their calls "consist chiefly of infantile sounds reserved by adult jackdaws for these occasions" (*King Solomon's Ring*). We and the birds have the same excuse. Different sorts of tenderness, are both tenderness and the language of the earliest tenderness we have ever known is recalled to do duty for the new sort.

One of the most remarkable by-products of Affection has not yet been mentioned. I have said that is not primarily an Appreciative Love. It is not discriminating. It can "rub along" with the most unpromising people. Yet oddly enough this very fact means that it can in the end make appreciations possible which, but for it, might never have existed. We may say, and not quite untruly, that we have chosen our friends and the woman we love for their various excellences—for beauty, frankness, goodness of heart, wit, intelligence, or what not. But it had to be the particular kind of wit, the particular kind of beauty, the particular kind of goodness that we like, and we have our personal tastes in these matters. That is why friends and lovers feel that they were "made for one another". The especial glory of Affection is that it can unite those who most emphatically, even comically, are not; people who, if they had not found themselves put down by fate in the same household or community, would have had nothing to do with each other. If Affection grows out of this—of course it often does not—their eyes begin to open. Growing fond of "old so-and-so", at first simply because he happens to be there, I presently begin to see that there is "something in him" after all. The moment when one first says, really meaning it, that though he is not "my sort of man" he is a very good man "in his own way" is one of liberation. It does not feel like that; we may feel only tolerant and indulgent. But really we have crossed a frontier. That "in his own way" means that we are getting beyond our own idiosyncracies, that we are learning to appreciate goodness or intelligence in themselves, not merely goodness or intelligence flavoured and served to suit our own palate.

"Dogs and cats should always be brought up together," said someone, "it broadens their minds so." Affection broadens ours; of all natural loves it is the most catholic, the least finical, the broadest. The people with whom you are thrown together in the family, the college, the mess, the ship, the religious house, are from this point of view a wider circle than the friends, however numerous, whom you have made for yourself in the outer world. By having a great many friends I do not prove that I have a wide appreciation of human excellence. You might as well say I prove the width of my literary taste by being able to enjoy all the books in my own study. The answer is the same in both cases—"You chose those books. You chose those friends. Of course they suit you." The truly wide taste in reading is that which enables a man to find something for his needs on the sixpenny tray outside any secondhand bookshop. The truly wide taste in humanity will similarly find something to appreciate in the cross-section of humanity whom one has to meet every day. In my experience it is Affection that creates this taste, teaching us first to notice, then to endure, then to smile at, then to enjoy, and finally to appreciate, the people who "happen to be there". Made for us? Thank God, no. They are themselves, odder than you could have believed and worth far more than we guessed.

And now we are drawing near the point of danger. Affection, I have said, gives itself no airs; charity, said St Paul, is not puffed up. Affection can love the unattractive: God and His saints love the unlovable. Affection "does not expect too much", turns a blind eye to faults, revives easily after quarrels; just so charity suffers long and is kind and forgives. Affection opens our eyes to goodness we could not have seen, or should not have appreciated without it. So does humble sanctity. If we dwelled exclusively on these resemblances we might be led on to believe that this Affection is not simply one of the natural loves but is Love Himself working in our human hearts and fulfilling the law. Were the Victorian novelists right after all? Is love (of this sort) really enough? Are the "domestic affections", when in their best and fullest development, the same thing as the Christian life? The answer to all these questions, I submit, is certainly No.

I do not mean simply that those novelists sometimes wrote as if they had never heard the text about "hating" wife and mother and one's own life also. That of course is true. The rivalry between all natural loves and the love of God is something a Christian dare not forget. God is the great Rival, the ultimate object of human jealousy; that beauty, terrible as the

Gorgon's, which may at any moment steal from me—or it seems like stealing to me—my wife's or husband's or daughter's heart. The bitterness of some unbelief, though disguised even from those who feel it as anti-clericalism or hatred of superstition, is really due to this. But I am not at present thinking of that rivalry; we shall have to face it in a later chapter. For the moment our business is more "down to earth".

How many of these "happy homes" really exist? Worse still; are all the unhappy ones unhappy because Affection is absent? I believe not. It can be present, causing the unhappiness. Nearly all the characteristics of this love are ambivalent. They may work for ill as well as for good. By itself, left simply to follow its own bent, it can darken and degrade human life. The debunkers and anti-sentimentalists have not said all the truth about it, but all they have said is true.

Symptomatic of this, perhaps, is the odiousness of nearly all those treacly tunes and saccharine poems in which popular art expresses Affection. They are odious because of their falsity. They represent as a ready-made recipe for bliss (and even for goodness) what is in fact only an opportunity. There is no hint that we shall have to do anything: only let Affection pour over us like a warm shower-bath and all, it is implied, will be well.

Affection, we have seen, includes both Need-love and Gift-love. I begin with the Need—our craving for the Affection of others.

Now there is a clear reason why this craving, of all love-cravings, easily becomes the most unreasonable. I have said that almost anyone may be the object of Affection. Yes; and almost everyone expects to be. The egregious Mr Pontifex in *The Way of All Flesh* is outraged to discover that his son does not love him; it is "unnatural" for a boy not to love his own father. It never occurs to him to ask whether, since the first day the boy can remember, he has ever done or said anything that could excite love. Similarly, at the beginning of *King Lear* the hero is shown as a very unlovable old man devoured with a ravenous appetite for Affection. I am driven to literary examples because you, the reader, and I do not live in the same neighbourhood; if we did, there would unfortunately be no difficulty about replacing them with examples from real life. The thing happens every day. And we can see why. We all know that we must do something, if not to merit, at least to attract, erotic love or friendship. But Affection is often assumed to be provided, ready made, by nature; "built-in", "laid-on", "on the house". We have a right to expect it. If the others do not give it, they are "unnatural".

This assumption is no doubt the distortion of a truth. Much has been "built-in". Because we are a mammalian species, instinct will provide at least some degree, often a high one, of maternal love. Because we are a social species familiar association provides a *milieu* in which, if all goes well, Affection will arise and grow strong without demanding any very shining qualities in its objects. If it is given us it will not necessarily be given us on our merits; we may get it with very little trouble. From a dim perception of the truth (many are loved with Affection far beyond their deserts) Mr Pontifex draws the ludicrous conclusion, "Therefore I, without desert, have a right to it." It is as if, on a far higher plane, we argued that because no man by merit has a right to the Grace of God, I, having no merit, am entitled to it. There is no question or rights in either case. What we have is not "a right to expect" but a "reasonable expectation" of being loved by our intimates if we, and they, are more or less ordinary people. But we may not be. We may be intolerable. If we are, "nature" will work against us. For the very same conditions of intimacy which make Affection possible also—and no less naturally—make possible a peculiarly incurable distaste; a hatred as immemorial, constant, unemphatic, almost at times unconscious, as the corresponding form of love. Siegfried, in the opera, could not remember a time before every shuffle, mutter, and fidget of his dwarfish foster-father had become odious. We never catch this kind of hatred, any more than Affection, at the moment of its beginning. It was always there before. Notice that *old* is a term of wearied loathing as well as of endearment: "at his old tricks", "in his old way", "the same old thing".

It would be absurd to say that Lear is lacking in Affection. In so far as Affection is Need-love he is half-crazy with it. Unless, in his own way, he loved his daughters he would not so desperately desire their love. The most unlovable parent (or child) may be full of such ravenous love. But it works to their own misery and everyone else's. The situation becomes suffocating. If people are already unlovable a continual demand on their part (as of right) to be loved—their manifest sense of injury, their reproaches, whether loud and clamorous or merely implicit in every look and gesture of resentful self-pity—produce in us a sense of guilt (they are intended to do so) for a fault we could not have avoided and cannot cease to commit. They seal up the very fountain for which they are thirsty. If ever, at some favoured moment, any germ of Affection for them stirs in us, their demand for more and still more, petrifies us again. And of course such people always desire the same proof of our love; we are to join their side, to hear and share their grievance against someone else. If my boy really loved me he would see how selfish his father is . . . if my brother loved me he would make a party with me against my sister . . . if you loved me you wouldn't let me be treated like this . . .

And all the while they remain unaware of the real road. "If you would be loved, be lovable," said Ovid. That cheery old reprobate only meant, "If you want to attract the girls you must be attractive," but his maxim has a wider application. The amorist was wiser in his generation than Mr Pontifex and King Lear.

The really surprising thing is not that these insatiable demands made by the unlovable are sometimes made in vain, but that they are so often met. Sometimes one sees a woman's girlhood, youth, and long years of her maturity up to the verge of old age all spent in tending, obeying, caressing, and perhaps supporting, a maternal vampire who can never be caressed and obeyed enough. The sacrifice—but there are two opinions about that—may be beautiful; the old woman who exacts it is not.

The "built-in" or unmerited character of Affection thus invites a hideous misinterpretation. So does its ease and informality.

We hear a great deal about the rudeness of the rising generation. I am an oldster myself and might be expected to take the oldsters' side, but in fact I have been far more impressed by the bad manners of parents to children than by those of children to parents. Who has not been the embarrassed guest at family meals where the father or mother treated their grown-up offspring with an incivility which, offered to any other young people, would simply have terminated the acquaintance? Dogmatic assertions on matters which the children understand and their elders don't, ruthless interruptions, flat contradictions, ridicule of things the young take seriously—sometimes of their religion—insulting references to their friends, all provide an easy answer to the question "Why are they always out? Why do they like every house better than their home?" Who does not prefer civility to barbarism?

If you asked any of these insufferable people—they are not all parents of course—why they behaved that way at home, they would reply, "Oh, hang it all, one comes home to relax. A chap can't be always on his best behaviour. If a man can't be himself in his own house, where can he? Of course we don't want Company Manners at home. We're a happy family. We can say *anything* to one another here. No one minds. We all understand."

Once again it is so nearly true yet so fatally wrong. Affection is an affair of old clothes, and ease, of the unguarded moment, of liberties which would be ill-bred if we took them with strangers. But old clothes are one thing; to wear the same shirt till it stank would be another. There are proper clothes for a garden party; but the clothes for home must be proper too, in their own different way. Similarly there is a distinction between public and domestic courtesy. The root principle of both is the same: "that no one give any kind of preference to himself". But the more public the occasion, the more our obedience to this principle has been "taped" or formalised. There are "rules" of good manners. The more intimate the occasion, the less the formalisation; but not therefore the less need of courtesy. On the contrary, Affection at its best practises a courtesy which is incomparably more subtle, sensitive, and deep than the public kind. In public a ritual would do. At home you must have the reality which that ritual represented, or else the deafening triumphs of the greatest egoist present. You must really give no kind of preference to yourself; at a party it is enough to conceal the preference. Hence the old proverb "come live with me and you'll know me". Hence a man's familiar manners first reveal the true value of his (significantly odious phrase!) "Company" or "Party" manners. Those who leave their manners behind them when they come home from the dance or the sherry party have no real courtesy even there. They were merely aping those who had.

"We can say *anything* to one another." The truth behind this is that Affection at its best can say whatever Affection at its best wishes to say, regardless of the rules that govern public courtesy; for Affection at its best wishes neither to wound nor to humiliate nor to domineer. You may address the wife of your bosom as "Pig!" when she has inadvertently drunk your cocktail as well as her own. You may roar down the story which your father is telling once too often. You may tease and hoax and banter. You can say, "Shut up. I want to read." You can do anything in the right tone and at the right moment—the tone and moment which are not intended to, and will not, hurt. The better the Affection the more unerringly it knows which these are (every love has its *art of love*). But the domestic Rudesby means something quite different when he claims liberty to say "anything". Having a very imperfect sort of Affection himself, or perhaps at that moment none, he arrogates to himself the beautiful liberties which only the fullest Affection has a right to or knows how to manage. He then uses them spitefully in obedience to his resentments;

or ruthlessly in obedience to his egoism; or at best stupidly, lacking the art. And all the time he may have a clear conscience. He knows that Affection takes liberties. He is taking liberties. Therefore (he concludes) he is being affectionate. Resent anything and he will say that the defect of love is on your side. He is hurt. He has been misunderstood.

He then sometimes avenges himself by getting on his high horse and becoming elaborately "polite". The implication is of course, "Oh! So we are not to be intimate? We are to behave like mere acquaintances? I had hoped—but no matter. Have it your own way." This illustrates prettily the difference between intimate and formal courtesy. Precisely what suits the one may be a breach of the other. To be free and easy when you are presented to some eminent stranger is bad manners; to practise formal and ceremonial courtesies at home ("public faces in private places") is—and is always intended to be—bad manners. There is a delicious illustration of really good domestic manners in *Tristram Shandy*. At a singularly unsuitable moment Uncle Toby has been holding forth on his favourite theme of fortification. "My Father", driven for once beyond endurance, violently interrupts. Then he sees his brother's face; the utterly unretaliating face of Toby, deeply wounded, not by the slight to himself—he would never think of that—but by the slight to the noble art. "My Father" at once repents. There is an apology, a total reconciliation. Uncle Toby, to show how complete is his forgiveness, to show that he is not on his dignity, resumes the lecture on fortification.

But we have not yet touched on jealousy. I suppose no one now believes that jealousy is especially connected with erotic love. If anyone does the behaviour of children, employees, and domestic animals ought soon to undeceive him. Every kind of love, almost every kind of association, is liable to it. The jealousy of Affection is closely connected with its reliance on what is old and familiar. So also with the total, or relative, unimportance for Affection of what I call Appreciative love. We don't want the "old, familiar faces" to become brighter or more beautiful, the old ways to be changed even for the better, the old jokes and interests to be replaced by exciting novelties. Change is a threat to Affection.

A brother and sister, or two brothers—for sex here is not at work—grow to a certain age sharing everything. They have read the same comics, climbed the same trees, been pirates or spacemen together, taken up and abandoned stamp-collecting at the same moment. Then a dreadful thing happens. One of them flashes ahead—discovers poetry or science or serious music or perhaps undergoes a religious conversion. His life is flooded with the new interest. The other cannot share it; he is left behind. I doubt whether even the infidelity of a wife or husband raises a more miserable sense of desertion or a fiercer jealousy than this can sometimes do. It is not yet jealousy of the new friends whom the deserter will soon be making. That will come; at first it is jealousy of the thing itself—of this science, this music, of God (always called "religion" or "all this religion" in such contexts). The jealousy will probably be expressed by ridicule. The new interest is "all silly nonsense", contemptibly childish (or contemptibly grown-up), or else the deserter is not really interested in it at all—he's showing off, swanking; it's all affectation. Presently the books will be hidden, the scientific specimens destroyed, the radio forcibly switched off the classical programmes. For Affection is the most instinctive, in that sense the most animal, of the loves; its jealousy is proportionately fierce. It snarls and bares its teeth like a dog whose food has been snatched away. And why would it not? Something or someone has snatched away from the child I am picturing his life-long food, his second self. His world is in ruins.

But it is not only children who react thus. Few things in the ordinary peacetime life of a civilised country are more nearly fiendish than the rancour with which a whole unbelieving family will turn on the one member of it who has become a Christian, or a whole lowbrow family on the one who shows signs of becoming an intellectual. This is not, as I once thought, simply the innate and, as it were, disinterested hatred of darkness for light. A church-going family in which one has gone atheist will not always behave any better. It is the reaction to a desertion, even to robbery. Someone or something has stolen "our" boy (or girl). He who was one of Us has become one of Them. What right had anybody to do it? He is *ours*. But once change has thus begun, who knows where it will end? (And we all so happy and comfortable before and doing no harm to no one!)

Sometimes a curious double jealousy is felt, or rather two inconsistent jealousies which chase each other round in the sufferer's mind. On the one hand "This" is "All nonsense, all bloody high-brow nonsense, all canting humbug". But on the other, "Supposing—it can't be, it mustn't be, but just supposing—there were something in it?" Supposing there really were anything in literature, or in Christianity? How if the deserter has really entered a new world which the rest of us never suspected? But, if so, how unfair! Why him? Why was it never opened to us? "A chit of a girl—a whipper-snapper of a boy—being shown things that are hidden from their elders?" And since that is clearly incredible and unendurable, jealousy returns to the hypothesis "All nonsense".

Parents in this state are much more comfortably placed than brothers and sisters. Their past is unknown to their children. Whatever the deserter's new world is, they can always claim that they have been through it themselves and come out the other end. "It's a phase," they say. "It'll blow over." Nothing could be more satisfactory. It cannot be there and then refuted, for it is a statement about the future. It stings, yet—so indulgently said—is hard to resent. Better still, the elders may really believe it. Best of all, it may finally turn out to have been true. It won't be their fault if it doesn't.

"Boy, boy, these wild courses of yours will break your mother's heart." That eminently Victorian appeal may often have been true. Affection was bitterly wounded when one member of the family fell from the homely *ethos* into something worse—gambling, drink, keeping an opera girl. Unfortunately it is almost equally possible to break your mother's heart by rising above the homely *ethos*. The conservative tenacity of Affection works both ways. It can be a domestic counterpart to that nationally suicidal type of education which keeps back the promising child because the idlers and dunces might be "hurt" if it were undemocratically moved into a higher class than themselves.

All these perversions of Affection are mainly connected with Affection as a Need-love. But Affection as a Gift-love has its perversions too.

I am thinking of Mrs Fidget, who died a few months ago. It is really astonishing how her family have brightened up. The drawn look has gone from her husband's face; he begins to be able to laugh. The younger boy, whom I had always thought an embittered, peevish little creature, turns out to be quite human. The elder, who was hardly ever at home except when he was in bed, is nearly always there now and has begun to reorganise the garden. The girl, who was always supposed to be "delicate" (though I never found out what exactly the trouble was), now has the riding lessons which were once out of the question, dances all night, and plays any amount of tennis. Even the dog who was never allowed out except on a lead is now a well-known member of the Lamp-post Club in their road.

Mrs Fidget very often said that she lived for her family. And it was not untrue. Everyone in the neighbourhood knew it. "She lives for her family," they said. "What a wife and mother!" She did all the washing; true, she did it badly, and they could have afforded to send it out to a laundry, and they frequently begged her not to do it. But she did. There was always a hot lunch for anyone who was at home and always a hot meal at night (even in midsummer). They implored her not to provide this. They protested almost with tears in their eyes (and with truth) that they liked cold meals. It made no difference. She was living for her family. She always sat up to "welcome" you home if you were out late at night; two or three in the morning, it made no odds; you would always find the frail, pale, weary face awaiting you, like a silent accusation. Which meant of course that you couldn't with any decency go out very often. She was always making things too; being in her own estimation (I'm no judge myself) an excellent amateur dressmaker and a great knitter. And of course, unless you were a heartless brute, you had to wear the things. (The Vicar tells me that, since her death, the contributions of that family alone to "sales of work" outweigh those of all his other parishioners put together). And then her care for their health! She bore the whole burden of that daughter's "delicacy" alone. The Doctor—an old friend, and it was not being done on National Health—was never allowed to discuss matters with his patient. After the briefest examination of her, he was taken into another room by the mother. The girl was to have no worries, no responsibility for her own health. Only loving care; caresses, special foods, horrible tonic wines, and breakfast in bed. For Mrs Fidget, as she so often said, would "work her fingers to the bone" for her family. They couldn't stop her. Nor could they—being decent people—quite sit still and watch her do it. They had to help. Indeed they were always having to help. That is, they did things for her to help her to do things for them which they didn't want done. As for the dear dog, it was to her, she said, "just like one of the children". It was in fact as like one of them as she could make it. But since it had no scruples it got on rather better than they, and though vetted, dieted and guarded within an inch of its life, contrived sometimes to reach the dustbin or the dog next door.

The Vicar says Mrs Fidget is now at rest. Let us hope she is. What's quite certain is that her family are.

It is easy to see how liability to this state is, so to speak, congenital in the maternal instinct. This, as we saw, is a Gift-love, but one that needs to give; therefore needs to be needed. But the proper aim of giving is to put the recipient in a state where he no longer needs our gift. We feed children in order that they may soon be able to feed themselves; we teach them in order that they may soon not need our teaching. Thus a heavy task is laid upon this Gift-love. It must work towards its own abdication. We must aim at making ourselves superfluous. The hour when we can say "They need me no longer" should be our reward. But the instinct, simply in its own nature, has no power to fulfil this law. The instinct desires the good of its object, but not simply; only the good it can itself give. A much higher love—a love which desires the good of the object as such, from whatever source that good comes—must step in and help or tame the instinct before it can make the abdication. And of course it often does. But where it does not, the ravenous need to be needed will gratify itself either by keeping its objects needy or by inventing for them imaginary needs. It will do this all the more ruthlessly because it thinks (in one sense truly) that it is a Gift-love and therefore regards itself as "unselfish".

It is not only mothers who can do this. All those other Affections which, whether by derivation from parental instinct or by similarity of function, need to be needed may fall into the same pit. The Affection of patron for *protégé* is one. In Jane Austen's novel, Emma intends that Harriet Smith should have a happy life; but only the sort of happy life which Emma herself has planned for her. My own profession—that of a university teacher—is in this way dangerous. If we are any good we must always be working towards the moment at which our pupils are fit to become our critics and rivals. We should be delighted when it arrives, as the fencing master is delighted when his pupil can pink and disarm him. And many are.

But not all. I am old enough to remember the sad case of Dr Quartz. No university boasted a more effective or devoted teacher. He spent the whole of himself on his pupils. He made an indelible impression on nearly all of them. He was the object of much well merited hero-worship. Naturally, and delightfully, they continued to visit him after the tutorial relation had ended—went round to his house of an evening and had famous discussions. But the curious thing is that this never lasted. Sooner or later—it might be within a few months or even a few weeks—came the fatal evening when they knocked on his door and were told that the Doctor was engaged. After that he would always be engaged. They were banished from him forever. This was because, at their last meeting, they had rebelled. They had asserted their independence—differed from the master and supported their own view, perhaps not without success. Faced with that very independence which he had laboured to produce and which it was his duty to produce if he could, Dr Quartz could not bear it. Wotan had toiled to create the free Siegfried; presented with the free Siegfried, he was enraged. Dr Quartz was an unhappy man.

This terrible need to be needed often finds its outlet in pampering an animal. To learn that someone is "fond of animals" tells us very little until we know in what way. For there are two ways. On the one hand the higher and domesticated animal is, so to speak, a "bridge" between us and the rest of nature. We all at times feel somewhat painfully our human isolation from the sub-human world—the atrophy of instinct which our intelligence entails, our excessive self-consciousness, the innumerable complexities of our situation, our inability to live in the present. If only we could shuffle it all off! We must not—and incidentally we can't—become beasts. But we can be *with* a beast. It is personal enough to give the word *with* a real meaning; yet it remains very largely an unconscious little bundle of biological impulses. It has three legs in nature's world and one in ours. It is a link, an ambassador. Who would not wish, as Bosanquet put it, "to have a representative at the court of Pan"? Man with dog closes a gap in the universe. But of course animals are often used in a worse fashion. If you need to be needed and if your family, very properly, decline to need you, a pet is the obvious substitute. You can keep it all its life in need of you. You can keep it permanently infantile, reduce it to permanent invalidism, cut it off from all genuine animal well-being, and compensate for this by creating needs for countless little indulgences which only you can grant. The unfortunate creature thus becomes very useful to the rest of the household; it acts as a sump or drain—you are too busy spoiling a dog's life to spoil theirs. Dogs are better for this purpose than cats: a monkey, I am told, is best of all. Also it is more like the real thing. To be sure, it's all very bad luck for the animal. But probably it cannot fully realise the wrong you have done it. Better still, you would never know if it did. The most down-trodden human, driven too far, may one day turn and blurt out a terrible truth. Animals can't speak.

Those who say "The more I see of men the better I like dogs"—those who find in animals a *relief* from the demands of human companionship—will be well advised to examine their real reasons.

I hope I am not being misunderstood. If this chapter leads anyone to doubt that the lack of "natural affection" is an extreme depravity I shall have failed. Nor do I question for a moment that Affection is responsible for nine-tenths of whatever solid and durable happiness there is in our natural lives. I shall therefore have some sympathy with those whose comment on the last few pages takes the form "Of course. Of course. These things do happen. Selfish or neurotic people can twist anything, even love, into some sort of misery or exploitation. But why stress these marginal cases? A little common sense, a little give and take, prevents their occurrence among decent people." But I think this comment itself needs a commentary.

Firstly, as to *neurotic*. I do not think we shall see things more clearly by classifying all these malefic states of Affection as pathological. No doubt there are really pathological conditions which make the temptation to these states abnormally hard or even impossible to resist for particular people. Send those people to the doctors by all means. But I believe that everyone who is honest with himself will admit that he has felt these temptations. Their occurrence is not a disease; or if it is, the name of that disease is Being a Fallen Man. In ordinary people the yielding to them—and who does not sometimes yield?—is not disease, but sin. Spiritual direction will here help us more than medical treatment. Medicine labours to restore "natural" structure or "normal" function. But greed, egoism, self-deception, and self-pity are not unnatural or abnormal in the same sense as astigmatism or a floating kidney. For who, in Heaven's name, would describe as natural or normal the man from whom these failings were wholly absent? "Natural", if you like, in a quite different sense; archnatural, unfallen. We have seen only one such Man. And He was not at all like the psychologist's picture of the integrated, balanced, adjusted, happily married, employed, popular citizen. You can't really be very well "adjusted" to your world if it says you "have a devil" and ends by nailing you up naked to a stake of wood.

But secondly, the comment in its own language admits the very thing I am trying to say. Affection produces happiness if—and only if—there is common sense and give and take and "decency". In other words, only if something more, and other, than Affection is added. The mere feeling is not enough. You need "common sense", that is, reason. You need "give and take"; that is, you need justice, continually stimulating mere Affection when it fades and restraining it when it forgets or would defy the *art* of love. You need "decency". There is no disguising the fact that this means goodness; patience, self-denial, humility, and the continual intervention of a far higher sort of love than Affection, in itself, can ever be.

That is the whole point. If we try to live by Affection alone, Affection will "go bad on us".

How bad, I believe we seldom recognise. Can Mrs Fidget really have been quite unaware of the countless frustrations and miseries she inflicted on her family? It passes belief. She knew—of course she knew—that it spoiled your whole evening to know that when you came home you would find her uselessly, accusingly, "sitting up for you". She continued all these practises because if she had dropped them she would have been faced with the fact she was determined not to see; would have known that she was not necessary. That is the first motive. Then too, the very laboriousness of her life silenced her secret doubts as to the quality of her love. The more her feet burned and her back ached, the better, for this pain whispered in her ear, "How much I must love them if I do all this!" That is the second motive. But I think there is a lower depth. The unappreciativeness of the others, those terrible, wounding words—anything will "wound" a Mrs Fidget—in which they begged her to send the washing out, enabled her to feel ill-used, therefore, to have a continual grievance, to enjoy the pleasures of resentment. If anyone says he does not know those pleasures, he is a liar or a saint. It is true that they are pleasures only to those who hate. But then a love like Mrs Fidget's contains a good deal of hatred. It was of erotic love that the Roman poet said, "I love and hate," but other kinds of love admit the same mixture. They carry in them the seeds of hatred. If Affection is made the absolute sovereign of a human life the seeds will germinate. Love, having become a god, becomes a demon.

IV

FRIENDSHIP

WHEN EITHER AFFECTION or Eros is one's theme, one finds a prepared audience. The importance and beauty of both have been stressed and almost exaggerated again and again. Even those who would debunk them are in conscious reaction against this laudatory tradition and, to that extent, influenced by it. But very few modern people think Friendship a love of comparable value or even a love at all. I cannot remember that any poem since *In Memoriam,* or any novel, has celebrated it. Tristan and Isolde, Antony and Cleopatra, Romeo and Juliet, have innumerable counterparts in modern literature: David and Jonathan, Pylades and Orestes, Roland and Oliver, Amis and Amile, have not. To the Ancients, Friendship seemed the happiest and most fully human of all loves; the crown of life and the school of virtue. The modern world, in comparison, ignores it. We admit of course that besides a wife and family a man needs a few "friends". But the very tone of the admission, and the sort of acquaintanceships which those who make it would describe as "friendships", show clearly that what they are talking about has very little to do with that *Philia* which Aristotle classified among the virtues or that *Amicitia* on which Cicero wrote a book. It is something quite marginal; not a main course in life's banquet; a diversion; something that fills up the chinks of one's time. How has this come about?

The first and most obvious answer is that few value it because few experience it. And the possibility of going through life without the experience is rooted in that fact which separates Friendship so sharply from both the other loves. Friendship is—in a sense not at all derogatory to it—the least *natural* of loves; the least instinctive, organic, biological, gregarious, and necessary. It has least commerce with our nerves; there is nothing throaty about it; nothing that quickens the pulse or turns you red and pale. It is essentially between individuals; the moment two men are friends they have in some degree drawn apart together from the herd. Without Eros none of us would have been begotten and without Affection none of us would have been reared; but we can live and breed without Friendship. The species, biologically considered, has no need of it. The pack or herd—the community—may even dislike and distrust it. Its leaders very often do. Headmasters and Headmistresses and Heads of religious communities, colonels and ships' captains, can feel uneasy when close and strong friendships arise between little knots of their subjects.

This (so to call it) "non-natural" quality in Friendship goes far to explain why it was exalted in ancient and medieval times and has come to be made light of in our own. The deepest and most permanent thought of those ages was ascetic and world-renouncing. Nature and emotion and the body were feared as dangers to our souls, or despised as degradations of our human status. Inevitably that sort of love was most prized which seemed most independent, or even defiant, of mere nature. Affection and Eros were too obviously connected with our nerves, too obviously shared with the brutes. You could feel these tugging at your guts and fluttering in your diaphragm. But in Friendship—in that luminous, tranquil, rational world of relationships freely chosen—you got away from all that. This alone, of all the loves, seemed to raise you to the level of gods or angels.

But then came Romanticism and "tearful comedy" and the "return to nature" and the exaltation of Sentiment; and in their train all that great wallow of emotion which, though often criticised, has lasted ever since. Finally, the exaltation of instinct, the dark gods in the blood; whose hierophants may be incapable of male friendship. Under this new dispensation all that had once commended this love now began to work against it. It had not tearful smiles and keepsakes and baby-talk enough to please the sentimentalists. There was not blood and guts enough about it to attract the primitivists. It looked thin and etiolated; a sort of vegetarian substitute for the more organic loves.

Other causes have contributed. To those—and they are now the majority—who see human life merely as a development and complication of animal life all forms of behaviour which cannot produce certificates of an animal origin and of survival value are suspect. Friendship's certificates are not very satisfactory. Again, that outlook which values the collective above the individual necessarily disparages Friendship; it is a relation between men at their highest level of individuality. It withdraws men from collective "togetherness" as surely as solitude itself could do; and more dangerously, for it withdraws them by two's and three's. Some forms of democratic sentiment are naturally hostile to it because it is selective and an affair of the few. To say "These are my friends" implies "Those are not". For all these reasons if a man believes (as I do) that the old estimate of Friendship was the correct one, he can hardly write a chapter on it except as a rehabilitation. This imposes on me at the outset a very tiresome bit of demolition. It has actually become necessary in our time to rebut the theory that every firm and serious friendship is really homosexual.

The dangerous word *really* is here important. To say that every Friendship is consciously and explicitly homosexual would be too obviously false; the wiseacres take refuge in the less palpable charge that it is *really*—unconsciously, cryptically, in some Pickwickian sense—homosexual. And this, though it cannot be proved, can never of course be refuted. The fact that no positive evidence of homosexuality can be discovered in the behaviour of two Friends does not disconcert the wiseacres at all: "That," they say gravely, "is just what we should expect." The very lack of evidence is thus treated as evidence; the absence of smoke proves that the fire is very carefully hidden. Yes—if it exists at all. But we must first prove its existence. Otherwise we are arguing like a man who should say, "If there were an invisible cat in that chair, the chair would look empty; but the chair does look empty; therefore there is an invisible cat in it."

A belief in invisible cats cannot perhaps be logically disproved, but it tells us a good deal about those who hold it. Those who cannot conceive Friendship as a substantive love but only as a disguise or elaboration of Eros betray the fact that they have never had a Friend. The rest of us know that though we can have erotic love and friendship for the same person yet in some ways nothing is less like a Friendship than a love-affair. Lovers are always talking to one another about their love; Friends hardly ever about their Friendship. Lovers are normally face to face, absorbed in each other; Friends, side by side, absorbed in some common interest. Above all, Eros (while it lasts) is necessarily between two only.

But two, far from being the necessary number for Friendship, is not even the best. And the reason for this is important.

Lamb says somewhere that if, of three friends (A, B, and C), A should die, then B loses not only A but "A's part in C", while C loses not only A but "A's part in B". In each of my friends there is something that only some other friend can fully bring out. By myself I am not large enough to call the whole man into activity; I want other lights than my own to show all his facets. Now that Charles is dead, I shall never again see Ronald's reaction to a specifically Caroline joke. Far from having more of Ronald, having him "to myself" now that Charles is away, I have less of Ronald. Hence true Friendship is the least jealous of loves. Two friends delight to be joined by a third, and three by a fourth, if only the newcomer is qualified to become a real friend. They can then say, as the blessed souls say in Dante, "Here comes one who will augment our loves." For in this love "to divide is not to take away". Of course the scarcity of kindred souls—not to mention practical considerations about the size of rooms and the audibility of voices—set limits to the enlargement of the circle; but within those limits we possess each friend not less but more as the number of those with whom we share him increases. In this, Friendship exhibits a glorious "nearness by resemblance" to Heaven itself where the very multitude of the blessed (which no man can number) increases the fruition which each has of God. For every soul, seeing Him in her own way, doubtless communicates that unique vision to all the rest. That, says an old author, is why the Seraphim in Isaiah's vision are crying "Holy, Holy, Holy" *to one another* (Isa. 6:3). The more we thus share the Heavenly Bread between us, the more we shall all have.

The homosexual theory therefore seems to me not even plausible. This is not to say that Friendship and abnormal Eros have never been combined. Certain cultures at certain periods seem to have tended to the contamination. In war-like societies it was, I think, especially likely to creep into the relation between the mature Brave and his young armour-bearer or squire. The absence of the women while you were on the warpath had no doubt something to do with it. In deciding, if we think we need or can decide, where it crept in and where it did not, we must surely be guided by the evidence (when there is any) and not by an *a priori* theory. Kisses, tears, and embraces are not in themselves evidence of homosexuality. The implications would be, if nothing else, too comic. Hrothgar embracing Beowulf, Johnson embracing Boswell (a pretty flagrantly heterosexual couple), and all those hairy old toughs of centurions in Tacitus, clinging to one another and begging for last kisses when the legion was broken up . . . all pansies? If you can believe that you can believe anything. On a broad historical view it is, of course, not the demonstrative gestures of Friendship among our ancestors but the absence of such gestures in our own society that calls for some special explanation. We, not they, are out of step.

I have said that Friendship is the least biological of our loves. Both the individual and the community can survive without it. But there is something else, often confused with Friendship, which the community does need; something which, though not Friendship, is the matrix of Friendship.

In early communities the co-operation of the males as hunters or fighters was no less necessary than the begetting and rearing of children. A tribe where there was no taste for the one would die no less surely than a tribe where there was no taste for the other. Long before history began we men have got together apart from the women and done things. We had to. And to like doing what must be done is a characteristic that has survival value. We not only had to do the things, we had to talk about them. We had to plan the hunt and the battle. When they were over we had to hold a *post mortem* and draw conclusions for future use. We liked this even better. We ridiculed or punished the cowards and bunglers, we praised the star-performers. We revelled in technicalities. ("He might have known he'd never get near the brute, not with the wind that way" . . . "You see, I had a lighter arrowhead; that's what did it" . . . "What I always say is——" . . . "stuck him just like that, see? Just the way I'm holding this stick" . . .). In fact, we talked shop. We enjoyed one another's society greatly: we Braves, we hunters, all bound together by shared skill, shared dangers and hardships, esoteric jokes— away from the women and children. As some wag has said, palaeolithic man may or may not have had a club on his shoulder but he certainly had a club of the other sort. It was probably part of his religion; like that sacred smoking-club where the savages in Melville's *Typee* were "famously snug" every evening of their lives.

What were the women doing meanwhile? How should I know? I am a man and never spied on the mysteries of the Bona Dea. They certainly often had rituals from which men were excluded. When, as sometimes happened, agriculture was in their hands, they must, like the men, have had common skills, toils and triumphs. Yet perhaps their world was never as emphatically feminine as that of their men-folk was masculine. The children were with them; perhaps the old men were there too. But I am only guessing. I can trace the pre-history of Friendship only in the male line.

This pleasure in co-operation, in talking shop, in the mutual respect and understanding of men who daily see one another tested, is biologically valuable. You may, if you like, regard it as a product of the "gregarious instinct". To me that seems a round-about way of getting at something which we all understand far better already than anyone has ever understood the word *instinct*—something which is going on at this moment in dozens of ward-rooms, bar-rooms, common-rooms, messes, and golf-clubs. I prefer to call it Companionship—or Clubbableness.

This Companionship is, however, only the matrix of Friendship. It is often called Friendship, and many people when they speak of their "friends" mean only their companions. But it is not Friendship in the sense I give to the word. By saying this I do not at all intend to disparage the merely Clubbable relation. We do not disparage silver by distinguishing it from gold.

Friendship arises out of mere Companionship when two or more of the companions discover that they have in common some insight or interest or even taste which the others do not share and which, till that moment, each believed to be his own unique treasure (or burden). The typical expression of opening Friendship would be something like, "What? You too? I thought I was the only one." We can imagine that among those early hunters and warriors single individuals—one in a century? one in a thousand years?—saw what others did not; saw that the deer was beautiful as well as edible, that hunting was fun as well as necessary, dreamed that his gods might be not only powerful but holy. But as long as each of these percipient persons dies without finding a kindred soul, nothing (I suspect) will come of it; art or sport or spiritual religion will not be born. It is when two such persons discover one another, when, whether with immense difficulties and semi-articulate fumblings or with what would seem to us amazing and elliptical speed, they share their vision—it is then that Friendship is born. And instantly they stand together in an immense solitude.

Lovers seek for privacy. Friends find this solitude about them, this barrier between them and the herd, whether they want it or not. They would be glad to reduce it. The first two would be glad to find a third.

In our own time Friendship arises in the same way. For us of course the shared activity and therefore the companionship on which Friendship supervenes will not often be a bodily one like hunting or fighting. It may be a common religion, common studies, a common profession, even a common recreation. All who share it will be our companions; but one or two or three who share something more will be our Friends. In this kind of love, as Emerson said, *Do you love me?* means *Do you see the same truth?*—Or at least, "Do you *care about* the same truth?" The man who agrees with us that some question, little regarded by others, is of great importance, can be our Friend. He need not agree with us about the answer.

Notice that Friendship thus repeats on a more individual and less socially necessary level the character of the Companionship which was its matrix. The Companionship was between people who were doing something together—hunting, studying, painting or what you will. The Friends will still be doing something together, but something more inward, less widely shared and less easily defined; still hunters, but of some immaterial quarry; still collaborating, but in some work the world does not, or not yet, take account of; still travelling companions, but on a different kind of journey. Hence we picture lovers face to face but Friends side by side; their eyes look ahead.

That is why those pathetic people who simply "want friends" can never make any. The very condition of having Friends is that we should want something else besides Friends. Where the truthful answer to the question *Do you see the same truth?* would be "I see nothing and I don't care about the truth; I only want a Friend", no Friendship can arise— though Affection of course may. There would be nothing for the Friendship to be *about;* and Friendship must be about something, even if it were only an enthusiasm for dominoes or white mice. Those who have nothing can share nothing; those who are going nowhere can have no fellow-travellers.

When the two people who thus discover that they are on the same secret road are of different sexes, the friendship which arises between them will very easily pass—may pass in the first half-hour—into erotic love. Indeed, unless they are physically repulsive to each other or unless one or both already loves elsewhere, it is almost certain to do so sooner or later.

And conversely, erotic love may lead to Friendship between the lovers. But this, so far from obliterating the distinction between the two loves, puts it in a clearer light. If one who was first, in the deep and full sense, your Friend, is then gradually or suddenly revealed as also your lover you will certainly not want to share the Beloved's erotic love with any third. But you will have no jealousy at all about sharing the Friendship. Nothing so enriches an erotic love as the discovery that the Beloved can deeply, truly, and spontaneously enter into Friendship with the Friends you already had: to feel that not only are we two united by erotic love but we three or four or five are all travellers on the same quest, have all a common vision.

The co-existence of Friendship and Eros may also help some moderns to realise that Friendship is in reality a love, and even as great a love as Eros. Suppose you are fortunate enough to have "fallen in love with" and married your Friend. And now suppose it possible that you were offered the choice of two futures: "*Either* you two will cease to be lovers but remain forever joint seekers of the same God, the same beauty, the same truth, *or else,* losing all that, you will retain as long as you live the raptures and ardours, all the wonder and the wild desire of Eros. Choose which you please." Which should we choose? Which choice should we not regret after we had made it?

I have stressed the "unnecessary" character of Friendship, and this of course requires more justification than I have yet given it.

It could be argued that Friendships are of practical value to the Community. Every civilised religion began in a small group of friends. Mathematics effectively began when a few Greek friends got together to talk about numbers and lines and angles. What is now the Royal Society was originally a few gentlemen meeting in their spare time to discuss things which they (and not many others) had a fancy for. What we now call "the Romantic Movement" once *was* Mr Wordsworth and Mr Coleridge talking incessantly (at least Mr Coleridge was) about a secret vision of their own. Communism, Tractarianism, Methodism, the movement against slavery, the Reformation, the Renaissance might perhaps be said, without much exaggeration, to have begun in the same way.

There is something in this. But nearly every reader would probably think some of these movements good for society and some bad. The whole list, if accepted, would tend to show, at best, that Friendship is both a possible benefactor and a possible danger to the community. And even as a benefactor it would have, not so much survival value, as what we may call "civilisation-value"; would be something (in Aristotelian phrase) which helps the community not to live but to live well. Survival value and civilisation value coincide at some periods and in some circumstances, but not in all. What at any rate seems certain is that when Friendship bears fruit which the community can use it has to do so accidentally, as a by-product. Religions devised for a social purpose, like Roman emperor-worship or modern attempts to "sell" Christianity as a means of "saving civilisation", do not come to much. The little knots of Friends who turn their backs on the "World" are those who really transform it. Egyptian and Babylonian Mathematics were practical and social, pursued in the service of Agriculture and Magic. But the free Greek Mathematics, pursued by Friends as a leisure occupation, have mattered to us more.

Others again would say that Friendship is extremely useful, perhaps necessary for survival, to the individual. They could produce plenty of authority: "bare is back without brother behind it" and "there is a friend that sticketh closer than a brother". But when we speak thus we are using *friend* to mean "ally". In ordinary usage *friend* means, or should mean, more than that. A Friend will, to be sure, prove himself to be also an ally when alliance becomes necessary; will lend or give when we are in need, nurse us in sickness, stand up for us among our enemies, do what he can for our widows and orphans. But such good offices are not the stuff of Friendship. The occasions for them are almost interruptions. They are in one way relevant to it, in another not. Relevant, because you would be a false friend if you would not do them when the need arose; irrelevant, because the role of benefactor always remains accidental, even a little alien, to that of Friend. It is almost embarrassing. For Friendship is utterly free from Affection's need to be needed. We are sorry that any gift or loan or night-watching should have been necessary—and now, for heaven's sake, let us forget all about it and go back to the things we really want to do or talk of together. Even gratitude is no enrichment to this love. The stereotyped "Don't mention it" here expresses what we really feel. The mark of perfect Friendship is not that help will be given when the pinch comes (of course it will) but that, having been given, it makes no difference at all. It was a distraction, an anomaly. It was a horrible waste of the time, always too short, that we had together. Perhaps we had only a couple of hours in which to talk and, God bless us, twenty minutes of it has had to be devoted to *affairs*!

For of course we do not want to know our Friend's affairs at all. Friendship, unlike Eros, is uninquisitive. You become a man's Friend without knowing or caring whether he is married or single or how he earns his living. What have all these "unconcerning things, matters of fact" to do with the real question, *Do you see the same truth?* In a circle of true Friends each man is simply what he is: stands for nothing but himself. No one cares twopence about anyone else's family, profession, class, income, race, or previous history. Of course you will get to know about most of these in the end. But casually. They will come out bit by bit, to furnish an illustration or an analogy, to serve as pegs for an anecdote; never for their own sake. That is the kingliness of Friendship. We meet like sovereign princes of independent states, abroad, on neutral ground, freed from our contexts. This love (essentially) ignores not only our physical bodies but that whole embodiment which consists of our family, job, past, and connections. At home, besides being Peter or Jane, we also bear a general character; husband or wife, brother or sister, chief, colleague or subordinate. Not among our Friends. It is an affair of disentangled, or stripped, minds. Eros will have naked bodies; Friendship naked personalities.

Hence (if you will not misunderstand me) the exquisite arbitrariness and irresponsibility of this love. I have no duty to be anyone's Friend and no man in the world has a duty to be mine. No claims, no shadow of necessity. Friendship is unnecessary, like philosophy, like art, like the universe itself (for God did not need to create). It has no survival value; rather it is one of those things which give value to survival.

When I spoke of Friends as side by side or shoulder to shoulder I was pointing a necessary contrast between their posture and that of the lovers whom we picture face to face. Beyond that contrast I do not want the image pressed. The common quest or vision which unites Friends does not absorb them in such a way that they remain ignorant or oblivious of one another. On the contrary it is the very medium in which their mutual love and knowledge exist. One knows nobody so well as one's "fellow". Every step of the common journey tests his metal; and the tests are tests we fully understand because we are undergoing them ourselves. Hence, as he rings true time after time, our reliance, our respect and our admiration blossom into an Appreciative Love of a singularly robust and well-informed kind. If, at the outset, we had attended more to him and less to the thing our Friendship is "about", we should not have come to know or love him so well. You will not find the warrior, the poet, the philosopher, or the Christian by staring in his eyes as if he were your mistress: better fight beside him, read with him, argue with him, pray with him.

In a perfect Friendship this Appreciative Love is, I think, often so great and so firmly based that each member of the circle feels, in his secret heart, humbled before all the rest. Sometimes he wonders what he is doing there among his betters. He is lucky beyond desert to be in such company. Especially when the whole group is together, each bringing out all that is best, wisest, or funniest in all the others. Those are the golden sessions; when four or five of us after a hard day's walking have come to our inn; when our slippers are on, our feet spread out towards the blaze, and our drinks at our elbows; when the whole world, and something beyond the world, opens itself to our minds as we talk; and no one has any claim on or any responsibility for another, but all are freemen and equals as if we had first met an hour ago, while at the same time an Affection mellowed by the years enfolds us. Life—natural life—has no better gift to give. Who could have deserved it?

From what has been said it will be clear that in most societies at most periods Friendships will be between men and men or between women and women. The sexes will have met one another in Affection and in Eros but not in this love. For they will seldom have had with each other the companionship in common activities which is the matrix of Friendship. Where men are educated and women not, where one sex works and the other is idle, or where they do totally different work, they will usually have nothing to be Friends about. But we can easily see that it is this lack, rather than anything in their natures, which excludes Friendship; for where they can be companions they can also become Friends. Hence in a profession (like my own) where men and women work side by side, or in the mission field, or among authors and artists, such Friendship is common. To be sure, what is offered as Friendship on one side may be mistaken for Eros on the other, with painful and embarrassing results. Or what begins as Friendship in both may become also Eros. But to say that something can be mistaken for, or turn into, something else is not to deny the difference between them. Rather it implies it; we should not otherwise speak of "turning into" or being "mistaken for".

In one respect our own society is unfortunate. A world where men and women never have common work or a common education can probably get along comfortably enough. In it men turn to each other, and only to each other, for Friendship, and they enjoy it very much. I hope the women enjoy their feminine Friends equally. Again, a world where all men and women had sufficient common ground for this relationship could also be comfortable. At present, however, we fall between two stools. The necessary common ground, the matrix, exists between the sexes in some groups but not in others. It is notably lacking in many residential suburbs. In a plutocratic neighbourhood where the men have spent their whole lives in acquiring money some at least of the women have used their leisure to develop an intellectual life—have become musical or literary. In such places the men appear among the women as barbarians among civilised people. In another neighbourhood you will find the situation reversed. Both sexes have, indeed, "been to school". But since then the men have had a much more serious education; they have become doctors, lawyers, clergymen, architects, engineers, or men of letters. The women are to them as children to adults. In neither neighbourhood is real Friendship between the sexes at all probable. But this, though an impoverishment, would be tolerable if it were admitted and accepted. The peculiar trouble of our own age is that men and women in this situation, haunted by rumours and glimpses of happier groups where no such chasm between the sexes exists, and bedevilled by the egalitarian idea that what is possible for some ought to be (and therefore is) possible to all, refuse to acquiesce in it. Hence, on the one hand, we get the wife as school-marm, the "cultivated" woman who is always trying to bring her husband "up to her level". She drags him to concerts and would like him to learn morris-dancing and invites "cultivated" people to the house. It often does surprisingly little harm. The middle-aged male has great powers of passive resistance and (if she but knew) of indulgence; "women will have their fads." Something much more painful happens when it is the men who are civilised and the women not, and when all the women, and many of the men too, simply refuse to recognise the fact.

When this happens we get a kind, polite, laborious, and pitiful pretence. The women are "deemed" (as lawyers say) to be full members of the male circle. The fact—in itself not important—that they now smoke and drink like the men seems to simple-minded people a proof that they really are. No stag-parties are allowed. Wherever the men meet, the women must come too. The men have learned to live among ideas. They know what discussion, proof, and illustration mean. A woman who has had merely school lessons and has abandoned soon after marriage whatever tinge of "culture" they gave her—whose reading is the Women's Magazines and whose general conversation is almost wholly narrative— cannot really enter such a circle. She can be locally and physically present with it in the same room. What of that? If the men are ruthless, she sits bored and silent through a conversation which means nothing to her. If they are better bred, of course, they try to bring her in. Things are explained to her: people try to sublimate her irrelevant and blundering observations into some kind of sense. But the efforts soon fail and, for manners' sake, what might have been a real discussion is deliberately diluted and peters out in gossip, anecdotes, and jokes. Her presence has thus destroyed the very thing she was brought to share. She can never really enter the circle because the circle ceases to be itself when she enters it— as the horizon ceases to be the horizon when you get there. By learning to drink and smoke and perhaps to tell *risqué* stories, she has not, for this purpose, drawn an inch nearer to the men than her grandmother. But her grandmother was far happier and more realistic. She was at home talking real women's talk to other women and perhaps doing so with great charm, sense, and even wit. She herself might be able to do the same. She may be quite as clever as the men whose evening she has spoiled, or cleverer. But she is not really interested in the same things, nor mistress of the same methods. (We all appear as dunces when feigning an interest in things we care nothing about.)

The presence of such women, thousands strong, helps to account for the modern disparagement of Friendship. They are often completely victorious. They banish male companionship, and therefore male Friendship, from whole neighbourhoods. In the only world they know, an endless prattling "Jolly" replaces the intercourse of minds. All the men they meet talk like women while women are present.

This victory over Friendship is often unconscious. There is, however, a more militant type of women who plans it. I have heard one say, "Never let two men sit together or they'll get talking about some *subject* and then there'll be no fun." Her point could not have been more accurately made. Talk, by all means; the more of it the better; unceasing cascades of the human voice; but not, please, a subject. The talk must not be about anything.

This gay lady—this lively, accomplished, "charming", unendurable bore—was seeking only each evening's amusement, making the meeting "go". But the conscious war against Friendship may be fought on a deeper level. There are women who regard it with hatred, envy, and fear as the enemy of Eros and, perhaps even more, of Affection. A woman of that sort has a hundred arts to break up her husband's Friendships. She will quarrel with his Friends herself or, better still, with their wives. She will sneer, obstruct, and lie. She does not realise that the husband whom she succeeds in isolating from his own kind will not be very well worth having; she has emasculated him. She will grow to be ashamed of him herself. Nor does she remember how much of his life lies in places where she cannot watch him. New Friendships will break out, but this time they will be secret. Lucky for her, and lucky beyond her deserts, if there are not soon other secrets as well.

All these, of course, are silly women. The sensible women who, if they wanted, would certainly be able to qualify themselves for the world of discussion and ideas, are precisely those who, if they are not qualified, never try to enter it or to destroy it. They have other fish to fry. At a mixed party they gravitate to one end of the room and talk women's talk to one another. They don't want us, for this sort of purpose, any more than we want them. It is only the riff-raff of each sex that wants to be incessantly hanging on the other. Live and let live. They laugh at us a good deal. That is just as it should be. Where the sexes, having no real shared activities, can meet only in Affection and Eros—cannot be Friends—it is healthy that each should have a lively sense of the other's absurdity. Indeed it is always healthy. No one ever really appreciated the other sex—just as no one really appreciates children or animals—without at times feeling them to be funny. For both sexes are. Humanity is tragi-comical; but the division into sexes enables each to see in the other the joke that often escapes it in itself—and the pathos too.

I gave warning that this chapter would be largely a rehabilitation. The preceding pages have, I hope, made clear why to me at least it seems no wonder if our ancestors regarded Friendship as something that raised us almost above humanity. This love, free from instinct, free from all duties but those which love has freely assumed, almost wholly free from jealousy, and free without qualification from the need to be needed, is eminently spiritual. It is the sort of love one can imagine between angels. Have we here found a natural love which is Love itself?

Before we rush to any such conclusion let us beware of the ambiguity in the word *spiritual*. There are many New Testament contexts in which it means "pertaining to the (Holy) Spirit", and in such contexts the spiritual is, by definition, good. But when *spiritual* is used simply as the opposite of corporeal, or instinctive, or animal, this is not so. There is spiritual evil as well as spiritual good. There are unholy, as well as holy, angels. The worst sins of men are spiritual. We must not think that in finding Friendship to be *spiritual* we have found it to be in itself holy or inerrant. Three significant facts remain to be taken into account.

The first, already mentioned, is the distrust which Authorities tend to have of close Friendships among their subjects. It may be unjustified; or there may be some basis for it.

Secondly, there is the attitude of the majority towards all circles of close Friends. Every name they give such a circle is more or less derogatory. It is at best a "set"; lucky if not a *coterie*, a "gang", a "little senate", or a "mutual admiration society". Those who in their own lives know only Affection, Companionship, and Eros, suspect Friends to be "stuck-up prigs who think themselves too good for us". Of course this is the voice of Envy. But Envy always brings the truest charge, or the charge nearest to the truth, that she can think up; it hurts more. This charge, therefore, will have to be considered.

Finally, we must notice that Friendship is very rarely the image under which Scripture represents the love between God and Man. It is not entirely neglected; but far more often, seeking a symbol for the highest love of all, Scripture ignores this seemingly almost angelic relation and plunges into the depth of what is most natural and instinctive. Affection is taken as the image when God is represented as our Father; Eros, when Christ is represented as the Bridegroom of the Church. Let us begin with the suspicions of those in Authority. I think there is a ground for them and that a consideration of this ground brings something important to light. Friendship, I have said, is born at the moment when one man says to another "What! You too? I thought that no one but myself . . ." But the common taste or vision or point of view which is thus discovered need not always be a nice one. From such a moment art, or philosophy, or an advance in religion or morals might well take their rise; but why not also torture, cannibalism, or human sacrifice? Surely most of us have experienced the ambivalent nature of such moments in our own youth? It was wonderful when we first met someone who cared for our favourite poet. What we had hardly understood before now took clear shape. What we had been half ashamed of we now freely acknowledged. But it was no less delightful when we first met someone who shared with us a secret evil. This too became far more palpable and explicit; of this too, we ceased to be ashamed. Even now, at whatever age, we all know the perilous charm of a shared hatred or grievance. (It is difficult not to hail as a Friend the only other man in College who really sees the faults of the Sub-Warden).

Alone among unsympathetic companions, I hold certain views and standards timidly, half ashamed to avow them and half doubtful if they can after all be right. Put me back among my Friends and in half an hour—in ten minutes—these same views and standards become once more indisputable. The opinion of this little circle, while I am in it, out-weighs that of a thousand outsiders: as Friendship strengthens, it will do this even when my Friends are far away. For we all wish to be judged by our peers, by the men "after our own heart". Only they really know our mind and only they judge it by standards we fully acknowledge. Theirs is the praise we really covet and the blame we really dread. The little pock-ets of early Christians survived because they cared exclusively for the love of "the brethren" and stopped their ears to the opinion of the Pagan society all round them. But a circle of criminals, cranks, or perverts sur-vives in just the same way; by becoming deaf to the opinion of the outer world, by discounting it as the chatter of outsiders who "don't under-stand", of the "conventional", "the bourgeois", the "Establishment", of prigs, prudes, and humbugs.

It is therefore easy to see why Authority frowns on Friendship. Every real Friendship is a sort of secession, even a rebellion. It may be a rebel-lion of serious thinkers against accepted clap-trap or of faddists against accepted good sense; of real artists against popular ugliness or of charla-tans against civilised taste; of good men against the badness of society or of bad men against its goodness. Whichever it is, it will be unwelcome to Top People. In each knot of Friends there is a sectional "public opinion" which fortifies its members against the public opinion of the community in general. Each therefore is a pocket of potential resistance. Men who have real Friends are less easy to manage or "get at"; harder for good Authorities to correct or for bad Authorities to corrupt. Hence if our masters, by force or by propaganda about "Togetherness" or by unob-trusively making privacy and unplanned leisure impossible, ever succeed in producing a world where all are Companions and none are Friends, they will have removed certain dangers, and will also have taken from us what is almost our strongest safeguard against complete servitude.

But the dangers are perfectly real. Friendship (as the ancients saw) can be a school of virtue; but also (as they did not see) a school of vice. It is ambivalent. It makes good men better and bad men worse. It would be a waste of time to elaborate the point. What concerns us is not to expatiate on the badness of bad Friendships but to become aware of the possible danger in good ones. This love, like the other natural loves, has its congenital liability to a particular disease.

It will be obvious that the element of secession, of indifference or deafness (at least on some matters) to the voices of the outer world, is common to all Friendships, whether good, bad, or merely innocuous. Even if the common ground of the Friendship is nothing more momentous than stamp-collecting, the circle rightly and inevitably ignores the views of the millions who think it a silly occupation and of the thousands who have merely dabbled in it. The founders of meteorology rightly and inevitably ignored the views of the millions who still attributed storms to witchcraft. There is no offence in this. As I know that I should be an Outsider to a circle of golfers, mathematicians, or motorists, so I claim the equal right of regarding them as Outsiders to mine. People who bore one another should meet seldom; people who interest one another, often.

The danger is that this partial indifference or deafness to outside opinion, justified and necessary though it is, may lead to a wholesale indifference or deafness. The most spectacular instances of this can be seen not in a circle of friends but in a Theocratic or aristocratic class. We know what the Priests in Our Lord's time thought of the common people. The Knights in Froissart's chronicles had neither sympathy nor mercy for the "outsiders", the churls or peasantry. But this deplorable indifference was very closely intertwined with a good quality. They really had, among themselves, a very high standard of valour, generosity, courtesy, and honour. This standard the cautious, close-fisted churl would have thought merely silly. The Knights, in maintaining it, were, and had to be, wholly indifferent to his views. They "didn't give a damn" what he thought. If they had, our own standard today would be the poorer and the coarser for it. But the habit of "not giving a damn" grows on a class. To discount the voice of the peasant where it really ought to be discounted makes it easier to discount his voice when he cries for justice or mercy. The partial deafness which is noble and necessary encourages the wholesale deafness which is arrogant and inhuman.

A circle of friends cannot of course oppress the outer world as a powerful social class can. But it is subject, on its own scale, to the same danger. It can come to treat as "outsiders" in a general (and derogatory) sense those who were quite properly outsiders for a particular purpose. Thus, like an aristocracy, it can create around it a vacuum across which no voice will carry. The literary or artistic circle which began by discounting, perhaps rightly, the plain man's ideas about literature or art may come to discount equally his idea that they should pay their bills, cut their nails, and behave civilly. Whatever faults the circle has—and no circle is without them—thus become incurable. But that is not all. The partial and defensible deafness was based on some kind of superiority—even if it were only a superior knowledge about stamps. The sense of superiority will then get itself attached to the total deafness. The group will disdain as well as ignore those outside it. It will, in effect, have turned itself into something very like a class. A *coterie* is a self-appointed aristocracy.

I said above that in a good Friendship each member often feels humility towards the rest. He sees that they are splendid and counts himself lucky to be among them. But unfortunately the *they* and *them* are also, from another point of view *we* and *us*. Thus the transition from individual humility to corporate pride is very easy.

I am not thinking of what we should call a social or snobbish pride: a delight in knowing, and being known to know, distinguished people. That is quite a different thing. The snob wishes to attach himself to some group because it is already regarded as an *élite*; friends are in danger of coming to regard themselves as an *élite* because they are already attached. We seek men after our own heart for their own sake and are then alarmingly or delightfully surprised by the feeling that we have become an aristocracy. Not that we'd call it that. Every reader who has known Friendship will probably feel inclined to deny with some heat that his own circle was ever guilty of such an absurdity. I feel the same. But in such matters it is best not to begin with ourselves. However it may be with us, I think we have all recognised some such tendency in those other circles to which we are the Outsiders.

I was once at some kind of conference where two clergymen, obviously close friends, began talking about "uncreated energies" other than God. I asked how there could be any uncreated things except God if the Creed was right in calling Him the "maker of all things visible and invisible". Their reply was to glance at one another and laugh. I had no objection to their laughter, but I wanted an answer in words as well. It was not at all a sneering or unpleasant laugh. It expressed very much what Americans would express by saying "Isn't he cute?" It was like the laughter of jolly grown-ups when an *enfant terrible* asks the sort of question that is never asked. You can hardly imagine how inoffensively it was done, nor how clearly it conveyed the impression that they were fully aware of living habitually on a higher plane than the rest of us, that they came among us as Knights among churls or as grown-ups among children. Very possibly they had an answer to my question and knew that I was too ignorant to follow it. If they had said in so many words, "I'm afraid it would take too long to explain," I would not be attributing to them the pride of Friendship. The glance and the laugh are the real point—the audible and visible embodiment of a corporate superiority taken for granted and unconcealed. The almost complete inoffensiveness, the absence of any apparent wish to wound or exult (they were very nice young men) really underline the Olympian attitude. Here was a sense of superiority so secure that it could afford to be tolerant, urbane, unemphatic.

This sense of corporate superiority is not always Olympian; that is, tranquil and tolerant. It may be Titanic; restive, militant, and embittered. Another time, when I had been addressing an undergraduate society and some discussion (very properly) followed my paper, a young man with an expression as tense as that of a rodent so dealt with me that I had to say, "Look, sir. Twice in the last five minutes you have as good as called me a liar. If you cannot discuss a question of criticism without that kind of thing I must leave." I expected he would do one of two things; lose his temper and redouble his insults, or else blush and apologise. The startling thing is that he did neither. No new perturbation was added to the habitual *malaise* of his expression. He did not repeat the Lie Direct; but apart from that he went on just as before. One had come up against an iron curtain. He was forearmed against the risk of any strictly personal relation, either friendly or hostile, with such as me. Behind this, almost certainly, there lies a circle of the Titanic sort—self-dubbed Knights Templars perpetually in arms to defend a critical Baphomet. We—who are *they* to them—do not exist as persons at all. We are specimens; specimens of various Age Groups, Types, Climates of Opinion, or Interests, to be exterminated. Deprived of one weapon, they coolly take up another. They are not, in the ordinary human sense, meeting us at all; they are merely doing a job of work—spraying (I have heard one use that image) insecticide.

My two nice young clergymen and my not so nice Rodent were on a high intellectual level. So were that famous set who in Edwardian times reached the sublime fatuity of calling themselves "the Souls". But the same feeling of corporate superiority can possess a group of much more commonplace friends. It will then be flaunted in a cruder way. We have all seen this done by the "old hands" at school talking in the presence of a new boy, or two Regulars in the Army talking before a "Temporary"; sometimes by very loud and vulgar friends to impress mere strangers in a bar or a railway carriage. Such people talk very intimately and esoterically in order to be overheard. Everyone who is not in the circle must be shown that he is not in it. Indeed the Friendship may be "about" almost nothing except the fact that it excludes. In speaking to an Outsider each member of it delights to mention the others by their Christian names or nicknames; not although, but because, the Outsider won't know who he means. A man I once knew was even subtler. He simply referred to his friends as if we all knew, certainly ought to know, who they were. "As Richard Button once said to me . . . ," he would begin. We were all very young. We never dared to admit that we hadn't heard of Richard Button. It seemed so obvious that to everyone who was anyone he must be a household word; "not to know him argued ourselves unknown." Only much later did we come to realise that no one else had heard of him either. (Indeed I now have a suspicion that some of these Richard Buttons, Hezekiah Cromwells, and Eleanor Forsyths had no more existence than Mrs Harris. But for a year or so we were completely over-awed.)

We can thus detect the pride of Friendship—whether Olympian, Titanic, or merely vulgar—in many circles of Friends. It would be rash to assume that our own is safe from its danger; for of course it is in our own that we should be slowest to recognise it. The danger of such pride is indeed almost inseparable from Friendly love. Friendship must exclude. From the innocent and necessary act of excluding to the spirit of exclusiveness is an easy step; and thence to the degrading pleasure of exclusiveness. If that is once admitted the downward slope will grow rapidly steeper. We may never perhaps become Titans or plain cads; we might— which is in some ways worse—become "Souls". The common vision which first brought us together may fade quite away. We shall be a *coterie* that exists for the sake of being a *coterie;* a little self-elected (and therefore absurd) aristocracy, basking in the moonshine of our collective self-approval.

Sometimes a circle in this condition begins to dabble in the world of practise. Judiciously enlarging itself to admit recruits whose share in the original common interest is negligible but who are felt to be (in some undefined sense) "sound men", it becomes a power in the land. Membership of it comes to have a sort of political importance, though the politics involved may be only those of a regiment, a college, or a cathedral close. The manipulation of committees, the capture of jobs (for sound men), and the united front against the Have-nots now become its principal occupation, and those who once met to talk about God or poetry now meet to talk about lectureships or livings. Notice the justice of their doom. "Dust thou art and unto dust shalt thou return," said God to Adam. In a circle which has thus dwindled into a coven of wanglers Friendship has sunk back again into the mere practical Companionship which was its matrix. They are now the same sort of body as the primitive horde of hunters. Hunters, indeed, is precisely what they are; and not the kind of hunters I most respect.

The mass of the people, who are never quite right, are never quite wrong. They are hopelessly mistaken in their belief that every knot of friends came into existence for the sake of the pleasures of conceit and superiority. They are, I trust, mistaken in their belief that every Friendship actually indulges in these pleasures. But they would seem to be right in diagnosing pride as the danger to which Friendships are naturally liable. Just because this is the most spiritual of loves the danger which besets it is spiritual too. Friendship is even, if you like, angelic. But man needs to be triply protected by humility if he is to eat the bread of angels without risk.

Perhaps we may now hazard a guess why Scripture uses Friendship so rarely as an image of the highest love. It is already, in actual fact, too spiritual to be a good symbol of Spiritual things. The highest does not stand without the lowest. God can safely represent Himself to us as Father and Husband because only a lunatic would think that He is physically our sire or that His marriage with the Church is other than mystical.

But if Friendship were used for this purpose we might mistake the symbol for the thing symbolised. The danger inherent in it would be aggravated. We might be further encouraged to mistake that nearness (by resemblance) to the heavenly life which Friendship certainly displays for a nearness of approach.

Friendship, then, like the other natural loves, is unable to save itself. In reality, because it is spiritual and therefore faces a subtler enemy, it must, even more whole-heartedly than they, invoke the divine protection if it hopes to remain sweet. For consider how narrow its true path is. It must not become what the people call a "mutual admiration society"; yet if it is not full of mutual admiration, of Appreciative love, it is not Friendship at all. For unless our lives are to be miserably impoverished it must be for us in our Friendships as it was for Christiana and her party in *The Pilgrim's Progress:*

> They seemed to be a terror one to the other, for that they could not see that glory each one on herself which they could see in each other. Now therefore they began to esteem each other better than themselves. For you are fairer than I am, said one; and you are more comely than I am, said another.

There is in the long run only one way in which we can taste this illustrious experience with safety. And Bunyan has indicated it in the same passage. It was in the House of the Interpreter, after they had been bathed, sealed and freshly clothed in "White Raiment" that the women saw one another in this light. If we remember the bathing, sealing, and robing, we shall be safe. And the higher the common ground of the Friendship is, the more necessary the remembrance. In an explicitly religious Friendship, above all, to forget it would be fatal. For then it will seem to us that we—we four or five—have chosen one another, the insight of each finding the intrinsic beauty of the rest, like to like, a voluntary nobility; that we have ascended above the rest of mankind by our native powers. The other loves do not invite the same illusion. Affection obviously requires kinships or at least proximities which never depended on our own choice. And as for Eros, half the love songs and half the love poems in the world will tell you that the Beloved is your fate or destiny, no more your choice than a thunderbolt, for "it is not in our power to love or hate". Cupid's archery, genes—anything but ourselves. But in Friendship, being free of all that, we think we have chosen our peers. In reality, a few years' difference in the dates of our births, a few more miles between certain houses, the choice of one university instead of another, posting to different regiments, the accident of a topic being raised or not raised at a first meeting—any of these chances might have kept us apart. But, for a Christian, there are, strictly speaking, no chances. A secret Master of the Ceremonies has been at work. Christ, who said to the disciples, "Ye have not chosen me, but I have chosen you," can truly say to every group of Christian friends, "You have not chosen one another but I have chosen you for one another." The Friendship is not a reward for our discrimination and good taste in finding one another out. It is the instrument by which God reveals to each the beauties of all the others. They are no greater than the beauties of a thousand other men; by Friendship God opens our eyes to them. They are, like all beauties, derived from Him, and then, in a good Friendship, increased by Him through the Friendship itself, so that it is His instrument for creating as well as for revealing. At this feast it is He who has spread the board and it is He who has chosen the guests. It is He, we may dare to hope, who sometimes does, and always should, preside. Let us not reckon without our Host.

Not that we must always partake of it solemnly. "God who made good laughter" forbid. It is one of the difficult and delightful subtleties of life that we must deeply acknowledge certain things to be serious and yet retain the power and will to treat them often as lightly as a game. But there will be a time for saying more about this in the next chapter. For the moment I will only quote Dunbar's beautifully balanced advice:

Man, please thy Maker, and be merry,
And give not for this world a cherry.

V

EROS

BY *EROS* I mean of course that state which we call "being in love"; or, if you prefer, that kind of love which lovers are "in". Some readers may have been surprised when, in an earlier chapter, I described Affection as the love in which our experience seems to come closest to that of the animals. Surely, it might be asked, our sexual functions bring us equally close? This is quite true as regards human sexuality in general. But I am not going to be concerned with human sexuality simply as such. Sexuality makes part of our subject only when it becomes an ingredient in the complex state of "being in love". That sexual experience can occur without Eros, without being "in love", and that Eros includes other things besides sexual activity, I take for granted. If you prefer to put it that way, I am inquiring not into the sexuality which is common to us and the beasts or even common to all men but into one uniquely human variation of it which develops within "love"—what I call Eros. The carnal or animally sexual element within Eros, I intend (following an old usage) to call Venus. And I mean by Venus what is sexual not in some cryptic or rarified sense—such as a depth-psychologist might explore—but in a perfectly obvious sense; what is known to be sexual by those who experience it; what could be proved to be sexual by the simplest observations.

Sexuality may operate without Eros or as part of Eros. Let me hasten to add that I make the distinction simply in order to limit our inquiry and without any moral implications. I am not at all subscribing to the popular idea that it is the absence or presence of Eros which makes the sexual act "impure" or "pure", degraded or fine, unlawful or lawful. If all who lay together without being in the state of Eros were abominable, we all come of tainted stock. The times and places in which marriage depends on Eros are in a small minority. Most of our ancestors were married off in early youth to partners chosen by their parents on grounds that had nothing to do with Eros. They went to the act with no other "fuel", so to speak, than plain animal desire. And they did right; honest Christian husbands and wives, obeying their fathers and mothers, discharging to one another their "marriage debt", and bringing up families in the fear of the Lord. Conversely, this act, done under the influence of a soaring and iridescent Eros which reduces the role of the senses to a minor consideration, may yet be plain adultery, may involve breaking a wife's heart, deceiving a husband, betraying a friend, polluting hospitality, and deserting your children. It has not pleased God that the distinction between a sin and a duty should turn on fine feelings. This act, like any other, is justified (or not) by far more prosaic and definable criteria; by the keeping or breaking of promises, by justice or injustice, by charity or selfishness, by obedience or disobedience. My treatment rules out mere sexuality—sexuality without Eros—on grounds that have nothing to do with morals; because it is irrelevant to our purpose.

To the evolutionist Eros (the human variation) will be something that grows out of Venus, a late complication and development of the immemorial biological impulse. We must not assume, however, that this is necessarily what happens within the consciousness of the individual. There may be those who have first felt mere sexual appetite for a woman and then gone on at a later stage to "fall in love with her". But I doubt if this is at all common. Very often what comes first is simply a delighted pre-occupation with the Beloved—a general, unspecified pre-occupation with her in her totality. A man in this state really hasn't leisure to think of sex. He is too busy thinking of a person. The fact that she is a woman is far less important than the fact that she is herself. He is full of desire, but the desire may not be sexually toned. If you asked him what he wanted, the true reply would often be, "To go on thinking of her." He is love's contemplative. And when at a later stage the explicitly sexual element awakes, he will not feel (unless scientific theories are influencing him) that this had all along been the root of the whole matter. He is more likely to feel that the incoming tide of Eros, having demolished many sandcastles and made islands of many rocks, has now at last with a triumphant seventh wave flooded this part of his nature also—the little pool of ordinary sexuality which was there on his beach before the tide came in. Eros enters him like an invader, taking over and reorganising, one by one, the institutions of a conquered country. It may have taken over many others before it reaches the sex in him; and it will reorganise that too.

No one has indicated the nature of that reorganisation more briefly and accurately than George Orwell, who disliked it and preferred sexuality in its native condition, uncontaminated by Eros. In *Nineteen Eighty-Four* his dreadful hero (how much less human than the four-footed heroes of his excellent *Animal Farm*!), before towsing the heroine, demands a reassurance, "You like doing this?" he asks. "I don't mean simply me; I mean the thing in itself." He is not satisfied till he gets the answer, "I adore it." This little dialogue defines the reorganisation. Sexual desire, without Eros, wants *it*, the *thing in itself;* Eros wants the Beloved.

The *thing* is a sensory pleasure; that is, an event occurring within one's own body. We use a most unfortunate idiom when we say, of a lustful man prowling the streets, that he "wants a woman". Strictly speaking, a woman is just what he does not want. He wants a pleasure for which a woman happens to be the necessary piece of apparatus. How much he cares about the woman as such may be gauged by his attitude to her five minutes after fruition (one does not keep the carton after one has smoked the cigarettes). Now Eros makes a man really want, not a woman, but one particular woman. In some mysterious but quite indisputable fashion the lover desires the Beloved herself, not the pleasure she can give. No lover in the world ever sought the embraces of the woman he loved as the result of a calculation, however unconscious, that they would be more pleasurable than those of any other woman. If he raised the question he would, no doubt, expect that this would be so. But to raise it would be to step outside the world of Eros altogether. The only man I know of who ever did raise it was Lucretius, and he was certainly not in love when he did. It is interesting to note his answer. That austere voluptuary gave it as his opinion that love actually impairs sexual pleasure. The emotion was a distraction. It spoiled the cool and critical receptivity of his palate. (A great poet; but "Lord, what beastly fellows these Romans were!")

The reader will notice that Eros thus wonderfully transforms what is *par excellence* a Need-pleasure into the most Appreciative of all pleasures. It is the nature of a Need-pleasure to show us the object solely in relation to our need, even our momentary need. But in Eros, a Need, at its most intense, sees the object most intensely as a thing admirable in herself, important far beyond her relation to the lover's need.

If we had not all experienced this, if we were mere logicians, we might boggle at the conception of desiring a human being, as distinct from desiring any pleasure, comfort, or service that human being can give. And it is certainly hard to explain. Lovers themselves are trying to express part of it (not much) when they say they would like to "eat" one another. Milton has expressed more when he fancies angelic creatures with bodies made of light who can achieve total interpenetration instead of our mere embraces. Charles Williams has said something of it in the words, "Love you? I *am* you."

Without Eros sexual desire, like every other desire, is a fact about ourselves. Within Eros it is rather about the Beloved. It becomes almost a mode of perception, entirely a mode of expression. It feels objective; something outside us, in the real world. That is why Eros, though the king of pleasures, always (at his height) has the air of regarding pleasure as a by-product. To think about it would plunge us back in ourselves, in our own nervous system. It would kill Eros, as you can "kill" the finest mountain prospect by locating it all in your own retina and optic nerves. Anyway, whose pleasure? For one of the first things Eros does is to obliterate the distinction between giving and receiving.

Hitherto I have been trying merely to describe, not to evaluate. But certain moral questions now inevitably arise, and I must not conceal my own view of them. It is submitted rather than asserted, and of course open to correction by better men, better lovers, and better Christians.

It has been widely held in the past, and is perhaps held by many unsophisticated people today, that the spiritual danger of Eros arises almost entirely from the carnal element within it; that Eros is "noblest" or "purest" when Venus is reduced to the minimum. The older moral theologians certainly seem to have thought that the danger we chiefly had to guard against in marriage was that of a soul-destroying surrender to the senses. It will be noticed, however, that this is not the Scriptural approach. St Paul, dissuading his converts from marriage, says nothing about that side of the matter except to discourage prolonged abstinence from Venus (1 Cor. 7:5). What he fears is pre-occupation, the need of constantly "pleasing"—that is, considering—one's partner, the multiple distractions of domesticity. It is marriage itself, not the marriage bed, that will be likely to hinder us from waiting uninterruptedly on God. And surely St Paul is right? If I may trust my own experience, it is (within marriage as without) the practical and prudential cares of this world, and even the smallest and most prosaic of those cares, that are the great distraction. The gnat-like cloud of petty anxieties and decisions about the conduct of the next hour have interfered with my prayers more often than any passion or appetite whatever. The great, permanent temptation of marriage is not to sensuality but (quite bluntly) to avarice. With all proper respect to the medieval guides, I cannot help remembering that they were all celibates, and probably did not know what Eros does to our sexuality; how, far from aggravating, he reduces the nagging and addictive character of mere appetite. And that not simply by satisfying it. Eros, without diminishing desire, makes abstinence easier. He tends, no doubt, to a pre-occupation with the Beloved which can indeed be an obstacle to the spiritual life; but not chiefly a sensual pre-occupation.

The real spiritual danger in Eros as a whole lies, I believe, elsewhere. I will return to the point. For the moment, I want to speak of the danger which at present, in my opinion, especially haunts the act of love. This is a subject on which I disagree, not with the human race (far from it), but with many of its gravest spokesmen. I believe we are all being encouraged to take Venus too seriously; at any rate, with a wrong kind of seriousness. All my life a ludicrous and portentous solemnisation of sex has been going on.

One author tells us that Venus should recur through the married life in "a solemn, sacramental rhythm". A young man to whom I had described as "pornographic" a novel that he much admired, replied with genuine bewilderment, "Pornographic? But how can it be? It treats the whole thing so seriously"—as if a long face were a sort of moral disinfectant. Our friends who harbour Dark Gods, the "pillar of blood" school, attempt seriously to restore something like the Phallic religion. Our advertisements, at their sexiest, paint the whole business in terms of the rapt, the intense, the swoony-devout; seldom a hint of gaiety. And the psychologists have so bedevilled us with the infinite importance of complete sexual adjustment and the all but impossibility of achieving it, that I could believe some young couples now go to it with the complete works of Freud, Kraft-Ebbing, Havelock Ellis, and Dr Stopes spread out on bed-tables all round them. Cheery old Ovid, who never either ignored a mole-hill or made a mountain of it, would be more to the point. We have reached the stage at which nothing is more needed than a roar of old-fashioned laughter. But, it will be replied, the thing *is* serious. Yes; quadruply so. First, theologically, because this is the body's share in marriage which, by God's choice, is the mystical image of the union between God and Man. Secondly, as what I will venture to call a sub-Christian, or Pagan or natural sacrament, our human participation in, and exposition of, the natural forces of life and fertility—the marriage of Sky-Father and Earth-Mother. Thirdly, on the moral level, in view of the obligations involved and the incalculable momentousness of being a parent and ancestor. Finally it has (sometimes, not always) a great emotional seriousness in the minds of the participants.

But eating is also serious; theologically, as the vehicle of the Blessed Sacrament; ethically in view of our duty to feed the hungry; socially, because the table is from time immemorial the place for talk; medically, as all dyspeptics know. Yet we do not bring bluebooks to dinner nor behave there as if we were in church. And it is *gourmets*, not saints, who come nearest to doing so. Animals are always serious about food.

We must not be totally serious about Venus. Indeed we can't be totally serious without doing violence to our humanity. It is not for nothing that every language and literature in the world is full of jokes about sex. Many of them may be dull or disgusting and nearly all of them are old. But we must insist that they embody an attitude to Venus which in the long run endangers the Christian life far less than a reverential gravity. We must not attempt to find an absolute in the flesh. Banish play and laughter from the bed of love and you may let in a false goddess. She will be even falser than the Aphrodite of the Greeks; for they, even while they worshipped her, knew that she was "laughter-loving". The mass of the people are perfectly right in their conviction that Venus is a partly comic spirit. We are under no obligation at all to sing all our love-duets in the throbbing, world-without-end, heart-breaking manner of Tristan and Isolde; let us often sing like Papageno and Papagena instead.

Venus herself will have a terrible revenge if we take her (occasional) seriousness at its face value. And that in two ways. One is most comically—though with no comic intention—illustrated by Sir Thomas Browne when he says that her service is "the foolishest act a wise man commits in all his life, nor is there anything that will more deject his cool'd imagination, when he shall consider what an odd and unworthy piece of folly he had committed". But if he had gone about that act with less solemnity in the first place he would not have suffered this "dejection". If his imagination had not been misled, its cooling would have brought no such revulsion. But Venus has another and worse revenge.

She herself is a mocking, mischievous spirit, far more elf than deity, and makes game of us. When all external circumstances are fittest for her service she will leave one or both the lovers totally indisposed for it. When every overt act is impossible and even glances cannot be exchanged—in trains, in shops, and at interminable parties—she will assail them with all her force. An hour later, when time and place agree, she will have mysteriously withdrawn; perhaps from only one of them. What a pother this must raise—what resentments, self-pities, suspicions, wounded vanities, and all the current chatter about "frustration"—in those who have deified her! But sensible lovers laugh. It is all part of the game; a game of catch-as-catch-can, and the escapes and tumbles and head-on collisions are to be treated as a romp.

For I can hardly help regarding it as one of God's jokes that a passion so soaring, so apparently transcendent, as Eros, should thus be linked in incongruous symbiosis with a bodily appetite which, like any other appetite, tactlessly reveals its connections with such mundane factors as weather, health, diet, circulation, and digestion. In Eros at times we seem to be flying; Venus gives us the sudden twitch that reminds us we are really captive balloons. It is a continual demonstration of the truth that we are composite creatures, rational animals, akin on one side to the angels, on the other to tom-cats. It is a bad thing not to be able to take a joke. Worse, not to take a divine joke; made, I grant you, at our expense, but also (who doubts it?) for our endless benefit.

Man has held three views of his body. First there is that of those ascetic Pagans who called it the prison or the "tomb" of the soul, and of Christians like Fisher to whom it was a "sack of dung", food for worms, filthy, shameful, a source of nothing but temptation to bad men and humiliation to good ones. Then there are the Neo-Pagans (they seldom know Greek), the nudists and the sufferers from Dark Gods, to whom the body is glorious. But thirdly we have the view which St Francis expressed by calling his body "Brother Ass". All three may be—I am not sure—defensible; but give me St Francis for my money.

Ass is exquisitely right because no one in his senses can either revere or hate a donkey. It is a useful, sturdy, lazy, obstinate, patient, lovable, and infuriating beast; deserving now the stick and now a carrot; both pathetically and absurdly beautiful. So the body. There's no living with it till we recognise that one of its functions in our lives is to play the part of buffoon. Until some theory has sophisticated them, every man, woman, and child in the world knows this. The fact that we have bodies is the oldest joke there is. Eros (like death, figure-drawing, and the study of medicine) may at moments cause us to take it with total seriousness. The error consists in concluding that Eros should always do so and permanently abolish the joke. But this is not what happens. The very faces of all the happy lovers we know make it clear. Lovers, unless their love is very short-lived, again and again feel an element not only of comedy, not only of play, but even of buffoonery, in the body's expression of Eros. And the body would frustrate us if this were not so. It would be too clumsy an instrument to render love's music unless its very clumsiness could be felt as adding to the total experience its own grotesque charm—a sub-plot or antimasque miming with its own hearty rough-and-tumble what the soul enacts in statelier fashion. (Thus in old comedies the lyric loves of the hero and heroine are at once parodied and corroborated by some much more earthy affair between a Touchstone and an Audrey or a valet and a chambermaid). The highest does not stand without the lowest. There is indeed at certain moments a high poetry in the flesh itself; but also, by your leave, an irreducible element of obstinate and ludicrous un-poetry. If it does not make itself felt on one occasion, it will on another. Far better plant it foresquare within the drama of Eros as comic relief than pretend you haven't noticed it.

For indeed we require this relief. The poetry is there as well as the un-poetry; the gravity of Venus as well as her levity, the *gravis ardor* or burning weight of desire. Pleasure, pushed to its extreme, shatters us like pain. The longing for a union which only the flesh can mediate while the flesh, our mutually excluding bodies, renders it forever unattainable, can have the grandeur of a metaphysical pursuit. Amorousness as well as grief can bring tears to the eyes. But Venus does not always come thus "entire, fastened to her prey", and the fact that she sometimes does so is the very reason for preserving always a hint of playfulness in our attitude to her. When natural things look most divine, the demoniac is just round the corner.

This refusal to be quite immersed—this recollection of the levity even when, for the moment, only the gravity is displayed—is especially relevant to a certain attitude which Venus, in her intensity, evokes from most (I believe, not all) pairs of lovers. This act can invite the man to an extreme, though short-lived, masterfulness, to the dominance of a conqueror or a captor, and the woman to a correspondingly extreme abjection and surrender. Hence the roughness, even fierceness, of some erotic play; the "lover's pinch which hurts and is desired". How should a sane couple think of this? or a Christian couple permit it?

I think it is harmless and wholesome on one condition. We must recognise that we have here to do with what I called "the Pagan sacrament" in sex. In Friendship, as we noticed, each participant stands for precisely himself—the contingent individual he is. But in the act of love we are not merely ourselves. We are also representatives. It is here no impoverishment but an enrichment to be aware that forces older and less personal than we work through us. In us all the masculinity and femininity of the world, all that is assailant and responsive, are momentarily focused. The man does play the Sky-Father and the woman the Earth-Mother; he does play Form, and she Matter. But we must give full value to the word *play*. Of course neither "plays a part" in the sense of being a hypocrite. But each plays a part or role in—well, in something which is comparable to a mystery-play or ritual (at one extreme) and to a masque or even a charade (at the other).

A woman who accepted as literally her own this extreme self-surrender would be an idolatress offering to a man what belongs only to God. And a man would have to be the coxcomb of all coxcombs, and indeed a blasphemer, if he arrogated to himself, as the mere person he is, the sort of sovereignty to which Venus for a moment exalts him. But what cannot lawfully be yielded or claimed can be lawfully enacted. Outside this ritual or drama he and she are two immortal souls, two free-born adults, two citizens. We should be much mistaken if we supposed that those marriages where this mastery is most asserted and acknowledged in the act of Venus were those where the husband is most likely to be dominant in the married life as a whole; the reverse is perhaps more probable. But within the rite or drama they become a god and goddess between whom there is no equality—whose relations are asymmetrical.

Some will think it strange I should find an element of ritual or masquerade in that action which is often regarded as the most real, the most unmasked and sheerly genuine, we ever do. Are we not our true selves when naked? In a sense, no. The word *naked* was originally a past participle; the naked man was the man who had undergone a process of *naking*, that is, of stripping or peeling (you used the verb of nuts and fruit). Time out of mind the naked man has seemed to our ancestors not the natural but the abnormal man; not the man who has abstained from dressing but the man who has been for some reason undressed. And it is a simple fact—anyone can observe it at a men's bathing place—that nudity emphasises common humanity and soft-pedals what is individual. In that way we are "more ourselves" when clothed. By nudity the lovers cease to be solely John and Mary; the universal He and She are emphasised. You could almost say they *put on* nakedness as a ceremonial robe—or as the costume for a charade. For we must still beware—and never more than when we thus partake of the Pagan sacrament in our love-passages—of being serious in the wrong way. The Sky-Father himself is only a Pagan dream of One far greater than Zeus and far more masculine than the male. And a mortal man is not even the Sky-Father, and cannot really wear his crown. Only a copy of it, done in tinselled paper. I do not call it this in contempt. I like ritual; I

like private theatricals; I even like charades. Paper crowns have their legitimate, and (in the proper context) their serious, uses. They are not in the last resort much flimsier ("if imagination mend them") than all earthly dignities.

But I dare not mention this Pagan sacrament without turning aside to guard against any danger of confusing it with an incomparably higher mystery. As nature crowns man in that brief action, so the Christian law has crowned him in the permanent relationship of marriage, bestowing—or should I say, inflicting?—a certain "headship" on him. This is a very different coronation. And as we could easily take the natural mystery too seriously, so we might take the Christian mystery not seriously enough. Christian writers (notably Milton) have sometimes spoken of the husband's headship with a complacency to make the blood run cold. We must go back to our Bibles. The husband is the head of the wife just in so far as he is to her what Christ is to the Church. He is to love her as Christ loved the Church—read on—*and gave his life for her* (Eph. 5:25). This headship, then, is most fully embodied not in the husband we should all wish to be but in him whose marriage is most like a crucifixion; whose wife receives most and gives least, is most unworthy of him, is— in her own mere nature—least lovable. For the Church has no beauty but what the Bridegroom gives her; He does not find, but makes her, lovely. The chrism of this terrible coronation is to be seen not in the joys of any man's marriage but in its sorrows, in the sickness and sufferings of a good wife or the faults of a bad one, in his unwearying (never paraded) care or his inexhaustible forgiveness: forgiveness, not acquiescence. As Christ sees in the flawed, proud, fanatical, or lukewarm Church on earth that Bride who will one day be without spot or wrinkle, and labours to produce the latter, so the husband whose headship is Christ-like (and he is allowed no other sort) never despairs. He is a King Cophetua who after twenty years still hopes that the beggar-girl will one day learn to speak the truth and wash behind her ears.

To say this is not to say that there is any virtue or wisdom in making a marriage that involves such misery. There is no wisdom or virtue in seeking unnecessary martyrdom or deliberately courting persecution; yet it is, none the less, the persecuted or martyred Christian in whom the pattern of the Master is most unambiguously realised. So, in these terrible marriages, once they have come about, the "headship" of the husband, if only he can sustain it, is most Christ-like.

The sternest feminist need not grudge my sex the crown offered to it either in the Pagan or in the Christian mystery. For the one is of paper and the other of thorns. The real danger is not that husbands may grasp the latter too eagerly; but that they will allow or compel their wives to usurp it. From Venus, the carnal ingredient within Eros, I now turn to Eros as a whole. Here we shall see the same pattern repeated. As Venus within Eros does not really aim at pleasure, so Eros does not aim at happiness. We may think he does, but when he is brought to the test it proves otherwise. Everyone knows that it is useless to try to separate lovers by proving to them that their marriage will be an unhappy one. This is not only because they will disbelieve you. They usually will, no doubt. But even if they believed, they would not be dissuaded. For it is the very mark of Eros that when he is in us we had rather share unhappiness with the Beloved than be happy on any other terms. Even if the two lovers are mature and experienced people who know that broken hearts heal in the end and can clearly foresee that, if they once steeled themselves to go through the present agony of parting, they would almost certainly be happier ten years hence than marriage is at all likely to make them—even then, they would not part. To Eros all these calculations are irrelevant— just as the coolly brutal judgment of Lucretius is irrelevant to Venus. Even when it becomes clear beyond all evasion that marriage with the Beloved cannot possibly lead to happiness—when it cannot even profess to offer any other life than that of tending an incurable invalid, of hopeless poverty, of exile, or of disgrace—Eros never hesitates to say, "Better this than parting. Better to be miserable with her than happy without her.

Let our hearts break provided they break together." If the voice within us does not say this, it is not the voice of Eros.

This is the grandeur and terror of love. But notice, as before, side by side with this grandeur, the playfulness. Eros, as well as Venus, is the subject of countless jokes. And even when the circumstances of the two lovers are so tragic that no bystander could keep back his tears, they themselves—in want, in hospital wards, on visitors' days in jail—will sometimes be surprised by a merriment which strikes the onlooker (but not them) as unbearably pathetic. Nothing is falser than the idea that mockery is necessarily hostile. Until they have a baby to laugh at, lovers are always laughing at each other.

It is in the grandeur of Eros that the seeds of danger are concealed. He has spoken like a god. His total commitment, his reckless disregard of happiness, his transcendence of self-regard, sound like a message from the eternal world.

And yet it cannot, just as it stands, be the voice of God Himself. For Eros, speaking with that very grandeur and displaying that very transcendence of self, may urge to evil as well as to good. Nothing is shallower than the belief that a love which leads to sin is always qualitatively lower—more animal or more trivial—than one which leads to faithful, fruitful, and Christian marriage. The love which leads to cruel and perjured unions, even to suicide-pacts and murder, is not likely to be wandering lust or idle sentiment. It may well be Eros in all his splendour; heartbreakingly sincere; ready for every sacrifice except renunciation.

There have been schools of thought which accepted the voice of Eros as something actually transcendent and tried to justify the absoluteness of his commands. Plato will have it that "falling in love" is the mutual recognition on earth of souls which have been singled out for one another in a previous and celestial existence. To meet the Beloved is to realise, "We loved before we were born". As a myth to express what lovers feel this is admirable. But if one accepted it literally one would be faced by an embarrassing consequence. We should have to conclude that in that heavenly and forgotten life affairs were no better managed than here. For Eros may unite the most unsuitable yokefellows; many unhappy, and predictably unhappy, marriages were love-matches.

A theory more likely to be accepted in our own day is what we may call Shavian—Shaw himself might have said "metabiological"—Romanticism. According to Shavian Romanticism the voice of Eros is the voice of the *élan vital* or Life Force, the "evolutionary appetite". In overwhelming a particular couple it is seeking parents (or ancestors) for the superman. It is indifferent both to their personal happiness and to the rules of morality because it aims at something which Shaw thinks very much more important: the future perfection of our species. But if all this were true it hardly makes clear whether—and if so, why—we should obey it. All pictures yet offered us of the superman are so unattractive that one might well vow celibacy at once to avoid the risk of begetting him. And secondly, this theory surely leads to the conclusion that the Life Force does not very well understand its (or her? or his?) own business. So far as we can see the existence or intensity of Eros between two people is no warrant that their offspring will be especially satisfactory, or even that they will have offspring at all. Two good "strains" (in the stockbreeders' sense), not two good lovers, is the recipe for fine children. And what on earth was the Life Force doing through all those countless generations when the begetting of children depended very little on mutual Eros and very much on arranged marriages, slavery, and rape? Has it only just thought of this bright idea for improving the species?

Neither the Platonic nor the Shavian type of erotic transcendentalism can help a Christian. We are not worshippers of the Life Force and we know nothing of previous existences. We must not give unconditional obedience to the voice of Eros when he speaks most like a god. Neither must we ignore or attempt to deny the god-like quality. This love is really and truly like Love Himself. In it there is a real nearness to God (by Resemblance); but not, therefore and necessarily, a nearness of Approach. Eros, honoured so far as love of God and charity to our fellows will allow, may become for us a means of Approach. His total commitment is a paradigm or example, built into our natures, of the love we ought to exercise towards God and Man. As Nature, for the Nature lover, gives a content to the word *glory*, so this gives a content to the word *Charity*. It is as if Christ said to us through Eros, "Thus—just like this—with this prodigality—not counting the cost—you are to love me and the least of my brethren." Our conditional honour to Eros will of course vary with our circumstances. Of some a total renunciation (but not a contempt) is required. Others, with Eros as their fuel and also as their model, can embark on the married life. Within which Eros, of himself, will never be enough—will indeed survive only in so far as he is continually chastened and corroborated by higher principles.

But Eros, honoured without reservation and obeyed unconditionally, becomes a demon. And this is just how he claims to be honoured and obeyed. Divinely indifferent to our selfishness, he is also demoniacally rebellious to every claim of God or Man that would oppose him. Hence as the poet says:

People in love cannot be moved by kindness,
And opposition makes them feel like martyrs.

Martyrs is exactly right. Years ago when I wrote about medieval love-poetry and described its strange, half make-believe, "religion of love", I was blind enough to treat this as an almost purely literary phenomenon. I know better now. Eros by his nature invites it. Of all loves he is, at his height, most god-like; therefore most prone to demand our worship. Of himself he always tends to turn "being in love" into a sort of religion.

Theologians have often feared, in this love, a danger of idolatry. I think they meant by this that the lovers might idolise one another. That does not seem to me to be the real danger; certainly not in marriage. The deliciously plain prose and business-like intimacy of married life render it absurd. So does the Affection in which Eros is almost invariably clothed. Even in courtship I question whether anyone who has felt the thirst for the Uncreated, or even dreamed of feeling it, ever supposed that the Beloved could satisfy it. As a fellow-pilgrim pierced with the very same desire, that is, as a Friend, the Beloved may be gloriously and helpfully relevant; but as an object for it—well (I would not be rude), ridiculous. The real danger seems to me not that the lovers will idolise each other but that they will idolise Eros himself.

I do not of course mean that they will build altars or say prayers to him. The idolatry I speak of can be seen in the popular misinterpretation of Our Lord's words "Her sins, which are many, are forgiven her, for she loved much" (Luke 7:47). From the context, and especially from the preceding parable of the debtors, it is clear that this must mean: "The greatness of her love for Me is evidence of the greatness of the sins I have forgiven her." (The *for* here is like the *for* in "He can't have gone out, *for* his hat is still hanging in the hall"; the presence of the hat is not the cause of his being in the house but a probable proof that he is.) But thousands of people take it quite differently. They first assume, with no evidence, that her sins were sins against chastity, though, for all we know, they may have been usury, dishonest shopkeeping, or cruelty to children. And they then take Our Lord to be saying, "I forgive her unchastity because she was so much in love." The implication is that a great Eros extenuates—almost sanctions—almost sanctifies—any actions it leads to.

When lovers say of some act that we might blame, "Love made us do it," notice the tone. A man saying, "I did it because I was frightened," or "I did it because I was angry," speaks quite differently. He is putting forward an excuse for what he feels to require excusing. But the lovers are seldom doing quite that. Notice how tremulously, almost how devoutly, they say the word *love*, not so much pleading an "extenuating circumstance" as appealing to an authority. The confession can be almost a boast. There can be a shade of defiance in it. They "feel like martyrs". In extreme cases what their words really express is a demure yet unshakable allegiance to the god of love.

"These reasons in love's law have passed for good," says Milton's Dalila. That is the point; *in love's law*. "In love", we have our own "law", a religion of our own, our own god. Where a true Eros is present, resistance to his commands feels like apostasy, and what are really (by the Christian standard) temptations speak with the voice of duties—quasi-religious duties, acts of pious zeal to Love. He builds his own religion round the lovers. Benjamin Constant has noticed how he creates for them, in a few weeks or months, a joint past which seems to them immemorial. They recur to it continually with wonder and reverence, as the Psalmists recur to the history of Israel. It is in fact the Old Testament of Love's religion; the record of love's judgments and mercies towards his chosen pair up to the moment when they first knew they were lovers. After that, its New Testament begins. They are now under a new law, under what corresponds (in this religion) to Grace. They are new creatures. The "spirit" of Eros supersedes all laws, and they must not "grieve" it.

It seems to sanction all sorts of actions they would not otherwise have dared. I do not mean solely, or chiefly, acts that violate chastity. They are just as likely to be acts of injustice or uncharity against the outer world. They will seem like proofs of piety and zeal towards Eros. The pair can say to one another in an almost sacrificial spirit, "It is for love's sake that I have neglected my parents—left my children—cheated my partner—failed my friend at his greatest need." These reasons in love's law have passed for good. The votaries may even come to feel a particular merit in such sacrifices; what costlier offering can be laid on love's altar than one's conscience?

And all the time the grim joke is that this Eros whose voice seems to speak from the eternal realm is not himself necessarily even permanent. He is notoriously the most mortal of our loves. The world rings with complaints of his fickleness. What is baffling is the combination of this fickleness with his protestations of permanency. To be in love is both to intend and to promise lifelong fidelity. Love makes vows unasked; can't be deterred from making them. "I will be ever true" are almost the first words he utters. Not hypocritically but sincerely. No experience will cure him of the delusion. We have all heard of people who are in love again every few years; each time sincerely convinced that "*this* time it's the real thing", that their wanderings are over, that they have found their true love and will themselves be true till death.

And yet Eros is in a sense right to make this promise. The event of falling in love is of such a nature that we are right to reject as intolerable the idea that it should be transitory. In one high bound it has overleaped the massive wall of our selfhood; it has made appetite itself altruistic, tossed personal happiness aside as a triviality, and planted the interests of another in the centre of our being. Spontaneously and without effort we have fulfilled the law (towards one person) by loving our neighbour as ourselves. It is an image, a foretaste, of what we must become to all if Love Himself rules in us without a rival. It is even (well used) a preparation for that. Simply to relapse from it, merely to "fall out of" love again, is—if I may coin the ugly word—a sort of *disredemption*. Eros is driven to promise what Eros of himself cannot perform.

Can we be in this selfless liberation for a lifetime? Hardly for a week. Between the best possible lovers this high condition is intermittent. The old self soon turns out to be not so dead as he pretended—as after a religious conversion. In either he may be momentarily knocked flat; he will soon be up again; if not on his feet, at least on his elbow, if not roaring, at least back to his surly grumbling or his mendicant whine. And Venus will often slip back into mere sexuality.

But these lapses will not destroy a marriage between two "decent and sensible" people. The couple whose marriage will certainly be endangered by them, and possibly ruined, are those who have idolised Eros. They thought he had the power and truthfulness of a god. They expected that mere feeling would do for them, and permanently, all that was necessary. When this expectation is disappointed they throw the blame on Eros or, more usually, on their partners. In reality, however, Eros, having made his gigantic promise and shown you in glimpses what its performance would be like, has "done his stuff". He, like a godparent, makes the vows; it is we who must keep them. It is we who must labour to bring our daily life into even closer accordance with what the glimpses have revealed. We must do the works of Eros when Eros is not present. This all good lovers know, though those who are not reflective or articulate will be able to express it only in a few conventional phrases about "taking the rough along with the smooth", not "expecting too much", having "a little common sense", and the like. And all good Christian lovers know that this programme, modest as it sounds, will not be carried out except by humility, charity, and divine grace; that it is indeed the whole Christian life seen from one particular angle.

Thus Eros, like the other loves, but more strikingly because of his strength, sweetness, terror, and high port, reveals his true status. He cannot of himself be what, nevertheless, he must be if he is to remain Eros. He needs help; therefore needs to be ruled. The god dies or becomes a demon unless he obeys God. It would be well if, in such case, he always died. But he may live on, mercilessly chaining together two mutual tormentors, each raw all over with the poison of hate-in-love, each ravenous to receive and implacably refusing to give, jealous, suspicious, resentful, struggling for the upper hand, determined to be free and to allow no freedom, living on "scenes". Read *Anna Karenina*, and do not fancy that such things happen only in Russia. The lovers' old hyperbole of "eating" each other can come horribly near to the truth.

VI

CHARITY

WILLIAM MORRIS WROTE a poem called "Love Is Enough" and someone is said to have reviewed it briefly in the words "It isn't." Such has been the burden of this book. The natural loves are not self-sufficient. Something else, at first vaguely described as "decency and common sense", but later revealed as goodness, and finally as the whole Christian life in one particular relation, must come to the help of the mere feeling if the feeling is to be kept sweet.

To say this is not to belittle the natural loves but to indicate where their real glory lies. It is no disparagement to a garden to say that it will not fence and weed itself, nor prune its own fruit trees, nor roll and cut its own lawns. A garden is a good thing but that is not the sort of goodness it has. It will remain a garden, as distinct from a wilderness, only if someone does all these things to it. Its real glory is of quite a different kind. The very fact that it needs constant weeding and pruning bears witness to that glory. It teems with life. It glows with colour and smells like heaven and puts forward at every hour of a summer day beauties which man could never have created and could not even, on his own resources, have imagined. If you want to see the difference between its contribution and the gardener's, put the commonest weed it grows side by side with his hoes, rakes, shears, and packet of weed killer; you have put beauty, energy, and fecundity beside dead, sterile things. Just so, our "decency and common sense" show grey and deathlike beside the geniality of love. And when the garden is in its full glory the gardener's contributions to that glory will still have been in a sense paltry compared with those of nature. Without life springing from the earth, without rain, light, and heat descending from the sky, he could do nothing. When he has done all, he has merely encouraged here and discouraged there, powers and beauties that have a different source. But his share, though small, is indispensable and laborious. When God planted a garden He set a man over it and set the man under Himself. When He planted the garden of our nature and caused the flowering, fruiting loves to grow there, He set our will to "dress" them. Compared with them it is dry and cold. And unless His grace comes down, like the rain and the sunshine, we shall use this tool to little purpose. But its laborious—and largely negative—services are indispensable. If they were needed when the garden was still Paradisal, how much more now when the soil has gone sour and the worst weeds seem to thrive on it best? But heaven forbid we should work in the spirit of prigs and Stoics. While we hack and prune we know very well that what we are hacking and pruning is big with a splendour and vitality which our rational will could never of itself have supplied. To liberate that splendour, to let it become fully what it is trying to be, to have tall trees instead of scrubby tangles, and sweet apples instead of crabs, is part of our purpose.

But only part. For now we must face a topic that I have long postponed. Hitherto hardly anything has been said in this book about our natural loves as rivals to the love of God. Now the question can no longer be avoided. There were two reasons for my delay. One—already hinted—is that this question is not the place at which most of us need begin. It is seldom, at the outset, "addressed to our condition". For most of us the true rivalry lies between the self and the human Other, not yet between the human Other and God. It is dangerous to press upon a man the duty of getting beyond earthly love when his real difficulty lies in getting so far. And it is no doubt easy enough to love the fellow-creature less and to imagine that this is happening because we are learning to love God more, when the real reason may be quite different. We may be only "mistaking the decays of nature for the increase of Grace". Many people do not find it really difficult to hate their wives or mothers. M. Mauriac, in a fine scene, pictures the other disciples stunned and bewildered by this strange command, but not Judas. He laps it up easily.

But to have stressed the rivalry earlier in this book would have been premature in another way also. The claim to divinity which our loves so easily make can be refuted without going so far as that. The loves prove that they are unworthy to take the place of God by the fact that they cannot even remain themselves and do what they promise to do without God's help. Why prove that some petty princeling is not the lawful Emperor when without the Emperor's support he cannot even keep his subordinate throne and make peace in his little province for half a year? Even for their own sakes the loves must submit to be second things if they are to remain the things they want to be. In this yoke lies their true freedom; they "are taller when they bow". For when God rules in a human heart, though He may sometimes have to remove certain of its native authorities altogether, He often continues others in their offices and, by subjecting their authority to His, gives it for the first time a firm basis. Emerson has said, "When half-gods go, the gods arrive." That is a very doubtful maxim. Better say, "When God arrives (and only then) the half-gods can remain." Left to themselves they either vanish or become demons. Only in His name can they with beauty and security "wield their little tridents". The rebellious slogan "All for love" is really love's death warrant (date of execution, for the moment, left blank).

But the question of the Rivalry, for these reasons long postponed, must now be treated. In any earlier period, except the nineteenth century, it would have loomed large throughout a book on this subject. If the Victorians needed the reminder that love is not enough, older theologians were always saying very loudly that (natural) love is likely to be a great deal too much. The danger of loving our fellow-creatures too little was less present to their minds than that of loving them idolatrously. In every wife, mother, child and friend they saw a possible rival to God. So of course does Our Lord (Luke 14:26).

There is one method of dissuading us from inordinate love of the fellow-creature which I find myself forced to reject at the very outset. I do so with trembling, for it met me in the pages of a great saint and a great thinker to whom my own glad debts are incalculable.

In words which can still bring tears to the eyes, St Augustine describes the desolation in which the death of his friend Nebridius plunged him (*Confessions IV*, 10). Then he draws a moral. This is what comes, he says, of giving one's heart to anything but God. All human beings pass away. Do not let your happiness depend on something you may lose. If love is to be a blessing, not a misery, it must be for the only Beloved who will never pass away. Of course this is excellent sense. Don't put your goods in a leaky vessel. Don't spend too much on a house you may be turned out of. And there is no man alive who responds more naturally than I to such canny maxims. I am a safety-first creature. Of all arguments against love none makes so strong an appeal to my nature as "Careful! This might lead you to suffering."

To my nature, my temperament, yes. Not to my conscience. When I respond to that appeal I seem to myself to be a thousand miles away from Christ. If I am sure of anything I am sure that His teaching was never meant to confirm my congenital preference for safe investments and limited liabilities. I doubt whether there is anything in me that pleases Him less. And who could conceivably begin to love God on such a prudential ground—because the security (so to speak) is better? Who could even include it among the grounds for loving? Would you choose a wife or a Friend—if it comes to that, would you choose a dog—in this spirit? One must be outside the world of love, of all loves, before one thus calculates. Eros, lawless Eros, preferring the Beloved to happiness, is more like Love Himself than this.

I think that this passage in the *Confessions* is less a part of St Augustine's Christendom than a hangover from the high-minded Pagan philosophies in which he grew up. It is closer to Stoic "apathy" or neo-Platonic mysticism than to charity. We follow One who wept over Jerusalem and at the grave of Lazarus, and, loving all, yet had one disciple whom, in a special sense, he "loved". St Paul has a higher authority with us than St Augustine—St Paul who shows no sign that he would not have suffered like a man, and no feeling that he ought not so to have suffered, if Epaphroditus had died (Philem. 2:27).

Even if it were granted that insurances against heartbreak were our highest wisdom, does God Himself offer them? Apparently not. Christ comes at last to say, "Why hast thou forsaken me?"

There is no escape along the lines St Augustine suggests. Nor along any other lines. There is no safe investment. To love at all is to be vulnerable. Love anything, and your heart will certainly be wrung and possibly be broken. If you want to make sure of keeping it intact, you must give your heart to no one, not even to an animal. Wrap it carefully round with hobbies and little luxuries; avoid all entanglements; lock it up safe in the casket or coffin of your selfishness. But in that casket—safe, dark, motionless, airless—it will change. It will not be broken; it will become unbreakable, impenetrable, irredeemable. The alternative to tragedy, or at least to the risk of tragedy, is damnation. The only place outside Heaven where you can be perfectly safe from all the dangers and perturbations of love is Hell.

I believe that the most lawless and inordinate loves are less contrary to God's will than a self-invited and self-protective lovelessness. It is like hiding the talent in a napkin and for much the same reason. "I knew thee that thou wert a hard man." Christ did not teach and suffer that we might become, even in the natural loves, more careful of our own happiness. If a man is not uncalculating towards the earthly beloveds whom he has seen, he is none the more likely to be so towards God whom he has not. We shall draw nearer to God, not by trying to avoid the sufferings inherent in all loves, but by accepting them and offering them to Him; throwing away all defensive armour. If our hearts need to be broken, and if He chooses this as the way in which they should break, so be it.

It remains certainly true that all natural loves can be inordinate. *Inordinate* does not mean "insufficiently cautious". Nor does it mean "too big". It is not a quantitative term. It is probably impossible to love any human being simply "too much". We may love him too much *in proportion to* our love for God; but it is the smallness of our love for God, not the greatness of our love for the man, that constitutes the inordinacy. But even this must be refined upon. Otherwise we shall trouble some who are very much on the right road but alarmed because they cannot feel towards God so warm a sensible emotion as they feel for the earthly Beloved. It is much to be wished—at least I think so—that we all, at all times, could. We must pray that this gift should be given us. But the question whether we are loving God or the earthly Beloved "more" is not, so far as concerns our Christian duty, a question about the comparative intensity of two feelings. The real question is, which (when the alternative comes) do you serve, or choose, or put first? To which claim does your will, in the last resort, yield?

As so often, Our Lord's own words are both far fiercer and far more tolerable than those of the theologians. He says nothing about guarding against earthly loves for fear we might be hurt; He says something that cracks like a whip about trampling them all under foot the moment they hold us back from following Him. "If any man come to me and hate not his father and mother and wife . . . and his own life also, he cannot be my disciple" (Luke 14:26).

But how are we to understand the word *hate*? That Love Himself should be commanding what we ordinarily mean by hatred—

commanding us to cherish resentment, to gloat over another's misery, to delight in injuring him—is almost a contradiction in terms. I think Our Lord, in the sense here intended, "hated" St Peter when he said, "Get thee behind me." To hate is to reject, to set one's face against, to make no concession to, the Beloved when the Beloved utters, however sweetly and however pitiably, the suggestions of the Devil. A man, said Jesus, who tries to serve two masters, will "hate" the one and "love" the other. It is not, surely, mere feelings of aversion and liking that are here in question. He will adhere to, consent to, work for, the one and not for the other. Consider again, "I loved Jacob and I *hated* Esau" (Mal. 1:2–3). How is the thing called God's "hatred" of Esau displayed in the actual story? Not at all as we might expect. There is of course no ground for assuming that Esau made a bad end and was a lost soul; the Old Testament, here as elsewhere, has nothing to say about such matters. And, from all we are told, Esau's earthly life was, in every ordinary sense, a good deal more blessed than Jacob's. It is Jacob who has all the disappointments, humiliations, terrors, and bereavements. But he has something which Esau has not. He is a patriarch. He hands on the Hebraic tradition, transmits the vocation and the blessing, becomes an ancestor of Our Lord. The "loving" of Jacob seems to mean the acceptance of Jacob for a high (and painful) vocation; the "hating" of Esau, his rejection. He is "turned down", fails to "make the grade", is found useless for the purpose. So, in the last resort, we must turn down or disqualify our nearest and dearest when they come between us and our obedience to God. Heaven knows, it will seem to them sufficiently like hatred. We must not act on the pity we feel; we must be blind to tears and deaf to pleadings. I will not say that this duty is hard; some find it too easy; some, hard almost beyond endurance. What is hard for all is to know when the occasion for such "hating" has arisen. Our temperaments deceive us. The meek and tender—uxorious husbands, submissive wives, doting parents, dutiful children—will not easily believe that it has ever arrived. Self-assertive people, with a dash of the bully in them, will believe it too soon. That is why it is of such extreme importance so to order our loves that it is unlikely to arrive at all.

How this could come about we may see on a far lower level when the Cavalier poet, going to the wars, says to his mistress:

I could not love thee, dear, so much
    Loved I not honour more.

There are women to whom the plea would be meaningless. *Honour* would be just one of those silly things that Men talk about; a verbal excuse for, therefore an aggravation of, the offence against "love's law" which the poet is about to commit. Lovelace can use it with confidence because his lady is a Cavalier lady who already admits, as he does, the claims of Honour. He does not need to "hate" her, to set his face against her, because he and she acknowledge the same law. They have agreed and understood each other on this matter long before. The task of converting her to a belief in Honour is not now—now, when the decision is upon them—to be undertaken. It is this prior agreement which is so necessary when a far greater claim than that of Honour is at stake. It is too late, when the crisis comes, to begin telling a wife or husband or mother or friend, that your love all along had a secret reservation—"under God" or "so far as a higher Love permits". They ought to have been warned; not, to be sure, explicitly, but by the implication of a thousand talks, by the principle revealed in a hundred decisions upon small matters. Indeed, a real disagreement on this issue should make itself felt early enough to prevent a marriage or a Friendship from existing at all. The best love of either sort is not blind. Oliver Elton, speaking of Carlyle and Mill, said that they differed about justice, and that such a difference was naturally fatal "to any friendship worthy of the name". If "All"—quite seriously all—"for love" is implicit in the Beloved's attitude, his or her love is not worth having. It is not related in the right way to Love Himself.

And this brings me to the foot of the last steep ascent this book must try to make. We must try to relate the human activities called "loves" to that Love which is God a little more precisely than we have yet done. The precision can, of course, be only that of a model or a symbol, certain to fail us in the long run and, even while we use it, requiring correction from other models. The humblest of us, in a state of Grace, can have some "knowledge-by-acquaintance" (*connaître*), some "tasting", of Love Himself; but man even at his highest sanctity and intelligence has no direct "knowledge about" (*savoir*) the ultimate Being—only analogies. We cannot see light, though by light we can see things. Statements about God are extrapolations from the knowledge of other things which the divine illumination enables us to know. I labour these deprecations because, in what follows, my efforts to be clear (and not intolerably lengthy) may suggest a confidence which I by no means feel. I should be mad if I did. Take it as one man's reverie, almost one man's myth. If anything in it is useful to you, use it; if anything is not, never give it a second thought. God is love. Again, "Herein is love, not that we loved God but that He loved us" (I John 4:10). We must not begin with mysticism, with the creature's love for God, or with the wonderful forestates of the fruition of God vouchsafed to some in their earthly life. We begin at the real beginning, with love as the Divine energy. This primal love is Gift-love. In God there is no hunger that needs to be filled, only plenteousness that desires to give. The doctrine that God was under no necessity to create is not a piece of dry scholastic speculation. It is essential. Without it we can hardly avoid the conception of what I can only call a "managerial" God; a Being whose function or nature is to "run" the universe, who stands to it as a headmaster to a school or a hotelier to a hotel. But to be sovereign of the universe is no great matter to God. In Himself, at home in "the land of the Trinity", he is Sovereign of a far greater realm. We must keep always before our eyes that vision of Lady Julian's in which God carried in His hand a little object like a nut, and that nut was "all that is made". God, who needs nothing, loves into existence wholly superfluous creatures in order that He may love and perfect them. He creates the universe, already foreseeing—or should we say "seeing"? there are no tenses in God—the buzzing cloud of flies about the cross, the flayed back pressed against the uneven stake, the nails driven through the mesial nerves, the repeated incipient suffocation as the body droops, the repeated torture of back and arms as it is time after time, for breath's sake, hitched up. If I may dare the biological image, God is a "host" who deliberately creates His own parasites; causes us to be that we may exploit and "take advantage of" Him. Herein is love. This is the diagram of Love Himself, the inventor of all loves.

God, as Creator of nature, implants in us both Gift-loves and Need-loves. The Gift-loves are natural images of Himself; proximities to Him by resemblance which are not necessarily and in all men proximities of approach. A devoted mother, a beneficent ruler or teacher, may give and give, continually exhibiting the likeness, without making the approach. The Need-loves, so far as I have been able to see, have no resemblance to the Love which God is. They are rather correlatives, opposites; not as evil is the opposite of good, of course, but as the form of the blancmange is an opposite to the form of the mould.

But in addition to these natural loves God can bestow a far better gift; or rather, since our minds must divide and pigeon-hole, two gifts.

He communicates to men a share of His own Gift-love. This is different from the Gift-loves He has built into their nature. These never quite seek simply the good of the loved object for the object's own sake. They are biased in favour of those goods they can themselves bestow, or those which they would like best themselves, or those which fit in with a pre-conceived picture of the life they want the object to lead. But Divine Gift-love—Love Himself working in a man—is wholly disinterested and desires what is simply best for the beloved. Again, natural Gift-love is always directed to objects which the lover finds in some way intrinsically lovable—objects to which Affection or Eros or a shared point of view attracts him, or, failing that, to the grateful and the deserving, or perhaps to those whose helplessness is of a winning and appealing kind. But Divine Gift-love in the man enables him to love what is not naturally lovable; lepers, criminals, enemies, morons, the sulky, the superior, and the sneering. Finally, by a high paradox, God enables men to have a Gift-love towards Himself. There is of course a sense in which no one can give to God anything which is not already His; and if it is already His, what have you given? But since it is only too obvious that we can withhold ourselves, our wills and hearts, from God, we can, in that sense, also give them. What is His by right and would not exist for a moment if it ceased to be His (as the song is the singer's), He has nevertheless made ours in such a way that we can freely offer it back to Him. "Our wills are ours to make them Thine." And as all Christians know there is another way of giving to God; every stranger whom we feed or clothe is Christ. And this apparently is Gift-love to God whether we know it or not. Love Himself can work in those who know nothing of Him. The "sheep" in the parable had no idea either of the God hidden in the prisoner whom they visited or of the God hidden in themselves when they made the visit. (I take the whole parable to be about the judgment of the heathen. For it begins by saying, in the Greek, that the Lord will summon all "the nations" before Him—presumably, the Gentiles, the *Goyim*.)

That such a Gift-love comes by Grace and should be called Charity, everyone will agree. But I have to add something which will not perhaps be so easily admitted. God, as it seems to me, bestows two other gifts; a supernatural Need-love of Himself and a supernatural Need-love of one another. By the first I do not mean the Appreciative love of Himself, the gift of adoration. What little I have to say on that higher—that highest—subject will come later. I mean a love which does not dream of disinterestedness, a bottomless indigence. Like a river making its own channel, like a magic wine which in being poured out should simultaneously create the glass that was to hold it, God turns our need of Him into Need-love of Him. What is stranger still is that He creates in us a more than natural receptivity of Charity from our fellow men. Need is so near greed and we are so greedy already that it seems a strange grace. But I cannot get it out of my head that this is what happens.

Let us consider first this supernatural Need-love of Himself, bestowed by Grace. Of course the Grace does not create the need. That is there already; "given" (as the mathematicians say) in the mere fact of our being creatures, and incalculably increased by our being fallen creatures. What the Grace gives is the full recognition, the sensible awareness, the complete acceptance—even, with certain reservations, the glad acceptance—of this Need. For, without Grace, our wishes and our necessities are in conflict.

All those expressions of unworthiness which Christian practise puts into the believer's mouth seem to the outer world like the degraded and insincere grovellings of a sycophant before a tyrant, or at best a *façon de parler* like the self-depreciation of a Chinese gentleman when he calls himself "this coarse and illiterate person". In reality, however, they express the continually renewed, because continually necessary, attempt to negate that misconception of ourselves and of our relation to God which nature, even while we pray, is always recommending to us. No sooner do we believe that God loves us than there is an impulse to believe that He does so, not because He is Love, but because we are intrinsically lovable. The Pagans obeyed this impulse unabashed; a good man was "dear to the gods" because he was good. We, being better taught, resort to subterfuge. Far be it from us to think that we have virtues for which God could love us. But then, how magnificently we have repented! As Bunyan says, describing his first and illusory conversion, "I thought there was no man in England that pleased God better than I." Beaten out of this, we next offer our own humility to God's admiration. Surely He'll like *that*? Or if not that, our clear-sighted and humble recognition that we still lack humility. Thus, depth beneath depth and subtlety within subtlety, there remains some lingering idea of our own, our very own, attractiveness. It is easy to acknowledge, but almost impossible to realise for long, that we are mirrors whose brightness, if we are bright, is wholly derived from the sun that shines upon us. Surely we must have a little—however little— native luminosity? Surely we can't be *quite* creatures?

For this tangled absurdity of a Need, even a Need-love, which never fully acknowledges its own neediness, Grace substitutes a full, child-like, and delighted acceptance of our Need, a joy in total dependence. We become "jolly beggars". The good man is sorry for the sins which have increased his Need. He is not entirely sorry for the fresh Need they have produced. And he is not sorry at all for the innocent Need that is inherent in his creaturely condition. For all the time this illusion to which nature clings as her last treasure, this pretence that we have anything of our own or could for one hour retain by our own strength any goodness that God may pour into us, has kept us from being happy. We have been like bathers who want to keep their feet—or one foot—or one toe—on the bottom, when to lose that foothold would be to surrender themselves to a glorious tumble in the surf. The consequences of parting with our last claim to intrinsic freedom, power, or worth, are real freedom, power, and worth, really ours just because God gives them and because we know them to be (in another sense) not "ours". Anodos has got rid of his shadow. But God also transforms our Need-love for one another, and it requires equal transformation. In reality we all need at times, some of us at most times, that Charity from others which, being Love Himself in them, loves the unlovable. But this, though a sort of love we need, is not the sort we want. We want to be loved for our cleverness, beauty, generosity, fairness, usefulness. The first hint that anyone is offering us the highest love of all is a terrible shock. This is so well recognised that spiteful people will pretend to be loving us with Charity precisely because they know that it will wound us. To say to one who expects a renewal of Affection, Friendship, or Eros, "I forgive you as a Christian" is merely a way of continuing the quarrel. Those who say it are of course lying. But the thing would not be falsely said in order to wound unless, if it were true, it would be wounding.

How difficult it is to receive, and to go on receiving, from others a love that does not depend on our own attraction, can be seen from an extreme case. Suppose yourself a man struck down shortly after marriage by an incurable disease which may not kill you for many years; useless, impotent, hideous, disgusting; dependent on your wife's earnings; impoverishing where you hoped to enrich; impaired even in intellect and shaken by gusts of uncontrollable temper, full of unavoidable demands. And suppose your wife's care and pity to be inexhaustible. The man who can take this sweetly, who can receive all and give nothing without resentment, who can abstain even from those tiresome self-depreciations which are really only a demand for petting and reassurance, is doing something which Need-love in its merely natural condition could not attain. (No doubt such a wife will also be doing something beyond the reach of a natural Gift-love, but that is not the point at present.) In such a case to receive is harder and perhaps more blessed than to give. But what the extreme example illustrates is universal. We are all receiving Charity. There is something in each of us that cannot be naturally loved. It is no one's fault if they do not so love it. Only the lovable can be naturally loved. You might as well ask people to like the taste of rotten bread or the sound of a mechanical drill. We can be forgiven, and pitied, and loved in spite of it, with Charity; no other way. All who have good parents, wives, husbands, or children, may be sure that at some times—and perhaps at all times in respect of some one particular trait or habit—they are receiving charity, are loved not because they are lovable but because Love Himself is in those who love them.

Thus God, admitted to the human heart, transforms not only Gift-love but Need-love; not only our Need-love of Him, but our Need-love of one another. This is of course not the only thing that can happen. He may come on what seems to us a more dreadful mission and demand that a natural love be totally renounced. A high and terrible vocation, like Abraham's, may constrain a man to turn his back on his own people and his father's house. Eros, directed to a forbidden object, may have to be sacrificed. In such instances, the process, though hard to endure, is easy to understand. What we are more likely to overlook is the necessity for a transformation even when the natural love is allowed to continue.

In such a case the Divine Love does not *substitute* itself for the natural—as if we had to throw away our silver to make room for the gold. The natural loves are summoned to become modes of Charity while also remaining the natural loves they were. One sees here at once a sort of echo or rhyme or corollary to the Incarnation itself. And this need not surprise us, for the Author of both is the same. As Christ is perfect God and perfect Man, the natural loves are called to become perfect Charity and also perfect natural loves. As God becomes Man "not by conversion of the Godhead into flesh, but by taking of the Manhood into God", so here; Charity does not dwindle into merely natural love but natural love is taken up into, made the tuned and obedient instrument of, Love Himself.

How this can happen, most Christians know. All the activities (sins only excepted) of the natural loves can in a favoured hour become works of the glad and shameless and grateful Need-love or of the selfless, unofficious Gift-love, which are both Charity. Nothing is either too trivial or too animal to be thus transformed. A game, a joke, a drink together, idle chat, a walk, the act of Venus—all these can be modes in which we forgive or accept forgiveness, in which we console or are reconciled, in which we "seek not our own". Thus in our very instincts, appetites and recreations, Love has prepared for Himself "a body".

But I said "in a favoured hour". Hours soon pass. The total and secure transformation of a natural love into a mode of Charity is a work so difficult that perhaps no fallen man has ever come within sight of doing it perfectly. Yet the law that loves must be so transformed is, I suppose, inexorable.

One difficulty is that here, as usual, we can take a wrong turn. A Christian—a somewhat too vocally Christian—circle or family, having grasped this principle, can make a show, in their overt behaviour and especially in their words, of having achieved the thing itself—an elaborate, fussy, embarrassing, and intolerable show. Such people make every trifle a matter of explicitly spiritual importance—out loud and to one another (to God, on their knees, behind a closed door, it would be another matter). They are always unnecessarily asking, or insufferably offering, forgiveness. Who would not rather live with those ordinary people who get over their tantrums (and ours) unemphatically, letting a meal, a night's sleep, or a joke mend all? The real work must be, of all our works, the most secret. Even as far as possible secret from ourselves. Our right hand must not know what our left is doing. We have not got far enough if we play a game of cards with the children "merely" to amuse them or to show that they are forgiven. If this is the best we can do we are right to do it. But it would be better if a deeper, less conscious, Charity threw us into a frame of mind in which a little fun with the children was the thing we should at that moment like best.

We are, however, much helped in this necessary work by that very feature of our experience at which we most repine. The invitation to turn our natural loves into Charity is never lacking. It is provided by those frictions and frustrations that meet us in all of them; unmistakable evidence that (natural) love is not going to be "enough"—unmistakable, unless we are blinded by egotism. When we are, we use them absurdly. "If only I had been more fortunate in my children (that boy gets more like his father every day) I could have loved them perfectly." But every child is sometimes infuriating; most children are not infrequently odious. "If only my husband were more considerate, less lazy, less extravagant" . . . "If only my wife had fewer moods and more sense, and were less extravagant" . . . "If my father wasn't so infernally prosy and close-fisted." But in everyone, and of course in ourselves, there is that which requires forbearance, tolerance, forgiveness. The necessity of practising these virtues first sets us, forces us, upon the attempt to turn—more strictly, to let God turn—our love into Charity. These frets and rubs are beneficial. It may even be that where there are fewest of them the conversion of natural love is most difficult. When they are plentiful the necessity of rising above it is obvious. To rise above it when it is as fully satisfied and as little impeded as earthly conditions allow—to see that we must rise when all seems so well already—this may require a subtler conversion and a more delicate insight. In this way also it may be hard for "the rich" to enter the Kingdom.

And yet, I believe, the necessity for the conversion is inexorable; at least, if our natural loves are to enter the heavenly life. That they can enter it most of us in fact believe. We may hope that the resurrection of the body means also the resurrection of what may be called our "greater body"; the general fabric of our earthly life with its affections and relationships. But only on a condition; not a condition arbitrarily laid down by God, but one necessarily inherent in the character of Heaven: nothing can enter there which cannot become heavenly. "Flesh and blood", mere nature, cannot inherit that Kingdom. Man can ascend to Heaven only because the Christ, who died and ascended to Heaven, is "formed in him". Must we not suppose that the same is true of a man's loves? Only those into which Love Himself has entered will ascend to Love Himself. And these can be raised with Him only if they have, in some degree and fashion, shared His death; if the natural element in them has submitted—year after year, or in some sudden agony—to transmutation. The fashion of this world passes away. The very name of nature implies the transitory. Natural loves can hope for eternity only in so far as they have allowed themselves to be taken into the eternity of Charity; have at least allowed the process to begin here on earth, before the night comes when no man can work. And the process will always involve a kind of death. There is no escape. In my love for wife or friend the only eternal element is the transforming presence of Love Himself. By that presence, if at all, the other elements may hope, as our physical bodies hope, to be raised from the dead. For this only is holy in them, this only is the Lord.

Theologians have sometimes asked whether we shall "know one another" in Heaven, and whether the particular love-relations worked out on earth would then continue to have any significance. It seems reasonable to reply: "It may depend what kind of love it had become, or was becoming, on earth." For, surely, to meet in the eternal world someone for whom your love in this, however strong, had been merely natural, would not be (on that ground) even interesting. Would it not be like meeting in adult life someone who had seemed to be a great friend at your preparatory school solely because of common interests and occupations? If there was nothing more, if he was not a kindred soul, he will now be a total stranger. Neither of you now plays conkers. You no longer want to swop your help with his French exercise for his help with your arithmetic. In Heaven, I suspect, a love that had never embodied Love Himself would be equally irrelevant. For Nature has passed away. All that is not eternal is eternally out of date.

But I must not end on this note, I dare not—and all the less because longings and terrors of my own prompt me to do so—leave any bereaved and desolate reader confirmed in the widespread illusion that reunion with the loved dead is the goal of the Christian life. The denial of this may sound harsh and unreal in the ears of the broken hearted, but it must be denied.

"Thou hast made us for thyself," said St Augustine, "and our heart has no rest till it comes to Thee." This, so easy to believe for a brief moment before the altar or, perhaps, half-praying, half-meditating in an April wood, sounds like mockery beside a deathbed. But we shall be far more truly mocked if, casting this way, we pin our comfort on the hope—perhaps even with the aid of *séance* and necromancy—of some day, this time forever, enjoying the earthly Beloved again, and no more. It is hard not to imagine that such an endless prolongation of earthly happiness would be completely satisfying.

But, if I may trust my own experience, we get at once a sharp warning that there is something wrong. The moment we attempt to use our faith in the other world for this purpose, that faith weakens. The moments in my life when it was really strong have all been moments when God Himself was central in my thoughts. Believing in Him, I could then believe in

Heaven as a corollary. But the reverse process—believing first in reunion with the Beloved, and then, for the sake of that reunion, believing in Heaven, and finally, for the sake of Heaven, believing in God—this will not work. One can of course imagine things. But a self-critical person will soon be increasingly aware that the imagination at work is his own; he knows he is only weaving a fantasy. And simpler souls will find the phantoms they try to feed on void of all comfort and nourishment, only to be stimulated into some semblance of reality by pitiful efforts of self-hypnotism, and perhaps by the aid of ignoble pictures and hymns and (what is worse) witches. We find thus by experience that there is no good applying to Heaven for earthly comfort. Heaven can give heavenly comfort; no other kind. And earth cannot give earthly comfort either. There is no earthly comfort in the long run.

For the dream of finding our end, the thing we were made for, in a Heaven of purely human love could not be true unless our whole Faith were wrong. We were made for God. Only by being in some respect like Him, only by being a manifestation of His beauty, lovingkindness, wisdom, or goodness, has any earthly Beloved excited our love. It is not that we have loved them too much, but that we did not quite understand what we were loving. It is not that we shall be asked to turn from them, so dearly familiar, to a Stranger. When we see the face of God we shall know that we have always known it. He has been a party to, has made, sustained, and moved moment by moment within, all our earthly experiences of innocent love. All that was true love in them was, even on earth, far more His than ours, and ours only because His. In Heaven there will be no anguish and no duty of turning away from our earthly Beloveds. First, because we shall have turned already; from the portraits to the Original, from the rivulets to the Fountain, from the creatures He made lovable to Love Himself. But secondly, because we shall find them all in Him. By loving Him more than them we shall love them more than we now do.

But all that is far away in "the land of the Trinity", not here in exile, in the weeping valley. Down here it is all loss and renunciation. The very purpose of the bereavement (so far as it affects ourselves) may have been to force this upon us. We are then compelled to try to believe, what we cannot yet feel, that God is our true Beloved. That is why bereavement is in some ways easier for the unbeliever than for us. He can storm and rage and shake his fist at the universe, and (if he is a genius) write poems like

Housman's or Hardy's. But we, at our lowest ebb, when the least effort seems too much for us, must begin to attempt what seem impossibilities.

"Is it easy to love God?" asks an old author. "It is easy," he replies, "to those who do it." I have included two Graces under the word Charity. But God can give a third. He can awake in man, towards Himself, a supernatural Appreciative Love. This is of all gifts the most to be desired. Here, not in our natural loves, nor even in ethics, lies the true centre of all human and angelic life. With this all things are possible.

And with this, where a better book would begin, mine must end. I dare not proceed. God knows, not I, whether I have ever tasted this love. Perhaps I have only imagined the tasting. Those like myself whose imagination far exceeds their obedience are subject to a just penalty; we easily imagine conditions far higher than any we have really reached. If we describe what we have imagined we may make others, and make ourselves, believe that we have really been there. And if I have only imagined it, is it a further delusion that even the imagining has at some moments made all other objects of desire—yes, even peace, even to have no more fears—look like broken toys and faded flowers? Perhaps. Perhaps, for many of us, all experience merely defines, so to speak, the shape of that gap where our love of God ought to be. It is not enough. It is something. If we cannot "practise the presence of God", it is something to practise the absence of God, to become increasingly aware of our unawareness till we feel like men who should stand beside a great cataract and hear no noise, or like a man in a story who looks in a mirror and finds no face there, or a man in a dream who stretches out his hand to visible objects and gets no sensation of touch. To know that one is dreaming is to be no longer perfectly asleep. But for news of the fully waking world you must go to my betters.

INDEX

References to particular books are indicated as follows: *Mere Christianity* (MC), *The Screwtape Letters* (SL), *Miracles* (M), *The Great Divorce* (GD), *The Problem of Pain* (PP), *A Grief Observed* (GO), *The Abolition of Man* (AM), and *The Four Loves* (FL).

(MC); "begotten not made," 129–30, 132, 145–47 (MC); on being like children, 70 (MC); as the Bridegroom, 794, 812–13 (FL); corn-king versus, 402–3, 405, 423 (M); crown of thorns, 813 (FL); "count the cost," 160–63 (MC); death of (Crucifixion), 52–56, 139 (MC), 345, 347, 429 (M), 609, 615, 627 (PP), 812, 827 (FL); on dying to live, 94, 145–47 (MC), 558, 600, 622 (PP); Eros and love of, 815 (FL); "Follow thou Me," 6 (MC); Gift-love and, 743, 828 (FL); historical Jesus, 251 (SL), 399 (M); Incarnation and, 398–404, 411, 418, 424 (M), 558 (PP), 746 (FL); lament over Jerusalem, 757, 823 (FL); on marriage, 90 (MC), 237–38 (SL); miracles and, 341, 420 (M); miracles, classification in Old and New Creation, and review, 420, 422–27, 429–46 (M); as New Man, 174 (MC), 422, 422n. 3 (M); as perfect God and perfect Man, 831 (FL); presence of, 155, 170 (MC), 194–96, 207, 239 (SL); rebirth, 401–4, 406, 408 (M); Resurrection, 429–47 (M); riches and poverty and, 168, 169 (MC), 614 (PP); as savior, 59–61 (MC); as Son of God, 141–43, 145, 152–53 (MC), 361, 367 (M); suffering of, 598 (PP); time and, 138–39 (MC); Transfiguration, and "whiteness," 437 (M); what He did, 50, 52–56, 145–47 (MC), 345, 407 (M), 622 (PP); who He is, 49, 50–51, 55, 57, 129–30, 134, 139 (MC), 251–53 (SL), 345, 398 (M)

Christendom, 762 (FL)

Christian, 8, 59–60 (MC), 744, 756, 767, 773, 790, 801, 815 (FL); the body and, 809 (FL); born again, 154 (MC), 454 (M); brotherhood, 136 (MC); charity, 828, 832 (FL); duty, 824 (FL); early, as circle of friends, 795 (FL); friendship and, 801–2 (FL); meaning of term, 8 (MC); marriage and, 802, 811, 814 (FL); martyrs, 813 (FL); miracles, 419–47 (M); nice people versus New Men, 164–70 (MC); society, 74–77 (MC); two discoveries of a, 118 (MC); as unworthy, 829 (FL); writers, 812 (FL)

Christian Behavior (Lewis), 5 (MC)

Christian life, 117, 121, 143, 155, 158 (MC), 218, 241, 254 (SL), 446 (M), 767, 808, 819, 820, 834 (FL); charity and, 832 (FL)

Christian Socialism, 289 (SL)

Christianity, 7 (MC), 253 (SL), 558 (PP), 756, 760, 788 (FL); baptism, belief, and communion, 57–58, 59 (MC); becoming Sons of God (a little Christ) and good infection, 129–31, 144, 147, 151–55, 156–59, 163, 176 (MC), 289 (SL), 420–23 (M); central belief of, 35–36, 52, 156–58 (MC), 429–47, 455 (M); comfort of, 36 (MC); complexity and profundity of, 43 (MC); conceptions of God, 39–41 (MC); contemporary fads of Christianity "and," 257–59 (SL); corn-religions versus, 403, 404, 423 (M); cosmology, 636 (PP); conversion to, 188–89, 191, 221, 224, 230, 253 (SL), 773 (FL); death in, 411–18 (M); doctrines of, 366–71, 413 (M), 618–21 (PP); Dualism and, 43–45 (MC); Dying God and, 403, 417–18 (M), 558, 622 (PP), 725 (AM); good deeds versus Faith, 122, 156 (MC); gospels of, 429–32 (M); as hard or easy, 156–59 (MC); hope for Heaven,

experience, 268 (SL)

extremism, 204–5 (SL)

Ezekiel, 404 (M); *1:26*, 368, 368n. 10 (M); *16:6–15, 573* (PP)

faith, 6–7, 109, 119–23 (MC), 211, 212, 228–29, 273 (SL), 834–35 (FL); as belief, 115–18 (MC)

Fall, Doctrine of the, 416–17, 420 (M), 588–600, 607–9, 631 (PP), 778 (FL)

family, 75 (MC), 191–93, 213–14, 236–38, 261 (SL); affection and, 747, 774–75, 779 (FL); Duties to Children and Posterity, 734 (AM); Duties to Parents, Elders, Ancestors, 734 (AM); jealousy and, 773 (FL); love and, 743, 758, 762, 777 (FL)

Farrar, Kay and Austin, 655 (GO)

Fascists, 727 (AM)

fashions or vogues, 258 (SL)

fasting, 616 (PP)

fate, 801–2 (FL)

fatigue, 272–74 (SL)

fear, 200, 228, 270, 271, 273 (SL), 509, 510 (GD); as *Numinous*, 553–57 (PP)

feelings, 195, 273 (SL); impermanence of, 94, 117 (MC), 754, 818, 819 (FL); sense experiences, 185–86, 233 (SL)

Fisher, John, 809 (FL)

flippancy, 215–17, 219 (SL)

forgiveness, 36, 98–102, 147 (MC), 481, 513 (GD), 626–27 (PP), 744, 812, 816, 832 (FL)

fortitude, 72 (MC)

Fox, Canon Adam, 404n. 2 (M)

Francis, Saint, 809 (FL)

Free Will, 47 (MC), 189, 207 (SL), 307, 410, 460 (M), 487, 506 (GD), 561, 565, 620, 626 (PP); human wickedness and, 579–87, 588–600 (PP); omni-

science and, 139–40 (MC), 264–65 (SL), 598 (PP)

freedom, 207, 290 (SL), 539 (GD), 562 (PP); submission to God and they "are taller when they bow," 822 (FL)

Freud, Sigmund, 78 (MC)

friendship, 213–14, 216, 251 (SL), 639 (PP), 747, 764, 766, 767, 780–802, 826, 830 (FL); affection and, 790, 793 (FL); allies and, 788 (FL); the Ancients and, 780, 781, 793, 796 (FL); Aristotle's *Philia*, 780 (FL); authorities distrust of, 794, 795 (FL); banishing of male companionship, by women, 792–93 (FL); basis of, 785, 786, 787, 789, 794–95, 801 (FL); Cicero's *Amicitia*, 780 (FL); circles of friends, 794, 797–800 (FL); co-existence of Friendship and Eros, 786–87 (FL); community and, 787–88 (FL); *coterie*, 797, 799 (FL); Dunbar's advice, 802 (FL); element of exclusion, 797–99 (FL); element of secession, 795, 796 (FL); envy and, 794 (FL); Eros versus, 782–83, 786, 789–90, 793 (FL); gender-based, 790–92, 793 (FL); homosexual theory, 782–84 (FL); individuality and, 762, 788, 811 (FL); as instrument of God, 801–2 (FL); jealousy and, 783, 793 (FL); in literature, 780 (FL); love between God and Man and, 794 (FL); male, in pre-history, 784–85 (FL); matrix of (companionship) and, 784–86 (FL); modern devaluing of, 780–83 (FL); multiple friends and, 783, 787 (FL); "mutual admiration society," 801 (FL); "non-natural" quality, 781, 784, 787, 789, 793 (FL); pride as danger of, 799, 800 (FL); school of virtue or school of vice, 796 (FL); social movements and, 787–88, 795 (FL); as spiritual, 793–94, 800 (FL); as uninquisitive, 789 (FL); "What! You too? I thought I was the only one," 785, 794 (FL)

Froissart's *Chronicles*, 796

fulfillment, 112–14 (MC), 228 (SL), 640–42 (PP)

fun, 215–16 (SL), 749, 785, 792, 808, 832 (FL)

Genesis, 329 (M), 589–90 (PP); *1:1*, 368 (M); *2:19*, 628 (PP); *3:19*, 800 (FL); *46:4*, 600 (PP)

gentleman, 8 (MC)

Giant-Land (Quizz), 305 (M)

Gift-love, 743, 745, 753, 763, 768, 775–76, 827, 828, 830–31 (FL); as charity, 828, 832 (FL); as image of God, 827–28 (FL)

glory, 755, 756, 815, 820–21 (FL)

gluttony, 233–35 (SL)

God, 366–67, 368, 375–84 (M), 644 (PP), 666–67, 684–85 (GO); Adam and, 800 (FL); adoration of, 828 (FL); begetting versus making, 129–30, 132, 141, 144, 148–149 (MC); as Beloved, 822, 835 (FL); charity as instrument of, 831–32 (FL); as comfort and terror, 36 (MC), *See also Numinous;* as creator, 28–32, 33–36, 41, 47, 49, 148, 162 (MC), 240, 252–53 (SL), 329, 340, 356–59, 367, 377, 395, 403, 408–10, 443, 446 (M), 553, 559, 569–70, 574, 594, 603, 632 (PP), 827, 834 (FL); demands of virtue by, 72–73, 116–22 (MC); as doer of miracles, 372–89 (M); end of the world and, 60 (MC); Eden and, 821 (FL); the Father,

141–43, 152 (MC), 360 (M), 794 (FL); "fear of," 755–56 (FL); friendship as instrument of, 801–2 (FL); Gift-love and, 827–28 (FL); giving to Man of everything, 118, 155 (MC), 606 (PP); good deeds and, 117–18 (MC); goodness, Divine, 35 (MC), 560–66, 567–78 (PP); as the great Rival, 767–68 (FL); help of, 88 (MC); imitation of, 746 (FL); Jahweh, 404–5 (M); as judge, 80 (MC); knowing, 134–36 (MC), 756–57, 826–27 (FL); as love (Love Himself), 142 (MC), 346–47, 383 (M), 562, 569 (PP), 743, 746, 747, 767, 826–27, 829, 830, 831, 833, 834, 835 (FL); love for, 744, 756, 767, 821, 822–23, 826–36 (FL); love of man, 110 (MC), 207, 240 (SL), 345 (M), 518, 569–77 (PP), 794 (FL); "managerial" God, 827 (FL); natural loves as rival to love of, 821 (FL); Nature-God versus, 403–5 (M); "nearness to God," 745–46, 748, 815 (FL); Need-love of, 828–29 (FL); omnipotence, 560–66, 611 (PP); omniscience of, 137–40 (MC), 263–65 (SL), 598, 609 (PP); personal, 132–36 (MC), 383–84 (M); pride and, 104–8 (MC); revelation of, 49 (MC); righteousness and, 558, 630 (PP); as "something behind" empirical life and Moral Law, 24–27, 30, 33–36, 41 (MC); suffering and, 560–66, 567–78 (PP); Supernaturalism and, 308, 324 (M); "Thy will be done," 200, 207 (SL), 506, 606–7 (PP), 659 (GO); time and, 137–40 (MC), 263–65 (SL); triune, 132–44, 145 (MC), 367 (M)

Golden Rule, 74–77, 98–102, 109 (MC), 712 (AM)

good deeds, 117–18, 120–21, 156 (MC)

good and good people, 20–23, 26, 43, 81, 160–63 (MC), 375 (M), 503 (GD), 567–68 (PP), 820, 829 (FL). *See also* God, goodness, Divine; perfection

Goethe, Johann Wolfgang von, 729 (AM)

grace, 94 (MC), 216, 221, 287 (SL), 571 (PP), 746, 758, 769, 817, 821, 826, 828, 829, 830, 836 (FL)

Grahame, Kenneth, 554 (PP), 764 (FL)

gratitude, 228 (SL), 788 (FL)

greed and avarice, 104 (MC), 228 (SL), 748, 778, 829 (FL)

Greeks, 76 (MC), 292 (SL), 308, 373 (M), 761, 763, 787, 788, 808 (FL)

Gresham, Douglas H., 652–56 (GO)

Gresham, Helen Joy, 652–56 (GO)

Gresham, W. L., 654 (GO)

grief, 651–88 (GO), 765, 810, 825, 834, 835–36 (FL)

happiness, 49, 73, 87 (MC), 219, 229, 263 (SL), 448 (M), 499, 531 (GD), 830, 834 (FL); affection and, 778–79 (FL); Eros and, 813–14 (FL); love of God and, 822–23 (FL)

Hardy, Thomas, 605 (PP), 836 (FL)

hatred, 100, 101, 110 (MC), 201, 230–32, 269 (SL), 748, 769, 779, 821, 824–25 (FL)

Havard, R., 645 (PP)

Heaven, 73, 112–14 (MC), 215, 246, 250, 268, 275–77 (SL), 439, 441–46 (M), 463, 465–66, 467–541 (GD), 638–44 (PP), 833 (FL); reunion with the loved ones in, 834–35 (FL)

Hebrews: *2:10,* 612 (PP); *9:22,* 610 (PP)

Hegel, Georg Wilhelm Friedrich, 40 (MC), 290 (SL), 373 (M)

Hell, 42, 68 (MC), 183, 215–16, 236, 246, 249, 271, 287 (SL), 463, 465, 467–75,

484, 503, 504, 506, 508, 536–39 (GD), 606, 620–27 (PP) , 824 (FL); road to, 220 (SL), 506–9 GD)

Hilton, Walter, 549 (PP)

Hinduism, 39 (MC), 360, 380, 408 (M)

Historical Point of View, 210, 265, 268 (SL)

Hobbes, Thomas, 604 (PP)

Holy Ghost (Spirit), 143–44 (MC), 600 (PP)

homosexuality, 782–84 (FL)

Hooker, Richard, 596n. 4, 608, 616 (PP)

Hope, 109, 112–14 (MC), 228 (SL), 446 (M)

Hosea *11:8,* 574 (PP)

Housman, A. E., 605 (PP), 836 (FL)

Humanitarianism, 580 (PP)

humanity (Man), 640n. 2 (PP); abolition of, 724–30 (AM); belief in God or gods, 39–41 (MC); Biological (*Bios*) versus Spiritual (*Zoë*) life, 131, 144–47, 153, 173 (MC), 453 (M); composite nature of, 408, 417 (M); creation of, 148–50 (MC), 239 (SL), 346 (M), 569–71 (PP); Death and rebellion, 415–18, 426 (M); fall of, 417, 421 (M), 588–600, 608–9 (PP); "good infection" of, 144 (MC); human nature, 743 (FL); illusions of, 581–84, 605 (PP), 745, 762, 801, 830, 834 (FL); individuals in, 149 (MC), 206–7 (SL); made in the likeness of God, 137 (MC), 539 (GD); Need-love and, 743–45 (FL); rational creature, uniqueness of, 410 (M); redeemed, 410–12, 421, 421n. 2 (M), 529 (GD), 615 (PP); relationship to God, 570–78 (PP); Something Beyond and, 29–32 (MC); study of, 29–30 (MC); wickedness of, 579–87 (PP); wrong direction of, 41 (MC)

miracles *(cont.)*
uralism and, 305, 310, 448 (M); Old
Testament, 421n. 1 (M); philosophical
beliefs and inquiry into, 303–4 (M);
prayer and, 459–60 (M); probability,
390–97, 398 (M); progress of science
and objections to, 343–48, 360, 362
(M); Resurrection, 395–97, 401, 428,
429–47 (M); "special providences,"
456–58 (M); Supernaturalism and,
305–10, 339 (M); Virgin Birth, 342,
343, 352, 424 (M); walking on water,
342, 428, 434 (M)
Mohammedanism, 39, 71, 95 (MC), 360
(M)
monarchy, 307 (M)
Monism, 449 (M), 588 (PP)
Montaigne, Michel Eyquem de, 588
(PP)
Moral Law, 19–22, 33–36 (MC). *See also*
Law of Human Nature
morality, 15–23, 34–35, 122, 156 (MC),
556–58, 567–69 (PP); Christian (love
thy neighbor), 74–77, 81, 98–102
(MC), 202, 226 (SL), 712 (AM), 758
(FL); Christian versus non-Christian,
69 (MC); moral choices, 78–81 (MC);
progress in, 21–22, 33–36, 83 (MC),
716 (AM); psychoanalysis and, 78–82
(MC), 203 (SL), 579 (PP); reason and,
330–34, 336 (M); sexual, 84–89 (MC);
social, 74–77 (MC); three parts of,
65–67 (MC). *See also* Law of Human
Nature
More, Thomas, 181 (SL)
Morris, William, 820 (FL)
music, 216, 249 (SL)
mystery, 812, 813 (FL)
mystics, 375–76, 378, 443 (M), 827 (FL)
myth, 593 (PP), 814, 826 (FL)

nakedness, 789, 809, 811–12 (FL)
Napoleon, 472 (GD), 620 (PP)
Naturalist and Naturalism, 305–21, 325,
326–29, 331–34, 335–39, 357, 395, 410,
415, 448 (M)
Nature, 24–27, 28–30, 130, 131, 148,
153, 159, 170, 175 (MC), 308–29, 337,
354, 360 (M), 725 (AM); conquest of,
and applied science, 718–20, 725
(AM); creation of, by God, 328, 332,
340, 354, 356–59, 377, 395, 405, 406
(M); definition, 306–7 (M); entropy
of, 437 (M); good and evil in, 358,
407, 408 (M), 628–37 (PP); iconography, 755 (FL); laws of, 377, 387, 395,
426, 456 (M), 562 (PP); laws of, and
miracles, 340, 349–55, 385, 422 (M);
love of, 754–57, 815 (FL); miracles
and obedience of, 436–38 (M); New,
438–40 (M); redemption of, 410–11,
434 (M); religions of, 403–5, 409 (M),
756, 757 (FL); "return to nature," 781
(FL); Romanticism and, 781 (FL); as
teacher, 755, 756 (FL); time and, 456–
58 (M); Uniformity of, 393 (M)
Nazism, 290 (SL)
Need-love, 743–45, 748, 750, 752, 753,
754, 763, 767, 769, 774, 788, 827, 828,
830, 831 (FL); as charity, 832 (FL); of
God, 828–29 (FL)
Need-pleasures, 750–51, 752, 753 (FL);
Eros and transformation of, 805 (FL)
Neo-Pagans, 809 (FL)
neo-Platonism, 745, 823 (FL)
New Man, 58, 146, 164–70, 171–77
(MC), 422, 422n. 3, 455n. 1 (M)
New Nature, 438–39, 441 (M)
New Testament, 52, 76, 142, 153 (MC),
402, 421n. 1, 448 (M), 599 (PP), 796
(FL)

submission or surrender (to God), 156–58, 176 (MC), 200, 221–23, 245 (SL), 479 (GD), 602, 617, 620 (PP), 659 (GO); they "are taller when they bow," 822 (FL)

Subnatural, 312 (M)

suffering, 197, 198, 221, 266 (SL), 406 (M), 503 (GD), 545, 549, 558, 559, 601–19 (PP); animal, 628–37 (PP); disease, 602n. 1 (PP); Divine Goodness and, 566, 567–77 (PP); grief, 651–88 (GO), 765, 810, 825, 834, 835–36 (FF); heroism and, 646 (PP); self-torture, 617, 617n. 1 (PP); six propositions on, 615–19 (PP)

superman, 815 (FL)

Supernaturalist and Supernaturalism, 305–10, 313, 324, 335–39, 356, 452, 453 (M)

superstition, 271 (SL)

Swedenborg, Emanuel, 541 (GD)

Symbolism and Belief (Bevan), 360, 362 (M), 626 (PP)

Tacitus, 509 (GD), 784 (FL)

Tantalus, 497 (GD)

Tao, 701, 702–17, 721, 723, 727, 728, 730 (AM); Duties to Children and Posterity, 734 (AM); Duties to Parents, Elders, Ancestors, 734 (AM); Law of General Beneficence, 731–33 (AM); Law of Good Faith and Veracity, 736 (AM); Law of Justice, 735–36 (AM); Law of Magnanimity, 737 (AM); Law of Mercy, 736–37 (AM); Law of Special Beneficence, 733–34 (AM)

Taylor, Jeremy, 502 (GD)

temperament, 109 (MC), 155, 166–70, 212, 233–35 (SL)

temperance, 72 (MC)

temptation, 117, 120 (MC), 212, 218–20, 223, 245, 271, 288 (SL), 586, 596 (PP), 778, 807, 809, 817 (FL)

Tennyson, Alfred Lord, 780, 828 (FL)

Theism, 320 (M), 562, 576 (PP), 715 (AM)

theodicy, 756 (FL)

theology, 128–29, 132, 134 (MC), 755, 756 (FL)

Theosophy, 374 (M)

They Asked for a Paper (Lewis), 282 (SL)

time, 207 (SL); "before all worlds," 129, 148–49 (MC); change and, 257 (SL); the dead and, 665–67 (GO); eternal, 522, 538 (GD); future, 227, 228, 259 (SL); God and, 139–40 (MC), 263–65 (SL), 456–58 (M); Nature and, 456–58 (M); past, 227 (SL); present, 227–28 (SL), 522 (GD); value of, 212 (SL)

1 Timothy *1:20*, 602n. 1 (PP)

"To Lucasta, Going to the Wars" (Lovelace), 825–26 (FL)

Tolkien, J. R. R., 652 (GO)

Tolstoy, Leo, 819 (FL)

Totalitarianism, 149 (MC)

Traherne, Thomas, 700 (AM)

transcendentalism, 815 (FL)

transfiguration, 437, 441 (M)

transformation, 171 (MC), 250 (SL); five steps of, 172–74 (MC)

transmutation, 833 (FL)

Treatise of Human Nature (Hume), 390 (M)

Trinity, 132–44, 145 (MC), 367, 370 (M), 561 (PP)

Tristram Shandy (Fielding), 764, 772 (FL)

Typee (Melville), 784 (FL)

undulation, 206–11 (SL)

Universalism, 539 (GD)

universe, 24, 28, 30, 39–41, 148 (MC), 551, 644 (PP); Materialist versus Religious view, 28, 31 (MC); progress of science and objections to Christianity and miracles, 343–48, 362 (M); redeemed, 615 (PP)

unselfishness, 260–62 (SL)

Unspoken Sermons, First Series (MacDonald), 545, 643 (PP)

usury, 76 (MC)

vanity, 106 (MC), 212–14, 219, 234, 242, 256 (SL), 678 (GO)

Venus (carnal element of Eros), 803, 804, 806, 807, 808–9, 810, 811, 813, 814, 818, 832 (FL)

veracity, 736 (AM)

vice, 228, 233, 269 (SL), 504 (GD), 579 (PP), 750, 796 (FL)

Victories of Love, The (Patmore), 429 (M)

Virgin Birth, 6–7, 130 (MC), 342, 343, 352, 425 (M)

Virgil, 552 (PP), 725 (AM)

virtue(s), 700, 727 (AM); Cardinal, 70–73, 83–89, 109 (MC); practice of, 72–73, 116–23 (MC), 202, 223, 224–26, 229, 269, 270 (SL), 408 (M), 579, 608 (PP); Theological, 70, 109–23 (MC)

von Hügel, Friedrich, 623n. 3, 624 (PP)

Wagner, Richard, 769 (FL)

Wain, John, 652 (GO)

war, 100 (MC), 197–99, 200, 204–5, 273 (SL), 761–62 (FL)

Way of All Flesh, The (Butler), 768, 769, 770 (FL)

"What! You too? I thought I was the only one" (Lewis), 785, 794 (FL)

Wells, H. G., 333, 344 (M)

Wesley, John, 633n. 2 (PP)

Western Islands (Johnson), 696 (AM)

White, Gilbert, 764 (FL)

Whitehead, Alfred North, 256 (SL), 395 (M)

Will, 202, 221–23 (SL), 617 (PP). *See also* Free Will

Williams, Charles, 398 (M), 806 (FL)

Williams, N. P., 592n. 1 (PP)

Wind in the Willows, The (Grahame), 554 (PP), 764 (FL)

witches, 22 (MC)

women: aging and vanity, 242–44 (SL); arthritis and, 646 (PP); banishing of male companionship, by, 792–93 (FL); Christian, 248 (SL); in early communities, 784 (FL); fatigue and, 274 (SL); friendship as gender-based, 783, 790–92, 793 (FL); imaginary, 244 (SL); maternal love and, 758, 769, 775, 776 (FL); unselfishness in, 260 (SL); as wives, 95–97 (MC)

Wordsworth, William, 373 (M), 554, 628 (PP), 696, 700, 702 (AM), 754–55, 757, 787 (FL)

World War I, 101–2 (MC)

World War II, 183, 204–5, 227, 256, 264, 266, 269, 272–73 (SL)

worldliness, 268 (SL)

worship, 753, 828 (FL)

Zeus, 574 (PP), 812 (FL)

Zoë, 131, 134, 144–147, 153, 173 (MC), 453 (M)